RPG IV at Work

About the At Work Series

Developed by Merrikay Lee, the *At Work* series gives work-ing professionals the tools, techniques, and usable code they need to craft streamlined solutions to everyday challenges.

Merrikay Lee is series editor for the MC Press line of profes-sional books, which comprises more than 75 titles. She has spent more than 20 years as a technical professional in the IBM midrange industry and 15 years in the publishing field. She is the author of four books and has worked with numer-ous IT technical professionals to develop titles for the IBM midrange community of IT professionals. She is president of Lee Publishing Services Inc. in Dallas, Texas, and can be reached at mlee@leepublishing.com.

RPG IV at Work

Doug Pence and Ron Hawkins

MIDRANGE COMPUTING
IIR PUBLICATIONS INC.

First Edition
First Printing—October 2000

The information in this book has been revised and expanded since it was first published by Midrange Computing © 1996 and titled *Power RPG IV: Advanced Concepts, Tips, & Techniques, Including ILE* by Doug Pence and Ron Hawkins.

© 1996, 2000 Midrange Computing
ISBN: 1-58347-023-9

Midrange Computing
5650 El Camino Real, Suite 225
Carlsbad, CA 92008–9711 USA
www.midrangecomputing.com

For information on translations or book distributors outside the USA or to arrange bulk-purchase discounts for sales promotions, premiums, or fund-raisers, please contact Midrange Computing at the above address.

V4R4 or higher

ACKNOWLEDGMENTS

First and foremost, we would like to thank our immediate families. It is family that serves as both the reason and the inspiration to take on projects like this.

We would like to express our gratitude to our parents. Now that we find ourselves parents of teenagers, we have much greater appreciation for what you went through. We are hopeful that someday you will be able to look back and feel that it was all worth it.

Doug would like to extend thanks to his wife, Cathy, and their kids, John, Rachel, and Sarah. Your patience and understanding is appreciated, even if my gratitude is not shown as often as it should be.

Ron would like to thank his wife, Darla, and their kids, Daniel, Nicholas, and Rebecca.

We would also like to thank Merrikay Lee. Without her, this project would not have happened. It is an honor to work with someone that is bright, personable, and consummately professional.

Thank you, Jon Paris. How could IBM ever have let you get away? We can think of no better representative of our beloved AS/400 than yourself. It is very comforting to know that you are only an email away.

Last, but not least, we would like to thank our co-workers at CPU Medical Management Systems. You tolerate our weaknesses and help us exploit our strengths. Your ongoing support is greatly appreciated.

Doug Pence and Ron Hawkins
San Diego, California

CONTENTS

PREFACE

*If a man empties his purse into his head no one can take it away from him. An investment
in knowledge always pays the best interest.*

—Benjamin Franklin

The authors of this book, Doug Pence and Ron Hawkins, have spent the better part
of the last two decades accumulating tips, tools, and techniques that will benefit
any AS/400 programmer. Our objective was to put together a collection that would serve
all RPG/400 programmers, whether they are junior programmers right out of school or
seasoned veterans with 10 years of experience.

Along with the announcement of V3R1 of the AS/400 operating system came RPG IV
and a virtual avalanche of new information and capabilities. This book will open doors
and unlock that information, helping you take full advantage of the wide range of AS/400
capabilities.

From designing software to attain maximum performance to learning how to use advanced problem-solving tools, this book presents a wide range of important topics. It offers in-depth coverage of basic subjects—like data structures, string handling, and
subfiles—and also tackles the more intricate areas like application program interfaces

(APIs), the Integrated Language Environment (ILE), and using journaling as a debugging tool. It covers built-in functions, data types, and ILE subprocedures. From coding to compiling, there are tips for RPG programmers of every level. There are numerous tools designed to improve programmer productivity and efficiency.

Knowing the best way to do the job is often a direct result of being familiar with all of the tools at your disposal. It is for this reason that this book should find its way into every RPG reference library.

1

PERFORMANCE STARTS
WITH PROGRAM DESIGN

Throughout this chapter, we focus on reducing I/O and maximizing the use of main memory. We discuss how the Integrated Language Environment (ILE) affects performance and how it should affect your design considerations. We compare the pros and cons of *dynamic* program calls and *static* program calls, and we give you numerous tips on how to maximize your system resources.

A THOUSAND-MILE JOURNEY BEGINS WITH A SINGLE STEP...

To understand how to write programs that perform well on the AS/400, you need to understand which functions most degrade system performance. The primary bottleneck on most midrange systems is related to either I/O processing or memory management. Creating, deleting, opening, closing, reading, and writing to data files drains system performance, making your software appear to run slowly. Over-utilization of system memory causes the system to "thrash" and spend the majority of its resources moving objects from memory to disk and vice versa. Most software on the AS/400 and its predecessors falls victim to one or the other of these problems.

I/O AND ITS EFFECT ON AS/400 PERFORMANCE

I/O processing is slow because it is still slave to a mechanical process. The data is stored on some form of magnetic media and must be retrieved or written using the moving parts of the storage device, whatever that happens to be.

Despite major technical achievements in this area within the last decade, I/O processing remains the culprit of most performance problems on the AS/400. Features like *journaling*, *RAID*, and *mirroring* have been added to the operating system for stability and to allow us to make software systems more reliable, but their use can further amplify the I/O processing bottleneck problem. The good news is that there are a number of things that you can do as a programmer to help alleviate this problem. Let's begin with the basics.

Don't Need It? Don't Use It!

From a performance standpoint, opening and closing files are two of the most time-consuming events that take place on the AS/400. When an RPG program is called, the data files are usually opened automatically by the system. If the programs you are working with have a large number of files (sometimes this is unavoidable), program initiation can seem to take forever while the program is loaded and all of the files are opened.

This delay can be reduced if the file opens are *user-controlled*, if the files are already open with a *shared data path,* or *both*.

User-Controlled File Opens

User-controlled file opens give you the option of only opening a file when you intend to use it. As you can see in in Figure 1.1, you can code your program to open files as you need them instead of when the program loads. With the announcement of V4R4 of OS/400, you can now use the %OPEN built-in function to tell whether a file is open. Another option would be to use an error indicator on the open statement, as shown in Figure 1.2. Failure to perform one step or the other results in a nasty little RPG error.

If you code your file opening routines at strategic points within your program, it is possible that certain files may never be opened at all. For example, if the program contains multiple screens that are processed conditionally depending on user response, the program could be coded to open only the files associated with the selected screens. There is a double bonus in this situation because files that are never opened obviously never need to be closed.

Perhaps more important from an overall performance standpoint, user-controlled files offer an excellent opportunity to distribute program overhead so it is less noticeable to the user.

```
FFilename++IPEASFRlen+LKlen+AIDevice+.Keywords++++++++++++++++++++++++Comments++++
FCustomer  IF   E           K Disk    UsrOpn

CLON01Factor1+++++++Opcode&ExtFactor2+++++++Result++++++++Len++D+HiLoEq...Comments
 * Open the file, if it is not already open
C                    If        not %Open(Customer)
C                    Open      Customer
C                    Endif
C         CustKey    Chain     Customer                               99
```

Figure 1.1: User-controlled opens using conditional flags.

```
FFilename++IPEASFRlen+LKlen+AIDevice+.Keywords++++++++++++++++++++++++Comments++++
FCustomer  IF   E           K DISK    USROPN

CLON01Factor1+++++++Opcode&ExtFactor2+++++++Result++++++++Len++D+HiLoEq...Comments
C                    Open      Customer                       99
C         CustKey    Chain     Customer                       99
```

Figure 1.2: User-controlled opens using error indicators.

The example in Figure 1.3 illustrates how you can code the program so the files are being opened at the same time the program is waiting for a response from the user. While Execute Format (EXFMT) was a wonderful addition to the RPG language, those of us who have been in the midrange market for a while remember when we had to code the display file as a primary or demand file. Separate steps were required to write and read each screen format.

```
FFilename++IPEASFRlen+LKlen+AIDevice+.Keywords++++++++++++++++++++++++Comments++++
FDisplay   CF   E           Workstn
FCustomer  IF   E           K DISK    UsrOpn
FSalesmen  IF   E           K DISK    UsrOpn

CLON01Factor1+++++++Opcode&ExtFactor2+++++++Result++++++++Len++D+HiLoEq...Comments
 * Write Display Format
C                    Write     Format
 * Open files, if needed
C                    If        not %Open(Customer)
C                    Open      Customer
C                    Endif
C                    If        not %Open(Salesmen)
C                    Open      Salesmen
C                    Endif
 * Wait for input from the display file
C                    Read      Format                              99
```

Figure 1.3: User-controlled opens between writing and reading display file format.

3

In this example, the WRITE and READ op codes replace EXFMT. Notice that several user-controlled file opens have been placed in between the WRITE and the READ. When this program executes, the screen panel displays and the files open while operator attention is focused on the screen. Coding the program this way creates a condition where the files are being opened while the program is waiting on the user, instead of the other way around.

When using this particular technique of writing and reading display formats, you must compile your display file as DFRWRT(*NO) so it does not defer writing a screen until a read operation is encountered. Failure to comply with this requirement results in a condition where the screen does not appear until the read operation is executed.

When using user-controlled file opens, you may choose to ignore the closing of the files and let the program handle that part of it when the last record indicator is encountered. If the pause caused when the program ends is causing unwanted delays, you may want to try using the RETURN op code instead of setting on LR. The RETURN operation code has its own set of potential pitfalls, however, which will be discussed in further detail later in this chapter under "").

The Shared Data Path

Another technique that helps you reduce program initiation overhead uses a method called *shared data paths*. This method can be very useful when programs and subprograms use the same data files. By opening the data or display files using shared open data paths, subsequent high-level language (HLL) programs can be opened in about half the time.

The example in Figure 1.4 is a sample initial program called when a user first signs on to the system. The Override Database File (OVRDBF) command specifies that the open data path is to be shared, and the Open Database File (OPNDBF) command opens the data files that are used by the application most often. The Monitor Message (MONMSG) command was added to prevent error messages from appearing if the files in question already had an open data path when the program was run.

When the sample program in Figure 1.4 is run, the files are opened with a shared data path and the menu is displayed. Program calls to application programs within this same session will then use the existing open data path instead of creating a new one.

```
PGM
MONMSG      CPF0000
            OVRDBF      FILE(CUSTOMER) SHARE(*YES)
            OVRDBF      FILE(SALESMEN) SHARE(*YES)
            OPNDBF      FILE(CUSTOMER) OPTION(*ALL)
            OPNDBF      FILE(SALESMEN) OPTION(*ALL)
            GO          CUSTMENU
ENDPGM
```

Figure 1.4: Sign-on CL program to pre-open files and display initial menu.

Another way to use the open data path methodology is to build or change the file so that the data path is always shared. Notice that the Create Physical File (CRTPF), Change Physical File (CHGPF), Create Display File (CRTDSPF), and Change Display File (CHGDSPF) commands give you the option of compiling the objects in such a manner that the data path is always shared.

You may want to share the open data path of a display file when you have several programs within a single job stream that happen to use the same display file. Employing this technique gives you the same advantages as if you used it with a database file.

RPG IV: The Next Generation

ILE was announced with OS/400 V3R1. From that point on, you have been allowed to read a record with one program and update it with another, as long as the open data path is shared within a job or activation group.

In other words, if your application uses the same physical or display files over and over, those files may be opened and closed many times within a single job stream. This can cause big delays in application program initiation and create a situation in which your overall system performance is significantly degraded. You may also have applications that open files that never get closed (for one reason or another), creating a condition where your job has multiple open data paths for the same file. Using shared data paths can help alleviate these problems and improve overall system throughput.

Another interesting twist ILE offered was the ability to share open data paths within an activation group (which is explained later in this chapter and in chapter 14). The activation group offers a little more security than sharing open data paths by job, but as we are about to discuss, there are still many dangerous pitfalls.

Words of Caution

If you are considering the use of shared open data paths, there are some very important considerations you need to think about. First, the term *shared* in this case may be somewhat misleading. Not all sessions have access to the open data paths. Only programs within the same session or job (or, optionally, activation group) share the open data path.

Most important, there is a critical warning to heed if you use the library list to manipulate which file you are going to use on the system. When a file has been pre-opened with a shared open data path, an application program uses that file whether or not it is currently in your library list. The program simply uses the open data path of the shared file. If you do not have files with the same name in multiple libraries, this is not a problem. But if you do have multiple libraries that have files with the same name, you must proceed with the utmost caution. Failure to heed this warning could result in reading or updating files in libraries that are not even in your library list! One way of minimizing this potential nightmare is to restrict the sharing of your data path within the activation group only. This is done using the OPNSCOPE parameter of the Override with Data Base File (OVRDBF) command.

Another important thing to remember when using open data paths is that the file is always in use as long as the session exists. It does not matter whether a program is actually running. This is a potential problem when a job needs dedicated access to a file (with file saves, for example). Files with shared data paths remain "in use" until the files are closed or the session is terminated.

The use of shared open data paths mean you cannot assume the file pointer will be where you want it to be when a program is initiated. If you are going to do any type of sequential read operation, remember to set your file pointer appropriately. You do not need to worry about this when the open data path is not shared because each program in the job stream will open and keep its own independent file pointer.

You also need to pay attention to how you open the file. In other words, you will experience problems if you open a file as *input only* and then try to update the file in a subsequent program.

There are other security and operational issues to consider before trying this particular method. More information on this technique is offered in the IBM AS/400 *Database Guide*, the *CL Reference Manual*, and the *ILE RPG/400 Programmer's Guide*.

THE PATH YOU CHOOSE MIGHT BE THE MOST IMPORTANT PART OF YOUR JOURNEY

The path you chose to take through your data is often the most critical decision you can make with regard to how an application performs. As stated earlier in this chapter, I/O has a dramatic effect on performance.

For example, if you choose to read a file by index instead of arrival sequence, you are making a choice to greatly increase the amount of work the system has to do. The AS/400 HLLs do not perform as well when reading a file by index as they do when they read data in arrival sequence. The reason? When a program reads a data file by an index key, the system must first read the key and then go get the physical data. As a result, the HLL program must double the I/O processing right off the bat. Also, because the physical data is being accessed in a random fashion, the data cannot be blocked (retrieving multiple records on every I/O operation) in the same manner as it would be when the file is processed in arrival fashion. This increases the system resources used when the HLL program is run.

When running one of your RPG programs, you may have noticed a message in your job log stating that the key was to be ignored and the data was being processed in arrival sequence. This occurred because, at compile time, the system noticed there was nothing in your RPG program that required the file to be processed randomly. In other words, there were no I/O operations, like CHAIN or SETLL (Set Lower Limits), that required a key. Consequently, the system decided that to be more efficient, the HLL program should process the data in arrival sequence and assigned a minimal blocking factor (more on blocking when we discuss reading files by the index).

Design Considerations with Regard to I/O Processing

When designing a new program, the choice is whether to read records in arrival sequence, to read by an index, or to use the Open Query File (OPNQRYF) or Format Data (FMTDTA) commands to sequence the data into the desired path. Unfortunately, the answer is: It depends. Answer these two, key questions before you decide which method to employ:

- Is the program interactive or will it run in batch?
- How big is the file being processed?

Most of the time, you do not have much of a choice when you are coding an interactive program. You will have a tough time trying to convince your salespeople they are better off working with a subfile of their prospects in arrival sequence. They will want the subfile presented in a sequence that makes them more productive, with little or no regard for system performance. Who can blame them? Addressing system performance is your job, not theirs.

Batch programs should almost always be written to use FMTDTA or OPNQRYF. Even if there is already an index available for the sequence you desire, the program is likely to run faster if you get the data into the proper arrival sequence prior to processing it.

Avoid Reading Files by the Index Whenever You Can

If the program you are writing involves a data file with a handful of records (in the hundreds), it may be more efficient to read the file by keyed index. This is because there is a certain amount of overhead required to run FMTDTA or OPNQRYF. However, if the file you are reading has 250,000 records, you will notice a definite performance improvement if you put the data into the appropriate sequence first. Two options available to perform this task are FMTDTA and OPNQRYF.

We should mention that both of these options apply only to batch jobs. Interactive jobs that include FMTDTA or OPNQRYF can severely impact performance. Any job requiring these tools (generally, where a large number of records are to be read) should be run in batch.

Since the addition of the ALLWCPYDTA(*OPTIMIZE) parameter to the OPNQRYF command, there are few reasons to use the FMTDTA (sort) command. This new option allows the system to decide whether to sort the data.

The use of OPNQRYF can be very simple or very complex. Let's say, for example, that you have a daily sales report that has been written to read a logical file over your 250,000-record customer file by customer name. The code in Figure 1.5 could be embedded into a CL driver program to put the customer file (CUST) into customer name sequence prior to running the RPG program. The RPG program could then be changed to read the CUST file in arrival sequence.

```
OVRDBF FILE(CUST) SHARE(*YES)
OPNQRYF FILE((CUST)) ALWCPYDTA(*OPTIMIZE) KEYFLD((CUSNAM))
```

Figure 1.5: Using OPNQRYF to sequence data into the appropriate arrival sequence.

The net result of this change is a significant performance improvement. Because the system does not need to read the index first and then go out and get the data, I/O is reduced. The system also automatically blocks the data, and multiple records are read each time the system has to go to the disk.

LOGICAL FILES ARE A VALUABLE TOOL, BUT DON'T OVERUSE THEM

The logical file is one of the most treasured gems in our toolbox, but most of us have abused the privilege of using it at one time or another. Why shouldn't we? The sales department asked us for a new report and we do not seem to have a data path that puts the data in the exact sequence it is looking for. It would be so easy to add that new logical file over the Customer Master file, write the report, and get the request off our desk...

Don't Do It!

Before adding a new logical file, consider the consequences of your actions. Depending on the DDS and compile options you use when you create the logical file, you are potentially creating additional system overhead for your AS/400 every time that the physical file is updated. Even if you build the file so index maintenance is delayed, the index still has to be built at some point.

The decision of whether you should create a new logical file should be based on the runtime environment (batch or interactive) for which it is required. Logical files should not be created for programs that will run in a batch environment.

There are also other disadvantages to logical files. Logical files require disk space for the index. File backups and restores take longer because they either have to save or rebuild the access path. There is also a certain amount of system overhead the system incurs when keeping track of logical files and the physical files with which they are associated.

BLOCKING DATA TO MAKE THE MOST OF I/O PROCESSING

A technique called record blocking is one of the most effective ways to take full advantage of the I/O processing in your programs. The principal concept of record blocking is that you tune your programs to go out and "grab" multiple records to process each time your program needs data instead of fetching records one at a time. Let's see if we can better illustrate this concept.

Do you do the weekly grocery shopping for your household? Why do you usually stop to get a shopping cart when you visit the grocery store? Can you imagine shopping for a family of five without a cart? You would have to bring the items to the front counter one or two at a time. It would take forever! As ridiculous as this idea sounds, that is precisely what many AS/400 programmers are asking their system to do when they do not take advantage of record blocking.

Record blocking is an effective tool anytime you are performing sequential read operations on a file. Record blocking is simply how you tell the system to put more than one item in the cart (a euphemism for the I/O buffer) before you return to the front counter (your program). The trick is to figure out how many items should go in the cart before they start falling all over the floor.

Regardless of whether you specify it, your system will perform a limited amount of record blocking. When your program performs a read operation, the system will check the I/O buffer to see if it needs to go read some records. If so, the system will go out and read enough records to fill the I/O buffer (the default size or block is usually 4K), and then return control to your program. How many records it reads to fill the buffer depends on the physical size of your records, as well as the size of the buffer. In many cases, performance can be enhanced if you select a buffer size that is closer to the amount of memory the system uses for an Open Data Path (ODP) (64K).

To calculate the optimal blocking factor for the file you are copying, divide the physical record length of the file into the size of the ODP for the job (64K).

When Your Cup Runneth Over

You may be asking yourself why you shouldn't just use a really big blocking factor and be done with it. We have seen this technique before and it seems like it should work well. The problem with this technique is that the system is only prepared to deal with a buffer size less than or equal to the size of the ODP. Any additional overflow is automatically written or "cached" out to disk. The end result of this technique is that the records would really have to be read twice, once from the database file and then from the overflow buffer.

As you can see, the best possible solution is to calculate a blocking factor that is close to the size of the ODP, without creating an overflow condition. You apply the newly calculated blocking factor using the OVRDBF command.

10

Let's take a look at the example in Figure 1.6. We calculated the optimal blocking factor by taking the record length of the CUST file (the record length was 58) and divided it into 65,535 (64K minus 1). The result was 1,129.91, so our optimal blocking factor was 1,129. We then issued the OVRDBF command to set our blocking factor and call our RPG program.

```
PGM

    OVRDBF      FILE(CUST) SEQONLY(*YES 1129)
    CALL        MYPROGRAM
    DLTOVR      FILE(CUST)

ENDPGM
```

Figure 1.6: Using OVRDBF to apply a blocking factor.

USING SETOBJACC TO REDUCE I/O AND MAXIMIZE MEMORY USAGE

Throughout this chapter, we have encouraged you to reduce the impact of the mechanical process of reading disk as it pertains to your application. One way to do this is to maximize the use of your system memory.

The Set Object Access (SETOBJACC) command is used to pull objects (primarily programs, database files, and their access paths) into memory to reduce the amount of disk I/O required by the system. If a database file's index and data can be processed from memory rather than disk, the mechanical part of the task is removed from the equation and the processing is performed significantly faster. Obviously, how well this works depends on the amount of main memory you have on your system, the time of day the job runs, and the size of the files or programs with which you are working.

For two reasons, the benefits of moving a physical file that must be processed randomly (by key) into memory will far outweigh the benefits of doing the same for a file that will be read in arrival sequence:

- When you compile your RPG program, the compiler checks to see if you are processing a file in arrival sequence. If so, the system automatically blocks records when the program is run. Blocking is a term used to describe when the system retrieves multiple blocks of your data on each I/O request because the system determined the order in which you will be reading the records. The number of data blocks retrieved depends on algorithms within the operating system.

> Blocking is not effective on randomly accessed files because the system must work overtime to load records into memory that are not in the sequence the program expects. In fact, blocking can actually degrade performance when it is applied to randomly accessed files.

- When you are reading a file by an index key, the system must first read the index record and then go out to seek the physical data.

You will attain the maximum advantage if you can put both the physical file and its access path into main memory simultaneously. All of the I/O requests from within your program occur in memory rather than on disk.

Using the SETOBJACC command to put a file into memory is like record blocking, except that you can bring the entire file into memory at once. In the case of randomly accessed files, you want to bring both the data and the access path into memory, if you can. This can have a tremendous impact on program performance because the mechanical process of the disk I/O has been eliminated. The SETOBJACC command may be run interactively or from within a program.

It should be noted that the SETOBJACC command is not useful when the file is specified as output only. This is because the output operations are already "buffered" in memory (remember that all records are added to the end of a file unless you are reusing deleted records) and do not cause high levels of I/O activity.

There are basically two flavors to the SETOBJACC command: plain vanilla and tutti-frutti. Plain vanilla is very simple and great to use when your system is dedicated to a single task (like month end or daily startup). Tutti-frutti is a little more involved, but the benefits derived can be substantial.

Make Mine Vanilla, Please

Most AS/400 shops have certain times of the day, week, or month when dedicated processing can occur. If you have this luxury, you may want to look at this flavor of SETOBJACC command to speed up the dedicated jobs that run at such times.

For our example in Figure 1.7, we take our customer physical file (CUST) in our library (FILES) and place it into main memory. Our job is to process the file randomly by key, so we also specify the MBRDATA parameter so both the data and the access path are pulled into main memory (we could have indicated that just the access path or data be brought in).

```
SETOBJACC OBJ(FILES/CUST) OBJTYPE(*FILE) POOL(*JOB) MBRDATA(*BOTH)
```

Figure 1.7: Using SETOBJACC to put objects into main storage.

When the SETOBJACC command is run, the system takes a "snapshot" of memory just prior to pulling your object into memory. It then sends a message to your job log that lets you know how much benefit you will gain from running the command. Figure 1.8 shows an example of what the message looks like.

```
19K of CUST brought to pool with 996K unused.
```

Figure 1.8: Message sent when running the SETOBJACC command, showing object size and the space available in the memory pool.

The message states that prior to bringing 19K of the CUST file into memory, 996K of memory was available. Because main storage is not cleared of objects when a job ends, memory may not be available. The objects in memory are left there until the space is needed for something else. If the message tells you that 0K was available prior to attempting to bring your object into memory, clear the memory pool first.

Clear the Pool!

For our example, let's assume the job is running interactively. In this case, the parameters for the Clear Memory Pool (CLRPOOL) command are very simple (Figure 1.9).

```
CLRPOOL POOL(*JOB)
```

Figure 1.9: Clearing the memory pool.

The CLRPOOL command clears all objects out of the main storage pool so there is plenty of room for the objects that we want to place there. The down side to this is that your job will be moved out of the main storage pool as well. We recommend signing off to end your job after running the CLRPOOL command. When you sign back on, the memory pool is cleared, and you will have initiated a new job.

With a clear memory pool, you are free to run the SETOBJACC command to put the objects you will be using into main memory. You can then run the rest of your job as you would normally. The only step left is to clear your objects from memory once your job is completed. There are two ways to do this. You can use the CLRPOOL command as we did prior to placing objects into memory, or you can use the SETOBJACC command with slightly different parameters (Figure 1.10).

```
SETOBJACC OBJ(FILES/CUST) OBJTYPE(*FILE) POOL(*PURGE)
```

Figure 1.10: Clearing objects from main storage after using SETOBJACC to put them there.

Time for Tutti-Frutti

The tutti-frutti method would be used in non-dedicated environments, but the same basic principles and advantages we experienced in the plain vanilla version apply. The difference with the tutti-frutti version is that you set up your own memory pools to store your most heavily used objects.

Memory Pools

Memory pool is simply a term used to describe the segregation of memory. When you install memory on the AS/400, it is automatically placed into the memory pool designated *BASE. If you leave your default system configuration alone, all of your subsystems will get their memory from this pool.

When processing in a non-dedicated environment, it is best to create your own subsystem. When you create a subsystem and allocate memory to it, the memory the new subsystem uses is taken from the *BASE storage pool. The command to allocate 500K to pool number 2 in the SETOBJS subsystem is shown in Figure 1.11. Ensure that you have enough memory in the *BASE memory pool before executing the command. If there is not enough, decrease the size of some other subsystem that will return the memory to the *BASE pool. This can be done while you are working in the Work with System Status (WRKSYSSTS) command display.

```
CRTSBSD SBSD(QGPL/SETOBJS) POOLS((1 *BASE)(2 500K 1))
```

Figure 1.11: Creating a subsystem for SETOBJACC.

The 500K figure is for the purposes of this example only. You need to adjust it based on the size of the objects you are going to put in it. When you run the SETOBJACC command, it displays a message (like the one shown in Figure 1.8) that tells you the size of the object put into memory as well as the available space in the pool before the object was put in.

The example in Figure 1.8 shows that the object CUST has a size of 19K and was put into a memory pool that had 996K available prior to the execution of the SETOBJACC command. If there is not enough space available for the whole file, it might still be advantageous for you to bring in as much of the file as you can. Obviously, it is better to fit the whole object in the pool if possible. But remember, it is not the size of the object that is important; it is the number of times the file is being accessed. You can still improve response time by bringing a 20K file (or half of a 40K file) into memory if that file is accessed a jillion times a day.

The next step is to start the subsystem and initialize the memory pool. You should automate this process by making it part of your daily startup routine. The command in Figure1.12 starts the subsystem and clears pool 2 in our SETOBJ subsystem, which is where we are going to load our files. Do not become confused by the numbering system of the pools. The AS/400 operating system divides memory into pools and numbers them. Pool 1 is the MACHINE pool and pool 2 is the *BASE pool. All other pools are numbered consecutively from there. In addition, each pool can be segregated up to 10 times. We segregate ours twice, and put the memory in pool 2.

```
STRSBS SBSD(QGPL/SETOBJS)
CLRPOOL POOL(SETOBJS 2)
```

Figure 1.12: Clearing the user-created private main storage memory pool.

We can now bring the file into memory using the command in Figure1.13. The SETOBJACC command executes extremely quickly, taking no more than a few seconds for most files.

```
SETOBJACC OBJ(FILES/CUST) OBJTYPE(*FILE) POOL(SETOBJS 2) MBRDATA(*BOTH)
```

Figure 1.13: Using SETOBJACC to put objects into a private main storage pool.

Memory Is Fast, Disk I/O Is Slow

Bringing a file or program into memory (which is done with relatively few I/Os) can eliminate thousands of disk accesses throughout the day and result in tremendous savings in transaction throughput. It requires some planning regarding which objects should be in memory, but the rewards can far exceed the effort.

As you can see, the difference between plain vanilla and tutti-frutti is not all that great. Enjoy the improved performance and *bon appétit*.

TOO MUCH OF A GOOD THING CAN KILL YOU

We stress that you should concentrate on reducing I/O and maximize the use of your system memory. But like many good things in life, it is easy to go overboard.

If your system does not have enough memory or you are over-using it in an effort to reduce I/O, your overall system performance can be degraded because your system is thrashing. In this case, there are too many objects contending for system memory and the system is trying to keep up by expending all of its resources moving pages temporarily from memory to disk and vice versa. This is similar to the drop-off in performance you notice on your PC when you do not have enough memory to run a job and "virtual memory" is used.

There are a variety of tools that can help you analyze if this is a problem on your system. We recommend that you take a class on work management if you think this may be an issue on your system.

REUSING DELETED RECORDS

Odds are pretty good that most of the physical files on your system can be broken down into three categories:

- Files that almost never change.
- Files that have records written to them regularly, but records that never get deleted.
- Files from which records are frequently written and deleted.

We concern ourselves with the second and third types in this section. Because the information in these types of files is not static, they can reach conditions that adversely affect performance if they are not maintained properly.

When you must read a file randomly by key, system performance is better when the physical data in the file is in the same order as the key by which you are reading it. This is because a single I/O operation is more likely to get a block of data that holds more than one record that must be processed. If the sequence of the data and the index do not match, the I/O operation will likely result in only a single record being processed before the system has to go out and get another block (and the same block may need to be read later). The end result is that many more I/O operations may need to take place for the job to complete.

When a record is added to a file, the data is normally added to the end of the file, unless the REUSEDLT parameter was specified for the file. When REUSEDLT has been specified for a physical file, the system attempts to "reuse" records that were previously deleted whenever you add new records to the file. This parameter must be specified when the file is built (CRTPF), or you can change the file using the Change Physical File (CHGPF) command.

Using the REUSEDLT parameter can adversely affect system performance. The system has to search for deleted records every time a new record is added. Depending on the size of the file, as well as the percentage of deleted records, this may not be a big deal. Additionally, because new records may be inserted into spots where deleted records previously existed, programs that were designed to process the file in arrival sequence may perform differently than initially intended.

THE RGZPFM COMMAND

Regardless of how records get added, if the index is added to randomly, the index and the data will not be in the same sequence after the add is performed. As we have repeatedly discussed, the greatest bottleneck for system performance is I/O. One way to combat this is to perform maintenance on files that experience heavy traffic. The Reorganize Physical File Member (RGZPFM) command can be used to put the data and index back into the same sequence and, at the same time, remove any records that are flagged for deletion. Any programs that process the file randomly benefit from this process because the I/O is likely to be reduced (record size can affect this too because it directly relates to how many records are retrieved on a single I/O process).

The primary functions of the RGZPFM command are to remove deleted records from a physical file and to change the sequence of the records to match a selected index (this is usually the primary key to the physical file). If you have a physical file that is usually read by a specific logical file, it may be advantageous to reorganize the records in the file so they match the key of that particular logical file.

It can be surprising how much disk space gets tied up in deleted records if your data files never get reorganized. When a record gets deleted on the AS/400, it still takes up the same amount of space on disk until the record gets reused (if the file was designated to use the Reuse Deleted Records [REUSEDLT] option) or the RGZPFM command is run. The file must not be in use when the RGZPFM command is run, so it may be a problem in some shops that do not schedule down time to perform system maintenance tasks.

If you do not specify any additional parameters, the RGZPFM command simply removes the deleted records from the physical file. The KEYFILE parameter can be used to resequence the data to match the key of the physical file or to match the path of a selected logical file. The examples in Figures1.14 through 1.16 respectively show our customer file being reorganized to remove deleted records only and to remove the deleted records, and then being resequenced into physical file key order. As a result, the data will be in customer name order (that is, the path of the CUSBYNAM logical file).

```
RGZPFM FILE(CUST)
```

Figure 1.14: Using RGZPFM to remove deleted records from a file.

```
RGZPFM FILE(CUST) KEYFILE(*FILE)
```

Figure 1.15: Using RGZPFM to remove deleted records and resequence the data to match the key to the physical file.

```
RGZPFM FILE(CUST) KEYFILE(CUSBYNAM)
```

Figure 1.16: Using RGZPFM to remove deleted records and resequence the data to match the key of a logical file.

Note: You do not want to use the KEYFILE parameter on a file that has no key. You will end up with an error message or a file that is not reorganized.

THE RGZPFFLTR COMMAND

The Reorganize Physical File Filter (RGZPFFLTR) command (explained in more detail in chapter 11) can be a valuable tool if your shop has the luxury of being able to schedule unattended down time to perform system maintenance. The command can be set up as an autostart job that automatically reviews all of the files on your system to determine which files need to be reorganized. How it determines whether the RGZPFM process is required is based on a percentage value you use when you call the RGZPFFLTR command.

The percentage refers to the level of deleted records in a file that you deem acceptable. For example, if you think that all files that have at least 10 percent of the records in them deleted should be reorganized, you would set the parameter at 10 percent.

In any case, the files that meet the prescribed percentage criteria are reorganized automatically into the order of the key of the physical file. This utility could take some time to run, depending on the number of files that meet the specified criteria and the speed of your system, but the overall impact on system performance and DASD utilization could be appreciable.

PERFORMANCE AND THE DYNAMIC PROGRAM CALL

The AS/400's ability to break down job streams into smaller subprograms is one of the wonderful things about the system. RPG and CL can be used to break down larger jobs into smaller, more manageable components that can be used elsewhere. These modular components can be thought of as *reusable code*. They can be called from a variety of places to perform the same function. We think it is a good idea to code your programs with this thought in mind!

One example of this type of module is our window subfile program, which is used to decide to which printer a report should be sent (this sample program is in chapter 2). You can call this program from any RPG or CL program, and the operator is able to select a printer. The selection values are returned to the calling program parameters.

The program can be called from any other program that has been designed to request printed output. The fact that the same program can be called from many different places makes the code reusable. The greatest value to reusable code is that every time you enhance it, you are enhancing the utilization of all programs that call it.

As with most good things, however, there is a price to pay. Breaking down longer job streams into smaller, more manageable components can have an adverse effect on system performance. As previously stated, IBM announced ILE with V3R1. For the first time in the history of IBM midrange systems, they gave us a choice between *dynamic* program calls and *static* program calls.

Pandora's Box

A *dynamic* call is a call to another program whose address is resolved at runtime. This is the type of call we have always used in OPM programs. It is very flexible because it can use the library list to locate the actual program to run, which means that it can be changed at runtime. It is also very slow to initiate, especially if you are calling a program written in a different language. You execute a static call with the standard CALL op code.

A *static* call is a call to another program whose address is resolved when the program is created. This type of call initiates very quickly—as much as four times faster than a dynamic call. In fact, it initiates almost as fast as if the called program were coded as a subroutine in the calling program. You execute a static call with the ILE Call Bound (CALLB) op code.

While static calls are much faster than dynamic calls, that speed can come with a heavy price tag. Static calls to programs other than service programs are *bound by copy*. That means a copy of the program being called is made in the calling program when it is compiled. That's why the called program can run almost as fast as if it were a subroutine in the calling program. And basically, it is!

Even given the dramatic performance improvement, binding by copy should be avoided unless you are in a very stable operational environment. It can indeed be the Pandora's Box of programming. It looks beautiful on the outside, but if you open it up, it can release plagues for the body and sorrow for the mind.

Making changes to programs that have been bound by copy to other programs can quickly become a cascading nightmare of never-ending changes. Each time you change a *module* (which we formerly referred to as a program) that happens to be bound by copy into multiple programs, each of those programs must be recompiled. Worse yet, some programs that call the changed program may be missed, causing different levels of the same program to exist on your system.

We have given you some tools in chapter 11 to help you avoid this problem, but if your system is still being updated on a regular basis, you can easily end up with a very volatile situation. Visions of your tired old body being dragged out of bed in the middle of the night to fix a program that you already corrected—but without the changes making it into the client's version—should flash before your eyes anytime you consider opening this box.

As you may know, there was one redeeming quality in Pandora's Box: hope. There is hope in the CALLB op code because it sets the stage for fast, multi-language programming. If you need a system function that is best coded in C, go ahead and use the CALLB. By performing the static call, you won't lose in the call overhead what you gained by coding in C in the first place.

Even without static program binding, a number of techniques can be employed to help you reduce the impact on dynamic call performance. In the next section, we discuss changes you can make to your CL and RPG programs to reduce the effect of program calls.

The bottom line is this: Even though there is hope in the box, we recommend you keep the lid at least partially on unless you are in a very stable operating environment.

CL Program Calls

CL program calls have a few downsides RPG does not have, so here are a few tips to keep in mind when you are working with CL programs:

- If your CL program is designed to contain a loop where a program is called multiple times, use a qualified program name (indicating the library and program name) on your call instead of letting the library list determine where the program resides. Unlike RPG, the CL program does not keep internal pointers telling it where the program was found originally.

- If you have a choice of calling a CL program or an RPG program that both perform the same function, choose the RPG program. A CL program requires more overhead to call than an RPG program.

- If programs within the job stream will use the same files, seriously consider sharing open data paths (as discussed earlier). Reduced I/O nets you the greatest gain in performance.

RPG Program Calls

There are also several tips you can use to reduce system overhead when performing program calls from RPG. Here are a few we came up with:

- If an RPG program is going to be dynamically called more than once in the job stream, consider using the return op code instead of setting on last record (LR). This keeps the program resident in memory so it does not need to repeatedly incur the overhead required for program initialization and file open and close operations. When making this change, however, you need to pay attention to file pointers, field usage, and indicator settings. Because the program does not terminate, these values are going to be what they were when you last exited the program.

- If you elect to employ this method, you should code a "last call" routine, which will call the program one last time to set on LR and release the resources the program is hanging on to. This will prevent you from having rogue programs hanging around and sucking up valuable system resources.

- As previously mentioned, if you have a choice of calling a CL program or an RPG program that both perform the same function, choose the RPG program. A CL program requires more overhead to initiate than an RPG program.

Again, focus on the reduction of I/O operations. User-controlled file opens and shared open data paths can be used to reduce the effect of file open and close operations. Appropriate use of the SETOBJACC command or sharing open data paths can be used to minimize the effect of I/O on your programs.

ILE PERFORMANCE ISSUES

All of the performance issues raised so far in this chapter apply to both OPM and ILE environments. But with ILE, there is even more to consider.

Never Buy at Retail Prices

The first thing you should consider when compiling an ILE program is the optimization level. The definition of the word "optimization" is "performance!" More specifically, it means maximizing the runtime performance of an object. The compiler does this amazing feat for you via the optimization techniques of the optimizing translator. These techniques look for processing shortcuts to reduce the amount of system resources used to produce the same output. Think of optimization as buying wholesale, not retail. You spend less money (resources) to get the same product (output).

You control the optimization level via the optimize parameter on the Create RPG Module (CRTRPGMOD), Create Program (CRTPGM), and Create Service Program (CRTSRVPGM) commands. Although you can specify optimizing on the CRTPGM command, the actual optimizing techniques are applied to the modules. The values allowed for the optimize parameter are as follows:

> *NONE — minimal optimizing
>
> *BASIC — some optimizing
>
> *FULL — maximum optimizing

When testing and debugging your programs, you should first compile with optimization *NONE. This is the fastest compiling option (we don't know anybody who actually gets a program up and running, bug free, in production on the first compile). Once you have the program debugged, compile it again with the *FULL optimization option and then run through your final testing before putting it into production.

There is another reason, aside from the lengthy compile time, you do not want to compile with the *FULL (or *BASIC) option while debugging a program. Because of the optimization techniques applied, you cannot change the value of a variable while in debug. Worse yet, you may not be able to display the value of a variable! And even if it shows you a value, you cannot rely on it being the correct, current value. We use debug 90 percent of the time to check on the value of a variable, so this negates the whole value of the debug process.

The reason for this inaccuracy is because the optimizer might have caused the current value of a data variable to be in a hardware register, and the debugger cannot access hardware registers. The factors used in making the determination to put a variable in a hardware register include how it is used, its size, and where in the code you have stopped. In short, you cannot rely on the value shown for a variable if you are running it with an optimization level other than *NONE.

Activation Group Therapy

The next parameter on the create commands that needs our attention is the activation group parameter, ACTGRP. This parameter accepts three options:

- ACTGRP (you name it) — You give the system the name of the activation group in which it is to run. If the activation group exists, it is used. If not, a new one is created. The activation group is not destroyed when the program ends.

- ACTGRP(*NEW) — The system creates an activation group when the program is called, and deletes it when the program ends.

- ACTGRP(*CALLER) — The program runs in the activation group in which the calling program runs.

You should *almost never* use the *NEW option. Use the user-named option instead.

The reason we say "almost never" (and not "never") is that the *NEW option does provide a method of simulating recursive calls in RPG. If Program A calls Program B, and Program B then calls Program A, the system would normally generate a recursive call error condition. If, however, Program A were compiled with the *NEW option, the call to Program A would generate a new activation group for the second copy of Program A to run in. No error message would be generated.

The Three Strategies

There are three different strategies to consider with regards to the activation group. The first option is to use a named activation group for all programs. If you create a name that is unique to your application, you provide a measure of insulation from other applications on the system.

An alternative to this method is to specify a named activation group only on the "outermost" programs (such as all programs called from the menu system). All called programs will use *CALLER, which will place them in the named activation group of the program that called them. This will put all programs in the named activation group anyway.

The third method is a variation of the second. You can use *NEW on all "outermost" programs and *CALLER on all called programs. This will get the system to generate the activation group name and all called programs to use the same generated name.

We prefer to use a named activation group because there are less maintenance worries. With methods two and three, you have to know which programs are the "outermost" and which are called. By running all programs in a uniquely named activation group, you have less chance of programmers making the wrong choice later on.

REDUCING THE SIZE OF YOUR PROGRAMS

One way to reduce memory utilization on your system is to reduce the size of the programs that are being run. Logic tells us that if the programs being loaded into memory were half the size, twice as many could fit in memory at once. There is a simple way to attain this goal without reprogramming or reducing the functionality of your system: remove program observability in your programs.

When a program is compiled, the system takes your source member and translates it into a program object the machine can read and execute. As part of the compile process, the system automatically adds in program overhead to allow the program to be debugged. This extra program overhead the compiler automatically built in is called *observabillity*.

Observability is a very valuable part of your toolbox when you are writing, implementing, and beta testing a new system. Without it, you would not be able to run Debug and it would take much longer to diagnose problems. But once a system goes into production, you are not as likely to be running Debug all of the time. Why not use the Change Program (CHGPGM) command to remove the observability and cut the size of your programs in half? You can always restore observability by recompiling the program.

The results of removing observability vary, but we have seen some programs shrink to 40 percent of their original size. To run a test for yourself, simply display the size of a program by running the Display Program (DSPPGM) command. Then use the CHGPGM command to remove observability. Running the DSPPGM command again reveals how much you were able to reduce the size of your program. In our example in Figure 1.17, we remove observability from the CUSPGM program in library TESTLIB by keying the CHGPGM command.

```
CHGPGM   PGM(TESTLIB/CUSPGM) RMVOBS(*ALL)
```

Figure 1.17: Removing program observability and reducing program size with CHGPGM.

It is not uncommon for us to run the CHGPGM command on an entire production library to remove observability. If the library is in a stable condition and is rarely changed, why would you need to retain observability? Our experience is that the end results can be somewhat dramatic on systems that do not have enough memory. How often have you worked on a system that had "too much" memory?

REDUCING SCREEN I/O IN YOUR INTERACTIVE PROGRAMS

Another way to improve overall system performance is to minimize the amount of data that must be passed to and from display panels from within your interactive programs. Rather than reduce the amount of information on the screens, you can move toward this goal by reducing redundant data.

Many interactive programs are designed to send an entire display panel full of data on every output to the screen. Sometimes, the data being sent to the screen is almost identical to the information that is already displayed, with only one or two fields or display attributes changing from the previous display. This can create a situation where there is a lot more system traffic than necessary. It is particularly noticeable if these programs are being run on terminals that are running over remote lines, where you can actually see the terminal "paint" the lines on the screen.

When a display panel is sent to the screen, display attributes, as well as the data, must be sent. These attributes control which fields are high-intensity, reverse-image, underlined, nondisplay, input-capable, and much more. There is a lot of data beyond what you see that must be sent for every screen operation.

There is a way you can code your interactive programs so only the data and attributes that have changed since the previous screen I/O operation are sent to the screen. This method involves the use of the Put with Explicit Override (PUTOVR), Override Data (OVRDTA), and Override Attribute (OVRATR) DDS keywords.

PUTOVR is a DDS record-level keyword that essentially allows the system to "look" before presenting a display panel to see what needs to be sent to the screen. If the system determines that the display panel being sent is not already on the screen, the entire panel is displayed. On the other hand, if the display panel is already displayed, only fields that have the OVRDTA or OVRATR keywords in effect are sent to the screen. Use of this technique can have a significant impact on how much data needs to be sent to the screen.

In Figure 1.18, we used the PUTOVR keyword on the FORMAT1 display panel. Note that our customer number and customer name fields both have been coded to use the OVRDTA keywords. The CUSNBR field also has been coded with the OVRATR keyword.

```
AAN01N02N03T.Name++++++RLen++TDpBLinPosFunctions++++++++++++++++++++++++++++
A          R FORMAT1
A                                    PUTOVR
A                                  1 35'Customer Lookup'
A            PGMNAM      35    B  4 25DSPATR(RI)
A                                  4  5'Customer Number:'
A            CUSNBR       5    B  4 22OVRDTA
A                                    OVRATR
A  40                                DSPATR(HI)
A            CUSNAM      35         +2OVRDTA
```

Figure 1.18: Using the PUTOVR, OVRDTA, and OVRATR DDS keywords.

When FORMAT1 is initially written to the screen, the entire display panel is sent because the system detects that FORMAT1 is not already on the screen. On subsequent output operations to the screen, only the CUSNBR and CUSNAM fields are sent because they have been coded with the OVRDTA fields. Note that the PGMNAM field has not been coded with the OVRDTA keyword because it will not change after the initial output to the screen.

Also in our example, only the CUSNBR field has been assigned the OVRATR keyword. This means that the only field on the screen with display attributes that may change after the initial display is the CUSNBR field. If the indicator controlling the High Intensity attribute (indicator 40) is turned on, the field is updated on the following output to the screen. If the OVRATR keyword was not coded with the CUSNBR field, the display attributes do not change, and the attributes in effect on the initial output operation remain in effect as long as the screen is displayed.

Indicators may be used to condition both the OVRDTA and OVRATR keywords. For that reason, you may want to go a step further than this example and condition these keywords so they are only active when the data or attributes are going to change.

SERVICE PROGRAMS CAN AFFECT PERFORMANCE

You should be aware of the performance implications involved in the use of service programs. Used correctly, they combine speed of execution with ease of maintenance. Used incorrectly, they can negatively impact performance.

Service programs load all modules in the service program into memory whenever the first module is called. The keyword here is ALL. It will even load modules into memory that are not used by the calling program! You should take this into consideration when designing a service program. The idea is to combine similar functions into a single, easy-to-maintain service program. You would not want to create a service program that contains 50 modules, even if they all performed the same functions! You could wait quite a long time for all of the modules to load. On the other hand, you would not want to create a service program with a single module either.

You need to balance the likelihood of all of the modules in a service program being needed by a calling program with the time it takes to load the modules up front. The good news is that once they are loaded, the modules stay active until the activation group ends. So even if the calling program ends, the modules are still in memory if the activation group is still active.

DO NOT OVERLOOK THE OBVIOUS

If your system is experiencing performance problems (and whose isn't?), there are a number of things you should look for prior to changing programs. Some of the same things that make the AS/400 such a wonderful computer to work on can also lead to degraded performance. Among the things that can cause degraded performance are the following:

- DASD (disk storage) that is more than 80 percent utilized. Check your utilization with the WRKDSKSTS command. The AS/400 operating system needs room to work. If it does not have enough room, the system has to work overtime trying to find the space.

- Running jobs interactively that are better suited for batch environments. This is especially true if the job in question requires heavy I/O processing. Any job that runs for more than 30 seconds and does not require operator intervention or action is a candidate for batch processing.

- Moving batch jobs to subsystems that were set up to run interactive jobs. These jobs run with the incorrect runtime attributes (priority, time-slice, and so on) and will adversely affect interactive performance.

- Inadequate memory. You are far better off having too much than too little. You may remember when 640K (640,000 bytes) was once considered to be enough for a personal computer. Just try to any of today's programs on 640K! These days, all computers require more memory in order to run. We have already shown you how to get more performance out of your system if you have enough main memory.

- Query and SQL. While these are wonderful tools, you need to ensure they are not regularly run in an interactive environment. You pay a huge performance price if users on your system abuse this privilege.

- Message logging levels. How much information is being written to your job logs? This can have an effect on system performance if more information is being recorded than is required. (You will learn all about message logging levels in chapter 10.)

- Journaling. If you use journaling, you pay a price for the overhead required. You are doubling (at least) the amount of the I/O operations required for the files undergoing journaling.

THE BLAME GAME

In the old days, we used to see numerous articles and publications that focused on the performance of RPG operation codes. These articles would give the impression that using one operation code over another would have a serious impact on system performance. While we certainly do not deny that the AS/400 performs some operations better than others, we think the dramatic increase in processing power we have seen in the last decade or so greatly offsets the minimal impact of changing RPG operation codes.

Admittedly, by competitive performance standards, the old CISC AS/400s did not perform multiplication and division functions very well. And the AS/400 can tend to lag when performing lookups on large arrays or when comparing very large fields to one another. Using file translation or the Translate (XLATE) operation code can cause delays.

But odds are that you would not be using the function if you did not need it. The time you spend searching for improved performance would be far better spent looking for I/O bottlenecks and memory over-utilization.

PERFORMANCE, PERFORMANCE, PERFORMANCE

Users simply will not be able to get fast enough performance. It is one of the rules in today's computing environment. The faster computers get, the more performance users expect. Who can blame them?

The simple truth is, the AS/400 is competing with lightning-fast, single-user systems that were not designed to run in a multi-user environment. They do not require all the excess overhead that is considered to be mandatory in the "midrange" market. Of course, they can be loaded with comparable layers of software to perform networking, database management, security, print spooling and spool management, and the multitude of other standard operating system functions we have come to expect from our beloved AS/400.

Unfortunately, most comparisons are not and will not be apples to apples. It is also difficult to imagine IBM ever aggressively marketing the AS/400. Therefore, the AS/400 will continue to be considered a dog by some in the computing world, and it probably will never get the industry-wide reputation it so richly deserves.

It is up to the people at our level to get everything out of the system that we possibly can. You should consider your quest for better performance to be your own personal search for the Holy Grail. It is not whether you arrive at your destination that is important; but instead, how much you learn along the way.

2

SUBFILES BELONG IN
EVERY PROGRAMMER'S TOOLBOX

The subfile originally appeared on the IBM System/38 as a simple method for storing data (usually a subset of a collection of database records) in memory for the purposes of presenting them as part of a display file. Like most of the System/38 operating system, the subfile was later migrated to the AS/400, where it has been greatly enhanced since that time.

A subfile is defined similarly to the way you define a database file. In fact, a subfile can be read, chained to, written to, or updated much like a database file. There are some characteristics that differentiate the subfile from the database file, however. With subfiles, you can store data in *hidden* fields—fields that are not displayed, but can be used when you process the file later. You can control which record the cursor is positioned at without having to keep track of a zillion indicators. You can present or process a group of records on the display at the same time with a single command. The list could go on and on, but the primary advantages of subfiles are speed, performance, ease of coding/maintenance, and the ability to select several records to be processed within a single operation to the workstation.

In this chapter, we cover subfile fundamentals as well as some advanced topics, and code four very different kinds of subfiles. If you are a novice programmer, you should feel comfortable working with subfiles when you complete this chapter. If you are an intermediate or advanced programmer, you may find a few gems within these pages.

THE BASICS

The two principle components of any subfile are the *control* record and the *subfile* record. Being true to its name, the control record is used to control the presentation of the subfile through a series of keywords, which are generally controlled with indicators. These keywords are used to indicate how many records are in the subfile, which function keys are allowed, how many records are displayed at one time, etc. The control record can also include input/output fields, just as with any other record format, and is often used to display the headings of each field in the subfile.

In Figure 2.1, we see a subfile presented in a DDS window. This subfile is used to help an operator select a printer when requesting a printed report or list. The control record (represented by the shaded area) presents the operator with five different options:

- Enter part or all of the printer description and press Enter to advance automatically to the description closest to the characters keyed.

- Enter a 1 in front of the desired printer record and press Enter to indicate the selected choice.

- Press the page keys to scroll forward or back through the printer description records.

- Press F12 to cancel and return to the previous screen.

- Press F3 to exit the application.

The subfile record is where we define each data field in the subfile. The fields can be specified as input, output, or hidden fields (not displayed). The example in Figure 2.2 shows that the subfile record (represented by the shaded area) has three visible fields:

- An input-capable option field (Opt) that allows the operator to indicate the desired selection.

- The printer ID (Code) that is coded as output only.

- Extended description of the printer (Description), also coded as output only.

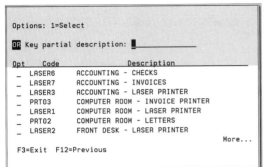

Figure 2.1: Subfile control record (shaded area).

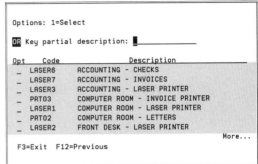

Figure 2.2: Subfile record (shaded area).

In the example in Figure 2.2, we easily could have coded the printer ID field (Code) as a hidden field and only displayed the description on the screen. The printer ID field would still be available when we went to process the subfile.

Another thing to notice in the preceding example is that the literal More... is displayed near the bottom of the screen. This indicates that pressing the Page Down key results in the presentation of a new page of subfile records. This feature is discussed in more detail under the heading "The Subfile End (SFLEND) Keyword."

THE SUBFILE RECORD FORMAT (SFL) DDS

When coding a subfile, you must always define the subfile first and then the control record. The DDS for the subfile record is similar to DDS for a database file, except that you are coding a file that will be presented to the screen and reside only in memory.

A subfile record format must have at least one display field (the exception to this rule is a message subfile, which we talk about later in this chapter). The field locations on the detail records represent the line and position of the fields as they appear on the first subfile record displayed. The system figures out where the subsequent records belong on the screen based on the value of the Subfile Page Size (SFLPAG), which is defined in the control record format.

Figure 2.3 shows the definition of a sample subfile record format. Note that the SFACCOUNT# field is defined as a hidden field with a use type of H and there are no line or position entries. This field stores data we can use later when processing the file, but the data in SFACCOUNT# is not displayed on the screen. The SFLSELECT and SFCUSTDESC fields are displayed beginning on the seventh line in positions 2 and 5, respectively.

```
.....AAN01N02N03T.Name++++++RLen++TDpBLinPosFunctions++++++++++++++++++++++++++++++
      A           R SFLRCD                   SFL
      A             SFACCOUNT#    10   H
      A             SFLSELECT     1A   B   7   2
      A             SFCUSTDESC    30A   O   7   5
```

Figure 2.3: DDS for a subfile record format.

THE SUBFILE CONTROL RECORD FORMAT (SFLCTL) DDS

The subfile control record gives you the ability to indicate how the subfile should be presented and react when various conditions present themselves. There are four record-level keywords that are mandatory for every subfile control record format (see Table 2.1).

Table 2.1: Mandatory DDS Keywords for a Subfile Control Record Format.

Keyword	Description
SFLCTL	Subfile Control. Indicates that the record format will control a subfile. It must be coded directly after the subfile record format that it is to control.
SFLDSP	Subfile Display. Indicates to the system that the subfile should be displayed when an output operation is performed on the subfile control record. An option indicator is usually coded with this keyword. If you perform an output operation to the subfile control record while this keyword is active and there are no subfile records to display, your program receives an error message. By indicating an option indicator on the SFLDSP keyword and only turning it on if there happen to be subfile records to display, you avoid the error message.
SFLPAG	Subfile Page. Describes the size of the subfile "page." Generally speaking, this keyword describes how many subfile records appear on the screen at one time. If each subfile record format takes up only one line of the screen, this number matches the number of lines on the screen taken up by the subfile (SFLPAG is 7 for the example in Figure 2.2). On the other hand, if each subfile record format uses two lines, sflpag is half the number of lines required by the display file. Note that not every subfile record must take up the same number of lines (a variable number of lines is allowed if you are using the field selection technique discussed later in this chapter).
SFLSIZ	Subfile Size. Defines the number of records in the subfile. How this keyword affects the operation of the subfile depends upon whether the Subfile Page (SFLPAG) and the Subfile Size (SFLSIZ) are equal (more on this subject later in the chapter). Depending on conditions we discuss later in this chapter, the system may change the value in this field.

The Subfile Display Control (SFLDSPCTL) keyword (described in the next section) is also required if you are performing any input operation with the subfile control record.

The rest of the keywords that can be used on a subfile control record cover a wide variety of functions. The length of the list may seem a little intimidating, but you will find that many of the keywords are rarely used. In this chapter, we cover the keywords that we feel are most pertinent. The optional subfile control keywords (as of V3R1) are listed in Table 2.2.

Table 2.2: Optional DDS Keywords for a Subfile Control Record Format.

Keyword	Description
SFLCLR	Subfile Clear. When you perform an output operation to the subfile control record with this keyword active (conditional indicators are advised), the subfile is cleared of all data. SFLCLR is similar to the Subfile Initialize (SFLINZ) keyword, except that no subfile records exist after execution of this keyword. You need to remember to turn off the conditioning indicator for the Subfile Display (SFLDSP) keyword after performing the SFLCLR operation. Failure to do so causes an error message if you try to perform a subsequent output operation to the subfile control record and you have not written any subfile records first.
SFLCSRRRN	Subfile Cursor Relative Record Number. This optional keyword is used to return (to the program) the relative record number of the subfile record where the cursor is currently positioned. The parameter for the keyword is the name of the signed numeric hidden field that you must define in the control record that is used to hold the subfile relative record number.
SFLDLT	Subfile Delete. This conditional keyword is used to delete a subfile. This operation normally is not required with most subfiles because closing the display file accomplishes the same goal. The exception to this rule is if you already have the maximum number of subfiles (12) on the screen, and you need to get rid of one to make room for another.
SFLDROP	Subfile Drop. This conditional keyword is used when the subfile record format requires more than one line on the display. When a subfile record takes more than one line on the display, it is *folded*. When an output operation is performed on the subfile control record with the SFLDROP keyword active, the subfile records are truncated so they fit on a single display line (the additional information does not appear) and more records will fit on a single page. Execution of the SFLDROP keyword on records that have already been truncated results in the display of the records in a folded state.

Table 2.2: Optional DDS Keywords for a Subfile Control Record Format (continued).

Keyword	Description
SFLDSPCTL	Subfile Display Control. This conditional keyword indicates whether the subfile control record format should be displayed when you send an output operation to it. You must use this keyword if you plan to perform any input operations on the subfile control record format (even if no fields are displayed).
SFLEND	Subfile End. Tells the system what action to take when the end of the subfile is encountered. Options on this keyword allow for a plus sign (+), More..., and Bottom, or a graphical scroll bar (on graphical displays only). We discuss SFLEND later in this chapter (see "The Subfile End (SFLEND) keyword").
CHCAVAIL	Choice Available. This option may be displayed with different attributes options that are not available. This generally only applies to graphical workstations.
CHCSLT	Choice Selected. This options may be displayed with different attributes than options that have not been selected.
CHCUNAVAIL	Choice Unavailable. This option is much like the previous two. You can control the attributes of choices that are not available to the operator.
SFLENTER	Subfile Enter. This optional keyword is used to indicate that the Enter key (or other function key) act as a Page Up key.
SFLFOLD	Subfile Fold. This optional keyword is similar to the SFLDROP keyword, except the multiple-line subfile records initially are brought up in a folded state (instead of truncated). Performing an output operation to the subfile control record format with this keyword actively switches the subfile records from a truncated to a folded state and vice versa.
SFLINZ	Subfile Initialize. Used to initialize a subfile to blanks, nulls, and zeros (depending upon the field type). The optional keyword is similar to the SFLCLR keyword, except that the subfile is initialized (records will exist) instead of cleared.
SFLLIN	Subfile Line. Used to describe multiple-column subfiles. This optional keyword can be used when you want to show more than one subfile record on a single display line. The additional parameter is used to specify how many spaces to place between the displayed records. When used, the records are written from top to bottom and then left to right. In other words, the first set of records appears top to bottom in the first column, the next set appears top to bottom in the next column, and so on.
SFLMLTCHC	Subfile Multiple Choice. Used to control the attributes of subfile selections when more than a single option is chosen. This option only applies to graphical workstations.

Table 2.2: Optional DDS Keywords
for a Subfile Control Record Format (continued).

Keyword	Description
SFLMODE	Subfile Mode. This optional keyword may be used in conjunction with the SFLDROP or SFLFOLD keywords. The required parameter is used to define a hidden field that returns whether or not the subfile is displayed presently in a folded or a truncated mode. You must define the parameter as a hidden, 1-byte alphanumeric field in the subfile control record format.
SFLMSG	Subfile Message. This conditional keyword displays a message when an output operation is performed on the subfile control record format. More on this subject later when we discuss error handling with a message subfile.
SFLMSGID	Subfile Message ID. Can be used to conditionally display messages from the specified message file when an output operation is performed on the subfile control record. We cover this in more depth when we discuss error handling with a message subfile.
SFLPGMQ	Subfile Program Queue. This optional keyword can be used in conjunction with the SFLINZ keyword to build a message subfile. The entire message subfile can be built with a single output operation on the subfile control record format. This keyword is unique because it may appear on the subfile record format or the subfile control record format.
SFLRCDNBR	Subfile Record Number. Allows you to indicate which page of the subfile should be displayed when an output operation is performed on the subfile control record format. If you do not specify this keyword, the system automatically presents the first page of the subfile to the screen. The field associated with this keyword must contain the relative record number of the subfile record you wish to see on the first page. The CURSOR parameter of this keyword can be used to indicate that the cursor is to be positioned automatically at the relative record number in question. The *TOP parameter can be used to indicate that the relative record number specified should represent the record that you wish to position at the top of the screen. If you omit this parameter, the SFLRCDNBR keyword ensures that the record specified appears somewhere on the screen.
SFLRNA	Subfile Records Not Active. Used in conjunction with the Subfile Initialize (SFLINZ) keyword to indicate that when the subfile is initialized, it is left with no active records.
SFLROLVAL	Subfile Roll Value. Used to describe an input field on the subfile control record. The operator uses the input field to indicate how many subfile records to page up or down. When this keyword is omitted, the system automatically pages the entire value specified in Subfile Page (SFLPAG).

Table 2.2: Optional DDS Keywords
for a Subfile Control Record Format (continued).

Keyword	Description
SFLSCROLL	Subfile Scroll. This field is used to return the relative record number of the subfile record at the top of the screen back to your program when scroll bars are being used. Scroll bars are an optional feature that can be specified on the Subfile End (SFLEND) keyword if you happen to be using graphical displays.
SFLSNGCHC	Subfile Single Choice. Used to control the display attributes of options that are available to be chosen. This option only applies to graphical workstations.

A sample subfile control record has been coded in Figure 2.4. Note that the SFLCTL, SFLDSP, SFLPAG, and SFLSIZ required keywords are all present. We have added SFLDSPCTL so our subfile control record is displayed when we write an output operation to the control record. Subfile End (SFLEND) was added so the literal More... or Bottom is displayed on our subfile depending on how indicator 41 is conditioned when we perform the output operation.

```
.....AAN01N02N03T.Name++++++RLen++TDpBLinPosFunctions+++++++++++++++++++++++++++++
A              R SFLCTL                        SFLCTL(SFLRCD)
A                                              SFLSIZ(0010)
A                                              SFLPAG(0010)
A                                              SFLDSP
A                                              SFLDSPCTL
A    41                                        SFLEND(*MORE)
```

Figure 2.4: DDS for a subfile control record format.

You are going to find that writing subfile programs is not that difficult. However, there are more issues that we need to discuss before we begin coding.

LOADING THE SUBFILE

You can employ two methods when loading subfiles. One method is to write enough records to fill a single page of the subfile and then execute the subfile control format. This type of subfile is generally referred to as a *page-at-a-time* subfile. The second method of loading a subfile is to write all database records to the subfile before executing the control format. We refer to this second type as a *load-all* subfile.

The load-all subfile type should *only* be used when there is a fixed, small number of records that will be displayed. Remember that these records are being written into main storage memory, and your program is not the only resource contending for that valuable space. If too many programs contend for main memory, the system spends all of its time moving objects in and out of main storage and performance suffers. Also, why perform the extra I/O required to fill the subfile? Remember that someone is sitting and waiting at the keyboard while this task is performed. Use the advice that your parents gave you and just take what you need.

If there is a large (or unknown) number of records to be written to the subfile, you should *always* use the page-at-a-time style of subfiles.

THE RELATIONSHIP BETWEEN
SUBFILE SIZE (SFLSIZ) AND SUBFILE PAGE (SFLPAG)

Regardless of whether you are employing page-at-a-time or load-all subfiles, there are two primary categories of subfiles. These types are distinguishable based on the relationship between the number of records allowed in the subfile (SFLSIZ) and the number of records to be displayed in a single subfile page (SFLPAG).

When *SFLSIZ* and *SFLPAG* Are the Same

When SFLSIZ and SFLPAG are the same, the maximum number of records allowed in the subfile can never exceed the number of records to be displayed on a single page. The SFLDROP, SFLFOLD, and SFLROLVAL keywords are invalid for this type of subfile because they refer to functions that require more than one page of records to exist in the subfile. Likewise, when an operator presses the Page Up or Page Down keys, control is always returned to the RPG program.

Field selection can be employed on this type of subfile where you use indicators to determine which fields appear in the subfile. But because the amount of data displayed is based on these indicators, the data displayed in the subfile can be inconsistent. Introducing this inconsistency in the data makes the SFLINZ, SFLLIN, SFLRCDNBR, and SFLRNA keywords invalid.

When *SFLSIZ* and *SFLPAG* Are Not Equal

When the values specified for SFLSIZ and SFLPAG are not the same, the system processes the Page Up and Page Down keys without returning control to the RPG program as long as there are records in the subfile to scroll through. When the beginning or end of the subfile is encountered within the scrolling process, control is returned to the RPG program, where the decision to write more records or perform some other function can be made.

With this type of subfile, you typically load enough records into the subfile to present a single page and then perform the output operation on the subfile control record format. If the operator presses Page Down, control is returned to the RPG program (there are no more records in the subfile to display), where your program writes an additional page of data to the subfile without clearing the original records and then repeats the process. Using this method, if the operator presses Page Up (after pressing Page Down at least once), the paging is handled entirely by OS/400 without control ever having to be returned to the RPG program until the beginning of the subfile is encountered.

Another characteristic of this type of subfile is that the subfile automatically extends itself to contain additional records if you write a subfile record with a relative record number greater than the value specified in the SFLSIZ keyword. It continues to extend itself up to 9,999 records, which is the maximum that can be specified for a subfile. It is for this reason that you want to make sure that the field you designate as the subfile relative record number is defined with enough digits to contain the potential end result.

Deciding the initial size of the subfile can be important. If SFLSIZ is too big, memory is wasted, which could hurt overall response time. If the SFLSIZ is too small, the system may be working overtime to extend the size of the subfile continuously. In general, we like to code the SFLSIZ as two or three times the SFLPAG.

THE PAGE KEYS AND THEIR RELATIONSHIP TO THE SUBFILE

As we discussed earlier, the system handles rolling when the page keys are pressed, as long as there are records remaining to be displayed. If you have coded the load-all style of subfile, you do not need to code anything to handle the page keys at all (including the ROLL and PAGE keywords in the subfile control record) because OS/400 performs the task for you.

On the other hand, if you have coded the preferred page-at-a-time subfile, you have a little more work to do. When the subfile hits the end or start of the file (depending on which page key is pressed), control is passed back to the RPG program so more records can be written.

The Page Down Key for Page-at-a-Time Subfiles

When the Page Down key is pressed and the last page of records that have been written to the subfile is displayed, control is returned to the RPG program. A new page of subfile records is then added (without clearing the previous records) and the subfile is displayed. This process continues as long as there is data left to be written to the subfile. Once the condition is reached and there is no more data with which to populate the subfile, the indicator that corresponds with the Subfile End (SFLEND) keyword is set on and the subfile is displayed once again. In Figure 2.4, indicator 41 represents the SFLEND indicator.

The Page Up Key for Page-at-a-Time Subfiles

If the user presses the Page Up key and the first page of the subfile is currently displayed, control is returned to the program. The database file must first be repositioned so the database file pointer corresponds to the first record in the subfile. To complete the setting of the database file pointer, the program must then read backwards until it has read enough records to fill a subfile page.

Because the program is rolling backwards through the data, the subfile must be cleared before writing a new set of subfile records. This is done so pages will not get out of sequence. You can do this by performing an output operation to the subfile control record with the indicators set so that either the Subfile Clear (SFLCLR) or the Subfile Initialize (SFLINZ) keyword is active at the time. You must remember to reset your indicators after clearing the subfile or you will experience problems with subsequent output requests.

After the database file pointer has been reset and the subfile has been cleared, we can loop back up as if the user had pressed the Page Down key.

CONTROLLING WHICH PAGE OF THE SUBFILE YOU SEE FIRST

When the last page of the subfile is not currently displayed and the Page Down key is pressed, the system rolls the screen to the next page in the subfile without ever returning control to the RPG program. On the other hand, if the user presses the Page Down key and the last page of the subfile is displayed, control is returned to the program. We simply continue reading the database records (as long as there are records to read) and writing to the subfile records.

Once we have loaded another page, we redisplay the subfile. The problem with this is that when a subfile is displayed, the default setting is to display the subfile from the beginning of the subfile. In other words, the first page is always initially displayed. Consequently, if we write additional pages to the subfile and perform an output operation on the subfile control record, the first page of the subfile is displayed again and it looks as if nothing happened. The user must press the Page Down key a second time (with control returning to the RPG program because subfile records already exist) to see the additional pages that were written. Fortunately, there is a solution to this problem. We can control which page of the subfile is displayed by using the Subfile Record Number (SFLRCDNBR) keyword.

To use the SFLRCDNBR keyword, define a four-character, zoned numeric field (with zero decimal positions) within the subfile control record that is used to store a subfile relative record number, as we have in Figure 2.5. Generally, we code this field as a hidden field. The program must load this field with the relative record number of a record that is in the page we want displayed. The system then displays that page, but the record corresponding to the relative record number we loaded into the SFLRCDNBR field is not necessarily at the top of the screen.

```
.....AAN01N02N03T.Name++++++RLen++TDpBLinPosFunctions+++++++++++++++++++++++++++++
A          R SFLCTL                        SFLCTL(SFLRCD)
A                                          SFLSIZ(0020)
A                                          SFLPAG(0010)
A                                          SFLDSP
A            SFLRCDNBR       4  0H         SFLRCDNBR
```

Figure 2.5: Using the SFLRCDNBR keyword.

Using the example in Figure 2.5, we can use the SFLRCDNBR keyword to control which page of the subfile is to be displayed. To use this option, we load the appropriate subfile relative record number into the SFLRCDNBR field prior to performing an output operation to the subfile control record format. If there are 30 records in the subfile and we want the third page to be displayed, we put any number between 21 and 30 into the SFLRRN field to attain our desired results.

If you want a specific record to appear at the top of the subfile screen, load the appropriate relative record number into the SFLRCDNBR field and use the *TOP parameter in the DDS. This gives you control over which specific record appears at the top of each screen.

By using the CURSOR parameter, you can also use the SFLRCDNBR field to control where the cursor is positioned within the subfile. This offers a good alternative to using the position cursor (PC) display attribute within your subfile. The problem with using the display attribute to position the cursor is that the position cursor attribute remains in effect until you update the subfile record with the conditioning indicator off. Subsequent output requests to the subfile control record may leave the cursor positioned where you no longer want it.

THE SUBFILE END (SFLEND) KEYWORD

The SFLEND keyword is used to indicate to the program operator whether there are more records that can be displayed in the subfile. This keyword is only activated when there are no more records to be written to the subfile.

When we are coding the load-all subfile, we can go ahead and set the conditioning indicator for the SFLEND keyword on from the outset because we know that all the records that will be written to the subfile are being written from the start.

But when we are coding page-at-a-time subfiles, we are only going to write records to the subfile as needed, so we do not turn the conditioning indicator on until there are no more records to write. In most cases, this means that we have reached an end-of-file condition on the database file that we happen to be loading into the subfile.

There are three different output options that can be employed when using the sflend keyword. The parameter used with the SFLEND keyword indicates to the system which output option you want to use. These optional parameters are *MORE, *PLUS, and *SCRBAR.

Using the SFLEND Keyword with the *MORE Parameter

The *MORE parameter of the SFLEND keyword is probably the most familiar because it is used to display the More... and Bottom literals on the screen. The *MORE keyword tells the system to display More... at the end of every page of the subfile unless the conditioning indicator is on *and* the last page of the subfile currently is displayed, in which case the literal Bottom is displayed. The drawback to using the *MORE parameter on the SFLEND keyword is that you must leave an entire unused line in place to display the More... or Bottom literals. This unused line directly follows the last record of the subfile (output line of the first subfile record + SFLPAG + 1 line). If you fail to leave the line blank when using the *MORE parameter, your display file will not compile.

Using the SFLEND Keyword with the *PLUS Parameter

The default option on the sflend keyword is *PLUS, where a plus sign (+) is displayed in lieu of the More... literal. When the last page of the subfile is displayed and the SFLEND conditioning indicator has been turned on, no plus sign (+) is displayed. This method can have an advantage because the extra blank display line that *MORE requires is not needed. Its intent is not as clear to some program operators, however. When present, the plus sign (+) automatically overlays the last three positions of the last subfile record on a page, which may cause a problem if you are not careful when laying out your subfile record on the screen.

Using the SFLEND Keyword with the *SCRBAR Parameter

The final output option parameter for the SFLEND keyword is *SCRBAR, where a graphical scroll bar can be utilized. This option was made available as part of V3R1 and, obviously, only applies to graphical workstations with device descriptions that support a pointer device (generally a mouse). When using the *SCRBAR parameter, you can also specify the *MORE or *PLUS parameter so the system knows which option to exercise when the application is run from a non-graphical workstation.

The scroll bar works much as it would with other graphical interfaces because it has a cursor to indicate how big the subfile is and where you are within it. The cursor can be moved with the pointing device, repositioning the subfile accordingly.

You must leave the three right-most characters in your subfile record blank to leave room for the scroll bar to appear on the screen. This restriction is similar to the extra blank line that must be left when you are using the *MORE parameter.

Figure 2.6 shows what a subfile scroll bar looks like. We code the program that presents this display later in this chapter.

The scroll bar option is a lot more attractive with load-all subfiles than with page-at-a-time subfiles. If you use page-at-a-time subfiles, the cursor within the scroll bar would represent the number of records that

```
Options: 1=Select or press ENTER to cancel

Option   State      Description
          AK       ALASKA                        ▲
  _       AL       ALABAMA
  _       AR       ARKANSAS
  _       AZ       ARIZONA
  _       CA       CALIFORNIA
  _       CO       COLORADO
  _       DE       DELAWARE                      ▼
```

Figure 2.6: Example of a subfile scroll bar.

are currently in the subfile and not those that could ultimately end up there. When used in a load-all subfile, the cursor is obviously a much better representation of where the operator is within the file.

CODING THE "CUSTOMER SUBFILE" DISPLAY FILE

Having said all that, writing the code necessary to create and display a subfile is actually fairly simple. The first subfile program we will code is a page-at-a-time subfile used to display a customer file in customer number sequence. This program is not all that functional, but it is a good example of a variety of the concepts we have been discussing.

As you can see in Figure 2.7, the program operator has the option of pressing the page keys to scroll through the customer file or pressing Enter to end the program. Every time the Page Down key is pressed, we add a new page of subfile records and perform an output/input operation (EXFMT) to the subfile control record. When the operator presses the Page Up key, our program clears the subfile (so subfile records are not written out of order), resets the database pointers, rebuilds the subfile, and performs the I/O operation.

```
                          Customer Subfile


        Press PAGE keys, or Enter to Cancel

        Customer Name            Customer Number
     JEFF'S COMPUTER CABLES          10
     SORRENTO ELECTRICAL SUPPLY      11
     ENCINITAS PAINT                 12
     BILLS MUFFLERS                  120
     JOLLYTIME LANDSCAPE             13
     RONS BUSINESS EQUIPMENT         130 015x621
     WESTONHILL PROPERTY MANAGEMENT  14
     NORTHERN LIGHTS                 140
     SOUTH BAY PLUMBING              15
     CHULA VISTA SPRINKLER SUPPLY    16
     SANTEE ELECTRICAL               17
     BAYSIDE REALTY                  18
                                                     More...
```

Figure 2.7: Sample "Customer Subfile" display.

Let's examine the subfile record and subfile control record as they have been defined in the DDS specifications shown in Figure 2.8. As required, the Subfile Record (SFLRCD) is defined before and directly prior to the Subfile Control Record (SFLCTL). The SFLCTL keyword indicates which subfile record (SFLRCD in this case) is being controlled by the subfile control record format.

```
A*****************************************************************************
A*  TO COMPILE:
A*     CRTDSPF FILE(XXXLIB/FIG28DS)
A*****************************************************************************

AAN01N02N03T.Name++++++RLen++TDpBLinPosFunctions++++++++++++++++++++++++++++++
A              R SFLRCD                     SFL
A                SFCUSTNAME   30A  0  7  2
A                SFCUSTNBR    10A  0  7 36
A              R SFLCTL                      SFLCTL(SFLRCD)
A                                            SFLSIZ(0024)
A                                            SFLPAG(0012)
A   21                                       SFLDSP
A   22                                       SFLDSPCTL
A   23                                       SFLCLR
A   24                                       SFLEND(*MORE)
A                                            ROLLDOWN(27)
A                                            ROLLUP(28)
A                SFLRCDNBR     4  OH         SFLRCDNBR
A                                        1 29'Customer Subfile'
A                                            DSPATR(HI UL)
A                                        4  5'Press PAGE keys, or Enter to-
A                                            Cancel'
A                                        6  2'   Customer Name          -
A                                            Customer Number'
A                                            DSPATR(HI UL)
```

Figure 2.8: DDS for the "Customer Subfile."

The subfile control record contains the four mandatory keywords required for every control record format: Subfile Control (SFLCTL), Subfile Display (SFLDSP), Subfile Size (SFLSIZ), and Subfile Page (SFLPAG).

Note that in our example SFLSIZ and SFLPAG have different values. SFLPAG has a value of 12 (meaning that up to 12 records appear on the screen at one time), and SFLSIZ contains 24 records (indicating that the subfile will usually consist of about two pages of data). If more than 24 records are written to the subfile, the system automatically extends the size of the subfile to the number of records needed. Users may notice, however, a slight pause in response time while the system performs this task.

We also conditioned the SFLDSP keyword (telling the system when to display the subfile records) with an indicator. If we fail to condition this keyword and an attempt is made to display subfile records when no records have been written to the subfile, the system responds with an error message. We only turn on the conditioning indicator (21) for the SFLDSP keyword if a record is written to the subfile.

The SFLDSPCTL keyword tells the system when to display the control record. This keyword is required on this subfile because we are performing input requests on the subfile control record format, and we have information on the subfile control record format that we want to display. We have conditioned the SFLDSPCTL on an indicator (22) because we do not want the subfile control record to be displayed when we perform an output operation on the subfile control record to clear the subfile.

An indicator (23) is used to condition the Subfile Clear (SFLCLR) keyword, which is only turned on when we want the subfile cleared. For the purposes of our program, this condition is met when the operator presses Page Up. Failure to properly condition this keyword could result in the subfile being cleared on each output operation to the control file record.

The status of the Subfile End (SFLEND) keyword is based on an indicator (24), which we turn on once we find the end of our customer database file. Turning on this indicator causes the Bottom literal to appear when the last page of the subfile is displayed. When all other pages are displayed, the Page Down key is enabled and the More... literal appears just below the last subfile record.

The ROLLDOWN and ROLLUP keywords are coded to set on indicators 27 and 28 (depending on which key is pressed). Note that the PAGEUP and PAGEDOWN keywords have been added as DDS keywords in place of the ROLLUP and ROLLDOWN keywords. They work exactly as their counterparts do, except that PAGEUP is the equivalent of ROLLDOWN and PAGEDOWN is the equivalent of ROLLUP.

We use the Subfile Record Number (SFLRCDNBR) field to control which subfile page is displayed. The subfile relative record number we load into the SFLRCDNBR field determines which subfile page is displayed. In this example, we have not specified any parameters for this keyword to indicate where the cursor should be (we have no input fields), and we do not care if the record we specify in the SFLRCDNBR field is at the top of the screen or not.

CODING THE "CUSTOMER SUBFILE" RPG PROGRAM

The RPG program in Figure 2.9 typifies what is involved in writing a page-at-a-time subfile. We read enough database records to fill a page of the subfile and then perform an Execute Format (EXFMT) on the subfile control record so the operator can decide what the next course of action should be. Using this approach, we are ensuring we have done the minimal number of disk I/O operations on the database file and that, initially, there is very little memory required to store our subfile. Because we cannot be absolutely certain how many records our customer database file can contain, this is the most logical method to use when designing this subfile.

```
*****************************************************************
*   TO COMPILE:
*       CRTBNDRPG PGM(XXXLIB/FIG209RG) SRCMBR(FG209RG)
*****************************************************************
FFilename++IPEASF.....L.....A.Device+.Keywords++++++++++++++++++++++++++
FFg208DS   cf   e              Workstn Sfile(SflRcd:SflRcdNbr)
FCustomer  if   e           k Disk

CLON01Factor1+++++++Opcode&ExtFactor2+++++++Result++++++++Len++D+HiLoEq
 * Setup subfile control indicators
c                     MoveA     '0100'       *In(21)

 * Stay in the loop until page keys are pressed...
c                     Dou       (*In27 = *Off) and (*In28 = *Off)
 * Load subfile
c                     Do        12
c                     Read      Customer
 * Write subfile record if valid record was read...
c                     If        not %Eof(Customer)
c                     Eval      SfCustName = CustName
c                     Eval      SfCustNbr  = Customer#
c                     Eval      SflRcdNbr  = SflRcdNbr + 1
c                     Eval      *In21 = *On
c                     Write     SflRcd
c                     Else
c                     Leave
c                     Endif
c                     EndDo
 * Determine the end-of-file condition
c     Customer#       Setgt     Customer
c                     If        not %Found(Customer)
c                     Eval      *In24 = *On
c                     endif
 * Fall out of loop and present the subfile to the display...
c                     Exfmt     SflCtl
 * If Page Up is pressed, go execute routine to reset file point
C     *IN27           CasEq     *On          RollBack
```

Figure 2.9: RPG program for the "Customer Subfile" (part 1 of 2).

```
C                       EndCs
C                       EndDO
   *
C                       Eval      *InLR = *On
   *
C      RollBack         BegSr
   * Reset DataBase File pointer using data from first record in the subf
C      1                Chain     SflRcd
C      SfCustNbr        Setll     Customer
   * Clear the subfile first...
C                       MoveA     '0010'         *In(21)
C                       Write     SflCtl
C                       MoveA     '0100'         *In(21)
C                       Clear                    SflRcdNbr
   * Read back through DataBase file to get enough records to fill a page
C                       Do        13
C                       ReadP     Customer
C                       If        %Eof(Customer)
   * Reset DataBase file pointer if beginning of file was encountered
C      *Loval           Setll     Customer
C                       Leave
C                       EndIf
C                       EndDo
C                       EndSr
```

Figure 2.9: RPG program for the "Customer Subfile" (part 2 of 2).

The first step performed in our example is to set the initial conditioning indicators for our subfile control record format. We set on the conditioning indicator (22) to display the subfile control record format so it appears on our first output operation.

We then enter a loop that populates the subfile with the first 12 records (that is, the size of our subfile page). The loop has been coded so the subfile remains active as long as the page keys are pressed. When the Enter key is pressed, the program exits the loop and the program terminates (indicator LR is set on).

By adding 1 to the SFLRCDNBR field each time we write a subfile record, we ensure that the most recent page of the subfile is always displayed. New pages of the subfile continue to be added to the subfile every time the Page Down key is pressed, until the end of the customer database file is reached. At that point, the SFLEND indicator (24) is turned on. This causes the Bottom literal to be displayed.

If the Page Up key is pressed, we execute the ROLLBACK subroutine, which clears out the subfile and repositions the database file pointer. If the subfile is not cleared, we are adding records to the subfile that are out of sequence.

To reposition the database file pointer, the ROLLBACK subroutine first chains to the very first record in the subfile that was written to get the record key that will be used to reposition the file. This is more efficient than reading backwards through either the database file or the subfile because we may have accumulated many pages of data in the subfile before the Page Up key was ever pressed. Remember that OS/400 handles the roll back process through the subfile records (without ever returning control to the RPG program) as long as there are subfile records to read.

That was not so difficult, was it? You have taken one of the most widely misunderstood and feared subjects among beginner and intermediate AS/400 programmers and made it look easy. Your confidence with subfiles should be soaring now.

Let's have some fun and move on to that window subfile with the scroll bar we saw back in Figure 2.6. But before we write our next subfile program, we need to cover a few more basic concepts. Because this is a window subfile, we will be dealing with a few DDS window keywords. We are also going to introduce you to a subfile in which the operator can perform input.

Writing Subfiles within a DDS Window

Finally! The ability to put subfiles within DDS windows was announced when V2R3 was released. Subfiles have become such a major component of our day-to-day programming that the ability to put them within a window was a very natural progression.

Even though we do not cover the DDS window keywords until the next chapter, do not let that deter you. As you can see in Figure 2.10, the code required for the purposes of this example involves only two new DDS keywords—and they are very simple. There are, however, some new issues we need to cover before getting into this next example.

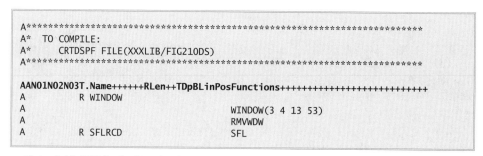

```
A*************************************************************************
A* TO COMPILE:
A*    CRTDSPF FILE(XXXLIB/FIG210DS)
A*************************************************************************

AAN01N02N03T.Name++++++RLen++TDpBLinPosFunctions+++++++++++++++++++++++++++++++
A          R WINDOW
A                                    WINDOW(3 4 13 53)
A                                    RMVWDW
A          R SFLRCD                  SFL
```

Figure 2.10: DDS for the State Lookup window subfile (part 1 of 2).

```
A   42                                      SFLNXTCHG
A              SFLRELRCD      4S 0H
A              SFLSELECT      1A  B  5   4DSPATR(HI)
A              SFLSTATE       2A  0  5 12
A              SFLDESCR      25A  0  5 19
A   R SFLCTL                               SFLCTL(SFLRCD)
A                                          OVERLAY
A                                          SFLDSP
A                                          SFLDSPCTL
A   24                                     SFLEND(*SCRBAR *MORE)
A                                          SFLSIZ(0050)
A                                          SFLPAG(0007)
A   42                                     SFLMSG('Invalid Selection Entry')
A                                          WINDOW(WINDOW)
A              SETCSRPOS      4S 0H        SFLRCDNBR(CURSOR)
A              CURCSRPOS      5S 0H        SFLSCROLL
A                                       2  2'Options:'
A                                       2 11'1=Select'
A                                          DSPATR(HI)
A                                       2 20'or press ENTER to cancel'
A                                       4  2'Option   State        Description  -
A                                            '
A                                          DSPATR(UL HI)
A   R DUMMY
A                                          KEEP
A                                          ASSUME
A                                       1  2' '
```

Figure 2.10: DDS for the State Lookup window subfile (part 2 of 2).

Reading Subfile Records That Have Changed

The fact that OS/400 can handle much of the rolling within the subfile without returning control to the RPG program poses a rather unique problem. If our subfile has more than one page of data in it, we do not know which page was displayed at the time input was performed. Nor do we know if input was performed on more than one subfile record.

We could address these potential problems by setting up a loop within our RPG program that chains through the subfile using the subfile relative record number to see if any input was keyed into our input fields. This is not very efficient, however, and does not help us if a record has been updated.

The Read Changed Record (READC) RPG op code is the answer to this particular problem. When used in conjunction with the Subfile Next Change (SFLNXTCHG) subfile record-level keyword, your program can be coded so that only modified subfile records are read.

The rub with this particular method of processing is that if your program detects an error in the entered data and the subfile is redisplayed, you will not read the record in error again unless the operator changes data on the record in error. If you condition this keyword on an indicator, you can beat this problem by setting on the option indicator and performing an UPDATE operation to the subfile record prior to the next EXFMT on the control file record format. This updates the modified data tag, and the record is read on the next READC loop whether or not the operator changes any data in the subfile record.

Don't Blank Out That Screen, Dummy!

When using the DDS window keywords, you may have already experienced the frustration of screens inexplicably being blanked out when you try to present your DDS window. If you call an external RPG program that displays a window over a previously displayed screen format, the screen displayed by the preceding program is blanked out before the window is displayed. This seems to defeat the purpose of using a window.

One solution to this problem is to add a dummy format containing the KEEP and ASSUME keywords to the display file that contains the window. Note that there is a DUMMY format in Figure 2.10 that is never called. Removing it, however, results in the problem described above.

Subfile Error Messages

This example in Figure 2.10 also uses one of the two simplest forms of subfile messages. We use the Subfile Message (SFLMSG) keyword to display error messages on the screen. When the conditioning indicator is turned on and an output operation is performed on the subfile control record format, the message text specified with the SFLMSG keyword is displayed in the message area at the bottom of the screen.

The Subfile Message ID (SFLMSGID) is the other simple subfile message method. This keyword is used like the SFLMSG keyword, except that you specify the message ID and the qualified name and location of the message file.

Because these methods include conditioning by indicators, they do not afford you a lot of flexibility. When you have programs with a large number of potential errors or you want to pass variable data into the messages, you are better off using message subfiles. We discuss these situations later in this chapter.

I'd Like Scroll Bars with That Subfile, if You Please...

As with the Subfile End (SFLEND) keyword, you can now use scroll bars for graphical workstations that have a pointing device. Because our State Lookup subfile is coded as a load-all type of subfile, it was a practical option for this example.

Notice in Figure 2.10 that we are using the *SCRBAR parameter on the SFLEND keyword. We also used the *MORE parameter so workstations that are incapable of showing the scroll bar use the More... and Bottom literals instead of the plus sign (+), which is less user friendly.

Because we are using the scroll bar, we can also demonstrate the field level Subfile Scroll (SFLSCROLL) keyword. This keyword returns the relative record number of the subfile record at the top of the screen back to your RPG program. The field to hold the returned relative record number must be coded as a five-digit, signed numeric hidden field.

CODING THE STATE LOOKUP WINDOW SUBFILE DISPLAY FILE

Let's examine the DDS in Figure 2.10 that we are using for our State Lookup window subfile program. You are already familiar with most of the keywords we will use.

This program is different from the ones we already looked at because it presents three different record formats (WINDOW, SFLCTL, and SFLRCD) to the screen at the same time.

The DDS for the WINDOW record format is simple. It only tells the system that we are using a DDS window that begins on line 3, in position 4, and that is 13 lines deep and 53 characters across. The RMVWDW keyword has been added so the system will remove existing DDS windows from the screen prior to presenting this one. Because the WINDOW keyword tells the AS/400 that this format is a DDS window, the system handles the rest of the work for you.

The Subfile Record (SFLRCD) in our example uses the Subfile Next Change (SFLNXTCHG) keyword just discussed. It also has a hidden field (SFLRELRCD) in which we store the subfile relative record number. This comes in handy when we want to control the positioning of our subfile. We then have an input-capable field called SFLSELECT, which a program operator can use to key a selection option. The other two fields are used to store the state code and description.

Our subfile control record has the standard required keywords (SFLSIZ, SFLPAG, SFLDSP, and SFLCTL). This particular subfile is coded as a load-all subfile because we know we have a small, fixed number of records that can be loaded into the subfile. The fact that there are only 50 states leaves us in a position to know the exact number of records contained in the subfile. By putting all of the records in the subfile up front, we are able to let the system handle all of the rolling for us when the page keys are pressed. Note that the Subfile Size (SFLSIZ) is 50 and the Subfile Page (SFLPAG) is 7.

We have also coded the SFLDSPCTL keyword into our control record. This is required because we will be requesting input from our subfile and because we have information in the control record we would like to display on the screen.

We use the SFLRCDNBR field to control which page of the subfile is displayed and, by loading the appropriate values into the SETCSRPOS field, where within the subfile the cursor is positioned.

The WINDOW keyword tells the system that the subfile should be presented within a window and identifies the name of the window.

CODING THE STATE LOOKUP
WINDOW SUBFILE RPG PROGRAM

As you see in Figure 2.11, it does not take very much code to get our window subfile program up and running. This window subfile routine may be called from any program you allow an operator to use to look up the valid state codes. The selected state code is returned to the calling program in the RETURNCODE parameter.

```
*****************************************************************************
*   TO COMPILE:
*      CRTBNDRPG PGM(XXXLIB/FIG211RG) SRCMBR(FG211RG)
*****************************************************************************
FFilename++IPEASF.....L.....A.Device+.Keywords+++++++++++++++++++++++++++++
FFg210DS   CF   E                  WORKSTN SFile(SflRcd:SflRelRcd)
FStates    IF   E            K DISK


DName++++++++++ETDsFrom+++To/L+++IDc.Keywords+++++++++++++++++++++++++++++++
D ReturnCode      s              2
D GetOut          s              1
```

Figure 2.11: RPG for the State Lookup window subfile program (part 1 of 2).

```
CLON01Factor1+++++++Opcode&ExtFactor2+++++++Result++++++++Len++D+HiLoEq
C     *Entry      Plist
C                 Parm                        ReturnCode

 * Perform preparatory functions
C                 Clear                       SflSelect
C                 Eval        SetCsrPos = 1
C                 Write       Window
 * Write subfile
C                 Do          50
C                 Read        States
C                 If          Not %Eof(States)
C                 Eval        SflState = State
C                 Eval        SflDescr = StateDesc
C                 Eval        SflRelRcd = SflRelRcd + 1
C                 Write       SflRcd
C                 EndIf
C                 EndDo
 * Process subfile
C                 Dou         Getout = *ON
 * Display/Read Subfile
C                 ExFmt       SFLCTL
C                 Eval        *In42 = *OFF
C                 Eval        SetCsrPos = CurCsrPos
C                 Dou         *In41 = *ON
 * Look for Record Selection Request
C                 ReadC       SflRcd
C                 If          %EOF
 * Enter was pressed without a Request
C                 Eval        GetOut = *ON
C                 Else
C                 Select
 * Record was selected
C                 When        SflSelect = '1'
C                 Eval        ReturnCode = SflState
C                 Eval        GetOut = *On
 * Record was not selected. Reposition cursor.
C                 When        SflSelect <> *Blanks
C                 Eval        *In42 = *On
C                 Eval        SetCsrPos = SflRelRcd
C                 Update      SflRcd
C                 Other
C                 Iter
C                 EndSl
C                 Leave
C                 EndIf
C                 EndDo
C                 EndDo
 *
C                 Eval        *InLR = *On
```

Figure 2.11: RPG for the State Lookup window subfile program (part 2 of 2).

The program initially writes the window record format to the screen, reads through the STATES database file, and then loads the subfile with each record read from the file. This is typical for a load-all style of subfile.

Once the subfile has been loaded, the program is ready to process and edit input from the operator. An I/O request is made of the subfile control record and the current cursor position is fed back into the SETCSRPOS field that represents our SFLRCDNBR field. This is done because we cannot know where the actual cursor position is at the time we read the control record. Remember that the system is controlling our rolling when page keys are pressed, so our current cursor position could be anywhere in the subfile.

Rather than reading all of our subfile records to see if the operator made a selection, we use READC to read only the records that have changed. If we find that no records have changed, we can assume that the operator wanted to terminate the program and simply pressed Enter without making a change.

If records have changed, there are only three possibilities:

- The operator made a valid selection by keying a 1 in front of the desired selection.

- An invalid selection was made (a value other than 1 was keyed).

- The selection field contains blanks. Note that if the operator presses Field Exit through the selection field to get down to the desired record, the selection field is tagged as having been changed even though the field has a blank in it. We account for this possibility by coding the program to ignore records in which a blank selection was made.

If the selection is determined to be in error, we set on the error indicator (42) so the SFLMSG keyword is activated and the error is displayed. We also load the relative record number of the incorrect subfile record (stored in the SFLRELRCD hidden field) into the SETCSRPOS (SFLRCDNBR) field. This causes the cursor to be positioned on the error record and ensures that the appropriate page of the subfile is displayed.

By performing an UPDATE operation on the subfile record that is in error, the record is flagged as changed the next time the subfile control record is read. If we fail to do this and the operator does not correct or change the record that we found in error, the record is not read the next time the READC operation is performed. The record remains in an error condition and is not edited again.

ERROR HANDLING WITH A MESSAGE SUBFILE

The message subfile is unique; it has been designed specifically to present error messages to the screen. It allows us to present multiple error messages in a single output operation and easily lends itself to allowing us to pass variable information into the error messages themselves. And for those of us who code a lot of subprograms, it also enables us to write an error message in one program and have it sent to the message queue of another.

In this next example, we look at an RPG program that prompts for and edits a customer number. If the customer number is deemed invalid, we use an API to send an error message to our program and output the message to our message subfile.

Figure 2.12 shows the DDS necessary to code an error message subfile. The SFLMSGRCD keyword tells the system on which line to display the error message. The SFLMSGKEY keyword tells the system if it is to display only messages with a certain message ID or all messages in the message queue. The field identified by the SFLPGMQ keyword indicates which program message queue to display. In Figure 2.13, we load this field with an asterisk (*) to indicate that the current program message queue is to be used.

```
A*******************************************************************************
A*   TO COMPILE:
A*      CRTDSPF FILE(XXXLIB/FIG212DS)
A*******************************************************************************

AAN01N02N03T.Name++++++RLen++TDpBLinPosFunctions++++++++++++++++++++++++++++++
A              R MSGSFL                      SFL
A                                            SFLMSGRCD(24)
A                MESSAGEKEY                   SFLMSGKEY
A                PROGRAMQUE                   SFLPGMQ
A              R MSGCTL                      SFLCTL(MSGSFL)
A                                            OVERLAY
A                                            SFLSIZ(3) SFLPAG(1)
A                                            SFLDSP SFLINZ
A   90                                       SFLEND
A                PROGRAMQUE                   SFLPGMQ
A              R FORMAT1
A   40                                       OVERLAY
A                                            CF03(03 'End of job')
A                                 21  3'                              -
A                                      '                              -
A                                            DSPATR(UL)
A                                 22  5'F3=Exit'
A                                  9 21'Customer Number:'
A                CUSTNUMBER    10A  B  9 38
A                                  1 27'Customer Inquiry'
A                                            DSPATR(HI)
A                                            DSPATR(UL)
```

Figure 2.12: DDS for a message subfile.

```
  ************************************************************************

  *  TO COMPILE:

  *     CRTBNDRPG PGM(XXXLIB/FIG213RG)

  ************************************************************************
  FFilename++IPEASF.....L.....A.Device+.Keywords+++++++++++++++++++++++++++++++Comments
  FFG212DS   CF  E               WORKSTN

  DName+++++++++++ETDsFrom+++To/L+++IDc.Keywords+++++++++++++++++++++++++++++++++Comments
  d Error           DS                    INZ
  d  BytesProv              1      4B 0 INZ(116)
  d  BytesAvail             5      8B 0
  d  ErrMsgId               9     15
  d  ERR###                16     16
  d  ErrMsgData            17    116

  d CowsCumHom      S               1    Inz(*off)
  d MessageKey      S               4B 0 Inz(0)
  d MsgData         S              50
  d MsgDataLen      S               4B 0 Inz(50)
  d MsgQueNbr       S               4B 0 Inz(0)
  d MessageId       S               7    Inz('CPF9898')
  d MessageFil      S              20
  d MessageTyp      S              10    INZ('*DIAG')
  d MessageQue      S              10    INZ('*')

  CLON01Factor1+++++++Opcode&ExtExtended-factor2+++++++++++++++++++++++++++++++++Comments
  c                 DoU       CowsCumHom = *On
   * Write error message subfile if error is found...
  c                 If        *In40 = *ON
  c                 Write     MsgCtl
  c                 EndIf
   * Present display file and turn off error indicator
  c                 Exfmt     Format1
  c                 Eval      *In40 = *OFF
   * Send error message to program message queue if error is found
  c                 If        CustNumber = *ALL'9'
  c                 Exsr      SendError
  c                 Else
   * Get out if no error is found
  c                 Leave
  c                 EndIf
  c                 EndDo

  c                 Eval      *InLr = *ON

   * Initialization subroutine
  csr   *InzSR      BegSr
  c                 Eval      ProgramQue = '*'
  c                 Eval      *In90 = *ON
```

Figure 2.13: RPG for a message subfile (part 1 of 2).

```
csr              EndSr

 * Send error to program message queue subroutine
csr    SendError  BegSr
c                 EVAL      MessageFil = 'QCPFMSG   ' + 'QSYS'
c                 EVAL      MsgData = 'Customer ' + CustNumber
c                           + ' is invalid.'
c                 EVAL      MsgDataLen = 50
 * Send Error Message
c                 CALL      'QMHSNDPM'
c                 PARM                  MessageId
c                 PARM                  MessageFil
c                 PARM                  MsgData
c                 PARM                  MsgDataLen
c                 PARM                  MessageTyp
c                 PARM                  MessageQue
c                 PARM                  MsgQueNbr
c                 PARM                  MessageKey
 * Error Code
c                 PARM                  Error
c                 Eval      *In40 = *ON
csr              EndSr
```

Figure 2.13: RPG for a message subfile (part 2 of 2).

Like all subfiles, the control record contains the required SFLSIZ, SFLPAG, SFLCTL, and
SFLDSP keywords. Our SFLPAG is set to 1, so only one error message line appears at a
time, but the user can position the cursor on that line and roll through any other messages
that may be in the subfile. A plus sign (+) appears on the message line if there is more
than one message.

We chose to use the SFLINZ keyword so all messages can be written to the message queue
in a single output operation. If we had not used the SFLINZ keyword, only one message at
a time could be written to the subfile message record.

The RPG code needed to write an error message to a message queue and display that
message on the screen is shown in Figure 2.13. Let's take a look at the initialization subroutine (*INZSR) first. The field PROGRAMQUE (which is the field specified on the
SFLPGMQ keyword) is loaded with an *. This indicates that the current program message
queue is to be used.

Next, the format that contains the customer input field that is to be edited is displayed. If the customer number does not pass our edit, the SENDERROR subroutine is executed, with the API sending an error to our program's message queue.

Substitution Variables in Error Messages

SENDERROR uses the global message CPF9898, which is found in every system-supplied QCPFMSG message file. It has only one data field, which is a vacant space used to supply the error to be displayed. Using the Evaluate (EVAL) op code, we construct an error message that contains the variable we want included in the body of the message.

Our program then uses the Send Program Message (QMHSNDPM) API to send the message to the message queue. The variable MessageQue contains an *, which indicates the message should be sent to this message queue. Message queue number (MsgQueNbr) indicates the number of invocation levels back you want the message sent. A 0 in this field indicates that the message is sent to the current program, a 1 means it should be sent to the previous calling program, and so on.

Once the message is written to the message queue, the write to MSGCTL format displays the error message subfile records. The Execute Format (EXFMT) of FORMAT1 redisplays the screen in error and waits for the correction from the user.

Note that the OVERLAY keyword needs to be optioned on when an error is being displayed. The normal routine the system employs when displaying a screen is to first remove everything currently on the screen and then display a new screen. Because this would erase the error message just displayed, we condition the OVERLAY keyword on the FORMAT1 screen, telling the system to leave the screen as it is and write over it with the new screen.

USING SEARCH FIELDS
IN THE SUBFILE CONTROL RECORD FORMAT

Most of the time, you want to allow the program operator the opportunity to search for or *lookup* a specific record when you want to present a database file in a subfile. This is particularly true in the case of large database files you present as page-at-a-time. Obviously, it is not productive for somebody to sit and scroll through page after page of data looking for the desired record. You may as well give him a printed list.

It is for this reason that search fields in the subfile control record format are so useful. The search field allows the program operator to key all or part of a search word/field. The keyed entry is used to reposition the database pointer so the subfile can be written with records that more closely match what the operator is looking for.

For our example (Figure 2.14), we have chosen a printer lookup window subfile program that could be easily inserted into any report or list request program. This window subfile presents the printer description records alphabetically on the screen (by printer description) and allows an end user to look up, or search for, the printer to which the printed output is sent. When a subfile record on the screen is selected (by keying the appropriate option), the printer ID is returned to the calling program in a parameter. If the operator does not see the desired record within the window, he may either press the page keys or key part of a printer description to reposition the database file (and consequently the subfile) appropriately.

For the purposes of our sample program (Figures 2.15 and 2.16), we created DDS for a physical file and a logical file that are used to describe the printers on your system. The physical file is called PRINTER, and the logical file that lets us view the file by description is called PRINTERS.

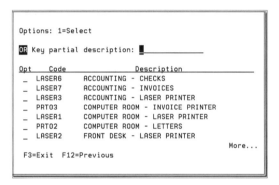

Figure 2.14: Lookup window for selecting a printer.

```
.. ..A..........T.Name++++++RLen++TDpB......Functions++++++++++++++++++++++++++++++
   A          R PRTREC                      TEXT('PRINTER DESCRIPTIONS')
   A            PRINTERID    10A             TEXT('PRINTER I.D.')
   A                                         COLHDG('PRINTER' 'I.D.')
   A            PRINTRDESC   35A             TEXT('PRINTER DESCRIPTION')
   A                                         COLHDG('PRINTER' 'DESCRIPTION')
```

Figure 2.15: DDS for the PRINTER physical file.

```
.....A..........T.Name++++++.Len++TDpB......Functions++++++++++++++++++++++++++++++
   A          R PRTREC                      PFILE(PRINTER)
   A          K PRINTRDESC
```

Figure 2.16: DDS for the PRINTERS logical file.

The DDS for this application, as seen in Figures 2.17 and 2.18, is very much the same as it would be for any window subfile you are coding. There are three basic ingredients required:

- The DDS window.
- The subfile record.
- The subfile control record.

```
A*******************************************************************************
A*  TO COMPILE:
A*    CRTDSPF FILE(XXXLIB/FIG217DS) SRCMBR(FG217DS)
A*******************************************************************************
AAN01N02N03T.Name++++++RLen++TDpBLinPosFunctions++++++++++++++++++++++++
A          R WINDOW
A                                      WINDOW(3 4 16 56)
A                                      RMVWDW
A                              15  2'F3=Exit  F12=Previous'
A                                      DSPATR(HI)
A          R SFLRECORD               SFL
A            HIDDENKEY1   12A  H
A            SFLOPTION     1A  B  7  2DSPATR(HI UL)
A            SFLPRINTID   10A  O  7  5
A            SFLDESCRIP   40A  O  7 16
A          R SFLCONTROL                SFLCTL(SFLRECORD)
A                                      ROLLUP(95)
A                                      ROLLDOWN(96)
A                                      CA03(03 'EOJ')
A                                      CA12(12 'PREVIOUS')
A                                      BLINK
A  40                                  ALARM
A                                      OVERLAY
A                                      PUTOVR
A  21                                  SFLDSP
A  22                                  SFLDSPCTL
A  23                                  SFLCLR
A  24                                  SFLEND(*MORE)
A                                      SFLSIZ(0007)
A                                      SFLPAG(0007)
A  40                                  SFLMSG('Invalid option selected'
A                                      WINDOW(WINDOW)
A                               2  1'Options:'
A                               2 10'1=Select'
A                                      DSPATR(HI)
A                               4  1'OR'
A                                      DSPATR(RI)
A                               4  4'Key partial description:'
A            SEARCHDESC   15A  B  4 29DSPATR(HI)
A  76                                  DSPATR(PC)
A                                      OVRATR
```

Figure 2.17: DDS for the printer lookup window (part 1 of 2).

```
A                           6 1'Opt    Code              ,     Desc
A                             tion                  ,
A                             DSPATR(UL)
A        R DUMMY
A                             KEEP
A                             ASSUME
A                           1 2' '
```

Figure 2.17: DDS for the printer lookup window (part 2 of 2).

```
*****************************************************************
*  TO COMPILE:
*     CRTBNDRPG PGM(XXXLIB/FIG218RG) SRCMBR(FG218RG)
*****************************************************************
FFilename++IPEASF.....L.....A.Device+.Keywords++++++++++++++++++++++++++++Comments
FFG217DS   CF  E              Workstn SFile(SflRecord:SflRelRec)
FPrinters  IF  E           K Disk    UsrOpn

DName+++++++++++ETDsFrom+++To/L+++IDc.Keywords++++++++++++++++++++++++++++Comments
D ReturnCode     S              2
D Filecode       S              4
D PassCode       S             10
D NextFormat     S              5
D Reset          S              1
D SflRelRec      S              7 0
D X              S              2 0
D Y              S              2 0

 * Parameter Descriptions
 *
 * ReturnCode: Code to return after lookup operation is performed.
 *             03 = End of Job Requested
 *             12 = Previous screen requested
 *             50 = Record was selected & record key is in the PASKEY
 *
 * FileCode:   File to perform lookup operation on
 *
 * PassCode:   Key Value to return if lookup operation is successful
 *
CL0N01Factor1+++++++Opcode&ExtExtended-factor2++++++++++++++++++Comments++
C      *ENTRY      PLIST
C                  PARM                    ReturnCode
C                  PARM                    FileCode
C                  PARM                    PassCode
 *
C                  DoU       ReturnCode <> *BLANKS
C      NextFormat  CasEQ     'FMT1 '       @Format1
C                  EndCS
```

Figure 2.18: RPG specifications for the LOOKUP program (part 1 of 4).

```
C                    EndDo
 **
C                    Eval      *InLr = *ON
 *
 *****   Subroutine: "*InzSr"  *****************************************
 ***   Process Initialization Routine  ******************************
CSR   *INZSR       BegSr
 * Only open the file you need
C                    If        FileCode = 'PRT'
C                    Open      Printers
C                    EndIf
 *
C                    Clear                 ReturnCode
 * Set DataBase File Pointers
C                    Eval      Reset = *ON
C                    ExSr      FileSet
 * Populate Subfile
C                    ExSr      LoadSfl
C                    MOVE      'FMT1 '       NextFormat
CSR                  EndSr

 *****   SUBROUTINE: "@Format1"  ***********************************
 ***   PROCESS SUBFILE FORMAT    ***********************************
CSR   @Format1     BegSr
 *
C                    If        (*In95 = *OFF) and (*In96 = *OFF)
C                    Write     Window
C                    EndIf
C                    MoveA     '10'          *IN(22)
C                    ExFmt     SflControl
C                    MoveA     '0000'        *IN(38)
 * If Page Up was pressed, page back through the DataBase records
C                    If        *In96 = *ON
C                    ExSr      RollBack
C                    LeaveSr
C                    EndIf
C                    Eval      *In97 = *OFF
 * If Page Down was pressed, page forward through the DataBase records
C                    If        *In95 = *ON
C                    If        *In24 = *OFF
C                    ExSr      LoadSfl
C                    EndIf
C                    LeaveSr
C                    EndIf
 * If a search description was keyed, reposition DataBase file pointer
C                    IF        SearchDesc <> *BLANKS
C                    ExSr      FileSet
C                    ExSr      LoadSfl
C                    LeaveSr
C                    END
 * If F3 was pressed, Exit program
C                    IF        *In03 = *ON
```

Figure 2.18: RPG specifications for the LOOKUP program (part 2 of 4).

```
C                    Eval        ReturnCode = '03'
C                    LeaveSr
C                    EndIf
 * If F12 was pressed, return to previous operation
C                    IF          *In12 = *ON
C                    Eval        ReturnCode = '12'
C                    LeaveSr
C                    EndIf
 * Read subfile for records changed to see if a record was selected
C                    Dou         *In47 = *ON
C                    Readc       SflRecord                       47
C                    If          not %EOF
 * Sound alarm & position cursor if option keyed is not a "1" or blanks
C                    If          (SflOption <> '1') and
C                                (SflOption <> ' ')
C                    Eval        *In40 = *ON
C                    Update      SflRecord
C                    Else
 * If a "1" was keyed, pass selection back to calling program. If blank
 * were keyed, return to calling program with no selection made.
C                    If          SflOption = '1'
C                    Eval        PassCode = HiddenKey1
C                    Eval        ReturnCode = '50'
C                    Leave
C                    EndIf
C                    EndIf
C                    EndIf
C   N40              EndDo
CSR                  EndSr

 *****    SUBROUTINE: "LoadSfl" **************************************
 ***   BUILD SUBFILE AND DISPLAY WITH SCREEN 1   ********************
CSR    LoadSfl       BegSr
 * Clear subfile
C                    Eval        SflRelRec = 0
C                    MoveA       '0010'        *IN(21)
C                    Write       SflControl
 * Read DataBase records and populate subfile
C      1            Do          7             X
C                    ExSr        ReadFwd
C                    If          *In24 = *OFF
C                    Eval        SflRelRec = SflRelRec + 1
C                    Eval        *In21 = *ON
C                    Eval        SflOption = *BLANKS
 * FileCode indicates which DataBase file is being processed
C                    If          FileCode = 'PRT '
C                    Eval        HiddenKey1 = PrtrID
C                    Eval        SflPrintId = PrtrID
C                    Eval        SflDescrip = PrtDsc
C                    EndIf
C                    WRITE       SflRecord
C                    EndIf
```

Figure 2.18: RPG specifications for the LOOKUP program (part 3 of 4).

```
C  N24              EndDo
C                   Clear                    SearchDesc
CSR                 EndSr
 *****     SUBROUTINE: "RollBack" ****************************************
 ***   ROLL DOWN PROCESSING FOR SUBFILE  ******************************
CSR    RollBack     BegSr
C                   Eval      *In24 = *OFF
C                   Eval      Y = SflRelRec + 8
C      1            Do        Y          X
C                   ExSr      ReadBack
C                   If        *In24 = *ON
C                   Eval      Reset = *ON
C                   ExSr      FileSet
C                   EndIf
C  N24              EndDo
C                   ExSr      LoadSfl
CSR                 EndSr
 *****     SUBROUTINE: "FileSet" *****************************************
 ***   SET READ POSITIONING FOR SUBFILE  ******************************
CSR    FileSet      BegSr
C                   If        FileCode = 'PRT '
 * If Reset is on, reset DataBase pointer to the beginning of the file
C                   If        Reset = *ON
C                   Clear                    SearchDesc
C                   EndIf
C                   Eval      PrtDsc = SearchDesc
C      PrtDsc       Setll     PRTREC
C                   EndIf
C                   Eval      Reset = *OFF
CSR                 EndSr
 *****     SUBROUTINE: "ReadFwd" *****************************************
 ***   READ FORWARD THROUGH THE FILE       *****************************
CSR    ReadFwd      BegSr
C                   If        FileCode = 'PRT '
C                   Read      PRTREC                              24
 * If end-of-file condition encountered, reset DataBase file pointer
 * to reset end-of-file condition
C                   If        %EOF
C      *HIVAL       SetGT     PRTREC
C                   EndIf
C                   EndIf
CSR                 EndSr
 *****     SUBROUTINE: "ReadBack" ****************************************
 ***   READ BACKWARDS THROUGH THE FILE       ***************************
CSR    ReadBack     BegSr
C                   If        FileCode = 'PRT '
C                   ReadP     PRTREC                              24
C                   EndIf
CSR                 EndSr
```

Figure 2.18: RPG specifications for the LOOKUP program (part 4 of 4).

Subfiles over Database Files with Keys That Are Not Unique

Sometimes it is necessary to write a subfile program over a file path where there is no key or where the key is not unique. If you have written a page-at-a-time subfile and you need to reset the database pointer because the Page Up key has been pressed, you have a problem.Because you probably do not know where the file pointer currently is, unless you count how many times the Page Down key is pressed, you cannot simply read backwards.

A file whose path is alphabetical by name is one instance in which there may be more than one record with the same key. After all, there are a lot of people named Jones. Because the first thing the roll back subroutine must do is position the pointer of the database file, this can present a problem when you are paging backwards and one of the duplicate keys is represented by the first record in the subfile. The question is, at which of the duplicate database records is the correct record to position the read/write heads? If you do not position the read/write heads to the correct record, database records are skipped or duplicated when you are rolling backwards.

The solution to this problem is to keep track of the relative record number of the database record at the time it is written to subfile. We do not want to display this number on the screen, but use it only when rolling. This is accomplished by using a hidden field in the subfile.

The relative record number of the database file can be found in positions 397 to 400 of the file information data structure (INFDS). In Figure 2.19, this field is named DBASERRN in the data structure INFO. (The file information data structure is defined by the INFDS line immediately following the file definition statement.) We then move this field into a hidden field in our subfile.

```
FFilename++IPEASF.....L.....A.Device+.Keywords++++++++++++++++++++++++++++Comments
FDISPLAY   CF  E                WORKSTN SFILE(SFLRCD:RRN)
FFILENAME  IF  E           K DISK     INFDS(INFO)
DName++++++++++ETDsFrom+++To/L+++IDc.Keywords++++++++++++++++++++++++++++++Comments
D INFO            DS
D  DBaseRRN              397    400B 0
```

Figure 2.19: Retrieving the relative record number of a database file.

During the roll back subroutine, chain to the first subfile record and then establish a loop to read the database file until the hidden field relative record number equals the relative record number of the database record. Once this is done, the read/write heads are positioned on the correct record.

HOORAY FOR SUBFILES!

Subfiles are one of the most powerful tools in the AS/400 programmer's arsenal. They are both versatile and effective, and we hope you appreciate and value them as much as we do.

3

WE DO WINDOWS
(AND MENU BARS, TOO)!

U nless you have had your head buried in the sand for the last five or 10 years, you
have noticed that while many RPG shops are still cranking our green-screen code,
everyone else is using sexy operating systems like Windows NT and Linux. Is character-based computing dead? Probably. But that is not such a bad thing. UI, or *user interface*, is not what the AS/400 does best, anyway. What it does do best is manage and
process data in a stable and reliable environment. We could go on and on about how almost every Fortune 1000 company has AS/400s or how Bill Gates does his billing on the
AS/400, but that is not what this chapter is all about.

What this chapter *is* about is telling you that there are millions of green-screen interactive
programs that are working just fine. As a matter of fact, they will be doing so for many
years to come. Why is that? The reason is simple. The cost of replacing thousands of
"dumb" terminals combined with the cost of rewriting all the user interfaces simply cannot be justified. Until it reaches a point where the gain in productivity outweighs the cost
of performing such a change, the status quo shall remain. It is a straightforward business
decision.

There are some things you can do to make your applications a little more up-to-date, however. You can employ "screen scraper" technologies that allow you to create GUI interfaces that are mapped to the 5250 data stream. Or you can write RPG applications that allow you, by generating HTML, to present your user interface through a browser. Both of these solutions let you run in a "mixed" environment, where dumb terminals co-exist with intelligent workstations.

But if you only wish to spice up your existing applications, you can do so by employing some of the DDS enhancements that have been introduced in the last several years.

HOW TO ENHANCE YOUR GREEN SCREENS

Since Version 2 of OS/400, we have seen the announcement of a variety of DDS keywords that support DDS windows, menu bars, scroll bars, radio buttons, and so on. This chapter demonstrates how to use a variety of the new DDS functions that have been announced over the last several years. A list of the topics covered includes the following:

- Hardware configuration and its effect on GUI applications:
  - The equipment you are using will determine what "look" you get.
  - What options work with which equipment?
- Pull-down menu bars:
  - Radio buttons.
  - Choice options.
  - Shortcut keys.
  - Accelerator keys.
  - Choice filters.
  - Setting choice defaults.
- DDS windows:
  - Borders and colors.
  - Window placement.
  - Message lines.
  - Restoring the display.
  - Sample DDS window program.
- Scroll bars:
  - Using scroll bars on your subfiles.

HARDWARE AND ITS EFFECT ON ENHANCED DDS APPLICATIONS

Before you begin writing enhanced DDS applications, you need to be aware that the actual format of the display presented to the user is dependent upon the hardware configuration. Older workstations and controllers were not designed or manufactured with a graphical user interface in mind.

When IBM began to employ the newer DDS functions in OS/400, it still had to make allowances for the millions of dollars worth of older equipment that was already in place. It was forced to consider the older workstations and workstation controllers attached to the 200,000 or 300,000 AS/400 systems that were already installed at the time (as we write this chapter, there are some 600,000 AS/400s installed worldwide).

Consequently, the look and feel of the new DDS functions vary widely depending on the equipment you happen to be running. We compiled a table of the equipment possibilities as of V3R1. Table 3.1 shows the possible configurations and how each function appears.

Table 3.1: Hardware Configurations and Workstations.

Configuration	Selection Fields	Selection Lists
GUI-Programmable Workstations[1]	GUI[2]	Bar selection cursor. Possible check boxes for multiple-choice lists. Possible radio buttons for single-choice lists.
InfoWindow II Display Stations[3] Attached to Enhanced Interface Controller[4]	Character-based GUI[5]	Bar selection cursor. Possible check boxes for multiple-choice lists. Possible radio buttons for single-choice lists.
3477 Display Station Attached to Enhanced Interface Controller[4]	Mnemonics (shortcut keys); bar selection cursor.	Bar selection cursor. Input field to left of list.
5250 Display Station Attached to Enhanced Interface Controller[4]	Bar selection cursor.	Bar selection cursor. Input field to left of list.
ASCII Display Station Attached to ASCII Controller Supporting Enhanced Interface[6]	Bar selection cursor.	Bar selection cursor. Input field to left of list.

Table 31.: Hardware Configurations and Workstations (continued).		
Configuration	**Selection Fields**	**Selection Lists**
Any Display Station Attached to Controller Not Supporting Enhanced Interface [7]	Entry field driven.	Input field to left of list.

NOTES:

[1] For example, RUMBA/400.

[2] GUI shows as solid-line window borders.

[3] InfoWindow II display stations: 3486, 3487, 3488.

[4] Twinaxial controllers: 5494 Release 1.1, features 6050, 2661, 9146, and 9148.

[5] Character-based GUI, except lines are created using characters.

[6] ASCII controllers that support enhanced interface: features 6041, 6141, 2637, 9145, and 9147.

[7] For example, 5250 display stations attached to 5294 and 5394 controllers or features 2638, 6040, and 6140. Another example: Client Access/400—PCs emulating a controller with an attached 5250 display station.

MY SCREEN STILL DOESN'T LOOK RIGHT

Normally, display files are created with the default for the ENHDSP, which is *YES. This means that if the display station is capable of enhanced interfaces, they are automatically used. In other words, window borders and menu bar separators are presented graphically on a graphical display. This parameter can be overridden or changed with the OVRDSPF and CHGDSPF commands, respectively. Make sure this parameter is *YES.

If you are showing formats that use ENHDSP *YES and ENHDSP *NO, all formats display as if ENHDSP *NO is active (no graphics).

If you are using User Interface Manager (UIM) help with a file that has ENHDSP(*YES) specified, the display changes from graphical to character-based.

A window is always displayed as though ENHDSP(*NO) is specified if the window is placed in the first or last column on the screen.

Some PCs ignore the window border and menu bar separator keywords, even if they support the enhanced interface.

THE MENU BAR

A menu bar is a horizontal row of keywords found at the top of your screen, as shown in Figure 3.1. Pressing a function key or using a mouse pointer device draws the cursor to

72

the top of the screen, and an operator can *pull down* a menu of functions that are generally associated with the selected keyword on the menu bar. An example of a pull-down menu is shown in Figure 3.2.

```
(FUNCTIONS)    (COMMUNICATE)    (PRINTING)


                       Customer Inquiry



                 Customer Number: _____








   F3=Exit  F12=Previous
```

Figure 3.1: Example of a GUI menu bar.

```
[FUNCTIONS]    (COMMUNICATE)    (PRINTING)

   Display Job
   Work W/Submitted    Customer Inquiry
   Joblogs
   Disconnect Job

                 Customer Number: _____








   F3=Exit  F12=Previous
```

Figure 3.2: Example of a pull-down menu.

73

The row of text at the top of the screen with the menu keywords (FUNCTIONS), (COMMU-NICATE), and (PRINTING) constitutes the menu bar in Figure 3.1. Positioning the cursor on one of these phrases (using a mouse pointer/mouse button or the F10 function key and pressing the Enter key) displays a pull-down menu of functions you can perform. An example of the result appears in Figure 3.2.

Functions on a pull-down menu are usually executed by positioning the cursor on one of the listed functions and pressing the Enter key or mouse button again (generally referred to as point and click).

DDS KEYWORDS FOR CODING THE MENU BAR

Table 3.2 contains DDS keywords that are associated with menu bars. While we have included all of the keywords, only a few are necessary to produce a workable menu bar. The rest provide more functionality, but are not necessarily required.

Table 3.2: Menu Bar DDS Keywords.

Keyword	Keyword Text	Description
CHCACCEL	Choice Accelerator Text	Specify text for accelerator function key.
CHCAVAIL	Choice Attribute Available	Specify the color or attribute when displaying choices.
CHCCTL	Choice Control	Control availability of the choices.
CHCSLT	Choice Selected Attribute	Specify the color or display attribute when a choice is selected.
CHCUNAVAIL	Choice Unavailable	Specify the color or display attribute for unavailable choices.
CHOICE	Selection Field Choice	Define a field for a selection choice.
MLTCHCFLD	Multiple Choice Selection Field	Define a multiple-choice selection field.
MNUBAR	Menu Bar	Define a menu bar.
MNUBARCHC	Menu Bar Choice	Define a choice for a menu bar field.
MNUBARDSP	Menu Bar Display	Display a menu bar.
MNUBARSEP	Menu Bar Separator	Specify the color, attribute, or character of the menu bar separator character.

Table 3.2: Menu Bar DDS Keywords (continued).

Keyword	Keyword Text	Description
MNUBARSW	Menu Bar Switch	Assign a function key to toggle between menu bar and user screen.
MNUCNL	Menu Cancel Key	Assign a function key to cancel the menu bar or pull-down menu.
PULLDOWN	Pull Down Menu	Define a format as a pull-down menu.
SNGCHCFLD	Single Choice Field	Define a single-choice selection field.

The DDS required to code the display file with the menu bar shown in Figures 3.1 and 3.2 is shown in Figure 3.3. We first coded a couple of file-level keywords that control access to the menu bar. MNUBARSW is a keyword that allows you to define a function key that, when pressed, toggles between your format and the menu bar.

```
A*******************************************************************************
A*  TO COMPILE:
A*     CRTDSPF FILE(XXXLIB/FIG303DS) SRCMBR(FG303DS)
A*******************************************************************************
AAN01N02N03T.Name++++++RLen++TDpBLinPosFunctions++++++++++++++++++++++++++
A                                      DSPSIZ(24 80 *DS3)
A                                      MNUBARSW(CA10)
A                                      MNUCNL(CA12 12)
A          R FMTC
A                                      CF03(03 'End of job')
A                                      OVERLAY
A                                      MNUBARDSP(MENUBAR1 &MENUCHOICE &PUL-
A                                      LINPUT)
A            MENUCHOICE     2Y OH
A            PULLINPUT      2S OH
A                                    4 27'Customer Inquiry'
A                                      DSPATR(HI)
A                                    9 21'Customer Number:'
A            CUSTNUMBER    10A  B   9 38DSPATR(PC)
A                                   22  5'F3=Exit'
A                                      COLOR(BLU)
A                                   22 14'F12=Previous'
A                                      COLOR(BLU)
A          R MESSAGESFL                SFL
A                                      SFLMSGRCD(24)
A            MESSAGEKEY                SFLMSGKEY
A            PROGRAMQUE                SFLPGMQ
A          R MESSAGECTL                SFLCTL(MESSAGESFL)
A                                      OVERLAY
```

Figure 3.3: Sample DDS for the menu bar in Figures 3.1 and 3.2 (part 1 of 2).

```
A                                          SFLSIZ(3) SFLPAG(1)
A                                          SFLDSP SFLINZ
A    90                                    SFLEND
A              PROGRAMQUE                  SFLPGMQ
A    R MENUBAR1
A                                          MNUBAR
A              MENUFIELD      2Y 0B  1 2CHCSLT((*COLOR TRQ))
A                                          MNUBARCHC(1 SYSREC '(FUNCTIONS)')
A                                          MNUBARCHC(2 COMREC '(COMMUNICATE)')
A                                          MNUBARCHC(3 PRTREC '(PRINTING)')
A    R SYSREC
A                                          PULLDOWN(*NOSLTIND)
A                                          WDWBORDER((*COLOR GRN) (*DSPATR RI)-
A                                          (*CHAR '           '))
A              SYSTEMFLD      2Y 0B  1 2SNGCHCFLD
A                                          CHECK(ER)
A                                          CHOICE(1 '>Display Job')
A                                          CHOICE(2 '>Work W/Submitted')
A                                          CHOICE(3 '>Joblogs')
A                                          CHOICE(4 'D>isconnect Job')
A    R COMREC
A                                          PULLDOWN
A              COMFIELD       2Y 0B  1 3MLTCHCFLD
A                                          CHOICE(1 '>Passthrough')
A                                          CHOICE(2 '>Establish Communication')
A                                          CHOICE(3 '>Send Message')
A                                          CHOICE(4 '>Delete Communication')
A                                          CHCCTL(1 &CHOICFLD1)
A                                          CHCCTL(2 &CHOICFLD2)
A                                          CHCCTL(3 &CHOICFLD3)
A                                          CHCCTL(4 &CHOICFLD4)
A              CHOICFLD1      1Y 0H
A              CHOICFLD2      1Y 0H
A              CHOICFLD3      1Y 0H
A              CHOICFLD4      1Y 0H
A    R PRTREC
A                                          PULLDOWN(*NOSLTIND)
A                                          WDWBORDER((*COLOR GRN) (*DSPATR RI)-
A                                          (*CHAR '           '))
A              PRINTFIELD     2Y 0B  1 2SNGCHCFLD
A                                          CHECK(ER)
A                                          CHOICE(1 '>Work Writers')
A                                          CHOICE(2 'Work >Spool Files')
A                                          CHOICE(3 'Work >Outqueues')
```

Figure 3.3: Sample DDS for the menu bar in Figures 3.1 and 3.2 (part 2 of 2).

In our example, the cursor automatically moves to the first phrase in the menu bar (FUNCTIONS) if the cursor is positioned on the customer number field and F10 is pressed. On the other hand, if the cursor is on the menu bar and F10 is pressed, it moves to the customer number field.

The MNUCNL keyword provides a function key that cancels a pull-down menu. In our example, pressing F12 cancels the pull-down menu request.

Next, we need to name the format on which we are going to place the menu bar. The keyword for that is MNUBARDSP. This keyword has two possible formats: one for records that have the MNUBAR keyword and one for records that do not have the MNUBAR keyword. Because we have chosen to define the menu bar as a separate record with the MNUBAR keyword on another format, we use the second format of the MNUBARDSP keyword:

```
MNUBARDSP(Menu bar record &Choice field &Pull down input)
```

or

```
MNUBARDSP(&Pull down input)
```

Parameter Definitions:

Menu bar record: The name of the menu bar format to be displayed when this record is written to the screen.

Choice field: Field name our RPG program can use to determine which option the user selected. This field must be defined on the format as a two-digit hidden field with a Y in position 35 and zero decimal positions.

Pull down input: Optional. If used, it must be defined as a two-digit, zoned numeric hidden field. It can be used to retrieve the option that was selected on the pull-down menu when the pull-down menu contains only a single-choice selection field.

You designate a format as a menu bar by using the MNUBAR keyword. A format with this keyword specified must also contain a field with at least one MNUBARCHC keyword:

```
MNUBAR(*Separator OR *Noseparator)
```

Parameter Definitions:

*SEPARATOR/*NOSEPARATOR: An optional parameter is available with this keyword to indicate whether a separator line should be placed below the last line of the menu bar choices. *SEPARATOR is the default.

The MNUBARCHC keyword does most of the work. The format for this keyword is:

```
MNUBARCHC(choice field, PullDown format name, choice text, return
field)
```

Parameter Definitions:

Choice field: Provides a number that is returned to the program (in the choice field) to indicate which option was selected.

PullDown format name: Names the window format that is presented if the user selects this choice.

Choice text: The phrase that is displayed to represent this choice.

Return field: Optional parameter. It specifies whether control is returned to the application when a menu bar choice is selected (instead of automatically presenting the pull-down format). The field must be defined as two-digit, zero-decimal, zoned, and hidden. Possible values are:

0   No selection made.

n   Choice number in the pull-down menu.

-1   Pull-down record contains something other than a single-choice selection field. Read the pull-down format to determine the actual selection made.

The actual pull-down menu that appears is a record format that has been coded with the PULLDOWN keyword.

```
PULLDOWN(*SLTIND OR *NOSLTIND *NORSTCSR OR *RSTCSR)
```

Parameter Definitions:

*SLTIND/*NOSLTIND: Specifies whether selection indicators (such as radio buttons) should be displayed. *SLTIND is the default.

*NORSTCSR/*RSTCSR: Specifies whether functions should be restricted when the cursor is outside the window. If *NORSTCSR is specified, the window function keys will operate regardless of where the cursor is located. If *RSTCSR is specified and a function key is pressed while the cursor is outside the window, you hear a beep and the cursor is placed inside the window. Control is not returned to the program at this time.

CODING RPG FOR MENU BARS AND PULL-DOWN MENUS

The RPG needed for processing a menu bar is straightforward, as shown in Figure 3.4. The field we named MenuChoice is checked to determine which format to read. Each format has a different choice field that is checked to determine which option was selected.

```
***********************************************************************
*   TO COMPILE:
*     CRTBNDRPG PGM(XXXLIB/FIG34RG)
***********************************************************************

FFilename++IPEASF.....L.....A.Device+.Keywords++++++++++++++++++++++++++++++Comments++
FFIG33DS   CF   E            WORKSTN

DName++++++++++ETDsFrom+++To/L+++IDc.Keywords++++++++++++++++++++++++++++++Comments++
D One             S         1

CLON01Factor1+++++++Opcode&ExtExtended-factor2+++++++++++++++++++++++++++++Comments++
C                   EVAL      ChoicFld1 = 0
C                   EVAL      ChoicFld2 = 0
C                   EVAL      ChoicFld3 = 0
C                   EVAL      ChoicFld4 = 0
C                   EXFMT     FMTC
C                   EXSR      MENUSL
C                   EVAL      *INLR = *ON
C     MENUSL        BEGSR
C                   SELECT
 * System functions
C                   WHEN      MenuChoice = 1
C                   READ      SYSREC                              68
 * Display Job
C                   IF        SystemFld = 1
C                   CALL      'SYSJOB'
C                   PARM      '1'         One
C                   ENDIF
 * Work with submitted jobs
C                   IF        SystemFld = 2
C                   CALL      'SYSJOB'
C                   PARM      '2'         One
C                   ENDIF
 * Work with job logs
C                   IF        SystemFld = 3
C                   CALL      'SYSJOB'
C                   PARM      '3'         One
C                   ENDIF
 * Disconnect job
C                   IF        SystemFld = 4
C                   CALL      'SYSJOB'
C                   PARM      '4'         One
```

Figure 3.4: The RPG program used to present a menu bar (part 1 of 2).

```
C                   ENDIF
 * Communications
C                   WHEN      MenuChoice = 2
C                   READ      COMREC                          68
 * Display station passthrough
C                   IF        ChoicFld1 = 1
C                   CALL      'COMJOB'
C                   PARM      '1'          One
C                   ENDIF
 * Establish communications
C                   IF        ChoicFld2 = 2
C                   CALL      'COMJOB'
C                   PARM      '2'          One
C                   ENDIF
 * Send message
C                   IF        ChoicFld3 = 3
C                   CALL      'COMJOB'
C                   PARM      '3'          One
C                   ENDIF
 * Delete commuications stuff
C                   IF        ChoicFld4 = 4
C                   CALL      'COMJOB'
C                   PARM      '4'          One
C                   ENDIF
 * Printing
C                   WHEN      MenuChoice = 3
C                   READ      PRTREC                          68
 * Work with writers
C                   IF        PrintField = 1
C                   CALL      'PRTJOB'
C                   PARM      '1'          One
C                   ENDIF
 * Work with spooled files
C                   IF        PrintField = 2
C                   CALL      'PRTJOB'
C                   PARM      '2'          One
C                   ENDIF
 * Work with output queues
C                   IF        PrintField = 3
C                   CALL      'PRTJOB'
C                   PARM      '3'          One
C                   ENDIF
C                   ENDSL
C                   ENDSR
```

Figure 3.4: The RPG program used to present a menu bar (part 2 of 2).

This program is presented for the purposes of this example only. The CL programs to actually provide the functions on the pull-down windows are not shown.

SINGLE-CHOICE, PULL-DOWN MENUS

A single-choice selection screen contains a fixed number of choices from which only one choice or option is allowed. The choices appear as a vertical list. You indicate a single-choice field by using the SNGCHCFLD keyword. The format is shown below:

```
SNGCHCFLD((*RSTCST OR *NORSTCSR) (*NOAUTOSLT OR *AUTOSLT OR
*AUTOSLTENH) (*NOSLTIND OR *SLTIND) (*NOAUTOENT OR *AUTOENT OR
*AUTOENTNN) (*NUMCOL NUMBER OF COLUMNS) (*NUMROW NUMBER OF ROWS)
(*GUTTER GUTTER WIDTH))
```

Parameter Definitions:

*RSTCST/*NORSTCSR: Optional parameter that indicates whether the arrow keys are allowed to move the cursor outside the selection field. The default is *NORSTCSR. This parameter is ignored if the display is attached to a controller that does not support an enhanced interface.

An exception to the restrictions imposed by this keyword occurs if the selection field is the only field contained in the pull-down window. If this is true, when the cursor is within the left-most or right-most columns, the respective arrow key closes the current window and opens the pull-down window associated with the menu bar choice to the left or right of the current menu bar choice.

*NOAUTOSLT: Optional parameter indicating whether the Enter key is allowed to select the current choice automatically, as determined by the cursor position. *NOAUTOSLT means the users must select the choice. *AUTOSLTENH means that autoselect is only in effect if the display is attached to an enhanced controller.

*NOSLTIND/*SLTIND: Optional parameter indicating whether selection indicators (push buttons, check boxes) should be displayed. *SLTIND is the default.

*NOAUTOENT: Indicates to what extent the autoenter feature should be enabled. The autoenter feature causes the record to be returned to the program as soon as a choice is selected, without the user having to press the Enter key. *NOAUTOENT disables the feature. *AUTOENT enables the feature. *AUTOENTNN enables the feature only if numeric selection of the choices is not required.

*NUMCOL: Optional parameter indicating that the selection field should be displayed in multiple columns sequenced from left to right across the columns, as shown below:

```
choice1   choice2   choice3
choice4   choice5   choice6
```

*NUMROW: Optional parameter indicating that the selection field should be displayed in multiple rows sequenced from top to bottom, as shown below:

> choice1   choice3   choice5
> choice2   choice4   choice6

*GUTTER: Optional parameter used to control the number of spaces between the columns of multiple-choice selection fields. Must have a minimum value of at least 2; default spacing is three characters.

The choices that appear on the pull-down format are defined with the CHOICE keyword. Similar to the MNUBARCHC keyword, the CHOICE keyword allows for a choice number to be keyed to select the option and displays the phrase on the pull-down menu. On nongraphical displays, the choice number is displayed next to the choice text.

```
CHOICE(Choice number Choice text *SPACEB)
```

Parameter Definitions:

Choice number: Indicates an identification number representing this choice. Valid values are from 1 to 99. Duplicate values within a selection field are not allowed.

Choice text: Defines the text that appears representing this choice. May be defined as a character string or as a program-to-system field.

*SPACEB: Optional parameter that inserts a blank line before this choice on the menu bar. Should be used to logically group choices that are numbered consecutively. If the choices are not numbered consecutively and you are using vertical selection fields (single column), a blank line is automatically placed between nonconsecutive choices.

RADIO PUSH BUTTONS

Before the advent of electronic switches and remote-controlled radios for cars, car radios were controlled by push buttons (we are not making this up). When you wanted to change the station, you pushed a button, which stayed depressed while that station was active. The computer industry borrowed this phrase and applied it to the GUI. When a user selects an option, it appears as if he pushed a button.

The PULLDOWN keyword accepts either the *SLTIND (which is the default) or *NOSLTIND parameters. If you use the *SLTIND option, a box is placed around the option when the user selects it, giving the illusion that a button is being pushed.

MULTIPLE-CHOICE, PULL-DOWN MENUS

In Figure 3.3, the COMREC format contained the keyword MLTCHCFLD, while the other formats contained the SNGCHCFLD keyword. The single-choice keyword SNGCHCFLD indicates that only one selection at a time is allowed from the pull-down window. The MLTCHCFLD keyword is used to indicate that more than one item can be selected. For example, you may need an application that can establish communications and pass-through at the same time. The format for the MLTCHFLD keyword is as follows:

```
MLTCHCFLD((*RSTCSR OR *NORSTCSR) (*NOSLTIND OR *SLTIND) (*NUMCOL
NUMBER OF COLUMNS) (*NUMROW NUMBER OF ROWS) (*GUTTER GUTTER WIDTH))
```

Parameter Definitions:

*RSTCSR/*NORSTCSR: Optional parameter that indicates whether the arrow keys are allowed to move the cursor outside of the selection field. The default is *NORSTCSR. This parameter is ignored if the display is attached to a controller that does not support an enhanced interface.

An exception to the restrictions imposed by this keyword occurs if the selection field is the only field contained in the pull-down window. If this is true, when the cursor is within the left-most or right-most columns, the respective arrow key closes the current window and opens the pull-down window associated with the menu bar choice to the left or right of the current menu bar choice.

*NOSLTIND/*SLTIND: Optional parameter indicating whether selection indicators (push buttons and check boxes, for example) should be displayed. *SLTIND is the default.

*NUMCOL: Optional parameter indicating that the selection field should be displayed in multiple columns sequenced from left to right across the columns, as shown below:

    choice1   choice2   choice3

    choice4   choice5   choice6

*NUMROW: Optional parameter indicating that the selection field should be displayed in multiple rows sequenced from top to bottom, as shown below:

    choice1   choice3   choice5

    choice2   choice4   choice6

*GUTTER: Optional parameter used to control the number of spaces between the columns of multiple-choice selection fields. Must have a minimum value of at least 2; the default spacing is three characters.

On a multiple-choice format, there must be one CHCCTL keyword for every CHOICE keyword used. The CHCCTL keyword contains the name of the field the program will use to determine if the choice was selected. As with the single-choice field, a 1 in the field on input indicates it was selected.

On output, you must load the field associated with each CHCCTL field with a 0, 1, or 2. A 0 in the field indicates the selection is available to be selected. A 1 indicates that the selection is available and is also the default selection. A 2 in the corresponding field indicates the selection is not available at this time.

The CHCCTL keyword optionally controls error handling when the user selects an invalid option. You can specify the error message number and the file in which it resides. The specified message is displayed if the user selects an invalid option.

You can also hard code the message. A third option is to load the error message into a field in your program and display that field.

```
CHCCTL(Choice number &Control field Msgid Msglib Msgfile)
```

Parameter Definitions:

Choice number: Required parameter that specifies the choice to which this keyword applies.

Control field: Required parameter that is the name of a 1-byte, numeric hidden field. On output, your program outputs the control value to indicate whether the field is available. On input, the field indicates if the field was selected. Possible values and their meanings are:

0 - Available.

1 - Selected.

2 - Unavailable; cursor not allowed here unless help is available for choice.

3 - Unavailable; placing cursor on choice is allowed.

4 - Unavailable; cannot place cursor on choice even if help is available.

<u>MSGID</u>: Message number to display if the user selects an unavailable choice. This field is optional. If not specified, the default message CPD919B is issued. This parameter can also be a program-to-system field, in which case it must be a 7-byte, alphanumeric field with a data type of P, and the field must exist in the record format you are defining.

<u>MSGLIB</u>: Library name containing the message file that contains the message displayed when the user selects an unavailable choice.

<u>MSGFILE</u>: Name of the message file containing the message that is displayed when the user selects an unavailable choice.

PULL-DOWN MENU SHORTCUT KEYS

You may have noticed the right angle bracket (>) symbol embedded in the functions displayed in the pull-down menu. This symbol designates a shortcut key that can be used to select the option. The highlighted character following the symbol is the shortcut key. Pressing the designated shortcut key while the cursor is positioned on the menu bar also selects the option.

Note: Shortcut keys only work on character-based graphical displays attached to a controller that supports an enhanced interface for nonprogrammable workstations.

PULL-DOWN MENU ACCELERATOR KEYS

An accelerator key is a function key that performs the same function as the selected phrase. It is displayed next to the pull-down menu choice (three spaces after the length of the longest choice text), but the pull-down menu does not have to be displayed for the accelerator key to be active. You define the key just as you define any other function key, at either the file or field level.

After you have defined the function key, you define the text that is displayed with the choice. Use the CHCACCEL keyword to accomplish this. It is up to you to code the program to operate correctly if the function key is pressed, just as you would with any other function key. All the CHCACCEL keyword does is provide a way to enter the text for the accelerator key to be displayed with the choice text.

```
CHCACCEL (Choice number Accelerator text)
```

Parameter Definitions:

Choice number: Specifies the number of the choice to which this keyword applies. Valid values are from 1 to 99.

Accelerator text: Specifies the text displayed to identify the accelerator key. This parameter may be entered in two ways:

- As a quoted character string.
- As a program-to-system field.

This text is placed three columns to the right of the longest choice text. The actual display length of the accelerator text is also determined by the length of the longest choice text. This is because the combination of the two cannot exceed the width of the smallest display size for the file.

CONTROLLING THE ATTRIBUTES
OF AVAILABLE/UNAVAILABLE CHOICES

We have already seen that the CHCCTL keyword controls whether a field is available when the pull-down menu appears. The CHCAVAIL keyword controls the color or display attribute of available selections in a menu bar or selection field. CHCUNAVAIL does the same thing for unavailable choices. The CHCSLT keyword specifies the color and display attributes of a selected choice.

```
chcavail (Color  Display attributes)
```

Parameter Definitions:

Color: Specifies the color of the choice text. It is expressed in the form *COLOR XXX, where XXX is:

BLU Blue	GRN Green	PNK Pink	RED Red
TRQ Turquoise	YLW Yellow	WHT White	

Display attributes: Specifies the display attribute of the choice text. It is expressed in the form (*DSPATR (VALUE1) (VALUE2)...), where *value* is:

BL Blink	CS Column separator	HI High intensity
ND Nondisplay	RI Reverse image	UL Underline

86

SETTING PULL-DOWN MENU DEFAULTS

If your program outputs a valid choice in the option field when the format is displayed, that choice becomes the default. If the user simply presses the Enter key without actually making a selection, the choice number in that field is executed. On output, regardless of how the user selects the option (i.e., entering a number, positioning the cursor, or using the shortcut key), this field is filled with the number corresponding to the selected option.

TO MENU BAR OR NOT TO MENU BAR

Using menu bars can give you the look and feel of a graphical user interface if you are on an enhanced controller. If you are not, the look is undesirable and the feel is anything but good. If the software you develop runs on systems with the enhanced controllers (as all newer systems do), menu bars provide a nice and easy interim interface, even for workstations that do not have a mouse.

WE DO WINDOWS

Windows have been with us for a long time. Clever prehistoric programmers (more commonly referred to as System/36 programmers) were able to code pop-up windows in their applications, but it took an extraordinary amount of effort to achieve and maintain this result.

Today's more contemporary programmers (which we of course define as AS/400 RPG programmers) are able to code windows with just a couple of simple DDS keywords. We can put subfiles in windows, move windows around on the fly, control the window border characteristics, put titles on the window, and much more. All of this functionality is achieved simply by using the correct keyword on the file format definition. We've come a long way, baby!

In case you have lived all of your life on the dark side of the moon and still think a window is a portal you look out of or open for fresh air, let's define the term. Simply put, a *window* is information that overlays an existing screen, with some form of border (or window) around the information to make it stand out. You can view both the information inside the window and the information outside the window so you do not lose your point of reference. However, only the information inside the window is active; you cannot work with the underlying display while the window is active.

WHO NEEDS WINDOWS?

Windows can do a lot to enhance the visual appeal and functionality of your programs. One of the most obvious uses for windows is to provide field-level help. Program operators should be able to place the cursor on a field, press the Help key, and have a pop-up window appear that tells them all about the field. You can see this application throughout the OS/400 operating system.

Another good use for a window interface is to provide a *subfile* list of records from which the user can choose. Let's say an operator needs to enter a salesperson's number in a field, but he only knows the salesperson's name. You could set up your program so that placing the cursor in the salesperson number field and pressing a function key cause a pop-up window to appear with an alphabetical list of all salespeople. A subfile selection field allows the operator to select the salesperson he wants, and the number is entered into the field automatically.

Another good example (demonstrated in this chapter) is to present a subfile of commands the user can execute by selecting a subfile record from the window. Creating a very user-friendly interface to the operating system, this is similar in function to the assist window, except that it gives you the ability to customize the options presented to each user.

These are just a few of the many uses for windows. We are sure you can come up with many more once you see how easy they are to code. The chart shown in Table 3.3 lists the five keywords that allow you to create and work with windows.

Table 3.3: DDS Window Keywords.

Keyword	Description
WINDOW	Defines a window, changes the contents of a window, or activates an inactive window.
WDWBORDER	Specifies the color, display attributes, and characters of the border around the window.
WDWTITLE	Specifies the text, color, and display attributes of the title of the window, which is embedded in the top or bottom border.
RMVWDW	Removes other windows from the display.
USRRSTDSP	Prevents the system from automatically saving and restoring the underlying display when a window is written or removed.

THE WINDOW KEYWORD

The WINDOW keyword has two different formats, as shown in the following examples. The first format defines a window, while the second format indicates that the system should place the record format into a window already defined in another record format.

In the first format, you tell the system where to put the window and how big it is going to be. The beginning line number and column fields control where the window is placed on the screen at execution time. For instance, if you are trying to present help text on a particular field, you can retrieve the cursor position and have the window appear one line below it.

But what if the cursor was on the last line, or column, of the screen? Where would you put the window? What if it was on the second-to-last line? You could, with a lot of code, determine the correct placement of the window based on how close the cursor is to the bottom or edge of the screen. But this would be rather tedious to code and very difficult to maintain if you had to change the screen later.

Wouldn't it be nice if the system could determine the best position of the window? Well, it can! (You knew we were leading up to that, didn't you?) Take a look at the special option *DFT. Instead of using the beginning line and column number parameters, you code the keyword *DFT and the system decides where to place the window.

To display a window, the first window record written must contain the window size and location parameters (or you can specify *DFT to let the system do it for you). A window containing the size and location information is called a *window definition record*. It is the record that actually creates the window and makes it visible. It is all you need to display a window.

It is possible to display the same window on a screen more than once. The second edition of the window, which has the same names as the first, becomes the active window. If you want to move the window, write the same window a second time with the RMVWDW keyword active. This keyword removes the first edition of the window from the screen and gives the appearance of moving the window from one location to another.

Here are two different examples of how you may use the WINDOW keyword:

```
WINDOW(Beginning line # OR Field containing beginning line #
Beginning column OR Field containing beginning column Number of lines
Number of columns *MSGLIN OR *NOMSGLIN *RSTCSR OR *NORSTCSR)
```

or

```
WINDOW(*DFT Number of lines Number of columns *MSGLIN OR *NOMSGLIN
*RSTCSR *OR *NORSTCSR)
```

Parameter Definitions:

Beginning line #: The line number at which you place the top of the window, or the field name containing the line number at which you place the top of the window. If a field name is used, it must exist in the record format as a signed numeric, program-to-system field, with a length no greater than 3.

Beginning column: The position of the uppermost left corner of the window, or the field name containing the position of the uppermost left corner of the window. If a field name is used, it must exist in the record format as a signed numeric, program-to-system field, with a length no greater than 3.

*DFT: Let the system decide where the starting line number and column number should be. The system uses a set order of rules when determining where to position the window. See the note following these definitions for the rules.

Number of lines: The total number of lines the window spans. Must be no greater than the number of lines in the display minus 2. The last line in a window is used for messages and cannot contain any fields.

Number of columns: The number of columns within the window. Cannot exceed four less than the available positions for the display.

*MSGLIN: Message line. Indicates that the message line is contained within the window. *MSGLIN is the default. *NOMSGLIN moves the message line out of the window and to the bottom of the screen (or wherever the MSGLOC keyword specifies).

*RSTCSR: Restricted cursor. Indicates that the user is limited in functions when the cursor is outside the window. When the cursor is outside the window, *NORSTCSR indicates that all the function keys are still available, as if the cursor were within the window.

System Rules for Automatic Window Placement

If you use the *DFT parameter and let the system decide where to place the window, it uses a set of rules to make the placement determination. These rules are as follows:

1. If the window fits below the cursor, with the top row of the window being one line below the cursor position, place it there. If it fits on the screen, beginning in the same column as the cursor, place it there. If it does not fit, place it as far to the left of the column as necessary to fit the complete window on the screen.

2. If the window does not fit below the cursor, see if it fits above. If so, place it there. The bottom of the window will be one line above the cursor. Position the window left to right according to the same criteria in rule 1.

3. If the window fits to the right of the cursor, place it there. The right border of the window is placed in the next-to-the-last column of the display. If possible, position the top row of the window on the same line as the cursor; otherwise, position the window only as far above as necessary so it still fits on the screen.

4. If the window fits to the left of the cursor, place it there. Position the right border of the window two columns to the left of the cursor. Position it vertically as described above.

5. Position the window in the lower-right-hand corner of the display if it does not fit anywhere else.

Window Border Keyword

The Window Border (WDWBORDER) keyword allows you to control the color, attributes, and characters used to create the border of the window. If you specify this keyword, at least one of the parameters must also be specified.

The Window Border keyword has the following format:

```
WDWDORDER((COLOR) (DISPLAY ATTRIBUTE) (CHARACTERS))
```

Parameter Definitions:

Color: Specify the color of the border. The default color is blue. The parameter is ignored on a monochrome display.

Display attribute: Specify the display attribute of the border. Use the form (*DSPATR (VALUE 1 (VALUE 2...))). If more than one attribute is coded, they are combined to form one attribute for the entire border.

Characters: Specify the characters that make up the border. Use the form (*CHAR 'characters'). This parameter must be an eight-character string, with each character specifying a different position of the window. The order is as follows:

Position 1: Top left corner.

Position 2: Top border.

Position 3: Top right corner.

Position 4: Left border.

Position 5: Right border.

Position 6: Bottom left corner.

Position 7: Bottom border.

Position 8: Bottom right corner.

WINDOW TITLE KEYWORD

The Window Title (WDWTITLE) keyword is used to assign a title that appears in the header of the window. The WDWTITLE keyword format is as follows:

```
WDWTITLE((Title text) (color) (display attribute) (*CENTER or
*RIGHT or *LEFT or *TOP or *BOTTOM))
```

Parameter Definitions:

Title text: Optional parameter specifying the text to be placed in the border. Use the form (*TEXT VALUE), where value can be either hard coded or a program-to-system field. If the title characters are blanks, a blank title is displayed. If the characters are nulls, then no title is displayed.

Color: Specify the color of the text title. Use the form (*COLOR VALUE). If no color is specified, it defaults to the color of the border. It is ignored on a monochrome display.

*CENTER, *LEFT, *RIGHT: Specify the alignment of the text field.

REMOVE WINDOW KEYWORD

There are no parameters for the Remove Window (RMVWDW) keyword. When you write to a format that has this keyword, all other windows currently on the display are removed. If there are no other windows on the display, the keyword is ignored.

If you have multiple windows on the screen and simply want to ensure that a certain one has the focus (i.e., it is the one most prominently displayed), read or write to the window. This causes the new window to display, and any windows overlaying it to become secondary or to be removed.

USER RESTORE DISPLAY KEYWORD

There are no parameters for the User Restore Display (USRRSTDSP) keyword. Writing to a format with this keyword causes the system to bypass the normal window save and restore processing. Use of the USRRSTDSP keyword will cause the system to suppress the standard Save and Restore operations that would normally occur with DDS window processing.

Normal window processing by the system creates a situation in which the current display is saved (including any windows not being removed) before any other window is displayed. When a window is removed, the system restores the display from its saved version. Because normal window processing is a resource-intensive function, use of the USRRSTDSP keyword is greatly encouraged. In fact, under the following conditions, the system actually performs *two* saves of the screen:

- When you are displaying only one window at a time.
- When the current display file is compiled with RSTDSP(*YES).
- When the window record overlaying the current display is in a different file.

The first save operation is performed because the display file is compiled with RSTDSP(*YES). The second save is performed because of normal window processing. Use of USRRSTDSP eliminates the second save operation. Be sure to specify the keyword on the window that follows the first window you do not want the system to save. The USRRSTDSP keyword is only allowed on records containing the window keyword. It is ignored on the window reference record.

Take a deep breath when reading the following: Although option indicators are allowed on the USRRSTDSP keyword, once the keyword is in effect, it remains in effect (even if the option indicator is set off) until you perform an I/O on either the initial display screen or the window that is two windows before the window on which the USRRSTDSP is specified. Whew!

Although the rules governing USRRSTDSP sound complicated, the reward is worth the effort. The AS/400 sometimes takes an undeserved beating when people talk about its response time. More often than not, it is programming and operation techniques that cause response problems, not the system itself.

WINDOWS AND RESPONSE TIME

Response time, as it pertains to windows, is dependent upon your communications setup and on the complexity of the window being displayed. For our purposes, complexity is defined as the amount of information that must be saved and restored. The slowest response time occurs when the first window is added to a display and the system must perform read and save operations.

A window of average size and complexity on a terminal attached to the AS/400 by twinaxial, local area network (LAN), TCP/IP, or other high-speed communications line should always have a response time of less than one second. If you are attached to a 5600-baud line, expect a little longer response time to perform the read and save operations and display the window. If you are on a 9600-baud line, well, you're probably not reading this section anyway because you obviously do not care about response time (but figure about one to two seconds to display a window).

THE SYSTEM REQUEST WINDOW PROGRAM

Now let's look at a sample window program that can be used to add some sizzle to your system. The AS/400 operating system is touted as one of the easiest operating systems to use (not as easy as a graphical user interface, but easy nonetheless). The AS/400 has a consistent command interface: All commands conform to the same naming conventions.

Once you learn the convention, it is relatively easy to find commands. But we think that it can be made even easier!

We have put together a System Request Window program that allows you to put all system-operation functions at the fingertips of your users. All system operations and special system-wide functions are made available by simply pressing the System Request key (Figure 3.5).

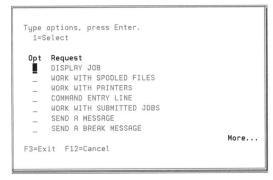

This program also allows you to customize the list of options each user should have available. You can establish a default template of options that is available to all users, or you can specify options per user ID for users you want to make exceptions for.

Figure 3.5: System Request Window program.

Figure 3.6 shows the DDS for a physical file that we have named REQUEST. This file holds a display field, a command to be executed, a user name, and a sequence number. A subfile program (shown in Figure 3.7) displays this file in a window. The DDS for the window is shown in Figure 3.8.

```
***********************************************************************
*   TO COMPILE:
*      CRTPF FILE(XXXLIB/REQUEST)
***********************************************************************
AAN01N02N03T.Name++++++RLen++TDpBLinPosFunctions+++++++++++++++++++++++++++++++
A            R REQREC
A              USERNAME      10         COLHDG('USER NAME')
A              DISPLAYFLD    45         COLHDG('DISPLAY FIELD')
A              SEQUENCE#      5 0       COLHDG('SEQUENCE #')
A              COMMAND      256         COLHDG('COMMAND')
A            K USERNAME
A            K SEQUENCE#
```

Figure 3.6: DDS for the REQUEST file.

```
*****************************************************************************
*   TO COMPILE:
*      CRTBNDRPG PGM(XXXLIB/FIG37RG)
*****************************************************************************

FFilename++IPEASF....L.....A.Device+.Keywords+++++++++++++++++++++++++++++Comments++
FFIG38DS   CF    E                  WORKSTN
F                                            SFILE(SFLRCD:SfRelRec)
FREQUEST   IF    E           K DISK

DName++++++++++ETDsFrom+++To/L+++IDc.Keywords+++++++++++++++++++++++++++++Comments++
D                   SDS
D  PARMS                 *PARMS
D   UserProfil             254    263
D ReturnCode      S                2
D CommandLen      S               15  5 INZ(256)

CL0N01Factor1+++++++Opcode&ExtFactor2+++++++Result++++++++Len++D+HiLoEq.Comments++
C     *ENTRY       PLIST
C                  PARM                      ReturnCode
C                  EVAL      SfSelect = *BLANKS
C                  EVAL      SetPosit = 1
C     UserProfil   SETLL     REQUEST                               24
C                  IF        *In24 = *OFF
C                  EVAL      UserProfil = *BLANKS
C     UserProfil   SETLL     REQUEST
C                  ENDIF
C                  DOU       *In24 = *ON
C     UserProfil   READE     REQUEST                               24
C                  IF        *In24 = *OFF
C                  EVAL      SfDesc = DisplayFld
C                  EVAL      HidSequenc = Sequence#
C                  EVAL      HidCommand = Command
C                  EVAL      SfRelRec = (SfRelRec + 1)
C                  WRITE     SFLRCD
C                  ENDIF
C                  ENDDO

C                  IF        SfRelRec <> *ZEROS
C                  EVAL      *IN21 = *ON
C                  ENDIF
C                  DOU       (*IN12 = *ON) or (*In03 = *ON)
C                  WRITE     WINDOW
*  Display & Read subfile
C                  EXFMT     SFLCTL
C                  IF        (*In12 = *OFF) and (*In03 = *OFF)
C                  EVAL      *IN42 = *OFF
*  Set cursor position and read changes looking for a selection request
C                  EVAL      SetPosit = CurrentPos
C                  DOU       *In41 = *ON
C                  READC     SFLRCD                                41
C                  IF        *In41 = *OFF
```

Figure 3.7: RPG Attention Window program (part 1 of 2).

```
C                   SELECT
* Process record and get out if a record was selected
C                   WHEN      SfSelect = '1'
C                   CALL      'QCMDEXC'                          99
C                   PARM                     HidCommand
C                   PARM                     CommandLen
* Reset cursor
C                   EVAL      SfSelect = *BLANKS
C                   UPDATE    SFLRCD
C                   WHEN      SfSelect <> *BLANKS
C                   EVAL      *IN42 = *ON
C                   EVAL      SetPosit = SfRelRec
C                   UPDATE    SFLRCD
C                   LEAVE
C                   OTHER
C                   ITER
C                   ENDSL
C                   ENDIF
C                   ENDDO
C                   ENDIF
C                   ENDDO

C                   EVAL      *INLR = *ON
```

Figure 3.7: RPG Attention Window program (part 2 of 2).

```
A*******************************************************************************
A* TO COMPILE:
A*    CRTDSPF FILE(XXXLIB/FIG38DS)
A*******************************************************************************

AAN01N02N03T.Name++++++RLen++TDpBLinPosFunctions+++++++++++++++++++++++++++++++
A                                      DSPSIZ(24 80 *DS3)
A                                      CA12(12)
A                                      CA03(03)
A            R WINDOW
A                                      WINDOW(*DFT 15 53 *NORSTCSR)
A                                      RMVWDW
A                              14  2'F3=Exit'
A                                      COLOR(BLU)
A                              14 11'F12=Cancel'
A                                      COLOR(BLU)
A            R SFLRCD                  SFL
A  42                                  SFLNXTCHG
A              SFSELECT    1A  B  6  4
A              SFDESC     45A  O  6  8
A              SFRELREC    4S  OH
A              HIDSEQUENC  5S  OH
A              HIDCOMMAND 256A  H
A            R SFLCTL                  SFLCTL(SFLRCD)
```

Figure 3.8: DDS for the System Request window (part 1 of 2).

97

```
A                                         SFLSIZ(0050)
A                                         SFLPAG(0007)
A                                         WINDOW(WINDOW)
A    21                                   SFLDSP
A                                         SFLDSPCTL
A    24                                   SFLEND(*MORE)
A    42                                   SFLMSG('Invalid Selection Entry')
A                                         OVERLAY
A                                         USRRSTDSP
A              SETPOSIT      4S OH        SFLRCDNBR(*TOP)
A              CURRENTPOS    5S OH        SFLSCROLL
A                                      2  2'Type options, press Enter.'
A                                         COLOR(BLU)
A                                      3  4'1=Select'
A                                         DSPATR(HI)
A                                         COLOR(BLU)
A                                      5  3'Opt  Request'
A                                         DSPATR(HI)
A         R DUMMY
A                                         KEEP
A                                         ASSUME
A                                      1  2' '
```

Figure 3.8: DDS for the System Request window (part 2 of 2).

This program allows a user to run commands by selecting a subfile record from within a window. The command to be run is stored in the REQUEST file and keyed by user name and sequence number. When the user selects a subfile record, the command is executed via QCMDEXC. What could be easier? No commands or parameters to memorize. Just read the screen, select a record based on a description of what the function is, and the command is executed.

To make our program even easier to use, it can be called when the Attention key is pressed. Assuming you have compiled the program shown in Figure 3.7 as REQ001RG, you can change the user profile by entering the following command:

```
CHGUSRPRF USRPRF(XXX) ATNPGM(REQ001RG)
```

Thereafter, whenever user XXX presses the Attention key, the window shown in Figure 3.8 appears. The actual functions that appear in the window are dependent upon the records entered into the REQUEST file. We have not provided a file maintenance program for this file. You can either write your own or use a product like the Data File Utility (DFU). Key the default records you want to make available to all users and leave the User ID field blank. Only specify the User ID for those users whom you want to set up as exceptions.

The code for the RPG subfile program is rather simple. We assume that there will not be many records per user in the REQUEST file, so we use the load-all technique of subfile processing to load the subfile. Because of this, we do not have to code any rolling routines; the system handles rolling for us.

First check to see if the user (taken from the Program Status Data Structure) has any records in the REQUEST file. If not, then use the default records, which are the ones with a blank user name. In addition to the fields being displayed in the subfile, load the command to be run into a hidden field so you can execute the hidden command when the user makes a selection.

After displaying the subfile, set up a loop and, looking for a 1 in the selection field, read all changed subfile records. Once one is found, the process subroutine retrieves the correct REQUEST file record and passes the command field to the QCMDEXC API (see chapter 6) to execute the command. All of the normal prompting characters (for example, ?? and ?*) can be used in the command field to prompt for the command.

SCROLL BARS AND SUBFILES

The ability to put subfiles into DDS windows was a welcome addition to OS/400 with the release of V2R3. At long last, we were able to add graphically oriented lookup capabilities to our interactive programs. Subfiles could be presented that would not wipe out the entire displayed screen.

And along with V3R1 came the ability for users to employ a scroll bar with their subfiles. The AS/400 scroll bar works much as it would with other graphical interfaces. It has a scroll block to indicate how big the subfile is and where you are within it. The scroll block can be moved with the pointing device (provided you are on a graphical workstation), and the subfile is repositioned accordingly.

You can use the scroll bar by using a keyword option on the Subfile End (SFLEND) DDS keyword. We cover this option in detail in chapter 2.

GUI THIS, AND GUI THAT

Sizzle, pizzazz, function, and ease of use. This is what the GUI craze is all about. So why shouldn't AS/400 programmers get in on the fun?

As you have seen, some of the enhanced DDS elements are so easy to code that they are actually irresistible! We have been coding windows in programs for more years than we care to admit, and the hoops we had to jump through to do it were numerous—PUTOVR, OVRDTA, OVERLAY, RSTDSP, etc., etc., etc. If you wanted a subfile in a window (and this was a very common request), you had to fake it. If you wanted a pull-down menu, you had to forget it!

Now there are just five keywords you can use to control a window, and you don't even have to know where the window is going to appear—the system decides for you! Want a subfile in a window? No problem. The system does it. Want a scroll bar displayed on that subfile? Piece of cake!

If you have not added enhanced DDS features to your green-screen applications yet, what in the world are you waiting for?

4

INFORMATION DATA STRUCTURES AND ERROR HANDLING

W hile it is true that the AS/400 operating system communicates mainly via messages, it is equally true that it communicates a wealth of information via user spaces and special data structures. Two such data structures are the File Information Data Structure and the Program Status Data Structure.

This chapter explains the information contained in these two very special data structures, and shows you how you can access them in your RPG programs. We also show you how to handle file and program errors by using the plethora of information that can be found in these data structures.

FILE INFORMATION DATA STRUCTURE

The first thing you should know about the data found in the File Information Data Structure is that it varies depending on the type of file you are processing. You can get detailed information on every I/O operation you perform in your program—if you know how to get to it.

A File Information Data Structure is maintained for every file your program uses, regardless of whether or not you code the data structure in your program. It is up to you to decide if you want to access the information. As you will see, this is not difficult to code and can be very advantageous in certain situations. Making the File Information Data Structure available for one of the files in your program is as simple as adding a File Description Specification Keyword to further describe the file in question. You can see two examples of this in Figure 4.1.

```
FFilename++IPEASF.....L.....A.Device+.Keywords+++++++++++++++++++++++++++
FFILE1     IF   E          K DISK     INFDS(File1Ds)
FFILE2     IF   E          K DISK     INFDS(File2Ds)

DName+++++++++++++ETDsFrom+++To/L+++IDc.Keywords+++++++Comments++++++++++++
D File1Ds          DS
D  F1FileName               1      8
D  F1Status               11     15 0
D File2Ds          DS
D  F2FileName               1      8
D  F2Status               11     15 0
```

Figure 4.1: Specifying the File Information Data Structure.

The File Description Specification Keyword for the Information Data Structure is the INFDS keyword followed by the name of an associated data structure enclosed in parentheses. In Figure 4.1, we see the INFDS keyword on the File Description Specification describing the database file named FILE1. The name of the File Information Data Structure for database file FILE1 is FILE1DS.

After any I/O operation to FILE1 (including opening the file), the data structure FILE1DS contains the requested information coded in the data structure. For our example in Figure 4.1, the file name (F1FileName) and the status code (F1Status) are coded into our data structure. We could name the fields anything because the fields are positionally stored in the data structure. The From and To positions of the field determine the information that is contained in the field.

For the example in Figure 4.1, we also created a File Information Data Structure for the FILE2 database file, named FILE2DS. The naming conventions are totally arbitrary, but because you cannot have the same field defined in two different data structures, we named them differently. We believe it is good practice to establish some kind of naming convention to help make the names easy to remember.

102

Special Keywords

IBM has determined that certain fields in the Information Data Structures are more likely to be requested by a program than others. Because of this, these fields have been assigned special keywords you use to reference the information. The idea is to free you from the hassle of having to remember the From and To positions in the Information Data Structures. The need for this feature could be ruled as questionable because you still have to remember the special keywords.

Table 4.1 contains a list of the special keywords in the File Information Data Structure. You code the keyword in the Input Specification for the data structure subfield in positions 44 to 51 in lieu of the field positions. Figure 4.2 shows an example of how to code a File Information Data Structure using one of the special keywords.

Table 4.1: Special Keywords in the File Information Data Structure.

Keyword	From Position	To Position	Decimal Positions	Description
*FILE	1	8	—	The first eight characters of the file name used by the RPG program associated with this data structure.
*INP	71	72	0	Type of keyboard being used.
*OUT	73	74	0	Type of display being used.
*OPCODE	16	21	—	RPG operation code last used to access the file. Note that op codes with six-letter names will be shortened to the five characters formerly used in the OPM version of RPG III. These include DELETE (DELET), EXCEPT (EXCPT), READPE (REDPE), UNLOCK (UNLCK), and UPDATE (UPDAT).
*SIZE	67	70	0	Total number of characters that can fit on the workstation device.
*STATUS	11	15	0	Status codes (defined later in this chapter).
*RECORD	38	45	—	Format name being processed.
*ROUTINE	22	29	—	RPG routine that was processing the file.

```
FFilename++IPEASF.....L.....A.Device+.Keywords+++++++++++++++++++++++++
FFILE1    IF  E          K DISK    INFDS(File1Ds)

DName++++++++++++ETDsFrom+++To/L+++IDc.Keywords+++++++Comments+++++++++++++
D File1Ds          DS
D  F1FileName            1     8
D  F1Status         *STATUS
```

Figure 4.2: Coding special keywords.

FIELD DEFINITIONS

Now that you have seen two ways to code a File Information Data Structure, let's take a look at all of the common fields in the File Information Data. Figure 4.3 shows a sample data structure for all of the common fields that can be accessed and field definitions. These fields are in the same positions, regardless of the file type. Some other portions of the data structure change based on the type of file being described.

```
DName++++++++++++ETDsFrom+++To/L+++IDc.Keywords+++++++Comments+++++++++++++
D File1Ds          DS
D  F1FileName            1     8
D  F1OpenInd             9     9
D  F1EndofFil           10    10
D  F1Status             11    15 0
D  F1OperCode           16    21
D  F1Routine            22    29
D  F1StmtNbr            30    37
D  F1SpeclRtn           38    42 0
D  F1RecordCd           38    45
D  F1MesageId           46    52
D  F1SorceID            53    54
D  F1Unused             53    66
D  F1WkstnSiz           67    70 0
D  F1KeyBdTyp           71    72 0
D  F1DispType           73    74 0
D  F1LangMode           75    76 0
```

Figure 4.3: Common fields in the File Information Data Structure.

Table 4.2 shows the common fields in the File Information Data Structure.

104

In Table 4.3, we list the possible status codes that may be contained in positions 11 to 15 of the File Information Data Structure. As previously noted, the *STATUS keyword can also be used to access the status codes.

Table 4.2: Common Fields in the File Information Data Structure.

Field Name	Description
F1FileName	First eight characters of the file name (as used by the RPG program).
F1OpenInd	File open indicator (1 = Open).
F1EndOfFil	File at end of file indicator (1 = End of File).
F1Status	Status codes. Very useful for error determination and handling (see Table 4.3 for complete list).
F1OperCode	RPG operation code last used to access the file. The first five characters specify the code while the sixth position is itself a code, where: F = Op code specified on a file name. R = Op code specified on a record format name. I = Last operation was implicit.
F1Routine	First eight characters of the name of the routine that was processing the file. The routine may be an ILE procedure or subprocedure.
F1StmtNbr	The source listing statement number where the last file operation occurred. In certain situations, this field may not be large enough to hold the entire statement number. In these cases, the overflow is stored in positions 53 and 54.
F1SpeclRtn	User-specified return code for SPECIAL files.
F1RecordCd	For an externally described file, the first eight characters of the name of the record format being processed when the error occurred. For internally described files, the record format indicator is left-justified into the field.
F1Mesageid	System message ID of the error (i.e., CPF9801).
F1SorceID	Source ID for the statement number in F1StmtNbr.
F1WkstnSiz	Number of rows and columns that fit on the workstation display.
F1KeybdTyp	Type of keyboard being used. Set to 00 if alphanumeric, and 10 if ideographic.
F1DispType	Type of display being used. Set to 00 if alphanumeric, 10 if ideographic, and 20 if DBCS.
F1LangMode	Always 00.

Table 4.3: File Information Data Structure Status Codes.

Code	Condition
00000	No exception/error occurred.
00002	Function key used to end display.
00011	Read to end of file.
00012	No record found on a CHAIN, SETLL, or SETGT operation.
00013	Subfile is full; trying to write another record.
01011	Undefined record type.
01021	Attempted to write duplicate record (either database or subfile).
01022	Referential constraint error detected on file member.
01023	Error in trigger program before file operation.
01024	Error in trigger program after file operation.
01031	Matching records out of sequence.
01041	Array or table load sequence error.
01042	Alternate collating sequence for table error.
01051	Too many entries in table or array.
01071	Numeric sequence error.
01121	Print key pressed, but no indicator specified in DDS for print.
01122	Rollup pressed, but no indicator specified in DDS.
01123	Rolldown pressed, but no indicator specified in DDS.
01124	Clear key pressed, but no indicator specified in DDS.
01125	Help key pressed, but no indicator specified in DDS.
01126	Home key pressed, but no indicator specified in DDS.
01201	Record mismatch detected on input.
01211	I/O operation to a closed file.
01215	Open issued to a file already opened.
01216	Error on an implicit OPEN/CLOSE operation.
01217	Error on an explicit OPEN/CLOSE operation.
01218	Record locked; unable to allocate.
01221	Update without prior read or chain.
01222	Record cannot be allocated due to referential constraint error.
01231	Error on SPECIAL file.
01235	Error in PRTCTL space or skip entries.

Table 4.3: File Information Data Structure Status Codes (cont.).	
01241	Record number not found in record address file.
01251	Permanent I/O error.
01255	Session or device error. Recovery may be possible.
01261	Attempted to exceed maximum number of acquired devices.
01271	Attempted to acquire unavailable device.
01281	Operation to device not yet acquired.
01282	Job ending with controlled option.
01284	Unable to acquire second device for single device file.
01285	Attempted to acquire a previously acquired device.
01286	Attempted to open shared file with SAVDS or IND file options.
01287	Response indicators overlap IND indicators.
01299	Other I/O error detected.
01331	Wait time exceeded for READ from WORKSTN file.

Open Feedback Information

By now, you may be feeling overwhelmed by the sheer volume of information stored in the File Information Data Structure. But wait! There's more! Remember, the data structure varies depending on the file type.

The open feedback area resides in positions 81 to 240. RPG copies the contents of the file Open Feedback area to the Information Data Structure whenever the associated file is opened (hence the name). Members in a multi-membered file opened with a READ operation to a member are also copied into this area .

The Data Management Guide contains a layout of all these fields, but if you go there, be prepared to do a little math. The fields are laid out in this book by the length, data type, and offset of each. You must calculate the actual From and To positions. To do so, you will need to use the following formula:

From = 81 + Offset

To = From -1 + Character Length (in bytes)

We have done the math for you, as shown in Figure 4.4. Table 4.4 shows the same information, plus a description of each field in a tabular form.

```
DName+++++++++++ETDsFrom+++To/L+++IDc.Keywords+++++++Comments+++++++++++++
D OpenFeedBk      DS
D   F1OdpType            81     82
D   F1FileName           83     92
D   F1FileLib            93    102
D   F1SpoolNam          103    112
D   F1SpoolLib          113    122
D   F1SpoolNbr          123    124B 0
D   F1RecordLn          125    126B 0
D   F1MaxKeyLn          127    128B 0
D   F1MbrName           129    138
D   F1FilTypCd          147    148B 0
D   F1NbrLines          152    153B 0
D   F1NbrColum          154    155B 0
D   F1RcdCnt            156    159B 0
D   F1AccesTyp          160    161
D   F1DupeKeys          162    162
D   F1Source            163    163
D   F1CntlBlck          164    173
D   F1CBlkOvr           174    183
D   F1VolIdOff          184    185B 0
D   F1BlockLmt          186    187B 0
D   F1OvrFlowL          188    189B 0
D   F1BlockOff          190    191B 0
D   F1ReqrName          197    206
D   F1OpenCnt           207    208B 0
D   F1NbrBased          211    212B 0
D   F1OpenId            214    215
D   F1MaxFmtLn          216    217B 0
D   F1CCSID             218    219B 0
D   F1NbrDefnd          227    228B 0
```

Figure 4.4: Open feedback area.

Table 4.4: Field Definitions of the Open Feedback Area.

Field Name	Description
F1OdpType	Open data path type. Possible values are:
	DB = Database.
	DS = Display device.
	SP = Spooled file.
F1FileName	File name as it is known to the system (which may be different than how the RPG program knows it).
F1FileLib	Library name in which the file resides.
F1SpoolNam	Spooled file name.
F1SpoolLib	Library name in which the spooled file resides.

Table 4.4: Field Definitions of the Open Feedback Area (continued).

Field Name	Description
F1SpoolNbr	Spooled file number.
F1RecordLn	Record length of the file associated with this data structure.
F1MaxKeyLen	Maximum key length.
F1MbrName	Member name.
F1FileTypCd	Type of file subtype code.
F1NbrLines	Number of lines on the workstation display.
F1NbrColum	Number of columns on the workstation display.
F1RcdCnt	Number of records in the file when the file was opened.
F1AccesTyp	Type of data-file access. Possible values are: AR = Arrival sequence. KF = Keyed fifo; duplicate keys allowed. KL = Keyed lifo; duplicate keys allowed. KU = Keyed unique.
F1DupeKeys	Duplicate keys indicator. Possible values are: D = Duplicate keys are valid. U = Unique keys only.
F1Source	Source file indicator (Y = This is a source file).
F1CntlBlck	User-file control block parameters.
F1CBlkOvr	User-file control block parameter overrides.
F1VolIdOff	Offset to the location of the volume ID on the tape.
F1BlockLmt	Blocked input/output limit.
F1OvrFlowL	Overflow line number.
F1BlockOff	Blocked input/output offset. The offset from this record to the next record.
F1ReqrName	Requester name.
F1OpenCnt	Open count.
F1NbrBased	Number of members based on file.
F1OpenId	Open identifier.
F1MaxFmtLn	Maximum record format length.
F1CCSID	Database CCSID.
F1NbrDefnd	Number of devices defined.

I/O Feedback Area

Positions 241 through 366 are used for the I/O feedback information area. The content of this area is copied by RPG to the File Information Data Structure:

- On every I/O operation if a POST operation for the file is not specified anywhere in your program.

- Only after a POST for the file, if a POST operation for the file is specified anywhere in your program.

Again, you must go to the Data Management Guide to get a breakdown of the information in the data structure. Use the same calculations to figure From and To positions for this area of the File Information Data Structure as you do for the open feedback area (using an offset position of 241 instead of 81). Or refer to Figure 4.5, where we have, once again, done the math for you. (See Table 4.5 for same information in tabular form.)

```
DName++++++++++++ETDsFrom+++To/L+++IDc.Keywords+++++++Comments+++++++++++++
D IOFeedBack      DS
D  F1NbrWrite           243    246B 0
D  F1NbrReads           247    250B 0
D  F1NbrBoth            251    254B 0
D  F1NbrOther           255    258B 0
D  F1CurOper            260    260
D  F1FmtName            261    270
D  F1DevClass           271    272
D  F1DevName            273    282
D  F1RcdLen             283    286B 0
```

Figure 4.5: I/O feedback area.

Table 4.5: Field Definitions of the I/O Feedback Area.

Field Name	Description
F1NbrWrite	Number of writes performed.
F1NbrReads	Number of reads performed.
F1NbrBoth	Number of writes and reads performed.
F1NbrOther	Number of other I/Os performed.
F1CurOper	Current operation.
F1FmtName	Record format name.
F1DevClass	Device class.
F1DevName	Device name.
F1IRcdLen	Record length.

Device-Specific Feedback Area

The length of the device-specific feedback area, which begins in position 367, is dependent on two factors: the device type and whether DISK files are keyed. The minimum length of the data area when device-specific feedback is used is 528 bytes:

- On every I/O operation, if a POST operation for the file is not specified anywhere in your program.

- Only after a POST for the file, if a POST operation for the file is specified anywhere in your program.

The offset position of the device-specific feedback areas begins in 367 (if you want to go to the Data Management Guide). We went ahead and did the math for you in Figures 4.6, 4.7, and 4.8 (as well as Tables 4.6, 4.7, and 4.8). Figure 4.6 shows this portion of the data structure for a printer file, Figure 4.7 reflects the data structure for a database file, and Figure 4.8 shows a breakdown of this part of the data structure for a workstation file.

```
DName+++++++++++ETDsFrom+++To/L+++IDc.Keywords+++++++Comments++++++++++++
D PrintFeedB      DS
D  F1CurLine#         367     368B 0
D  F1CurPage#         369     372B 0
D  F1MajorCod         401     402
D  F1MinorCod         403     404
```

Figure 4.6: Device-specific feedback area—printers.

Table 4.6: Field Definitions of the Printer Device-Specific Feedback Area.

Field Name	Description
F1CurLine#	Current line number.
F1CurPage#	Current page number.
F1MajorCod	Major return code.
F1MinorCod	Minor return code.

```
DName+++++++++++ETDsFrom+++To/L+++IDc.Keywords+++++++Comments++++++++++++
D DBFilFeedB      DS
D   F1FeedBSiz         367    370B 0
D   F1JoinFile         371    374
D   F1NbrLockd         377    378B 0
D   F1MaxField         379    380B 0
D   F1BitMapOf         381    384B 0
D   F1FPosBits         385    385  0
D   F1CurRecDl         386    386  0
D   F1NbrKeys          387    388B 0
D   F1LenKeys          393    394B 0
D   F1MbrNbr           395    396B 0
D   F1RelRec#          397    400B 0
D   F1KeyValue         401    2400
```

Figure 4.7: Device-specific feedback area—database file.

Table 4.7: Field Definitions of the Database File Device-Specific Feedback Area.

Field Name	Description
F1FeedBSiz	Size of database feedback area.
F1JoinFile	Joined file indicator.
F1NbrLockd	Number of locked records.
F1MaxField	Maximum number of fields.
F1BitMapOf	Offset to error bit map.
F1FPosBits	File position bits.
F1CurRecDl	Current record deleted indicator.
F1NbrKeys	Number of keys.
F1LenKeys	Length of keys
F1MbrNbr	Member number.
F1RelRec#	Relative record number.
F1KeyValue	Key value (maximum length 2,000 characters).

```
DName+++++++++++ETDsFrom+++To/L+++IDc.Keywords+++++++Comments++++++++++++
D WkStnFeedB      DS
D  F1DspFlags          367   368
D  F1AidKey            369   369
D  F1CursrLoc          370   371
D  F1DataLen           372   375B 0
D  F1SfRelRec          376   377B 0
D  F1SfMinRrn          378   379B 0
D  F1SfNbrRec          380   381B 0
D  F1WinCsrLc          382   383
D  F1MajorCod          401   402
D  F1MinorCod          403   404
```

Figure 4.8: Device-specific feedback area—workstation file.

Table 4.8: Field Definitions of the Workstation File Device-Specific Feedback Area.

Field Name	Description
F1DspFlags	Display flags.
F1AidKey	AID byte.
F1CursrLoc	Cursor location.
F1DataLen	Actual data length.
F1SfRelRec	Subfile relative record number.
F1SfMinRrn	Subfile minimum relative record number.
F1SfNbrRec	Number of records in the subfile.
F1WinCsrLoc	Active window cursor location.
F1MajorCod	Major return code.
F1MinorCod	Minor return code.

In Figure 4.9 (and Table 4.9), we show the fields required to get device-specific attribute feedback information. Attribute information can be retrieved for a display device or ICF communication session. The actual operation to retrieve the device-specific attributes will be performed when a POST operation is performed with a program device specified for Factor 1.

```
DName+++++++++++ETDsFrom+++To/L+++IDc.Keywords+++++++++++++++++++++++++++++Comments++
D WkStnAtrFB        DS
D  ProgramDev       241    250
D  DeviceDesc       251    260
D  UserId           261    270
D  DeviceCls        271    271
D  DeviceType       272    277
D  Requester        278    278
D  AcquireSts       279    279
D  InviteSts        280    280
D  DataAvail        281    281
D  NbrRows          282    283B 0
D  NbrCols          284    285B 0
D  Blink            286    286
D  LineSts          287    287
D  DisplayLoc       288    288
D  DisplayTyp       289    289
D  KeybdType        290    290
D  CntrlrInfo       342    342
D  ColorCapbl       343    343
D  GridCapbl        344    344
```

Figure 4.9: Device-specific attribute feedback area—workstation file.

Table 4.9: Field Definitions of the Workstation File Device-Specific Attribute Feedback Area.

Field Name	Description
ProgramDev	Workstation device.
DeviceDesc	Workstation description.
UserId	User Profile ID signed on to workstation.
DeviceCls	Workstation device Class.
DeviceType	Workstation device Type.
Requester	Requesting workstation?
AcquireSts	Workstation acquire status.
InviteSts	Workstation invite status.
DataAvail	Data available.
NbrRows	Number of rows on workstation.
NbrCols	Number of columns on workstation.
Blink	Workstation capable of using blink attribute?
LineSts	Workstation online or offline?
DisplayLoc	Display location.
DisplayTyp	Display type.
KeybdType	Type of keyboard on workstation.
CntrlrInfo	Workstation controller information.
ColorCapbl	Workstation color enabled?
GridCapbl	Workstation capable of displaying a grid?

Figure 4.9 shows this portion of the data structure for a workstation file, and Figure 4.10 (and Table 4.10) reflects the data structure for an ICF ISDN communication session.

```
DName++++++++++++ETDsFrom+++To/L+++IDc.Keywords++++++++++++++++++++++++++++++Comments++
D ISDNFeedBk        DS
D   ISDNLength           385     386B 0
D   ISDNType             387     388
D   ISDNPlan             389     390
D   ISDNNbr              391     430
D   ISDNSubLen           435     436B 0
D   ISDNSubTyp           437     438
D   ISDNSubAdr           439     478
D   ISDNConect           480     480
D   ISDNRmtLen           481     482B 0
D   ISDNRmtAdr           483     514
D   ISDNExtLen           519     520
D   ISDNExtTyp           521     521
D   ISDNExtNum           522     561
D   ISDNX25              566     566
```

Figure 4.10: Device-specific attribute feedback area—ISDN ICF communication session.

Table 4.10: Field Definitions of the ISDN ICF Communication Session Device-Specific Attribute Feedback Area.

Field Name	Description
ISDNLength	Remote number length.
ISDNType	Remote number type.
ISDNPlan	Remote number plan.
ISDNNbr	Remote number.
ISDNSubLen	Remote sub-address length.
ISDNSubTyp	Remote sub-address type.
ISDNSubAdr	Remote sub-address.
ISDNConect	Connection.
ISDNRmtLen	Remote address length.
ISDNRmtAdr	Remote address.
ISDNExtLen	Extension length.
ISDNExtTyp	Extension type.
ISDNExtNum	Extension number.
ISDNX25	X.25 call type.

PROGRAM STATUS DATA STRUCTURE

The Program Status Data Structure is similar to the File Information Data Structure, except that its purpose is to provide exception/error information about an RPG program. While a File Information Data Structure can be defined for each file, a Program Status Data Structure is defined once per program. Even though we show all of the fields in our example, you only need to code the elements you need for your purposes. As shown in Figure 4.11, the data structure is extremely easy to define. Table 4.11 shows the same information, plus a description of each field in a tabular form.

```
DName+++++++++++ETDsFrom+++To/L+++IDc.Keywords+++++++Comments++++++++++++
D                    SDS
D   ProcName           1     10
D   StatusCode        11     15
D   PrevStatus        16     20
D   SourcStmt#        21     28
D   ErrRoutine        29     36
D   NbrParms          37     39  0
D   ExcType           40     42
D   ExcNumber         43     46
D   MIObjDefTm        47     50
D   MsgWrkArea        51     80
D   PgmLibName        81     90
D   MessageDta        91    170
D   PrevMsgId        171    174
D   ErrFileID        175    184
D   DateStartd       191    198
D   Century          199    200  0
D   ErrFilName       201    208
D   ErrFileSts       209    243
D   JobName          244    253
D   UserProfil       254    263
D   JobNumber        264    269  0
D   RunDate          270    275  0
D   SystemDate       276    281  0
D   RunTime          282    287  0
D   CompilDate       288    293  0
D   CompilTime       294    299  0
D   CompilLevl       300    303
D   SourceFile       304    313
D   SourceLib        314    323
D   SourceMbr        324    333
D   ProgramNam       334    343
D   ModuleName       344    353

D   CurrUserId       358    367
D   Unused2          368    429
```

Figure 4.11: Defining a Program Status Data Structure.

Table 4.11: Field Definitions of the Program Status Data Structure.

Field Name	Description
ProcName	Procedure name.
StatusCode	Status codes. See Figure 4.12 and Table 4.3.
PrevStatus	Previous status code.
SourceStmt#	RPG IV source statement sequence number.
ErrRoutine	RPG routine in which the exception/error occurred.
NbrParms	Number of parms passed to this program.
ExcType	Exception type (CPF or MCH).
ExcNumber	Exception number.
MIObjDefTm	Machine instruction object definition template number.
MsgWrkArea	Work area for messages. Used internally by the compiler.
PgmLibName	Library name in which the program resides.
MessageDta	Error message data. CPF messages are placed here when status contains 09999.
PrevMsgId	Previous message ID. Identifies the exception that caused RPG9001 (the called program failed) to be signaled.
ErrFileID	File name on which the last file operation occurred. Updated only when error occurs. This contains the full file name.
DateStard	Date the job actually started. Same format as *DATE.
Century	First two digits of four-digit year.
ErrFilName	File name on which the last file operation occurred. Updated only when error occurs. Could be truncated if long file name is used.
ErrFileSts	File status on the last file used. Includes status code, routine name, statement number, and record name. Updated only when error occurs.
JobName	Job name.
UserProfil	User profile name.
JobNumber	Job number.
RunDate	Date program started running in the system. UDATE is derived from this date.
SystemDate	System date.
RunTime	Time of program running.
CompilDate	Date program was compiled.
CompilTime	Time program was compiled.
CompilLevl	Level of the compiler.
SourceFile	Source file name used to compile the program.
SourceLib	Source library name.
SourceMbr	Source file member name used to compile the program.
ProgramNam	Name of program containing procedure.
ModuleName	Name of module containing procedure.
CurrUserID	ID of the current user.

117

All you need to do to define the Program Status Data Structure is code an S in position 23 followed by DS in positions 24 and 25, then define the subfields you want to make accessible to your program. The Program Status Data Structure and all of the possible subfields are shown in Figure 4.11.

Just as the File Information Data Structure has predefined keywords for frequently used fields, so does the Program Status Data Structure. You can access these fields either by providing the From and To positions in the data structure or by coding the special keyword in the From and To positions.

Figure 4.12 shows examples of both methods. Table 4.12 shows all of the special keywords in the Program Status Data Structure.

```
DName+++++++++++ETDsFrom+++To/L+++IDc.Keywords+++++++Comments++++++++++++
D                     SDS
D   ProgramNam           1    10
D   StatusCode       *STATUS
D   PrevStatus          16    20
```

Figure 4.12: Defining subfields with special keywords.

Table 4.12: Special Keywords in the Program Status Data Structure.

Keyword	From Position	To Position	Decimal Positions	Description
*PROC	1	10	—	Name of this procedure. [1]
*STATUS	11	15	—	Status codes. See Table 4.4.
*ROUTINE	29	36	—	Error routine. [2]
*PARMS	37	39	—	Number of parameters passed to this program.

Notes:

[1] If the module is running and someone compiles it, the module is renamed and put in library QRPLLIB. This parameter maintains the original name of the program.

[2] Possible error routines:

*INIT	Program initialization
*DETL	Detail lines
*GETIN	Get an input record
*TOTC	Total calculations
*DETC	Detail calculations
*OFL	Overflow lines
*TERM	Program ending

[3] Parameters expected by the program, but not passed by the calling program, do not cause a problem until the program attempts to access the field. If you first check the number of parameters passed to the program and do not use the field if it was not passed, you can have a variable number of parameters.

118

In Table 4.13, we list the possible status codes that can be contained in positions 11 to 15 of the Program Status Data Structure. Remember that the *STATUS keyword also can be used to access the status codes.

Table 4.13: Program Status Data Structure Status Codes.

Code	Condition
00000	No exception/error occurred.
00001	Called program returned with the last record (LR) indicator on.
00050	Conversion resulted in substitution.
00100	Out-of-range condition occurred on a string operation.
00101	A negative square root was encountered on a mathematic operation.
00102	Divide-by-zero condition detected.
00103	Intermediate result field is not large enough to contain the result (occurs in free-form arithmetic operations).
00112	Invalid Date, Time, or Timestamp value has been detected.
00113	Invalid date calculation resulting in a date less than *LOVAL or greater than *HIVAL encountered.
00114	Date mapping error from a four-digit year to a two-digit year where the mapped date does not fall between 1940 and 2039.
00115	Variable-length field has an invalid length.
00120	Array or table load sequence error.
00121	Array index is not valid.
00122	OCCUR operation is being performed on element outside of the data structure boundaries.
00123	Reset was attempted during program initialization.
00202	Called program or procedure failed and the halt indicators (H1 through H9) are not on.
00211	Error encountered trying to call a program or procedure.
00221	Called program tried to use a parameter that was not passed to it.
00222	Pointer or parameter error.
00231	Called program or procedure returned with one of the halt indicators (H1 through H9) on.
00232	Halt indicator is on.
00233	Halt indicator is on when the RETURN operation is run.
00299	RPG IV formatted dump failed.
00333	Error encountered on DSPLY operation.

Table 4.13: Program Status Data Structure Status Codes (continued).

Code	Condition
00401	Data area that is specified on IN or OUT operation could not be found.
00402	The Program Data Area (*PDA) not valid for a non-prestart job.
00411	Data area type or length does not match definition.
00412	Data area was not locked for an output operation.
00413	Error encountered on a data area IN or OUT operation.
00414	User is not currently authorized to use data area.
00415	User is not currently authorized to update data area.
00421	Error encountered on an UNLOCK operation.
00425	Length requested for storage allocation is not valid.
00426	Error during storage management operation.
00431	Data area was previously locked by another program.
00432	Data area was previously locked by the current program.
00450	Character field is not entirely enclosed by shift-out and shift-in characters.
00501	Failure to retrieve the sort sequence.
00502	Failure to convert the sort sequence.
00802	Commitment control is not active.
00803	Commitment control roll back operation failed.
00804	Error occurred on the COMMIT (commitment control) operation.
00805	Error occurred on the ROLBAK (commitment control) operation.
00907	Data decimal error was encountered. The sign or digit was not valid.
00970	The RPG IV compiler used to create the program does not match the level number of the run-time subroutines encountered.
09998	Internal failure encountered in RPG IV compiler or internal subroutines.
09999	Program exception encountered in system routine.

Error Handling

If you have been programming on the AS/400 for longer than a day, you undoubtedly have experienced the frustration of having a program blow up. It is bad enough that some user has figured out a way to cause a perfectly good program to crash, but it is another thing when the system then issues a useless message that only means something to someone buried deep within the halls of IBM.

Adding insult to injury, the user is sometimes given options to continue! Now, when was the last time you met a user who, when presented with a choice of options, would choose the correct one? (Does option C mean "Continue" or "Cancel?")

Wouldn't it be nice if you could tell the system what to do anytime it encounters an error, even if you hadn't thought of the error when you wrote the program? Well, one method of error prevention is called a *PSSR subroutine.

IMPLEMENTING THE *PSSR SUBROUTINE

A *PSSR subroutine is a user-written subroutine that receives control when the system detects an error in a program. You identify the subroutine by coding (surprise!) *PSSR in factor one of the BEGSR statement. You can access a *PSSR subroutine in three different ways:

- When you code a file access statement (such as CHAIN), and you do not specify an error indicator in positions 73 and 74, control is transferred by the system to the subroutine when an error occurs.

- You can code an error indicator in positions 73 and 74. When the error indicator comes on, execute the subroutine by coding *PSSR in Factor 2 of the EXSR statement.

- You can use the INFSR keyword on the File Definition Specification, specifying *PSSR as the subroutine name.

With the advent of subprocedures, the scope of the *PSSR subroutine has changed. A *PSSR subroutine is local to the procedure that contains it. If you code a *PSSR subroutine in the main procedure and an error occurs in a subprocedure, the *PSSR subroutine will not get called. You would need to code another *PSSR subroutine in the subprocedure to make this work.

The first thing you should be aware of when coding a *PSSR subroutine is the possibility of creating a permanently endless loop. In our experience, we have found that this situation tends to slow other users' response times and totally destroy yours.

A *PSSR subroutine is called by the system whenever an error occurs. If an error occurs while you are in the *PSSR subroutine, the *PSSR subroutine gets called again, which could cause the *PSSR error again, which again calls the *PSSR subroutine, which again causes the error... Well, you get the picture.

To ensure this does not occur, the first thing you need to do in the *PSSR subroutine is make sure you have not come from an error inside the subroutine itself. You can do this very simply by checking a field for blanks. If it is not blank, let the system take over and display its own error messages. If it is blank, continue with the subroutine and make the field nonblank. This flagging routine is very basic coding that must be done in every *PSSR subroutine you write. The program compiles and runs without this code, but you will pay the price if you leave it out.

Now you are inside the *PSSR subroutine, past the endless loop check, so you know an error has occurred in your program. But *what* happened? You can interrogate the *STATUS field of the File Information Data Structure or the MSGDTA field of the Program Status Data Structure to find out.

Another thing you could do at this point is call a generic error-handling program and pass it the File Information Data Structure and the Program Status Data Structure. This program could then log the error information to a database file and present an error screen with a message like, "An error has occurred - CALL Ron or Doug at 123-4567." This is a very nice technique that eliminates IBM's cryptic messages. It also provides a log of every error that occurs.

How you designate the return point of *PSSR subroutine depends on where you have coded the subroutine. If the subroutine is coded in the main procedure, you have one set of options available that depends on the RPG cycle. But because subprocedures do not use the RPG cycle, you must use a different set of options to designate a return point. Let's look at both methods.

Main Procedure Return Points

Regardless of what you do inside the subroutine, you have some options as to where to return control of the program. Factor 2 of the ENDSR statement of a *PSSR subroutine can be a field name that contains the control return point. Table 4.14 lists the valid values and their meanings. If the field contains an invalid entry, no error is indicated, and the system acts as if the field is blank.

Table 4.14: Error Return Points.

Value	Description
*CANCL	Cancel program.
*DETC	Detail calculations.
*DETL	Detail lines.
*GETIN	Get an input record.
*OFL	Overflow lines.
*TOTC	Continue at beginning of total calculations.
*TOTL	Continue at beginning of total lines.
blanks	Return control to the system. This is true if field is blanks or not specified, or if field contains an invalid entry. If routine was called explicitly, control returns to the next sequential statement.

If the *PSSR subroutine is called explicitly via the EXSR statement and no return point is indicated, control returns to the statement following the EXSR statement.

If the subroutine is called implicitly (via INFSR on an F-Specification or a CHAIN op code with no error indicator specified), a system error message is probably issued. An error message is not issued if the status code ranges from 1121 to 1126 because these error codes indicate that an invalid key was pressed on the keyboard (Print or Roll Up, for example). In this case, control returns to the next sequential statement.

Returning from *PSSR within a Subprocedure

You cannot specify return points for *PSSR subroutines coded in subprocedures. Factor 2 of the ENDSR statement for the *PSSR subroutine must be blank if the subroutine is contained in a subprocedure. If the ENDSR statement is reached under these conditions, the subprocedure will terminate abnormally.

You have two options to indicate where control processing returns from *PSSR subroutines coded in subprocedures. The method that offers the most flexibility is guaranteed to offend your programming sensibilities. It involves the use of the dreaded GOTO op code, which you use to return to a tag line within the subprocedure.

The other option is to end the subprocedure completely by issuing a RETURN when an error is found. Because the error happened within the subprocedure, this does not take you back to where the error occurred. Instead, the RETURN statements takes you back to where the subprocedure was executed.

Points to Remember

After the *PSSR subroutine is run, the system resets the field specified in Factor 2 of the ENDSR statement to blanks. This means that your program should set the value of the field each time the subroutine is executed. If an error occurs during the start or end of the program, control passes to the system and not to the *PSSR subroutine.

Do not let *PSSR subroutines in subprocedures reach the ENDSR statement. The subprocedure will terminate abnormally.

OPM/ILE Differences in Error Handling

The main difference between the way the OPM and ILE handle errors is in the way they treat "unhandled" exceptions. An "unhandled" error is an error for which you have not instructed the system what to do with. In OPM, if an "unhandled" error occurs, the system will issue an inquiry message. In ILE, the system will first give programs higher up the stack a chance to handle the message. If no program does handle the message, the system will then issue the inquiry message.

Let's say Program A calls Program B, which in turn calls Program C with an error indicator on the CALL. In the old days (OPM), if an error occured in Program C, you would get an error message even though you have an error indicator coded on the CALL statement. With ILE, the error indicator on the call handles the error, and no error message is sent.

We should point out that in the old days, inquiry messages started with RPG. Nowadays, they start with RNQ. This could cause problems if you are using the Message Reply List to monitor for messages. We should also point out that correct use of a *PSSR subroutine in Program C would handle the error so no inquiry message is sent in either OPM or ILE.

Record Locks

Every good programmer knows how to code the functions of accessing a file so the system does not maintain a lock on the record until the programmer actually needs it (and every programmer has a different and "proper" way to do it). But what about all those other guys who access the record and keep it locked so your program cannot get at it?

Wouldn't it be nice if, when you chained to a file to get a record and some other program had that record locked, you could send a message to your user giving them the name of the bonehead who is keeping your program from running? Well, the File Information Data Structure can tell you if a record is locked on the file, and the Program Status Data Structure can tell you the name of the job that has the lock! The sample programs in Figures 4.13 and 4.14 demonstrate this technique.

```
A*****************************************************************************
A*  TO COMPILE:
A*     CRTDSPF FILE(XXXLIB/FIG413DS)
A*****************************************************************************

AAN01N02N03T.Name++++++RLen++TDpBLinPosFunctions+++++++++++++++++++++++++++++
A                                       DSPSIZ(24 80 *DS3)
A          R FMTC
A                                       CF03(03 'End of job')
A                                       CF12(12 'Return to Previous')
A                                       OVERLAY
A                          21  3'                                          -
A                                   '                                      -
A                                       DSPATR(UL)
A                          22  5'F3=Exit'
A                          22 19'F12=Previous'
A                           9 21'Customer Number:'
A          CUSTNUMBER   10A  B  9 38
A 99                                     ERRMSGID(CPF9898 QSYS/QCPFMSG 99 &M-
A                                       ESSAGEHLD)
A                           1 27'Customer Update'
A                                       DSPATR(HI)
A                                       DSPATR(UL)
A          MESSAGEHLD   80A  P
```

Figure 4.13: DDS for sample record lock program.

```
*****************************************************************************
*  TO COMPILE:
*     CRTBNDRPG PGM(XXXLIB/FIG414RG) SRCMBR(FG414RG)
*****************************************************************************

FFilename++IPEASF.....L.....A.Device+.Keywords+++++++++++++++++++++++++++++
FFIG413DS  CF  E             WORKSTN
FCUSTOMER  UF  E           K DISK
F                                       INFDS(Info)

DName+++++++++++++ETDsFrom+++To/L+++IDc.Keywords+++++++++++++++++++++++++++++
D Info            DS
```

Figure 4.14: Sample RPG program for record locks (part 1 of 2).

```
D   Status              *STATUS
D               SDS
D   MessageDta          91    170
D   InB4        S              1
D   MessageHld  S             80


CLON01Factor1+++++++Opcode&ExtExtended-factor2++++++++++++++++++++++++++++
C                       DOU       *In99 = *OFF
C                       EXFMT     FMTC
C       CustNumber      CHAIN     CUSTOMER                             6899
C                       IF        *in99 = *on
C                       EXSR      *PSSR
C                       ENDIF
C                       ENDDO
C                       EVAL      *INLR   = *ON
CSR     *PSSR           BEGSR
C                       IF        InB4 = *on
C                       EVAL      *INLR   = *ON
C                       RETURN
C                       ELSE
C                       EVAL      InB4   = *ON
  * Record Lock
C                       IF        Status = 01218
C                       EVAL      MessageHld = MessageDta
C                       ENDIF
C                       ENDIF
C                       EVAL      InB4   = *OFF
CSR                     ENDSR
```

Figure 4.14: Sample RPG program for record locks (part 2 of 2).

The program in our example first brings up a screen asking for a customer number. It then attempts to get the record via the CHAIN op code. Because the file is coded as an update file in the File Specification, the system checks to see that the record is not being held for update elsewhere. If some other job (or even a previous job step within your job) has a lock on the record, indicator 99 comes on. Be aware that the amount of time the system waits for a record is determined by the RCDWAIT parameter on the CRTPF or CHGPF commands. The normal default is 60 seconds, but if this is changed to *NOMAX, you could be waiting until you are old and gray.

When indicator 99 comes on, the *PSSR subroutine is called explicitly. The first thing it does is make sure it is not taking part in an endless loop by checking the INB4 field. If it is, it terminates. If it is not, it interrogates the status field for code 1218—record locked, unable to allocate.

If a record lock problem exists, it moves the message data field from the Program Status Data Structure into the program-to-system field MessageHld. This field is defined on an

ERRMSGID keyword, so the message data from the Program Status Data Structure is displayed as an error message at the bottom of the screen when the record format is output.

We then fall out of the *PSSR subroutine (after blanking out our endless loop protection field). Because we have not coded a return point in Factor 2 of the ENDSR statement and the subroutine was called explicitly, control returns to the next sequential statement after the EXSR statement. Because indicator 99 is still on, we loop back up and redisplay the format with the error message indicating which job has the record locked.

INFORMATION IS POWER

The File Information Data Structure and the Program Status Data Structure can provide a wealth of information to your programs. The special keywords provided in each structure make accessing essential information a very easy task.

You can use the information, such as program name, instead of hard coding the data in your program. The obvious advantage is that the program does not have to be changed when the information changes (such as when a program is renamed or cloned).

When combined with the *PSSR subroutine, these information data structures can provide your program with a great deal of flexibility when it handles errors. You can elect to present your own global error screen whenever an unexpected error occurs. You can monitor for particular errors, take appropriate action on them, and let the system handle any other unexpected errors.

The bottom line is: The choice is yours. Information is power!

5

TIPS AND TECHNIQUES
FOR THE RPG/400 PROGRAMMER

The fact that you bought this book and are reading this chapter indicates one of three things:

A. You are an experienced programmer who is always looking for ways to improve.

B. You are a beginning programmer who is always looking for ways to improve.

C. You are a family member or close friend.

If you are reading this book for reasons A or B, we trust you will find something here to add to your toolbox. If you are reading this for reason C, thank you. Your obligation has been met and you may now stop reading.

In this chapter, we cover a little something for everyone. We start off by reviewing some basic RPG operation codes to perform routine tasks. For instance, did you know you can left-justify a field with only two statements of code? Check it out! There are a couple of ways we know of to translate lowercase to uppercase. We demonstrate how to do it using the Translate (XLATE) operation code.

The BITON/BITOFF operation codes have been around for a long time and are still very useful tools to have around, even though they can be a "bit" cumbersome to use. The example in this chapter shows how they are used to control the display attributes of embedded fields. This can be useful if you need to highlight or reverse image a key word or phrase within a line of text.

We follow this information with some techniques to make routine file maintenance tasks a little easier. Did you know, for example, that with the proper use of the RTNDTA keyword, you can eliminate all of the tedious MOVE statements that are usually coded to move fields from a database file to a display file? We not only demonstrate this technique, but also show you how to use multiple views of the same file in a program.

We will also cover parameters, asking the eternal question, "To pass or not to pass?" (please forgive us, William Shakespeare). And the answer is... Who cares? If you code the receiving program correctly, it will not blow up, even if the calling program does not pass the parameters it expects.

RPG IV is a great language, but it has one big drawback. If an RPG program written prior to RPG IV fails and the system issues an error message, it will include the source line number of the program that has the error. This is an incredibly useful piece of information when you are trying to determine what went wrong. Would you believe that RPG IV programs will not give up the source line number! We'll cover the keywords in the header specification that will take care of this problem.

Boycott indicators! The current trend in programming is to avoid using indicators whenever possible. We'll show you a technique for coding display attributes without having to use indicators.

Triggers are a great way to track changes to a database file. A trigger can monitor any method you can think of to change data in a file. And almost any information about the change can be recorded in a file, such as who made it, when it was made, and the program that was used to make it. Whoops! Did we say "the program that was used to make it?" The trigger does not keep that bit of information, but we will show you a small program that will get the job done.

130

REMOVING LEADING BLANKS (LEFT JUSTIFY)

The CHECK op code is very useful for removing leading blanks. When used in conjunction with the Substring (SUBST) op code, leading blanks can be removed from a field with two simple statements (see Figure 5.1).

```
CLON01Factor1+++++++Opcode&ExtFactor2+++++++Result++++++++Len++D+HiLoEq..Comments
C        ' '              CHECK     NAME          X                     2 0
C                         SUBST(P)  NAME:X        NAME
```

Figure 5.1: Using the CHECK op code to remove leading blanks.

The example in Figure 5.1 uses the CHECK op code to find the first nonblank character in the NAME field, storing the address of that field in a numeric variable called X. The Substring (SUBST) function is then used to move the nonblank characters NAME into the left-most characters of the NAME field. It then pads the remaining positions of the NAME field with blanks.

As an example, let's apply the code in Figure 5.1 to the following NAME field:

```
0...+... 1 ...+... 2 ...+... 3
          SMITH
```

The results after the operation in Figure 5.1 look like this:

```
0...+... 1 ...+... 2 ...+... 3
SMITH
```

TRANSLATE (XLATE) PERFORMS SINGLE-CHARACTER SUBSTITUTION WITHIN CHARACTER STRINGS

The Translate (XLATE) op code is a handy tool when you need to perform character substitution within a character string. You can specify From and To characters or entire strings of characters that need to be translated.

One of the more popular uses for this op code is to translate a lowercase character string to uppercase. This is a frequent requirement when you are importing data from an external source. Figure 5.2 shows an example of how to address this issue.

```
DName++++++++++++ETDsFrom+++To/L+++IDc.Keywords+++++++++++++++++++++++++++Comments++++
DLower           C                   'abcdefghijklmnopqrstuvwxyz'
DUpper           C                   'ABCDEFGHIJKLMNOPQRSTUVWXYZ'

CLON01Factor1+++++++Opcode&ExtFactor2++++++Result++++++++Len++D+HiLoEq...Comments
C     Lower:Upper   XLATE     LowerField    UpperField
```

Figure 5.2: Using XLATE to translate lowercase character strings to uppercase.

USING BITON/BITOFF OPERATION CODES

BITON and the converse op code BITOFF allow you to change the status of the bits in a single-byte field. The BITON op code changes the specified bits from a 0 (off) to a 1 (on) (Figure 5.3). The BITOFF op code does just the opposite.

Factor 1	Op Code	Factor 2	Result Field	Ext	HI	LO	EQ
—	BITON	'bit pattern'	1 byte field	—	N/A	N/A	N/A

Figure 5.3: Example of the BITON RPG op code.

In both of these operation codes, Factor 1 is left blank. Factor 2 can contain either a single-byte character field or a named constant containing a bit pattern. If a field is used in Factor 2, the bits that are on in that field are set off in the results field. The bits that are off in the field in Factor 2 are ignored.

You should be aware of the horizontal method of addressing bits used in RPG. There are 8 bits in a byte. The bits are numbered from left to right, beginning with 0.

One of our favorite uses of these operation codes is to change a display attribute of some portion of a text field. The DSPATR keyword is easy to use, but works on the complete field. You cannot use it to highlight a single word inside a text field. You can, however, use the BITON/BITOFF operation codes to accomplish this. Let's take at look at the code in Figure 5.4.

We first use the BITOFF op code to set off all of the bits in our field named HighLight. This is similar to initializing a field. We then use the BITON op code to set on bits 2 and 6. When sent to a display device, this combination of bits translates into a command character that tells the system to turn on highlighting.

```
CLON01Factor1+++++++Opcode&ExtFactor2+++++++Result++++++++Len++D+HiLoEq...Comments
C                    BITOFF  '01234567'     HighLight       1
C                    BITON   '26'           HighLight       1
C                    BITOFF  '01234567'     Normal          1
C                    BITON   '2'            Normal          1
C                    BITOFF  '01234567'     ReversImag      1
C                    BITON   '27'           ReversImag      1
C                    MOVEL   HighLight      Field
C                    MOVE    Normal         Field
```

Figure 5.4: Using BITON/BITOFF to change display attributes .

We will now use the BITON/BITOFF op codes to set on bit 2 in a field called Normal. (You might notice that we have included the bit pattern for the field named ReversImag, which is short for *reverse image*. We are not using it in this example, but we thought you might find it useful.) We use the Normal field to turn off the highlighting function. Next we move the HighLight field to the beginning of the field we want highlighted and move the Normal field to the end of the field we want highlighted. When this field, named (cleverly enough) FIELD, is displayed on a device, it is highlighted. This field can then be embedded in an array, or *substringed* (you will not find this word in your dictionary, but consider it a derivative of the Substring op code) together with other text that would be normally displayed.

When using this technique, be sure to use the normal pattern to shut off the display attribute you set. If you do not, the attribute remains in effect until the end of the displayed line.

Using RTNDTA in File Maintenance

A file maintenance program is like a sewer; it performs a very necessary function, but nobody likes to work there. Let's face it, file maintenance programs are boring and tedious. Every one of them performs pretty much the same routines—read a record, move the fields from the record to the screen, display the screen, edit the fields, move the fields back to the record, update the record. This a standard, low-tech, boring job that must be done.

There is a DDS keyword, RTNDTA, that can eliminate a lot of code. While it cannot actually make you *like* doing file maintenance programs, it simplifies the task by eliminating a lot of tedious move statements.

Figure 5.5 shows a typical file maintenance task. It reads a record, moves the fields in the record to the screen, and waits for the user to enter some data. The record is not locked at this point because we do not know how long the user will be at lunch while this record is on the screen. When the user comes back from his break and presses the Enter key, we get the database record (this time locking the record for update), and the fields are moved from the screen to the record and the database record is updated.

```
CL0N01Factor1+++++++Opcode&ExtFactor2+++++++Result++++++++Len++D+HiLoEq...Comments
C        CustKey        CHAIN(N)  Customer                        68
C                       EVAL      DispName = CustName
C                       EVAL      DispAddr1 = CustAddr1
C                       EVAL      DispAddr2 = CustAddr2
C                       EVAL      DispCity = CustCity
C                       EVAL      DispState = CustState
C                       EVAL      DispZip = CustZip
C                       EXFMT     Format1
C        CustKey        CHAIN     Customer                        68
C                       EVAL      CustName = DispName
C                       EVAL      CustAddr1 = DispAddr1
C                       EVAL      CustAddr2 = DispAddr2
C                       EVAL      CustCity = DispCity
C                       EVAL      CustState = DispState
C                       EVAL      CustZip = DispZip
C                       UPDATE    CustRec
```

Figure 5.5: Routine file maintenance task.

Figure 5.6 shows the same function as in Figure 5.5, but it uses the RTNDTA DDS keyword in the display file. All of the fields in the display file have the same names as the fields in the database file. This eliminates you having to code all of the MOVE statements to get them from the database record to the display file record format.

```
CL0N01Factor1+++++++Opcode&ExtFactor2+++++++Result++++++++Len++D+HiLoEq...Comments
C        CustKey        CHAIN(N)  Customer                        68
C                       EXFMT     Format1
C        CustKey        CHAIN     Customer                        68
C                       READ      Format1                             68
C                       UPDATE    CustRec
```

Figure 5.6: Maintenance function with the RTNDTA keyword.

But wait a minute, you say, when my program chains back out to the database record to get it for update, it will lose any of the data keyed into the fields in the display format. This is true, so we have coded another read to the display file record format (Format1). The RTNDTA keyword is coded on this record format and because this was the last record format written to the screen, the system gets the fields from the screen again, as the user

134

keyed them. But wait another minute, you say, the READ Format1 statement will cause the program to wait for input from the user. Normally, this would be true, but the RTNDTA keyword also prevents this from happening.

This is a very powerful technique that can potentially eliminate tons of code and reduce the amount of maintenance that must be performed later. In this very simple example, we eliminated a lot of extraneous code. And remember the programmer's motto: Less code, fewer errors.

PROCESSING MULTIPLE VIEWS OF THE SAME DATABASE FILE

Options, options, and more options. We are really in the business of providing people with options. The more the merrier. One of the options every user seems to demand is the ability to display the records from a database file in a sequence other than the database designer intended. With DB/400's support of logical files, this does not present much of a problem. Remember the performance considerations when using this technique, however (see chapter 1).

In Figure 5.7, we present our usual method of handling multiple views of the same file in a single program. The first step is to define the files in the File Description Specifications. The compiler frowns on using two file definitions with the same record format, so we need to rename one of the record formats. This is accomplished using the RENAME keyword. We name the actual record format and then give it an alias we can use to refer to it inside the RPG program.

```
FFilename++IPEASFRlen+LKlen+AIDevice+.Keywords++++++++++++++++++++++++++Comments++++
FFile1      IF   E           K DISK
FFile1LogicIF   E           K DISK     Rename(FileRec:LogicRec)


CLON01Factor1+++++++Opcode&ExtFactor2+++++++Result++++++++Len++D+HiLoEq...Comments
C                   SELECT
C                   WHEN      *IN71 = *ON
C                   READ      File1                               68
C                   WHEN      *IN72 = *ON
C                   READ      File1Logic                          68
```

Figure 5.7: Multiple views of the same file in a single program.

Now that the compiler is happy, we can continue on our merry way and read whichever view of the database file the user is happy with. The system keeps two independent file pointers for each "view" of your data. You do, however, need to be careful when you are handling the contents of individual fields.

One of our complaints with RPG is that its file access operation codes (READ and CHAIN, for example) do not allow a field name in Factor 2. This would greatly simplify the amount of code necessary to deal with multiple view of the same database file. We hear that this capability might—just might—make it into a future release.

PASS THE PARAMETER, IF YOU PLEASE

There are numerous ways to handle passing information between programs on the AS/400. You can use files, data queues, message queues, data areas, parameters, pointers, exports/imports, and so on.

Parameters are defined in a program using a Parameter List (PLIST) statement, with *EN-TRY defined in Factor 1. A PLIST statement must be followed by at least one Parameter (PARM) statement that defines the data being received by the program.

We see an example of this in Figure 5.8. Two parameters are being passed to this program: a two-character, alphanumeric return code and a two-digit, numeric location code.

```
DName+++++++++++ETDsFrom+++To/L+++IDc.Keywords+++++++++++++++++++++++++Comments++++
D                SDS
DParms              *PARMS

CL0N01Factor1+++++++Opcode&ExtFactor2+++++++Result++++++++Len++D+HiLoEq...Comments
C     *ENTRY       PLIST
C                  PARM                      ReturnCode      2
C                  PARM                      PasLocCode      2 0
C                  IF         Parms >= 1
C                  EVAL       ReturnCode = *blanks
C                  ENDIF
C                  IF         Parms >= 2
C                  EVAL       WrkLocCode = PasLocCode
C                  ENDIF
```

Figure 5.8: Passing a variable number of parameters between programs.

The thing to remember about parameter passing is that the program neither checks nor cares about any of the parameters until it actually tries to use them. This means that if a program calls another program and does not pass all of the parameters that the called program is expecting, nothing happens until—and if—the called program tries to access one of the passed parameters. If the called program does try to use a parameter and the program that initiated the call did not pass the field, you get introduced to one of the operating system's nifty little error handling routines.

There is a simple method of avoiding this error. Code the Program Status Data Structure and use the keyword *PARMS, as we did in Figure 5.8. The PARMS field contains the number of parameters the calling program passed to the called program. If the PARMS field tells us that a parameter was passed to this program, we move the parameter to a work field. Unless the program is passing data back to the calling program, the program only works with the work fields. If it is passing data back to the calling program, it must check the PARMS field again. At no time does the program attempt to access a parameter without first checking the PARMS field to see if the field was passed to it.

If you are on a recent release of OS/400, you can use the built-in function %PARMS to determine the number of parameters passed to the program. This eliminates the need for you to code the program status data structure. The following code example can be used to test for the number of parameters passed:

```
CLON01Factor1+++++++Opcode&ExtFactor2+++++++Result++++++++Len++D+HiLoEq
C                   IF        %PARMS > 2
```

USING A RTNCOD PARAMETER BETWEEN PROGRAMS

We all know the problems associated with using one big program to do many different functions. The program is slow to load into memory, difficult to follow, and hard for others to maintain. In large and complex applications, it is far better to design many smaller programs controlled by one *driver* program. These smaller programs are generally referred to as *subprograms*. The subprograms only get loaded into memory when they are needed. Maintenance can usually be isolated to one small, easy-to-follow subprogram.

This technique can present something of a problem, however, because the calling program often needs to know what happened in the called program. The driver program must know if it calls a subprogram that presents the user with a screen and the user presses F3 to exit in order to end the job step. As usual, there are many ways to accomplish this, one of which is to use a parameter to pass the function key that was pressed. Figure 5.9 illustrates this technique.

```
CLON01Factor1+++++++Opcode&ExtFactor2+++++++Result++++++++Len++D+HiLoEq....Comment
s+
C        *ENTRY        PLIST
C                      PARM                     ReturnCode        2
C                      EXFMT        Format1
C                      IF           *INKC = *On
C                      EVAL         ReturnCode = '03'
C                      EVAL         *InLr = *On
C                      ENDIF
C                      IF           *INKL = *On
C                      EVAL         ReturnCode = '12'
C                      ENDIF
```

Figure 5.9: Using a RTNCOD parameter between programs.

USING THE INDICATOR ARRAY

One technique we often take for granted is one new programmers might not yet be aware of. You can use the array handling operation code Move Array (MOVEA) to simultaneously set many indicators on and off. We use this technique quite often at the beginning of edit routines to set off all of the error indicators. Figure 5.10 demonstrates this technique.

```
DName+++++++++++ETDsFrom+++To/L+++IDc.Keywords+++++++++++++++++++++++++Comments++++
DIndicatSet       C                   '001100111100001111-
D                                      00000000'

CLON01Factor1+++++++Opcode&ExtFactor2+++++++Result++++++++Len++D+HiLoEq...Comments
C                      EXFMT        Format1
C                      MOVEA        *ALL'0'         *IN(40)
C                      EXFMT        Format2
C                      MOVEA        '000000'        *IN(32)
C                      EXFMT        Format3
C                      MOVEA        IndicatSet      *IN(50)
```

Figure 5.10: Using the indicator array.

After displaying FORMAT1, the MOVEA operation code is used to set off indicators 40 through 99. The reserved word *ALL is used to indicate the settings of the indicators. We could just as easily specify *ALL(1) to set all the indicators on.

After displaying FORMAT2, the MOVEA operation code is used to set off indicators 32 through 37. Factor 2 is only eight characters long, so this version of the technique is limited in the number of indicators affected by the operation code.

The example in Figure 5.10 also uses a named constant to set the status of indicators 50 through 75. This version of the technique can handle as many indicators as you want, and set them to any required status.

When you use this technique, be aware that the indicators affected by the movea statement do not show up in the RPG compile listing as having been used. This is because they are individual elements in an array.

USING INDICATORS AS FIELD NAMES

You can also refer to an indicator as a named field. Every indicator has its own name using the format *INXX, where XX is the indicator number. The first two statements shown in Figure 5.11 are basically equal. You can, and should, test the status of indicators by using the indicator name, either in Factor 1 on an IFEQ statement or anywhere in an EVAL statement.

```
CL0N01Factor1+++++++Opcode&ExtFactor2+++++++Result++++++++Len++D+HiLoEq...Comments
C                   SETON                                         01
C                   EVAL      *IN01 = *ON
C                   IF        *IN01 = *ON
C                   MOVE      *ON           *INLR
C                   ENDIF
```

Figure 5.11: Indicators as named fields.

We have a strong aversion to using indicators to condition Calculation Specifications. While it's easier to code, it's harder to read, follow, and—especially—maintain.

RETRIEVING THE PROGRAM NAME

One very useful bit of information you can extract from the Program Status Data Structure is the name of the running program. Why is this useful, you ask? After all, you wrote the program and know its name. Why do you need the Program Status Data Structure to tell you this?

The obvious answer is maintenance. After you have been programming for some time, you should find that you rarely write programs from scratch. More likely, you find something similar in your toolbox and start there.

139

But there is another, less obvious, answer. The system sometimes changes the name of the program! If a program is executing and some inattentive programmer compiles it, the system moves it into the QRPLLIB library. As it does this, it renames the object. The net result is that the running program still runs the old code, while any new instances of the program run the newly compiled version.

While that program is running in QRPLLIB, it has a different name. If you hard coded the name of the program into any fields (such as message queue name), you might experience the system-handling error routine. This is kind of like meeting the Master Control Program (for all you TRON fans)—a very nasty experience.

The best way to code the name of the program is to retrieve it from the Program Status Data Structure. An example of this is shown in Figure 5.12. The program name is retrieved using the *PROC keyword. In our example, we have assigned it a field name of ProgramNam. (You should note that RPG III used the *PROGRAM keyword and RPG IV uses *PROC.)

```
DName+++++++++++ETDsFrom+++To/L+++IDc.Keywords+++++++++++++++++++++++++++Comments++++
D                SDS
DProgramNam          *PROC
```

Figure 5.12: Extracting the program name.

USING MULTIPLE FORMAT FILES

The AS/400 uses a very strong relational database file manager. File definitions are external to programs processing the data, thus ensuring consistency and relieving the programmer of the necessity of defining the data.

But some people believe that this file management system cannot handle multiple format files. While it is true that a single file can only contain one format, it is also true that a logical file can be built over multiple files (each file having a different format). The net result appears to be a multiple format file. This is especially useful in a header/detail-type file relationship.

If you perform a read on the logical file, you get a record from either file (which could be the header record or the detail record), depending on which was next in sequence. From a programming perspective, the problem becomes determining the record format that was

140

just read. This information can be obtained from the File Information Data Structure. Figure 5.13 shows the RPG code that demonstrates this technique.

```
FFilename++IPEASFRlen+LKlen+AIDevice+.Keywords+++++++++++++++++++++++++Comments++++
FLogical   IF   E         K DISK     INFDS(InfoDs)

DName++++++++++ETDsFrom+++To/L+++IDc.Keywords+++++++++++++++++++++++++Comments++++
DInfoDs           DS
DFormatName       *RECORD

CLON01Factor1++++++Opcode&ExtFactor2+++++++Result++++++++Len++D+HiLoEq....Comment
s+
C                 READ     Logical                             68
C                 SELECT
C                 WHEN     FormatName = 'HEADER'
C                 EXSR     Header
C                 WHEN     FormatName = 'DETAIL'
C                 EXSR     Detail
C                 ENDSL
```

Figure 5.13: Processing a multiple-format logical file.

You must be sure to read the file and not the record format. If you specify the file name on the read statement, you read either the header record or the detail record. On the other hand, if you specify a record format name on the read statement, you only read records that are in that format. Once we have read the file, the field we named FORMAT, which has been named with the special keyword *RECORD, contains the name of the record format we just read. We use this field to determine whether we have read a header or detail record.

LOCALIZED INDICATORS

It is unfortunate, but true—indicators are still a fact of life in RPG. We still need them to communicate to I/O devices. Complex programs can still use quite a few indicators. One way to hold down the number of indicators used in a program is to use the concept of localized indicators.

A localized indicator has a value that is only seen within the subroutine in which it is being used. It is as if each subroutine had its own indicator array. While RPG IV does not support this concept, you can fake it.

141

When we enter a subroutine, we save the contents of the indicator array. We then clear the array. This allows the subroutine to use any indicator it needs without disturbing the normal flow of the program. At the end of the subroutine, we restore the indicator array to its original state.

The net effect of this technique is to make the entire subroutine "indicatorless." This can prove very useful if the subroutine will be used in many places. Figure 5.14 shows an example of this technique.

```
CLON01Factor1+++++++Opcode&ExtFactor2+++++++Result++++++++Len++D+HiLoEq...Comments
C                    EXSR      Example
C        Example     BEGSR
C                    MOVEA     *IN(1)         SaveIndic         99
C                    MOVEA     *OFF           *IN(1)
 ** Processing stuff goes here
C                    MOVEA     SaveIndic      *IN(1)
C                    ENDSR
```

Figure 5.14: Code sample for localized indicators.

DISPLAY ATTRIBUTES WITHOUT INDICATORS

There is a strong aversion in the RPG community to using indicators, and they should be avoided whenever possible. One rational for using indicators was in the area of display-file communications. If you have to display a field with attributes other than normal (highlight, reverse image, etc), you have to use an indicator, right? Wrong!

The code shown in Figure 5.15 shows you how to code a field in a display file that will get its display attributes from the value of a field in a program. The NAMEATR field is defined with a P in the type position, indicating that it is a program to system field. The DSPATR keyword on the NAME field specifies &NAMEATR as a parameter. This means that the value of the NAMEATR field will control the actual display attribute of the NAME field.

The NAMEATR field must contain a valid hexadecimal value the DSPATR keyword understands. The code in Figure 5.16 demonstrates how you can accomplish this. We have included in this example the hexadecimal values for many commonly used attributes.

```
.AAN01N02N03T.Name++++++RLen++TDpBLinPosFunctions+++++++++++++++++
A          R FORMAT1
A            NAMEATR      1A  P
A                                 4  3'Ins Company Name:'
A            NAME        31A  O   4 22DSPATR(&NAMEATR)
```

Figure 5.15: DDS forcontrolling DSPATR without indicators.

```
FFilename++IPEASF.....L.....A.Device+.Keywords++++++++++++++++++++++++++
fHexAttrDs cf   e              workstn
DName++++++++++ETDsFrom+++To/L+++IDc.Keywords++++++++++++++++++++++++++
d Normal       s              1   inz(x'20')
d ReverseImg   s              1   inz(x'21')
d HighLight    s              1   inz(x'22')
d UnderLine    s              1   inz(x'24')
d NonDisplay   s              1   inz(x'27')
d Blink        s              1   inz(x'28')
d ColumnSeps   s              1   inz(x'30')
d Protect      s              1   inz(x'A0')

CL0N01Factor1+++++++Opcode&ExtFactor2+++++++Result++++++++Len++D+HiLoEq
c              Eval      NameAtr = Highlight
c              Eval      Name = 'JOHN'
c              Exfmt     Format1
c              Eval      *inlr = *on
```

Figure 5.16: RPG forcontroling DSPATR without indicators.

USING THE CLEAR OP CODE

We have already seen how the use of the RTNDTA keyword can eliminate a bunch of te-dious MOVE statements when you want to update fields. The CLEAR op code can do the same thing when you want to blank out all of the fields on a screen.

Normally, you blank out the input fields before you present an input screen so that what-ever the user entered into those fields the last time the screen was displayed will not show up the next around. If there are 10 fields on the screen, 10 move statements are required to clear them. You can clear all 10 fields with one CLEAR statement. And best of all, if someone comes along later and adds a new field to the screen, it too is cleared with the same CLEAR statement

Figure 5.17 shows the CLEAR op code. If you specify a format name in Factor 2, all fields in the format are cleared. You can also use the CLEAR op code to clear a field or all fields in a database file record format. Fields that are numeric are set to all zeros; alphanumeric fields are set to all blanks. While this in itself does nothing to help future maintenance (after all, it's not likely that the field will change from alphanumeric to numeric), it does relieve you from having to know which type of field you are clearing.

Factor 1	Op Code	Factor 2	Result Field
—	CLEAR	Format Name	—

Figure 5.17: The CLEAR op code.

SOFT CODING FUNCTION KEYS

The soft coding of function keys refers to a technique of determining the function key the user presses without the use of indicators. In place of indicators, you assign meaningful field names to the function key that was pressed.

The main advantage to soft coding keys is ease of maintenance. This makes it much easier to read the code and understand the intent of the original programmer. Look at the following program, and then you be the judge:

```
If (*IN13 = *ON)

If (*INKM = *ON)

If (WhatKey = F13)
```

The WhatKey=F13 line is the only line that immediately tells you that what follows is to be executed if the user presses the F13 function key. The IF *INKM line comes close, but then you have to translate the KM into the correct function key.

Figure 5.18 shows you how to soft code function keys. The File Information Data Structure (see chapter 4) contains information about the function key the user pressed in position 369. Using the hexadecimal code generated by each key, we then set up named constants for each key that could be pressed. After assigning meaningful names to each key, all we have to do is compare byte 369 of the File Information Data Structure with the each of the named constants. The result? Clear, concise, colorful, captivating code. (Sounds like a soft drink commercial, doesn't it?)

144

```
FFilename++IPEASFRlen+LKlen+AIDevice+.Keywords+++++++++++++++++++++++++Comments++++
FDsplayFileCF   E              WORKSTN INFDS(InfoDs)

DName++++++++++ETDsFrom+++To/L+++IDc.Keywords+++++++++++++++++++++++++Comments++++
DInfoDs         DS
DWhatKey                  369      369
DF01            C                       CONST(X'31')
DF02            C                       CONST(X'32')
DF03            C                       CONST(X'33')
DF04            C                       CONST(X'34')
DF05            C                       CONST(X'35')
DF06            C                       CONST(X'36')
DF07            C                       CONST(X'37')
DF08            C                       CONST(X'38')
DF09            C                       CONST(X'39')
DF10            C                       CONST(X'3A')
DF11            C                       CONST(X'3B')
DF12            C                       CONST(X'3C')
DF13            C                       CONST(X'B1')
DF14            C                       CONST(X'B2')
DF15            C                       CONST(X'B3')
DF16            C                       CONST(X'B4')
DF17            C                       CONST(X'B5')
DF18            C                       CONST(X'B6')
DF19            C                       CONST(X'B7')
DF20            C                       CONST(X'B8')
DF21            C                       CONST(X'B9')
DF22            C                       CONST(X'BA')
DF23            C                       CONST(X'BB')
DF24            C                       CONST(X'BC')
DClearKey       C                       CONST(X'BD')
DEnterKey       C                       CONST(X'F1')
DHelpKey        C                       CONST(X'F3')
DPageDown       C                       CONST(X'F5')
DPageUp         C                       CONST(X'F4')
DPrintKey       C                       CONST(X'F6')

CL0N01Factor1+++++++Opcode&ExtFactor2+++++++Result+++++++Len++D+HiLoEq....Comment
s+
C                        EXFMT     Format1
C                        SELECT
C                        WHEN      WhatKey = F01
 *   Function key F1 pressed
C                        WHEN      WhatKey = F02
 *   Function key F2 pressed
C                        WHEN      WhatKey = EnterKey
 *   Enter key pressed
C                        ENDSL
C                        ENDSR
```

Figure 5.18: Soft coding function keys.

145

HEADER SPECIFICATION COMPILE OPTIONS

The ILE RPG header specification has been greatly enhanced since the days of the old OPM model of RPG. The good old H-Spec is freeform and keyword based. It can also be automatically inserted into your program. If you want the same set of keywords to be automatically inserted into every one of your RPG IV programs, you should use the RPGLEHSPEC data area.

If you put the keywords in the RPGLEHSPEC data area, they will be automatically inserted into your program at compile time. You can create this data area (of any size you want) in any library you choose. Please note that if you already have a header specification coded in the program, the keywords will not be retrieved into the program. You should also ensure that only valid keywords are in the data area.

If the compiler does not find a header specification in the program, or the RPGLEHSPEC data area in the library list, it will look for another data area called DFTLEHSPEC in the QRPGLE library. If it finds this data area, it will use the header specifications found there.

THE HEADER SPECIFICATION AND ITS EFFECT ON DEBUG

Speaking of valid keywords in the header specification, here are two OPTION keywords you should be aware of. Your programs must be recompiled with these keywords in a header specification.

The first is OPTION(*SRCSTMT), which ensures that statement numbers for the listing match the SEU source member sequence numbers. Source code pulled into the program from other source members has a source member number concatenated onto the front of the SEU sequence number. Without this option specified, error messages sent by the system do not match the source statement number. This would force you to keep a copy of the compile listing for every program you have, or to recompile the program to get the compile listing of the program having the problem. Neither alternative is good. OP-TION(*SRCSTMT) should be inserted into every program you have.

The other option keyword you should be aware of is OPTION(*NODEBUGIO). This option stops a debug from issuing a break for each field in a database file when you put a break point on a file access line. Let's say you chain to a file with three fields in it. If you put a break point on that chain statement, the debugger would break three times! With OP-TION(*NODEBUGIO), it only breaks once.

These two options are available in V4R4. They are also available in prior releases via PTFs. You need a separate PTF for both the runtime version and the compiler version. If you go to the IBM Web site at *www.as400service.rochester.ibm.com*, you can get to a list of the relevant PTFs for your release.

WHO PULLED THE TRIGGER?

No, this is not a murder mystery. But triggers do hide a secret. The system will not willingly give up the name of the program that caused the trigger to fire. It will tell you every other thing you could possibly want to know about the transaction, but it will not tell you the name of the program that caused it to happen.

We are not going to give a tutorial on using triggers (there are plenty of fine books on the subject already). So if you do not already know how to use triggers, you can probably skip this technique. But if you do use them (and you should), the procedure shown in Figure 5.19 will return the name of the program that caused the trigger to fire. This procedure should be called from the trigger program.

The procedure uses the Send Program Message (QMHSNDPM) API, which will send a message up the program stack. Once the message has been sent up the program stack, we receive the message using the Receive Program Message (QMHRCVPM) API. The name of the program we are receiving the message from is contained in position 111 of the message. This could be the name of the program that caused the trigger to fire—but it might not be.

Some programs in the call stack belong to IBM. Weed these programs out by checking to see if the program (or module) exists in either the QPDA or QSYS library. If it does, assume these are IBM programs and subtract one from the stack counter. We then send another message to a program one step farther up the call stack and repeat the process.

We use another procedure to see if the program exists. That procedure is aptly called *Exists*. To create this object, you must use the CRTMOD command to create a module. You can then either bind the module directly to a program or put it in a service program. See chapter 14—for an explanation of this procedure or if you need help with procedures in general.

```
* To Create:  CRTRPGMOD MODULE(GETTRGPGM)

HNOMAIN
*
*  procedure name:    GetTrgPgm
*
*  procedure function: Return name of program that caused trigger
*                      to fire.

d  GetTrgPgm       PR              20

d  Exists          PR               1
d   Object                         10       const
d   Objecttype                     10       const
d   ObjectLib                      10       const options(*nopass)

P  GetTrgPgm       B                        export
d  GetTrgPgm       PI              20

d  MsgAction       s               10
d  MsgData         s                9
d  MsgDtaLen       s                6 0 inz(%size(MsgData))
d  MsgFileLib      s               20
d  MsgId           s               10
d  MsgKey          s                9b 0
d  MsgQueue        s               10
d  MsgQueNbr       s                9b 0
d  MsgType         s               10
d  RcvData         s             1000
d  RcvDtaLen       s                6 0 inz(%size(RcvData))
d  RcvFormat       s                8
d  RcvKey          s                9b 0 inz
d  StackNbr        s                6 0 inz(3)
d  TestPgm         s               10
d  WaitTime        s                9b 0
d  WhoCalled       s               20
*

D  ErrorDs         DS                       INZ
D   BytesProv               1       4B 0 inz(116)
D   BytesAval               5       8B 0
D   MessageId               9      15
D   Err###                 16      16
D   MessageDta             17     116

c                  movel   'QCPFMSG   '  MsgFileLib
c                  move    'QSYS      '  MsgFileLib

c                  dou     WhoCalled <> *blanks
* send a message to a program up the job stack
C                  CALL    'QMHSNDPM'
C                  PARM                    MsgId
```

Figure 5.19 : The program that caused the trigger to fire (part 1 of 3).

```
C                       PARM                          MsgFileLib
C                       PARM                          MsgData
C                       PARM                          MsgDtaLen
C                       PARM        '*RQS'            MsgType
C                       PARM        '*'              MsgQueue
C                       PARM        StackNbr          MsgQueNbr
C                       PARM                          RcvKey
C                       PARM                          ErrorDs

 * cpf2904 call stack not found
c                       if          MessageId = 'CPF2904'
c                       eval        WhoCalled = MessageId
c                       endif

c                       if          WhoCalled = *blanks
c                       move        RcvKey          MsgKey
 * receive (and remove) the message you sent
C                       CALL        'QMHRCVPM'
C                       PARM                          RcvData
C                       PARM                          RcvDtaLen
C                       PARM        'RCVM0200'        RcvFormat
C                       PARM        '*'              MsgQueue
C                       PARM        StackNbr          MsgQueNbr
C                       PARM        '*RQS'            MsgType
C                       PARM                          MsgKey
c                       parm        0                 WaitTime
c                       parm        '*REMOVE'         MsgAction
C                       PARM                          ErrorDs

c                       eval        StackNbr = StackNbr + 1

 * extract the program name that received the message you sent
c                       eval        TestPgm = %subst(RcvData:111:10)

 * ignore programs in QSYS or QPDA as these are most likely IBM's
c                       if          Exists(TestPgm:'*PGM':'QSYS') = 'Y' OR
c                                   Exists(TestPgm:'*MOD':'QSYS') = 'Y' OR
c                                   Exists(TestPgm:'*PGM':'QPDA') = 'Y' OR
c                                   Exists(TestPgm:'*MOD':'QPDA') = 'Y'
c                       iter
c                       endif

c                       eval        WhoCalled = TestPgm
c                       endif
c                       enddo

c                       return      WhoCalled
P   GetTrgPgm   E
P   Exists      B                          export
d   Exists      PI          1
d   Object                  10    const
d   ObjectType              10    const
```

Figure 5.19 : The program that caused the trigger to fire (part 2 of 3).

```
d  ObjectILib                        10     const options(*nopass)

d  ReceiveVar     s                 100
d  ReceiveLen     s                  9b 0  inz(100)
d  ObjdFormat     s                  8     inz('OBJD0100')
d  ObjectLib      s                 20     inz('          *LIBL     ')
d  ObjectTypF     s                 10
d  Valid          s                  1
D  ErrorDs        DS               116     INZ
D  BytesPrv               1          4B 0  inz(116)
D  BytesAvl               5          8B 0  inz(0)
D  MessageId              9         15
D  ERR###               16         16
D  MessageDta           17        116
   *

c                        movel     Object        ObjectLib
c                        eval      ObjectTypF = ObjectType
c                        if        %parms = 3
c                        move      ObjectILib    ObjectLib
c                        endif
   * Attempt to retrieve object description
C                        CALL      'QUSROBJD'
C                        PARM                    ReceiveVar
C                        PARM                    ReceiveLen
C                        PARM                    ObjdFormat
C                        PARM                    ObjectLib
C                        PARM                    ObjectTypF
C                        PARM                    ErrorDs

c                        select
   * If not authorized, then object exists
c                        when      MessageId = 'CPF9821'
c                        eval      Valid = 'Y'
   * Otherwise, error trying to get object description, means not valid
c                        when      MessageDta <> *blanks
c                        eval      Valid = 'N'
c                        other
c                        eval      Valid = 'Y'
c                        endsl

c                        return    Valid
P  Exists         E
```

Figure 5.19 : The program that caused the trigger to fire (part 3 of 3).

A DIVERSE ARSENAL IS YOUR BEST DEFENSE

Regardless of how long you remain in this business, you can never have too many tools in your toolbox. Knowing where to get them is usually the most important step in programming.

6

THE POWER OF
COMMAND PROCESSING APIs

This chapter is primarily dedicated to covering two very special API programs: Command Execute (QCMDEXC) and Process Commands (QCAPCMD). Both of these APIs can be used to reduce the amount of code you use and greatly increase the flexibility of your RPG programs.

The QCMDEXC API is used to call AS/400 commands from within your RPG or CL programs. It is a powerful tool and should certainly be in every RPG programmer's arsenal. Almost anything you would ever want to do with a single command can be done right from within your program! We'll also show you how to prototype the call to this API.

The QCAPCMD API allows you to edit a command string for validity, allows for prompting, and returns the command parameters to your RPG program.

Yet another way to execute commands from within a program is to use the C function "system." C functions come standard with your machine and are easily accessible with RPG IV. We will show you how easy this C function is to use.

THE WHAT, THE WHY, AND THE HOW OF COMMAND EXECUTE (QCMDEXC)

Think about the possibilities. With QCMDEXC, you can submit jobs, manipulate library lists, override printer parameters, sort database files, and a veritable plethora of other tasks, all from within your RPG program.

In this chapter, we give you three sample ways to use the API to get more flexibility from your RPG programs, including:

- Running the Open Query File (OPNQRYF) command from within a print program to sequence a file into the order you want before listing it.

- Overriding printer parameters within an RPG program to allow you to send printed output to a specific printer and change the number of copies.

- Submitting a job from within an RPG program.

The QCMDEXC API is not only versatile, it is also very easy to use. All you need to do is call the program and pass it two parameters: the command you want to run and the length of the command (you can even fudge a little on this one because the system does not seem to mind if you pad the back end of your command with blanks). The length of the second parameter, which specifies the command length, must be a 15-digit field with five decimal positions. It is that easy!

The example in Figure 6.1 shows you how to embed the Work with Spool Files (WRKSPLF) command into an RPG program. Let's get into some more practical examples of the QCMDEXC API.

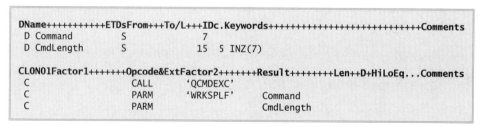

```
DName+++++++++++ETDsFrom+++To/L+++IDc.Keywords+++++++++++++++++++++++++++++++Comments
D Command           S              7
D CmdLength         S             15   5 INZ(7)

CLON01Factor1+++++++Opcode&ExtFactor2+++++++Result++++++++Len++D+HiLoEq...Comments
C                   CALL      'QCMDEXC'
C                   PARM      'WRKSPLF'      Command
C                   PARM                     CmdLength
```

Figure 6.1: Using QCMDEXC to run WRKSPLF from within an RPG program.

Running OPNQRYF
to Sort a Database File from within an RPG Program

If your system has multiple report programs that produce the same output, odds are pretty good that the reason they are different programs is because they have different sequence or selection criteria. When output change requests are made, you may be asked to make the same changes to all of them. By sequencing and selecting your data dynamically, you can add a great deal of flexibility to your programs and reduce the amount of maintenance you perform.

The first sample program in this chapter gives you the ability to do just that. The RPG program is a simple file listing program that prints our customer (CUST) file in customer-name or customer-number order. When the program is called, a parameter is passed that determines the sequence in which the records are printed. If a 1 is passed to the program, the list is printed in customer-name sequence. Otherwise, the list prints in customer-number order.

Note the User Controlled Open (USROPN) keyword specified on the File Description Specification for the CUST file. This tells the system that the file open and close to our CUST file is user-controlled within the program (see chapter 1 for more information on user-controlled file opens). Before we can open the file, we must perform file overrides on it. The override we use tells the system that we want our RPG program and the OPNQRYF command to share the same data path of our CUST file. We do this by using the Override Data Base File (OVRDBF) command.

Also note that the program uses QCMDEXC to call the commands, specifying that the program use a shared access path for the CUST file and then again to perform the OPNQRYF operation to sequence the data. The ALLWCPYDTA(*OPTIMIZE) option is specified to enhance the performance of the OPNQRYF function (this option allows OPNQRYF to make the decision as to whether the file should be sorted). An Evaluate (EVAL) expression operation is used to concatenate the primary element of the OPNQRYF command to the appropriate KEYFLD parameter. The KEYFLD parameter chosen is dependent on the value within the parameter passed to the program. Once the OPNQRYF command has been performed, the CUST file can be opened for use within our RPG program.

The QCMDEXC program is called on three different times in the example in Figure 6.2. First, it is used to run the OVRDBF command so the system knows to share the open data path between the OPNQRYF command and the RPG program. Second, QCMDEXC is used to perform the OPNQRYF command, and the data is then sequenced. And third, the

QCMDEXC API is used to close the CUST file once we are finished with the list. Failure to close the file could cause some interesting and unintended results in subsequent programs using the CUST file.

```
*************************************************************************
*  TO COMPILE:
*     CRTBNDRPG PGM(XXXLIB/FIG62RG)
*************************************************************************
FFilename++IPEASF.....L.....A.Device+.Keywords++++++++++++++++++++++++++++Comments
FCUSTOMER  IF  E               DISK    USROPN
FQSYSPRT   O   F 132           PRINTER OFLIND(*INOF)


DName+++++++++++ETDsFrom+++To/L+++IDc.Keywords++++++++++++++++++++++++++++Comments
D CmdAry          S                  80     DIM(5) CTDATA PERRCD(1)
D Sequence#       S                   1
D Command         S                  80
D CmdLength       S                  15  5 INZ(80)


CLON01Factor1+++++++Opcode&ExtFactor2+++++++Result++++++++Len++D+HiLoEq...Comments
C     *ENTRY       PLIST
C                  PARM                      Sequence#
 * Over-ride the Open Data Path of the CUSTOMER file
C                  MOVEL     CmdAry(1)       Command
C                  CALL      'QCMDEXC'
C                  PARM                      Command
C                  PARM                      CmdLength
C     Sequence#    IFEQ      '1'
 * Perform OPNQRYF to sequence records into customer name order
C                  EVAL      Command = %TRIMR(CmdAry(2))
C                            + ' ' + CmdAry(3)
C                  ELSE
 * Perform OPNQRYF to sequence records into customer number order
C                  EVAL      Command = %TRIMR(CmdAry(2))
C                            + ' ' + CmdAry(4)
C                  ENDIF
C                  CALL      'QCMDEXC'
C                  PARM                      Command
C                  PARM                      CmdLength
 * Now that OPNQRYF has been performed, the file may be opened
C                  OPEN      CUSTOMER
C                  EXCEPT    HEDING
 * Read and print records
C                  DOU       *In50 = *ON
C                  READ      CUSREC                               50
C     *IN50        IFEQ      *OFF
C                  EXCEPT    DETAIL
C                  ENDIF
C                  ENDDO
 * Close the CUSTOMER file
C                  EVAL      Command = CmdAry(5)
```

Figure 6.2: Using QCMDEXC to run OPNQRYF from within an RPG program (part 1 of 2).

```
C                       CALL      'QCMDEXC'
C                       PARM                  Command
C                       PARM                  CmdLength
C                       EVAL      *InLr = *ON

OFilename++DF..N01N02N03Excnam++++B++A++Sb+Sa+.............................Comment
s++
OQSYSPRT   E            HEDING        2 02
O          OR    OF
O                                     72 'CUSTOMER LIST'
O          E            HEDING        1
O          OR    OF
O                                     15 'CUSTOMER NUMBER'
O                                     45 'CUSTOMER NAME'
O          EF           DETAIL        1
O                       Customer#     15
O                       Custname      65

** CmdAry compile time array
OVRDBF FILE(CUSTOMER) SHARE(*YES)
OPNQRYF FILE((CUSTOMER)) ALWCPYDTA(*OPTIMIZE)
KEYFLD((CUSTNAME))
KEYFLD((CUSTOMER#))
CLOF CUSTOMER
```

Figure 6.2: Using QCMDEXC to run OPNQRYF from within an RPG program (part 2 of 2).

Employing this methodology, we create a listing program to dynamically sequence the data. This may eliminate the need for you to have to code and maintain additional programs with similar output. It also allows us to process the data in the CUST file in arrival sequence, rather than the less-efficient method of reading the file by key (see chapter 1).

Overriding Printer Parameters from within an RPG Program

Allowing users to decide where they want a report printed is pretty standard stuff. Odds are good that you already have found a way to handle this request. But if you are not familiar with the QCMDEXC program, you may want to check out this next example.

In Figure 6.3, we use the QCMDEXC program from within our RPG print program to change printers and the number of copies printed. Parameter one of our program is the number of copies we want to print, and parameter two is the printer device to which we want to direct the output.

```
**************************************************************************
 *   TO COMPILE:
 *      CRTBNDRPG PGM(XXXLIB/FIG63RG)
**************************************************************************
FFilename++IPEASF.....L.....A.Device+.Keywords+++++++++++++++++++++++++++Comments
FCUSTOMER  IF   E              DISK
FQSYSPRT   O    F   132        PRINTER OFLIND(*INOF)
F                                      USROPN

DName+++++++++++ETDsFrom+++To/L+++IDc.Keywords++++++++++++++++++++++++++++Comments
D CmdAry          S             70    DIM(1) CTDATA PERRCD(1)
D INbrCopies      S              2
D IPrinter        S             10
D CmdLength       S             15  5 INZ(70)
D TotRecords      S              5  0
 *
D                 DS
D Command                       70
D  NbrCopies                     2    OVERLAY(Command:30)
D  Printer                      10    OVERLAY(Command:38)
 *
D                 SDS
D  Parameters      *PARMS

CLON01Factor1+++++++Opcode&ExtFactor2+++++++Result++++++++Len++D+HiLoEq...Comments
C     *ENTRY       PLIST
C                  PARM                      INbrCopies
C                  PARM                      IPrinter
 * Perform the printer over-rides
C     Parameters   IFGT     *ZEROS
C                  MOVEA    CmdAry(1)     Command
C                  EVAL     NbrCopies = INbrCopies
C                  EVAL     Printer = IPrinter
C                  CALL     'QCMDEXC'
C                  PARM                  Command
C                  PARM                  CmdLength
C                  ENDIF
 * Open printer file and begin output operations
C                  OPEN     QSYSPRT
C                  EXCEPT   HEDING
 * Read and print customer file records
C                  DOU      *In50 = *ON
C                  READ     CUSREC                              50
C     *IN50        IFEQ     *OFF
C                  EVAL     TotRecords = (TotRecords + 1)
C                  EXCEPT   DETAIL
C                  ENDIF
C                  ENDDO
C                  EXCEPT   TOTALS
C                  CLOSE    QSYSPRT
C                  EVAL     *InLr = *ON
```

Figure 6.3: Using QCMDEXC to override printer attributes (part 1 of 2).

```
OFilename++DF..N01N02N03Excnam++++B++A++Sb+Sa+..........................Comments
OQSYSPRT    E               HEDING           3 02
O          OR    OF
O                                            5 'DATE:'
O                            UDATE         Y 14
O                                           70 'CUSTOMER LIST'
O                                          121 'PAGE:'
O                            PAGE          Z 127
O          E                HEDING           1
O          OR    OF
O                                           20 'CUSTOMER NUMBER'
O                                           46 'CUSTOMER NAME'
O          EF               DETAIL           1
O                            Customer#        20
O                            CustName         66
O          E                TOTALS      2  1
O                            TotRecords   1  14
O                                           35 'TOTAL RECORDS LISTED'

** Cmdary compile time array
OVRPRTF FILE(QSYSPRT) COPIES( ) DEV(           ) OUTQ(*DEV)
```

Figure 6.3: Using QCMDEXC to override printer attributes (part 2 of 2).

As in our previous example, the file we are overriding must remain closed while we perform the overrides. Notice the USROPN keyword specified on the File Description Specification of the printer file (QSYSPRT), which tells the system it is a user-controlled file. Once we have performed our desired file overrides, we code the open and close of QSYSPRT ourselves.

We choose to use the PARMS field in the Program Status Data Structure to indicate to the program whether parameters are passed to the program (the Program Status Data Structure is discussed in chapter 4). If the customer file listing program is called with parameters 1 and 2 specified (the PARMS field is greater than zero), we perform printer file overrides to specify our desired printer and the number of copies we want. If no parameters are passed to the program, the override is not performed.

The only element of the CMDARY compile time array (which is defined in the Definition Specification in Figure 6.3) holds the shell of the Override Printer File (OVRPRTF) command. We choose to use a data structure as a tool to load the parameters of the OVRPRTF command because it is generally easier to follow than using the CAT command to concatenate the various components. We begin by loading the CMDARY compile time array element into our data structure and then overlaying it with the values passed into the program as parameters 1 and 2. The net result is a complete OVRPRTF command that is ready to be executed. This is done by calling the QCMDEXC API. Once the override to the

157

printer file is performed, the printer file is opened and the rest of the simple list program is completed.

Submitting a Job
to the Job Queue from within an RPG Program

As an RPG programmer on the AS/400, you may have wondered why there is no SMBJOB op code that allows you to submit jobs from within your RPG program. We have too. But the good news is that by using the QCMDEXC API, you can do just that.

For our next example, we use a little RPG prompt program that prompts for a printer ID and the number of copies, validates the values entered, and then submits a program to the job queue. The program we are submitting is the customer list program, which we wrote in our previous example (Figure 6.3). The display file coded in Figure 6.4 is used to present the prompt screen shown in Figure 6.5.

```
A*******************************************************************************
A*  TO COMPILE:
A*     CRTDSPF FILE(XXXLIB/FIG64DS)
A*******************************************************************************
.....AAN01N02N03T.Name++++++RLen++TDpBLinPosFunctions+++++++++++++++++++++++++++
A              R FORMAT1
A                                        CHGINPDFT
A                                        CF03
A                                    1 26'List Customer File'
A                                        DSPATR(UL HI)
A                                    8  7'Printer to send report to.........-
A                                        ................'
A              PRINTER      10   B  8 58DSPATR(HI UL)
A   41                                   ERRMSG('Invalid Printer Id Entered')
A   43                                   ERRMSG('Your list was submitted...')
A                                   10  7'Number of copies to print.........-
A                                        ................'
A              NBRCOPIES   2D  OB 10 58DSPATR(HI)
A                                        CHECK(RZ)
A   42                                   ERRMSG('Invalid Number of Copies')
A                                   21  3'                                   -
A                                        '                                   -
A                                        DSPATR(UL)
A                                   23  4'F3=Exit'
```

Figure 6.4: Customer list prompt screen display file.

```
                          List Customer File




         Printer to send report to........................ _____

         Number of copies to print........................ 01








         F3=Exit
```

Figure 6.5: Customer list prompt screen.

In the RPG program in Figure 6.6, we first establish the default values for the number-of-copies field and then present our prompt screen. The program has been coded to continue presenting the prompt screen until F3 is pressed. If the entries keyed pass the edits, the print job is submitted to the job queue and a confirmation message is sent to the screen.

```
****************************************************************************
*   TO COMPILE:
*       CRTBNDRPG PGM(XXXLIB/FIG66RG)
****************************************************************************

FFilename++IPEASF.....L.....A.Device+.Keywords++++++++++++++++++++++++++++Comments
FLCUSTDSP  CF   E               WORKSTN

DName+++++++++++ETDsFrom+++To/L+++IDc.Keywords++++++++++++++++++++++++++++Comments
D CmdAry          S              80     DIM(1) CTDATA PERRCD(1)
D Library         S              10     INZ('*LIBL')
D ObjectType      S              10     INZ('*DEVD')
D ObjIsValid      S               1
D CmdLength       S              15  5 INZ(80)
 *
D                 DS                     INZ
```

Figure 6.6: Using QCMDEXC to submit jobs from within an RPG program (part 1 of 2).

```
D Command                         80
D PassCopies                       2       OVERLAY(Command:35)
D PassPrintr                      10       OVERLAY(Command:40)

CLON01Factor1+++++++Opcode&ExtFactor2+++++++Result++++++++Len++D+HiLoEq...Comments
 *   Establish defaults
C                        MOVEA     Cmdary(1)       Command
C                        Eval      NbrCopies = 1
 *   Do until an EOJ request is encountered
C                        DOU       *InKC = *ON
C                        EXFMT     FORMAT1
C                        MOVEA     '000'           *IN(41)
 *   Validate printer ID
C        *INKC           IFEQ      *OFF
C                        CALL      'FIG67RG'
C                        PARM                      Printer
C                        PARM                      Library
C                        PARM                      ObjectType
C                        PARM                      ObjIsValid
 *   Send error message if entry is not valid
C        ObjIsValid      IFNE      'Y'
C                        Eval      *In41 = *ON
C                        ITER
C                        ENDIF
 *   Must specify the number of copies
C        NbrCopies       IFEQ      *ZEROS
C                        Eval      *In42 = *ON
C                        ITER
C                        ENDIF
 *   Submit Customer List
C                        Eval      *In43 = *ON
C                        MOVE      NbrCopies       PassCopies
C                        Eval      PassPrintr = Printer
C                        CALL      'QCMDEXC'
C                        PARM                      Command
C                        PARM                      CmdLength
C                        ENDIF
C                        ENDDO
 **
C                        Eval      *InLr = *ON

 ** Cmdary compile time array
SBMJOB CMD(CALL PGM(LSTCUS) PARM('99' 'Printer ID')) JOB(LISTCUST)
```

Figure 6.6: Using QCMDEXC to submit jobs from within an RPG program (part 2 of 2).

The next step is to edit the printer ID keyed by the program operator. We use the FIG67RG API program (shown in Figure 6.7), which is explained in further detail when we cover system APIs in chapter 9. The purpose of the API program is to make sure the device description of the printer ID keyed does, in fact, exist on the system.

```
*****************************************************************************
*   TO COMPILE:
*      CRTBNDRPG PGM(XXXLIB/FIG67RG)
*****************************************************************************

DName+++++++++++ETDsFrom+++To/L+++IDc.Keywords+++++++++++++++++++++++++++++++Comments
D ErrorDs         DS                        INZ
D  BytesProvd               1      4B 0
D  BytesAvail               5      8B 0
D  MessageId                9     15
D  ERR###                  16     16
D  MessageDta              17    116
D Receiver         S              100
D ReceivrLen       S               4B 0 INZ(100)
D Object           S               10
D ObjLibrary       S               10
D ObjType          S                8
D ExistYesNo       S                1
D FileLib          S               20
D FileFormat       S                8     INZ('OBJD0100')

CLON01Factor1+++++++Opcode&ExtFactor2+++++++Result++++++++Len++D+HiLoEq...Comments
C     *ENTRY        PLIST
C                   PARM                    Object
C                   PARM                    ObjLibrary
C                   PARM                    ObjType
C                   PARM                    ExistYesNo
C     ObjLibrary    IFEQ      *BLANKS
C                   EVAL      ObjLibrary = 'LIBL'
C                   ENDIF
C                   EVAL      FileLib = Object + ObjLibrary
* Attempt to retrieve object description
C                   CALL      'QUSROBJD'
C                   PARM                    Receiver
C                   PARM                    ReceivrLen
C                   PARM                    FileFormat
C                   PARM                    FileLib
C                   PARM                    ObjType
C                   PARM                    ErrorDs
C                   EVAL      ExistYesNo = 'Y'
C     MessageId     IFNE      *BLANKS
C                   EVAL      ExistYesNo = 'N'
C                   ENDIF
C                   EVAL      *InLr = *ON
```

Figure 6.7: RPG API program used to validate printer existence.

If either the printer ID or the number-of-copies field is deemed invalid, the prompt screen is redisplayed with the appropriate error message indicator on. The operator may then press Error Reset, correct the value in error, and press Enter; or press F3 to terminate the program.

If the keyed field entries pass the edits, the QCMDEXC API is called and the program is submitted to the job queue, passing along the printer ID and number of copies keyed as parameters. The confirmation indicator (*IN43) is then turned on and the screen is redisplayed. A message is displayed indicating that the requested job was submitted to the job queue.

QCMDEXC: AN API FOR ALL SEASONS

As you have seen in the preceding examples, the QCMDEXC API is a very powerful and easy-to-use tool. Once you have the hang of it, you may be surprised at how many different uses you can find for it.

THE COMMAND PROCESSING (QCAPCMD) API

You now have a pretty good understanding of the QCMDEXC API, and that it can be used to execute almost any command from within your program. But what if you simply wanted the operator to press a function key to get a window where a command could be keyed? You would probably want to edit that command for validity, rather than presenting one of those nasty CPF errors if an invalid command is keyed. And would you ever want to trap the information that the user keyed in response to that prompt?

The way to accomplish these goals is via the QCAPCMD API. It allows you to edit a command string for validity, allows for prompting, and returns the command parameters to your program.

The first step to doing this would be to prompt the user with an entry line where a command could be keyed. You would then pass that field (filled with whatever the user had entered) to the QCAPCMD API, which would verify that a proper command was entered, prompt for that command (if requested to do so), and return the changed command string to your program (updated with whatever the user had entered into the prompted fields). The QCAPCMD API can either process the keyed command or simply verify that the command is valid and let you pass the changed command on to the QCMDEXC API to run it.

Let's take a closer look at the QCAPCMD API. You first give it the command string to be processed (trailing blanks are allowed), followed by the length of the command string field. The next three parameters (option control block, block length, and block format) are used to control the various functions the API can perform (run the command or just verify that it is a valid command, prompt, etc.). Parameter 6 will return the updated command string with any variable information the user may have entered. Parameter 7 is the length of the changed command string, and the last parameter is the standard error code data structure described in chapter 9. Table 6.1 shows the input parameters needed to use this API.

Table 6.1: Required Input Parameters for the Command Processing (QCAPCMD) API.

Parameter	Description	Type	Size
1	Source command string	Input	Char(*)
2	Command string length	Input	Binary(4)
3	Option control block	Input	Char(*)
4	Option control block length	Input	Char(20)
5	Option control block format	Input	Char(8)
6	Changed command string	Output	Char(*)
7	Length available for changed command string	Input	Binary(4)
8	Error code data structure	Both	Char(*)

Parameter Definitions:

Source command string: The command string that is to be processed, either prompted for or run.

Command string length: The length of the source command string. Valid values are between 1 and 6,000. Trailing blanks in the command string can count in the length.

Option control block: Currently there is only one format allowed. See Table 6.2 for the format of this structure.

Control block length: The length of the option control block parameter. Must be a minimum of 20 bytes.

Control block format name: The name of the data structure defining the data in the control block. Currently, the only valid entry is CPOP0100.

Changed command string: The updated command string. This may be considerably longer than the source command string because it contains the keywords. No padding is performed on this field; you must use the length of changed command string field to determine the number of characters returned. This field will not be changed if an error occurred during the execution of the QCAPCMD API.

Length available to changed command string: Total number of bytes the QCAPCMD API has to return the changed command string. If the string is larger than this number, the returned command string will be truncated to fit.

Error Data Structure: The standard error code data structure as described in chapter 9.

Table 6.2: Format of the Option Control Block (CPOP0100).

Offset	Type	Description
0	Binary(4)	Type of command processing
4	Char(1)	DBCS handling
5	Char(1)	Prompter action
6	Char(1)	Command string syntax
7	Char(4)	Message retrieve key
11	Char(9)	Reserved

Parameter Definitions:

Source command string: The command string that is to be processed.

Type of processing: Type of command processing to be performed. Valid values and their meaning are as follows:

0 - Command running. Processes in the same way as QCMDEXC.

1 - Command syntax check. Processes in the same way as QCMDCHK.

2 - Command line running. Processes in the same way as QCMDEXC except that limited user checking and prompting for missing required parameters are performed.

3 - Command line syntax checking. Complement of type 2.

4 - CL program statement. Checked according to the same rules as SEU for CL. Variable names are allowed.

5 - CL input stream. Checked according to the same rules as input batch stream.

6 - Command definition statements.

7 - Binder definition statements. Checked according to the same rules as SEU for BND.

8 - User-defined option. Allows user to create commands similar to those used in PDM.

9 - ILE CL programs source. Checked according to the rules of SEU for ILE CL.

DBCS data handling: Determines whether the command analyzer should handle the SO/SI characters as DBCS.

0 - Ignore DBCS.

1 - Handle DBCS.

Prompter action: Should the prompter be called for the command string? Valid values are:

0 - Never call the prompter, even if prompting characters (?, *?, etc.) are embedded in the command string.

1 - Always call the prompter, even if there are no prompting characters embedded in the string.

2 - Prompt only if prompting characters are present. Error code CPF3CF1 is issued if this code is used with command processing types 4 through 8.

3 - Show help. Provide help display for the command.

Command string syntax: Specifies whether the command is in the AS/400 syntax (library/object) or the System 38 syntax (object.library).

Message retrieve key: The message retrieve key of the request message that contains the source command statements to process.

C FUNCTION: SYSTEM

Another method of executing commands from within programs takes advantage of RPG IV's ability to execute system-provided C functions. In this case, the function is called *system*. It provides the same capability as QCMDEXC, except that you do not have to pass the size of the command. Just pass the command you want executed as a parameter, and the function will figure out the length of the command.

Figure 6.8 shows all the code necessary to execute the system function. When dealing with C functions, the case of the characters really does matter. This function must be keyed in all lowercase characters.

The call to the system function is prototyped and accessed using the EXTPROC keyword. It accepts one parameter: the command to be executed. As we have noted, the length of the command does not have to be passed to this function. Both the VALUE and OP-TIONS(*STRING) keywords must be used on the command parameter. C functions expect strings to be null terminated, and the OPTIONS(*STRING) keyword handles this requirement for you.

The next thing you should notice is the definition of the CPFMSGID field. Defining the field with the IMPORT('_EXCP_MSGID') will cause the field to be loaded with the contents of the global variable EXCP-MSGID. This will be the CPF message number of any error encountered while the command is executed . This is a big advantage over QCMDEXC.

Because this program is only intended to demonstrate how to code using the system function, its logic is very simple. The program accepts a command as a parameter and passes that command to the system function. If any errors are encountered, it will display the CPF message number. If not, the command is executed.

The main trick to using this function lies in how the program should be compiled. To access system-provided C functions, you need to compile the program using the QC2LE binding directory.

```
DName++++++++++ETDsFrom+++To/L+++IDc.Keywords+++++++++++++++++++++++++++++
d System           PR              10i 0 extproc('system')
d  Cmd                               *   value options(*string)
d CpfMsgId         s                7    import('_EXCP_MSGID')
d RunCmdIn         s               50


CLON01Factor1+++++++Opcode&ExtFactor2+++++++Result++++++++Len++D+HiLoEq
c     *entry        Plist
c                   Parm                      RunCmdIn

 * execute the command passed to the program
c                   If        System(RunCmdIn) <> 0

 * If procedure returned not zero, display the error msgid
c     CpfMsgId      dsply
c                   endif

c                   eval      *inlr = *On
```

Figure 6.8: How to use 'system.'

PROTOTYPING THE CALL TO QCMDEXC

It is a good idea to prototype all calls to any API. This allows errors to be caught at compile time instead of execution time. A prototyped call to QCMDEXC can be seen in Figure 6.9. Use the EXTPGM keyword to call the API.

Prototyping calls provide another feature. It allows you to "name" the command to be executed, which provides a form of self-documentation. You can see in this example that the "name" on the prototype to call QCMDEXC is DSPPFM. This feature makes it abundantly clear that you are executing the DSPPFM command. Of course, the command to be executed can be a variable or a constant.

```
d DspPfm          PR                    extpgm('QCMDEXC')
d   Cmd                      32727      options(*VARSIZE) const
d   Len                         15    5 const

 * execute the command
c                  Callp      DspPfm('DSPPFM FILE(FAMLY)':18)
```

Figure 6.9: Prototyped call to QCMDEXC.

COMMAND PERFORMANCE

The QCAPCMD API is much more flexible than the QCMDEXC API. But as usual, with flexibility comes complexity. Despite this, this API performs a very useful function. It allows you to provide a command entry line in your programs that you can use to both validate and execute the requested user action. As an added bonus, you have the capability of "trapping" what the user entered. Take the time to learn how to use these two very special APIs. You may surprise yourself with how much power is at your command.

Prototyping the calls to APIs performs a very useful function. It allows more errors to be caught at compile time instead of runtime. You should begin using this feature wherever you can.

Do not be afraid to learn about and use C functions. The system function is very useful and provides more error feedback than QCMDEXC. Try it, you might like it.

7

ARRAY AND STRING HANDLING

Dictionaries define an array as "an orderly grouping." While that definition does describe an array in RPG, perhaps a better description for our purposes is found in the IBM *RPG/400 Reference Guide*. The guide refers to an array as "a systematic program-internal arrangement of data fields (array elements) with the same field length, data type (character or numeric), and number of decimal positions (if numeric)."

WHAT IS AN ARRAY?

As the description indicates, an array consists of a consecutive set of like data elements that are stored in main memory while your RPG program is running. Prior to V3R1 and RPG IV, arrays required a fixed amount of main storage that was defined to the system when your program was compiled. Arrays always had a fixed number of elements, and each element had to (and still must) be the same size and data type.

New functions and features were introduced with V3R1 that removed most of the inflexibility that used to be associated with arrays. Even though the role of arrays has changed, you will see that arrays still have their place on the AS/400. We begin by defining the different types of arrays and giving you a couple of examples so you can see how useful they are.

WHAT WOULD YOU USE AN ARRAY FOR?

Up until the introduction of the string handling op codes and built-in functions, arrays were a major component of every RPG programmer's toolbox. Whether you needed to pack a name into Last name, First or pack city, state, and zip code together, arrays were the best tool available for the job.

The introduction of the string handling op codes and built-in functions in RPG changed all that. Arrays were instantly outdated for this purpose because they required too much coding compared to their successors. What used to take 10 or more lines of code could now be done in one or two. Less code meant fewer opportunities for error.

But as you will see, arrays are still a valuable tool. They are great for accumulating totals when printing a report. They are useful for validating data in your interactive programs. They can be used to pull like data elements together so they can be processed from within a loop. They are often without peer when it comes to formatting data that appears on reports and screens.

ARRAY BASICS

Within your RPG program, you define the field size, the data type, and the maximum number of data elements that will exist within the array. Also within your program, you manage the sequence and content of the data elements with techniques that we demonstrate in this chapter.

Prior to ILE RPG and V3R1, the only way to define an array was with an Extension Specification. The Extension Specification has now been replaced with the Definition Specification. The Definition Specification tells the system the name of your array and how many elements it has, as well as the size and type of the elements. If your array happens to be numeric, this specification also tells the system the number of decimal positions that belong to each element.

RPG IV allows you to address arrays wholly or as individual array elements. When you use the array name followed by a numeric field or value enclosed in parentheses, you are addressing an individual array element. This field or value is commonly referred to as an *array index*.

Array indices must contain valid array address values when used. If a statement is encountered in which an array index is zero or greater than the maximum number of array elements allowed, the result is an *array index error*, which causes the program to be interrupted. You need to use care when coding arrays to make sure these conditions cannot possibly exist. We will show you some tips you can employ that will help you make sure this error condition does not occur.

RPG IV allows you to specify *compile-time*, *runtime*, and *dynamic arrays*. As its name implies, the data for a compile-time array is loaded when the program is compiled. The runtime array is loaded and managed from within the RPG program while it is running. The dynamic array allows you to use dynamic memory allocation to control the amount of memory required from within your program.

It is the runtime array we will initially focus on. But before we get too carried away with runtime arrays, we need to mention that there is a fourth type of array, which we like to call the *two-dimensional array*. The two-dimensional array is not just an array. It is a hybrid combination of a Multiple-occurrence Data Structure and multiple arrays. It differs from arrays because each element is itself a data structure with fields of varying size and data type. Refer to chapter 8 for more details about this special type of array.

THE RUNTIME ARRAY

In Figure 7.1, we define two runtime arrays. The first is called StateCode. It has 50 array elements, each of which is two characters long. This array is used to hold the two-character abbreviation of each U.S. state. Because there are only 50 states, we are able to set the size of the array at a maximum size of 50. We also know that the size of the field we use as an index only needs to be two digits because it is highly unlikely there will ever be more than 99 states (which is the maximum number that will fit in a two-digit field).

```
DName+++++++++++ETDsFrom+++To/L+++IDc.Keywords++++++++++++++++++++++++++++++++Comments
D StateCode      S              2    DIM(50)
D StateTot       S              5  0 DIM(50)
```

Figure 7.1: Defining runtime arrays with a Definition Specification.

Setting the size of your array can be something of a science. The idea is to not only set a size that is at least as large as the maximum number of elements you could possibly encounter, but also keep the number of elements to a minimum because main storage (memory) is being allocated every time your program is run. The number of elements multiplied by the size of each element translates into how much main storage is being allocated each time your program is run.

Prior to V3R1, the number of array elements in memory could not be increased from within your program. We will show you later in this chapter how to use dynamic arrays to tell your program the maximum number of array elements it could possibly encounter and only allocate the storage in memory for the elements that you use.

The second array in Figure 7.1 is called StateTot, which is used to store the total number of customers that reside in each state. Each StateTot array element contains five digits with zero decimal positions. In Figure 7.2, we use the arrays defined in the previous example to accumulate and store the total number of customers we have in each state. This method to accumulate totals is especially valuable if you cannot control the sequence of the records being read.

```
CLON01Factor1+++++++Opcode&ExtFactor2+++++++Result++++++++Len++D+HiLoEq...Comments

    * Read all customer records and accumulate totals by state
C                     Dou       %EOF
C                     Read      CUSREC                              50
C                     If        Not %EOF
C                     Eval      X = 1
C        State        Lookup    StateCode(X)                        68
    * If current state is not already in the array, find a spot for it
C                     If        Not %Found
C        '  '         Lookup    StateCode(X)                        68
C                     EndIf
    * Increment total for current state
C                     Eval      StateCode(X) = State
C                     Eval      StateTot(X) = StateTot(X) + 1
C                     EndIf
C                     EndDo
```

Figure 7.2: Accumulating totals in runtime arrays.

For example, let's say you need to write a Customer List RPG program that is to be printed alphabetically by customer name, but you also need to print summary totals at the bottom of the report showing how many customers are in each state. The totals will be printed twice. They will print first in the sequence of the two-character abbreviation for each state, and a second time by the number of customers in each state.

This poses a potential problem. Reading the customer records in a sequence that presents the records alphabetically by customer name will, in all likelihood, result in totals that are recorded in a sequence that does not match our desired output for the summary by state. And what about when we print the totals by the number of customers in each state?

Do you resequence the file into state order and read all of the records a second time just to print the totals in the desired sequence? Probably not. As we discussed in chapter 1, reducing I/O can have a big impact on overall system performance.

Do you create a totals-output field for each of the 50 states? This would be very tedious, and the repetition creates a situation that leaves room for error. Would this solution even be viable if we were talking about 500 totals-output fields? Probably not.

Figure 7.2 demonstrates a technique that allows us to accumulate totals into array elements that may be processed for output later. By accumulating the totals as you read the records, you are prepared to output a summary later without making another pass through the data. In Figure 7.2, we read and print the customer file records as we process them in alphabetical order and, at the same time, store our totals in the StateTot array. We use the StateCode array to keep track of which state the corresponding StateTot array element represents. After the totals have been accumulated, the final result looks something like this:

StateCode Array:

CA	NV	AZ	OR	ID	NY

StateTot Array:

451	103	55	28	12	1033

A quick glance at the arrays tells us that we have 451 customers in California, 55 in Arizona, 12 in Idaho, and so on. Each data element in the StateTot array directly corresponds to the element in the StateCode array.

USING RUNTIME ARRAYS TO STORE AND ACCUMULATE TOTALS

Let's analyze the code in Figure 7.2 to see how our totals are accumulated. If the first customer record read is from California, the program uses the LOOKUP op code to perform a lookup in the StateCode array to see if we have already processed a customer record from California.

The LOOKUP op code is unique to tables and arrays. Its name aptly describes its function. It performs a lookup operation to see if the search argument specified in Factor 1 already exists somewhere within the array. If the search argument does exist, the indicator *IN68 specified in position 75 (the = column) is turned on and the number of the element in which the search argument was found is returned to the index field (X in this case). The index field is enclosed in parentheses directly after the name of the array specified in Factor 2 (positions 36 through 49). The index field is a numeric field enclosed in parentheses that follows the name of the array in the LOOKUP statement. Note that prior to the LOOKUP operation, the index was reset to 1. This must be done because the search begins from where the index happens to be set. If X was greater than 1, the LOOKUP operation may not return the results we are looking for.

Back to our example. Let's assume that this was the first record read. The lookup failed to find an array element of CA and needs to add it. We have coded the program to look for the first available array element in the StateCode array by performing another lookup using the LOOKUP op code to find the first array element filled with blanks.

Once the first available blank element is found, the CA state code is moved into the StateCode array and a count of 1 is added to the corresponding array element in the StateTot array. After reading our first customer record and processing the record, our arrays look like this:

StateCode Array:

CA					

StateTot Array:

1					

If the next customer record read is from Nevada, the StateCode array lookup is performed with the NV state code. As before, the NV code is added when NV is not initially found. After reading and processing our second customer record from Nevada, our arrays look like this:

StateCode Array:

CA	NV				

StateTot Array:

1	1				

Let's assume that the third customer record read is again from California. In this case, the lookup in the StateCode array for CA is successful (as indicated when indicator 68 comes on) and the appropriate array index is returned and stored in the field X.

This time, we simply add 1 to the StateTot array element that directly corresponds to the StateCode array element we found in the lookup operation. After reading and processing the third customer record, our arrays look like this:

StateCode Array:

CA	NV				

StateTot Array:

2	1				

When all of the customer records have been read and processed, we end up with a StateCode array that contains state codes for each and every customer record in our file. The StateTot array contains a count representing the number of customers we have in each state.

SEQUENCING RUNTIME ARRAYS FOR OUTPUT OPERATIONS

We now have the data needed to print our summary totals at the bottom of our report. But there is a problem. How are we going to get the totals to print out in state or customer count order? Our arrays have been built based on the customer name arrival sequence of the records because our report specifications called for printing the detail in that order. The solution to this problem lies in a technique demonstrated in Figure 7.3.

```
 ********************************************************************
 *   TO COMPILE:
 *      CRTBNDRPG PGM(XXXLIB/FIG703RG) SRCMBR(FG703RG)
 ********************************************************************
 FFilename++IPEASF.....L.....A.Device+.Keywords+++++++++++++++++++++++++
 fCustomer  IF   E              Disk
 fStates    IF   E            K Disk
 fQsysprt   O    F  132         Printer OFLind(*InOF)

 DName+++++++++++ETDsFrom+++To/L+++IDc.Keywords+++++++++++++++++++++++++
 d                   ds
 d State_Info                     7    Dim(50)
 d  StateCode                     2    Overlay(State_Info)
 d  StateTot                      5  0 Overlay(State_Info:3) INZ
 *
 d Total            S             7  0
 d X                S             3  0

 CL0N01Factor1++++++++Opcode&ExtFactor2+++++++Result++++++++Len++D+HiLoEq
 * Print report heading
 c                     Except    Heading

 * Read customer file and accumulate totals by state
 c                     Dou       %Eof
 c                     Read      CusRec
 c                     If        not %Eof
 c                     Eval      X = 1
 c      State          Lookup    StateCode(X)                       68
 c                     If        not %Found
 c      ' '            Lookup    StateCode(X)                       68
 c                     EndIf
 * Increment total for current state
 c                     Eval      StateCode(X) = State
 c                     Eval      StateTot(X) = StateTot(X) + 1
 c                     EndIf
 c                     EndDo

 * Sort the entire State_Info array alphabetically into state sequence
 c                     SortA     StateCode

 * Run through the State_Info array and print totals
 c                     Do        50          X
 c                     If        StateCode(X) <> *BLANKS
 c      StateCode(X)   Chain     STATES                            68
 c                     Eval      Total = Total + StateTot(X)
 c                     Except    DETAIL
 c                     EndIf
 c                     EndDo
 * Print array totals
 c                     Except    TOTALS

 * Print report heading again
```

Figure 7. 3: Using the Sort Array (SORTA) op code to resequence array elements (part 1 of 2).

```
C                         Except    Heading

 * Sort the State_Info array numerically by the number of customers per
C                         SortA     StateTot

 * Repeat the process of printing the State_Info array
C                         Do        50        X
C                         If        StateCode(X) <> *BLANKS
C         StateCode(X)    Chain     STATES                              68
C                         Except    DETAIL
C                         EndIf
C                         EndDo

 * Print array totals
C                         Except    TOTALS
C                         Eval      *INLR = *ON

O..............N01N02N03Field+++++++++YB.End++PConstant/editword/DTform
oQsysprt    E             Heading        3 02
o           OR    OF
o                                            70 'Summary by State'

o           E             Heading        1
o           OR    OF
o                                            16 'State'
o                                            42 'Total'

o           EF            Detail         1
o                         StateCode(X)       4
o                         StateDesc         31
o                         StateTot(X)    1  40

o           E             Totals       2 1
o                         Total          1  14
o                                            30 'Total Customers'
```

Figure 7. 3: Using the Sort Array (SORTA) op code to resequence array elements (part 2 of 2).

In Figure 7.3, we code a print program that simply prints the customer-summary-by-state report, which is similar to the summary we have been talking about. We employ a loop to load the arrays, much as we did in the previous example.

Take a look at the Definition Specifications for the State_Info array. By defining the State_Info array within a data structure, we are able to use the OVERLAY keyword to embed the StateCode and StateTot arrays within the State_Info array. By defining the arrays this way, each element of the State_Info array is actually seven characters. The first two characters of each State_Info array element compose the state code and the last five digits are the customer totals for each state. Coding it this way allows us to use both the

StateCode and StateTot arrays independently, as if they were defined as standalone arrays.

In order to print our totals in state code order, we need to sort the State_Info array. The Sort Array (SORTA) op code is perfect for this purpose, except that sorting the State_Info array would result in totals sequenced by state code only (because the first two characters of the State_Info array are the state code). But RPG IV allows us to use the data structure subfields to sort the array. (Note: This is *way* cool!)

In Figure 7.3, we used our loop to compile our totals first. We then used the SORTA op code to sort our array into state code sequence and then a loop to print the array contents. We then printed a new heading, used the SORTA op code again to sort our array into our totals sequence, and used a loop to print the contents again. Figure 7.4 shows how the resulting output looked:

```
                     Summary by State

              State                    Total
        AZ   ARIZONA                     2
        CA   CALIFORNIA                  9
        ID   IDAHO                       3
        NV   NEVADA                      1
        OR   OREGON                      1
        WA   WASHINGTON                  2

               18 Total Customers

                     Summary by State

              State                    Total
        NV   NEVADA                      1
        OR   OREGON                      1
        WA   WASHINGTON                  2
        AZ   ARIZONA                     2
        ID   IDAHO                       3
        CA   CALIFORNIA                  9

               18 Total Customers
```

Figure 7.4: Resulting output after using the Sort Array (SORTA) op code to resequence array elements.

Using Runtime Arrays to Format Data for Output

In our next example, we are going to use arrays to solve a common output problem. We want to print a customer phone list, but it needs to be a three-column alphabetical list, much like a phone book. This desired output is multicolumn, alphabetical reports because they are easier to read.

Our customer phone list program in Figure 7.5 uses a compile-time array (which we will explain later in this chapter) and two arrays to store data that will be printed. The program uses OPNQRYF to sequence the customer file first. The file is then read and the fields we are going to print are saved in the Names and Numbers arrays. The Names array holds the customer name, and the Numbers array holds the phone number. Storing the data in the arrays gives us the flexibility to produce the list in the desired format.

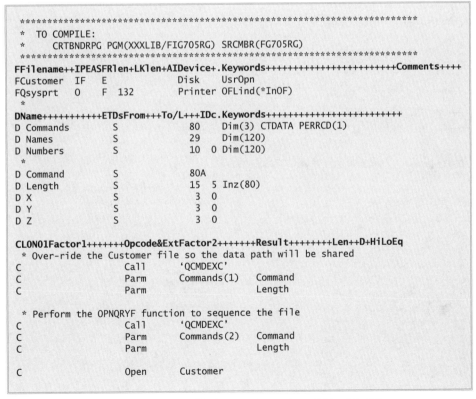

```
**********************************************************************
*   TO COMPILE:
*       CRTBNDRPG PGM(XXXLIB/FIG705RG) SRCMBR(FG705RG)
**********************************************************************
FFilename++IPEASFRlen+LKlen+AIDevice+.Keywords+++++++++++++++++++++++++Comments++++
FCustomer  IF   E               Disk    UsrOpn
FQsysprt   O    F   132         Printer OFLind(*InOF)
*
DName++++++++++++ETDsFrom+++To/L+++IDc.Keywords+++++++++++++++++++++++++
D Commands        S              80     Dim(3) CTDATA PERRCD(1)
D Names           S              29     Dim(120)
D Numbers         S              10   0 Dim(120)
*
D Command         S              80A
D Length          S              15   5 Inz(80)
D X               S               3   0
D Y               S               3   0
D Z               S               3   0

CLON01Factor1+++++++Opcode&ExtFactor2+++++++Result++++++++Len++D+HiLoEq
 * Over-ride the Customer file so the data path will be shared
C                   Call      'QCMDEXC'
C                   Parm      Commands(1)   Command
C                   Parm                    Length

 * Perform the OPNQRYF function to sequence the file
C                   Call      'QCMDEXC'
C                   Parm      Commands(2)   Command
C                   Parm                    Length

C                   Open      Customer
```

Figure 7.5: Using arrays to format a multicolumn customer phone list (part 1 of 3).

```
C                       Dou       %Eof
C                       Read      CusRec
 * If end of file is encountered, print array contents and get out of loop
C                       If        %Eof
C         X             CaSGT     *Zeros         Output
C                       EndCS
C                       Leave
C                       EndIf
 * Put names in arrays until there are enough entries for a page
C                       Eval      X = X + 1
C                       MoveL     CustName       Names(X)
C                       Move      PhoneNbr       Numbers(X)
C         X             CaSEQ     120            Output
C                       EndCs
C                       EndDo
 * Close the file
C                       Call      'QCMDEXC'
C                       Parm      Commands(3)    Command
C                       Parm                     Length
C                       Eval      *InLR = *ON

CSR       Output        BegSr
C                       Except    Heading
C         1             Do        40             X
C                       Eval      Y = X + 40
C                       Eval      Z = X + 80
C                       Except    Detail
C                       EndDo
C                       Eval      X = 0
C                       Clear                    Names
C                       Clear                    Numbers
CSR                     EndSR

OFilename++DF..N01N02N03Excnam++++B++A++Sb+Sa+........
OQsysprt    E                     Heading        2 02
O           OR    OF
O                                                78 'Customer Phone List'

O           E                     Heading        1
O           OR    OF
O                                                15 'Customer'
O                                                40 'Phone#'
O                                                59 'Customer'
O                                                84 'Phone#'
O                                               103 'Customer'
O                                               128 'Phone#'

O           EF                    Detail         1
O                                 Names(X)       29
O                                 Numbers(X)     42 '  /   -  0'
O                                 Names(Y)       73
O                                 Numbers(Y)     86 '  /   -  0'
```

Figure 7.5: Using arrays to format a multicolumn customer phone list (part 2 of 3).

```
0                   Names(Z)           117
0                   Numbers(Z)         130 ' / - 0'
**
OVRDBF FILE(CUSTOMER) SHARE(*YES)
OPNQRYF FILE((CUSTOMER)) ALWCPYDTA(*OPTIMIZE) KEYFLD((CUSTNAME))
CLOF CUSTOMER
```

Figure 7.5: Using arrays to format a multicolumn customer phone list (part 3 of 3).

The program first runs OPNQRYF from within the RPG program to sequence the customer file into customer name order. We use the QCMDEXC API program in conjunction with the Commands compile-time array to perform the OPNQRYF operation (we first examined this technique in chapter 6).

Once our file is in the desired sequence, we load our output arrays accordingly. The Names array is loaded alphabetically by customer name because that is the sequence in which we are reading the file. The customer phone numbers are loaded into the corresponding Numbers array elements.

Our program specifications call for a phone list that prints three columns across and 40 records deep. To be able to output the data in our desired sequence, we fill all 120 array elements (three columns multiplied by 40 records deep) and then use a print loop to dump the array contents. Because we also need to print the partially filled arrays when our end-of-file is reached, we have separated the output operation into a subroutine called OUTPUT (seems appropriate enough, does it not?).

In the output subroutine, we use three separate array indices to stagger the output to meet our desired format. In other words, we want the first array element to print on the same line as the 41st and the 81st array elements. The end result is a list you can use to look for a customer name alphabetically down the first column and, if it is not found there, down the second column, and so on.

The X index is used to print array elements 1 through 40, which are listed in the first column. The Y index is used to print elements 41 through 80 (the second column), and Z is used to print elements 81 through 120 (column three).

By using this technique, our list prints alphabetically top to bottom and then left to right. This phone-book style of output is made easy thanks to the use of arrays.

THE %ELEM BUILT-IN FUNCTION
PREVENTS ARRAY INDEX ERRORS

In Figure 7.5, the "do loop" we use to print our array elements was hard coded to perform 40 iterations of the loop. If the number of array elements was ever changed and the iteration on the do loop was not, the likely result would be an array index error or some other negative result. Prior to the announcement of built-in functions (which we will discuss later in this chapter), this was about the only way you could tell the system how many times a loop should be performed.

But there is a new built-in function called %ELEM, which returns the number of elements in a table, array, or Multiple-occurrence Data Structure. Figure 7.6 reflects the traditional way to program a processing loop.

```
CLON01Factor1+++++++Opcode&ExtFactor2+++++++Result++++++++Len++D+HiLoEq...Comments
c     1            Do         100          X
 * array processing goes here
c                  EndDo
```

Figure 7.6: Standard do loop processing.

With the %ELEM built-in function, you can build your do loop so it will always perform the code iteration for each element defined in your array, as seen in Figure 7.7.

```
CLON01Factor1+++++++Opcode&ExtFactor2+++++++Result++++++++Len++D+HiLoEq...Comments
c     1            Do         %ELEM(Array)  X
 * array processing goes here
c                  EndDo
```

Figure 7.7: Using the %ELEM built-in function to prevent array index errors.

By coding the program in this fashion, you prevent errors when you are writing and performing maintenance on your programs. If the number of array elements needs to be increased or decreased, you may not have to modify the code processing the array. By using the %ELEM built-in function to limit the number of iterations, the loop will automatically be performed for each array element, regardless of the number of elements in the array.

It should be noted that the %ELEM function can be used in the Definition Specifications as well. If you have several arrays with the same number of elements, you only need to indicate the number of elements once, and then use the %ELEM function to define the rest.

RUNTIME ARRAY HANDLING RPG OP CODES

Now that we have defined and discussed the value of runtime arrays, we need to look at how the various RPG op codes affect arrays. Some of these op codes only apply to arrays, and others work differently than you might expect.

Most of the arithmetic op codes work with numeric arrays. You specify that you are performing the operations on the entire array or just on a specific array element through the use of an array index. If you specify the index (by following the array reference with a number or numeric field enclosed in parentheses), the operation is performed on the specified array element. If you do not specify an index, the operation is performed on the entire array.

Using the MOVE and Move Left (MOVEL) op codes on single-array elements (by specifying the array index) works in the same fashion as if you had specified individual fields. Using these operations on whole arrays may not produce the kind of results you expect. Performing a MOVE or MOVEL from a field, constant, or data structure into an entire array completes the move as if it is being done with a single field, but the same results are recorded into all elements of the array.

For example, let's say we wanted to move the literal smith into an array of single, one-character elements. We call our array Name. If we simply perform a MOVEL:

```
CLON01Factor1+++++++Opcode&ExtFactor2+++++++Result++++++++
C                   MOVEL     'SMITH'       Name
```

the results in the Name array look like this:

S	S	S	S	S

While this may, in fact, be our intended result, it is more likely that we wanted to put each character of our constant into an element of the array.

That is where the Move Array (MOVEA) op code comes in. MOVEA was introduced to allow you to perform moves that cross the boundaries of the array. If we perform the same operation using MOVEA in place of MOVEL:

```
CLON01Factor1+++++++Opcode&ExtFactor2+++++++Result++++++++
C                   MOVEA     'SMITH'        Name
```

the results of the NAME array look like this:

Table 7.1 outlines the op codes that are used specifically with arrays (with the exception of the LOOKUP op code, which can also be used for tables).

THE COMPILE-TIME ARRAY

Another type of array is the compile-time array. As its name implies, data is loaded into this type of array when a program is compiled. The data used to load the array is coded right into the source of your RPG program.

This type of array can be useful when you need to work with a small number of data elements that always remain constant. An example of this type of data is days of the week. There are a limited number of days in a week and they are not likely to change. Rather than store them in a file or data area, it is easier to simply store them in a compile-time array at the end of a program.

Compile-time array data is actually stored *after* the source to your program, and there are two ways it can be stored. The first way is to use one of three special keywords that are used to tell the compiler that compile-time array data is about to follow. These keywords are **CTDATA (compile-time data), **ALTSEQ (compile-time data follows with an alternating collating sequence), and **FTRANS (compile-time file translation data follows).

If you choose to use these three new keywords, your compile-time array data can be placed in any order following your program source (as long as the array data directly follows the keyword describing the array). If you do not use these new keywords, your compile-time array data needs to directly follow the last source statement (generally an Output or Calculation Specification) and must match the same sequence with which the arrays were defined. In other words, if your program has multiple compile-time arrays and you do not choose to use the keywords, the array data must be defined in the program in the same sequence as the Definition Specifications describing them.

Table 7.1: Op Codes Used Specifically with Arrays.	

Op Code	Description
LOOKUP	The Lookup (LOOKUP) op code can actually be used for tables or arrays. It is used to perform a "seek and find" operation to determine if the search argument specified in Factor 1 exists in the table or array. If the search argument is found, the EQ indicator (in position 75) is turned on and the address of the array element found is returned to the index field of Factor 2 (position 36) if the index field was specified. When an index is specified, the LOOKUP begins at the array element initially specified in the index.
	If you want the search to begin at the start of the array, you must make sure the index is set to 1. You may also use the LOOKUP operation to perform high or low lookups that seek out the array elements that are closest to the search argument specified, but still satisfy the search conditions. The high or low lookups are done by using the indicators in positions 71 and 72 (HI) or 73 and 74 (LO), depending upon the desired search criteria.
MOVEA	Move Array (MOVEA) is used to move values to and from arrays. This op code may be used to move an array to a field, a field to an array, or an array to another array. In this case, a data structure or any constant qualifies as a field too. MOVEA may be used for alphanumeric or numeric arrays and fields, but the Factor 2 and Result field types must match. An index may be specified in Factor 2 or the Result field, and the move operation begins at the point of the index. The move that is performed is similar to a Move Left (MOVEL) because the move begins with the left-most point of Factor 2 and begins loading the value into the left-most portion of the Result field. If Factor 2 and the Result fields are not equal in length, the move is performed for the length that matches the shorter of the two.
SORTA	Sort Array (SORTA) performs the function that the name of the op code implies. The name of the array you want to sort goes into Factor 2. The array elements are automatically resequenced into an order that coincides with the value of the array elements. If array elements include blanks or zeros, these entries appear first after SORTA is executed. If the SORTA is performed on a field that happens to be a subfield in a data structure, the entire array is sequenced in the order of the subfield specified as Factor 2 of the SORTA statement (see Figure 7.3).
XFOOT	Cross Foot (XFOOT) sums all of the values of a numeric array in a single command. The Result field must contain a valid numeric field or array element where the total is placed when the operation is performed.

The data of each compile-time array will be designated and separated beginning with two asterisks (**) keyed into positions 1 and 2 of the source statement directly following your program source. The two asterisks act as a trigger record to tell the compiler that table or compile-time-array data follows.

The source records that follow the trigger record represent the data for the compile-time array. Figure 7.8 shows two examples of what compile-time-array data looks like. In the first example, the compile-time array is designated without any keyword. In the second example, the **CTDATA keyword was used to designate that compile-time data follows.

```
...+... 1 ...+... 2 ...+... 3 ...+... 4 ...+... 5 ...+... 6 ...+... 7
**
AL
AK
AZ


...+... 1 ...+... 2 ...+... 3 ...+... 4 ...+... 5 ...+... 6 ...+... 7
**CTDATA States
AL
AK
AZ
```

Figure 7.8: Examples of compile-time-array data.

In Figure 7.9, we have defined a compile-time array with a Definition Specification. Our array is named States, has 50 total elements that are each two characters in length (representing each of the 50 states), and there is one entry per source record. The CTDATA keyword tells the compiler that this array represents compile-time data. The PERRCD keyword tells the compiler that there is only one array entry per source record. Figure 7.8 shows the trigger record and the first few array entry source records.

```
DName++++++++++ETDsFrom+++To/L+++IDc.Keywords++++++++++++++++++++++++++++++Comments
D States            S              2   DIM(50) CTDATA PERRCD(1)
```

Figure 7.9: Defining a compile-time array with a Definition Specification.

This array can be used to validate the state entered on a data entry screen. You can use the LOOKUP op code with the value entered on the screen against the States array to see if the keyed value exists in the array. If the keyed value is not found, you can issue an error message so the program operator can correct the field before the keyed data is accepted.

ALTERNATIVE DEFINITION OF ARRAYS

The most common way to load an array is with some form of logic loop, as in our previous examples. But there are some other very useful ways to load data into arrays that will help you at input, output, and calculation time.

You can use File Input Specifications to redefine data fields into array elements. The specifications can be used to take entire fields from a file and split them up into array elements. They can also be used to take individual fields and redefine them so the system considers them to be part of an array.

In Figure 7.10, we define an array called AGE. The array is used to store and process aged accounts receivable amounts that are stored in our customer file. We could load each aging field stored in the customer file into our array, perform the necessary processing, and then move the fields back prior to output. But this would be time-consuming and tedious.

```
DName+++++++++++ETDsFrom+++To/L+++IDc.Keywords++++++++++++++++++++++++++++++Comments
D AGE             S              9  2 DIM(6)
I..............Ext-field+.................Field++++++++++L1M1..P1MnZr.....Comments
ICUSREC
I             CUS000                  AGE(1)
I             CUS030                  AGE(2)
I             CUS060                  AGE(3)
I             CUS090                  AGE(4)
I             CUS120                  AGE(5)
I             CUS150                  AGE(6)
```

Figure 7.10: Redefining runtime arrays using input specifications.

A better way is to tell the system at file-definition time that each of the aging fields in our customer file represents a specific array element. The example in Figure 7.10 does exactly that. Even though our customer file is externally described, we use an internal definition of the CUSREC record format to tell the system that field CUS000 is the first array element in the AGE array, CUS030 is the second element, and so on.

Another example of how to redefine input file data fields into array elements is shown in Figure 7.11. While our first example uses field names from our externally described customer file, this second example uses the field positions within the file to tell the system which fields in our customer file to use as array elements. We use the array name, along with the index that is used to describe which element within the array represents the specified field positions, in place of the field names that exist in the external description of the file. This method is less desirable than the method demonstrated in Figure 7.10 because changes in the size and type of data can cause a lot of extra, tedious work.

```
DName+++++++++++ETDsFrom+++To/L+++IDc.Keywords++++++++++++++++++++++++++++++++Comments
D AGE            S              9  2 DIM(6)
I....................Fmt+SPFrom+To+++DcField++++++++++L1M1FrP1MnZr.....Comments
ICUSREC
I                         P   101  105   AGE(1)
I                         P   106  110   AGE(2)
I                         P   111  115   AGE(3)
I                         P   116  120   AGE(4)
I                         P   121  125   AGE(5)
I                         P   126  130   AGE(6)
```

Figure 7.11: Redefining runtime arrays with multiple input specifications.

Note that there are no decimal positions specified on the Input Specifications, even though the array definition reflects the array elements as being nine digits with two decimal places. The compiler will not allow you to specify decimal positions at the input level when you are redefining array elements. Instead, it takes the definition from the Definition Specification describing the array.

Interestingly, the compiler insists that you handle the data type in the opposite manner. The example in Figure 7.11 shows that the data in our customer file is in a packed format, as specified in column 36 of the Input Specifications, but the compiler will not let you specify that the array is packed on the Definition Specification. The compiler takes the data type definition from the Input Specification describing the input file.

The aging fields from the customer file shown in the example in Figure 7.11 are contiguous fields (stored consecutively in the file). It is easier to redefine the array elements with a single Input Specification, as shown in Figure 7.12.

```
DName+++++++++++ETDsFrom+++To/L+++IDc.Keywords++++++++++++++++++++++++++++++++Comments
D AGE            S              9  2 DIM(6)
I....................Fmt+SPFrom+To+++DcField++++++++++L1M1FrP1MnZr.....Comments
ICUSREC
I                         P   101  130   AGE
```

Figure 7.12: Redefining multiple runtime array elements with a single input specification.

You can also use data structures to redefine arrays as you do with file input specifications. If you choose to use this method, however, you must be careful to initialize your numeric data structures before your program tries to use them. As we discuss in chapter 8, numeric data structures are considered to have blanks in them until you initialize or load data into them. If you fail to perform one of these options, your program will likely result in a Data Decimal Error, which occurs when the system encounters non-numeric data in a numeric field.

ARRAYS CAN BE VERY DYNAMIC

A new type of array, introduced with V3R1, has the ability to dynamically allocate storage. It is logically referred to as a *dynamic* array. The idea behind it is that you define the array to initially take very little main memory, and then size your array on the fly, using only the memory that you need.

To code a dynamic array, you need to use three new system APIs: CEEGTST (get heap storage), CEECZST (reallocate storage), and CEEFRST (free storage).

Coding this type of array can get involved. Because there is a very good example of how to code a program using this type of array in IBM's *ILE RPG/400 Programmers Guide*, we decided not to duplicate the efforts here. But if you have a situation where you need to code a runtime array where you cannot predict the ultimate number of elements, you may want to look this one up.

STRING HANDLING
ISN'T JUST FOR PEOPLE WITH YO-YOS ANYMORE

String handling op codes were a significant (and long-awaited) announcement as part of OS/400 Version 2. When Version 3 was announced, string handling was further enhanced with the new built-in functions. These new tools allow us to concatenate, scan, and parse results from data fields without having to load them into arrays first.

Even though the string handling operation codes are largely outdated at this stage, we have listed them in Table 7.2. All of the operations listed in there make the process of string manipulation a far more palatable task.

Op Code	Description
	Table 7.2: String Handling Op Codes.
CAT	Concatenates (joins) two character or constant fields into a single Result field. You can specify how many (if any) blanks you want to have between the two fields once they have been concatenated.
CHECK	Used primarily to validate data in one string of data, and checks to see if all of the characters from the string being checked happen to exist in another string. If invalid characters exist in the string being searched, the address position(s) of illegal characters can be returned to a field or array.
CHECKR	Functions similarly to the CHECK op code, except the check for character validity is performed from the right-most character to the left. Just like the CHECK op code, checking is discontinued once an illegal character is found, unless the Result field specified happens to be a numeric array.
SCAN	Scans (searches) a data field or array for a specific search argument and returns the positional address(es) of where within the searched field or array the search argument is found. No positional address is returned if the search argument is not found. If the Result field of this op code is a numeric array, multiple positional addresses may be returned if there are multiple occurrences of the search argument within the field or array being searched.
SUBST	Substrings (extracts) a portion of a character field, array element, or data structure element and places it into another. You specify the start position of the extract and the size of the Result field is used to determine how many characters are moved. This op code generally is used in conjunction with the SCAN or CHECK op codes.
XLATE	Translates characters of a field, array element, or data structure from one value (or set of values) to another. An example of how to use this op code is the translation of fields from lowercase to uppercase.

With the advent of the EVAL operation code and freeform expressions, RPG IV evolved into a language for the 21st century. At long last, RPG programmers were able to use tools that had long been available to programmers that worked in other languages. For the first time, we were able to address pointers in memory and convert data types on the fly. We were now able to write extensive numeric calculations using a wide variety of data types that were originally not available to RPG. And one of the best things to come out of the evolution was the advent of the built-in function.

Built-in functions can be readily identified because they begin with a percent (%) sign. Unlike operation codes that may only be used in Calculation Specifications, built-in functions may also be placed in Definition Specifications. Another way built-in functions are not like operation codes is that they return a value, rather than place function results in a Result field.

Table 7.3 contains an extensive list of the built-in functions available as of V4R4 of OS/400. Because we are mainly focusing on the string handling capabilities of RPG IV in this chapter, we are not going to try to address how to use all of them here. You will also find the release with which each of the built-in functions was announced and made part of the RPG IV language.

Table 7.3: Built-in Functions Available as of V4R4.

Function Name	Description	Value Returned	Release
%ABS	Return the absolute value of expression	Absolute value of expression	V3R7
%ADDR	Return the address of variable	Address of variable	V3R1
%CHAR	Convert alternative data types to a character format	Value in character format	V4R1
%DEC	Convert alternative data types to a decimal format	Value in packed numeric format	V3R7
%DECH	Convert alternative data types to a decimal format with half adjust	Half-adjusted value in packed	V3R7
%DECPOS	Obtain the number of decimal positions of a numeric value	Number of decimal digits	V3R7
%DIV	Performs the same function as the DIV (divide) op code	Quotient	V4R4
%EDITC	Apply an edit code to a numeric value	String with edit code applied	V3R7
%EDITFLT	Convert a numeric variable to a float external representation	Character representation of floating format	V3R7
%EDITW	Apply an edit word to a numeric variable	String with edit word applied	V3R7
%ELEM	Obtain the number of elements of an array, table, or multiple occurrence data structure	Number of elements or occurrences	V3R1
%EOF	Indicate when an end-of-file condition exists	'1' if beginning or end of file	V4R2
%EQUAL	Used with SETLL and LOOKUP to indicate when an exact match was found	'1' if SETLL/LOOKUP found exact match	V4R2

Table 7.3: Built-in Functions Available as of V4R4 (continued).

Function Name	Description	Value Returned	Release
%ERROR	Used in conjunction with the E operation code extender. Indicates when an error condition exists	'1' if op code is in error	V4R2
%FLOAT	Convert alternative data type to floating format	Value in floating format	V3R7
%FOUND	Was the record found in an I/O operation? Valid op codes are: CHAIN, SETLL, SETGT, DELETECHECK, CHECKR, SCAN, LOOKUP	'1' if record or match found	V4R2
%GRAPH	Convert numeric value to graphic value	Value in graphic format	V4R4
%INT	Convert alternative data type to integer format	Value in integer format	V3R7
%INTH	Convert alternative data type to Integer format, half adjust	Half-adjusted value in integer format	V3R7
%LEN	Obtain the length of a variable or set the length of a variable length field	Length in digits or characters	V3R7
%NULLIND	Query or set null indicator	'1' or '0', indicating null setting	V3R7
%OPEN	Is the database file open?	'1' if file is open	V4R2
%PADDR	Obtain the address of a procedure	Address of procedure	V3R1
%PARMS	Return number of parameters passed to a program	Number of parameters passed in	V3R2
%REM	Return remainder after a %DIV operation	Remainder from the division	V4R4
%REPLACE	Replace "target" character string with a "source" character string	String with replaced value inserted	V4R2
%SCAN	Scan for characters	First position of search argument, or 9	V3R7
%SIZE	Return size of variable in bytes	Size of variable or literal	V3R1
%STATUS	Return file or program status	If error, value set for program or file status.	V4R2
%STR	Get or store null terminated string	Characters addressed by pointer	V3R7
%SUBST	Perform a substring operation, equivalent to the SUBST operation code	Subset of a string	V3R1

Table 7.3: Built-in Functions Available as of V4R4 (continued).

Function Name	Description	Value Returned	Release
%TRIM	Trim leading and trailing blanks from an alphanumeric variable	String with blanks trimmed front/back	V3R1
%TRIML	Trim leading blanks from an alpha-numeric variable	String with leading blanks trimmed	V3R1
%TRIMR	Trim trailing blanks from an alpha-numeric variable	String with trailing blanks trimmed (replaced with null characters)	V3R1
%UCS2	Convert alternative data types to UCS-2 value (Unicode)	Value in UCS-2 format	V4R4
%UNS	Convert alternative data types to unsigned format	Value in unsigned format	V3R7
%UNSH	Convert alternative data types to unsigned format, half-adjust	Half-adjusted unsigned value	V3R7
%XFOOT	Sum array expression elements, equivalent to the XFOOT operation code	Sum of the elements of array	V4R4

EVERYBODY WANTS TO BE A CAT

For many years, arrays were the only tool RPG programmers could use for string handling and manipulation. As you can see in Figure 7.13, array handling was not always terribly efficient.

```
E....FromfileTofile++Name++N/rN/tbLenPDSArrnamLenPDSComments+++++++++......
E                 WRK       40 1                    WORKING ARRAY
*
CLON01N02N03Factor1+++OpcdeFactor2+++ResultLenDHHiLoEqComments+++++++......
C                 MOVE *BLANKS   WRK
C                 MOVEACITY      WRK
C        WRK,X    DOWEQ*BLANKS                       FIND LAST NON-BLANK
C                 SUB  1         X           68      CHARACTER
C    68           END
C                 ADD  1         X
C                 MOVEA','       WRK,X              ADD A COMMA
C                 ADD  2         X
C                 MOVEASTATE     WRK,X              ADD THE STATE
C                 ADD  3         X
C                 MOVEAZIPCOD    WRK,X              ADD THE ZIP
C                 ADD  5         X
C                 MOVE '-'       WRK,X
C                 ADD  1         X
C                 MOVEAZIP4      WRK,X              ADD ZIP + 4
C                 MOVEAWRK       CSZ   40           MOVE RESULT TO FIELD
```

Figure 7.13: Using RPG III arrays to pack city, state, and zip code.

The objective of this routine is to take the contents of the following fields and pack them together into one field:

Field	Size and Attributes	Contents
CITY	15A	San Diego
STATE	2A	CA
ZIPCOD	5A	92126
ZIP4	4A	4440

The result after the routine is run looks something like this:

```
San Diego, CA 92126-4440
```

As you can see from the example in Figure 7.14, the CAT op code requires significantly less code to perform the same operation shown in Figure 7.13. As you already know, less code means less maintenance and fewer chances for error.

```
DName++++++++++++ETDsFrom+++To/L+++IDc.Keywords+++++++++++++++++++++++++++++++Comments
D CSZ             S          40A

CLON01Factor1+++++++Opcode&ExtFactor2+++++++Result++++++++Len++D+HiLoEq...Comments
C     CITY        CAT(P)    ',':0         CSZ
C                 CAT       STATE:1       CSZ
C                 CAT       ZIPCOD:1      CSZ
C                 CAT       '-':0         CSZ
C                 CAT       ZIP4:0        CSZ
```

Figure 7.14: Using the CAT op code to pack city, state, and zip code.

The first statement in Figure 7.14 uses the CAT op code to concatenate the contents of the CITY field in Factor 1 to a constant comma (,) found in Factor 2. Because the P extender is specified directly after the CAT op code, our Result field (CSZ) is *padded*, or filled with blanks, prior to placing the results of our CAT operation there. After filling the CSZ field with blanks, the results of the concatenation are placed into the Result field:

Factor 1	Op Code	Factor 2	Result Field
[1st character string]	CAT[P]	2nd string[:# of blanks]	concatenation result

Placing a colon (:) and a numeric value or field after the constant or field specified in Factor 2 tells the system how many blanks to use between the Factor 1 and Factor 2 values once the concatenation is complete. On the first line of the example in Figure 7.14, we tell the system that we want a comma (represented by the constant specified in Factor 2) to directly follow the field value of Factor 1, with no spaces between them. The results recorded in the CSZ field after the first line of the example in Figure 7.14 looks like this:

```
San Diego,
```

The second line of our example is used to concatenate the STATE field to the current value of the CSZ field, leaving a single space between the two values. Factor 1 is left blank here because the system automatically assumes, unless you specify otherwise, that Factor 1 is the same as the Result field.

The remaining statements concatenate the ZIPCOD, a dash (-), and the ZIP4 field to the end of the CSZ field to attain the desired results. We are able to accomplish our goal with approximately one quarter the number of statements. Another advantage is that we did not need to worry about array index errors because arrays are no longer part of the equation.

Note that this operation was made simpler because the zip code is stored as an alphanumeric field. If it were stored as numeric, we would either have to move the code to an alphanumeric field before performing the CAT operation or use the new %CHAR built-in function that was recently announced in RPG IV.

String handling has gotten even easier as the RPG language has evolved. As you can see in Figure 7.15, far less code is needed to pack the city, state, and zip code into a single field.

The code in Figure 7.15 performs essentially the same function as the previous two examples, but there is also additional functionality. This example shows how to convert fields of a different data type to be converted to alphanumeric using a built-in function. Because the zip code fields in our database are generally numeric, we will use the %CHAR built-in function to change its value. The %CHAR built-in function allows you to treat a field as alphanumeric, even though the field has another data type.

```
DName++++++++++ETDsFrom+++To/L+++IDc.Keywords++++++++++++++++++++++++++++++Comments
D CSZ            S            40A

CLON01Factor1+++++++Opcode&ExtExtended-factor2+++++++++++++++++++++++++++++Comments
C                   EVAL      CSZ = %TRIM(CITY) + ', ' +
C                             STATE + ' ' + %CHAR(ZIPCOD) +
C                             '-' + %CHAR(ZIP4)
```

Figure 7.15: Using freeform expressions to pack city, state, and zip code.

In Figure 7.15, we used the EVAL op code to pull our city, state, and zip code fields together. We first specified the %TRIM function on the CITY field to trim off the leading and trailing blanks (we could have used %TRIMR because only trailing blanks are likely to be present in this field). We then used the plus sign (+) to concatenate the result of our %TRIM function to the literal that includes a comma (,) and a trailing blank that will appear after the city and before the state.

The first line of our EVAL statement ended with a plus sign (indicating a pending concatenation), so the next two lines serve as a continuation of our EVAL statement. We then used the plus sign to concatenate the state and zip code fields to our CSZ field. Note that we used the %CHAR built-in function to designate the numeric ZIP and ZIP4 fields as characters, even though they are stored in our database as numeric fields.

The net result of the code in Figure 7.15 was the same as the code in Figures 7.13 and 7.14, except that we also converted our zip code fields from numeric to alphanumeric fields. Figure 7.16, shows how to use the CAT op code to pack a first name, a middle initial, and a last name into a single field.

```
CLON01Factor1+++++++Opcode&ExtFactor2+++++++Result++++++++Len++D+HiLoEq...Comments
C     FIRST         CAT(P)    INIT:1         NAME
C                   CAT       LAST:1         NAME
```

Figure 7.16: Using CAT to pack first name, middle initial, and last name.

The same "packing" operation as the one performed in 7.16 was made much simpler when we used the newer built-in functions, as shown in Figure 7.17.

```
CLON01Factor1++++++Opcode&ExtExtended-factor2+++++++++++++++++++++++++++Comments
C                   EVAL      NAME = %Trim(First) + ' ' + %Trim(Init) +
C                             ' ' + %Trim(Last)
```

Figure 7.17: Using freeform expressions to pack first name, middle initial, and last name.

Note that in Figure 7.17, we used the %TRIM built-in function to strip leading and trailing blanks from each of the name fields. Using the %TRIM on the one-character field for initial was performed so names missing the middle initial would still be packed correctly.

CHECK, PLEASE

The CHECK op code is a useful tool for validating data in a string. Figure 7.18 uses the CHECK op code to validate data in the alphanumeric field called TSTAMT to ensure the data is entirely numeric. If the test determines that all characters in the field are numeric, it moves the value in TSTAMT to the field called AMOUNT. Otherwise, the AMOUNT field is filled with zeros.

```
DName++++++++++ETDsFrom+++To/L+++IDc.Keywords+++++++++++++++++++++++++++++Comments
D Number         C                    CONST('0123456789')
D Amount         S             9 2
CLON01Factor1++++++Opcode&ExtFactor2+++++++Result++++++++Len++D+HiLoEq...Comments
C     Number     CHECK     Tstamt                          68
C                IF        *IN68
C                EVAL      Amount = 0
C                ELSE
C                EVAL      Amount = Tstamt
C                ENDIF
```

Figure 7.18: Using CHECK to validate a numeric field.

You may have occasion to perform this test to avoid Data Decimal Errors. As you are aware, the AS/400 is very particular about data types. If a field is defined as being numeric, the AS/400 tends to get a little upset if it finds data other than numbers in it. Unfortunately, data imported into the AS/400 often comes from other systems (including some of the AS/400's predecessors) that are not nearly as good at checking the validity of their data.

197

You can also specify a Result field with the CHECK op code that will be used to store the address(es) of the digits that were found to be invalid. The Result field can be a numeric field or array.

Factor 1	Op Code	Factor 2	Result Field	HI	LO	EQ
validation string	CHECK	string to check[:start position]	[posi-tion(s)]	—	[Err]	[Found]

If the specified Result field happens to be a numeric array, the CHECK operation checks the entire contents of the string specified in Factor 2, and returns the address of the fields found to be invalid to the Result field array.

CHECKR VALIDATES CHARACTER STRINGS FROM RIGHT TO LEFT

The CHECKR op code serves basically the same function as the CHECK op code, except that the string is validated from the right-most characters of the string back to the left-most character.

Factor 1	Op Code	Factor 2	Result Field	HI	LO	EQ
validation string	CHECK R	string to check[:start position]	[posi-tion(s)]	—	[Err]	[Found]

If you choose to use indexing on Factor 2 (the string being searched), the CHECKR operation begins at the character address specified by the index field and searches from right to left, back to the beginning character of the string.

USING THE %TRIM BUILT-IN FUNCTION TO REMOVE LEADING AND TRAILING BLANKS

You may find that you need to remove leading and trailing blanks from a field to strip out the pertinent data. The %TRIM built-in function will perform this service. The example in Figure 7.19 shows how to use it to remove both leading and trailing blanks in the NAME field and put the results in a field called LAST.

```
CL0N01Factor1+++++++Opcode&ExtExtended-factor2+++++++++++++++++++++++++++Comments
C                   EVAL        LAST = %TRIM(NAME)
```

Figure 7.19: Using %TRIM to remove leading and trailing blanks.

Let's apply the code in Figure 7.19 to the following NAME field:

```
0...+... 1 ...+... 2 ...+... 3
         SMITH
```

After the operation, the results in the field called LAST look like this:

```
0...+... 1
SMITH
```

USING THE %TRIML BUILT-IN FUNCTION TO REMOVE LEADING BLANKS

If you want to remove only leading blanks, %TRIML, which was designed for this purpose, is the built-in function to use. The example in Figure 7.20 shows how to use the %TRIML built-in function to ensure that any leading blanks in the NAME field are removed. Another way to describe this particular function would be to say that we are using the %TRIML built-in function to left-justify the NAME field.

```
CL0N01Factor1+++++++Opcode&ExtExtended-factor2+++++++++++++++++++++++++++Comments
C                   EVAL        NAME = %TRIML(NAME)
```

Figure 7.20: Using %TRIML to remove leading blanks.

You will notice that the results look very similar to those of the previous example:

```
0...+... 1 ...+... 2 ...+... 3
         SMITH
```

After the operation, the results look like the following:

```
0...+... 1 ...+... 2 ...+... 3
SMITH
```

REMOVING TRAILING BLANKS

Sometimes you need to right-justify a field by removing trailing blanks. As described in the *ILE RPG for AS/400 Reference* manual, we felt that the %TRIMR built-in function was designed to perform this function. But this was not the case. As a matter of fact, if you apply the code seen in in Figure 7.21, you will see no difference in the resulting NAME field at all. The reason for this is that the %TRIMR built-in function simply changes the trailing blanks to null characters. It does not physically remove them from the field .

```
CLON01Factor1+++++++Opcode&ExtExtended-factor2+++++++++++++++++++++++++++++++Comments
C                   EVAL      NAME = %TRIMR(NAME)
```

Figure 7.21: Using %TRIMR to "remove" trailing blanks.

If you wish to physically remove blanks and right-justify a field, you need to get a little more creative than that. While showing you how to perform this task, we will also introduce you to some new built-in functions. See Figure 7.22.

```
CLON01Factor1+++++++Opcode&ExtExtended-factor2+++++++++++++++++++++++++++++++Comments
C                   Eval      FieldLen = %len(Input)
C                   Eval      InputLen = %len(%trimr(Input))
C                   If        FieldLen > InputLen
C                   Eval      Output = %subst(Input :
C                               InputLen + 1 : FieldLen - Inputlen) +
C                               Input
C                   Else
C                   Eval      Output = Input
C                   Endif
```

Figure 7.22: How to remove trailing blanks.

As an example, let's apply the code in Figure 7.22 to the following INPUT field:

```
0...+... 1 ...+... 2 ...+... 3
      SMITH
```

The results after the operation would be placed in OUTPUT and would look like this:

```
0...+... 1 ...+... 2 ...+... 3
                SMITH
```

The example in Figure 7.22 works by calculating the number of trailing blanks in the field named INPUT, extracting them from the INPUT field, and then concatenating extracted blanks onto the front of the field.

The routine first calculates the length of the field by using the %LEN (return length) built-in function, which will return a numeric value corresponding to the length of the field. In the next step, we calculate the length of the actual data in the field by using %TRIMR to "remove" the trailing blanks from the data before returning the length of the field.

Once you know the actual length of the field, as well as the length of the data in the field, the rest is easy. We simply use the %SUBST built-in function to extract the trailing blanks from the input field and concatenate them to the front of the input field itself. You will notice that we first checked to see that the two values are not the same (they would be if the data in the field went all the way to the end of the field). Failure to perform this step would have resulted in a runtime error.

Journey to the Center of the Earth

In Figure 7.22, we showed you how to remove the trailing blanks. With minor modifications, you can use pretty much the same code to center text within a field. Let's take a look at the example in Figure 7.23.

```
CLON01Factor1+++++++Opcode&ExtExtended-factor2++++++++++++++++++++++++++++++Comments
C                   Eval      FieldLen = %len(Input)
C                   Eval      InputLen = %len(%trim(Input))
C                   Eval      NbrBlanks = ((FieldLen - InputLen) / 2)
C                   If        FieldLen > InputLen
C                   Eval      Output = %subst(Output : NbrBlanks :
C                                      NbrBlanks) + %Trim(Input)
C                   Else
C                   Eval      Output = Input
C                   Endif
```

Figure 7.23: Centering text within a field.

The code in Figure 7.23 is very similar to the code we used in Figure 7.22. We begin by calculating the length of the field, but using the %LEN built-in function. We then calculate the length of the actual input by applying the same operation, but trimming off the leading and trailing blanks (using %TRIM). We then figure out the total number of blanks in the field by subtracting the length of the input, INPUTLEN, from the length of the field, FIELDLEN, and then cutting them in half by dividing by 2.

Our NBRBLANKS variable now contains half the number of blanks that were left in our IN-PUT field. All we really need to do at this point is concatenate the number of blanks (in NBRBLANKS) to the front of the input data. We perform this by using the substring (%SUBST) built-in function

As an example, let's apply the code in Figure 7.23 to the following INPUT field:

```
0...+... 1 ...+... 2 ...+... 3
SMITH
```

The results after the operation would be placed in OUTPUT and look like this:

```
0...+... 1 ...+... 2 ...+... 3
            SMITH
```

SEEK AND YE SHALL FIND—WITH SCAN

Scan allows you to search a character string for a specific search argument, and then return a character address if the search argument is found. For example, let's say we want to know how many of the customers in our customer file are corporations. We could search the customer names for the characters INC and get a pretty good idea. The code looks something like that in Figure 7.24.

```
CLON01Factor1+++++++Opcode&ExtFactor2+++++++Result++++++++Len++D+HiLoEq...Comments
C     'INC':3      Scan      CustName                              68
 * If a corporation was found, go print the record...
C     *In68        CasEQ     *ON           Print
C                  EndCS
```

Figure 7.24: Using SCAN to find customers with INC in the customer name field.

The search argument of the SCAN op code is always specified in Factor 1. The argument can be a constant, all or part of a field, an array element, or a table name. You can specify that you only want to use the first portion of a field by indicating the field length in Factor 1. The field length is specified by following the value in Factor 1 with a colon (:) and a numeric field or constant.

Factor 1	Op Code	Factor 2	Result Field	HI	LO	EQ
search argument[:length]	SCAN	string to scan[:start position]	[position(s)]	—	[Err]	[Found]

Factor 2 contains the string you want searched. The string must be a character, but it can be a field, constant, array element, or table.

If you choose to specify the optional Result field, it is loaded with the positional address of the search argument if it happens to be found. If you choose to omit the Result field, you must specify an indicator in position 75. The indicator is turned on if the search argument is found and turned off if it is not.

Note that the SCAN op code is case sensitive. Using SCAN to detect an uppercase character string does not detect the same string in lowercase, and vice versa. If you want to perform a search that crosses the case boundaries, you can do so if you use the SCAN op code in conjunction with the Translate (XLATE) op code, which is discussed later in this chapter.

There is also a %SCAN built-in function that is very similar to the SCAN operation code. You need to note, however, that the %SCAN built-in function does not have the ability to return an array of all of the occurrences like the SCAN operation code can.

SUBSTRING (SUBST) TIES THE WHOLE STRING-HANDLING THING TOGETHER

You can use the Substring (SUBST) operation or the %SUBST built-in function to extract a value or values from a character string and move the results to the desired target character string, all from within a single operation. The character strings involved must be alphanumeric data. These elements may be arrays, array elements, and data structures, to name a few possibilities.

Factor 1	Op Code	Factor 2	Result Field	HI	LO	EQ
[Length to be extracted]	SUBST[P]	base string[:start]	Target string	—	[Err]	—

The substring function really performs two or three functions at the same time. It extracts the data you desire and then performs a "move left" function into the Result field. If you specify a P in the extender field (directly following the SUBST op code), the remainder of the Result field is padded with blanks.

The character string from which you want to extract data is specified in Factor 2. Optionally, you can indicate the position within the string where you want the extraction to begin by following the string specified in Factor 2 with a colon (:) and a number or numeric field that contains the character address where the search should begin.

You tell the system how many characters to extract by the numeric value or numeric field you specify in Factor 1. If Factor 1 is omitted, the system calculates the length of the extraction based on the start position and the length of the string that was specified in Factor 2.

The %SUBST operation serves essentially the same function. It can be used within your definition specifications or accompany a freeform calculation specification, as in the following example:

Op Code	Extended-factor2
Eval	Result=%SUBST(string:start{:length})

Let's take a look at how the %SUBST built-in function can be used in conjunction with the %SCAN built-in function to create a powerful combination. In Figure 7.25, we use the two built-in functions to literally find a needle in a haystack. Let's say you have the following literal:

```
HaystackHaystackHaystackNeedleHaystackHaystack
```

In our example, we want find our needle in a haystack and separate the wheat from the chaff. In Figure 7.25, we accomplish this goal with two lines of code.

```
CLON01Factor1+++++++Opcode&ExtFactor2+++++++Result++++++++Len++D+HiLoEq...Comments
 * Find the needle
 c                    Eval      Start = %Scan('Needle' : Input)

 * Move results to output
 c                    Eval      Output = %Subst(Input : Start:
 c                              %Len('Needle'))
```

Figure 7.25: Using %SCAN and %SUBST to find a needle amongst the haystacks.

In Figure 7.25, we use the %SCAN built-in function to find the literal "Needle." The first parameter to this built-in function is the character string we are looking for. The second parameter is the input search string we wish to have "scanned." We omitted the third parameter, length, because it is assumed when you specify the character string we are searching for.

Once we identify the starting position of the "Needle" literal, we extract it from the string using the %SUBST built-in function. The first parameter for the %SUBST function is the input search string. Next we specify the start position of our "Needle" character string that we extrapolated using the %SCAN function. And even though we obviously know the length of the literal "Needle," we use the %LEN built-in function to specify the length of our literal.

TRANSLATE (XLATE) PERFORMS SINGLE-CHARACTER SUBSTITUTION WITHIN CHARACTER STRINGS

The XLATE op code is a handy tool when you need to perform character substitution within a character string. You can specify From and To characters to translate or entire strings of characters that need to be translated.

Factor 1	Op Code	Factor 2	Result Field	HI	LO	EQ
From value: To value	XLATE[P]	base string[:start]	Target string	—	[Err]	—

One of the more popular uses for this op code is to translate a lowercase character string to uppercase. This is a frequent requirement when you are importing data from an external source. Figure 7.26 shows an example of how to address this issue.

```
DName++++++++++++ETDsFrom+++To/L+++IDc.Keywords++++++++++++++++++++++++++++++++Comments
D Lower           C                  CONST('abcdefghijklmnopqrst-
D                                    uvwxyz')
D Upper           C                  CONST('ABCDEFGHIJKLMNOPQRST-
D                                    UVWXYZ')
CL0N01Factor1+++++++Opcode&ExtFactor2+++++++Result++++++++Len++D+HiLoEq...Comments
C       Lower:Upper   XLATE(P)  InName       OutName
```

Figure 7.26: Using XLATE to translate lowercase character strings to uppercase.

In Figure 7.26, we take an input field named InName that may or may not contain lower-case characters, and translate the characters to uppercase, placing the end results in a field called OutName. To do this, we use a named constant field Lower that contains all the lowercase characters we want to translate. We use another named constant, Upper, that holds the corresponding uppercase characters.

The XLATE operation looks for characters in the InName field that happen to exist in the Lower named constant and replaces them with the corresponding character found in the Upper named constant.

In Figure 7.27, we use the XLATE op code to translate brackets in the field called InField to parentheses.

```
CL0N01Factor1+++++++Opcode&ExtFactor2+++++++Result++++++++Len++D+HiLoEq...Comments
C       '{':'('     XLATE(P)  InField      InField
C       '}':')'     XLATE(P)  InField      InField
```

Figure 7.27: Using XLATE to translate brackets to parentheses.

FINAL WORDS ABOUT ARRAY AND STRING HANDLING

As you have seen while reading this chapter, array and string handling are a vital part of RPG programming. Array handling is invaluable for performing data validation, format-ting output, and storing totals that will be output later in a program. The string handling op codes make difficult character manipulation chores much easier to perform.

Take the time to become familiar with the tools discussed in this chapter. You will find it time well spent.

8

DATA STRUCTURES, DATA AREAS, AND THE LOCAL DATA AREA

In this chapter, we discuss three valuable components that are used for definition, composition, and transportation of data elements both to and from your RPG programs. As the AS/400 has continued its logical evolution, these three components have become a bigger part of the overall scheme of things. We have seen a myriad of APIs announced that use data structures to pass system data back and forth to our programs. Multiple-occurrence Data Structures have been added to reduce the number of fields and arrays required, as well as to give us a method for creating *two-dimensional* arrays. And the local data area (LDA) is still one of the best ways to pass localized data from one program to the next.

You will find that a thorough knowledge of these tools can give you a distinct competitive advantage over your programming counterparts. Once you have mastered these techniques, you will be able to write more efficient code that also performs better. Let's continue on our path of education by example to discuss the merit and functions of each of these methods.

THE DATA STRUCTURE

Data structures are used primarily to define and redefine data elements. In its simplest form, you can consider a data structure to be a sum of all of its parts. It is used to subdivide larger fields into smaller subfields, or compose smaller fields into larger ones.

By allowing you to create subdivisions in the data, a unique condition is created where data in the lesser subfields is dynamically bound to the larger fields that are being divided. If data in the subfield is changed, the value of the larger field is changed as well. Consequently, if values in the larger field are changed, the subdivided data is changed at the same time. This can eliminate an awful lot of code that would otherwise be needed to move data back and forth.

Let's begin by looking at a hypothetical point-of-sale transaction. In the following example, we look at a stock-keeping unit (SKU) number that might be used in a retail application. SKU numbers are used to identify a particular product or service.

The SKU number usually can be parsed out into codes that represent the department, manufacturer, vendor, model number, and stock number. As a general rule, the SKU number is used to record and track sales as well as to help manage the inventory.

When we read a SKU number from our hypothetical point-of-sale transaction, we could perform a series of MOVE and MOVEL operations to parse, or separate out, our department, manufacturer, vendor, model, and stock numbers. But this is time-consuming to code and involves setting up a series of work fields. Another option is to use the new string handling op codes that we covered in chapter 7. But these methods involve several steps, which leaves more room for error.

A much simpler way to perform this same task is to use a data structure to subdivide the number for you. Every time the SKU number changes, the subfields that make up the data structure defining the SKU number change as well.

In the following example, our sample SKU number is 22502807224089123491A405. Whew! While this number appears to be large and unwieldy, it is not nearly as overwhelming if you break it down as follows:

Sample SKU number:

Department	Manufacturer	Vendor	Model	Stock Number
22	502	80722	4089123491A	405

Figure 8.1 shows two different data structures that break down the SKU number for us. Note that the subfields (Department, Manufactur, Vendor, ModelNbr, and StockNbr) are all subsets of the field positions that make up the SKUNumber field.

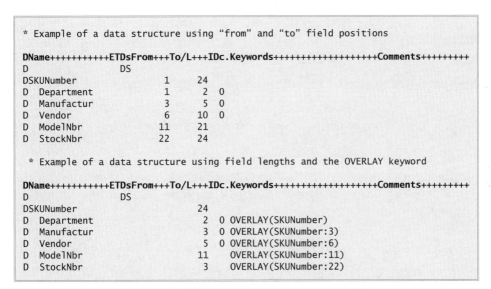

```
* Example of a data structure using "from" and "to" field positions

DName++++++++++ETDsFrom+++To/L+++IDc.Keywords+++++++++++++++++++Comments+++++++++
D                   DS
DSKUNumber           1     24
D  Department        1      2 0
D  Manufactur        3      5 0
D  Vendor            6     10 0
D  ModelNbr         11     21
D  StockNbr         22     24

 * Example of a data structure using field lengths and the OVERLAY keyword

DName++++++++++ETDsFrom+++To/L+++IDc.Keywords+++++++++++++++++++Comments+++++++++
D                   DS
DSKUNumber                 24
D  Department               2 0 OVERLAY(SKUNumber)
D  Manufactur               3 0 OVERLAY(SKUNumber:3)
D  Vendor                   5 0 OVERLAY(SKUNumber:6)
D  ModelNbr                11   OVERLAY(SKUNumber:11)
D  StockNbr                 3   OVERLAY(SKUNumber:22)
```

Figure 8.1: Using data structure definition specifications to break down a SKU number.

The first example in Figure 8.1 shows a data structure that is defined using From and To field positions, much as it was defined in the Input Specifications when we worked with RPG III.

The second example in Figure 8.1 shows how RPG IV allows us to simply code the length of the field(s); the compiler will calculate the From and To lengths for us. Note that the OVERLAY keyword was specified on the subfields that make up the SKU number, so the system would know that the subfields are subsets of the SKUNumber field. The OVERLAY keyword did not require a starting position for Department because the overlay began in position 1 of the SKU number. The OVERLAY keyword for the manufacturer number did require a start position, however, because the manufacturer number represents the third, fourth, and fifth characters of the SKU number field.

Either of these data structures, in effect, redefines the SKU number field into the various subfields we desire. Note that we have told the system that the first three fields

(Department, Manufactur, and Vendor) are all numeric fields, even though they are sub-elements of a larger alphanumeric field (SKUNUMBER).

If our retail point-of-sale application reads a database or display file record that contains the field called SKUNumber, our program could address and use the various subfields without having to worry about any additional overhead or work to extract the subfields. In this particular case, the SKUNumber field in the database or display file needs to contain 24 alphanumeric characters, just as it is defined in the data structure. The compiler gives you a hard time if you try to define it otherwise.

In the next example, we do not define the length of the SKUNumber field in our data structures. Instead, we simply name the data structure and define just the subfields.

The data structures in Figure 8.2 serve essentially the same function as the data structures in Figure 8.1. The difference is that instead of defining the field SKUNumber down in the Definition Specifications with the subfields, SKUNumber has been used as the name of the data structure.

```
 * Example of a data structure using "from" and "to" field positions

DName++++++++++++ETDsFrom+++To/L+++IDc.Keywords+++++++++++++++++++++Comments+++++++++
D SKUNumber       DS
D   Department          1        2  0
D   Manufactur          3        5  0
D   Vendor              6       10  0
D   ModelNbr           11       21
D   StockNbr           22       24

  * Example of a data structure using field lengths

DName++++++++++++ETDsFrom+++To/L+++IDc.Keywords+++++++++++++++++++++Comments+++++++++
D                 DS
DSKUNumber
D   Department               2  0
D   Manufactur               3  0
D   Vendor                   5  0
D   ModelNbr                11
D   StockNbr                 3
```

Figure 8.2: Alternate data structure definitions used to break down a SKU number.

In Figure 8.2, we do not need to specify the size of the SKUNumber field. In this instance, it is assumed that the size of the data structure is merely a sum of all its parts. As a general rule, if you do not specify the size of a data structure, the compiler defines the length of it by computing the length of all of the subfields within the structure. However, if the name of the data structure also happens to be an input field from a file, the definition comes from the file instead.

For the first example in Figure 8.2, we defined the buffer positions within the SKUNumber data structure that represent the various subfields. In the second example, we merely specified the lengths of the subfields and let the system calculate the buffer positions for us.

Rules Regarding Data Structures

Data structures, which can be externally described or program-described (as shown in Figures 8.1 and 8.2), are defined in the Definition Specifications of your RPG program. They support character, graphic, date, time, timestamp, basing-pointer, procedure-pointer, zoned-decimal, packed, and binary data types. Data types are defined in the same manner, and they generally follow the same rules you adhere to when coding data files.

The definition of a data structure begins with the characters DS in positions 24 and 25 of a Definition Specification. If your data structure is internally described, you may optionally name your data structure in columns 7 through 21 of the same Definition Specification. When a data structure is externally described (we discuss this in more detail when we cover "Externally Defined Data Structures" later in this chapter), you must either specify the name in positions 7 through 21 or use the EXTNAME keyword.

The fields for a data structure and its subfields must all appear together within the Definition Specifications (they may not be mixed in with file definitions or other data structures). The compiler does not allow field names within a data structure to exist in any other data structures within the program. As shown in the previous example, however, they may exist in database or display file definitions.

A data structure can go all the way up to 32,767 characters in size, which happens to be the same as the maximum size of an alphanumeric field in RPG IV.

Special Data Structures

There are four very unique data structures on the AS/400 that are used for special purposes:

- **File Information Data Structure.** Serves as a feedback area used to retrieve additional information about a file from the system. This data structure is initiated by the use of a special keyword that is specified in the File Description Specifications. This data structure is used primarily for error detection and prevention (i.e., record lock conditions or errors trying to open a database file). Chapter 4 offers a detailed explanation of the File Information Data Structure and its potential uses.

- **Program Status Data Structure.** Used to retrieve information about the program that is running. This information includes procedure name, job number, user ID, library name where the program resides, and a variety of other job information that may be pertinent to the task at runtime. Chapter 4 illustrates examples of the information that can be retrieved and where you might want to use it within your programs.

- **Data Area Data Structure.** Used to describe the information inside a data area. A data area is kind of like a single-record data file that happens to come in two flavors: local and global. The local data area (LDA) is unique to each program session and is used primarily to pass information from one job stream component to the next. On the other hand, global data areas can reside in any library and can be accessed by programs and CL alike. Data Area Data Structures can be used to describe and define both types of data areas. Examples of this type of data structure are covered later in this chapter.

- **Multiple-occurrence Data Structure**. Offers a way to define multiple like-data structures at once within your RPG program. The Multiple-occurrence Data Structure introduces flexibility into your RPG programs that may be used to eliminate arrays, fields, and work files from your RPG programs. If you eliminate work files, you are also eliminating unnecessary I/O processing. We cover the topic of Multiple-occurrence Data Structures a little later in the chapter.

There are also other special data structures like the Program Initialization (PIP) Data Structure and those involving system APIs (which are covered in detail in chapter 9).

Dynamics of Data Structures

As stated, one of the advantages of using data structures is that when you change data in one of the components, it can dynamically change the data fields or subfields being used to redefine the component. In Figure 8.1, we saw how reading a database or display file record with the SKUNumber field in it dynamically changed the values of the data structure subfields to redefine the SKUNumber field.

What happens when the situation is reversed? Let's calculate a follow-up date that might be used in an accounts receivable application. The objective of this routine is to create a follow-up date that is the 15th of the following month. To perform this function, begin by using the data structure shown in Figure 8.3.

```
DName++++++++++++ETDsFrom+++To/L+++IDc.Keywords++++++++++++++++++++++++++++++Comments
D                         DS
D  MonDayYear                        D   DATFMT(*MDY) INZ
D  Month                         2       OVERLAY(MonDayYear:1)
D  Day                           2       OVERLAY(MonDayYear:4)
D  Year                          2       OVERLAY(MonDayYear:7)
```

Figure 8.3: Using data structure input specifications to break down a date field.

Although there are a number of ways to perform this type of operation, we are going to use a data structure to help us perform this simple calculation. The first step is to load today's date into our data structure field.

You will note that the MonDayYear field has a data type (specified on column 40) of D, indicating that the field is a date data type. The DATFMT keyword is used to further describe the date field to the system. In this case, *MDY indicates that the date is stored in a Month-Day-Year format (see chapter 12 for a much more detailed explanation of date data types). The date data type includes separator characters, so the date of December 31, 1996, would be stored as 12/31/96. Also note that we did not need to specify the size of the field. The system knows that a field with a date data type in conjunction with a date format of *MDY will appear as eight characters to your RPG IV program.

The Month, Day, and Year fields have been specified in the data structure using the aforementioned OVERLAY keyword. The month is in the first two positions of the field, a separator character in the third position, the day in the fourth and fifth positions, and so on.

The task of retrieving the current date could easily be performed in a variety of ways. Our options include using the TIME op code; loading UYEAR, UMONTH, and UDAY into the appropriate subfields (Year, Month, and Day); moving UDATE into the MonDayYear data structure field (if your system date format is Month/Day/Year); or using the *DATE keyword. Whatever the method, it is unimportant for our example.

Let's say that our current date is December 31, 2000.

After loading our MonDayYear data structure field, the value of the MonDayYear field is 12/31/00. The values of the various subfields are:

Month	Day	Year
12	31	00

Applying the code shown in Figure 8.4 results in a date field in the MonDayYear data structure that represents the 15th of the month following the original date.

```
CLON01Factor1+++++++Opcode(E)+Factor2+++++++Result++++++++Len++D+HiLoEq...Comments
C                   MOVE      UDATE          MonDayYear
C                   ADDDUR    1:*M           MonDayYear
C                   MOVE      '15'           Day
```

Figure 8.4: RPG code using the data structure in Figure 8.3 to add a month to a date field.

In Figure 8.4, we moved UDATE (the system date) into our MonDayYear date field and then used the Add Duration (ADDDUR) op code to increase the date by one month. We could have accomplished the same thing by incrementing the Month field, but then we would have had to worry about whether the month had rolled over to an invalid month (in this case it would have been 13) and write code to increment the Year field and restore the Month field to a valid value. The ADDDUR op code is a much cleaner way to deal with a date field.

We then moved 15 into the Day field, replacing whatever happened to be there.

After applying the code in Figure 8.4, the MonDayYear data structure field contains a value of 01/15/01, and the subfield values are:

Month	Day	Year
01	15	01

There are other ways we could have found our desired follow-up date, but as you can see, the data structure gives us an easy way to use data structure subfields to dynamically change data.

The Data Structure and the Data Decimal Error

As you are no doubt aware, your AS/400 is terribly picky about data types. If you define a field as signed numeric, then that is exactly what the AS/400 expects to see. If it encounters blanks or alphanumeric data where it expects to see numeric data, the system complains very loudly in the form of a Data Decimal Error.

Data structures are one area of RPG in which it is very easy to create a condition for Data Decimal Errors to occur. This is because data structures are initially assumed to be alphanumeric data, regardless of the data type of the subfields defined within.

This potential error condition exists because data structures are not automatically initialized at program initiation unless you instruct your program to do so. If the data defined in your data structure is defined as signed numeric, and your program tries to refer to the numeric field prior to initializing or loading numeric data into the field, your program experiences a Data Decimal Error condition.

For example, let's say your program contains the data structure shown in Figure 8.5. If your program refers to the Amount, Dollars, or Cents numeric fields prior to loading data or moving zeros into them, you have a Data Decimal Error on your hands when the program is run.

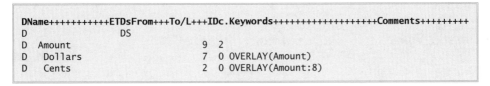

```
DName+++++++++++ETDsFrom+++To/L+++IDc.Keywords+++++++++++++++++++++Comments+++++++++
D                      DS
D   Amount                      9 2
D     Dollars                   7 0 OVERLAY(Amount)
D     Cents                     2 0 OVERLAY(Amount:8)
```

Figure 8.5: Example of a Data Decimal Error waiting to happen.

One way to address this potential problem is to always load data into the field(s) prior to using the field(s). An even safer way to address this problem is to instruct the system to automatically initialize the data structure at program initiation time.

To initialize a data structure at program initiation time, simply use the INZ keyword in the Definition Specification that defines the data structure. The INZ keyword should appear with other keywords beginning in position 44 of the Definition Specification.

Figure 8.6 provides an example of the same data structure shown in Figure 8.5, except that this one is initialized automatically at program runtime just prior to running the optional Initialize (*INZSR) subroutine. When this subroutine is present in your RPG program, it runs before the execution of all other Calculation Specifications.

```
DName+++++++++++ETDsFrom+++To/L+++IDc.Keywords+++++++++++++++++++++Comments+++++++++
D                       DS
D   Amount                        9  2 INZ
D     Dollars                     7  0 OVERLAY(Amount)
D     Cents                       2  0 OVERLAY(Amount:8)
```

Figure 8.6: Performing data structure initialization.

The data structure in Figure 8.6 has the INZ keyword in position 44 of the Definition Specification of the Amount field, so there are no Data Decimal Errors associated with the Amount, Dollars, or Cents fields unless the same fields happen to be defined in a database file with invalid numeric data. It should be noted that this initialization could also have been accomplished by using the INZ keyword on the Definition Specification. The subfields would automatically have been dynamically initialized either way.

Because we did not specify otherwise, the three numeric fields in our example are initialized as zeros. Data structure initialization is performed based on data type. In other words, alphanumeric fields are initialized to blanks and numeric fields are initialized to zeros, unless you specify otherwise. Because zeros are invalid in a field designated as a date data type, date fields would be initialized with a month of 01, a day of 01, and a year of 0001. The next section deals with situations where we want fields initialized to values other than the data type default values.

Default Values and Data Subfield Initialization

As we saw in the previous example, data structure initialization is a handy way to clear the fields in an entire data structure. But subfields within a data structure can also be initialized, and not necessarily to values dictated by the data type.

To initialize subfields in a data structure, simply put an INZ keyword in the Definition Specification describing the data structure subfield. Figure 8.7 shows the same data structure as in the previous two examples, except the initialization is performed on a subfield level instead of the entire data structure.

```
DName+++++++++++ETDsFrom+++To/L+++IDc.Keywords+++++++++++++++++++++Comments+++++++++
D   Amount                        9  2
D     Dollars                     7  0 INZ OVERLAY(Amount)
D     Cents                       2  0 INZ OVERLAY(Amount:8)
```

Figure 8.7: Data structure subfield initialization.

This example serves essentially the same purpose as the example in Figure 8.6. The Dollars and Cents fields are initialized to zeros because their data types are signed numeric, and an INZ has been specified as a keyword in the Definition Specifications. The subfields make up the entire Amount field, so initializing the subfields also initialized the Amount field.

What sets subfield initialization apart from data structure initialization is that default values may be established for each subfield. The default values are placed in parentheses following the INZ keyword when you are using the Definition Specification to define the subfield. As with Calculation Specifications, defaults for alphanumeric fields are placed in quotes, while numeric values are not.

In Figure 8.8, we choose to use both forms of data structure initialization at the same time. We specify an INZ keyword in the data structure Definition Specification telling the system to initialize the entire data structure based on data type. We then place a default value in parentheses following the INZ keyword when defining the Dollars subfield with a default value of 5.

```
DName++++++++++++ETDsFrom+++To/L+++IDc.Keywords+++++++++++++++++++++Comments+++++++++
D                      DS                    INZ
D   Amount                          9 2
D     Dollars                       7 0 INZ(5) OVERLAY(Amount)
D     Cents                         2 0 OVERLAY(Amount:8)
```

Figure 8.8: Data structure subfield initialization with default values.

In this example, the entire data structure is initialized according to data type (in this case, zeros) and then the default value of 5 is placed in the Dollars subfield. Consequently, the value of the Amount field after initialization is 5.00.

This same technique can be applied to alphanumeric fields. For instance, let's say we could initialize a description field with the value of Not on File, with the assumption that we probably will replace the initial value with a valid description later.

The example in Figure 8.9 establishes the definition of the field called Descriptn and initializes the original value of the field as Not on File (by placing the literal in parentheses following the INZ keyword).

```
DName++++++++++++ETDsFrom+++To/L+++IDc.Keywords+++++++++++++++++++++Comments+++++++++
D   Descriptn                      35    INZ('Not on File')
```

Figure 8.9: Alphanumeric subfield initialization with default values.

In place of the literal default value in parentheses, we could have specified the name of a named constant, figurative constant, or built-in function. The value in the named constant, figurative constant (i.e., *ALL 'a'), or built-in function would then serve as the default entry.

> **Note:** Default values may be reestablished by using the RESET op code.

In Figure 8.9, we established the initial value of the field called Descriptn as Not on File, with the idea that we would replace the value once a valid entry was made. If the RESET op code is specified later in the program, the default values are reestablished at that time. The RESET op code may be specified for a single field or for an entire data structure, as shown in Figure 8.10.

```
DName++++++++++++ETDsFrom+++To/L+++IDc.Keywords+++++++++++++++++++++Comments+++++++++
D ResetData       DS                  INZ
D  Amount                       9 2
D   Dollars                     7 0 INZ(5) OVERLAY(Amount)
D   Cents                       2 0 OVERLAY(Amount:8)
D   Descriptn                  35   INZ('Not on File')
```

Figure 8.10: Data structure subfield initialization with default values.

If RESET is applied to the ResetData data structure, all of the subfields in the data structure are reinitialized to their original values. The Dollars and Descriptn fields are reset to include the default values specified, and the Cents field is reinitialized to zeros because of its numeric data type.

The Amount field in this example is simply a redefinition of the Dollars and Cents fields, so the value of the Amount field is reset to 5.00 and the Descriptn field is reset to Not on File.

Externally Described Data Structures

Externally Described Data Structures can be used to define LDAs, data areas, program-described files, and parameter lists. We will discuss these topics more as this chapter progresses.

Many of the same attributes that make externally described data files such a powerful tool on the AS/400 also apply to Externally Described Data Structures. Because they are defined in a single place, there is consistency in definition. Programs using the data structure are easier to maintain because they do not necessarily need to be modified when the data structure changes, unless the program happens to use the fields within the data structure that were changed.

If an external data structure does change, programs using the data structure only need to be recompiled, with two notable exceptions. The first exception is if the program uses one or more of the fields in the data structure that was changed. The second exception is if new fields are added to the end of the data structure. In this case, only the programs using the newly added field(s) need to be modified or compiled.

As with any other data file, external data structure definitions are coded with DDS. In fact, an external definition is really just a physical file, and you can use other physical file specifications as external data structures. This technique can come in handy when your program uses a work file that exactly matches another physical file.

Basically, it does not matter whether the external definition you refer to in your Definition Specifications ever has data. The physical file specifications are simply being used as a data structure that is used to describe and define your data.

Figure 8.11 shows the DDS for a simple externally defined data structure. Figure 8.12 shows the RPG Input Specifications for the external definition called ExternlDef.

```
A..........T.Name++++++RLen++TDpB......Functions++++++++++++++++++++++++++++++
A          R ExternlDef                TEXT('External Data Structure')
A            CompanyNum    3S 0        COLHDG('Company Number')
A            CompanyNam    40A         COLHDG('Company Name')
```

Figure 8.11: DDS for an Externally Described Data Structure.

```
DName++++++++++++ETDsFrom+++To/L+++IDc.Keywords++++++++++++++++++++Comments+++++++++
D Definition     E DS                    EXTNAME(ExternlDef)
```

Figure 8.12: RPG Input Specifications for an Externally Described Data Structure.

The name of the data structure defined by the RPG IV Definition Specifications in Figure 8.12 is Definition. The data structure subfields called CompanyNum and CompanyNam are defined and ready for use from within the RPG IV program, just as if you had defined the data structure from within the program.

To get a full appreciation for the value of the Externally Described Data Structure, we really need to see how this methodology applies when used in conjunction with data areas, LDAs, program-described files, and parameter lists.

DATA AREAS

As their name implies, data areas are areas on disk that are used to store data. They are similar to data files in that they reside in a library, are used to store data, and may be externally or program-described. They are unlike files in that they may not have multiple record formats or multiple records.

As we mentioned earlier in this chapter, data areas come in two flavors: local and global. Data kept in the LDA is temporary in nature and is pertinent only to the session with which it is associated. In other words, the LDA is unique to each program session and is used primarily to pass information from one job stream component to the next. Consequently, workstation sessions may not share the LDA, and the information is unique to each workstation session. The information in the LDA is only available until the session is terminated.

Data kept in a global data area is permanent in nature and is available to all. This type of data area can reside in any library and can be accessed by RPG IV programs (and other languages) and CL. Data areas can be accessed by any job and may be shared throughout the system.

You can have your RPG IV program automatically open, close, and lock global data areas, or you can perform these functions yourself. Similar to record-level locks for data files, you can lock a data area to prevent another program from updating it while you need it.

Global Data Areas

Global data areas are generally created on demand by keying the Create Data Area (CRTDTAARA) command or from within a CL program. We discuss three ways your RPG IV programs can define data areas. These three ways consist of using a Data Area Data Structure, using an externally described data area, or simply using a program-described data area.

Data Area Data Structures

Data Area Data Structures are the easiest of the three to code, but they are less flexible than the other two methods already mentioned. Defining a Data Area Data Structure instructs your RPG IV program to read and lock the data area at program initialization and then perform an update to the data area and release the lock at last record time.

Unless you use the Unlock (UNLOCK) or Write Data Out to a Data Area (OUT) operation codes within your RPG IV program, the initial lock on the data area remains in effect until your program ends. This is not always practical when other programs throughout the system share your data area.

Data Area Data Structures are defined by placing a U in position 23 of the Definition Specification that defines the data structure. We see an example of this in Figures 8.13 and 8.14. In Figure 8.13, we define a Data Area Data Structure named DataDef. As you can see, the DDS resembles specifications you would use for any physical file.

```
A..........T.Name++++++RLen++TDpB......Functions++++++++++++++++++++++++++++
A          R DATADEF
A            DEVICE         10A        COLHDG('Tape Device')
A            PRINTER        10A        COLHDG('Printer Name)
A            OUTQUEUE       10A        COLHDG('OutQueue')
```

Figure 8.13: DDS for a Data Area Data Structure.

```
DName++++++++++ETDsFrom+++To/L+++IDc.Keywords++++++++++++++++++++++Comments+++++++++
D             EUDS                    EXTNAME(DATADEF)
```

Figure 8.14: Input Specifications for a Data Area Data Structure.

By specifying a U in position 23 of the Definition Specification (as seen in Figure 8.14), we are telling the system to read in and lock the DATADEF data area when the program is initialized, and then write out and unlock the data area when the program ends. The data stored in the data area is available throughout the program, and the field values may be updated as needed. The results of the update are recorded when the program ends.

Externally Described Data Areas

Externally described data areas are very similar to the Data Area Data Structure. The principle difference is that they offer a little more flexibility with regard to lock state conditions and when data is retrieved or written to the data area. You will find this to be true of the program-described data areas as well, but you lose the rigidity and standardization with regard to data area definition.

Externally described and program-described data areas offer more control over when the data area is read, locked, written to, and released. Unlike Data Area Data Structures, data areas are not automatically read and locked during program initiation and written to at Last Record (LR) time.

Instead, there are four specific operation codes that you use in your RPG IV program when working with data areas. These are Define (DEFINE), Read IN Data from a Data Area (IN), Write Data Out to a Data Area (OUT), and Unlock a Data Area or Other Object (UNLOCK).

The DEFINE op code is useful for a variety of definition functions, but we want to discuss how it relates to data areas.

Factor 1	Op Code	Factor 2	Result Field
*DTAARA	DEFINE	[Data Area Name]	Data Structure Name

Specifying *DTAARA in Factor 1 of the DEFINE statement tells the system we are defining a data structure to represent the data area. We may optionally put the name of the data area in Factor 2, but for our examples we use the Definition Specifications to indicate the name of our data area. The Result field contains the field or data structure name that is used to represent the data area.

The IN operation code is used to perform a controlled read of a single data area or all data areas defined in the program. If you specify *LOCK as Factor 1 of the IN operation code, the data areas in Factor 2 are locked until they are unlocked using the UNLOCK or OUT operation codes, or the job is terminated.

Factor 1	Op Code	Factor 2
[*LOCK]	IN	Data Area or *DTAARA

Factor 2 of the IN operation code is either the name of the data area in question or the literal *DTAARA. Choosing the *DTAARA option causes all data areas defined in the program to be read. Also, the data areas are all locked if they are specified to do so in Factor 1.

The OUT operation code is used to perform a controlled update of a data area.

Factor 1	Op Code	Factor 2
[*LOCK]	OUT	Data Area or *DTAARA

If you specify *LOCK as Factor 1 of the OUT op code, the locks on the data areas in Factor 2 remain in effect after data has been written to them. The locks remain in effect until the data areas are unlocked using the UNLOCK op code, using a subsequent OUT operation code that does not have *LOCK specified, or when the job is terminated.

Factor 2 of the OUT op code is either the name of a data area or the literal *DTAARA. As with the IN operation code, the *DTAARA option specified in Factor 2 causes all data areas defined in the program to be written to. The locks then either remain in effect or are released, depending on the contents of Factor 1.

The UNLOCK operation code is used to release a data area or record of a file that has been opened for update.

Op Code	Factor 2
UNLOCK	Data Area or File Name

Note: When used with data areas, the IN, OUT, and UNLOCK op codes may only refer to data areas that have been defined with the DEFINE statement.

In Figure 8.15, we look at the same data structure contained in Figures 8.13 and 8.14. This time, however, we use the definition for an Externally Described Data Structure.

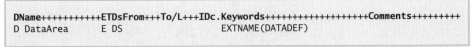

```
DName++++++++++ETDsFrom+++To/L+++IDc.Keywords+++++++++++++++++++Comments+++++++++
D DataArea      E DS                EXTNAME(DATADEF)
```

Figure 8.15: Input specifications for an externally described data area.

In the following example, we define a data structure named DataArea. By specifying an E in column 22 of our Definition Specification, we tell the compiler that this data structure is externally defined and the name of the external definition can be found in parentheses following the EXTNAME keyword (DATADEF in this case). The name identified in the parentheses refers to a physical file found somewhere in the library list at the time the RPG IV program is compiled. Figure 8.16 shows the Calculation Specifications that define, lock, read, write, and unlock the DTADEF data area.

```
CLON01Factor1+++++++Opcode(E)+Factor2+++++++Result++++++++Len++D+HiLoEq...Comments
* Read and Lock Data Area
C     *DTAARA      DEFINE                    DataArea          30
C     *LOCK        IN          DataArea
C                  MOVE        Print         Printer
C                  MOVE        Tape          Device
 * Write changes out to the data area
C                  OUT         DataArea
```

Figure 8.16 : Calculation Specifications for opening, locking, and updating an externally described data area.

By using *DTAARA in the DEFINE statement, we tell the system that we are defining a data area. In this case, we did not put the name of the data area in Factor 2, but instead put the name of a data structure in the Result field (DataArea). This definition (in conjunction with the Definition Specifications) tells the system that we are using the DataArea data structure to redefine the DATADEF data area. The process of redefining the data area is similar to when we redefined the SKUNumber earlier in this chapter.

In the next step, we read the data from the DATADEF data area using the IN op code, placing a lock on the data area at that time. Remember that the IN operation is a destructive read, and whatever was in the fields defined by the DATADEF data structure is replaced with the data from the data area. Consequently, as long as the IN operation is performed prior to any reference to the fields specified in the data structure, we do not need to worry about data structure initialization.

After performing our IN operation, we move data into the externally described fields that we want to change and write the data back out to the data area. We did not specify otherwise on the OUT statement, so the lock we previously placed on the data area when performing the IN operation is released.

224

Program-Described Data Areas

The last category of global data areas to cover is program-described data areas. In the following example, we use a data area that has no external definition. We have instead decided to define the data area and then move it to an internal Program-described Data Structure for processing. Once we are finished manipulating the data, we move data defined by our Program-described Data Structure back into the data area.

In Figure 8.17, we define a data area variable named DataArea using the DEFINE statement. The fact that we used *DTAARA in Factor 1 of this statement tells the system we are defining a variable that is to be supported by a data area.

```
CLON01Factor1+++++++Opcode(E)+Factor2+++++++Result++++++++Len++D+HiLoEq...Comments
 * Read the data area and put the data in a data structure
C       *DTAARA     DEFINE                    DataArea        30
C       *LOCK       IN          DataArea
C                   MOVE        DataArea      DataDs
```

Figure 8.17: RPG Calculation Specifications to lock and read a data area.

We then read and lock our data area and move the data area contents to a data structure named DataDS, as seen in Figure 8.18. It should be noted that a lock remains in effect on DataArea until we perform an OUT or an UNLOCK operation (on the data area), or until our job terminates. As with file record locks, no other job is able to obtain a lock on the data area until we have released our lock.

```
DName++++++++++++ETDsFrom+++To/L+++IDc.Keywords++++++++++++++++++++++++++++++Comments
D DataDS          DS
D  Device                     10
D  Printer                    10
D  OutQueue                   10
```

Figure 8.18: Program-described Data Structure used to define a data area.

In Figure 8.19, we move the contents of our DataDS data structure back into our variable (DataArea) and then write the contents back out to the data area. Because we did not specify *LOCK in Factor 1 of our OUT statement, the lock is released automatically at this time. If we had used *LOCK as Factor 1 of our OUT statement, the data area would have been updated and the lock would have remained in effect.

```
CLON01Factor1+++++++Opcode(E)+Factor2+++++++Result++++++++Len++D+HiLoEq...Comments
* Put the contents of the data structure back into the data area
C                   MOVE      DataDS        DataArea
C                   OUT       DataArea
```

Figure 8.19: RPG Calculation Specifications to write to and unlock a data area.

THE LOCAL DATA AREA

For those of you who were around for IBM's System/34 and System/36, you will recognize the local data area as one of the most powerful tools that could be used for passing limited amounts of data from one program to the next. The data in the LDA is special because it is "local" and only available for the current job. Submitted jobs, jobs in other workstation sessions, and jobs running on other workstations each have their own unique LDAs.

In the case of the AS/400, the size of the LDA has been expanded to 1K, or 1,024 bytes. You can use any or all of the LDA from any of your programs.

LDA on the AS/400 is still a powerful tool for program-to-program communications. It can be externally described with a data structure and is useful for reducing the number of parameters that must be passed from one program to the next. This is especially true if the data only needs to be accessible to a few links within a chain of programs. Instead of using the same parameters from one program to the next, you can place the data in LDA and only access or update it in the programs that need it.

In the case of submitted jobs, the LDA originally consists of the same contents the LDA of the workstation that submitted the job consists of. Once the submitted job is running, however, the LDA takes on a life of its own. Changes occurring to the data in the LDA are isolated within the submitted job only, and the data is only held in the system as long as the submitted job is still running.

Program-Described Local Data Area

The designation of LDA is very similar to the data area definitions we just studied. In Figure 8.20, we show the simplest form of LDA. In this case, we used a Data Area Data Structure to describe LDA.

```
DName++++++++++ETDsFrom+++To/L+++IDc.Keywords++++++++++++++++++++++++++++++++Comments
D                UDS
D   Device                    10
D   Printer                   10
D   OutQueue                  10
```

Figure 8.20: Program-described input specifications defining the LDA.

The U in position 23 of the data structure Definition Specification tells the system we are defining a Data Area Data Structure. The system knows we are defining the LDA (as opposed to a global data area) because positions 7 through 21 of that same statement are blank.

In Figure 8.20, we define the first 30 bytes of LDA. The total size of LDA is 1024 bytes of character data, but your program only needs to define the portion of the LDA it will use. Notice that we only specified the length of the subfields and let the system calculate the From and To positions for us.

Using a Program-Described Data Structure to Define the LDA

In Figures 8.21, 8.22, and 8.23, we read the LDA in our Calculation Specifications and then move the data into our LoclDtaAra data structure. We write that data back out to the LDA using our Program-described Data Structure (LoclDtaAra).

```
DName++++++++++ETDsFrom+++To/L+++IDc.Keywords++++++++++++++++++++++++++++++++Comments
D LoclDtaAra       DS
D   Device                    10
D   Printer                   10
D   Outqueue                  10
```

Figure 8.21: Program-described Data Structure used to redefine the LDA.

```
CLON01Factor1+++++++Opcode(E)+Factor2+++++++Result++++++++Len++D+HiLoEq...Comments
 * Read data from LDA and place it in a data structure
C     *DTAARA    DEFINE    *LDA          LoclDtaAra
C                IN        LoclDtaAra
```

Figure 8.22: RPG Calculation Specifications used to read the LDA and move it to a Program-described Data Structure.

```
CLON01Factor1+++++++Opcode(E)+Factor2+++++++Result++++++++Len++D+HiLoEq...Comments
* Read data from LDA and place it in a data structure
C                   OUT       LoclDtaAra
```

Figure 8.23: RPG Calculation Specifications used to write data to the LDA via a Program-described Data Structure.

In Figure 8.22, we define LDA to our program using the special keyword *LDA in Factor 2 of the DEFINE statement. At the same time, we tell the system we are using the LoclDtaAra data structure to redefine LDA within our program. Note that we did not use the *LOCK parameter of the IN op code in our example because the LDA is unique to the current session and may not be accessed by any other job. On the subsequent statement, we read in LDA and consequently move the data into our data structure.

Later in our program, we write the contents of our data structure back out to the LDA by performing the code in Figure 8.23. The changed data in the LDA is then available to any subsequent programs in the job stream.

Using Externally Described Data Structures to Define the LDA

External data structures also can be useful for defining your LDA. By using an external definition, you assure consistent definitions from program to program, and also reduce the amount of maintenance required when the definition of LDA must change. This is especially true when you have many programs that use the same definitions of LDA. In Figures 8.24 through 8.27, you can see an example of using an external data structure (LOCALDEF) to define the LDA.

```
A..........T.Name++++++RLen++TDpB......Functions++++++++++++++++++++++++++++++
A           R LOCALDEF
A             CUSTNBR      10A         COLHDG('CUSTOMER NUMBER')
A             CUSTNAME     40A         COLHDG('CUSTOMER NAME')
A             CUSTADDRS    30A         COLHDG('CUSTOMER ADDRESS')
A             CUSTCITY     30A         COLHDG('CUSTOMER CITY')
A             CUSTSTATE     2A         COLHDG('CUSTOMER STATE')
A             CUSTZIPCOD    9A         COLHDG('CUSTOMER ZIP CODE')
A             SALESMAN      5A         COLHDG('CUSTOMER SALESMAN')
A             CUSTPHONE    10S 0       COLHDG('CUSTOMER PHONE#')
```

Figure 8.24: DDS for an external data structure used to define the LDA.

228

```
DName++++++++++++ETDsFrom+++To/L+++IDc.Keywords++++++++++++++++++++++++++++++Comments
D LoclDtaAra     EUDS               EXTNAME(LOCALDEF)
```

Figure 8.25: Input Specifications designating an external data structure used to define the LDA.

```
CLON01Factor1+++++++Opcode(E)+Factor2+++++++Result++++++++Len++D+HiLoEq...Comments
 * Read and initialize local data area
 C     *DTAARA      DEFINE    *LDA          LoclDtaAra
 C                  IN        LoclDtaAra
 C                  CLEAR                   LoclDtaAra
```

Figure 8.26: Calculation Specifications defining and reading the LDA via an external data structure.

```
CLON01Factor1+++++++Opcode(E)+Factor2+++++++Result++++++++Len++D+HiLoEq...Comment
 * Update Local Data Area
 C                  OUT       LoclDtaAra
```

Figure 8.27: Calculation Specifications writing data to the LDA via an external data structure.

USING EXTERNALLY DESCRIBED DATA
STRUCTURES TO DEFINE PROGRAM-DESCRIBED DATA FILES

Externally Described Data Structures also offer a viable alternative to program-described files. This is of particular interest to programmers working on legacy systems that happen to be running in the System/36 environment.

Instead of internally describing all of the fields in a file within the RPG program, you can use an Externally Described Data Structure to define the data fields within the file. This allows you to define the file in a single place and simply call on that definition each time you use the file. Changes in the file definition are made once, and programs requiring that change only need to be recompiled.

This method is particularly useful when you wish to store multiple formats of data in the same file. You can use a record-type code to determine which data structure to move the data to and create your own multiple-format data file.

229

The biggest benefit to this method must be field name and size consistency. You do not have to worry about a field being named something different in every program. Consistency helps eliminate errors.

This method is certainly not a substitute for externally described files, but it is definitely a step up from leaving all of the file definitions as program-described. You are unable to use any of the database tools like query or Display File Field Description (DSPFFD) because the system file definition still does not have that level of detail.

In Figure 8.28, we see a conventional program-described file. Figures 8.29 and 8.30 represent the same file, but with an external data structure used for file definition.

```
IFilename++SqNORiPos1+NCCPos2+NCCPos3+NCC................................Comments
ICustomer   NS
I.............Ext_field+Fmt+SPFrom+To+++DcField+++++++++L1M1FrP1MnZr.....Comments
I                             1   10   CustNbr
I                            11   50   CustName
I                            51   80   CustAddrs
I                            81  110   CustCity
I                           111  112   CustState
I                           113  121   CustZipCod
I                           122  126   Salesman
I                           127  136   0CustPhone
```

Figure 8.28: Program-described customer file .

```
A..........T.Name++++++RLen++TDpB......Functions++++++++++++++++++++++++++
A          R CUSTREC
A            CUSTNBR      10A          COLHDG('CUSTOMER NUMBER')
A            CUSTNAME     40A          COLHDG('CUSTOMER NAME')
A            CUSTADDRS    30A          COLHDG('CUSTOMER ADDRESS')
A            CUSTCITY     30A          COLHDG('CUSTOMER CITY')
A            CUSTSTATE     2A          COLHDG('CUSTOMER STATE')
A            CUSTZIPCOD    9A          COLHDG('CUSTOMER ZIP CODE')
A            SALESMAN      5A          COLHDG('CUSTOMER SALESMAN')
A            CUSTPHONE    10S 0        COLHDG('CUSTOMER PHONE#')
```

Figure 8.29: DDS for an external data structure describing the customer file.

```
DName+++++++++++ETDsFrom+++To/L+++IDc.Keywords++++++++++++++++++++++++++++++Comments
D CustData       E DS                  EXTNAME(CUSTREC)
```

Figure 8.30: Input Specifications designating an external data structure used to describe the customer file.

By using the data structure in Figure 8.29 to redefine the data in the customer file, all of the fields defined by the Externally Described Data Structure become available.

USING DATA STRUCTURES
TO REDUCE PROGRAM PARAMETERS

Programs that pass too many parameters are a common problem in many AS/400 systems. Programs that are initially written with two or three parameters end up with 10, 12, or even more.

When you have that many parameters being passed back and forth between programs, you have plenty of room for error. The programs being called, and those doing the calling, must be in constant synchronization. When a subprogram is called by multiple calling programs, the room for error gets multiplied. Program maintenance can become a nightmare.

A simple solution to this problem is to use an external data structure as a parameter in lieu of a parameter list. The data structure can hold many fields and, because the definition is external, you have consistency between the various programs.

In Figure 8.31, we define a data structure for use as a parameter in Figure 8.32. The data description specifications in Figure 8.31 are compiled as a physical file, even though the "file" will not contain data.

```
A..........T.Name++++++RLen++TDpB......Functions++++++++++++++++++++++++++++++
A          R DATADEF
A            DEVICE       10A          COLHDG('Tape Device')
A            PRINTER      10A          COLHDG('Printer Name')
A            OUTQUEUE     10A          COLHDG('OutQueue')
```

Figure 8.31: DDS for a parameter data structure.

```
CLON01Factor1+++++++Opcode(E)+Factor2+++++++Result+++++++++Len++D+HiLoEq...Comments
C     *ENTRY        PLIST
C                   PARM                     ParmDtaStr
```

Figure 8.32: Calculation Specifications defining a parameter data structure .

231

Figure 8.33 shows the Definition Specifications necessary to define the external data structure to our program. The PLIST in Figure 8.32 refers the program to the ParmDtaStr data structure for a list of the parameters that are passed between the programs.

```
DName++++++++++ETDsFrom+++To/L+++IDc.Keywords+++++++++++++++++++++++++++++Comments
D ParmDtaStr     E DS                  EXTNAME(DATADEF)
```

Figure 8.33: Input Specifications for a parameter data structure .

In the example here, we only have a few fields in our DATADEF external data structure, but you can use your imagination. Instead of using extensive parameter lists, your programs could simply reference the ParmDtaStr Externally Defined Data Structure. The length of the parameter does not need to be specified because the length of the Externally Defined Data Structure is used instead.

Maintenance could be made considerably easier. No matter how many fields in the Externally Defined Data Structure get changed, the program does not require additional maintenance (unless the program in question uses the fields that have changed; see "Externally Described Data Structures" in this chapter).

MULTIPLE-OCCURRENCE DATA STRUCTURES AND THE TWO-DIMENSIONAL ARRAY

A Multiple-occurrence Data Structure is a data structure like any other, except it has multiple copies (referred to as *occurrences*), each containing different data. Each occurrence or copy is actually treated as a separate, self-contained data structure, except that you do not have to define each occurrence separately. The occurrences are accessed with an index, much as you would access an array.

Figure 8.34 shows an example of the Definition Specification necessary to define a multiple-occurring data structure. The name of the data structure (DtaStrName) is specified in positions 7 through 21, and the OCCURS keyword is used to indicate how many occurrences of the data structure exist. Columns 33 through 39 are used for the length of the data structure, but as with all data structures, this field is optional. If you do not specify the length, the system automatically assigns the data structure the length of the accumulated subfields within it.

```
DName++++++++++++ETDsFrom+++To/L+++IDc.Keywords++++++++++++++++++++++Comments+++++++++
D DtaStrName     DS                  OCCURS(5)
D  TotalAmt           1      7 2
D  TotalCount         8     13 0
D  LocCode           14     15 0
D  LocName           16     45
```

Figure 8.34: Input specifications defining a Multiple-occurrence Data Structure.

In our example, we have indicated that our data structure has five occurrences. Because we did not specify the length of the data structure in columns 33 through 39, the length assigned to this data structure is 45 characters (where the last subfield ends).

Table 8.1 represents the DtaStrName Multiple-occurrence Data Structure defined in Figure 8.34 after data has been loaded into it. As you can see in the example, it is almost as if we had defined five separate data structures with the same four fields defined for each.

Table 8.1: Example of Data Stored in a Multiple-Occurrence Data Structure.				
Occurrence	TotalAmt	TotalCount	LocCode	LocName
1	50.00	1	01	Store number 1
2	150.00	3	05	Store number 5
3	250.00	5	19	Store number 19
4	150.00	3	14	Store number 14
5	50.00	1	12	Store number 12

The data structure index is either set or retrieved using the OCCUR op code. When setting the data structure index, the OCCUR statement tells the system which copy of the structure to use. The OCCUR statement can also be used to retrieve the current index and return it to a variable.

Factor 1	Op Code	Factor 2	Result Field
[index pointer]	OCCUR	Data Structure Name	[Occurrence Value]

If you want to set the occurrence (i.e., index) of a Multiple-occurrence Data Structure named DtaStrName to 1, you can do so by employing the following code:

233

```
CLON01Factor1+++++++Opcode(E)+Factor2+++++++Result++++++++++
C     1              OCCUR      DtaStrName
```

In effect, you are telling the system that you want to work with the first occurrence of the Multiple-occurrence Data Structure. Using the previous example, all references to subfields within the data structure refer to the first occurrence of the data structure. This remains the case until the OCCUR operation is performed again with a different index specified.

The index you use for the OCCUR operation could be a numeric literal, as specified in the previous example, or it could be any other numeric field. You need to make sure, however, that the specified index falls within the range of the number of elements (occurrences) that are defined for the Multiple-occurrence Data Structure.

The OCCUR operation allows you to retrieve the index value of where the index pointer is currently set. If your goal is to find the occurrence to which the data structure is pointing, use code that is somewhat like the following:

```
CLON01Factor1+++++++Opcode(E)+Factor2+++++++Result++++++++++
C                    OCCUR      DtaStrName    X
```

In this example, the current occurrence pointer value is retrieved from the system and written to the variable X.

Initializing the Multiple-Occurrence Data Structure

As we previously stated, data structures are considered to be alphanumeric, regardless of the data type specified in the subfields within. If you attempt to access a numeric subfield within a data structure prior to initializing it or loading it with numeric data, you find yourself with a Data Decimal Error. Multiple-occurrence Data Structures are no exception to this rule.

Using the INZ keyword on the Definition Specification used to define the Multiple-occurrence Data Structure causes all occurrences within the data structure to be initialized when the program is run. If you specify default subfield values (by using the INZ keyword on the subfield Definition Specification), the default is copied automatically to all occurrences.

234

If you need to reinitialize the Multiple-occurrence Data Structure (to be reused, for example), you find that the system does not automatically initialize each copy of the structure for you. Using the CLEAR or RESET operations simply clears or resets the occurrence where the index happens to be set.

If you want to clear the entire data structure, you need to establish a loop. In Figure 8.35, we have coded a loop to step through the occurrences of the data structure and reset the subfields within all of the occurrences of the Multiple-occurrence Data Structure.

```
DName++++++++++++ETDsFrom+++To/L+++IDc.Keywords++++++++++++++++++++++++++Comments++++
D DtaStrName     DS                  OCCURS(5)
D  TotalAmt               1      7 2
D  TotalCount             8     13 0
D  LocCode               14     15 0
D  LocName               16     45     INZ('Not on File')


CLON01Factor1+++++++Opcode(E)+Factor2+++++++Result++++++++Len++D+HiLoEq...Comments
C                    DO        5                X                      1 0
C        X           OCCUR     DtaStrName
C                    RESET                      DtaStrName
C                    ENDDO
```

Figure 8.35: Resetting a Multiple-occurrence Data Structure to its original values.

The numeric fields are cleared and reset to zero because there are no default values coded for them. The LocName field, however, is initialized to Not on File in each occurrence of the data structure. The INZ keyword on the Definition Specification defining the LocName subfield tells the system to initialize the field with the constant specified in the parentheses following the INZ keyword. We could have used a named constant for this purpose instead of the literal.

The Two-Dimensional Array

Reproducing the function of the Multiple-occurrence Data Structure coded in Figure 8.35 could be easily accomplished by replacing each field in the structure with its own array. But this would require four arrays, each with five elements, instead of the Multiple-occurrence Data Structure. Both methods work, but the data structure is probably easier to manage. The power of Multiple-occurrence Data Structures, however, is unmatched when you combine it with the power of arrays to create the two-dimensional array. By defining an array within the Multiple-occurrence Data Structure, you are, in effect, creating a two-dimensional array.

For an example of the two-dimensional array in action, let's establish a scenario we might encounter when we are asked to write a sales analysis report. Say we want to create a 31-element array, called AR$, that holds the total dollar amount of goods sold for each day of the month. Further, let's create another 31-element array called AR# to hold the number of sales transactions performed for each day of the month. On top of that, we want to keep each month's totals separate within the fiscal year.

Twenty-four arrays are needed to code this without multiple-occurring data structures! You need one array to represent the total dollar amount sold for each month of the year as well as an array to represent the number of sales for each month. That is quite a bit of code to write and maintain.

By using a simple multiple-occurring data structure with 12 occurrences (one for each month), we are able to considerably trim down the amount of code required for this operation. In the following example, we code two arrays called ARAmount (dollar amount sold per month) and ARCount (number of sales per month). These arrays exist as separate copies within each occurrence of the Multiple-occurrence Data Structure. As you can see from the code in Figure 8.36, it is not difficult to code this two-dimensional structure.

```
DName+++++++++++ETDsFrom+++To/L+++IDc.Keywords+++++++++++++++++++++++++++Comments++++
D DtaStrName      DS                        OCCURS(12) INZ
D   ARAmount            1     217 2
D                                           DIM(31)
D   ARCount            218    372 0
D                                           DIM(31)

CLON01Factor1+++++++Opcode(E)+Factor2+++++++Result++++++++Len++D+HiLoEq...Comments
C      Month         OCCUR     DtaStrName
* Amount sold
C                    ADD       AMOUNT        ARAmount(Day)
 * Count sold
C                    ADD       1             ARCount(Day)
```

Figure 8.36: Creating two-dimensional arrays with Multiple-occurrence Data Structures.

The first dimension of our structure, indexed using the month of the sales transaction, is used to set the occurrence of the structure. The second dimension, indexed by the day of the sale, is used as the index for each of the arrays.

In Figure 8.36, the Month field represents the month of the sale. In our example, we use this field to set the occurrence of the data structure prior to adding any data to the arrays.

This, in effect, tells the system which copy of the arrays to use. The Day field was used as the index to the arrays that were selected as a result of the OCCUR op code.

If the code specified in the Calculation Specifications of our example is run against all sales transactions that meet our report criteria, the net result is that we have 24 arrays potentially filled with data. We can then establish a loop to step through the data structure occurrences and print the data from each.

YOUR RPG TREASURE CHEST

By now, you realize all of the power that can be at your disposal when you are well-versed on the components covered in this chapter. Scenarios in which you can exhibit this new-found power are only limited by your imagination.

Using these tools properly results in far more efficient code (and far less of it). Ultimately, this results in less program maintenance and more time to work on the projects you like.

9

SYSTEM APIs

You are about to enter a brave new world—that of application program interface (APIs). You will find that it is a world of speed, efficiency, and information—*lots* of information.

In this chapter, we unravel some of the mystery and confusion surrounding APIs. We cover Retrieve, Message, Spool Files, ILE, and List APIs. We explain the ins and outs of user spaces. APIs can involve some complex parameter handling routines that makes them difficult to use. So we will demonstrate a technique called "wrapping" that involves using a procedure to mask the complexities of the API. We will cover some APIs that provide the capability to encrypt user passwords. And last, but not least, we show you how APIs are used in one of our favorite programming utilities.

If you do not know how to use APIs, if they are not part of your toolbox, a whole world of information remains behind closed doors. The good news is that opening those doors is not very difficult once you have the key, which we are confident you will find in this chapter.

WHAT IS AN API?

The "interface" referred to in API is the missing link between your programs and the IBM operating system. It is an IBM program you can call from within your RPG programs to perform work. This work includes, but is not limited to, retrieving system information. Your program passes parameters to indicate the work you want performed, and the API returns the data you requested in the form of a parameter or data structures placed into a user space (which we discuss in detail later in this chapter). Understanding these parameters and data structures serves as your master key that opens many doors inside your system.

The information provided for and returned from APIs is usually defined in a data structure or series of data structures. One of the principle advantages of using APIs is that IBM will not change the data structure in future releases. If it decides to alter an API in order to show more information, it will add another data structure and leave the existing data structures intact. We define these data structures in detail as we go along.

To find all the APIs available on the AS400 involves dealing with the online manuals. IBM is currently in the process of moving all of its manuals to its AS/400 Information Center Web page, which can be located at:

```
http://publib.boulder.ibm.com/html/as400/infocenter.html
```

Once you are there, you can choose your language and operating version and select GO. This will take you to the Information Center Welcome page. Under the programming link, you will find a heading for OS400 APIs. From here, you can choose between listing all of the APIs by category or by description. There is also a link to the *System Programmer's Interface Reference Manual* (QBKA8402, SC41-8223).

This manual contains all the APIs that have not yet been moved to the Information Center Web page. If you are just getting started with APIs, this site is a great place to start. Be sure to check out the Related Internet Links, which direct you to a lot of good information.

Many APIs return information into a variable data structure (or structures), which can be quite complex and tedious to code. However, many of these structures are defined in various source files in the System Include (QSYSINC) library, which comes free with every AS400. If you look in QSYSINC/QRPGLESRC, you will find quite a list of members that

240

contain the definitions of the data structures used by the APIs (over 280 at last count). You can copy these data structures right into your programs and save quite a bit of time.

Many APIs are not all that complex. In fact, some APIs are very simple. The Command Execute (QCMDEXC) program, covered in chapter 6, is probably the most powerful, but at the same time, it is one of the most basic. It allows you to run any command from within your RPG program. The QCMDEXC program is simple because it only needs two parameters. The first parameter consists of the command to be executed and the second parameter defines the length of the command within the first parameter.

Even easier to use than QCMDEXC is the Command Line (QUSCMDLN) API. This API has no parameters; you simply call it and a command entry window appears on your screen.

After reading this chapter, you should feel comfortable navigating through any of the APIs you need to perform your job. Although Table 9.1 lists the many APIs we cover, there are hundreds more.

Table 9.1: APIs Covered in Chapter 9.

API Name	Description
QBNLPGMI	List ILE program information
QCLRPGMI	Retrieve program information
QCMDEXC	Command execute
QDBLDBR	List database relations
QDBRTVFD	Retrieve file description
QMHRMVPM	Remove program message
QMHSNDPM	Send program message
QSPMOVSP	Move spooled file
QSYADDVALIDATIONLSTENTRY	Add validation list entry
QSYREMOVEVALIDATIONLSTENTRY	Remove validation list entry
QSYVALIDATEVALIDATIONLSTENTRY	Validate validation list entry
QUSCMDLN	Command entry line
QUSCRTUS	Create user space
QUSLFLD	List fields
QUSLSPL	List spooled file
QUSROBJD	Retrieve object description
QUSPTRUS	Retrieve pointer to user space
QUSRTVUS	Retrieve user space

RETRIEVE APIS

As their name implies, Retrieve APIs are used to extract information from the system. These APIs have both input and output parameters. You pass information to tell the APIs what kind of information you are trying to retrieve, and the APIs retrieve the requested information into a variable for you.

Before the advent of APIs, this type of programming was performed with a CLP command that directed its output to an outfile (usually with all the speed of a fast turtle). You then had to process the outfile to get the information you wanted.

With APIs, you can execute one quick call within an RPG program, and the information you are looking for is loaded into a data structure. Another advantage to APIs is that you have some measure of control over the speed of the API. As you would expect, the more information you ask for, the longer it takes to retrieve. Asking for just the information you need speeds up the process.

When using Retrieve APIs, the format name parameter is where you indicate the type of information you want returned. In general, APIs in which the lower-numbered format names are specified run faster than those in which the higher-numbered formats are specified. The variation in speed is due primarily to the amount of information involved. The Retrieve Job Information (QUSRJOBI) API is one notable exception to this rule—its formats have nothing to do with performance.

PUTTING THE POWER OF RETRIEVE APIS TO USE

Suppose we want to issue a warning error message to the system operator reminding him to back up his files. If we send the message every day, it becomes familiar and tends to get ignored. If we send it only when the files have not been backed up within a prescribed time frame, it will be more effective. In order to do this, we need to know the last time the files were saved.

To find the date a file was last saved, use the Retrieve Object Description (QUSROBJD) API. The chart in Table 9.2 shows the parameters for this specific API. You can find a similar chart for every API in the aforementioned *System Programmer's Interface Reference Manual* or online at the Information Center Web page.

Table 9.2: Required Parameter Group for the QUSROBJD API.

Parameter	Parameter Description	Type	Size
1	Receiver variable	Output	Char(*)
2	Length of receiver variable	Input	Binary(4)
3	Format name	Input	Char(8)
4	Object and library name	Input	Char(20)
5	Object type	Input	Char(10)
Optional Error Data Structure Parameter			
Parameter	Parameter Description	Type	Size
6	Error	Output	Char(*)

Parameter Definitions:

Receiver variable: This parameter represents the variable, or data structure, into which the system returns the requested information. Note that the field is output in nature and the size column contains CHAR(*), which indicates that the field length can vary every time you call the API.

Length of receiver variable: The second parameter of the API is the receiver variable length, which defines the length of the preceding parameter. This field, of input type, is where that we tell the system the length of the receiver variable parameter we want returned.

Format name: The third parameter of this API is the format name. The format parameter is where we indicate to the system exactly what information we are looking for. The format name we enter here tells the system how to format the data returned in the receiver variable parameter.

Object and library name: This is where we specify the name and library of the object about which we are requesting information.

Object type: Defines the object type.

Error structure: The sixth parameter of this API is the optional error data structure we are about to discuss.

THE OPTIONAL API ERROR CODE PARAMETER

Most APIs include an optional error code parameter. It is a variable-length data structure, but do not let that deter you. The fact that it is variable in length simply means that, the larger you define the data structure, the more information there is to return to you. The required components of the Optional API Error Code Parameter are shown in Table 9.3.

Table 9.3: Required Parameter Group for the Optional API Error Code Data Structure.

Parameter	Description	Type	Size
1	Bytes provided	Input	Binary(4)
2	Bytes available	Output	Binary(4)
3	Message identification code	Output	Char(7)
4	Error number	Output	Char(1)
5	Message data	Output	Char(*)

Parameter Definitions:

Bytes provided: A field whereby we tell the API the length of the message data we want returned in the Message Data field.

Bytes available: The actual length of the data returned if an error occurs. If this field is 0, you can safely assume the API executed properly. If its value is greater than 0, an error occurred and the parameter returns the number of bytes returned to your program.

Message ID: If an error was detected and the Bytes Available field is greater than zero, the Message Identification field contains the message identifier of the detected error.

Error number: The fourth parameter, Error Number, is reserved by the system and should be ignored.

Message data: If an error occurs, this parameter contains the substitution variables for the system message ID.

If the error code parameter is available to the API and you do *not* include it in the call, the API returns both diagnostic and escape messages. This means you get the normally cryptic system error message screen.

On the other hand, if you do code the program to use the error code parameter, only escape messages are returned to the program and the system does not present an error message screen. In general, if the error code parameter is available, use it. Once you have performed the error routine's initial deployment, the structure is easily cloned from program to program.

USING APIS TO RETRIEVE OBJECT DESCRIPTIONS

Output from the OBJD0300 format of the Retrieve Object Description (QUSROBJD) API is depicted in Table 9.4. Data is returned in this format if the format name in parameter 3 of the input parameters is specified as OBJD0300.

Table 9.4: USROBJD API Output Descriptions for Format OBJD0300.

Dec	Hex	Type	Description
—	—	—	Everything from OBJD0100/OBJD0200 formats
180	B4	Char(13)	Source file updated date and time
193	C1	Char(13)	Object saved date and time
206	CE	Char(13)	Object restored date and time
219	DB	Char(10)	Creator's user profile
229	E5	Char(8)	System where object was created
a237	ED	Char(7)	Reset date
244	F4	Binary(4)	Save size
248	F8	Binary(4)	Save sequence number
252	FC	Char(10)	Storage
262	106	Char(10)	Save command
272	110	Char(71)	Save volume ID
343	157	Char(10)	Save device
353	161	Char(10)	Save file name
363	16B	Char(10)	Save file library name
373	175	Char(17)	Save label
390	186	Char(9)	System level
399	18F	Char(16)	Compiler
415	19F	Char(8)	Object level
423	1A7	Char(1)	User changed
424	1A8	Char(16)	Licensed program
440	1B8	Char(10)	Program temporary fix (PTF)
450	1C2	Char(10)	Authorized program analysis report (APAR)

The QUSROBJD API returns data in one of the four possible formats seen in Table 9.5. We chose the OBJD0300 format for the following example because it contains the date and time an object was last saved.

Table 9.5: Formats for the QUSROBJD API.	
QUSROBJD API Format	Description
OBJD0100	Basic information
OBJD0200	Information similar to PDM
OBJD0300	Service information
OBJD0400	Full information

As is the case with input parameters, output parameters are defined in the SPI manual. Note that the offsets in the table begin at 0, so you must add 1 to the given decimal position when you define it in an RPG Input Specification.

For example, suppose we want to know the volume ID of the tape that holds the last copy of this file. The chart in Table 9.4 shows that the save volume ID resides in position 272, for a length of 71 bytes. The RPG Input Specifications needed to access that field are shown in Figure 9.1 and begin in 273.

```
DName++++++++++ETDsFrom+++To/L+++IDc.Keywords++++++++++++++++++++++++++Comments++++
D Offset           DS
D   VolumeID              273    343
```

Figure 9.1: Sample input specifications representing an API data structure offset.

Figure 9.2 shows the FIG92RG RPG program, which has all the code needed to use the QUSROBJD API. The FIG92RG program has the file and library names as input parameters, and the date and time last saved as an output parameter.

246

```
***********************************************************************
*   TO COMPILE:
*      CRTBNDRPG PGM(XXXLIB/FIG92RG)
***********************************************************************

DName++++++++++++ETDsFrom+++To/L+++IDc.Keywords+++++++++++++++++++++++++Comments++++
D ErrorDs          DS                    INZ
D  BytesProvd            1      4B 0 INZ(116)
D  BytesAvail            5      8B 0
D  MessageId             9     15
D  ERR###               16     16
D  MessageDta           17    116
D                  DS
D Receiver               206
D  DateSaved             13     OVERLAY(Receiver:194)
D ReceiveLen       S      4B 0 INZ(206)
D FileLib          S     20
D PassInFile       S     10
D PassInLib        S     10
D PassDateSv       S     13
D FormatName       S      8     INZ('OBJD0300')
D ObjectType       S     10     INZ('*FILE')

CL0N01Factor1+++++++Opcode&ExtFactor2+++++++Result++++++++Len++D+HiLoEq...Comments
C     *ENTRY       PLIST
C                  PARM                    PassInFile
C                  PARM                    PassInLib
C                  PARM                    PassDateSv
C                  EVAL      FileLib = PassInFile + PassInLib
C                  CALL      'QUSROBJD'
C                  PARM                    Receiver
C                  PARM                    ReceiveLen
C                  PARM                    FormatName
C                  PARM                    FileLib
C                  PARM                    ObjectType
C                  PARM                    ErrorDs
C                  IF        DateSaved <> *BLANKS
C                  EVAL      PassDateSv = DateSaved
C                  ENDIF
C                  EVAL      *InLr = *ON
```

Figure 9.2: Sample of the QUSROBJD API.

When reviewing the FIG92RG program, you see that if the Error Message ID field is blank after the call to QUSROBJD, the DateSaved field contains the date and time the file was last saved. In turn, the FIG92RG program returns the date last saved to the calling program in the PassDateSv parameter. The calling program can then use the returned parameter information to determine how many days have elapsed since the file was last saved. If the number of days that have elapsed is considered to be too many, the warning message is sent to the program operator.

CHECKING FOR OBJECTS USING
THE RETRIEVE OBJECT DESCRIPTION (QUSROBJD) API

With slight variations to the previous program used in Figure 9.2, we could use the same API to create a program that checks for the existence of any object. And that is exactly what we've done in the FIG93RG RPG program shown in Figure 9.3.

```
******************************************************************************
*  TO COMPILE:
*     CRTBNDRPG PGM(XXXLIB/FIG93RG)
******************************************************************************

DName+++++++++++ETDsFrom+++To/L+++IDc.Keywords+++++++++++++++++++++++++++Comments++++
D ErrorDs         DS                    INZ
D  BytesProvd              1      4B 0 INZ(116)
D  BytesAvail              5      8B 0
D  MessageId               9     15
D  ERR###                 16     16
D  MessageDta             17    116
D  Receiver       S             100
D  ReceivrLen     S               4B 0 INZ(100)
D  Object         S              10
D  ObjLibrary     S              10
D  ObjType        S               8
D  ExistYesNo     S               1
D  FileLib        S              20
D  FileFormat     S               8       INZ('OBJD0100')

CLON01Factor1+++++++Opcode&ExtFactor2+++++++Result++++++++Len++D+HiLoEq...Comments
C     *ENTRY        PLIST
C                   PARM                      Object
C                   PARM                      ObjLibrary
C                   PARM                      ObjType
C                   PARM                      ExistYesNo
C                   IF        ObjLibrary = *BLANKS
C                   EVAL      ObjLibrary = 'LIBL'
C                   ENDIF
C                   EVAL      FileLib = Object + ObjLibrary
* Attempt to retrieve object description
C                   CALL      'QUSROBJD'
C                   PARM                      Receiver
C                   PARM                      ReceivrLen
C                   PARM                      FileFormat
```

Figure 9.3: Sample RPG program to validate object existence (part 1 of 2).

```
C                     PARM                      FileLib
C                     PARM                      ObjType
C                     PARM                      ErrorDs
C                     EVAL      ExistYesNo = 'Y'
C                     IF        MessageId <> *BLANKS
C                     EVAL      ExistYesNo = 'N'
C                     ENDIF
C                     EVAL      *InLr = *ON
```

Figure 9.3: Sample RPG program to validate object existence (part 2 of 2).

An example of where you might want to use the FIG93RG program is when you are prompting for a report or list. If you ask the operator which printer to direct the output to, you should check the device to see if it exists and if it is the correct device type. Checking the response at time of entry prevents potential errors down the line.

When running the program in Figure 9.3, you pass it the object name, library, and object type. The program, in turn, passes back a Yes/No parameter indicating whether an object with the specified name, type, and library exists. If you choose not to specify a library name for the object being validated, the program uses the library list.

In the example, we modify the FileFormat parameter so the QUSROBJD API returns the data defined by format OBJD0100. The objective in this case is simply to know if the object exists (we don't really care what information is returned). We choose to use the format with the smallest number of fields for maximum API performance.

The FIG93RG RPG program in Figure 9.3 can be called from other application programs to verify the existence, type, and library of an object. To see this same function performed as a procedure, see chapter 14.

MESSAGE APIS

Let's continue our lessons by example and demonstrate how to send a message to a program message queue using the Send Program Message (QMHSNDPM) API. Message APIs provide a method for you to design your programs to work with AS/400 messages.

Examine the RPG program shown in Figure 9.4 to see how to use the QMHSNDPM API. The DDS for the program in Figure 9.5 is shown so you can compile and run this utility.

```
*****************************************************************************
*   TO COMPILE:
*      CRTBNDRPG PGM(XXXLIB/FIG94RG)
*****************************************************************************

HKeywords+++++++++++++++++++++++++++++++++++++++++++++++++++++++++++++++++Comments++++
H DATFMT(*YMD)

FFilename++IPEASFRlen+LKlen+AIDevice+.Keywords+++++++++++++++++++++++++++++Comments++++
FFIG95DS   CF  E               WORKSTN

DName+++++++++++ETDsFrom+++To/L+++IDc.Keywords+++++++++++++++++++++++++++++Comments++++
D ErrorDs        DS                      INZ
D  BytesProvd             1      4B 0 INZ(116)
D  BytesAvail             5      8B 0
D  MessageId              9     15
D  Err###                16     16
D  MessageDta            17    116

D StartPosit     S               8B 0
D StartLen       S               8B 0
D SpaceLen       S               8B 0
D ReceiveLen     S               8B 0
D MsgDtaLen      S               8B 0 INZ(60)
D MsgQueNbr      S               8B 0 INZ(0)
D MessageQue     S              10     INZ('*')
D MessageKey     S               4
D MessageFil     S              20
D MsgRemove      S              10     INZ('*ALL')
D ProgramQue     S              10     INZ('*')
D FileName       S              10     INZ('CUSTOMER')
D Library        S              10     INZ('QBOOK')
D MessageTyp     S              10     INZ('*DIAG')

D                DS
D PassDate                      13
D  PassYMDA                      6     OVERLAY(PassDate:2)

D PassYMD        S               6 0
D DateSaved      S               D     DATFMT(*YMD) INZ(D'40/01/01')
D Today          S               D     DATFMT(*YMD)
D MessageDat     S              10A
D CompareMDY     S               D     DATFMT(*MDY)

D DateErrCon     C                     'WARNING - Customer file last backed+
D                                      up on '

CLON01Factor1+++++++Opcode&ExtFactor2+++++++Result++++++++Len++D+HiLoEq...Comments
C                    EVAL      *In90 = *ON
C                    CALL      'FIG92RG'
```

Figure 9.4: Sample RPG program using the QMHSNDPM API (part 1 of 2).

```
C                   PARM                    FileName
C                   PARM                    Library
C                   PARM                    PassDate

C                   MOVE      PassYMDA      PassYMD
C         *YMD      TEST(D)                 PassYMD                  01
C                   MOVE      UDATE         CompareMDY
C                   SUBDUR    2:*D          CompareMDY
C                   IF        *In01 <> *ON
C         *YMD      MOVEL     PassYMD       DateSaved
C                   ENDIF
* If file was not saved in the last two days, send a warning message
C                   IF        DateSaved < CompareMDY
C                   EXSR      SNDMSG
C                   WRITE     MSGCTL
C                   ENDIF
C                   EXFMT     FMTC
C                   EXSR      CLRMSG
C                   EVAL      *InLr = *ON
CSR  CLRMSG         BEGSR
* Remove message API
C                   CALL      'QMHRMVPM'
C                   PARM                    MessageQue
C                   PARM                    MsgQueNbr
C                   PARM                    MessageKey
C                   PARM                    MsgRemove
C                   PARM                    ErrorDs
C                   ENDSR
C    SNDMSG         BEGSR
C                   EVAL      MessageFil = ('QCPFMSG   ' + 'QSYS')
C                   EVAL      MessageID  = 'CPF9898'
C                   IF        *In01 <> *ON
C                   MOVE      DateSaved     MessageDat
C                   ELSE
C                   EVAL      MessageDat = '000000    '
C                   ENDIF
C                   EVAL      MessageDta  = DateErrCon + MessageDat
* Send error message
C                   CALL      'QMHSNDPM'
C                   PARM                    MessageId
C                   PARM                    MessageFil
C                   PARM                    MessageDta
C                   PARM                    MsgDtaLen
C                   PARM                    MessageTyp
C                   PARM                    MessageQue
C                   PARM                    MsgQueNbr
C                   PARM                    MessageKey
C                   PARM                    ErrorDs
C                   ENDSR
```

Figure 9.4: Sample RPG program using the QMHSNDPM API (part 2 of 2).

```
A****************************************************************************
A*  TO COMPILE:
A*     CRTDSPF FILE(XXXLIB/FIG95DS)
A****************************************************************************

AAN01N02N03T.Name++++++RLen++TDpBLinPosFunctions++++++++++++++++++++++++++++++
A                                          DSPSIZ(24 80 *DS3)
A              R FMTC
A                                          CF03(03 'End of job')
A                                          CF12(12 'Return to Previous')
A                                          OVERLAY
A                                  21  3'                                 -
A                                          '                              -
A                                          DSPATR(UL)
A                                  22  5'F3=Exit'
A                                  22 19'F12=Previous'
A                                   9 21'Customer Number:'
A                CUSTOMER#   10A  B  9 38
A                                   1 27'Customer Inquiry'
A                                          DSPATR(HI)
A                                          DSPATR(UL)
A              R MSGSFL                     SFL
A                                          SFLMSGRCD(24)
A                SFLMSGKEY                 SFLMSGKEY
A                PROGRAMQUE                SFLPGMQ
A              R MSGCTL                     SFLCTL(MSGSFL)
A                                          OVERLAY
A                                          SFLSIZ(3) SFLPAG(1)
A                                          SFLDSP SFLINZ
A 90                                       SFLEND
A                PROGRAMQUE                SFLPGMQ
```

Figure 9.5: DDS for the FIG94RG RPG program using the QMHSNDPM API.

In Figure 9.4, the FIG92RG program is called to find the date the customer file was last saved. This function is performed prior to bringing up a screen format. (See Figure 9.2 for the code to the FIG92RG program.)

If the current date happens to be greater than the date last saved, we can safely assume that the customer file has not been saved today. When this happens, our warning is sent to the program operator via the FIG94RG program we just examined. It is in the FIG94RG program that the SNDMSG subroutine is then executed. The SNDMSG subroutine uses the QMHSNDPM API to send the message. The required parameter group for the QMHSNDPM API is shown in Table 9.6.

Table 9.6: Required Parameter Group for the QMHSNDPM API.

Parameter	Description	Type	Size
1	Message ID	Input	Char(7)
2	Message file name and library	Input	Char(20)
3	Message data	Input	Char(*)
4	Message data length	Input	Binary(4)
5	Message type	Input	Char(10)
6	Message queue name	Input	Char(10)
7	Job invocation number	Input	Binary(4)
8	Message key	Input	Char(4)
9	Error data structure	Both	Char(*)

Parameter Definitions:

Message ID: The message identification code of the message to be sent, or blanks for an immediate message. If you specify a message ID code, you must also specify the message file name and library in parameter 2.

Message file name and library: The name of the file and library that contain the message ID specified in parameter 1. The first 10 characters of the parameter are file name, and the last 10 characters are the library name. You may also specify the following special values: Current Library (*CURLIB) or Library List (*LIBL).

Message data: If you are using a predefined Message ID in parameter 1, this parameter is used to pass the data inserted into the message substitution variables. If you are sending an immediate message (indicated by sending blanks in parameter 1), this parameter field is the complete text of the immediate message.

Message data length: The number of bytes occupied by the message data field in the preceding parameter.

Message type: One of the following values: Completion (*COMP), Diagnostic (*DIAG), Escape (*ESCAPE), Informational (*INFO), Inquiry (*INQ), Notify (*NOTIFY), Request (*RQS), or Status (*STATUS). The Inquiry (*INQ) message type is only valid if the message is sent to the external message queue.

Message queue name: The name of the external message queue, the call stack entry to which to send the message, or the name of the entry to start counting from if job invocation number is 0.

Job invocation number: The location (invocation number) in the call stack that identifies the target entry of the message queue to which the message is sent. The number is relative to the message queue name parameter, indicating how many calls up the stack the target entry is from the message queue name entry.

Message key: The key to the message being sent. This parameter is ignored if the message type is specified as *STATUS.

Error data structure: The standard Optional Error Code Data Structure.

For the program in Figure 9.4, we choose to use the system-provided Message ID CPF9898 in message file QCPFMSG in library QSYS. This is a useful, general-purpose message that can be used to format any message on the fly, including any variable you want displayed with the message.

The CPF9898 message has no incoming text associated with it, and only one data field. We create our message using the free format EVAL op code to embed the date the file was last saved into our message and put it in the message data field for the system to display.

We have loaded an asterisk (*) in the message queue parameter indicating that the message is to be sent to the current job's message queue. The job invocation stack is 0, so the message is sent to the current program's message queue. Any other number put in this field causes the message to be sent back up the invocation stack. The number placed in the job invocation number parameter determines how far back in the stack the message is sent.

Our FIG94RG program issues a warning message to the program operator. It is displayed via the write to the MSGCTL format, and then followed by a general input screen (FMTC in this case).

To prevent the error from reappearing after you have entered data on the screen (this is only an informational warning message), the program executes the clear message subroutine. This subroutine uses another useful API—the Remove Program Messages (QMHRMVPM) API.

In this particular example, it is really not necessary to remove the messages from the program message queue because the program is going to set on the last record indicator and terminate. But in a working application, you would probably edit the data entered on the screen and loop back up to issue any error messages. You want to clear the message queue before issuing new messages so the old ones do not redisplay.

The QMHRMVPM API accepts five input parameters and two sets of optional parameters. For our purposes, we only cover the required entries, as shown in Table 9.7.

Table 9.7: Required Parameter Group for the QMHRMVPM API.

Parameter	Description	Type	Size
1	Message queue.	Input	Char(10)
2	Call stack counter relative to parameter 1. Indicates how many entries up the stack to go to find the message queue to remove.	Input	Binary(4)
3	Message key.	Input	Binary(4)
4	Messages to remove.	Input	Char(10)
5	Error.	Both	Char(*)

Parameter Definitions:

Message queue: The name of the call stack entry to which the message is sent, or the name of the entry to start counting from if the job invocation number is 0. You can also specify the external message queue, or *, for the current job's message queue.

Call stack counter: The location in the call stack identifying the entry to whose message queue the message is to be sent. The number is relative to the message queue name parameter, indicating how many calls up the stack the target entry is from the message queue name entry. Special values are:

*	The message queue of the current call stack.
*ALLINACT	All message queues for inactive call stack entries.
*EXT	The external message queue.

Message key: The message file key to the message being removed.

Messages to remove: The message or group of messages being removed. Valid values are:

*ALL	All messages in the message queue.
*BYKEY	Only the message specified by the key parameter.
*KEEPRQS	All messages except request messages.
*NEW	All new messages in the queue.
*OLD	All old messages in the queue.

Error: The standard Optional Error Code Data Structure.

We code an asterisk (*) in the Message Queue (MSGQ) field indicating that we want to clear this job's message queue. We also place a 0 in the call stack counter indicating that we want to clear the message queue of the program in which this command is coded. The Message Key (MSGKY) field is left blank. The Message Type to Remove (MSGRMV) is coded with *ALL to indicate that all messages are to be removed from the message queue.

USER SPACES

A user space is an area created and defined by the user. It is used for storing any kind of information you want to put in it. You can use user spaces to pass data from job to job or system to system. All of the list APIs direct their output to a user space that must exist at the time the API runs. Consequently, you must be able to use the Create User Space (QUSCRTUS) API if you intend to use any of the list APIs.

The maximum size of a user space is 16MB (as opposed to 2,000 bytes for a data area). If you create a space that is too small to hold the complete list from the API, it is extended to the nearest memory page boundary. If the space is still too small to hold the list, the API puts as much data as possible in the space and returns an error message in the Optional Error Code parameter.

Creating User Spaces

An example of how to create a user space is shown in Figure 9.6. After this code is executed, the QTEMP library contains an object called SPACENAM (of type *USRSPC) that is 1,024 bytes long. The user space is initialized to value X'00', which allows the creation of the user space to execute faster than the default of *BLANKS.

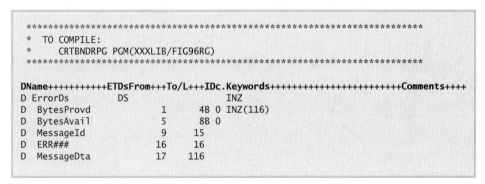

```
 ************************************************************************
 *   TO COMPILE:
 *      CRTBNDRPG PGM(XXXLIB/FIG96RG)
 ************************************************************************

DName+++++++++++ETDsFrom+++To/L+++IDc.Keywords+++++++++++++++++++++++++Comments++++
D ErrorDs          DS                  INZ
D  BytesProvd               1      4B 0 INZ(116)
D  BytesAvail               5      8B 0
D  MessageId                9     15
D  ERR###                  16     16
D  MessageDta              17    116
```

Figure 9.6: Sample RPG code to create a user space (part 1 of 2).

```
D InputDs         DS                    INZ
D  UserSpace                    20
D   SpaceName                   10      OVERLAY(UserSpace:1)
D                                       INZ('SPACENAME')
D   SpaceLib                    10      OVERLAY(UserSpace:11)
D                                       INZ('QTEMP')
D  SpaceLen       S             8B 0    INZ(1024)
D  SpaceAttr      S             10
D  SpaceValue     S              1
D  SpaceAuth      S             10       INZ('*CHANGE')
D  SpaceText      S             50
D  SpaceReplc     S             10       INZ('*YES')

CLON01Factor1+++++++Opcode&ExtFactor2+++++++Result+++++++Len++D+HiLoEq...Comments
 *  Create a user space named SPACENAM in library QTEMP
C                   CALL      'QUSCRTUS'
C                   PARM                    UserSpace
C                   PARM      *BLANKS       SpaceAttr
C                   PARM      1024          SpaceLen
C                   PARM      *BLANKS       SpaceValue
C                   PARM      '*CHANGE'     SpaceAuth
C                   PARM      *BLANKS       SpaceText
C                   PARM      '*YES'        SpaceReplc
C                   PARM                    ErrorDs
C                   EVAL      *InLr = *ON
```

Figure 9.6: Sample RPG code to create a user space (part 2 of 2).

Retrieving Data from a User Space

There are two APIs that you can use to retrieve information from a user space. The Retrieve User Space (QUSRTVUS) API gets information from the user space and puts it in a data area. It is usually called repeatedly with different starting points to obtain different structures from the user space. The second method to obtain data from a user space involves using the Retrieve Pointer to User Space (QUSPTRUS) API to get a pointer to the space and basing a data structure on that pointer. You then use pointer math (a fancy term for adding offset numbers relative to the beginning of the space) to look at different structures in the user space. We will show you both methods.

Which method you use depends upon a couple of things. In general, we prefer to use the pointer method to access a user space because it is much faster. You only need to call the API once to get started and then use simple math to access different areas. Once you get the hang of using it, it is actually easier to use. However, the QUSPTRUS API will return a pointer to an object even if that object is subject to an exclusive lock! This means you can get a user space at the same time another user is accessing the same location in the same user space. You would have to supply the code to ensure that this does not happen.

257

Another consideration is that the QUSPTRUS API does not update the object usage information. If you intend to update information in a user space, and this information, such as Last Used Date or Last Changed Date, is important to your application, you should not use the QUSPTRUS API. You would use the QUSRTVUS API instead.

One final limitation of the QUSPTRUS API concerns security. If the system value QALWUSRDMN contains the value QTEMP, some limits are placed on the API. You can only use the QUSRPTRUS API on user spaces that exist in QTEMP. This is necessary for the AS400 to maintain its government C2 security rating.

Using the Retrieve Pointer to User Space API

All that being said, we feel the best method of retrieving data from a user space is by using a pointer. A pointer is a data type that contains an address that points to a location in storage. To get a pointer that points to the user space, we need to use the QUSPTRUS API. Figure 9.7 shows an example of this easy-to-use API. Just call the API, giving it the name of the user space as the first parameter, and it will return a pointer to that user space in the second parameter.

Note that the pointer returned from the API is being used with the keyword BASE on the data structure definition line. The result of this simple technique is that not only did we get a pointer to the user space, but we also populated the fields in the data structure with the data in the user space. The field "Pointer" is not defined in this example, nor do you have to define it. Because the field is used with the BASE keyword and only pointers can be used with this keyword, the system defines the field for us.

```
DName+++++++++++ETDsFrom+++To/L+++IDc.Keywords+++++++++++++++++++++++++++Comments++++
DDataStruct       ds                based(Pointer)
D DataField1                 4b 0
D DataField2                 4b 0
DSpaceName        s          20   inz('NAME      QTEMP')

CLON01Factor1+++++++Opcode&ExtFactor2+++++++Result++++++++Len++D+HiLoEq...Comments
 * Retrieve the pointer to the user space, and overlay the
 * data structure
c                 call      'QUSPTRUS'
c                 parm                    SpaceName
c                 parm                    Pointer
 * After this call, datafield1 and datafield2 would contain the
 *  values from the first 8 positions of the user space
```

Figure 9.7: Accessing user space via QUSPTRUS.

Using the Retrieve User Space API

You extract data from a user space by using the QUSRTVUS API. This API gets information from the user space and puts it in a data area. It is relatively easy to use.

The QUSRTVUS API accepts four parameters: The name and the library that contain the user space, the starting position, the length of the data to extract, and the name of the data structure for the retrieved data.

Figure 9.8 shows an example of the code necessary to use this API. After the call to the QUSRTVUS API, the data structure GeneralDS contains whatever was in the user space beginning at location 1 for 140 bytes.

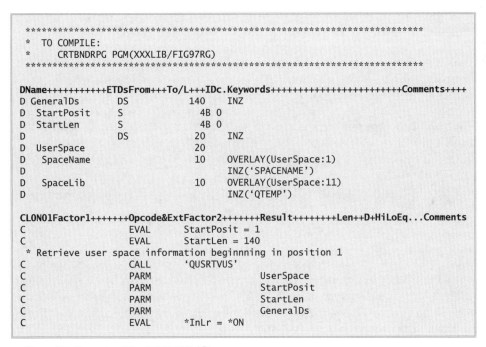

```
 ***********************************************************************
 *   TO COMPILE:
 *      CRTBNDRPG PGM(XXXLIB/FIG97RG)
 ***********************************************************************

DName+++++++++++ETDsFrom+++To/L+++IDc.Keywords+++++++++++++++++++++++Comments++++
D GeneralDs       DS              140    INZ
D  StartPosit     S                4B 0
D  StartLen       S                4B 0
D                 DS               20    INZ
D  UserSpace                       20
D   SpaceName                      10    OVERLAY(UserSpace:1)
D                                        INZ('SPACENAME')
D   SpaceLib                       10    OVERLAY(UserSpace:11)
D                                        INZ('QTEMP')

CL0N01Factor1+++++++Opcode&ExtFactor2+++++++Result++++++++Len++D+HiLoEq...Comments
C                   EVAL      StartPosit = 1
C                   EVAL      StartLen = 140
 * Retrieve user space information beginnning in position 1
C                   CALL      'QUSRTVUS'
C                   PARM                    UserSpace
C                   PARM                    StartPosit
C                   PARM                    StartLen
C                   PARM                    GeneralDs
C                   EVAL      *InLr = *ON
```

Figure 9.8: Example of the QUSRTVUS API.

LIST APIs

The List APIs generate list information and output into a user space. You must create and maintain the user space yourself (see "User Spaces" in this chapter). The challenge when using List APIs lies in extracting the generated list from the user space. This is because it

259

sometimes requires several steps to retrieve the correct fields and data structures you need to get the list. It is not uncommon to have to step through several data structures to get to the information retrieved with the List APIs.

Each List API follows the same general format when putting data into a user space. For each of the List APIs, there is an input section, a general header section, and a list section.

General Header Section

The general header section is the same for each List API. It contains general information about the objective of the API, but more important, it contains pointers to information about the list data within the user space. In other words, the header section serves as the information directory for the information you request.

The data structure in Figure 9.9 shows the field definitions required to find the data in the user space. Table 9.8 shows all of the fields included in the general header section.

```
DName++++++++++ETDsFrom+++To/L+++IDc.Keywords++++++++++++++++++++++++Comments++++
D GenHeadDs      DS            140     INZ
D  InputSize           113     116B 0
D  ListOffset          125     128B 0
D  NumberList          133     136B 0
D  EntrySize           137     140B 0
```

Figure 9.9: Data structure including primary fields for the general header of the List APIs.

As you can see, the RPG Input Specifications in Figure 9.9 differ from the chart definition in Table 9.8 by one character. This is because the chart starts at offset 0 while the Input Specifications must start at position 1. This is very common in most of the API charts in the SPI manual, so be aware. Also notice that the data type is specified as a B, indicating that the data is stored in a binary format.

Dec	Type	Field
0	Char(64)	User area
64	Binary(4)	Size of generic header
68	Char(4)	Structure's release and level
72	Char(8)	Format name
80	Char(10)	API used
90	Char(13)	Date and time used
103	Char(1)	Information status
104	Binary(4)	Size of user space used
108	Binary(4)	Offset to input parameter section
112	Binary(4)	Size of input parameter section
116	Binary(4)	Offset to header section
120	Binary(4)	Size of header section
124	Binary(4)	Offset to list data section
128	Binary(4)	Size of list data section
132	Binary(4)	Number of list entries
136	Binary(4)	Size of each entry

Table 9.8: General Header of the List APIs—All Fields.

List Section

The list section begins in the user space at the position indicated by the ListOffSet field in Figure 9.9. The number of entries in the list is indicated in NumberList and the size of each entry is in EntrySize. Generally speaking, when using these fields, you set up a do loop to step through the user space, extracting an item on the list for each step.

The data residing in the list section varies, depending on the API used. Its structure is defined in the aforementioned SPI manual for each API. In general, you base the list section data structure on a pointer that is first populated with the ListOffset field and incremented with the EntrySize field for each iteration of the loop. Alternatively, the lists can be extracted with the QUSRTVUS API and moved to the data structure describing the information retrieved.

Handles—Internal Identification

Some APIs require (as input) information that can only be received from other APIs. This type of parameter information is usually referred to as a *handle*. A handle is a temporary, system-generated identification number used to decrease the time it takes to locate information. You can think of a handle as an address the system places in its own temporary system address book.

DISPLAY ACCESS PATH COMMAND

Now let's examine one of our favorite utilities that uses many of the different types of APIs, including a List API—the List Database Relations (QDBLDBR) API. This utility is an enhanced form of the Display Database Relations (DSPDBR) command.

To find the existing data paths that are available over a physical file on the AS/400, you generally perform the following steps:

1. Run the DSPDBR command over the physical file in question.

2. Write down the file and library names of each logical file found on the DSPDBR display.

3. Run the Display File Description (DSPFD) command over each logical file to see if the data path you need already exists.

These steps are time-consuming and cut into your productivity as a programmer. We have written the DSPPATH command to combine the steps for you.

The DSPPATH command output looks like the example in Figure 9.10 (the code for the command is in Figure 9.13). The path for the physical file is listed first. Key fields and sequence (ascending or descending) are shown, followed by any select omit statements used. Then the path information is listed for each logical file built over the physical file (even if the logical file is built in a different library than where the physical file resides).

```
                        Display Access Paths
Physical File  . . . . . . . .:  CUSTOMER    Number of logicals. . . . .:  0013
Library  . . . . . . . . . . .:  *LIBL

Library    File       Format     Key Field Seq Select/Omit Values
FILES      CUSTOMER   CUSREC     CUSTNO    A   CUSTOMER NUMBER

FILES      CLACT3     JBYCLS     FMCLAS    A   FINANCIAL CLASS

FILES      CUSTL      CSTREC     CUSNAM    A   CUSTOMER NAME
                                 CUSDLT        O EQ '*'

FILES      CUSTLA     CSTREC     CUSNAM    A   CUSTOMER NAME
                                 CUSNUM    A   CUSTOMER NUMBER
                                 CUSDLT        O EQ '*'

FILES      CUSTLO     CSTREC     CULPMT    A   DATE OF LAST PAYMENT
                                                                    More...



   F3=Exit        F12=Previous
```

Figure 9.10: Output from the DSPPATH command.

Breaking Down the Code in the DSPPATH Program

Examine the code in Figures 9.11, 9.12, and 9.13. After creating some work fields, including a user space, the program calls the GETFIL subroutine to retrieve the key field information for the physical file.

```
    ********************************************************************
    *  TO COMPILE:
    *     CRTRPGPGM PGM(XXXLIB/FIG910RG)
    ********************************************************************
FFilename++IPEASFRlen+LKlen+AIDevice+.Keywords++++++++++++++++++++++++++Comments++++
     FFig911Ds CF   E            WORKSTN
     F                                     SFILE(SFLRCD:RelRecNbr)


DName+++++++++++ETDsFrom+++To/L+++IDc.Keywords++++++++++++++++++++++++++Comments++++
     D AR           S             1    DIM(4096)
     D A2           S             1    DIM(28)
     D ARYF         S            10    DIM(1000)
```

Figure 9.11: FIG910RG RPG program (part 1 of 9).

263

```
D ARYT            S              40        DIM(1000)
D SaveStart       S               9B 0
D SaveLen         S               9B 0
D OutFile         S              10
D OutLibrary      S              10
D First           S               1
D ObjFileFmt      S               8
D ObjectType      S              10
D LstOutFmt       S               8
D Ignore          S              10
D MessageFil      S              20
D MessageTyp      S              10
D MessageQue      S              10
D FileFmt         S               8
D RecordFmt       S              10
D OverRide        S               1
D System          S              10
D FmtType         S              10
D ListFormat      S              10
D TestType        S               1
D SpaceAttr       S              10
D SpaceValue      S               1
D SpaceText       S              50
D SpaceAuth       S              10        INZ('*CHANGE')
D SpaceReplc      S              10        INZ('*YES')
D C               S               4 0
D S               S               4 0
D I               S               4 0
D I1              S               4 0
D I2              S               4 0
D B               S               4 0
D RelRecNbr       S               4 0
D SfCompare       S               2
D SfRule          S               1
D SfValue         S              28
D SFileLib        S              20
D RFileLib        S              20
D ObjReceivr      S             100
D StartPosit      S               9B 0
D StartLen        S               9B 0
D ReceiveLen      S               9B 0
D MessageKey      S               9B 0
D MsgDtaLen       S               9B 0
D MsgQueNbr       S               9B 0
D FilStartP       S               9B 0
D FilStartL       S               9B 0
D SpaceLen        S               9B 0 INZ(1024)
D InFileLib       S              20
D InputDs         DS
D  UserSpace                  1  20
D   SpaceName                    10        OVERLAY(UserSpace:1)
D   SpaceLib                     10        OVERLAY(UserSpace:11)
```

Figure 9.11: FIG910RG RPG program (part 2 of 9).

```
D   OutFormat                   21    28
D   FileLib                     29    48
D    FileName                         10    OVERLAY(FileLib:1)
D    FileLibr                         10    OVERLAY(FileLib:11)
D ListDs           DS
D   MainFileLb                   1    20
D   MainFile                          10    OVERLAY(MainFileLb:1)
D   MainLib                           10    OVERLAY(MainFileLb:11)
D   DependFil                   21    30
D   DependLib                   31    40
D                DS
D   FieldSpace                   1    20
D   FSpaceName                        10    OVERLAY(FieldSpace:1)
D   FSpaceLib                         10    OVERLAY(FieldSpace:11)
D ErrorDs          DS                       INZ
D   BytesProvd                   1     4B 0
D   BytesAvail                   5     8B 0
D   MessageId                    9    15
D   Err###                      16    16
D   MessageDta                  17   116
D KeyData          DS
D   DependKey                    1    10
D   AscendDes                   14    14
D FindSelect       DS               150     INZ
D   FindFormat                  70    79
D   NbrKeys                    117   118B 0
D   NbrSelOmit                 130   131B 0
D   OffSelOmit                 132   135B 0
D   OffSet                     136   139B 0
D KeySelect        DS               150     INZ
D   Rule                         3     3
D   Compare                      4     5
D   CompName                     6    15
D   NbrSO                       16    17B 0
D   OffsetSO                    29    32B 0
D KeySOS           DS               150     INZ
D   POffset                      1     4B 0
D   NL                           5     6B 0
D   SelectVar                   21    48
D                DS
D   FFileLib                     1    20
D   FFileLibr                         10    OVERLAY(FFileLib:1)
D   FFileName                         10    OVERLAY(FFileLib:11)
D FGeneralDs       DS                       INZ
D   FSizeInput                 113   116B 0
D   FOffsetHed                 117   120B 0
D   FSizeHead                  121   124B 0
D   FOfftoList                 125   128B 0
D   FNbrInList                 133   136B 0
D   FSizeEntry                 137   140B 0
D FListDs          DS
D   FFieldName                   1    10
```

Figure 9.11: FIG910RG RPG program (part 3 of 9).

```
D FFieldText                33    82
D GenHeadDs        DS                  INZ
D InputSize              113   116B 0
D ListOffset             125   128B 0
D NumberList             133   136B 0
D EntrySize              137   140B 0
D Receiver         DS          4096    INZ
D NbrFormats              62    63B 0
D DBFileOffS             317   320B 0
D AccessType             337   338
D Requester       C                    CONST('*REQUESTER*LIBL')

CL0N01Factor1+++++++Opcode&ExtFactor2+++++++Result++++++++Len++D+HiLoEq
C     *ENTRY      PLIST
C                 PARM                     InFileLib
C                 EVAL      OutFile = %SUBST(InFileLib:1:10)
C                 EVAL      OutLibrary = %SUBST(InFileLib:11:10)
C                 EVAL      SpaceName = 'USRSPC'
C                 EVAL      SpaceLib = 'QTEMP'
C                 EVAL      FileName = OutFile
C                 EVAL      FileLibr = OutLibrary
C                 EVAL      BytesProvd = 116
C                 EVAL      MessageFil = ('QCPFMSG   ' + 'QSYS')
C                 EVAL      *IN53 = *ON
 * Create user space
C                 CALL      'QUSCRTUS'
C                 PARM                     UserSpace
C                 PARM                     SpaceAttr
C                 PARM      1024           SpaceLen
C                 PARM                     SpaceValue
C                 PARM                     SpaceAuth
C                 PARM                     SpaceText
C                 PARM                     SpaceReplc
C                 PARM                     ErrorDs
 * Attempt to retrieve object description
C                 CALL      'QUSROBJD'
C                 PARM                     ObjReceivr
C                 PARM      100            ReceiveLen
C                 PARM      'OBJD0100'     ObjFileFmt
C                 PARM                     InFileLib
C                 PARM      '*FILE'        ObjectType
C                 PARM                     ErrorDs
 * If file doesn't exist, send message and get out
C                 IF        MessageId <> *BLANKS
C                 EXSR      SNDMSG
C                 GOTO      END
C                 ENDIF
 * Create user space for fields
C                 EXSR      SPACE1
 *
C                 EVAL      SFileLib = InFileLib
C                 EVAL      First = *ON
```

Figure 9.11: FIG910RG RPG program (part 4 of 9).

```
     *  Write access path
     C                 EXSR      GETFIL
     C       MessageId CABEQ     'CPF5715'    NORECS
     C       MessageId CABEQ     'CPF3210'    END
     C                 EVAL      First = *OFF
     C                 EVAL      SpaceName = 'USRSPC'
     C                 EVAL      SpaceLib = 'QTEMP'
     *  List database relations to user space
     C                 CALL      'QDBLDBR'
     C                 PARM                   UserSpace
     C                 PARM      'DBRL0100'   LstOutFmt
     C                 PARM                   SFileLib
     C                 PARM      '*FIRST'     RecordFmt
     C                 PARM      *BLANKS      Ignore
     C                 PARM                   ErrorDs
     C       MessageId CABEQ     'CPF5715'    NORECS
     C                 EVAL      StartPosit = 1
     C                 EVAL      StartLen = 140
     C                 EVAL      SpaceName = 'USRSPC'
     C                 EVAL      SpaceLib = 'QTEMP'
     *  Retrieve user space general information
     C                 CALL      'QUSRTVUS'
     C                 PARM                   UserSpace
     C                 PARM                   StartPosit
     C                 PARM                   StartLen
     C                 PARM                   GenHeadDs
     C                 EVAL      StartPosit = 1
     C                 EVAL      StartLen = InputSize
     C                 EVAL      SpaceName = 'USRSPC'
     C                 EVAL      SpaceLib = 'QTEMP'
     *  Retrieve user space detail information
     C                 CALL      'QUSRTVUS'
     C                 PARM                   UserSpace
     C                 PARM                   StartPosit
     C                 PARM                   StartLen
     C                 PARM                   InputDs
     C                 EVAL      StartPosit = (ListOffset + 1)
     C                 EVAL      StartLen = EntrySize
     C                 EVAL      SaveLen = EntrySize
     C                 EVAL      NbrLogics = NumberList
     *  Retrieve the list by walking through the user space
  B1 C                 DO        Nbrlogics
     C                 EVAL      SpaceName = 'USRSPC'
     C                 EVAL      SpaceLib = 'QTEMP'
     C                 EVAL      SaveStart = StartPosit
     C                 CALL      'QUSRTVUS'
     C                 PARM                   UserSpace
     C                 PARM                   StartPosit
     C                 PARM                   StartLen
     C                 PARM                   ListDs
     C       DependFil CABEQ     '*NONE'      NORECS
     C                 EVAL      SpaceName = 'USRSPC'
```

Figure 9.11: FIG910RG RPG program (part 5 of 9).

267

```
        C                      EVAL      SpaceLib = 'QTEMP'
        C                      EVAL      SFileLib = DependFil
        C                      EVAL      %SUBST(SFileLib:11:10) = DependLib
        C                      EXSR      GETFIL
        C                      EXSR      CLEAR
        C                      EVAL      StartPosit = (SaveStart + SaveLen)
   E1   C                      ENDDO
        C        NORECS        TAG
        C                      IF        RelRecNbr > 0
        C                      EVAL      *In21 = *ON
   E1   C                      ENDIF
        C                      WRITE     FORMAT1
        C                      EXFMT     SFLCTL
        C        END           TAG
        C                      EVAL      *InLr = *ON
        *
        C        SNDMSG        BEGSR
        * Send error message
        C                      CALL      'QMHSNDPM'
        C                      PARM                    MessageId
        C                      PARM                    MessageFil
        C                      PARM                    InFileLib
        C                      PARM      20            MsgDtaLen
        C                      PARM      '*STATUS'     MessageTyp
        C                      PARM      '*EXT'        MessageQue
        C                      PARM      1             MsgQueNbr
        C                      PARM                    MessageKey
        C                      PARM                    ErrorDs
        C                      ENDSR

        C        GETFIL        BEGSR
        * Retrieve key field information for each logical file
        C                      CALL      'QDBRTVFD'
        C                      PARM                    Receiver
        C                      PARM      4096          ReceiveLen
        C                      PARM                    RFileLib
        C                      PARM      'FILD0100'    FileFmt
        C                      PARM                    SFileLib
        C                      PARM                    RecordFmt
        C                      PARM      '0'           OverRide
        C                      PARM      '*LCL'        System
        C                      PARM      '*EXT'        FmtType
        C                      PARM                    ErrorDs
        C        MessageId     CABEQ     'CPF5715'     ENDGET
        C                      MOVEA     Receiver      AR(1)
        C                      IF        First = *ON
        * File must be a physical file
        C                      MOVE      AR(9)         TestType
        C                      TESTB     '2'           TestType              01
        C                      IF        *In01 = *ON
        C                      EVAL      MessageId = 'CPF3210'
        C                      EXSR      SNDMSG
```

Figure 9.11: FIG910RG RPG program (part 6 of 9).

```
       C                    GOTO      ENDGET
E2     C                    ENDIF
E1     C                    ENDIF

       C                    EVAL      I = DbFileOffs
B1     C                    DO        NbrFormats
       C                    MOVEA     AR(I)           FindSelect
       C                    EVAL      S = (Offset + 1)
       C                    IF        First = *OFF
       *  Write blank line for clarity
       C                    EXSR      CLEAR
       C                    EVAL      RelRecNbr = RelRecNbr + 1
       C                    WRITE     SFLRCD
E2     C                    ENDIF
       C                    EVAL      SfLibrary = %SUBST(RFileLib:1:10)
       C                    EVAL      SfFileName = %SUBST(RFileLib:11:10)
       C                    EVAL      SfFormat = FindFormat
       C                    EXSR      GETTXT
B2     C                    DO        NbrKeys
       C                    MOVEA     AR(S)           KeyData
       C                    TESTB     '0'             AscendDes              79
B3     C                    SELECT
       C                    WHEN      *In79 = *OFF
       C                    EVAL      SfAsendDec = 'A'
       C                    WHEN      *In79 = *ON
       C                    EVAL      SfAsendDec = 'D'
E3     C                    ENDSL
       C                    EVAL      SfKeyField = DependKey
       C                    DO        B               C
       C                    IF        ARYF(C) = DependKey
       C                    EVAL      SfValue = Aryt(C)
       C                    LEAVE
       C                    ENDIF
E3     C                    ENDDO
       C                    EVAL      SfText = SfValue
       C                    EVAL      RelRecNbr = RelRecNbr + 1
       C                    WRITE     SFLRCD
       C                    EVAL      SfLibrary = *BLANKS
       C                    EVAL      SfFileName = *BLANKS
       C                    EVAL      SfFormat = *BLANKS
       C                    EVAL      SfValue = *BLANKS
       C                    EVAL      S = S + 32
E2     C                    ENDDO
       *  If select/omit statements exist
       C                    IF        NbrSelOmit <> *ZEROS
       C                    EXSR      SELOMT
E2     C                    ENDIF
       C                    EVAL      SfCompare = *BLANKS
       C                    EVAL      SfRule = *BLANKS
       C                    EVAL      I = I + 160
E1     C                    ENDDO
       C         ENDGET     TAG
```

Figure 9.11: FIG910RG RPG program (part 7 of 9).

```
        C                   ENDSR

        C     SELOMT        BEGSR
        C                   EVAL      I1 = (OffSelOmit + 1)
B1      C                   DO        NbrSelOmit
        C                   MOVEA     AR(I1)          KeySelect
        C                   IF        Compare = 'AL'
        C                   ITER
E2      C                   ENDIF
        C                   EVAL      SfCompare = Compare
        C                   EVAL      SfRule = Rule
        C                   EVAL      I2 = OffsetSo + 1
        C                   DO        NbrSO
        C                   MOVEA     AR(I2)          KeySOS
        C                   MOVEA     SelectVar     A2
        C                   EVAL      NL = NL - 19
        C                   IF        NL > *ZEROS
        C                   MOVEA     *BLANKS         A2(NL)
        C                   ENDIF
        C                   MOVEA     A2(1)           SfValue
        C                   EVAL      SfKeyField = CompName
        C                   EVAL      RelRecNbr = RelRecNbr + 1
        C                   EVAL      SfAsendDec = *BLANKS
        C                   EVAL      SfText = (SfRule + ' ' + SfCompare +
        C                             ' ' + SfValue)
        C                   EVAL      *In59 = *ON
        C                   WRITE     SFLRCD
        C                   EVAL      *In59 = *OFF
        C                   EVAL      I2 = POffset + 1
        C                   ENDDO
        C                   EVAL      I1 = (I1 + 32)
E1      C                   ENDDO
        C                   ENDSR

        C     CLEAR         BEGSR
        C                   EVAL      SfLibrary = *BLANKS
        C                   EVAL      SfFileName = *BLANKS
        C                   EVAL      SfFormat = *BLANKS
        C                   EVAL      SfKeyField = *BLANKS
        C                   EVAL      SfText = *BLANKS
        C                   EVAL      SfCompare = *BLANKS
        C                   EVAL      SfRule = *BLANKS
        C                   EVAL      SfAsendDec = *BLANKS
        C                   ENDSR
        * Get text for each field
        C     GETTXT        BEGSR
        C                   EVAL      FFileName = SfFileName
        C                   EVAL      FFileLibr = SfLibrary
        C                   EVAL      FSpaceName = 'FLDSPC'
        C                   EVAL      FSpaceLib = 'QTEMP'

        * List fields to user space
```

Figure 9.11: FIG910RG RPG program (part 8 of 9).

```
        C                     CALL      'QUSLFLD'
        C                     PARM                  FieldSpace
        C                     PARM      'FLDL0100'  ListFormat
        C                     PARM                  FFileLib
        C                     PARM      SfFormat    RecordFmt
        C                     PARM      '1'         OverRide
        C                     Z-ADD     1           FilStartP
        C                     Z-ADD     140         FilStartL
        C                     EVAL      FSpaceName = 'FLDSPC'
        C                     EVAL      FSpaceLib = 'QTEMP'
        * Retrieve user space general information
        C                     CALL      'QUSRTVUS'
        C                     PARM                  FieldSpace
        C                     PARM                  FilStartP
        C                     PARM                  FilStartL
        C                     PARM                  FGeneralDs
        C                     EVAL      FilStartP = FOffsetHed + 1
        C                     EVAL      FilStartL = FSizeHead
        C                     EVAL      FSpaceName = 'FLDSPC'
        C                     EVAL      FSpaceLib = 'QTEMP'
        C                     EVAL      FilStartP = FOfftoList + 1
        C                     EVAL      FilStartL = FSizeEntry
        * Retrieve the list by walking through the user space
B1      C                     DO        FNbrInList
        C                     EVAL      FSpaceName = 'FLDSPC'
        C                     EVAL      FSpaceLib = 'QTEMP'
        C                     CALL      'QUSRTVUS'
        C                     PARM                  FieldSpace
        C                     PARM                  FilStartP
        C                     PARM                  FilStartL
        C                     PARM                  FListDs
        C                     EVAL      B = B + 1
        C                     EVAL      ARYF(B) = FFieldName
        C                     EVAL      ARYT(B) = FFieldText
        C                     EVAL      FilStartP = FilStartP + FSizeEntry
E1      C                     ENDDO
        C                     ENDSR
        * Create user space for listing fields
        C       SPACE1        BEGSR
        C                     EVAL      FSpaceName = 'FLDSPC'
        C                     EVAL      FSpaceLib = 'QTEMP'
        C                     CALL      'QUSCRTUS'
        C                     PARM                  FieldSpace
        C                     PARM      *BLANKS     SpaceAttr
        C                     PARM      1024        SpaceLen
        C                     PARM      *BLANKS     SpaceValue
        C                     PARM      '*CHANGE'   SpaceAuth
        C                     PARM      *BLANKS     SpaceText
        C                     PARM      '*YES'      SpaceReplc
        C                     PARM                  ErrorDs
        C                     ENDSR
```

Figure 9.11: FIG910RG RPG program (part 9 of 9).

```
A*******************************************************************************
A*  TO COMPILE:
A*     CRTDSPF FILE(XXXLIB/FIG911DS)
A*******************************************************************************
AAN01N02N03T.Name++++++RLen++TDpBLinPosFunctions+++++++++++++++++++++++++
A                                             CF03    CF12
A            R SFLRCD                         SFL
A              SFLIBRARY      10A  0  7  2
AAN01N02N03T.Name++++++RLen++TDpBLinPosFunctions+++++++++++++++++++++++++
A              SFFILENAME     10A  0  7 13
A              SFKEYFIELD     10A  0  7 35
A              SFFORMAT       10A  0  7 24
A              SFASENDDEC      1  0  7 46
A              SFTEXT         32  0  7 48
A 59                                          DSPATR(HI)
A            R SFLCTL                         SFLCTL(SFLRCD)
A                                             SFLSIZ(0024)  SFLPAG(0012)
A                                             OVERLAY
A 21                                          SFLDSP
A                                             SFLDSPCTL
A 53                                          SFLEND(*MORE)
A                                      1 29'Display Access Paths' DSPATR(HI)
A                                      3  2'Physical File . . . . . . . .:'
A              OUTFILE        10A  0  3 35DSPATR(HI)
A                                      4  2'Library . . . . . . . . . .:'
A              OUTLIBRARY     10A  0  4 35DSPATR(HI)
A                                      6  2'Library    '   DSPATR(HI)
A                                      6 13'File       '   DSPATR(HI)
A                                      6 35'Key Field'     DSPATR(HI)
A                                      6 49'Select/Omit Values'  DSPATR(HI)
A                                      6 24'Format'        DSPATR(HI)
A                                      6 45'Seq'           DSPATR(HI)
A                                      3 47'Number of logicals. . . . .:'
A              NBRLOGICS       4  00 3 77DSPATR(HI)
A            R FORMAT1
A                                     23  4'F3=Exit'    COLOR(BLU)
A                                     23 18'F12=Previous'  COLOR(BLU)
```

Figure 9.12: FIG911DS display file.

```
/*=============================================================*/
/* To compile:                                                 */
/*                                                             */
/*        CRTCMD   CMD(XXX/DSPPATH)  PGM(XXX/FIG910RG)         */
/*                 SRCMBR(FIG912CM)                            */
/*                                                             */
/*=============================================================*/
          CMD      PROMPT('DISPLAY ACCESS PATH')
          PARM     KWD(FILE) TYPE(NAME1) MIN(1) PROMPT('File +
                     Name:')
NAME1:    QUAL     TYPE(*NAME) LEN(10)
          QUAL     TYPE(*CHAR) LEN(10) DFT(*LIBL) SPCVAL((' ' +
                     *LIBL)) CHOICE('Name, *LIBL') +
                     PROMPT('Library Name:')
```

Figure 9.13: The DSPPATH command.

272

The GETFIL subroutine calls the Retrieve File Description (QDBRTVFD) API to return all of the needed information in one variable, called Receiver. This variable contains different data structures, which can be in a different offset each time you run the command. The variable also contains offset pointers to indicate where each data structure is located. The Receiver field data is loaded into one long, generic array. Parts of the array are then (using the offset pointer fields) moved into the correct data structure.

Two loops are established to get all the key field information. The first loop uses NbrFormats, which is the number of formats in the file (logical files can have more than one format). The field DBFileOffs contains the offset location to key field information defined in the FindSelect data structure.

Before we use the information in the FindSelect data structure, we need to get the text description of each field in the file. This has not been included in any of the APIs we have used so far, but the List Fields (QUSLFLD) API does allow us to get at this information. So we call GETTXT subroutine, which lists the fields in the file into another user space. We walk through and load the file names and descriptions into two arrays. When it is time to write the subfile record, these arrays are used to retrieve the field descriptions. Then we use the FindSelect structure information.

The FindSelect structure contains the Offset field, which points to an array of key field names. The field NbrKeys indicates how many key fields exist, and is used as the index for the second loop. One subfile record is written for each key field in the array.

The next step is to determine whether there are any select or omit statements used in the path. The FindSelect structure also contains pointers to get at this information. NbrSelOmit is the number of select/omit statements while OffSelOmit is the offset to the array.

To get a list of all of the logicals over the physical file, the program uses the List Database Relations (QDBLDBR) API. This API produces its list in the user space that was created earlier. The QUSRTVUS API is then used to extract the file information for each of the logical files. This is done by first retrieving a generic header structure, which contains pointers to the space that has the file information, and then walking through the list stored in the user space until each file has been processed. For each file in the list, the GETFIL subroutine is called to perform the same functions as those performed on the physical file. Once the entire list has been processed, the information is written to the screen.

By running this command, you now have in instant road map of all of the paths that exist over any physical file on your system. This tool can be a real time saver when you are designing new programs.

SPOOL FILE APIS

The Spool File APIs allow you to manipulate spool files. Use them to generate a list of spool files based on a given selection criteria. You can access a specific spooled file and get the attribute or data within it.

A chart of all spool files and descriptions of their functions are shown in Table 9.9. We use some of the Spool File APIs in a utility that moves all spool file entries from one spool file to another. These APIs use user spaces, and we have chosen to demonstrate the technique of retrieving information using pointers and pointer math.

Table 9.9: Spool File APIs and Their Functions.

Name	Title	Description
QSPCLOSP	Close Spooled File	Close an open spool file.
QSPCRTSP	Create Spooled File	Create a spool file. When it is created, it does not contain any data.
QSPGETSP	Get Spooled File	Get data from an existing spool file, previously opened by the Open Spooled File (QSPOPNSP) API.
QUSLSPL	List Spooled File	Generate a list of spooled files into a user space. Selection criteria can be specified to filter the list.
QSPMOVSP	Move Spooled File	Move the spooled file to a different position within the output queue, or move it to another output queue.
QSPOPNSP	Open Spooled File	Open an existing spooled file for the Get Spooled File (QSPGETSP) API, which puts the data in a user space.
QSPPUTSP	Put Spooled File	Put the data into a spooled file that was created using the Create Spooled File (QSPCRTSP) API.
QUSRSPLA	Retrieve Spooled File Attributes	Put specific information about a spooled file into a field. The bigger the field, the greater the amount of information returned.

Moving Spool Files

Why would you want to move spool files? Spool file manipulation can be used to help ensure that all spool files for a particular job are kept together. This is a feature (as shown in Figure 9.14) you may find handy.

```
 ******************************************************************
 *   TO COMPILE:
 *      CRTBNDRPG PGM(XXXLIB/FIG914RG) SRCMBR(FIG914RG)
 *         DFTACTGRP(*NO)
 ******************************************************************

DName+++++++++++ETDsFrom+++To/L+++IDc.Keywords++++++++++++++++++++++++++++
 * Prototype for create user space procedure
d CrtUsrSpc       PR                    *
d   CrtSpcName                    20        const

D GeneralHed      DS                       based(GeneralPtr)
D  Offset                   125   128B 0
D  NumberList               133   136B 0
D  EntrySize                137   140B 0
D                 DS
D  OutSpool                   1    20
D  OutputQue                       10       OVERLAY(OutSpool:1)
D  QueLibrary                      10       OVERLAY(OutSpool:11)
D Receiver        DS                       Based(RcvPointer)
D  NbrReturnd                 1    4B 0
D  Retrieved                  5   204
D KeyData         DS
D  FldRtnLen                  1    4B 0
D  KeyReturn                  5    8B 0
D  KeyField                  17    26
D                 DS
D  KeyField1                  1    10
D  SflNbr                     1    4B 0
D ErrorDs         DS                       INZ
D  BytesProvd                 1    4B 0 inz(116)
D  BytesAvail                 5    8B 0
D  MessageId                  9    15
D  Err###                    16    16
D  MessageDta                17   116
D Keys            DS
D  Key1                       1    4B 0 inz(201)
D  Key2                       5    8B 0 inz(202)
D  Key3                       9   12B 0 inz(203)
D  Key4                      13   16B 0 inz(204)
D  Key5                      17   20B 0 inz(205)
D MoveDS          DS
D  MsJobName                  1    10
```

Figure 9.14: Move spool file utility (part 1 of 5).

```
D  MsJobUsr                  11    20
D  MsJobNbr                  21    26
D  MsJHandle                 27    42
D  MsSplHndle                43    58
D  MsSpoolNam                59    68
D  MsSplNbr                  69    72B 0
D  MsOutQue                  73    82
D  MsQueLib                  83    92
D  FromQueL      ds
D  FromQue                         10
D  FromLib                         10
D  ToQueL        ds
D  ToQue                           10
D  ToLibrary                       10

D  FormatName    S                  8
D  FormType      S                 10
D  FromUser      S                 10
D  I             S                  3  0
D  JobName       S                 26
D  MsgFileLib    s                 20     inz('QCPFMSG   *LIBL')
D  MsgDtaLen     s                  6  0 inz(100)
D  MsgType       s                 10     inz('*DIAG')
D  MsgQueue      s                 10
D  MsgQueNbr     s                  9b 0
D  MsgId         s                  7
D  MsgKey        s                  9b 0
D  MovFormat     S                  8
D  MoveLen       s                  9B 0
D  NbrOfKeys     s                  9B 0 inz(5)
D  Storage       S                  1
D  UserData      S                 10
D  UserSpace     s                 20     inz('SPLSPACE  QTEMP')

CLON01Factor1+++++++Opcode&ExtFactor2+++++++Result++++++++Len++D+HiLoEq
D  UserName      S                 10
C        *Entry        plist
C                      parm                        FromQueL
C                      parm                        ToQueL
C                      parm                        FromUser
c                      parm                        Formtype
c                      parm                        UserData

 * Set defaults for values not specified
c                      if          FromQue = '*ALL'
c                      eval        FromLib = *blanks
c                      endif
c                      if          (FromUser = *BLANKS)
c                      eval        FromUser = '*ALL'
c                      endif
c                      if          (Formtype = *BLANKS)
C                      eval        FormType = '*ALL'
```

Figure 9.14: Move spool file utility (part 2 of 5).

```
C                    endif

C                    eval       OutputQue = FromQue
C                    eval       QueLibrary = FromLib
C                    eval       MsOutQue = ToQue
C                    eval       MsQueLib = ToLibrary

 *  Create user space for output of spool file list
C                    eval       GeneralPtr = CrtUsrSpc(UserSpace)

 * List spool file entries to user space
C                    call       'QUSLSPL'
C                    parm                  UserSpace
C                    parm       'SPLF0200' FormatName
C                    parm       FromUser   UserName
C                    parm                  OutSpool
C                    parm                  FormType
C                    parm                  UserData
C                    parm                  ErrorDs
C                    parm                  JobName
C                    parm                  Keys
C                    parm                  NbrOfKeys

 * If no errors with the list API, process the user space
C                    if         MessageId = *blanks

C                    eval       RcvPointer = GeneralPtr + Offset
C                    Do         NumberList
C                    eval       I = 1

 * Process the five keys, loading each key to it's appropriate field
C                    do         5
C                    eval       KeyData = %subst(retrieved:i)
C                    select
C                    when       (KeyReturn = 201)
C                    eval       MsSpoolNam = KeyField
C                    when       (KeyReturn = 202)
C                    eval       MsJobName = KeyField
C                    when       (KeyReturn = 203)
C                    eval       MsJobUsr = KeyField
C                    when       (KeyReturn = 204)
C                    eval       MsJobNbr = KeyField
C                    when       (KeyReturn = 205)
C                    eval       KeyField1 = KeyField
C                    eval       MsSplNbr = SflNbr
C                    endsl
C                    eval       I = I + FldRtnLen
C                    enddo

C                    eval       MsOutQue = ToQue
C                    eval       MsQueLib = ToLibrary
 * Move the spooled file
```

Figure 9.14: Move spool file utility (part 3 of 5).

```
C                    call      'QSPMOVSP'
C                    parm                    MoveDs
C                    parm      92            MoveLen
C                    parm      'MSPF0100'    MovFormat
C                    parm                    ErrorDs

 * If errors with the move API, forward the error and leave
c                    if        MessageId <> *blanks
c                    exsr      SndErr
c                    leave
c                    endif

 * Increment pointer to get the next spooled file
C                    eval      RcvPointer = RcvPointer + EntrySize
C                    enddo

 * If errors with the list API, forward it back
c                    else
c                    exsr      SndErr
c                    endif

C                    eval      *InLr = *ON
 *
 * Send error message subroutine
c       snderr       begsr

C                    call      'QMHSNDPM'
C                    parm                    MessageId
C                    parm                    MsgFileLib
C                    parm                    MessageDta
C                    parm                    MsgDtaLen
C                    parm                    MsgType
C                    parm      '*'           MsgQueue
C                    parm      2             MsgQueNbr
C                    parm                    MsgKey
C                    parm                    ErrorDs

c                    endsr

 *
 *  Procedure to create extendable user space, return pointer to it.
 *
P  CrtUsrSpc      B
d  CrtUsrSpc      PI            *
d    CrtSpcName               20      const

 * Local Variables
D PasSpcName      DS           20
D  SName                    1  10
D  SLib                    11  20
D ChgAttrDs       DS
D  NumberAttr                   9B 0 inz(1)
```

Figure 9.14: Move spool file utility (part 4 of 5).

```
D  KeyAttr                       9B 0 inz(3)
D  DataSize                      9B 0 inz(1)
D  AttrData                      1    inz('1')
D  ListPtr        S                *
D  RetrndLib      S              10
D  SpaceAttr      S              10    inz
D  SpaceAuth      S              10    INZ('*CHANGE')
D  SpaceLen       S               9B 0 INZ(2048)
D  SpaceReplc     S              10    INZ('*YES')
D  SpaceText      S              50
D  SpaceValue     S               1

 * Create the user space
C                    move      CrtSpcName   PasSpcName
C                    call      'QUSCRTUS'
C                    parm                   PasSpcName
C                    parm                   SpaceAttr
C                    parm                   SpaceLen
C                    parm                   SpaceValue
C                    parm                   SpaceAuth
C                    parm                   SpaceText
C                    parm      '*YES'       SpaceReplc
C                    parm                   ErrorDs
 * Get pointer to user space
C                    call      'QUSPTRUS'
C                    parm                   PasSpcName
C                    parm                   ListPtr
 * Change user space to be extendable
C                    call      'QUSCUSAT'
C                    parm                   RetrndLIb
C                    parm                   PasSpcName
C                    parm                   ChgAttrDs
C                    parm                   ErrorDs

C                    return    ListPtr
P  CrtUsrSpc      E
```

Figure 9.14: Move spool file utility (part 5 of 5).

Take a look at the code in the program we used to move all spool file entries from one output queue to another. The program appears in Figure 9.14.

The program accepts the output queue name and output queue library from which to perform the move. It also accepts the user name that can be used to filter the selection. It then executes the subprocedure CrtUsrSpc to create a user space into which the List Spooled File API can put its data. (See "User Spaces" in this chapter for a detailed description of these APIs. Refer to chapter 14 if you need help understanding subprocedures.) The CrtUsrSpc procedure returns a pointer (GeneralPtr) that we have used to base the data structure GeneralHed. Because of this, this data structure will automatically be populated when the List Spooled File (QUSLSPL) API returns its information into the user space,.

The QUSLSPL API is then called. We use a data structure of codes to tell the API exactly what information about the spooled file we would like it to retrieve for us. See the data structure "KEYS" in the example. Table 9.10 shows a complete list of the codes this API accepts.

	Table 9.10: Code Table for Spool File APIs.	
Code	Type	Description
201	Char(10)	Spooled file name
202	Char(10)	Job name
203	Char(10)	User name
204	Char(6)	Job number
205	Binary(4)	Spooled file number
206	Char(10)	Output queue name
207	Char(10)	Output queue library name
208	Char(10)	Device name
209	Char(10)	User-specified data
210	Char(10)	Status
211	Binary(4)	Total number of pages
212	Binary(4)	Current page printing
213	Binary(4)	Number of copies left to print
214	Char(10)	Form type
215	Char(2)	Priority code
216	Char(7)	Date file was opened
217	Char(6)	Time file was opened
218	Char(16)	Internal job name (handle)
219	Char(16)	Internal spooled file identifier (handle)
220	Chart(10)	Device type

The input parameter group for the QUSLSPL API is shown in Table 9.11. All spooled files in the designated output queue are included in the list. Because of the list of keys we sent to the API, only the spooled file name (201), job name (202), user name (203), job number (204), and spooled file number (205) are returned for each spooled file.

Table 9.11: Input Parameter Group for the QUSLSPL API.

Parameter	Description	Type	Size
1	User space name	Input	Char(20)
2	Format name	Input	Char(8)
3	User name	Input	Char(10)
4	Output queue name	Input	Char(20)
5	Form type	Input	Char(10)
6	User-specified data	Input	Char(10)
Optional Parameter Group 1			
Parameter	Description	Type	Size
7	Error code	Both	Char(*)
Optional Parameter Group 2			
Parameter	Description	Type	Size
8	Job name	Input	Char(26)
9	Array of codes for return data	Input	Array(*) of Binary(4)
10	Number of fields in array in parameter 9	Input	Binary(4)

Parameter Definitions:

User space name: Object name and library name of the user space that will receive the generated list. Special values for library name are Current Library (*CURLIB) or Library List (*LIBL).

Format name: The format name of the system data structure that defines the format of the returned data. Valid format name values are SPLF0100 or SPLF0200.

User name: The name of the user whose spooled files should be included in the list. Part of the filtering criteria to generate the list. It must be blank if the job name parameter is specified. Special values are All Users (*ALL) or the Current User ID (*CURRENT).

Output queue name: Object name and library name of the output queue whose files are to be searched to determine if they are to be included in the list. These values are used as part of the filtering criteria to generate the list. Special values are *ALL (in which case the library part must be blank), Current Library (*CURLIB), or Library List (*LIBL) for the library part of the output queue name.

Form type: All files whose form type attribute matches this are to be included in the list. This field is also used as part of the filtering criteria to generate the list. Special values are *ALL (all form types) or *STD (the system default form type).

User-specified data: All files whose user-specified data attribute matches this are included in the list. Again, this value can be part of the filtering criteria to generate the list. Special value is *ALL.

Error code: The standard Optional Error Code Data Structure.

Job name: All files whose job name matches this value are to be included in the list. Job name can also be used as part of the filtering criteria to generate the list. This parameter must be blank if the user name, output queue name, form type, or user-specified data are not blank. The job name comprises three parts:

- Job Name: Char(10) - Specific name or * (indicates current job).
- User ID: Char(10) - User profile name or blanks if job name is *.
- Job Number: Char(6) - Specific job number or blanks if job name is specified as *.

Array of codes for return data: Array of codes indicating which attributes to return in format SPLF0200. Only the data represented by the codes are returned by the API. The valid codes are represented in Table 9.6. If the number of keys parameter is 0, this parameter is ignored.

Number of fields in array in parameter 9: The number of entries in the array of codes parameter. Must be 0 if the SPLF0100 format is being used. If this parameter is omitted, 0 is assumed.

After the call to the List Spooled File (QUSLSPL) API, the user space contains the information we are looking for. As with all List APIs, the format of the data contains a generic header, an input parameters section, a specific header section, and, finally, the list data section. The generic header section contains pointers to the other sections. See the List APIs in Table 9.8 for a complete description of this section.

The generic header data structure has already been populated through the use of the basing pointer technique. The field called OFFSET points us to the list section while the field called NumberList tells us how many entries are in the list. We use that number, NumberList, to establish a loop to walk through the user space (beginning at the start of the user space plus the offset position), extracting each entry in the list. See Table 9.12 for the format of the list section. Each entry in the list contains the five fields we are looking for, so we extract each field separately.

Table 9.12: Format of Lists from the QUSLSPL API.

SPLF0100

Offset	Type	Description
0	Char(10)	User name
10	Char(10)	Output queue name
20	Char(10)	Library name
30	Char(10)	Form type
40	Char(10)	User specified data
50	Char(16)	Internal job identifier (handle)
66	Char(16)	Internal spooled file identifier (handle)

SPLF0200

Offset	Type	Description
0	Binary(4)	Number of fields returned

These fields repeat for each code requested, so the offsets varies.

Offset	Type	Description
	Binary(4)	Length of field information returned
	Binary(4)	Code for data returned
	Char(1)	Type of data
	Char(3)	Reserved
	Binary(4)	Length of data returned
	Char(*)	Data returned for specified code
	Char(*)	Reserved

Having obtained all the fields necessary to move a spool file, we now call the Move Spool File (QSPMOVSP) API to actually move the spool file to the target output queue. The required input parameters for this API are shown in Table 9.13.

Table 9.13: Input Parameter Group for the QSPMOVSP API.

Parameter	Description	Type	Size
1	Move information data structure	Input	Char(20)
2	Length of move data structure	Input	Binary(4)
3	Format name of data structure	Input	Char(8)
4	Standard error code data structure	Both	Char(*)

Parameter Definitions:

Move information data structure: The information required by the system to perform the move. It must be specified in either the MSPF0100 or MSPF0200 format. See Table 9.10 for more information on these data structures.

Length of move data structure: The length of the information data structure. The minimum length for MSPF0100 is 92 and 144 for the MSPF0200 format.

Format name of data structure: The name of the format that describes the information data structure. Specify either MSPF0100 or MSPF0200 (see Table 9.14).

Standard error code data structure: The standard Optional Error Code Data Structure.

We chose to use the MSPF0100 format, which provides the function for moving the spooled file ahead of all other spooled files on the target output queue. We are reading the source output queue in one order and moving each spooled file to the top of the target output queue, resulting in the net effect of reversing the order of the spooled files on the target output queue.

If the order of the spooled files is of importance, we use the MSPF0200 format, which puts the spooled files *after* the target spooled file, thus keeping the original sequence of spooled files.

Table 9.14: Information Formats for the QSPMOVSP API.

MSF0100 Format

Offset	Type	Description
0	Char(10)	From job name
10	Char(10)	From job user name
20	Char(6)	From job number
26	Char(16)	From internal job identifier (handle)
42	Char(16)	From internal spooled file identifier (handle)
58	Char(10)	From spooled file name
68	Binary(4)	From spooled file number
72	Char(10)	To output queue name
82	Char(10)	To output queue library name

MSF0200 Format

Offset	Type	Description
0	Char(10)	From job name
10	Char(10)	From job user name
20	Char(6)	From job number
26	Char(16)	From internal job identifier (handle)
42	Char(16)	From internal spooled file identifier (handle)
58	Char(10)	From spooled file name
68	Binary(4)	From spooled file number
72	Char(10)	To job name
82	Char(10)	To job user name
92	Char(10)	To job number
98	Char(16)	To internal job identifier (handle)
114	Char(16)	To internal spooled file identifier (handle)
130	Char(10)	To spooled file name
140	Binary(4)	To spooled file number

Restrictions on Moving a Spooled File

There are a number of restrictions you must consider when moving a spooled file, including:

- You cannot move a spooled file that is being held by the HLDJOB SPLFILE(*YES) command.

- You cannot move a spooled file that is already printing.

- You cannot move a spooled file to follow a spooled file with an open status.

- You cannot move a spooled file to follow a spooled file with a closed status, unless both spooled files are part of the same job.

- You cannot move a spooled file to follow a spooled file with a deferred status, unless both spooled files are part of the same job.

- The target output queue must be defined as *FIFO (first in, first out).

- You cannot move a spooled file to follow a spooled file that is printing, unless the target spooled file is the last spooled file selected by the writer. The system considers a spooled file to be printing if it is in any of the following status conditions: PND (pending), WTR (at the writer), PRT (printing), SND (being sent), or MSGW (message waiting).

- A spooled file that is at the ready, open, closed, or deferred status is changed to the held status if it is moved to follow a spooled file that is held or saved.

- A spooled file that has a status of held, open, closed, or saved is changed to ready status when it is moved to the top of an output queue.

- A spooled file that has a status of held, open, closed, or saved is changed to ready status when it is moved to follow a spooled file that has a ready status.

PROGRAM APIS FOR ILE

Modular programming has both an upside and a downside. On the upside—small, easily maintainable modules. You do not write programs anymore; you write modules and then tell the compiler to gather (bind) these modules into a program. Maintenance, as well as testing, should be easier when you are working with small subsections of a program.

There are two ways to gather these modules into a program: bind by reference and bind by copy. If you bind by reference, links between the module and the program are completed when the program is executed, which causes a delay the first time the program is executed. This is very similar to the Original Program Model (OPM).

If you bind by copy, a copy of the module is placed in the program, which means the module will execute as if it were a subroutine. Bind by copy was not an available option in OPM. It is new for ILE.

The downside comes when you make a change to a module that has been bound by copy into more than one program. (We do not recommend that you copy a module into more than one program, but if you do, we're here to help. For more on this topic, see "Service Programs" in chapter 13.) Unless those programs are recompiled, they will not see the change you made to the module.

For example, suppose Program A is created from Module 1, Module 2, and Module3. Program B is created from Module 2, Module 4, and Module 5. Further, assume that all modules were bound to their respective programs using bind by copy. Now, while running Program A, a user discovers and reports a bug in Module 2. Being the astute programmer that you are, you quickly discover and correct the error in Module 2. You then recreate Program A, which now works correctly. Program B, however, still has the old copy of Module 2 and will not work correctly.

DISPLAY MODULE PROGRAMS (DSPMODPGM)

So the problem becomes, how do you know which programs use which modules? The Display Program (DSPPGM) command will list all modules a program uses, but not all programs that use a given module. In chapter 11, we have included a utility that does just that. We call it Display Module Programs (DSPMODPGM).

You can refer to chapter 11 for the complete code to this program. For now, we are going to take a look at the List ILE Program Information (QBNLPGMI) API. This API will list all modules that are contained in a given program. If we run this API over all the programs in a given library, we will get a list of all programs and their modules. Like all List APIs, the output is produced into a user space we then "walk through," retrieving each item in the list (the format name parameter controls the information contained in the list). We can then compare each item with our search criteria and display (or print) any that match.

Table 9.15 shows the input requirements needed to use the API. This is basically the qualified name of the user space, the format name to control the list information, the generic name of the programs to list, and the standard error code data structure. Table 9.16

shows a partial listing of the format of the returned data we used to create this utility (for a complete listing, refer to the *System Programmer's Interface Reference Manual*).

Parameter	Description	Type	Size
1	User space name	Input	Char(20)
2	Format name	Input	Char(8)
3	ILE Program Name	Input	Char(20)
4	Error data structure	Both	Char(*)

Table 9.15: Required Input Parameters for the QBNLPGMI API.

Parameter Definitions

User space name: The name and library of the user space where the requested information is to be placed. The first 10 characters are the name of the user space. The last 10 characters are the name of the library.

Format name: Format name of the system data structure that defines the format of the returned data. Valid format names are:

> PGML0100 - Module listing
>
> PGML0200 - Service program information
>
> PGML0300 - Export information
>
> PGML0400 - Import information
>
> PGML0500 - Copyright information

ILE program name: The name of the program that is to be listed. The first 10 characters contain the program name, and the last 10 characters contain the library name. The program name can contain *ALL or generic*. This allows us to list all programs in a particular library. If you provide the name of an OPM program, an error will be returned.

Error Code: The standard error code data structure.

Table 9.16: Format PGML0100.

Offset	Type	Description
0	Char(10)	Program name
10	Char(10)	Library name
20	Char(10)	Bound module name
30	Char(10)	Bound module library name
40	Char(10)	Source file name
50	Char(10)	Source file library name
60	Char(10)	Source member name
70	Char(10)	Module attribute
80	Char(13)	Module created date/time

WORKING WITH SERVICE PROGRAMS

If you are using service programs in your applications but are not using a binder language (see chapter 13) to keep track of changes to the public interface of the service program, you can quickly find yourself in a predicament. Say you have discovered that you made a change to an existing service program that changed the public interface. You now need to know all programs that use this service program so you can recompile them.

We have included a utility in chapter 11 that will list all programs that use a given service program. The program performs the same function as DSPMODPGM but for service programs. In fact, it even uses the same QBNLPGMI API to produce the list of programs. We simply use a different format name, PGML0200, to get a list of all service programs the program uses. Table 9.17 shows this output format.

Table 9.17: Format PGML0200.

Offset	Type	Description
0	Char(10)	Program name
10	Char(10)	Library name
20	Char(10)	Bound service program name
30	Char(10)	Bound service program library
40	Char(16)	Service program signature

We also thought it would be useful to show the date and time the program was created. We use the QCLRPGMI API to retrieve this information. Like all retrieve APIs, this one returns the information in a variable field, not a user space. Table 9.18 shows the required Input Specifications for this API, while Table 9.19 shows a partial listing of the PGMI0100 format our utility is using.

Table 9.18: Required Input Parameters for the QCLRPGMI API.

Parameter	Description	Type	Size
1	Receiver name	Output	Char(*)
2	Receiver length	Input	Binary(4)
3	Format name	Input	Char(8)
4	Qualified program name	Input	Char(20)
5	Error code	Both	Char(*)

Parameter Definitions:

Receiver name: The name of the variable that will contain the results of the call to the API. The amount of information returned is limited by the size of this variable.

Receiver length: The length of the receiver name parameter.

Format name: Format name of the system data structure that defines the format of the returned data. Valid format names are PGMI0100 (Basic OPM or ILE information), PGMI0200 (Basic plus SQL for OPM), or PGMI0300 (ILE program size).

Program name: The name of the program that will be listed. The first 10 characters contain the program name and the last 10 characters contain the library name.

Error Code: The standard error code data structure.

Table 9.19: Format PGMI0100 (partial).

Offset	Type	Description
0	Binary(4)	Bytes returned
4	Binary(4)	Bytes available
8	Char(10)	Program name
18	Char(10)	Program library
28	Char(10)	Program owner
38	Char(10)	Program attribute
48	Char(13)	Created date/time

ENCRYPTION APIS

The AS400 provides a suite of APIs that can be used to encrypt data. We know what you are thinking: "What the heck does encryption have to do with me? I don't work for the CIA." Encryption is not just for Big Brother anymore. As the ever-expanding Internet gobbles up more and more companies, it forces us to take a look at security measures we did not have to worry about before. Getting onto the Internet is easy. Retrofitting legacy code that was designed to work in house to work securely while running around the world is a different issue. Encryption is a tool to help retrofit applications. Tightened security is a small price to pay for the advantages of global computing.

Most applications have some kind of built-in security requiring a password. A menu system wants a password before you can run an option, or a pop up window that asks for a password to perform a special function. These passwords are usually stored in a data area or a file that can be viewed with easily accessible, system-provided commands. In other words, somebody who knows what he is doing has a good chance of discovering them. If you encrypt the passwords, they cannot be viewed by anybody!

The program shown in Figure 9.15 will encrypt passwords for you. If you are not yet familiar with prototyping procedures, read chapter 14. We are going to concentrate on the APIs that make this function work.

The program will allow you to add users to the system (with their password), remove the user from the system, and validate the user/password combination. This program is written as an external program you call to verify passwords. It is strongly recommended that you use this program as a guide and clone the code into your program so the password does not have to be passed as a parameter. Passing a password as a parameter is a security violation in itself, but it is better than storing it in a file.

The first step in the process is to create a validation list. This is an object on the AS400 (type *VLDL) that will store the encrypted password. You use the Create Validation List (CRTVLDL) command to create a list. You must have security clearance to operate this command. Just give the list a meaningful name and designate a library for it to reside in. To use the provided program, you must create a validation list called PWLIST in library QGPL.

Now you need to add a user to the list. The first three parameters the program expects is an action code, user profile, and password to encrypt. Use action code "A" to add the user and password to the list. Use "D" to delete the user from the list and "V" to verify that the password is correct.

The next two parameters, return code and error text, returning error information regarding your request. The return code field will be set to "N" if the request failed, and the error text will give the information from the API as to why it failed. The description parameter is used only when you are adding a new user to the list. It allows you to further describe the entry.

Let's take a closer look at the code. The ADDPW subroutine executes the ADDPASS function. If we look at the prototype for ADDPASS, we see that it executes the external procedure Add Validation List Entry, QsyAddValidationLstEntry. Note that the procedure name is coded in both upper- and lowercase characters. When calling external procedures, the case of the characters is important. The procedure wants five parameters, four of which are mandatory and one of which is optional. The OPTIONS(*OMIT) keyword on the ATRIBDSH parameter indicates that we do not have to pass this parameter. The first parameter is the name of validation list and is hard coded to QGPL/PWLIST. The next three parameters are data structures.

The ENTRYIDDS data structure contains the name of the user profile, preceded by two 4-byte binary fields that contain the length of the user profile data and the CCSID code. The user profile length is 10, and we use zero for the CCSID code, which means: Store the default CCSID for the current user. The user profile name does not have to exist on the system. This means that you could devise some kind of coding scheme to encrypt data based on something other than user profile. Valid values for the profile length are from 1 through 100.

The ENCRIPDS data structure follows the same format as the ENTRYIDDS data structure. But this data structure contains the password. Valid values for the length of the encrypted data are 1 through 600. The ENTRYDS data structure also follows the same format and contains your description of the ENTRYID field. Valid values for the length of the description are 1 through 1,000.

We have elected to omit the fifth parameter, which is an attribute data structure that allows you to change default values. By default, encrypted passwords cannot be viewed in their original form. This means you cannot look at the decrypted password using any method. You can verify a password, but you cannot see it. There are APIs that will return the data in its original, decrypted state, but only if you enable this function when you first add the entry to the validation list. This attribute data structure parameter provides the ability to enable this function. Because we are accepting the default value for this option, we can omit the parameter.

If the entry is successfully added to the validation list, the ADD field will contain a 0. If it was not successful, the field will contain a negative 1 and the errno global value (which is maintained by the system that contains the error number that occurred) will be set to indicate the error. Most APIs use an optional error data structure as a parameter to pass back error conditions. The C language-type APIs are different and, like the C language itself, much more difficult to follow.

The global value errno is accessed in an RPG program through the external procedure '__errno' which we have defined on the prototype C_Errno. It returns a pointer that can be used to retrieve a text description of the error.

The validation function is provided through the VLDPW subroutine. If you pass a "V" in the action code, this subroutine gets executed. It in turn executes the Verify Validation List Entry (QsyVerifyValidationLstEntry) API. While this is a relatively simple API, it makes the whole encryption process work. You simply give it the name of the validation list, the name of the user profile (or key), and the password to verify. You use the ENTRYIDDS data structure and the ENCRIPDS data structure to pass these values. If the password is invalid, the procedure returns a negative 2. The program will then set the RTNCODE field to "N" so the calling program knows the password was invalid.

The delete function is provided through the DLTPW subroutine. Pass in a "D" in the action code, and this subroutine gets executed. It uses the QsyRemoveValidationLstEntry API to accomplish this task. Pass this procedure the name of the validation list and the name of the user profile (again through the ENTRYIDDS data structure), and it will remove the user from the list.

```
*
*   Compile as QSECOFR *OWNER,Default Activation Group *NO,
*      Binding directory QC2LE, V4R1M0 or later
*
*   VLD016Rg = Program performs 3 functions:
*      Action code A = Add encrypted password to system
*                   D = Delete encrypted password from system
*                   V = Validate password passed to system
*
d AddPass           PR            10i 0 ExtProc('QsyAddValidation+
d                                            LstEntry')
d  ListName                       20
d  EntryIdDsH                     18
d  EncriptDsH                     18
```

Figure 9.15: Validation List APIs (part 1 of 3).

```
d   EntryDSH                        58
d   AtribDsH                        47      options(*omit)

d  Action          s                1
d  Add             s                10i 0 inz(0)
d  Description      s                50
d  Dlt             s                10i 0 inz(0)
d  ErrorText       s                70
d  ErrorVal        s                10i 0 based(@errorVal)
d  PassWord        s                10
d  Rtncode         s                1
d  UserId          s                10

  * Validation list name
d  ListNameA       s                20      inz('PWLIST    QGPL      ')

  * Prototype for validation API
d ValidPass        PR               10i 0 ExtProc('QsyVerifyValidation+
d                                         LstEntry')
d   ListName                        20
d   EntryIdDs                       18
d   EncriptDs                       18

  * Prototype for remove API
d DeletePass       PR               10i 0 ExtProc('QsyRemoveValidation+
d                                         LstEntry')
d   ListName                        20
d   EntryIdDs                       18

  * Prototype for error retrieval
d C_Errno          PR               *     extproc('__errno')
d C_Strerror       PR               *     extproc('strerror')
d   errno                           10i 0 value

  * Entry Id list (user profile name or key value)
D EntryIdDs        DS                     INZ
D   IdLength             1           4b 0 inz(10)
D   CCSIDLen             5           8b 0 inz(0)
D   EntUserId            9          18

  * Password to encript
D EncriptDs        DS                     INZ
D   EncripLen            1           4b 0 inz(10)
D   CCSIDEnc             5           8b 0 inz(0)
D   EncripData           9          18

  * Free-form description of item
D EntryDs          DS                     INZ
D   EntryLen             1           4b 0 inz(50)
D   CCSIDEnt             5           8b 0 inz(0)
D   EntryData            9          58
```

Figure 9.15: Validation List APIs (part 2 of 3).

```
c       *entry      plist
c                   parm                    Action
c                   parm                    UserId
c                   parm                    PassWord
c                   parm                    RtnCode
c                   parm                    ErrorText
c                   parm                    Description

c                   eval        EntUserId = UserId
c                   eval        EncripData = Password

c       Action      caseq       'A'         AddPw
c       Action      caseq       'D'         DltPw
c       Action      caseq       'V'         VldPw
c                   endcs

* Trap any errors that may have occurred
c                   eval        @errorval = C_Errno
c                   if          errorval <> 0
c                   if          %parms > 4
c                   eval        ErrorText = %str(C_Strerror(ErrorVal))
c                   eval        RtnCode = 'N'
c                   endif
c                   endif

c                   eval        *inlr = *on

* Add password to system
c       AddPw       Begsr
c                   eval        EntryData = Description
c                   eval        Add = (AddPass(ListnameA:
c                               EntryIdDs:EncriptDs:
c                               EntryDS:*omit))
c                   endsr
* Validate password
c       VldPw       Begsr
c                   If          (ValidPass(ListnameA:
c                               EntryIdDs:EncriptDs)) <> 0
c                   eval        RtnCode = 'N'
c                   endif
c                   endsr
* Delete password
c       DltPw       Begsr
c                   eval        Dlt = (DeletePass(ListnameA:
c                               EntryIdDs))
c                   endsr
```

Figure 9.15: Validation List APIs (part 3 of 3).

DON'T WORRY, BE API!

APIs provide a wide variety of functions not normally available to the RPG programmer. As with all things in life, variety breeds complexity, but that should not deter you from using these valuable tools. If you do your homework and become proficient in using APIs, you will become a much better programmer in the process.

This chapter has provided you with some tools, Display Path (DSPPATH) and Move Spooled Files (MOVSPL), that can help you in your everyday tasks. Using DSPPATH improves functions already provided by the operating system. Using MOVSPL provides a way for you to automate spool file handling. And the encryption APIs can help secure your applications as you move towards the Internet.

As you become proficient in using APIs, you will almost certainly generate your own tools. When you do, feel free to contact us. We would love to hear from you.

10

TRACKING DOWN PROBLEMS

If your programs don't have bugs, you don't need to read this chapter. Because you're still reading means you're probably in the same boat as the rest of us.

No matter how long you have been programming, how smart you are, or how carefully you code your programs, you are going to make mistakes. We are not stating anything that you do not already know, and it should not be discouraging to find out that you are only human.

One of the things that separates good programmers from those who go through their professional lives in mediocrity is how quickly they can find and fix problems that inevitably occur. The topics covered in this chapter include learning how to debug interactive and batch jobs (OPM only), using journaling as a debugging tool, and how to interpret and change the amount of information written to your job logs.

FINDING DEBUG IN DE PROGRAM

Debug is often the last place programmers go when they are trying to solve problems in their RPG programs. They look at the data and the code until their eyes are bugging out, trying to solve the problem before going to that *last* resort.

We are here to tell you that this is the worst possible approach you can take. You need to make Debug your best friend. It should be the *first* step you take when trying to solve a programming problem. It is generally a good idea to place a brand new program under Debug the very first time you run it so you can step through the code and make sure the program is doing what it was intended to do. As a matter of fact, we recommend placing *every* new program that has any degree of complexity under Debug when you first run it. This will allow you to perform the ultimate "desk check" as you step your way through your program.

Have you ever heard the expression "An ounce of prevention is worth a pound of cure?" Nothing could hit closer to home than this old adage as it applies to RPG programming. Solving a problem in a program is usually 10 times harder once the program is in production. This is especially true if the program with the error happens to update database files.

The amount of programming time lost to pride and stubbornness is simply staggering. And if your excuse has been that you do not know how to use Debug, you are about to have to find a new one.

DEBUG 101

AS/400 Debug is a process whereby you take a program or programs and place them under a microscope while they run. You can define points in the program where the program must take a break (cleverly called breakpoints), giving you time to examine and change variables within your program while it is running. You can also add, modify, or remove breakpoints, depending on your needs at the time. You can *step* through the code as the program runs to see its progress. You can even step into other programs, modules, and service programs. You can even run Debug on OPM programs that run in batch, but more on that later in this chapter.

Before we get too carried away, let's start at the beginning.

The first thing you need to know about debugging an RPG IV program is that you must tell the system, when you compile the program, that you are want to debug it. The reason for this is that the compiler then keeps a copy of the source within the compiled object. This makes the object much bigger, but it allows you to see program variables, line statements, and so forth.

The recommended method of debugging is to compile your programs with the debug option enabled, then test, test, and test some more. When you are ready to put the program into production, compile it one last time with the debug option disabled. If you employ this methodology and have to debug a program while it is in production, you will need to recompile the program before you can run Debug on it.

When compiling RPG IV programs, you first set the debug option using the DBGVIEW parameter on the Create Bound RPG Program (CRTBNDRPG) command. This parameter accepts six possible options, as detailed in Table 10.1.

Table 10.1: DBGVIEW Options.

Option	Description
*STMNT	Uses the line numbers shown on the compile listing to debug the program. This is the compile default.
*SOURCE	Uses the source member, saved at compile time, to debug the program.
*LIST	Uses the listing view to debug the program.
*COPY	Uses the source view and include any /COPY statements.
*ALL	Uses the source, listing, and /COPY views to debug the program.
*NONE	Disables all the debug options for the program.

DEBUG HEADER SPECIFICATIONS

How well debug works for you is dependent upon a couple of keywords in the header specification in the program. The OPTION keyword has two parameters that are of particular interest to the debug process.

The first OPTION(*NODEBUGIO) keyword to be aware of is *NODEBUGIO. This option stops debug from issuing a break for each field in a database file when you put a breakpoint on a file access line. Let's say you chain to a file with three fields in it. If you put a breakpoint on that chain statement, the debugger would break three times! With OPTION(*NODEBUGIO), it only breaks once.

The other parameter is OPTION(*SRCSTMT). This ensures that statement numbers for the listing match the SEU source member sequence numbers. Source code pulled into the program from other source members has a source member number concatenated onto the front of the SEU sequence number. Without this option specified, error messages sent by the system do not match the source statement number! In OPM, the numbers always matched. In ILE, you have to have this keyword to make it happen.

These two options are available in V4R4. They are also available in prior releases via PTFs. You need a separate PTF for both the runtime and the compiler versions. If you go to the IBM Web site at *www.as400service.rochester.ibm.com,* you can get a list of relevant PTFs for your release.

IN DE BEGINNING

Like most things in life, you can make the debugging process as simple or as complicated as you like. But even the most simple Debug functions can offer you a tremendous amount of information and insight into the function of your programs.

When you execute the Start Debug (STRDBG) command on an RPG IV program that has been compiled with the DBGVIEW option enabled (set to anything other than *NONE), the first thing you will see is a screen similar to that shown in Figure 10.1. The Display Module Source panel will show the source for the program. This panel will appear both when you define your initial debug criteria to the system and when you actually run your program under Debug.

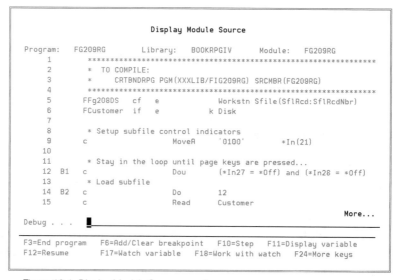

Figure 10.1: Display Module Source panel.

ADDING DE BREAKPOINT

The most common task to perform at this time is to set a breakpoint. The principle reason for this is that breakpoints give the programmer more control over looking at or changing variables as well as performing other debugging functions while the program is still running.

Once you have started Debug using the STRDBG command, you will be presented with the source from your module, as seen in Figure 10.1. You set the breakpoint by positioning the cursor on the line of source at which you want to set the breakpoint and then pressing F6. This will highlight the selected line, indicating where your breakpoint is set.

When you actually run the program, the breakpoint display will appear just before executing the selected line. The breakpoint display will show the module source on the screen, much as shown in Figure 10.1. All of the Debug function keys available to you on the Display Module Source display panel are illustrated in Table 10.2. However, the most common task you need to complete when you are defining your debug criteria is setting a breakpoint or two and getting out. We will discuss what happens to your program when it is run under Debug later in this chapter, but first, let's take a look at the various debugging options that are available.

Table 10.2: Function Keys for Display Module Source Display.

Function Key	Name	Description
F1	Help	Provides additional help.
F3	End	Stops the source debugger. If the program was running, the program ends.
F5	Refresh	Update the screen.
F6	Add/Remove Breakpoint	Add a breakpoint on the line at which the cursor is positioned. If a breakpoint already exists on that line, remove it.
F9	Retrieve	Retrieve last command entered on the command line.
F10	Step Over	Process one line and show the display module source screen again.
F11	Display Variable	Display the variable at which the cursor is now positioned.

	Table 10.2: Function Keys for Display Module Source Display (continued).	
Function Key	**Name**	**Description**
F12	Resume	Resume processing. If program is running, continue running until the next breakpoint is encountered or until end of program.
F13	Work with Module Breakpoints	Display the Work with Module breakpoints panel.
F14	Work with Module List	Display the Work with Module list panel
F15	Select View	Display the Select View panel.
F16	Set Debug Options	Display the Set Debug options panel.
F19	Left	Shift the display 40 characters to the left.
F20	Right	Shift the display 40 characters to the right.
F21	Command Line	Display the command entry line.
F22	Step Into	Process one line and display the Display Module Source panel again. Will execute call statements and take you into other programs.
F24	More Keys	Display more function keys

When selecting a source statement for your breakpoint, select one that you *know* will be executed. Selecting a statement that does not get executed results in no breakpoint. It is easy to add, change, or remove breakpoints later while the program is running (provided you are at a breakpoint). Also note that the breakpoint event always occurs just *prior* to the execution of the statement where you are adding the breakpoint.

DE CONDITIONAL BREAKPOINT

Sometimes, it is necessary to set what is known as a *conditional* breakpoint. This is a breakpoint that will not cause the program to stop until some condition has been met. Say, for example, the error you are trying to fix does not occur except when a particular customer record is processed. You would want your program breakpoint to occur only when it had read that particular customer record.

To set a conditional breakpoint, press F13 from the Display Module Source display panel. A screen similar to the one depicted in Figure 10.2 will be displayed. On the Work with Module Breakpoints display, you use the add option (option 1) to add the breakpoint to the line number you specify. In addition, you put the condition that must exist before the breakpoint will cause the program to stop in the column called, appropriately enough, Condition.

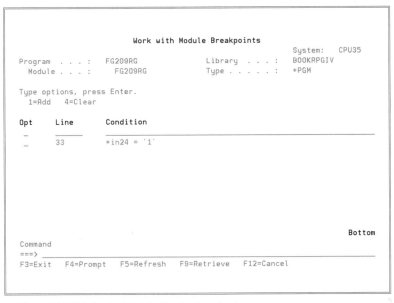

Figure 10.2: Work with Module Breakpoints display.

Another wrinkle you might encounter at this time is having a program that is composed of more than one module. If this is the case, you might want to debug more than one module at a time. If you need to debug more than one module, you need the Work with Module List panel (Figure 10.3) that appears when you press F14 from the Display Module Source panel seen in Figure 10.1. From the Work with Module List panel, you can work with all the modules that comprise the program being debugged.

DEBUGGING SERVICE PROGRAMS

In Figure 10.3, note that the CPUBASICS program has a type of *SRVPGM. You will not see a service program on this screen unless you specify it on the SRVPGM parameter of the STRDBG command. To get the screen shown in Figure 10.3, we entered the following command:

```
STRDBG PGM(OPNTRDRVRG) SRVPGM(CPUBASICS)
```

If you want to debug modules within the service program, use option 5 next to the module you want to debug. This will execute the DSPMODSRC command for that module and display the screen shown in Figure 10.1.

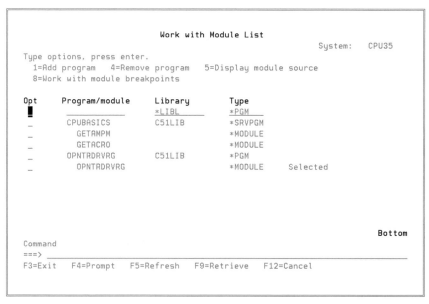

```
                          Work with Module List
                                                   System:    CPU35
     Type options, press enter.
       1=Add program    4=Remove program    5=Display module source
       8=Work with module breakpoints


     Opt    Program/module      Library       Type
       ▋      _____       *LIBL_____    *PGM___
       _      CPUBASICS         C51LIB        *SRVPGM
       _        GETAMPM                       *MODULE
       _        GETACRO                       *MODULE
       _      OPNTRDRVRG        C51LIB        *PGM
       _        OPNTRDRVRG                    *MODULE     Selected




                                                                   Bottom
     Command
     ===> _____
     F3=Exit    F4=Prompt    F5=Refresh    F9=Retrieve    F12=Cancel
```

Figure 10.3: Work with Module List display.

If you compiled the program using the DBGVIEW(*ALL) option, you could have different views to work with. Pressing F15 from the Display Module Source panel (Figure 10.1) will cause the Select View Display screen depicted in Figure 10.4 to appear. From the Select View Display, you can set which Debug view you want to work with.

Another option you might want to work with at this time is shown in Figure 10.5. Keying the SET keyword from the Display Module Source panel (Figure 10.1) and pressing the Enter key will cause the Set Debug Options panel to appear. The Set Debug Options panel lets you toggle between update production *YES and *NO.

```
                        Display Module Source
    ......................................................................
    :                         Select View                               :
    :                                                                    :
    : Current View . . . :    ILE RPG Source View                       :
    :                                                                    :
    : Type option, press Enter.                                         :
    :   1=Select                                                        :
    :                                                                    :
    : Opt     View                                                      :
    :  █        ILE RPG Listing View                                    :
    :  _        ILE RPG Source View                                     :
    :  _        ILE RPG Copy View                                       :
    :                                                                    :
    :                                                          Bottom   :
    : F12=Cancel                                                        :
    :                                                                    :
    :...................................................................:
                                                              More...
    Debug . . .   _____

    F3=End program    F6=Add/Clear breakpoint   F10=Step   F11=Display variable
    F12=Resume        F17=Watch variable   F18=Work with watch   F24=More keys
```

Figure 10.4: Select View Display screen.

```
                        Display Module Source
    ......................................................................
    :                       Set Debug Options                 : ********
    :                                                          :
    : Type changes, press Enter.                               :
    :                                                          :
    : Update production files . . . . . .  Y___   Y=Yes, N=No  : ********
    : Case (for FIND) . . . . . . . . . .  I___   I=Ignore, M=Match : Nbr)
    : OPM source debug support . . . . . .  N___   Y=Yes, N=No  :
    :                                                          :
    : F12=Cancel                                               :
    :                                                          :
    :.........................................................:
      11          * Stay in the loop until page keys are pressed...
      12  B1   c              Dou        (*In27 = *Off) and (*In28 = *Off)
      13          * Load subfile
      14  B2   c              Do         12
      15       c              Read       Customer
                                                              More...
    Debug . . .   set_____

    F3=End program    F6=Add/Clear breakpoint   F10=Step   F11=Display variable
    F12=Resume        F17=Watch variable   F18=Work with watch   F24=More keys
```

Figure 10.5: Set Debug Options panel.

If you are not familiar with the concept of Test and Production files and libraries, read on. When you create a library on the AS/400, the Create Library (CRTLIB) command has a parameter called TYPE. This parameter accepts either *TEST or *PROD. Your production libraries should be created with the parameter set to *PROD, while your testing libraries should be set to *TEST. What this type of arrangement affords you is the ability to make absolutely sure your testing steps do not update production files.

If you set the debug option to update production *NO and then run a program that attempts to update, write, or delete a record in a file that is in a library with type *PROD, the system will not perform the function. Instead it will issue an error message. This creates complete protection of your production files! Try it. You might like it.

RUNNING DE PROGRAM

Now that we have covered many of the principle Debug functions, we are ready to call our program. Unfortunately, there is no way to run the program directly from the Display Module Source display panel. You must end the task and then start the program. Press either F12 or F3 to do so. Now, call the program.

When the program reaches the point where the source statement specified in our breakpoint is about to be executed, the breakpoint display appears on our screen. It looks similar to the Display Module Source panel in Figure 10.1.

Most of the options that were available when you started Debug are also available here. However, the source shown in the panel should now be positioned to the first breakpoint the system encountered when running the program.

DISPLAYING DE VARIABLE

Probably the most common task at this point is displaying a variable. You can accomplish this in a variety of ways. The easiest way is to position the cursor on the field in the displayed source and press F11. This will cause the value of the field to be displayed on the line below the Debug entry line. In Figure 10.6, the Display Program Variables display panel shows the result of positioning the cursor on the field CUSTNAME, referenced at statement 18, and pressing F11.

If you display the value of an array or data structure, the system will return the values of the entire array or the values of all subfields in the data structure. Because these values probably will not fit on a single line, a new panel is displayed, as shown in Figure 10.7. The Evaluate Expression display panel is used to display multiple program values at once.

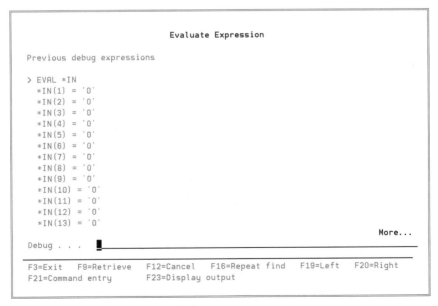

```
                        Display Module Source

Program:   FG209RG      Library:   BOOKRPGIV      Module:   FG209RG
    14  B2   c                     Do        12
    15       c                     Read      Customer
    16         * Write subfile record if valid record was read...
    17  B3   c                     If        not %Eof(Customer)
    18       c                     Eval      SfCustName = █ustName
    19       c                     Eval      SfCustNbr  = Customer#
    20       c                     Eval      SflRcdNbr  = SflRcdNbr + 1
    21       c                     Eval      *In21 = *On
    22       c                     Write     SflRcd
    23       c                     Else
    24       c                     Leave
    25  E3   c                     Endif
    26  E2   c                     EndDo
    27         * Determine the end-of-file condition
    28       c     Customer#   Setgt     Customer
                                                          More...
Debug . . .   _____

_____
F3=End program    F6=Add/Clear breakpoint    F10=Step   F11=Display variable
F12=Resume    F17=Watch variable   F18=Work with watch   F24=More keys
CUSTNAME = 'JEFF'S COMPUTER CABLES
```

Figure 10.6: Display Program Variables display.

```
                        Evaluate Expression

Previous debug expressions

> EVAL *IN
  *IN(1) = '0'
  *IN(2) = '0'
  *IN(3) = '0'
  *IN(4) = '0'
  *IN(5) = '0'
  *IN(6) = '0'
  *IN(7) = '0'
  *IN(8) = '0'
  *IN(9) = '0'
  *IN(10) = '0'
  *IN(11) = '0'
  *IN(12) = '0'
  *IN(13) = '0'
                                                          More...
Debug . . .   █_____

_____
F3=Exit   F9=Retrieve   F12=Cancel   F16=Repeat find   F19=Left   F20=Right
F21=Command entry        F23=Display output
```

Figure 10.7: Evaluate Expression display.

307

The Debug entry line provides another method for communicating with the debugger. In Table 10.3, we see a table of the Debug commands you can issue from this line. All of the capabilities provided by the function keys are also available via the Debug entry line. You can enter commands either by typing in the command name or using the abbreviated version of the command.

There are a number of commands you can use to position the source module on the screen. UP (or its incredibly abbreviated version, U) will move the source module up X number of lines. DOWN or (D) will do the opposite. LEFT, RIGHT, TOP, and BOTTOM all do pretty much what you expect.

The FIND (F) command searches through the source module for the designated string or line number. The search begins at the current cursor location. You can add a direction indicator at the end of the command (P for Previous, N for Next), as in FIND FieldName P. Another shortcut you can use is to simply key FIND, with no parameters. The command will then use the parameters used the last time you ran FIND.

Probably the most interesting and useful command is EVAL (E). This command allows you to display the contents of a variable as if you had positioned the cursor on a variable field name and pressed F11. If you want to see the hexadecimal value of a field, you would key EVAL FIELDNAME: X.

You can also use the EVAL command to change the value of a variable. Let's say you have a program that is using a field (Index) as an index to an array. The program is blowing up when it tries to use the Index field and you cannot tell why. So you put the program under Debug and place a breakpoint on the line causing the error message. When the Display Module Source panel appears, you key EVAL Index and see that the field is 0. So now you see how to correct the code so the Index field can never be 0, but will the program work if the index is set to the correct number? Using the EVAL command, you can set the Index to a valid number, continue the program, and check to see if the rest of your code is correct. You simply enter EVAL Index = 1 and then press F12 to resume the running of the program. The program will continue with the statement that had the breakpoint, with the field Index set to the value of 1 (or whatever number you set it to). This is a very powerful ability for any debugging tool.

Another useful command to be aware of is STEP, which allows you to walk through a program (or section of code) and stop at each line of code. Each time it stops, it displays the Display Module Source panel, awaiting your command. If you want to stop at every fifth line, you would key STEP 5.

Table 10.3: Debug Commands.

Command	Abbreviation	Description
ATTR	A	Display the attributes of a variable.
BREAK	BR	Enter breakpoints.
CLEAR	C	Remove breakpoints.
DISPLAY	DI	Display the names and definitions assigned by using the EQUATE command. Also allows you to display a different module.
EQUATE	EQ	Assign an expression, variable, or debug command to a name for shorthand use.
EVAL	EV	Display or change the value of a variable. Display the value of arrays, expressions, records, or structures.
SET	SE	Set debug options. Update production Yes/No, ignore case when using find function, and allow OPM programs to be used. Also can be set from the window displayed with this command.
STEP	S	Run one or more of the statements of the program being debugged.
FIND	F	Find a target line number, string, or text in the current module.
UP	U	Move the source member up the specified number of lines.
DOWN	D	Move the source member down the specified number of lines.
LEFT	L	Move the source member to the left the specified number of lines.
RIGHT	R	Move the source member to the right the specified number of lines.
TOP	T	Position the source member at the first line of source.
BOTTOM	B	Position the source member at the last line.
NEXT	N	Position the view to the next breakpoint in the source module.
PREVIOUS	P	Position the view to the previous breakpoint in the source module.
HELP	H	Show the online help.

In addition to this, the STEP command accepts two reserved words: OVER and INTO. These two reserved words refer to how to count the statements being executed. If you enter the command STEP 5 INTO and one of the lines in the next five statements calls another program, the system will go into that other program and continue counting lines until it has executed (in total) the number of lines indicated on the STEP command. It will then stop (even if it is in the called program) and display the Display Module Source panel. (This is true *only* if the called program also has debug data enabled within it.)

If you enter STEP 5 OVER and one of the lines in the next five statements calls another program, it will still execute the other program, but it will not count any of the lines in the other program. The CALL statement will count as only one line.

USING DEBUG TO DECIPHER I/O PROBLEMS

If your questions or problems involve I/O processing, you may find that running the Display Job (DSPJOB) command is useful while you are at a breakpoint. If you press F21 while on the Display Module Source panel, you will get a command line.

From the command line, key the DSPJOB command. You will then see the familiar Display Job menu of options. If you choose option 14 (Display Open Files, if active), you see all of the files that are open in your job stream.

By pressing a function key, you can see all of the I/O details for each file that is currently open (this includes your display files too!). These details include the file type, the I/O count (how many reads and writes), how the file was opened (input only or update, for example), the relative record number of the last record read (indicating where the current file pointer is), and whether the file was opened with a shared data path.

Depending on where your breakpoint is set, this information can help you solve a number of problems in your program. If the I/O count looks unusually high, you may be reading records that you did not intend to read. If the file was opened with a shared data path, you may have forgotten to reset your file pointer prior to your first read. When you are trying to solve data problems, this technique can often help you in your detective work.

DE SMALL PRINT

Source debugging is a powerful tool, but it has some limitations. The most serious of these is its inability to debug batch programs. It is hard to believe that IBM would leave this feature out. Hopefully, it will be added by the time this book is printed. If not, this is definitely another *requirement* for your next users' group.

DEBUGGING BATCH JOBS

Now that we have discussed the basics of starting Debug, setting breakpoints, and displaying program variables, it is time to talk about batch jobs. As we stated, to our knowledge, there is currently no way to debug ILE batch programs. But if you still have batch programs written in OPM, you may find this section of the chapter useful.

As you have probably noticed, all of the Debug data we displayed was brought up to the screen. That is great when we are talking about an interactive program, but what do we do when a batch program needs to be diagnosed?

Starting the Service Job

To run Debug on a batch program, you need to use a feature called a *service job*. Before initiating the service job, you need three components that describe the job you are debugging: the job name, the user, and the job number.

Finding this information is easy if the program happens to be at an error message or is already running (does the phrase "in a loop" come to mind?). You can use the Work with Active Jobs (WRKACTJOB) or Work with Submitted Jobs (WRKSBMJOB) commands to find the job in question and then take the option that reads "Work with Job." You will find all three parameters you need displayed at the top of the screen, as shown in Figure 10.8.

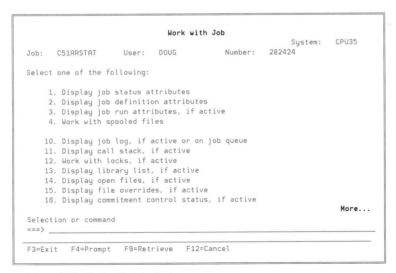

```
                              Work with Job
                                                    System:     CPU35
      Job:   C51ARSTAT      User:   DOUG        Number:   282424

      Select one of the following:

           1. Display job status attributes
           2. Display job definition attributes
           3. Display job run attributes, if active
           4. Work with spooled files

          10. Display job log, if active or on job queue
          11. Display call stack, if active
          12. Work with locks, if active
          13. Display library list, if active
          14. Display open files, if active
          15. Display file overrides, if active
          16. Display commitment control status, if active
                                                               More...
      Selection or command
      ===> _____

       F3=Exit   F4=Prompt   F9=Retrieve   F12=Cancel
```

Figure 10.8: Work with Job display.

If the job is already running, you need to put the job on hold. This is easily accomplished by using the WRKACTJOB or WRKSBMJOB commands and simply following the prompts on the screen.

On the other hand, if the job you want to debug is not already running, you need to go about it a little differently. You do not want the job to begin running until you have initiated the service job.

Place the job queue on hold with the Hold Job Queue (HLDJOBQ) command and then submit the job. Placing the job queue on hold does not stop existing programs from running, but it will keep new jobs in the queue from being initiated.

The next step is to submit your job. You can then use the WRKSBMJOB command to get the job identification parameters so you can start the service job.

By now, you should have written the job name, user, and number down. Key in STRSRVJOB and press F4. You should see a screen that looks like the one in Figure 10.9.

Figure 10.9: Starting a service job.

You may want to use a shortcut by keying the Start Service Job (STRSRVJOB) command while you are on the Work with Job display. The parameters you need to run the STRSRVJOB command are already at the top of your screen and can be entered from right to left. For example, if you are at the display seen in Figure 10.8 and you want to start your service job, key:

```
STRSRVJOB 282424/DOUG/C51ARSTAT
```

Using this method, you begin your service job from the command line on the Work with Job display. Let's move on to the next step.

Starting Debug on the Batch Job

Now that you have started the service job, you need to put the program into Debug. You can now use the STRDBG command just as if you are putting an interactive program into Debug. Note, though, that the system will not let you add your breakpoints until the job actually begins.

It is time to release the job queue using the Release Job Queue (RLSJOBQ) command. The system sends a break message when your job is ready to begin.

Defining Your Breakpoints

At this point, you must key F10 to get to a command entry screen. Your program is in Debug, but you have not told the system where you want it to break. To do that, use the ADDBKP or Add Trace (ADDTRC) functions to define where you want your program to stop, just as you would if you were debugging an interactive OPM job.

Perform the rest of the Debug functions as if the program is an interactive OPM program. That is all there is to it! When the job is complete, you get another break message informing you that the job being serviced has ended (do not confuse this with ending the service job).

Once the message has been delivered, you need to end both Debug and the service job. This can be done with the End Debug (ENDDBG) and End Service Job (ENDSRVJOB) commands, respectively. Failure to perform these cleanup functions could result in some rather unintentional and undesirable results later in your session.

JOURNALING AS A DEBUG TOOL

Every once in a while, we hear about a data file that mysteriously changes by itself. There seems to be no rhyme or reason to it. And because 24 different programs in seven different libraries are used to update this file, tracking down this anomaly is no small task. But wait! There is hope. You can use journaling to narrow down your search for the culprit.

Journaling is a process that records changes made to a physical file in an object called (appropriately enough) a *journal receiver*. These changes are recorded as journal entries, and are much like the journal entries you would find in a general ledger. The purpose of each is the same—recording a path that can be followed if you ever have to backtrack.

Generally speaking, journaling is used for automatic error recovery and is necessary if you use commitment control. For our purposes, we use it to help us track down the source of our wayward data.

But before you get too far into this subject, be aware that this technique can often consume quite a bit of disk space. Depending on how much activity occurs with the file in question, and how far it is between the intermittent data error you are looking for, the journal of file changes can get quite large. The journal not only records what has changed in the record, but also copies the entire record and the who, when, and where of the change. You obviously incur additional I/O while journaling is active, which may impact overall system performance. Like most things in life, you need to determine whether the potential benefits outweigh the cost.

Journaling 101

To perform journaling, you need to concern yourself with two principle components: the journal receiver and the journal itself. On the AS/400, it is the journal receiver that actually holds the journal entries (changes to the file, in our case). The journal itself is more like a directory of the file being journaled, the receivers that exist in the journal, and a variety of other information that describes the journal itself. Think of the journal as the header file when you have a system that has a header/detail record relationship (where the receiver is the detail record).

You need to create the journal receiver and then the journal. In the past, it was up to programmers and operators to maintain the journal receivers. Failure to do so would result in a situation where disk space would get gobbled up rapidly.

With the announcement of V3R1 came an improvement to the Create Journal (CRTJRN) command. You can now elect to have the journal receivers managed by the system itself. If you specify a threshold size when the journal receiver is created, and use the Manage Receiver (MNGRCV) parameter when the journal is created, the system cleans up the journal receivers for you. The operating system checks to see if your receiver has reached its threshold size at system IPL time. If the threshold is reached, the system detaches the active receiver from the journal and automatically creates and attaches a new receiver in its place. Once this action has been performed, the freshly deactivated journal may be saved (if desired) and deleted from the system to free up valuable disk space.

Before creating the journal, we must first create the receiver that will initially contain our journal entries. In the first example, we create a journal receiver called CUSTRCV in a library called TESTLIB. We do this by keying the following command:

```
CRTJRNRCV JRNRCV(TESTLIB/CUSTRCV)
```

We then create a journal named CUSTJRN in the TESTLIB library by keying the following command:

```
CRTJRN JRN(TESTLIB/CUSTJRN) JRNRCV(TESTLIB/CUSTRCV)
```

Note that we have indicated in the CRTJRN command the name of the initial receiver we will use to store our journal entries.

After those two simple commands, you are ready for your detective work. All you have to do to activate journaling is run the Start Journal Physical File (STRJRNPF) command. To begin the journaling of our CUSTOMER file in the TESTLIB library, we simply key:

```
STRJRNPF FILE(TESTLIB/CUSTOMER) JRN(CUSTJRN)
```

Now that journaling is active, our journal records everything that happens to our CUSTOMER file. This includes information about every time the file is opened, closed, or saved, and every time a record is written, deleted, or updated. In other words, every time the file is touched!

Reading the Journaling Results

Anytime we want to see all of the recorded journal entries for our CUSTOMER file, we key the following command:

```
DSPJRN JRN(TESTLIB/CUSTJRN)
```

A display similar to that shown in Figure 10.10 appears on screen. For the purposes of our example, though, we see a little too much information. We do not really care when the file was opened, closed, or saved. We are more interested in knowing the whos, whats, and whens of a program updating our file. Thankfully, the Display Journal (DSPJRN) command allows us to filter out the journal entries we do not want to see.

```
                      Display Journal Entries

 Journal  . . . . . . :   CUSTJRN       Library  . . . . . . :   TESTLIB

 Type options, press Enter.
  5=Display entire entry


 Opt   Sequence  Code  Type  Object    Library   Job         Time
  █           1  J     PR                         QPADEV0006  13:12:50
  _           2  D     JF    CUSTOMER  TESTLIB    QPADEV0006  13:13:19
  _           3  F     JM    CUSTOMER  TESTLIB    QPADEV0006  13:13:19
  _           4  F     OP    CUSTOMER  TESTLIB    QPADEV0006  13:13:36
  _           5  F     OP    CUSTOMER  TESTLIB    QPADEV0006  13:14:07
  _           6  R     UP    CUSTOMER  TESTLIB    QPADEV0006  13:14:07
  _           7  R     UP    CUSTOMER  TESTLIB    QPADEV0006  13:14:19
  _           8  R     UP    CUSTOMER  TESTLIB    QPADEV0006  13:14:22
  _           9  R     UP    CUSTOMER  TESTLIB    QPADEV0006  13:14:24
  _          10  R     UP    CUSTOMER  TESTLIB    QPADEV0006  13:14:26
  _          11  R     UP    CUSTOMER  TESTLIB    QPADEV0006  13:14:29
  _          12  R     UP    CUSTOMER  TESTLIB    QPADEV0006  13:14:30   +

 F3=Exit   F12=Cancel
```

Figure 10.10: Output from the DSPJRN command.

If you want to see only journal entries in which a record was changed, key the following command:

```
DSPJRN JRN(TESTLIB/CUSTJRN) JRNCDE((R))
```

The output from the DSPJRN command results in a screen similar to the one shown in Figure 10.10. Note that all entries under the Code heading are an R, indicating that we are looking at journal entries where a record has been changed. Under the Type heading, you see codes specifying the type of update that was performed. PT indicates that a record was added or posted, UP indicates an update, DL indicates where a record was deleted, and so on. You can place the cursor on the Type field and press Help to get a more complete list of the possible codes.

If you see an entry that piques your interest, you can key a 5 in front of that entry and press Enter to see a more detailed accounting of the journal entry. You are presented with a display that is similar to the one shown in Figure 10.11.

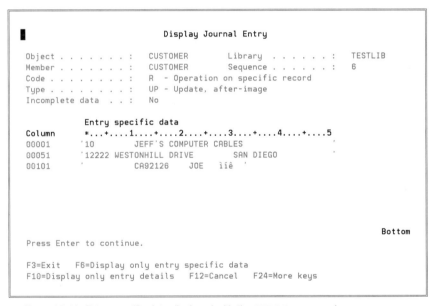

Figure 10.11: Entry-specific data displayed with the DSPJRN command.

The entry-specific data that is displayed may look scrambled if packed data exists in the record. If you want your "detective" to tell you the whos, whats, whens, and wheres, simply press F10 (Display only entry details). You are presented with a display similar to the one shown in Figure10.12, which tells you all of the above.

```
                        Display Journal Entry Details

  Journal  . . . . . . :   CUSTJRN         Library  . . . . . . :   TESTLIB
  Sequence . . . . . . :   6

  Code . . . . . . . . :   R  - Operation on specific record
  Type . . . . . . . . :   UP - Update, after-image

  Object . . . . . . . :   CUSTOMER        Library  . . . . . . :   TESTLIB
  Member . . . . . . . :   CUSTOMER        Flag . . . . . . . . :   0
  Date . . . . . . . . :   05/06/00        Time . . . . . . . . :   13:14:07
  Count/RRN  . . . . . :   1               Program  . . . . . . :   PFE0100

  Job  . . . . . . . . :   282417/DOUG/QPADEV0006
  User profile . . . . :   DOUG            Ref Constraint . . . :   No
  Commit cycle ID  . . :   0               Trigger  . . . . . . :   No


  Press Enter to continue.

  F3=Exit   F10=Display entry   F12=Cancel   F14=Display previous entry
  F15=Display only entry specific data
```

Figure 10.12: Entry details displayed via the DSPJRN command.

It is entirely possible that your journal contains too many entries to make this particular method practical, or that the data you are looking for is contained in a packed field. In either of these situations, you may want to display the information to an outfile. You could then code an RPG program that processes the outfile and, from there, narrow down your search.

When displaying a journal to an outfile, the DSPJRN command puts the first 100 bytes per record of your data into a single field that is a default length of 100 bytes. If you need to see more than the first 100 bytes of your file (we need 126 bytes in our CUSTOMER file example), use the Entry Data Length (ENTDTALEN) parameter of the DSPJRN command. If you do not, your data is automatically truncated.

To send our CUSTOMER file journal entries to an outfile named JOURNOUT in library TESTLIB, key:

```
DSPJRN JRN(TESTLIB/CUSTJRN) JRNCDE((R)) OUTPUT(*OUTFILE)
OUTFILE(TESTLIB/JOURNOUT) ENTDTALEN(126)
```

The *after* picture of the complete record is stored in a single field named JOESD (Journal Entry Specific Data). We could use the substring function of QRYDTA to parse out the data we are looking for, but we have found that looking at individual fields in the after picture is easier if you use an RPG program.

We do this by moving the JOESD field to an external data structure that has the same name as the file being journaled. For the example in Figure 10.13, we simply use our CUSTOMER physical file as an external data structure within our program. We did not code a File Specification for the customer file because our program uses the description of the customer file and not the actual file itself.

```
FFilename++IPEASFRlen+LKlen+AIDevice+.Keywords+++++++++++++++++++++++++Comments++++
FJOURNOUT  IF   E            DISK

DName++++++++++ETDsFrom+++To/L+++IDc.Keywords+++++++++++++++++++++++++Comments++++
D OUTFMT        E DS                  EXTNAME(CUSTOMER)

CLON01Factor1+++++++Opcode&ExtFactor2+++++++Result++++++++Len++D+HiLoEq...Comments
C                   READ     JOURNOUT                            50
C         *IN50     IFEQ     *OFF
C                   MOVEL    JOESD          OUTFMT
C                   ENDIF
```

Figure 10.13: RPG code to process a DSPJRN outfile .

The RPG program in Figure 10.13 could be used to read and interpret the data from the journal entries. Our example is incomplete because you would probably want to perform some sort of selective process to narrow down your search and then either send the data to a database file or to the printer.

Changing Receivers

Receivers can have voracious appetites. If left alone, one receiver can easily eat up your disk space without even belching. You can only curb its appetite by killing it. But before you can kill it (by deleting the journal receiver), you must detach it from the journal. To do this, issue the following command:

```
CHGJRN JRN(CUSTJRN) JRNRCV(*GEN)
```

This command detaches the Current Receiver (CUSTRCV), creates a new journal receiver, and attaches the new receiver to the journal. The name of the new receiver is the name of the old receiver with a four-digit sequence number attached to the end of the name. In our example, the name of the new receiver is CUSTRC0001. Notice that the sequence number automatically replaces the last digit of the receiver name because the original receiver name was seven characters long. If you prefer, make up your own name for the new receiver and enter it in the place of *GEN.

You are now free to kill the beast and get back all the storage it ate. Issue the following command:

```
DLTJRNRCV RCV(TESTLIB/CUSTRCV)
```

If you have not saved the receiver, you get the following error message:

```
CPA7025 - Receiver CUSTRCV in TESTLIB never fully saved. (I C).
```

After you reply to the message with an "I" to ignore it, the receiver is deleted.

Remember to Clean Up Your Mess

Once you have isolated your problem, you need to end journaling and clean up your disk. Before you can delete the journal, you must tell the system to stop journaling the file. You do that by issuing the following command:

```
ENDJRNPF FILE(TESTLIB/CUSTOMER)
```

You can then delete the journal by issuing the following command:

```
DLTJRN JRN(TESTLIB/CUSTJRN)
```

If you have created other receivers, do not forget to delete them.

JOB LOGS AND PROBLEM DETERMINATION

Job streams can get incredibly long and complex. Tracking down problems can become very difficult when you are dealing with these types of jobs. Sometimes your problem is hidden, and solving it is mostly a matter of figuring out how to retrieve more information from your system than is currently being offered. This is where the job log comes in.

Every job has a job log. If you are signed on and running an interactive session, your job log can keep track of the commands you are running, the messages you get, and the commands that are run from within the CL programs you call. The amount of information written to your job log is generally controlled by the job description you are currently running (more on this later in the chapter when we discuss logging levels).

When you are in an interactive session, your job log is maintained while your session is active and then is generally deleted when you sign off (depending on how your system is configured and the parameters you specify when you are running the SIGNOFF command). A batch job has its own job log that can be seen via the WRKSBMJOB command when you choose the option to review spooled files.

The job log can be the key to solving a problem that may not result in a visible error message. To see what is in your own job log, simply key DSPJOBLOG and press Enter, as in Figure 10.14. Note that you can display additional details by pressing F10 to see a screen similar to that shown in Figure 10.15. You are probably already familiar with these displays because they are accessible from so many other commands, such as WRKSBMJOB, WRKACTJOB, and DSPJOB.

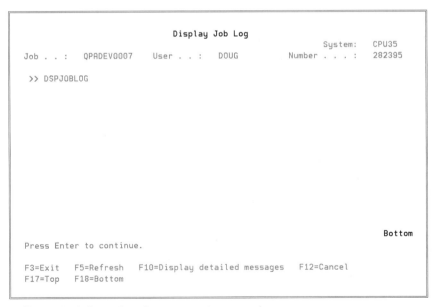

```
                            Display Job Log
                                                  System:    CPU35
 Job . . :    QPADEV0007   User . . :   DOUG      Number . . . :   282395

   >> DSPJOBLOG











                                                                   Bottom
   Press Enter to continue.

   F3=Exit    F5=Refresh    F10=Display detailed messages    F12=Cancel
   F17=Top    F18=Bottom
```

Figure 10.14: Output from the DSPJOBLOG command.

```
                          Display All Messages
                                                     System:    CPU35
 Job . . :   QPADEV0007    User . . :   DOUG       Number . . . :   282395

 2 >
     Last request at level 1 ended.
 2 >
     Last request at level 1 ended.
   > ENDDBG
   > WJ
   > DSPJRN JRN(CPUJRN)
     Object CPUJRN in library *LIBL not found.
   > C51LIB/LIBLIST C51
     Library list changed.
     Current library changed to C51CUSTOM.
   > DSPJRN JRN(CPUJRN)
     156 entries converted from journal CPUJRN in C51FILES.
   > DSPJOBLOG
                                                              More...
 Press Enter to continue.

 F3=Exit   F5=Refresh   F12=Cancel   F17=Top   F18=Bottom
```

Figure 10.15: Detailed messages displayed from the DSPJOBLOG command.

The Display Detailed Messages screen (which is displayed when you press F10 on the Display Job Log screen) shows the various commands that were run by the job. The job invocation level is also displayed directly before each command. The invocation level tells you how deeply nested a command is within a job. You can also use the DSPJOBLOG command to look at job logs of other users or jobs other than those of your current session (depending upon your security configuration) by specifying additional parameters. You can see the parameters when you press F4 after keying the command.

How Much Information Is Being Recorded in My Job Log?

The level of detail recorded in your job log is primarily a function of your message logging level and whether your job is recording CL program commands. Most systems are configured to record relatively little information because there is a performance hit that occurs when all commands and messages are being recorded.

Finding out how much information is currently being recorded in your job log is simple. Just run the DSPJOB command and choose the Display Job Definition Attributes option. You should see a display similar to the one shown in Figure 10.16.

```
                    Display Job Definition Attributes
                                                System:   CPU35
      Job:    QPADEV0007    User:   DOUG      Number:    282395

      Job description . . . . . . . . . . . . . . . . :   RONJOBD
        Library . . . . . . . . . . . . . . . . . . . :     RON
      Job queue . . . . . . . . . . . . . . . . . . . :
        Library . . . . . . . . . . . . . . . . . . . :
      Job priority (on job queue) . . . . . . . . . . :   5
      Output priority (on output queue) . . . . . . . :   5
      End severity  . . . . . . . . . . . . . . . . . :   30
      Message logging:
        Level . . . . . . . . . . . . . . . . . . . . :   4
        Severity  . . . . . . . . . . . . . . . . . . :   0
        Text  . . . . . . . . . . . . . . . . . . . . :   *NOLIST
      Log CL program commands . . . . . . . . . . . . :   *NO
      Printer device  . . . . . . . . . . . . . . . . :   NOPRINT
      Default output queue  . . . . . . . . . . . . . :   *DEV
        Library . . . . . . . . . . . . . . . . . . . :
                                                                  More...
      Press Enter to continue.

      F3=Exit   F5=Refresh   F12=Cancel   F16=Job menu
```

Figure 10.16: Determining message and CL program command logging levels.

As we mentioned before, the information displayed here is a byproduct of the job description (in this case, the JOBDESC job description in the QGPL library). As is the case with most things on the AS/400, these parameters may be overridden. Our areas of interest for the purposes of this topic are whether your job records CL program commands and what the message logging level settings for your jobs happen to be.

Logging Commands within CL Programs

If your job has been defined to log CL program commands, commands within CL programs are recorded in your job log when they are encountered. This is handy because it establishes an audit trail in your job log similar to that of the trace feature of Debug.

Message Logging

The message logging settings are based on three principle components: the message logging level, message severity, and message text level. The relationship of these three components determines the messages that are filtered from the job log and the ones that remain.

Parameter Definitions:

Message logging level: This parameter is used to tell the system how severe a message should be before it is logged into your job log. The possible values are 0 through 4.

0 - No messages are logged.

1 - Job start, completion, and completion status messages are logged. Also, all messages with a severity level greater than or equal to that indicated in the message severity parameter.

2 - All information recorded at level 1 plus any keyed commands or commands within a CL program that result in a message with a severity level greater than or equal to that indicated in the message severity parameter.

3 - All information recorded at level 2, plus any keyed commands or commands called from within a CL program.

4 - All information recorded at level 3, plus any trace messages.

Message severity: This parameter is used in conjunction with the previous message logging level parameter to indicate how severe an error should be before it is logged into the job log.

Message text level: This parameter is used to indicate how much data should be recorded in the job log when an error occurs that meets the criteria specified with the two prior parameters. These are:

*MSG   Only the message text of the error is recorded.

*SECLVL   The message text and the help text associated with the error are recorded in the job log.

*NOLIST   A job log is not produced unless the job ends abnormally. If a job log is created, the message text and the associated help text are recorded in the job log.

Changing Job Logging Levels

Depending on your needs, the logging level of a job may be changed on a temporary or permanent basis. If you want to change the logging level of your interactive session so it will record the most information possible, key:

```
CHGJOB LOG(4 0 *SECLVL) LOGCLPGM(*YES)
```

On the other hand, you can permanently change the logging level by changing the level set in the job description. To find out the job description under which you are running, you can use the DSPJOB command, as in Figure 10.17.

Be aware that changing the job description to record more information in the job log affects other jobs running under the job description. System performance is ultimately affected. Obviously, system overhead is required to log additional information. On the other hand, if your system is reasonably stable, you may want to reduce your default logging levels to help enhance performance.

If your desire is for the system to record more information so you can more easily track down problems, increasing the logging levels may help. You could change a job description named JOBDESC in QGPL to record the maximum information by keying:

```
CHGJOBD JOBD(QGPL/JOBDESC) LOG(4 0 *SECLVL) LOGCLPGM(*YES)
```

Another place where you may want to change your job logging levels is in a submitted job. You can actually change them with the SBMJOB command itself. To submit a job calling program XXX with the maximum logging level, key:

```
SBMJOB CMD(CALL PGM(XXX)) LOG(4 0 *SECLVL) LOGCLPGM(*YES)
```

Job logs for interactive sessions disappear when a user signs off using the default parameters of the Signoff command. The LOG parameter of the SIGNOFF command is usually set to the *NOLIST default, which tells the system the session job log is not needed after a user signs off. Changing the LOG parameter to *LIST causes the job log to be spooled to the printer.

Unfortunately, it is difficult to train many operators to change the sign-off parameters if they had problems during their session. Consequently, the problems encountered during the session are lost forever. One solution to this problem is to change the default for the SIGNOFF command. But this generates job logs for sessions where no problems are encountered, as well as for sessions that do have problems.

Perhaps a more sensible solution to this problem is a very useful program found in the *OS/400 Work Management Guide* (SC41-3306-00). The program (Figure 10.17) allows you to set up an initial menu program that only keeps the job logs if errors are encountered in the session. We find this to be a very useful program and well worth publishing again.

```
PGM
          DCLF MENU
          DCL &SIGNOFFOPT TYPE(*CHAR) LEN(7)
             VALUE(*NOLIST)
             .
             .
             .
          MONMSG MSG(CPF0000) EXEC(GOTO ERROR)
 PROMPT:  SNDRCVF RCDFMT(PROMPT)
          CHGVAR &IN41 '0'
             .
             .
             .
          IF (&OPTION *EQ '90') SIGNOFF
             LOG(&SIGNOFFOPT)
             .
             .
             .
          GOTO PROMPT
  ERROR:  CHGVAR &SIGNOFFOPT '*LIST'
          CHGVAR &IN41 '1'
          GOTO PROMPT
          ENDPGM
```

Figure 10.17: CL menu program to help manage job logs.

SOLUTIONS ARE BEST
FOUND BY THOSE WHO KNOW HOW TO LOOK FOR THEM

It seems painfully obvious, but it is a constant surprise to us how many programmers fail to learn to use the tools that are at their disposal. Programming is a lot more than just learning a programming language and writing code.

The best programmers are those who know how to use all of the tools in the toolbox. This includes the utilities that are shipped as part of the OS/400 operating system, the programming tools in this book, and the tools that are found within QUSRTOOL. The QUSRTOOL library, which was included with all releases of OS/400 prior to V3R1 (when it became a product available for purchase), should be required reading for AS/400 RPG programmers.

Take the time to learn how to use all of the tools at hand, and you may just become a master in your trade.

11

TOOLS FOR THE TOOLBOX

W e dedicate this chapter to explaining and detailing 11 of our favorite program-mer utilities (Table 11.1). We think they have made our job easier and are hopeful that others will also find this to be the case.

Table 11.1: A Summary of Tools for the Toolbox.

Command	Description
DSPPTH	The Display Path command is designed to help you instantly find all of the various keyed access paths that exist for a specific physical file. Specify the name and library of the physical file, and a display is presented that shows all of the various access paths that currently exist over the file. The utility displays the number of logical views that exist over the file and the keyed access path of each.
DSPFLD	The Display Field command gives you an instant, online look at all of the fields in a physical or logical file. The record length, number of fields, key fields, and file type are identified, as well as detail information on each field. The field-level detail includes field name, buffer positions, description text, size, and data type.
RGZPFFLTR	The Reorganize Physical File Filter command is designed to free up space on your system that is occupied by deleted records. The utility looks at all physical files on your system and automatically runs the Reorganize Physical File Member (RGZPFM) command on any file for which the percentage of deleted records in the file exceeds the threshold percentage you set when you run the RGZPFFLTR command.

Table 11.1: A Summary of Tools for the Toolbox (continued).

Command	Description
FNDDSPLF	The Find Displaced Logical Files command is designed to help you find logical files that do not reside in the same library as the physical file(s) they are over. This condition has the potential to be dangerous, particularly when libraries are saved or restored.
WRKOBJREF	The Work with Object Reference command is designed to allow you to display all references to a specified object in an online display. Some object types that may be displayed are files, programs, and data areas. If the object type happens to be a physical file, references to the logical files over it may be displayed as well.
SERPGMUSAG	The Service Program Usage command is a tool designed to help you manage programs written under the Integrated Language Environment (ILE). It is designed to help you identify those programs which were compiled referencing a specific service program.
MODUSAG	The Module Usage command is another ILE tool that will help you to identify which programs were compiled referencing a particular module (modules were formerly known as programs in the Original Program Model or OPM).
WRKFLD	The Work with Fields command will help you to identify fields in your system and their characteristics (i.e., field size, decimal positions, or name). It was originally designed to help programmers identify where date fields were being used in their systems to plan for the 21st century conversions.
DSPFILDSC	The Display File Description command is a slimmed down version of IBM's DSPFD command. The tool displays more concise information on a single screen with some DSPOBJD information thrown in as well.
SCNJOBLOG	The Scan Job Log command offers a consistent interface for scanning interactive and batch job logs. Information is displayed using filters by severity level and allows operator to scan for character strings.
FNDSRC	The Find Source command allows operators to search all source files on the system for a particular source member. It also allows the operator to perform a generic search over name or text description.

THE DISPLAY PATH (DSPPTH) COMMAND

When you sit down to write a new program on the AS/400, one of the first steps you need to take is to determine which paths are available for the data you need to process. To find the existing data paths over a physical file on the AS/400, you generally perform the following steps:

1. Run the Display Database Relations (DSPDBR) command over the physical file in question.

2. Write down the file and library names of each logical file found on the DSPDBR display.

3. Run the Display File Description (DSPFD) command over each logical file to see if the data path you need already exists.

These three steps can be time-consuming and cut into your productivity as a programmer. Some creative programmers have developed tools that perform these steps automatically, saving a lot of time along the way. These tools write the results of the DSPDBR command to an *outfile* and then either print them or bring them up on a display. Our Display Path (DSPPTH) command, however, goes one step further by using the system APIs discussed in chapter 9, bringing the information to the screen much more quickly.

The DSPPTH command output looks like the example shown in Figure 11.1. The path for the physical file is listed first. Key fields and sequence (ascending or descending) are shown, followed by any select omit statements used. Then the path information is listed for each logical file built over the physical file (even if the logical file is built in a different library).

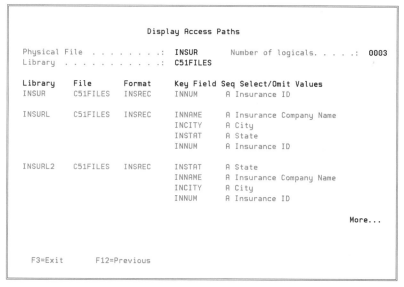

```
                         Display Access Paths

Physical File  . . . . . . . .:   INSUR        Number of logicals. . . . .:   0003
Library  . . . . . . . . . . .:   C51FILES

Library    File       Format    Key Field Seq Select/Omit Values
INSUR      C51FILES   INSREC     INNUM       A Insurance ID

INSURL     C51FILES   INSREC     INNAME      A Insurance Company Name
                                 INCITY      A City
                                 INSTAT      A State
                                 INNUM       A Insurance ID

INSURL2    C51FILES   INSREC     INSTAT      A State
                                 INNAME      A Insurance Company Name
                                 INCITY      A City
                                 INNUM       A Insurance ID

                                                              More...



   F3=Exit        F12=Previous
```

Figure 11.1: Output from the DSPPTH command.

329

As you can see from the preceding example, the various access paths for a file are easily found using the DSPPTH utility. There are three components that make up this utility: the DSPPTH command in Figure 11.2, the DSPPTHDS display file in Figure 11.3, and the DSPPTHRG RPG program in Figure 11.4.

```
/*==============================================================*/
/* To compile:                                                  */
/*                                                              */
/*          CRTCMD       CMD(XXX/DSPPTH) PGM(XXX/FIG1104RG)      */
/*                       SRCMBR(FIG1102CM)                       */
/*                                                              */
/*==============================================================*/
             CMD          PROMPT('DISPLAY ACCESS PATH')
             PARM         KWD(FILE) TYPE(NAME1) MIN(1) PROMPT('File +
                            Name:')
NAME1:       QUAL         TYPE(*NAME) LEN(10)
             QUAL         TYPE(*CHAR) LEN(10) DFT(*LIBL) SPCVAL((' ' +
                            *LIBL)) CHOICE('Name, *LIBL') +
                            PROMPT('Library Name:')
```

Figure 11.2: Source for the DSPPTH command.

```
**********************************************************************************
*  TO COMPILE:
*     CRTDSPF FILE(XXXLIB/FIG1103DS)
**********************************************************************************
AAN01N02N03T.Name++++++RLen++TDpBLinPosFunctions++++++++++++++++++++++++++++++
A                                        CF03     CF12
A           R SFLRCD                     SFL
A             SFLIBRARY    10A  O  7  2
A             SFFILENAME   10A  O  7 13
A             SFKEYFIELD   10A  O  7 35
A             SFFORMAT     10A  O  7 24
A             SFASENDDEC    1   O  7 46
A             SFTEXT       32   O  7 48
A  59                                    DSPATR(HI)
A           R SFLCTL                     SFLCTL(SFLRCD)
A                                        SFLSIZ(0024)   SFLPAG(0012)
A                                        OVERLAY
A  21                                    SFLDSP
A                                        SFLDSPCTL
A  53                                    SFLEND(*MORE)
A                                     1 29'Display Access Paths' DSPATR(HI)
A                                     3  2'Physical File . . . . . . . .:'
A             OUTFILE      10A  O  3 35DSPATR(HI)
```

Figure 11.3: Source for the FIG1103DS display file (part 1 of 2).

```
A                                 4  2'Library . . . . . . . . . . .:'
A           OUTLIBRARY   10A  0   4 35DSPATR(HI)
A                                 6  2'Library    '   DSPATR(HI)
A                                 6 13'File        '   DSPATR(HI)
A                                 6 35'Key Field'      DSPATR(HI)
A                                 6 49'Select/Omit Values'  DSPATR(HI)
A                                 6 24'Format'          DSPATR(HI)
A                                 6 45'Seq'             DSPATR(HI)
A                                 3 47'Number of logicals. . . . .:'
A           NBRLOGICS     4  00   3 77DSPATR(HI)
A         R FORMAT1
A                                23  4'F3=Exit'    COLOR(BLU)
A                                23 18'F12=Previous' COLOR(BLU)
```

Figure 11.3: Source for the FIG1103DS display file (part 2 of 2).

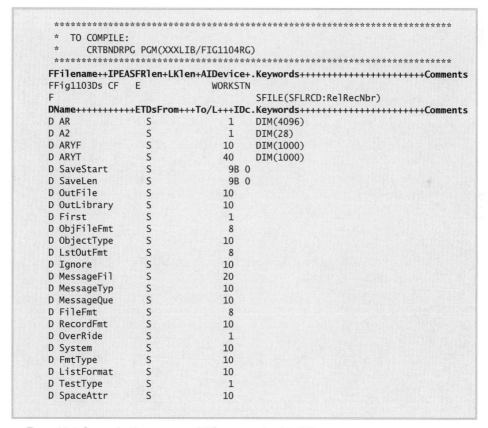

```
    ****************************************************************************
    *   TO COMPILE:
    *       CRTBNDRPG PGM(XXXLIB/FIG1104RG)
    ****************************************************************************
    FFilename++IPEASFRlen+LKlen+AIDevice+.Keywords++++++++++++++++++++++++++Comments
    FFig1103Ds CF   E                WORKSTN
    F                                         SFILE(SFLRCD:RelRecNbr)
    DName+++++++++++ETDsFrom+++To/L+++IDc.Keywords++++++++++++++++++++++++++Comments
    D AR            S               1    DIM(4096)
    D A2            S               1    DIM(28)
    D ARYF          S              10    DIM(1000)
    D ARYT          S              40    DIM(1000)
    D SaveStart     S               9B 0
    D SaveLen       S               9B 0
    D OutFile       S              10
    D OutLibrary    S              10
    D First         S               1
    D ObjFileFmt    S               8
    D ObjectType    S              10
    D LstOutFmt     S               8
    D Ignore        S              10
    D MessageFil    S              20
    D MessageTyp    S              10
    D MessageQue    S              10
    D FileFmt       S               8
    D RecordFmt     S              10
    D OverRide      S               1
    D System        S              10
    D FmtType       S              10
    D ListFormat    S              10
    D TestType      S               1
    D SpaceAttr     S              10
```

Figure 11.4: Source for the FIG1104RG RPG program (part 1 of 9).

```
D SpaceValue     S              1
D SpaceText      S             50
D SpaceAuth      S             10      INZ('*CHANGE')
D SpaceReplc     S             10      INZ('*YES')
D C              S              4 0
D S              S              4 0
D I              S              4 0
D I1             S              4 0
D I2             S              4 0
D B              S              4 0
D RelRecNbr      S              4 0
D SfCompare      S              2
D SfRule         S              1
D SfValue        S             28
D SFileLib       S             20
D RFileLib       S             20
D ObjReceivr     S            100
D StartPosit     S             9B 0
D StartLen       S             9B 0
D ReceiveLen     S             9B 0
D MessageKey     S             9B 0
D MsgDtaLen      S             9B 0
D MsgQueNbr      S             9B 0
D FilStartP      S             9B 0
D FilStartL      S             9B 0
D SpaceLen       S             9B 0 INZ(1024)
D InFileLib      S             20
D InputDs        DS
D  UserSpace                1   20
D   SpaceName               10      OVERLAY(UserSpace:1)
D   SpaceLib                10      OVERLAY(UserSpace:11)
D  OutFormat              21   28
D  FileLib                29   48
D   FileName                10      OVERLAY(FileLib:1)
D   FileLibr                10      OVERLAY(FileLib:11)
D ListDs         DS
D  MainFileLb               1   20
D  MainFile                 10      OVERLAY(MainFileLb:1)
D  MainLib                  10      OVERLAY(MainFileLb:11)
D  DependFil              21   30
D  DependLib              31   40
D                DS
D  FieldSpace               1   20
D  FSpaceName               10      OVERLAY(FieldSpace:1)
D  FSpaceLib                10      OVERLAY(FieldSpace:11)
D ErrorDs        DS                  INZ
D  BytesProvd               1    4B 0
D  BytesAvail               5    8B 0
D  MessageId                9   15
D  Err###                  16   16
D  MessageDta              17  116
```

Figure 11.4: Source for the FIG1104RG RPG program (part 2 of 9).

```
D KeyData          DS
D DependKey                 1        10
D AscendDes                14        14
D FindSelect       DS               150        INZ
D  FindFormat               70        79
D  NbrKeys                 117       118B 0
D  NbrSelOmit              130       131B 0
D  OffSelOmit              132       135B 0
D  OffSet                  136       139B 0
D KeySelect        DS               150        INZ
D  Rule                      3         3
D  Compare                   4         5
D  CompName                  6        15
D  NbrSO                    16        17B 0
D  OffsetSO                 29        32B 0
D KeySOS           DS               150        INZ
D  POffset                   1         4B 0
D  NL                        5         6B 0
D  SelectVar                21        48
D                 DS
D  FFileLib                  1        20
D  FFileLibr                          10        OVERLAY(FFileLib:1)
D  FFileName                          10        OVERLAY(FFileLib:11)
D FGeneralDs       DS                          INZ
D  FSizeInput              113       116B 0
D  FOffsetHed              117       120B 0
D  FSizeHead               121       124B 0
D  FOfftoList              125       128B 0
D  FNbrInList              133       136B 0
D  FSizeEntry              137       140B 0
D FListDs          DS
D  FFieldName                1        10
D  FFieldText               33        82
D GenHeadDs        DS                          INZ
D  InputSize               113       116B 0
D  ListOffset              125       128B 0
D  NumberList              133       136B 0
D  EntrySize               137       140B 0
D Receiver         DS              4096        INZ
D  NbrFormats               62        63B 0
D  DBFileOffS              317       320B 0
D  AccessType              337       338
D Requester        C                           CONST('*REQUESTER*LIBL')

CLON01Factor1+++++++Opcode&ExtFactor2+++++++Result++++++++Len++D+HiLoEq......
C     *ENTRY       PLIST
C                  PARM                        InFileLib
C                  EVAL        OutFile = %SUBST(InFileLib:1:10)
C                  EVAL        OutLibrary = %SUBST(InFileLib:11:10)
C                  EVAL        SpaceName = 'USRSPC'
C                  EVAL        SpaceLib = 'QTEMP'
```

Figure 11.4: Source for the FIG1104RG RPG program (part 3 of 9).

```
C                    EVAL      FileName = OutFile
C                    EVAL      FileLibr = OutLibrary
C                    EVAL      BytesProvd = 116
C                    EVAL      MessageFil = ('QCPFMSG   ' + 'QSYS')
C                    EVAL      *IN53 = *ON
 *  Create user space
C                    CALL      'QUSCRTUS'
C                    PARM                      UserSpace
C                    PARM                      SpaceAttr
C                    PARM      1024            SpaceLen
C                    PARM                      SpaceValue
C                    PARM                      SpaceAuth
C                    PARM                      SpaceText
C                    PARM                      SpaceReplc
C                    PARM                      ErrorDs
 *  Attempt to retrieve object description
C                    CALL      'QUSROBJD'
C                    PARM                      ObjReceivr
C                    PARM      100             ReceiveLen
C                    PARM      'OBJD0100'       ObjFileFmt
C                    PARM                      InFileLib
C                    PARM      '*FILE'          ObjectType
C                    PARM                      ErrorDs
 *  If file doesn't exist, send message and get out
C                    IF        MessageId <> *BLANKS
C                    EXSR      SNDMSG
C                    GOTO      END
C                    ENDIF
 *  Create user space for fields
C                    EXSR      SPACE1
 *
C                    EVAL      SFileLib = InFileLib
C                    EVAL      First = *ON
 *  Write access path
C                    EXSR      GETFIL
C     MessageId      CABEQ     'CPF5715'        NORECS
C     MessageId      CABEQ     'CPF3210'        END
C                    EVAL      First = *OFF
C                    EVAL      SpaceName = 'USRSPC'
C                    EVAL      SpaceLib = 'QTEMP'
 *  List database relations to user space
C                    CALL      'QDBLDBR'
C                    PARM                      UserSpace
C                    PARM      'DBRL0100'       LstOutFmt
C                    PARM                      SFileLib
C                    PARM      '*FIRST'         RecordFmt
C                    PARM      *BLANKS          Ignore
C                    PARM                      ErrorDs
C     MessageId      CABEQ     'CPF5715'        NORECS
C                    EVAL      StartPosit = 1
C                    EVAL      StartLen = 140
```

Figure 11.4: Source for the FIG1104RG RPG program (part 4 of 9).

```
C                     EVAL      SpaceName = 'USRSPC'

C                     EVAL      SpaceLib = 'QTEMP'
  * Retrieve user space general information
C                     CALL      'QUSRTVUS'
C                     PARM                     UserSpace
C                     PARM                     StartPosit
C                     PARM                     StartLen
C                     PARM                     GenHeadDs
C                     EVAL      StartPosit = 1
C                     EVAL      StartLen = InputSize
C                     EVAL      SpaceName = 'USRSPC'
C                     EVAL      SpaceLib = 'QTEMP'
  * Retrieve user space detail information
C                     CALL      'QUSRTVUS'
C                     PARM                     UserSpace
C                     PARM                     StartPosit
C                     PARM                     StartLen
C                     PARM                     InputDs
C                     EVAL      StartPosit = (ListOffset + 1)
C                     EVAL      StartLen = EntrySize
C                     EVAL      SaveLen = EntrySize
C                     EVAL      NbrLogics = NumberList
  * Retrieve the list by walking through the user space
B1 C                  DO        Nbrlogics
C                     EVAL      SpaceName = 'USRSPC'
C                     EVAL      SpaceLib = 'QTEMP'
C                     EVAL      SaveStart = StartPosit
C                     CALL      'QUSRTVUS'
C                     PARM                     UserSpace
C                     PARM                     StartPosit
C                     PARM                     StartLen
C                     PARM                     ListDs
C        DependFil    CABEQ     '*NONE'        NORECS
C                     EVAL      SpaceName = 'USRSPC'
C                     EVAL      SpaceLib = 'QTEMP'
C                     EVAL      SFileLib = DependFil
C                     EVAL      %SUBST(SFileLib:11:10) = DependLib
C                     EXSR      GETFIL
C                     EXSR      CLEAR
C                     EVAL      StartPosit = (SaveStart + SaveLen)
E1 C                  ENDDO
C        NORECS       TAG
C                     IF        RelRecNbr > 0
C                     EVAL      *In21 = *ON
E1 C                  ENDIF
C                     WRITE     FORMAT1
C                     EXFMT     SFLCTL
C        END          TAG
C                     EVAL      *InLr = *ON
  *
```

Figure 11.4: Source for the FIG1104RG RPG program (part 5 of 9).

```
      C     SNDMSG      BEGSR
      *  Send error message
      C                 CALL      'QMHSNDPM'
      C                 PARM                    MessageId
      C                 PARM                    MessageFil
      C                 PARM                    InFileLib
      C                 PARM      20            MsgDtaLen
      C                 PARM      '*STATUS'     MessageTyp
      C                 PARM      '*EXT'        MessageQue
      C                 PARM      1             MsgQueNbr
      C                 PARM                    MessageKey
      C                 PARM                    ErrorDs
      C                 ENDSR

      C     GETFIL      BEGSR
      *  Retrieve key field information for each logical file
      C                 CALL      'QDBRTVFD'
      C                 PARM                    Receiver
      C                 PARM      4096          ReceiveLen
      C                 PARM                    RFileLib
      C                 PARM      'FILD0100'    FileFmt
      C                 PARM                    SFileLib
      C                 PARM                    RecordFmt
      C                 PARM      '0'           OverRide
      C                 PARM      '*LCL'        System
      C                 PARM      '*EXT'        FmtType
      C                 PARM                    ErrorDs
      C     MessageId   CABEQ     'CPF5715'     ENDGET
      C                 MOVEA     Receiver      AR(1)
      C                 IF        First = *ON
      *  File must be a physical file
      C                 MOVE      AR(9)         TestType
      C                 TESTB     '2'           TestType              01
      C                 IF        *In01 = *ON
      C                 EVAL      MessageId = 'CPF3210'
      C                 EXSR      SNDMSG
      C                 GOTO      ENDGET
E2    C                 ENDIF
E1    C                 ENDIF

      C                 EVAL      I = DbFileOffs
B1    C                 DO        NbrFormats
      C                 MOVEA     AR(I)         FindSelect
      C                 EVAL      S = (Offset + 1)
      C                 IF        First = *OFF
      *  Write blank line for clarity
      C                 EXSR      CLEAR
      C                 EVAL      RelRecNbr = RelRecNbr + 1
      C                 WRITE     SFLRCD
E2    C                 ENDIF
      C                 EVAL      SfLibrary = %SUBST(RFileLib:1:10)
```

Figure 11.4: Source for the FIG1104RG RPG program (part 6 of 9).

```
     C                    EVAL      SfFileName = %SUBST(RFileLib:11:10)
     C                    EVAL      SfFormat = FindFormat
     C                    EXSR      GETTXT
B2   C                    DO        NbrKeys
     C                    MOVEA     AR(S)          KeyData
     C                    TESTB     '0'            AscendDes                  79
B3   C                    SELECT
     C                    WHEN      *In79 = *OFF
     C                    EVAL      SfAsendDec = 'A'
     C                    WHEN      *In79 = *ON
     C                    EVAL      SfAsendDec = 'D'
E3   C                    ENDSL
     C                    EVAL      SfKeyField = DependKey
     C                    DO        B          C
     C                    IF        ARYF(C) = DependKey
     C                    EVAL      SfValue = Aryt(C)
     C                    LEAVE
     C                    ENDIF
E3   C                    ENDDO
     C                    EVAL      SfText = SfValue
     C                    EVAL      RelRecNbr = RelRecNbr + 1
     C                    WRITE     SFLRCD
     C                    EVAL      SfLibrary = *BLANKS
     C                    EVAL      SfFileName = *BLANKS
     C                    EVAL      SfFormat = *BLANKS
     C                    EVAL      SfValue = *BLANKS
     C                    EVAL      S = S + 32
E2   C                    ENDDO
     *   If select/omit statements exist
     C                    IF        NbrSelOmit <> *ZEROS
     C                    EXSR      SELOMT
E2   C                    ENDIF
     C                    EVAL      SfCompare = *BLANKS
     C                    EVAL      SfRule = *BLANKS
     C                    EVAL      I = I + 160
E1   C                    ENDDO
     C        ENDGET      TAG
     C                    ENDSR

     C        SELOMT      BEGSR
     C                    EVAL      I1 = (OffSelOmit + 1)
B1   C                    DO        NbrSelOmit
     C                    MOVEA     AR(I1)         KeySelect
     C                    IF        Compare = 'AL'
     C                    ITER
E2   C                    ENDIF
     C                    EVAL      SfCompare = Compare
     C                    EVAL      SfRule = Rule
     C                    EVAL      I2 = OffsetSo + 1
     C                    DO        NbrSO
     C                    MOVEA     AR(I2)         KeySOS
```

Figure 11.4: Source for the FIG1104RG RPG program (part 7 of 9).

```
       C                    MOVEA     SelectVar    A2
       C                    EVAL      NL = NL - 19
       C                    IF        NL > *ZEROS
       C                    MOVEA     *BLANKS      A2(NL)
       C                    ENDIF
       C                    MOVEA     A2(1)           SfValue
       C                    EVAL      SfKeyField = CompName
       C                    EVAL      RelRecNbr = RelRecNbr + 1
       C                    EVAL      SfAsendDec = *BLANKS
       C                    EVAL      SfText = (SfRule + ' ' + SfCompare +
       C                              ' ' + SfValue)
       C                    EVAL      *In59 = *ON
       C                    WRITE     SFLRCD
       C                    EVAL      *In59 = *OFF
       C                    EVAL      I2 = POffset + 1
       C                    ENDDO
       C                    EVAL      I1 = (I1 + 32)
   E1  C                    ENDDO
       C                    ENDSR

       C      CLEAR         BEGSR
       C                    EVAL      SfLibrary = *BLANKS
       C                    EVAL      SfFileName = *BLANKS
       C                    EVAL      SfFormat = *BLANKS
       C                    EVAL      SfKeyField = *BLANKS
       C                    EVAL      SfText = *BLANKS
       C                    EVAL      SfCompare = *BLANKS
       C                    EVAL      SfRule = *BLANKS
       C                    EVAL      SfAsendDec = *BLANKS
       C                    ENDSR
        * Get text for each field
       C      GETTXT        BEGSR
       C                    EVAL      FFileName = SfFileName
       C                    EVAL      FFileLibr = SfLibrary
       C                    EVAL      FSpaceName = 'FLDSPC'
       C                    EVAL      FSpaceLib = 'QTEMP'
        * List fields to user space
       C                    CALL      'QUSLFLD'
       C                    PARM                   FieldSpace
       C                    PARM      'FLDL0100'   ListFormat
       C                    PARM                   FFileLib
       C                    PARM      SfFormat     RecordFmt
       C                    PARM      '1'          OverRide
       C                    Z-ADD     1            FilStartP
       C                    Z-ADD     140          FilStartL
       C                    EVAL      FSpaceName = 'FLDSPC'
       C                    EVAL      FSpaceLib = 'QTEMP'
        *  Retrieve user space general information
       C                    CALL      'QUSRTVUS'
       C                    PARM                   FieldSpace
       C                    PARM                   FilStartP
       C                    PARM                   FilStartL
       C                    PARM                   FGeneralDs
```

Figure 11.4: Source for the FIG1104RG RPG program (part 8 of 9).

```
        C                     EVAL      FilStartP = FOffsetHed + 1
        C                     EVAL      FilStartL = FSizeHead
        C                     EVAL      FSpaceName = 'FLDSPC'
        C                     EVAL      FSpaceLib = 'QTEMP'
        C                     EVAL      FilStartP = FOfftoList + 1
        C                     EVAL      FilStartL = FSizeEntry
        *    Retrieve the list by walking through the user space
   B1   C                     DO        FNbrInList
        C                     EVAL      FSpaceName = 'FLDSPC'
        C                     EVAL      FSpaceLib = 'QTEMP'
        C                     CALL      'QUSRTVUS'
        C                     PARM                    FieldSpace
        C                     PARM                    FilStartP
        C                     PARM                    FilStartL
        C                     PARM                    FListDs
        C                     EVAL      B = B + 1
        C                     EVAL      ARYF(B) = FFieldName
        C                     EVAL      ARYT(B) = FFieldText
        C                     EVAL      FilStartP = FilStartP + FSizeEntry
   E1   C                     ENDDO
        C                     ENDSR
        *   Create user space for listing fields
        C          SPACE1     BEGSR
        C                     EVAL      FSpaceName = 'FLDSPC'
        C                     EVAL      FSpaceLib = 'QTEMP'
        C                     CALL      'QUSCRTUS'
        C                     PARM                    FieldSpace
        C                     PARM      *BLANKS       SpaceAttr
        C                     PARM      1024          SpaceLen
        C                     PARM      *BLANKS       SpaceValue
        C                     PARM      '*CHANGE'     SpaceAuth
        C                     PARM      *BLANKS       SpaceText
        C                     PARM      '*YES'        SpaceReplc
        C                     PARM                    ErrorDs
        C                     ENDSR
```

Figure 11.4: Source for the FIG1104RG RPG program (part 9 of 9).

THE DISPLAY FIELD (DSPFLD) COMMAND

If you ever use the Display File Field Description (DSPFLD) command, you will want to consider this utility. The DSPFLD command provides an easy-to-read subfile display that shows all fields in a file. Buffer positions, key field identification, field description, record format length, and record format name are all condensed onto a single screen. The file field information also can be printed simply by pressing a function key. Figure 11.5 is an example of the DSPFLD command when it is run over our customer file.

```
                          Display File Fields
                                    Position to . . . . . . .:  _____
    Physical File  . . . . .: CUSTOMER     File Type . . . . . . .:        PF
    Library  . . . . . . . .: BOOKRPGIV    Record Length . . . . .:       132
    Record Format. . . . . .: CUSREC       Number of fields. . . .:         8

    Key Field      Length Dec Type From    To Text
    K1  CUSTOMER#      10       A     1     10 CUSTOMER#
        CUSTNAME       40       A    11     50 CUSTOMER NAME
        ADDRESS        30       A    51     80 CUSTOMER ADDRESS
        CITY           30       A    81    110 CUSTOMER CITY
        STATE           2       A   111    112 CUSTOMER STATE
        ZIP             9       A   113    121 ZIP CODE
        SALESMAN        5       A   122    126 SALESMAN
        PHONENBR       10    0  P   127    132 PHONE NUMBER



                                                                    Bottom


    F3=Exit      F12=Previous      F8=Print
```

Figure 11.5: Output from the DSPFLD command.

The DSPFLD utility consists of three source members: the DSPFLD command in Figure 11.6, the DSPFLDDS display file in Figure 11.7, and the DSPFLDRG RPG program in Figure 11.8.

```
/*===============================================================*/
/* To compile:                                                   */
/*                                                               */
/*          CRTCMD      CMD(XXX/DSPFLD) PGM(XXX/FIG1108RG)        */
/*                      SRCMBR(FIG1106CM)                         */
/*                                                               */
/*===============================================================*/
            CMD         PROMPT('List Fields')

            PARM        KWD(FILE) TYPE(QUAL) MIN(1) PROMPT('File')
            PARM        KWD(RCDFMT) TYPE(*NAME) DFT(*FIRST) +
                        SPCVAL((*FIRST)) PROMPT('Record format')

QUAL:       QUAL        TYPE(*NAME) LEN(10)
            QUAL        TYPE(*NAME) LEN(10) DFT(*LIBL) +
                        SPCVAL((*LIBL)) PROMPT('Library')
```

Figure 11.6: The DSPFLD command source.

```
A**********************************************************************
A*  TO COMPILE:
A*     CRTDSPF FILE(XXXLIB/FIG1107DS)
A**********************************************************************
AAN01N02N03T.Name++++++RLen++TDpBLinPosFunctions+++++++++++++++++++++++++++++++
A                                        CF03 CF12
A           R SFLRCD                     SFL
A             SFFLD        10A  O   8  6
A             SFLEN         5Y 0O   8 17EDTCDE(3)
A             SFTYPE        1A  O   8 28
A             SFFROM        5Y 0O   8 31EDTCDE(3)
A             SFTO          5Y 0O   8 37EDTCDE(3)
A             SFTEXT       38A  O   8 43
A             SFDEC         1A  O   8 25
A             SFKEY         3A  O   8  2DSPATR(HI)
A           R SFLCTL                     SFLCTL(SFLRCD)
A                                        SFLSIZ(0024) SFLPAG(0012)
A                                        CF08(08 'print')
A                                        OVERLAY
A 21                                     SFLDSP
A                                        SFLDSPCTL
A 53                                     SFLEND(*MORE)
A             RELRECPOS     4S 0H        SFLRCDNBR(*TOP)
A                                      1 28'Display File Fields'
A                                        DSPATR(HI)
A                                      3  2'Physical File . . . . .:'
A             OUTFILENAM   10A  O      3 28DSPATR(HI)
A                                      4  2'Library . . . . . . . .:'
A             OUTLIBNAME   10A  O      4 28DSPATR(HI)
A                                      7  6'Field' DSPATR(HI)
A                                      7 16'Length'  DSPATR(HI)
A                                      7 32'From'    DSPATR(HI)
A                                      7 43'Text'    DSPATR(HI)
A                                      7 40'To'      DSPATR(HI)
A                                      5  2'Record Format. . . . . .:'
A             OUTFORMAT    10A  O      5 28DSPATR(HI)
A                                      3 43'File Type . . . . . . .:'
A             OUTTYPE       5A  O      3 73DSPATR(HI)
A                                      7 23'Dec'     DSPATR(HI)
A                                      4 43'Record Length . . . . .:'
A             OUTRECLEN     6Y 0O      4 72DSPATR(HI) EDTCDE(3)
A                                      5 43'Number of fields. . . .:'
A             RELRECNBR     4Y 0O      5 74DSPATR(HI) EDTCDE(3)
A                                      7  2'Key'     DSPATR(HI)
A                                      7 27'Type'    DSPATR(HI)
A                                      2 43'Position to . . . . . .:'
A             POSITIONFL   10  B      2 68
A           R FORMAT1
A                                     23  4'F3=Exit'       COLOR(BLU)
A                                     23 18'F12=Previous' COLOR(BLU)
A                                     23 35'F8=Print'      COLOR(BLU)
```

Figure 11.7: The FIG1107DS display file source.

```
*******************************************************************************
*   TO COMPILE:
*       CRTBNDRPG PGM(XXXLIB/FIG1108RG)
*******************************************************************************
FFilename++IPEASFRlen+LKlen+AIDevice+.Keywords+++++++++++++++++++++++++Comments
FFIG1107DS CF   E                    WORKSTN
F                                             SFILE(SFLRCD:RelRecNbr)
FQSYSPRT   O    F   132               PRINTER OFLIND(*INOF)

DName++++++++++++ETDsFrom+++To/L+++IDc.Keywords+++++++++++++++++++++++++Comments
D AR              S               1    DIM(4096)
D AKEY            S              10    DIM(20)
D AK#             S               2  0 DIM(20)
D J               S               2  0
D JJ              S               2  0
D I               S               7  0
D S               S               7  0
D RelRecNbr       S               4  0
D RelRecHi#       S               4  0
D XX              S               7  0
D I1              S               1
D I2              S               2
D GENDS           DS
D  OffsetHdr          117       120B 0
D  SizeHeader         121       124B 0
D  OffsetList         125       128B 0
D  NbrInList          133       136B 0
D  SizeEntry          137       140B 0
D HeaderDs         DS
D  OutFileNam           1        10
D  OutLibName          11        20
D  OutType             21        25
D  OutFormat           31        40
D  RecordLen           41        44B 0
D InputDs          DS
D  UserSpace            1        20
D  SpaceName            1        10
D  SpaceLib            11        20
D  InpFileLib          29        48
D  InpFFilNam          29        38
D  InpFFilLib          39        48
D  InpRcdFmt           49        58
D ListDs           DS
D  SfFld                1        10
D  SfType              11        11
D  BufferOut           13        16B 0
D  FieldLen            21        24B 0
D  Digits              25        28B 0
D  Decimals            29        32B 0
D  FieldDesc           33        82
D ErrorDs          DS                  INZ
D  BytesPrv             1         4B 0
D  BytesAvl             5         8B 0
```

Figure 11.8: The FIG1108RG RPG program source (part 1 of 7).

```
D   MessageId                  9     15
D   ERR###                    16     16
D   MessageDta                17    116
D   ReceiveVr2      S               100
D   ReceiveVar      DS             4096
D   NbrOfFmts                 62     63B 0
D   DBFileOff                317    320B 0
D   FindSelDs       DS              150
D   NbrOfKeys                117    118B 0
D   KeyOffset                136    139B 0
D   KeyDataDs       DS
D   DependKey                  1     10
D                   DS
D   StartPosit                 1      4B 0
D   StartLen                   5      8B 0
D   SpaceLen                   9     12B 0
D   ReceiveLen                13     16B 0
D   MessageKey                17     20B 0
D   MsgDtaLen                 21     24B 0
D   MsgQueNbr                 25     28B 0
DGenSpcPtr                            *
DLstSpcPtr                            *
DHdrPtr                               *

CL0N01Factor1+++++++Opcode&ExtFactor2+++++++Result++++++++Len++D+HiLoEq......
C     *ENTRY      PLIST
C                 PARM                        FileLib         20
C                 PARM                        EntryFmt        10
C                 MOVEL(P)   'FFDSPC'         SpaceName
C                 MOVEL(P)   'QTEMP'          SpaceLib
C                 MOVEL      FileLib          InpFFilNam
C                 MOVE       FileLib          InpFFilLib
C                 EVAL       BytesPrv = 116
C     'QCPFMSG'   CAT        'QSYS':3         MSGF
C                 SETON                                                   53
 * Create the user space
C                 CALL       'QUSCRTUS'
C                 PARM                        UserSpace
C                 PARM       *BLANKS          SpaceAttr       10
C                 PARM       4096             SpaceLen
C                 PARM       *BLANKS          SpaceVal         1
C                 PARM       '*CHANGE'        SpaceAuth       10
C                 PARM       *BLANKS          SpaceText       50
C                 PARM       '*YES'           SpaceRepl       10
C                 PARM                        ErrorDs
 * Attemp to retrieve object description
C                 CALL       'QUSROBJD'
C                 PARM                        ReceiveVr2
C                 PARM       100              ReceiveLen
C                 PARM       'OBJD0100'       FileFormat       8
C                 PARM                        FileLib
C                 PARM       '*FILE'          ObjectType      10
C                 PARM                        ErrorDs
```

Figure 11.8: The FIG1108RG RPG program source (part 2 of 7).

```
      * If file doesn't exist, send message and get out
      C           IF        MessageId <> *BLANKS
      C           EXSR      SNDMSG
      C           GOTO      END
      C           ENDIF
      *
      C           EXSR      GETKEY
      * List fields to user space
      C           CALL      'QUSLFLD'
      C           PARM                  UserSpace
      C           PARM      'FLDL0100'  ListFormat        8
      C           PARM                  InpFileLIb
      C           PARM      EntryFmt    InpRcdFmt
      C           PARM      '1'         OverRide          1
      C           Eval      StartPosit = 1
      C           Eval      StartLen = 140
      C           CALL      'QUSRTVUS'
      C           PARM                  UserSpace
      C           PARM                  StartPosit
      C           PARM                  StartLen
      C           PARM                  GENDS
      C           EVAL      StartPosit = OffsetHdr + 1
      C           EVAL      StartLen = SizeHeader
      C           CALL      'QUSRTVUS'
      C           PARM                  UserSpace
      C           PARM                  StartPosit
      C           PARM                  StartLen
      C           PARM                  HeaderDs
      C           EVAL      SpaceName = 'FFDSPC'
      C           EVAL      SpaceLib = 'QTEMP'
      C           EVAL      StartPosit = OffsetList + 1
      C           EVAL      StartLen = SizeEntry
      * Do for number of fields
  B1  C           DO        NbrInList
      C           CALL      'QUSRTVUS'
      C           PARM                  UserSpace
      C           PARM                  StartPosit
      C           PARM                  StartLen
      C           PARM                  ListDs
      * Write the record to the subfile
      C           EXSR      WRITER
      C           EVAL      StartPosit = StartPosit + SizeEntry
  E1  C           ENDDO
      C           IF        RelRecNbr > 0
      C           EVAL      *IN21 = *ON
  E1  C           ENDIF
      C           EVAL      OutRecLen = RecordLen
      C     ' '   CHECKR    OutType     Z               1 0
      C           MOVEL(P)  OutType     F5                5
      C     5     SUB       Z           Z
      C           IF        Z < 5
      C           EVAL      OutType = *BLANKS
      C           CAT       F5:Z        OutType
```

Figure 11.8: The FIG1108RG RPG program source (part 3 of 7).

```
          C                    ENDIF
          C                    WRITE     FORMAT1
          C                    EVAL      RelRecPos = 1
          C          RESHOW    TAG
          C                    EXFMT     SFLCTL
          C                    IF        PositionFl <> *BLANKS
          C                    EXSR      REPOS
          C                    GOTO      RESHOW
          C                    ENDIF
          *   Print loop
B1        C                    IF        *IN08 = *ON
          C                    EXCEPT    HEDING
B2        C          1         DO        9998      X              4 0
          C          X         CHAIN     SFLRCD                     68
B3        C                    IF        *IN68 = *OFF
          C                    EXCEPT    DETAIL
E3        C                    ENDIF
E2        C   N68              ENDDO
E1        C                    ENDIF
          C          END       TAG
          C                    EVAL      *INLR = *ON
          *
          C          WRITER    BEGSR
          C                    EVAL      SFLEN = Digits
          C                    MOVE      Decimals      SFDEC
          C                    IF        SFLEN = *ZEROS
          C                    EVAL      SFLEN = FieldLen
          C                    EVAL      SFDEC = *BLANKS
E1        C                    ENDIF
          C                    EVAL      SFFROM = BufferOut
          C                    EVAL      SFTO = ((SFFROM + Fieldlen) - 1)
          C                    MOVEL     FieldDesc    SFTEXT
          C                    EVAL      SFKEY = *BLANKS
B1        C                    DO        20        I
          C                    IF        AKEY(I) = SFFLD
          C                    IF        AK#(I) < 10
          C                    MOVE      AK#(I)       I1          1
          C          'K'       CAT(P)    I1:0         SFKEY
X3        C                    ELSE
          C                    MOVE      AK#(I)       I2          2
          C          'K'       CAT(P)    I2:0         SFKEY
E3        C                    ENDIF
          C                    LEAVE
E2        C                    ENDIF
E1        C                    ENDDO
          C                    EVAL      RelRecNbr = (RelRecNbr + 1)
          C                    WRITE     SFLRCD
          C                    EVAL      RelRecHi# = RelRecNbr
          C                    ENDSR
          *
          C          REPOS     BEGSR
          C                    SELECT
          C                    WHEN      PositionFl = '*TOP'
```

Figure 11.8: The FIG1108RG RPG program source (part 4 of 7).

```
C                   EVAL      RelRecPos = 1
C                   WHEN      PositionFl = '*BOTTOM'
C                   EVAL      RelRecPos = (RelRecHi# - 10)
C                   IF        RelRecPos <= 0
C                   EVAL      RelRecPos = 1
C                   ENDIF
C                   OTHER
C                   DO        RelRecHi#     XX
C        XX         CHAIN     SFLRCD                              68
C                   IF        *IN68 = *OFF
C        ' '        CHECKR    PositionFl    P           2 0      68
C        PositionFl:P SCAN    SFTEXT                              60
C                   IF        (SFFLD = PositionFl) or (*IN60 = *ON)
C                   EVAL      RelRecPos = XX
C                   LEAVE
C                   ENDIF
C                   ENDIF
C                   ENDDO
C                   ENDSL
C                   EVAL      PositionFl = *BLANKS
C                   ENDSR
*
C        GETKEY     BEGSR
* Get key field information into ReceiveVar
C                   CALL      'QDBRTVFD'
C                   PARM                    ReceiveVar
C                   PARM      4096          ReceiveLen
C                   PARM                    InpFileLib
C                   PARM      'FILD0100'    FileFormat    8
C                   PARM                    FileLib       20
C                   PARM      EntryFmt      RecordFmt     10
C                   PARM      '0'           OverRide
C                   PARM      '*LCL'        System        10
C                   PARM      '*EXT'        FormatType    10
C                   PARM                    ErrorDs
C        MessageId  CABEQ     'CPF5715'     ENDGET
C                   MOVEA     ReceiveVar    AR(1)
C                   EVAL      I = DBFileOff
B1  C               DO        NbrofFmts
C                   MOVEA     AR(I)         FindSelDs
C                   EVAL      S = (KeyOffset + 1)
* Don't exceed array size
C                   IF        NbrOfKeys > 20
C                   EVAL      NbrOfKeys = 20
E2  C               ENDIF
C                   EVAL      JJ = 0
* Do for number of key fields
B2  C               DO        NbrOfKeys
C                   MOVEA     AR(S)         KeyDataDs
C                   EVAL      J = (J + 1)
C                   EVAL      JJ = (JJ + 1)
C                   MOVEA     DependKey     AKEY(J)
C                   MOVEA     JJ            AK#(JJ)
```

Figure 11.8: The FIG1108RG RPG program source (part 5 of 7).

```
      C                     EVAL      S = (S + 32)
E2    C                     ENDDO
      C                     EVAL      I = (I + 160)
E1    C                     ENDDO
      C     ENDGET          TAG
      C                     ENDSR
       *
      C     SNDMSG          BEGSR
       *  Send error message
      C                     CALL      'QMHSNDPM'
      C                     PARM                    MessageId
      C                     PARM                    MSGF           20
      C                     PARM                    FileLib
      C                     PARM      20            MsgDtaLen
      C                     PARM      '*DIAG'       MessageTyp     10
      C                     PARM      '*'           MessageQue     10
      C                     PARM      1             MsgQueNbr
      C                     PARM                    MessageKey
      C                     PARM                    ErrorDs
      C                     ENDSR

      O..............N01N02N03Field+++++++++YB.End++PConstant/editword/DTformat...
      OQSYSPRT   E          HEDING           3 02
      O             OR   OF
      O                                         5 'DATE:'
      O                     UDATE         Y    14
      O                                        75 'PAGE:'
      O                     PAGE          Z    80
      O                                        48 'DISPLAY FIELD FOR FILE'
      O                     OutFileNam         59
       *
      O          E          HEDING           1
      O             OR   OF
      O                                        24 'PHYSICAL FILE...........'
      O                     OutFileNam         35
      O                                        64 'FILE TYPE..............'
      O                     OutType            75
       *
      O          E          HEDING           1
      O             OR   OF
      O                                        24 'LIBRARY................'
      O                     OutLibName         35
      O                                        64 'RECORD LENGTH..........'
      O                     OutRecLen     Z    75
       *
      O          E          HEDING           3
      O             OR   OF
      O                                        24 'RECORD FORMAT..........'
      O                     OutFormat          35
      O                                        64 'NUMBER OF FIELDS........'
      O                     RelRecNbr     Z    78
       *
      O          E          HEDING           1
```

Figure 11.8: The FIG1108RG RPG program source (part 6 of 7).

```
O        OR    OF
O                                            22 'KEY    FIELD    LENGTH'
O                                            45 'DEC  TYPE  FROM    TO'
O                                            75 'TEXT...................'
 *
O        EF        DETAIL        1
O                  SFKEY                   4
O                  SFFLD                  16
O                  SFLEN        Z         20
O                  SFDEC                  27
O                  SFTYPE                 32
O                  SFFROM       Z         39
O                  SFTO         Z         45
O                  SFTEXT                 88
 *
```

Figure 11.8: The FIG1108RG RPG program source (part 7 of 7).

THE REORGANIZE PHYSICAL FILE FILTER (RGZPFFLTR) COMMAND

Those of us whose career paths closely paralleled the development of the family of IBM midrange systems initially found the AS/400 to be a bit of an enigma. All of the rules with which we were familiar regarding the placement of data had changed. Our trusty CATALOG was replaced with a variety of tools we could use to determine how much disk was used and where the files were stored, but the days of using a single command to determine what had gobbled up all of our DASD were long gone.

In Search of Missing DASD...

Many improvements made to the AS/400 operating system make the task of tracking down the missing DASD easier. Print Disk Information (PRTDSKINF) can be used to help reveal some of the disk utilization. But the very nature of the AS/400 operating system can make tracking down overall disk usage a difficult thing to expose.

One area where lost DASD can reside is in deleted records. When you delete a record on the AS/400, the record is simply blanked out or, more specifically, changed to *null* characters when the delete operation occurs. The deleted record is then ignored on subsequent I/O operations for that file. The significance of this point is that the "deleted" record still takes up the same amount of space on disk. This may not matter very much if the file was built to reuse deleted records (reusing deleted records is one of the options in the Create

Physical File [CRTPF] and Change Physical File [CHGPF] commands), but most files are not configured in this way because it can negatively impact performance.

Deleted records continue to take up space on the DASD until the file is reorganized. This occurs when, and if, RGZPFM is run. Depending on your AS/400 software, you may have hidden DASD that could be recovered on your system. Many AS/400 software packages do not reorganize physical files on a regular basis. Some do not perform this file maintenance at all.

If you are curious as to whether files on your system contain deleted records, you can use the DSPFD command over a few of the files to find out. You may be in for a little surprise.

The Reorganize Physical File Filter (RGZPFFLTR) command identifies files on your system that contain deleted records and automatically reorganizes them for you. It prints a status report informing you of how much DASD was regained using the utility. You can also specify the percentage of deleted records that must exist in each file before file reorganization occurs.

The Long and the Short of It

We employed the RGZPFFLTR command to greatly reduce the length of time our month-end process took to complete. Our month-end used to reorganize all of the major files in the system whether or not they needed it. This was primarily because there was no easy way to tell which files had deleted records in them.

Because this utility selectively reorganizes the files based on the percentage of deleted records, our month-end process now only reorganizes the files that need it. The amount of time our this process takes is reduced by more than 50 percent.

What's Under the Hood?

The command in Figure 11.9 accepts three parameters. The first, library name, also accepts the value *ALL, which causes the program to look at all files in the system. The second parameter is the percentage of deleted records that must exist in the file before the reorganization is performed. If a Y (for yes) is entered as the last parameter, the files that meet the established criteria are listed, but the reorganization is not performed.

```
/*================================================================*/
/* To compile:                                                    */
/*                                                                */
/*          CRTCMD    CMD(XXX/RGZPFFLTR) PGM(XXX/FIG1110RG)        */
/*                    SRCMBR(FIG1109CM)                            */
/*                                                                */
/*================================================================*/
            CMD       PROMPT('Reorganize Files Filter)')
            PARM      KWD(LIBRARY) TYPE(*CHAR) LEN(10) MIN(1) +
                        CHOICE('Name, *ALL') PROMPT('Library  . . +
                        . . . . . . . . .')
            PARM      KWD(PERCENT) TYPE(*DEC) LEN(2) DFT(10) +
                        MIN(0) PROMPT('Percent . . . . . . . . . +
                        . .')
            PARM      KWD(PRONLY) TYPE(*CHAR) LEN(1) RSTD(*YES) +
                        DFT(N) VALUES(Y N) MIN(0) +
                        PROMPT('Print only ? . . . . . . . . .') +
                        CHOICE('Y, N')
```

Figure 11.9: The RGZPFFLTR command source.

The RPG program for the RGZPFFLTR utility is shown in Figure 11.10. The CL program is represented in Figure 11.11.

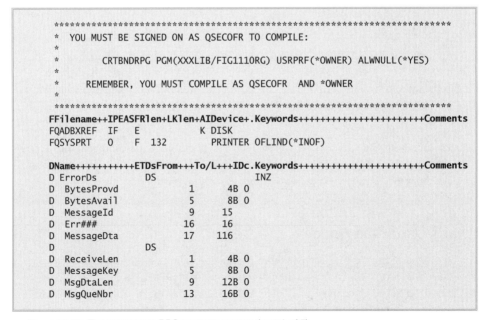

```
    ********************************************************************
    *   YOU MUST BE SIGNED ON AS QSECOFR TO COMPILE:
    *
    *          CRTBNDRPG PGM(XXXLIB/FIG1110RG) USRPRF(*OWNER) ALWNULL(*YES)
    *
    *   REMEMBER, YOU MUST COMPILE AS QSECOFR  AND *OWNER
    *
    ********************************************************************
    FFilename++IPEASFRlen+LKlen+AIDevice+.Keywords+++++++++++++++++++++++++Comments
    FQADBXREF  IF   E          K DISK
    FQSYSPRT   O    F 132         PRINTER OFLIND(*INOF)

    DName+++++++++++++ETDsFrom+++To/L+++IDc.Keywords+++++++++++++++++++++++++Comments
    D ErrorDs          DS                   INZ
    D  BytesProvd              1      4B 0
    D  BytesAvail              5      8B 0
    D  MessageId               9     15
    D  Err###                 16     16
    D  MessageDta             17    116
    D                  DS
    D  ReceiveLen              1      4B 0
    D  MessageKey              5      8B 0
    D  MsgDtaLen               9     12B 0
    D  MsgQueNbr              13     16B 0
```

Figure 11.10: The RGZPFFLTR RPG program source (part 1 of 5).

```
D Variable        DS          500
D  TotalBytes             1     4B 0
D  AvailBytes             5     8B 0
D  NbrRecords           141   144B 0
D  NbrDeleted           145   148B 0
D  DtaStrkSiz           149   152B 0
D  AccPathSiz           153   156B 0
D AfterTotal      S            10  0
D AllTotals       S            10  0
D B4AccPath       S            10  0
D B4AccSize       S            10  0
D B4Total         S            10  0
D DiffTotal       S            10  0
D Err             S             1A
D FileFormat      S             8A
D                 DS
D FileLibr                     20A
D  FLibrary                    10A   overlay(FileLibr:11)
D FormatName      S             8A
D Library         S            10A
D MemberName      S            10A
D MessageFil      S            20A
D MessageQue      S            10A
D MessageTyp      S            10A
D ObjectType      S            10A
D OverPerc        S             1A
D Percent         S             2  0
D PrintOnly       S             1A
D Reorg           S             1A
D Result          S             7  2
D TotalFile       S             7  0
D TotalOut        S             5  1
D TotalRecrd      S             9  0
D TotalReorg      S             7  0
D TotalType       S             2A
D TestPerc        S             2  0
D KeyField        S             5

CLON01Factor1+++++++Opcode&ExtFactor2+++++++Result++++++++Len++D+HiLoEq......
C     *ENTRY      PLIST
C                 PARM                      Library
C                 PARM                      Percent
C                 PARM                      PrintOnly
C                 EVAL      BytesProvd = 116
C                 SELECT
C                 WHEN      Library = '*ALL'
C     *LOVAL      SETLL     QADBXREF
C                 OTHER
C                 EXSR      EXIST
C     Library     SETLL     QADBXREF
C                 ENDSL
C                 IF        Err <> *ON
C                 EXCEPT    HEADNG
```

Figure 11.10: The RGZPFFLTR RPG program source (part 2 of 5).

```
C                       DOU       *In41
C                       IF        Library = '*ALL'
C                       READ      QADBXREF                               41
C                       ELSE
C       Library         READE     QADBXREF                               41
C                       ENDIF
C                       IF        *In41 = *OFF
C                       IF        (DBXATR = 'PF') AND (DBXTYP = 'D')
C                       EVAL      Reorg = *OFF
C                       EVAL      TotalFile = TotalFile + 1
C                       EXSR      RGZCHK
C                       IF        Reorg = *ON
C                       EVAL      B4AccSize = DtaStrkSiz
C                       EVAL      B4AccPath = AccPathSiz
C                       IF        PrintOnly <> 'Y'
C                       EXSR      RGZFIL
C                       ENDIF
C                       EXSR      PRINT
C                       EVAL      TotalReorg = TotalReorg + 1
C                       ENDIF
C                       ENDIF
C                       ENDIF
C                       ENDDO
C                       IF        AllTotals > 1000000
C       AllTotals       DIV(H)    1000000      TotalOut
C                       EVAL      TotalType = 'MB'
C                       ELSE
C                       IF        AllTotals > 1024
C       AllTotals       DIV(H)    1024         TotalOut
C                       EVAL      TotalType = 'KB'
C                       ENDIF
C                       ENDIF
C                       EXCEPT    TOTAL
C                       ENDIF
C                       EVAL      *InLr = *ON
* Ensure that requested library exists
C       EXIST           BEGSR
C                       MOVEL     Library      FileLibr
C                       MOVEL     'QSYS'       FLibrary
C                       CALL      'QUSROBJD'
C                       PARM                   Variable
C                       PARM      500          ReceiveLen
C                       PARM      'OBJD0100'   FileFormat
C                       PARM                   FileLibr
C                       PARM      '*LIB'       ObjectType
C                       PARM                   ErrorDs
C                       IF        MessageId <> *BLANKS
C       'QCPFMSG'       CAT       'QSYS':3     MessageFil
C                       CALL      'QMHSNDPM'
C                       PARM                   MessageId
C                       PARM                   MessageFil
C                       PARM                   Library
C                       PARM      10           MsgDtaLen
```

Figure 11.10: The RGZPFFLTR RPG program source (part 3 of 5).

```
C                      PARM      '*STATUS'     MessageTyp
C                      PARM      '*EXT'        MessageQue
C                      PARM      1             MsgQueNbr
C                      PARM                    MessageKey
C                      PARM                    ErrorDs
C                      EVAL      Err = *ON
C                      ENDIF
C                      ENDSR
 * Call CL program to perform reorg of file
C     RGZFIL          BEGSR
C                      IF        DBXNKF = 0
C                      EVAL      KeyField = '*NONE'
C                      ELSE
C                      EVAL      KeyField = '*FILE'
C                      ENDIF
C                      CALL      'FIG1111CL'
C                      PARM                    DBXLIB
C                      PARM                    DBXFIL
C                      PARM                    KeyField
 * Get new sizes
C                      EXSR      RTVMBR
C                      ENDSR
 * See if reorg needs to be done
C     RGZCHK          BEGSR
C                      EVAL      Reorg = *OFF
C                      MOVEL     DBXFIL        FileLibr
C                      MOVE      DBXLIB        FileLibr
C                      EVAL      ReceiveLen = 500
C                      EXSR      RTVMBR
C                      IF        (NbrRecords = 0) AND (NbrDeleted  0)
C                      EVAL      Reorg = *ON
C                      ENDIF
C                      IF        (NbrRecords <> 0) AND (NbrDeleted <> 0)
C                      EVAL      TotalRecrd = NbrDeleted + NbrRecords
C                      IF        TotalRecrd <> 0
C     NbrDeleted      DIV       TotalRecrd    Result
C     Result          MULT      100           TestPerc
C                      IF        TestPerc > Percent
C                      EVAL      Reorg = *ON
C                      ENDIF
C                      ENDIF
C                      ENDIF
C                      ENDSR
 * Accumulate totals and print detail
C     PRINT           BEGSR
C                      EVAL      B4Total = B4AccSize + B4AccPath
C                      EVAL      AfterTotal = DtaStrkSiz + AccPathSiz
C                      EVAL      DiffTotal = B4Total - AfterTotal
C                      EVAL      AllTotals = AllTotals + DiffTotal
C                      EXCEPT    DETAIL
C                      ENDSR
 * Retreive member description
C     RTVMBR          BEGSR
```

Figure 11.10: The RGZPFFLTR RPG program source (part 4 of 5).

```
C                       CALL      'QUSRMBRD'
C                       PARM                    Variable
C                       PARM                    ReceiveLen
C                       PARM      'MBRD0200'    FormatName
C                       PARM                    FileLibr
C                       PARM      '*FIRST'      MemberName
C                       PARM      '0'           OverPerc
C                       PARM                    ErrorDs
C                       ENDSR


O..............N01N02N03Field+++++++++YB.End++PConstant/editword/DTformat++.+
OQSYSPRT    E            HEADNG        1 01
O           OR    OF
O                                               9 'LIBRARY'
O                                              18 'FILE'
O                                              39 'BEFORE SIZE'
O                                              54 'AFTER SIZE'
O                                              69 'FILE SAVED'
O                                              84 'TOTAL SAVED'
OQSYSPRT    EF           DETAIL        1
O                        DBXLIB               12
O                        DBXFIL               24
O                        B4Total       1      39
O                        AfterTotal    1      54
O                        DiffTotal     1      69
O                        AllTotals     1      84
OQSYSPRT    EF           TOTAL         2 2
O                                              24 'TOTAL BYTES SAVED.......'
O                        TotalOut      1      39
O                        TotalType            42
OQSYSPRT    EF           TOTAL         1
O                                              24 'PHYSICAL FILES PROCESSED'
O                        TotalFile     Z      39
OQSYSPRT    EF           TOTAL         1
O                                              24 'FILES REORGANIZED.......'
O                        TotalReorg    Z      39
```

Figure 11.10: The RGZPFFLTR RPG program source (part 5 of 5).

```
/***********************************************************************/
/*   TO CREATE:                                                        */
/*        CRTCLPGM PGM(XXXLIB/FIG1111CL)                               */
/***********************************************************************/
PGM (&LIB &FILE &KEYFIELD)
DCL &LIB  *CHAR 10
DCL &FILE *CHAR 10
DCL &KEYFIELD *CHAR 5
MONMSG CPF0000
          RGZPFM    FILE(&LIB/&FILE) KEYFILE(&KEYFIELD)
ENDPGM
```

Figure 11.11: The RGZPFFLTR CL program source.

THE FIND DISPLACED LOGICAL FILE (FNDDSPLF) COMMAND

If a logical file resides in a different library than the physical file(s) it is over, you can end up with some rather unintentional and undesirable results. This tool helps you identify the *outlaw logical* file and do what it takes to bring it to justice.

We have all done it at one time or another. Our object library option in PDM is not what we think it is, or our library list was messed up when we compiled that new logical file. In many cases, we end up with a job that does not complete normally and we go on to correct the situation.

But what if the conditions are such that the job does complete normally? The end result is that we create an outlaw logical file that resides in a different library than the physical file it is over.

This condition is potentially dangerous for a number of reasons. Among them are nasty little error messages that come up when a program is called that is looking for a logical file that is nowhere to be found in the library list. Your update program could inadvertently update the wrong data file! Another reason could be revealed during the Save/Restore process. If the physical file does not already reside on disk when the system attempts to restore the outlaw logical file, the system gives you an error message and the logical file is not restored.

What makes this situation alarming is that you may have an outlaw on your system and not even know it. It may be lurking around the next corner waiting to pounce upon some poor unsuspecting user at the worst possible time.

The good news is that you can do something about it. You can use this utility to sniff out those nasty varmints and put them back where they belong.

Finding the Bad Guys

The Find Displaced Logical File (FNDDSPLF) command can be run over a specific library, library list, or all libraries on your system. The program finds all outlaw logical files in the libraries specified and brings them up in a subfile display, as seen in Figure 11.12.

```
                         Find Displaced Logical Files

    Physical     Library      Logical      Library      Created By    Created On
    RFINS        C51FILES     REFNOL3      C51WORK      LORI           1/27/00
    ECSTYP       DAKBAS5      ECSTYPL1     DAKFILES     KATHY          1/04/99
    AA@ARGLR     DALFILES     AA@ARGL1     DALBAS5      DEEV           2/07/00
    AA@ARGLR     DALFILES     AA@ARGR1     DALBAS5      DEEV           2/07/00
    AA@SHFT      DBSFILES     AA@SHFT1     DBSBAS5      KATHY         11/15/99
    APAPT        DM2WORK      APLDRORD     POINT40      KATHY          4/30/98
    DOCTR        FDMBAS5      DOCTRL5      FDMFILES     MARK           3/25/99
    FCLAS        FDMBAS5      FCLASL1      SATFILES     MONICA         1/31/00
    FCLAS        FDMBAS5      FCLASL1      FDMFILES     MONICA         1/31/00
    COLAGNCY     GHGFILES     COLAGNCYL    GHGBASE      ANDREY         2/01/00
    COLAGNCY     HCRFILES     COLAGNCYL    HCRBAS5      QSECOFR        3/14/00
    ACCES        HEPWORK      ACCES        HEPHOLDLIB   QSECOFR        8/20/99
    ACRWRKPF     HEPWORK      ACRWRKPF     HEPHOLDLIB   QSECOFR        8/20/99
    ADAY         HEPWORK      ADAY         HEPHOLDLIB   QSECOFR        8/20/99
    AGEFAM       HEPWORK      AGEFAM       HEPHOLDLIB   QSECOFR        8/20/99
    AMEMO        HEPWORK      AMEMO        HEPHOLDLIB   QSECOFR        8/20/99
                                                                      More...

    F3=Exit
```

Figure 11.12: Output from the FNDDSPLF command.

The program displays outlaw logical files even if the physical file they are over is not in the specified libraries. If the physical file and the logical file meet the designated search criteria, you see the record listed twice in the subfile.

How It Is Done

The program is a simple subfile display program over the system file QADBLDNC. This file is the *dependency logical multiple-format file* over the QADBFDEP file that can be found in the QSYS library. The QADBLDNC file is used to define the relationship between all of the physical and logical files on your system.

The command (Figure 11.13), display file (Figure 11.14), and RPG program (Figure11.15) that follow are all you need for this handy utility. Refer to the compile notes found in the source members for instructions.

```
/*==========================================================*/
/* To compile:                                              */
/*                                                          */
/*          CRTCMD    CMD(XXX/FNDDSPLF) PGM(XXX/FIG1115RG)   */
/*                    SRCMBR(FIG1113CM)                      */
/*                                                          */
/*==========================================================*/
            CMD       PROMPT('Find Displaced Logical Files')
            PARM      KWD(LIBRARY) TYPE(*CHAR) LEN(10) DFT(*LIBL) +
                      SPCVAL((*ALL)) MIN(0) CHOICE('Name, +
                      *LIBL, *ALL') PROMPT(Library:)
```

Figure 11.13: The FNDDSPLF command.

```
    ************************************************************************
    *   TO COMPILE:
    *       CRTDSPF FILE(XXXLIB/FIG1114DS)
    ************************************************************************
    AAN01N02N03T.Name++++++RLen++TDpBLinPosFunctions++++++++++++++++++++++++++
    A                                       CA03(03 'End of Program')
    A                                       PRINT(*LIBL/QSYSPRT)
    A           R SFLRCD                     SFL
    A             DBFFIL      10A  O  4  5
    A             DBFLIB      10A  O  4 18
    A             DBFFDP      10A  O  4 31
    A             DBFLDP      10A  O  4 44
    A             CRE8BY      10   O  4 57
    A             WHEN        6Y 00  4 70EDTCDE(Y)
    A           R SFLCTL                     SFLCTL(SFLRCD)
    A                                        SFLSIZ(0032)
    A                                        SFLPAG(0016)
    A                                        OVERLAY
    A 21                                     SFLDSP
    A                                        SFLDSPCTL
    A 41                                     SFLEND(*MORE)
    A                                      1 26'Find Displaced Logical Files'
    A                                        DSPATR(HI)
    A                                      3  5'Physical'
    A                                        DSPATR(HI)
    A                                      3 18'Library'
    A                                        DSPATR(HI)
    A                                      3 31'Logical'
    A                                        DSPATR(HI)
    A                                      3 44'Library'
    A                                        DSPATR(HI)
    A                                      3 57'Created By'
    A                                        DSPATR(HI)
    A                                      3 70'Created On'
    A                                        DSPATR(HI)
    A           R FMT1
    A                                     22  6'F3=Exit'
    A                                        COLOR(BLU)
```

Figure 11.14: The FIG1114DS display file source.

```
*****************************************************************************
*  TO COMPILE:
*     CRTBNDRPG PGM(XXXLIB/FIG1115RG)
*****************************************************************************

FFilename++IPEASFRlen+LKlen+AIDevice+.Keywords+++++++++++++++++++++++++++Comments
FFIG1114DS CF   E                    WORKSTN
F                                             SFILE(SFLRCD:RelRecNbr)
FQADBLDNC  IF   E           K DISK

DName+++++++++++ETDsFrom+++To/L+++IDc.Keywords++++++++++++++++++++++++++++Comments
D AR            S                 1   DIM(4096)
D ALIB          S                10   DIM(50)
D ErrorDs       DS                    INZ
D  BytesProvd          1      4B 0
D  BytesAvail          5      8B 0
D  MessageId           9     15
D  Err###             16     16
D  MessageDta         17    116
D              DS
D  ReceiveLen          1      4B 0
D  MessageKey          5      8B 0
D  MsgDtaLen           9     12B 0
D  MsgQueNbr          13     16B 0
D ReceivedDs    DS          4096
D  TotalBytes          1      4B 0
D  TotalAvail          5      8B 0
D  NbrSysLibs         65     68B 0
D  NbrPrdLibs         69     72B 0
D  NbrCurLibs         73     76B 0
D  NbrUsrLibs         77     80B 0
D Receiver1     DS           460
D  WHENYR             66     67 0
D  WHENMD             68     71 0
D  CRE8BY            220    229
D              DS
D  FFileLibr                 20
D   FLibrary                 10   OVERLAY(FFileLibr:1)
D   FSystem                  10   OVERLAY(FFileLibr:11)
D NoneFound     C                 CONST('No outlaw logicals f-
D                                 ound in')
D NowSearch     C                 CONST('Now searching files -
D                                 for outlaw logicals')
D Err           S                1A
D FileFormat    S                8A
D FileLibr      S               20A
D I             S                4 0
D PassInLibr    S               10A
D InternlJob    S               16A
D J             S                4 0
D JobName       S               26A
D Library       S               10A
D MData         S               50A
D MessageFil    S               20A
```

Figure 11.15: The FIG1115RG RPG program (part 1 of 4).

```
D MessageQue       S             10A
D MessageTyp       S             10A
D ObjectType       S             10A
D RelRecNbr        S              4 0

CLON01Factor1+++++++Opcode&ExtFactor2+++++++Result++++++++Len++D+HiLoEq.....
C     *ENTRY        PLIST
C                   PARM                    PassInLibr
C     'QCPFMSG'     CAT          'QSYS':3    MessageFil
C                   EVAL         BytesProvd = 116
C                   EVAL         Err = *OFF
C                   EVAL         Library = PassInLibr
 *    Make sure library exists
C                   IF           (Library <> '*ALL') AND (Library <> '*LIBL')
C                   EXSR         EXIST
C                   ENDIF
C                   IF           Err = *OFF
C                   EVAL         MsgDtaLen = 40
C                   EVAL         MData = NowSearch
C                   EVAL         MessageId = 'CPF9898'
C                   EVAL         MessageTyp = '*STATUS'
C                   EVAL         MessageQue = '*EXT'
C                   EVAL         MsgQueNbr = 0
C                   EXSR         SNDERR
C                   SELECT
C                   WHEN         Library = '*ALL'
C     *LOVAL        SETLL        QDBFDEP
C                   WHEN         Library = '*LIBL'
C                   EXSR         LIBLST
C     Library       SETLL        QADBLDNC
C                   OTHER
C     Library       SETLL        QADBLDNC
C                   ENDSL
C                   DOU          *In41
C                   IF           (Library = '*ALL') OR (Library = '*LIBL')
C                   READ         QDBFDEP                               41
C                   ELSE
C     Library       READE        QADBLDNC                              41
C                   ENDIF
C                   IF           *In41 = *OFF
C                   IF           DBFLIB <> DBFLDP
C                   EVAL         MessageID = *BLANKS
 * Get created information
C                   EXSR         GETCRT
C                   IF           MessageId = 'CPF9812'
C                   ITER
C                   ENDIF
C                   Z-ADD        0              WHEN
C                   MOVEL        WHENMD         WHEN
C                   MOVE         WHENYR         WHEN
C                   EVAL         RelRecNbr = RelRecNbr + 1
C                   WRITE        SFLRCD
C                   ENDIF
C                   ELSE
```

Figure 11.15: The FIG1115RG RPG program (part 2 of 4).

```
C                   IF        (PassInLibr = '*LIBL')
C                   EVAL      I = I + 1
C                   IF        ALIB(I) <> *BLANKS
C                   MOVEA     ALIB(I)        Library
C       Library     SETLL     QADBLDNC
C                   EVAL      *In41 = *OFF
C                   ENDIF
C                   ENDIF
C                   ENDIF
C                   ENDDO
 *
C                   IF        RelRecNbr <> 0
C                   EVAL      *In21 = *ON
C                   WRITE     FMT1
C                   EXFMT     SFLCTL
C                   ELSE
 *  No libraries found with outlaw logicals
C                   EVAL      MsgDtaLen = 38
C                   EVAL      MData = NoneFound + ' ' + Library
C                   EVAL      MessageId = 'CPF9898'
C                   EVAL      MessageTyp = '*STATUS'
C                   EVAL      MessageQue = '*EXT'
C                   EVAL      MsgQueNbr = 1
C                   EXSR      SNDERR
C                   ENDIF
C                   ENDIF
C                   EVAL      *InLr = *ON
 *  Get who created logical file and when
C       GETCRT      BEGSR
C                   EVAL      FLibrary = DBFFDP
C                   EVAL      FSystem = DBFLDP
C                   CALL      'QUSROBJD'
C                   PARM                    Receiver1
C                   PARM      460           ReceiveLen
C                   PARM      'OBJD0300'    FileFormat
C                   PARM                    FFileLibr
C                   PARM      '*FILE'       ObjectType
C                   PARM                    ErrorDs
C                   ENDSR
 *  Make sure requested library exists
C       EXIST       BEGSR
C                   EVAL      FLibrary = Library
C                   EVAL      FSystem = 'QSYS'
C                   CALL      'QUSROBJD'
C                   PARM                    ReceivedDs
C                   PARM      5000          ReceiveLen
C                   PARM      'OBJD0100'    FileFormat
C                   PARM                    FFileLibr
C                   PARM      '*LIB'        ObjectType
C                   PARM                    ErrorDs
C                   IF        MessageId <> *BLANKS
C                   EVAL      MsgDtaLen = 10
C                   EVAL      MData = Library
C                   EVAL      MessageTyp = '*DIAG'
```

Figure 11.15: The FIG1115RG RPG program (part 3 of 4).

```
C                         EVAL       MessageQue = '*       '
C                         EVAL       MsgQueNbr = 1
C                         EXSR       SNDERR
C                         ENDIF
C                         ENDSR
 * Send error back to caller
C       SNDERR            BEGSR
 * Send error message
C                         CALL       'QMHSNDPM'
C                         PARM                   MessageId
C                         PARM                   MessageFil
C                         PARM                   MData
C                         PARM                   MsgDtaLen
C                         PARM                   MessageTyp
C                         PARM                   MessageQue
C                         PARM                   MsgQueNbr
C                         PARM                   MessageKey
C                         PARM                   ErrorDs
C                         EVAL       Err = *ON
C                         ENDSR
 * Get library list
C       LIBLST            BEGSR
C                         CALL       'QUSRJOBI'
C                         PARM                   ReceivedDs
C                         PARM       5000        ReceiveLen
C                         PARM       'JOBI0700'  FileFormat
C                         PARM       '*'         JobName
C                         PARM                   InternlJOb
C                         MOVEA      ReceivedDs  AR(1)
C                         EVAL       I = (NbrSysLibs * 11) + 81
C                         EVAL       J = 1
 * Product libraries
C                         DO         NbrPrdLIbs
C                         MOVEA      AR(I)       ALIB(J)
C                         EVAL       J = J + 1
C                         EVAL       I = I + 11
C                         ENDDO
 * Current libraries
C                         DO         NbrCurLibs
C                         MOVEA      AR(I)       ALIB(J)
C                         EVAL       J = J + 1
C                         EVAL       I = I + 11
C                         ENDDO
 * User libraries
C                         DO         NbrUsrLibs
C                         MOVEA      AR(I)       ALIB(J)
C                         EVAL       J = J + 1
C                         EVAL       I = I + 11
C                         ENDDO
C                         MOVEA      ALIB(1)     Library
C                         EVAL       I = 1
C                         ENDSR
```

Figure 11.15: The FIG1115RG RPG program (part 4 of 4).

THE WORK WITH
OBJECT REFERENCE (WRKOBJREF) COMMAND

The following is a basic law of programming: Program complexity grows until it exceeds the capability of the programmer to maintain it. Change management systems (costing tens of thousands of dollars) have been created to help address this particular problem.

The Art of Change Management

One common problem with change management is trying to locate all the programs that reference a file, a data area, or even another program. Changing an object can be a scary thing if you do not know how many other objects in the system may be affected. Wouldn't it be nice to have a command that shows all objects that reference another?

In order to have such a command, you need to build a reference file. The Build Object Reference (BLDOBJREF) command submits a program to build an object reference file that shows all objects that reference another object. The program creates one record in the file for each reference. An inquiry program can be written to access the reference file, with the result being a very useful change management tool. The Work with Object Reference (WRKOBJREF) command is designed to perform just such a function.

Before you take the time to implement this tool, be aware that it is not perfect. Its reference file is created using the Display Program Reference (DSPPGMREF) command, which cannot pick up programs called using the QCMDEXC API. If your programs use the QCMDEXC command extensively, this tool may not be as useful as you would like.

Running the WRKOBJREF Command

All you need to do to run the WRKOBJREF command is key WRKOBJREF and press F4 (you need to build your object reference summary file prior to the execution of this command). After completing this, you see a prompt screen similar to that in Figure11.16.

Fill in the prompt with the library name, object name, and object type (*FILE, *PGM, *DTAARA, for example), and press Enter. If the type you specify happens to be a file, you are prompted for an extra set of parameters, as shown in Figure 11.17. These parameters are necessary to determine whether the object you specify happens to be a physical file. If it is, you can specify that the search of reference occurrences include any logical files that may be related to the physical file.

```
                    WORK with OBJECT REFERENCES (WRKOBJREF)

   Type choices, press Enter.

   OBJRFPF Library: . . . . . . . .    _____    Name
   Object name: . . . . . . . . . .    _____    Name
   Object type: . . . . . . . . . .    _____      Character value










                                                         Bottom
   F3=Exit   F4=Prompt   F5=Refresh   F12=Cancel   F13=How to use this display
   F24=More keys
```

Figure 11.16: Running the WRKOBJREF command.

```
                    WORK with OBJECT REFERENCES (WRKOBJREF)

   Type choices, press Enter.

   OBJRFPF Library: . . . . . . . . > BOOKRPGIV    Name
   Object name: . . . . . . . . . . > CUSTOMER     Name
   Object type: . . . . . . . . . . > *FILE        Character value
   Is Object a Physical File?: . . > Y             Y, N
   Include logicals over file?: . .   Y             N, Y
   Physical file library: . . . . .   *LIBL        Character value










                                                         Bottom
   F3=Exit   F4=Prompt   F5=Refresh   F12=Cancel   F13=How to use this display
   F24=More keys
```

Figure 11.17: Running the WRKOBJREF command on physical files.

Once you establish your search criteria and press Enter, you see an Object Reference display similar to that shown in Figure 11.18.

```
                         Work with Object References

   Object name. . . . CUSTOMER




       Name      Library    Text                                Useage  Logical
       FG209RG   BOOKRPGIV  RPG program for customer subfile     INPUT   PHYSICAL
       FG414RG   BOOKRPGIV  Sample RPG program for record locks  UNKNOWN PHYSICAL
       FG703RG   BOOKRPGIV  Using Sort Array (SORTA)             INPUT   PHYSICAL
       FG704RG   BOOKRPGIV  Multi column customer phone list using INPUT PHYSICAL
       FIG1155CL BOOKRPGIV  Display joblog spooled file with Scan OUTPUT PHYSICAL
       FIG1162CL BOOKRPGIV  Find source members retrieve library l       PHYSICAL




                                                                         Bottom

       F3=Exit      F12=Previous
```

Figure 11.18: Sample output from the WRKOBJREF command.

Getting Started with the WRKOBJREF Command

Because of the number of source members required to make the BLDOBJREF and WRKOBJREF commands work, we put together a CL program that builds all of the required objects for you. The first thing you need to do is get all of the source members into your desired library, put them in a physical source file named SOURCE (if needed, you can use the CRTSRCPF command to create the file), and then compile and call the OBJMAKECL program. The OBJMAKECL program builds everything you need to run these two commands.

Compile the OBJMAKECL program as follows:

```
CRTCLPGM PGM(XXXLIB/OBJMAKECL) SRCMBR(FG1123CL)
```

To run the OBJMAKECL program, simply key:

```
CALL OBJMAKECL PARM('XXXLIB')
```

Once the OBJMAKECL program has been run, you are ready to build your Object Reference pointer file. To do this, simply key BLDOBJREF and press F4. You are prompted for the libraries you want to include in your Object Reference pointer file and the date and time at which you want the command to execute.

Note: XXXLIB is the library where you have put the OBJREF source members.

How often you need to run the BLDOBJREF command depends on how much your programs change. If you are in a development environment like ours, you may want to incorporate this command into your daily startup programs, as we have. The data in your Object Reference pointer files can obviously only be current to the last time you ran the BLDOBJREF command. It is important to note that BLDOBJREF will replace data from any previous BLDOBJREF jobs that met the same criteria.

The Value of the WRKOBJREF Command

We find this tool to be tremendously valuable when we have to change existing objects in our system. The command provides a quick way to determine what is involved in the task, as well as a list of the source members that need to be changed. There are two commands in this utility: BLDOBJREF and WRKOBJREF. BLDOBJREF (Figure 11.19) is used to build the work files. Figures 11.20 through 11.28 make up the display files, RPG programs, and CL programs used to build or work with the files created by the BLDOBJREF command. WRKOBJREF (Figure 11.29) is used to display the object reference instances. Even though compile notes have been added in the remarks sections of these source members, the previously described OBJMAKECL program should take care of all of this for you.

```
/*==========================================================*/
/* To compile:                                              */
/*                                                          */
/*          CRTCMD    CMD(XXX/BLDOBJREF) PGM(XXX/FIG1125CL)  */
/*                    SRCMBR(FIG1119CM)                      */
/*                                                          */
/*==========================================================*/
          CMD       PROMPT('BUILD OBJECT REFERENCE')
          PARM      KWD(LIB) TYPE(*NAME) PROMPT('LIBRARY FOR FILE:') MIN(1)
          PARM      KWD(LIST) TYPE(LIST1) MIN(1) MAX(100) +
                    PROMPT('LIST OF LIBRARIES:')
          PARM      KWD(JOBQ) TYPE(*CHAR) LEN(10) DFT(QBATCH) +
                    PMTCTL(*PMTRQS) PROMPT('JOB QUEUE:')
          PARM      KWD(SCDATE) TYPE(*CHAR) LEN(6) DFT(*CURRENT) +
                    SPCVAL((*CURRENT 000000)) PMTCTL(*PMTRQS) +
                    PROMPT('SCHEDULE DATE:')
          PARM      KWD(SCTIME) TYPE(*CHAR) LEN(4) DFT(*CURRENT) +
                    SPCVAL((*CURRENT 0000)) PMTCTL(*PMTRQS) +
                    PROMPT('SCHEDULE TIME (MILITARY):')
          PARM      KWD(JOBN) TYPE(*CHAR) LEN(10) DFT(BUILDREF) +
                    PMTCTL(*PMTRQS) PROMPT('JOB NAME:')
LIST1:    ELEM      TYPE(*NAME) LEN(10) MIN(1) EXPR(*YES) +
                    PROMPT('LIBRARY NAME')
```

Figure 11.19: The BLDOBJREF command.

```
/****************************************************************************/
/*    TO CREATE:                                                            */
/*         CRTCLPGM PGM(XXXLIB/FIG1120CL                                    */
/****************************************************************************/
PGM (&FILE &LIB)

DCL VAR(&FILE) TYPE(*CHAR) LEN(10)
DCL VAR(&LIB) TYPE(*CHAR) LEN(10)

MONMSG CPF0000

          IF        COND(&LIB *EQ '          ') THEN(DO)
          CHGVAR    VAR(&LIB) VALUE('*LIBL')
          ENDDO

          CLRPFM    FILE(QTEMP/OBJRFLOG)

          DSPDBR    FILE(&LIB/&FILE) OUTPUT(*OUTFILE) +
                    OUTFILE(QTEMP/OBJRFLOG)

ENDPGM
```

Figure 11.20: The FIG1120CL CL program.

```
     ***************************************************************************
     *   TO COMPILE:
     *      CRTBNDRPG PGM(XXXLIB/FIG1121RG)
     ***************************************************************************
     *
     *     PROGRAM NAME - FIG1121RG
     *     FUNCTION     - TAKE FILE FROM DSPPGMREF AND WRITE PERTINENT
     *                    INFO TO SCANABLE FILE.
     *

     FFilename++IPEASFRlen+LKlen+AIDevice+.Keywords++++++++++++++++++++++++Comments
     FPGMREFO   IF  E             DISK
     FOBJRFPF   O   E             DISK

     CLON01Factor1++++++Opcode&ExtFactor2++++++Result+++++++Len++D+HiLoEq......
        C       1             SETLL     PGMREFO
B1      C                     DOU       *IN50 = *ON
        C                     READ      PGMREFO                                50
B2      C                     IF        *IN50 = *ON
        C                     LEAVE
E2      C                     ENDIF
        C                     EVAL      OBJLIB = WHLIB
        C                     EVAL      OBJNAM = WHPNAM
        C                     EVAL      OBJTXT = WHTEXT
        C                     EVAL      OBRNAM = WHFNAM
        C                     EVAL      OBRLIB = WHLNAM
        C                     MOVEL     WHFUSG        OBRUSE
        C                     EVAL      OBRTYP = WHOTYP
        C                     WRITE     OBJREC
E1      C                     ENDDO
        *
        C                     EVAL      *INLR = *ON
```

Figure 11.21: The FIG1121RG RPG program.

```
/*****************************************************************************/
/*    TO CREATE:                                                             */
/*        CRTCLPGM PGM(XXXLIB/FIG1122CL                                      */
/*****************************************************************************/
PGM  (&LIBRARY &REPADD &REFLIB)

DCL &LIBRARY *CHAR 10
DCL &REPADD *CHAR 1
DCL &REFLIB  *CHAR 10

            DSPPGMREF  PGM(&LIBRARY/*ALL) OUTPUT(*OUTFILE) +
                       OUTFILE(QTEMP/PGMREFO) OUTMBR(*FIRST)
```

Figure 11.22: The FIG1122CL CL program (part 1 of 2).

367

```
               OVRDBF    FILE(OBJRFPF) TOFILE(&REFLIB/OBJRFPF)
               OVRDBF    FILE(PGMREFO) TOFILE(QTEMP/PGMREFO)

IF COND(&REPADD *EQ 'R') THEN(DO)
CLRPFM &REFLIB/OBJRFPF
ENDDO

CALL FIG1121RG

               DLTOVR PGMREFO
               DLTOVR OBJRFPF

ENDPGM
```

Figure 11.22: The FIG1122CL CL program (part 2 of 2).

```
/*****************************************************************************/
/*    TO CREATE:                                                             */
/*         CRTCLPGM PGM(XXXLIB/FIG1123CL)                                    */
/*****************************************************************************/
PGM (&LIB)

DCL &LIB *CHAR 10
DCL &MSGDTA *CHAR 50
DCL &NOADD *CHAR 1

               ADDLIBLE   &LIB
               MONMSG     MSGID(CPF2103) EXEC(DO)
               CHGVAR     &NOADD '1'
               ENDDO

               CHGVAR     VAR(&MSGDTA) VALUE('Creating OBJRFPF file')
               SNDPGMMSG  MSGID(CPF9898) MSGF(QSYS/QCPFMSG) +
                            MSGDTA(&MSGDTA) TOPGMQ(*EXT) MSGTYPE(*STATUS)
               CRTPF      FILE(&LIB/OBJRFPF) SRCFILE(&LIB/SOURCE) +
                            SRCMBR(FIG1128)

               CHGVAR     VAR(&MSGDTA) VALUE('Creating PGMREFO file')
               SNDPGMMSG  MSGID(CPF9898) MSGF(QSYS/QCPFMSG) +
                            MSGDTA(&MSGDTA) TOPGMQ(*EXT) MSGTYPE(*STATUS)
               DSPPGMREF  PGM(&LIB/*ALL) OUTPUT(*OUTFILE) +
                            OUTFILE(QTEMP/PGMREFO) OUTMBR(*FIRST)

               CHGVAR     VAR(&MSGDTA) VALUE('Creating OBJRFLOG file')
               SNDPGMMSG  MSGID(CPF9898) MSGF(QSYS/QCPFMSG) +
                            MSGDTA(&MSGDTA) TOPGMQ(*EXT) MSGTYPE(*STATUS)
               DSPDBR     FILE(&LIB/OBJRFPF) OUTPUT(*OUTFILE) +
                            OUTFILE(QTEMP/OBJRFLOG)
```

Figure 11.23: The FIG1123CL CL program (part 1 of 2).

```
CHGVAR      VAR(&MSGDTA) VALUE('Creating OBJRFDSP display file')
SNDPGMMSG   MSGID(CPF9898) MSGF(QSYS/QCPFMSG) +
              MSGDTA(&MSGDTA) TOPGMQ(*EXT) MSGTYPE(*STATUS)
CRTDSPF     FILE(&LIB/FIG1127DS) SRCFILE(&LIB/SOURCE)

CHGVAR      VAR(&MSGDTA) VALUE('Creating OBJRF RPG program     ')
SNDPGMMSG   MSGID(CPF9898) MSGF(QSYS/QCPFMSG) +
              MSGDTA(&MSGDTA) TOPGMQ(*EXT) MSGTYPE(*STATUS)
CRTBNDRPG   PGM(&LIB/FIG1126RG) SRCFILE(&LIB/SOURCE)

CHGVAR      VAR(&MSGDTA) VALUE('Creating OBJHS RPG program     ')
SNDPGMMSG   MSGID(CPF9898) MSGF(QSYS/QCPFMSG) +
              MSGDTA(&MSGDTA) TOPGMQ(*EXT) MSGTYPE(*STATUS)
CRTBNDRPG   PGM(&LIB/FIG1121RG) SRCFILE(&LIB/SOURCE)

CHGVAR      VAR(&MSGDTA) VALUE('Creating OBJCRLGL CLP program ')
SNDPGMMSG   MSGID(CPF9898) MSGF(QSYS/QCPFMSG) +
              MSGDTA(&MSGDTA) TOPGMQ(*EXT) MSGTYPE(*STATUS)
CRTCLPGM    PGM(&LIB/FIG1120CL) SRCFILE(&LIB/SOURCE)

CHGVAR      VAR(&MSGDTA) VALUE('Creating OBJHSTCL CLP program ')
SNDPGMMSG   MSGID(CPF9898) MSGF(QSYS/QCPFMSG) +
              MSGDTA(&MSGDTA) TOPGMQ(*EXT) MSGTYPE(*STATUS)
CRTCLPGM    PGM(&LIB/FIG1122CL) SRCFILE(&LIB/SOURCE)

CHGVAR      VAR(&MSGDTA) VALUE('Creating OBJREFBLDS CLP program ')
SNDPGMMSG   MSGID(CPF9898) MSGF(QSYS/QCPFMSG) +
              MSGDTA(&MSGDTA) TOPGMQ(*EXT) MSGTYPE(*STATUS)
CRTCLPGM    PGM(&LIB/FIG1124CL) SRCFILE(&LIB/SOURCE)

CHGVAR      VAR(&MSGDTA) VALUE('Creating OBJREFBSBM CLP program ')
SNDPGMMSG   MSGID(CPF9898) MSGF(QSYS/QCPFMSG) +
              MSGDTA(&MSGDTA) TOPGMQ(*EXT) MSGTYPE(*STATUS)
CRTCLPGM    PGM(&LIB/FIG1125CL) SRCFILE(&LIB/SOURCE)

CHGVAR      VAR(&MSGDTA) VALUE('Creating WRKOBJREF command     ')
SNDPGMMSG   MSGID(CPF9898) MSGF(QSYS/QCPFMSG) +
              MSGDTA(&MSGDTA) TOPGMQ(*EXT) MSGTYPE(*STATUS)
CRTCMD      CMD(&LIB/WRKOBJREF) PGM(&LIB/FIG1126RG) +
              SRCFILE(&LIB/SOURCE) SRCMBR(FIG1129CM)

CHGVAR      VAR(&MSGDTA) VALUE('Creating BLDOBJREF command     ')
SNDPGMMSG   MSGID(CPF9898) MSGF(QSYS/QCPFMSG) +
              MSGDTA(&MSGDTA) TOPGMQ(*EXT) MSGTYPE(*STATUS)
CRTCMD      CMD(&LIB/BLDOBJREF) PGM(&LIB/FIG1125CL) +
              SRCFILE(&LIB/SOURCE) SRCMBR(FIG1119CM)


IF          COND(&NOADD *NE '1') THEN(DO)
RMVLIBLE    &LIB
ENDDO

ENDPGM
```

Figure 11.23: The FIG1123CL CL program (part 2 of 2).

```
/******************************************************************************/
/*    TO CREATE:                                                              */
/*        CRTCLPGM PGM(XXXLIB/FIG1124CL)                                      */
/******************************************************************************/
PGM (&LIB &LIST)

              DCL        VAR(&LIB) TYPE(*CHAR) LEN(10)
              DCL        VAR(&BLDLIB) TYPE(*CHAR) LEN(10)
              DCL        VAR(&REPADD) TYPE(*CHAR) LEN(1) VALUE('R')
              DCL        VAR(&LIST) TYPE(*CHAR) LEN(1902)
              DCL        VAR(&X) TYPE(*DEC) LEN(3 0) /* Count of nbr */
              DCL        VAR(&Y) TYPE(*DEC) LEN(5 0) VALUE(1) /* +
                           Displacement */
              DCL        VAR(&Z) TYPE(*DEC) LEN(5 0) /* Pos of values */
              DCL        VAR(&WORK) TYPE(*CHAR) LEN(2)
              DCL        VAR(&LSTCNT) TYPE(*DEC) LEN(5 0)
              DCL        VAR(&DISPCNT) TYPE(*DEC) LEN(5 0)

/*  GLOBAL MONITOR MESSAGE    */
              MONMSG     MSGID(CPF0000)

/*  IF REFERENCE FILE DOESN'T EXIST, CREATE IT FROM BASE COPY IN QGPL    */
              CHKOBJ     OBJ(&LIB/OBJRFPF) OBJTYPE(*FILE)
              MONMSG     MSGID(CPF9801) EXEC(DO)
              CRTDUPOBJ  OBJ(OBJRFPF) FROMLIB(QGPL) OBJTYPE(*FILE) +
                           TOLIB(&LIB)
              ENDDO

              OVRDBF     FILE(OBJRFPF) TOFILE(&LIB/OBJRFPF)
              CLRPFM     FILE(&LIB/OBJRFPF)

              CHGVAR     VAR(&WORK) VALUE(%SST(&LIST 1 2)) /* Nbr of +
                           lists */
              CHGVAR     VAR(&LSTCNT) VALUE(%BIN(&WORK 1 2))

/*  BEGIN LOOP FOR EACH LIST                                          */
LOOP:
              CHGVAR     VAR(&X) VALUE(&X + 1) /* Next list */
              CHGVAR     VAR(&Y) VALUE(&Y + 2) /* Next displacement */

/*  EXTRACT DISPLACEMENT VALUE    */
              CHGVAR     VAR(&WORK) VALUE(%SST(&LIST &Y 2))
              CHGVAR     VAR(&DISPCNT) VALUE(%BIN(&WORK 1 2))

              CHGVAR     VAR(&Z) VALUE(&DISPCNT + 3) /* Bgn pos +
                           within list */

/*  GET LIBRARY NAME              */
              CHGVAR     VAR(&BLDLIB) VALUE(%SST(&LIST &Z 10))

/*  DISPLAY PROGRAM REFERENCES TO WORK FILE IN QTEMP */
              DSPPGMREF  PGM(&BLDLIB/*ALL) OUTPUT(*OUTFILE) +
                           OUTFILE(QTEMP/PGMREFO) OUTMBR(*FIRST *ADD)

              IF         (&X *LT &LSTCNT) GOTO LOOP /* Loop back */
```

Figure 11.24: The FIG1124CL CL program (part 1 of 2).

```
/*  CALL PROGRAM TO WRITE RECORDS TO REFERENCE FILE   */
            OVRDBF     FILE(OBJRFPF) TOFILE(&LIB/OBJRFPF)
            OVRDBF     FILE(PGMREFO) TOFILE(QTEMP/PGMREFO)
            CALL       PGM(FIG1121RG)
            DLTOVR PGMREFO
            DLTOVR OBJRFPF

ENDPGM
```

Figure 11.24: The FIG1124CL CL program (part 2 of 2).

```
/******************************************************************************/
/*   TO CREATE:                                                             */
/*        CRTCLPGM PGM(XXXLIB/FIG1125CL)                                    */
/******************************************************************************/
PGM (&LIB &LIST &JOBQ &SCCDATE &SCCTIME &JOBN)

            DCL        VAR(&LIST) TYPE(*CHAR) LEN(1902)
            DCL        VAR(&LIB) TYPE(*CHAR) LEN(10)
            DCL        VAR(&JOBQ) TYPE(*CHAR) LEN(10)
            DCL        VAR(&JOBN) TYPE(*CHAR) LEN(10)
            DCL        VAR(&SCCDATE) TYPE(*CHAR) LEN(6)
            DCL        VAR(&SCCTIME) TYPE(*CHAR) LEN(4)
            DCL        VAR(&SCCDATE8) TYPE(*CHAR) LEN(8) +
                         VALUE(*CURRENT)
            DCL        VAR(&SCCTIME8) TYPE(*CHAR) LEN(8) +
                         VALUE(*CURRENT)

/*   GLOBAL MONITOR MESSAGE   */
            MONMSG     MSGID(CPF0000)

/*   IF SUBMITTING ON DATE OTHER THAN CURRENT THEN USE THAT DATE   */
            IF         COND(&SCCDATE *NE '000000') THEN(DO)
            CHGVAR     VAR(&SCCDATE8) VALUE(&SCCDATE)
            ENDDO

/*   IF SUBMITTING ON TIME OTHER THAN CURRENT THEN USE THAT TIME   */
            IF         COND(&SCCTIME *NE '0000') THEN(DO)
            CHGVAR     VAR(&SCCTIME8) VALUE(&SCCTIME)
            ENDDO

/*   SUBMIT THE JOB TO CREATE THE FILE                           */
            SBMJOB     CMD(CALL PGM(FIG1124CL) PARM(&LIB &LIST)) +
                         JOB(&JOBN) JOBQ(&JOBQ) SCDDATE(&SCCDATE8) +
                         SCDTIME(&SCCTIME8)

/*   SEND JOB SUBMITTED MESSAGE BACK TO USER                     */
            SNDPGMMSG  MSGID(CPF9898) MSGF(QCPFMSG) MSGDTA('JOB' +
                         *BCAT &JOBN *TCAT ' has been submitted +
                         to batch.') MSGTYPE(*DIAG)
ENDPGM
```

Figure 11.25: The FIG1125CL CL program.

```
    ***********************************************************************
    *  TO COMPILE:
    *     CRTBNDRPG PGM(XXXLIB/FIG1126RG)
    ***********************************************************************
    FFilename++IPEASFRlen+LKlen+AIDevice+.Keywords+++++++++++++++++++++++++Comments
    FFIG1127DS CF   E                    WORKSTN
    F                                            SFILE(SFLRCD:RelRecNbr)
    F                                            INFDS(InfoDs)
    FOBJRFPF    IF  E            K DISK          USROPN
    FOBJRFLOG   IF  E              DISK          USROPN

    DName+++++++++++ETDsFrom+++To/L+++IDc.Keywords+++++++++++++++++++++++++Comments
    D InfoDs          DS
    D  WorkStatID             197    206
    D  FirstLine              378    379B 0
    D ErrorDs          DS                   INZ
    D  BytesProv                1      4B 0
    D  BytesAval                5      8B 0
    D  MessageId                9     15
    D  ERR###                  16     16
    D  MessageDta              17    116
    D                  DS
    D  MsgDtaLen                1      4B 0
    D  MsgQueNbr                5      8B 0
    D  MsgKey                   9     12B 0
    D  RelRecNbr       S               4  0
    D  Found           S               1
    D  Duplicate       S              20
    D  PassLibNam      S              10
    D  PassObjNam      S              10
    D  PassType        S               8
    D  PhysicalFl      S               1
    D  LogicalYN       S               1
    D  LogicalLib      S              10
    D  ProgramQue      S              10
    D  Command         S              50
    D  Length          S              15  5 INZ(50)
    D  F20             S              20
    D  MoreLogics      S               1
    D                  SDS
    D  UserName               254    263
    D  NbrParms             *PARMS
    D RestOfCmd        C                   CONST('OVRDBF FILE(OBJRFPF)-
    D                                       TOFILE(')
    D FileNamCon       C                   CONST('/OBJRFPF)')
    D NoRefernce       C                   CONST('NO REFERENCES EXIST -
    D                                       FOR THIS OBJECT  - P-
    D                                       RESS ENTER')

    CLON01Factor1+++++++Opcode&ExtFactor2+++++++Result++++++++Len++D+HiLoEq......
    C     *ENTRY      PLIST
    C                 PARM                      PassLibNam
    C                 PARM                      PassObjNam
```

Figure 11.26: The FIG1126RG RPG program (part 1 of 4).

```
      C                      PARM                           PassType
      C                      PARM                           PhysicalFl
      C                      PARM                           LogicalYN
      C                      PARM                           LogicalLib
      C                      MOVEL      '*'                  ProgramQue
      C                      MOVEL(P)   RestOfCmd     Command
      C                      CAT        PassLibNam:0  Command
      C                      CAT        FileNamCon:0  Command
      C                      CALL       'QCMDEXC'
      C                      PARM                           Command
      C                      PARM                           Length
      C                      OPEN       OBJRFPF                              99
      C                      Eval       ScanName = PassObjNam
      C                      IF         (PassType = '*FILE') and (LogicalYN = 'Y')
      C                                 and (PhysicalFl = 'Y')
      C                      CALL       'OBJCRLGL'
      C                      PARM                           ScanName
      C                      PARM                           LogicalLib
      C                      OPEN       OBJRFLOG                             99
      C                      If         *IN99 = *OFF
      C                      EVAL       *IN82 = *ON
   E2 C                      ENDIF
   E1 C                      ENDIF
      C        ScanName      SETLL      OBJRFPF
      C                      EXSR       LODSFL
      C                      EVAL       *IN21 = *OFF
      C                      If         RelRecNbr <> 0
      C                      EVAL       *IN21 = *ON
      C                      EVAL       PosRelRec = 1
   X1 C                      ELSE
      C                      EXSR       ERRSR
      C                      WRITE      MSGCTL
      C                      EVAL       *IN03 = *ON
   E1 C                      ENDIF
      C                      DOU        (*IN03 = *ON) or (Found  'Y')
      C                      IF         *IN03 = *OFF
      C                      WRITE      FORMAT1
   E2 C                      ENDIF
      C                      EXFMT      SFLCTL
      C                      EVAL       Found = *Blanks
   E1 C                      ENDDO
      C                      EVAL       *INLR = *ON
      * Load the subfile
      CSR      LODSFL        BEGSR
      C                      DOU        MoreLogics = *blanks
      C                      EVAL       MoreLogics = *blanks
      C                      DOU        (*IN51 = *ON)
      C        ScanName      READE      OBJRFPF                              51
      C                      IF         *IN51 = *ON
      C                      LEAVE
   E3 C                      ENDIF
      *
      * If object referenced more than once in same progeram, only want it shown
```

Figure 11.26: The FIG1126RG RPG program (part 2 of 4).

373

```
       *   in the subfile once
       *
       C                    MOVEL     OBJLIB         F20              20
       C                    MOVE      OBJNAM         F20
       C                    IF        F20 = Duplicate
       C                    ITER
E3     C                    ENDIF
       C                    EVAL      Duplicate = F20
       C                    MOVE      OBJNAM         DOBJNM
       C                    MOVE      OBJLIB         DOBJLB
       C                    MOVEL     OBJTXT         DOBJTX
       C                    MOVE      *BLANKS        DUSEDS
       C                    IF        ObrTyp = '*FILE'
       C                    MOVEL(P)  'UNKNOWN'      DUSEDS
B4     C                    SELECT
       C                    WHEN      ObrUse = '01'
       C                    MOVEL(P)  'INPUT'        DUSEDS
       C                    WHEN      ObrUse = '02'
       C                    MOVEL(P)  'OUTPUT'       DUSEDS
       C                    WHEN      ObrUse = '03'
       C                    MOVEL(P)  'WRKSTN'       DUSEDS
       C                    WHEN      ObrUse = '04'
       C                    MOVEL(P)  'UPDATE'       DUSEDS
       C                    WHEN      ObrUse = '06'
       C                    MOVEL(P)  'UPD/ADD'      DUSEDS
       C                    WHEN      (ObrUse = '09') or (ObrUse = '11')
       C                    MOVEL(P)  'DEL/CRT'      DUSEDS
E4     C                    ENDSL
E3     C                    ENDIF
       C                    IF        (DLogNm = *blanks) and (*IN82 = *ON)
       C                    MOVEL     'PHYSICAL'     DLOGNM
E3     C                    ENDIF
       C                    EVAL      RelRecNbr = (RelRecNbr + 1)
       C                    WRITE     SFLRCD
E2     C                    ENDDO
       * If logicals are included in search, put next logical name and loop to th
       C                    IF        *IN82 = *ON
       C                    READ      OBJRFLOG                         52
       C                    IF        *IN52 = *OFF
       C                    MOVEL(P)  WHREFI         ScanName
       C                    MOVEL(P)  WHREFI         DLOGNM
       C                    EVAL      MoreLogics = 'X'
       C       ScanName     SETLL     OBJRFPF
E3     C                    ENDIF
E2     C                    ENDIF
E1     C                    ENDDO
       C                    ENDSR
       C       ERRSR        BEGSR
       C                    EVAL      BytesProv = 116
       C       'QCPFMSG'    CAT       'QSYS':3       MSGF
       C                    MOVE      'CPF9898'      MessageId
       C                    MOVEL(P)  NoRefernce     MessageDta
       C                    Z-ADD     60             MsgDtaLen
```

Figure 11.26: The FIG1126RG RPG program (part 3 of 4).

```
C                Z-ADD    0            MsgQueNbr
* Send error message
C                CALL     'QMHSNDPM'
C                PARM                  MessageId
C                PARM                  MSGF        20
C                PARM                  MessageDta
C                PARM                  MsgDtaLen
C                PARM     '*DIAG'      MessageTyp   10
C                PARM     '*'          MessageQue   10
C                PARM                  MsgQueNbr
C                PARM                  MsgKey
C                PARM                  ErrorDs
C                ENDSR
```

Figure 11.26: The FIG1126RG RPG program (part 4 of 4).

```
A***********************************************************************
A*  TO COMPILE:
A*     CRTDSPF FILE(XXXLIB/FIG1127DS)
A***********************************************************************
AAN01N02N03T.Name++++++RLen++TDpBLinPosFunctions++++++++++++++++++++++++++++++
A                                     DSPSIZ(24 80 *DS3)
A                                     PRINT
A                                     CA03(03)
A                                     CA12(03)
A          R SFLRCD                   SFL
A  40                                 SFLNXTCHG
A            DOBJNM     10A  O  9  4
A            DOBJLB     10A  O  9 15
A            DOBJTX     38A  O  9 26
A            DUSEDS      7A  O  9 65
A            DLOGNM      8A  O  9 73
A          R SFLCTL                   SFLCTL(SFLRCD)
A                                     CHGINPDFT
A                                     SFLSIZ(0024)
A                                     SFLPAG(0012)
A                                     OVERLAY
A  21                                 SFLDSP
A                                     SFLDSPCTL
A  51                                 SFLEND(*MORE)
A            POSRELREC   4S OH         SFLRCDNBR
A                                   1 26'Work with Object References'
A                                     DSPATR(HI)
A                                     DSPATR(UL)
A                                   3  3'Object name. . . .'
A N21                                 DSPATR(ND)
A            SCANNAME    10A  O  3 22
A N21                                 DSPATR(ND)
A  21N82                            8  2' Name        Library    Text      -
```

Figure 11.27: The FIG1127DS display file (part 1 of 2).

```
A                                                                  Useage-
A                                            ,
A                                            DSPATR(HI)
A   21 82                              8  2' Name      Library   Text    -
A                                                                  Useage-
A                                            Logical'
A                                            DSPATR(HI)
A           R FORMAT1
A                                            TEXT('Command keys')
A                                    23  4'F3=Exit'
A                                            COLOR(BLU)
A                                    23 17'F12=Previous'
A                                            COLOR(BLU)
A           R MSGSFL                         SFL
A                                            SFLMSGRCD(24)
A             MESSAGEKEY                      SFLMSGKEY
A             PROGRAMQUE                      SFLPGMQ
A           R MSGCTL                         SFLCTL(MSGSFL)
A                                            OVERLAY
A                                            ALARM
A                                            SFLSIZ(3) SFLPAG(1)
A                                            SFLDSP SFLINZ
A   90                                       SFLEND
A             PROGRAMQUE                      SFLPGMQ
```

Figure 11.27: The FIG1127DS display file (part 2 of 2).

```
A*****************************************************************************
A*  TO COMPILE:
A*     CRTPF FILE(XXXLIB/OBJRFPF) SRCMBR(FIG1128)
A*****************************************************************************
AAN01N02N03T.Name++++++RLen++TDpBLinPosFunctions+++++++++++++++++++++++++++++++
A           R OBJREC
A             OBJNAM        10         COLHDG('OBJECT NAME')
A             OBJLIB        10         COLHDG('OBJECT LIBRARY')
A             OBJTXT        40         COLHDG('OBJECT TEXT')
A             OBRNAM        10         COLHDG('REFERENCED OBJECT')
A             OBRLIB        10         COLHDG('REFERENCED LIBRARY')
A             OBRTYP        10         COLHDG('REFERENCED TYPE')
A             OBRUSE         2         COLHDG('FILE USEAGE')
A           K OBRNAM
A           K OBRLIB
A           K OBJNAM
A           K OBJLIB
```

Figure 11.28: The OBJRFPF physical file.

```
/*===============================================================*/
/* To compile:                                                   */
/*                                                               */
/*          CRTCMD    CMD(XXX/WRKOBJREF) PGM(XXX/FIG1126RG)       */
/*                    SRCMBR(FIG1129CM)                           */
/*                                                               */
/*===============================================================*/
          CMD         PROMPT('WORK with OBJECT REFERENCES')
          PARM        KWD(LIB) TYPE(*NAME) PROMPT('OBJRFPF Library:') +
                      MIN(1)
          PARM        KWD(NAME) TYPE(*NAME) PROMPT('Object name:') +
                      MIN(1)
          PARM        KWD(TYPE) TYPE(*CHAR) LEN(8) PROMPT('Object type:') +
                      MIN(1)
          PARM        KWD(PHYFIL) TYPE(*CHAR) LEN(1) RSTD(*YES) +
                      VALUES(Y N) DFT(N) PMTCTL(TYPE) PROMPT('Is +
                      Object a Physical File?:')
          PARM        KWD(LOGYN) TYPE(*CHAR) LEN(1) RSTD(*YES) +
                      DFT(Y) VALUES(N Y) PMTCTL(ATTR) +
                      PROMPT('Include logicals over file?:')
          PARM        KWD(LOGLIB) TYPE(*CHAR) LEN(10) DFT(*LIBL) +
                      PMTCTL(ATTR) PROMPT('Physical file library:')
TYPE:     PMTCTL      CTL(TYPE) COND((*EQ *FILE))
ATTR:     PMTCTL      CTL(PHYFIL) COND((*EQ Y))
```

Figure 11.29: The WRKOBJREF command.

THE SERVICE PROGRAM USAGE (SERPGMUSAG) COMMAND

Service programs were introduced as part of ILE. We discuss the pros and cons of service programs in chapter 13. In the meantime, suffice it to say that this command will help you to identify all programs in your system that call a service program.

This tool will list all programs in a given library that use the given service program. When running this tool, you enter the search library name and, optionally, a generic program name. In addition, you specify the service program and library that is the object of the search. The library name accepts the special value *ANY, which means exactly what it says: The tool will look for *any* program that uses a service program with the indicated name, regardless of the library the service program is in.

You can see an example of the output from this command in Figure 11.30. The display file, RPG program, and command that make it all work are in Figures 11.31 through 11.33, respectively.

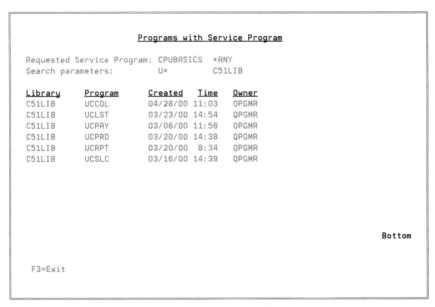

```
                    Programs with Service Program

Requested Service Program: CPUBASICS   *ANY
Search parameters:         U*          C51LIB


Library    Program    Created    Time    Owner
C51LIB     UCCOL      04/28/00  11:03    QPGMR
C51LIB     UCLST      03/23/00  14:54    QPGMR
C51LIB     UCPAY      03/06/00  11:56    QPGMR
C51LIB     UCPRD      03/20/00  14:38    QPGMR
C51LIB     UCRPT      03/20/00   8:34    QPGMR
C51LIB     UCSLC      03/16/00  14:39    QPGMR




                                                       Bottom


   F3=Exit
```

Figure 11.30: Output from the SERPGMUSAG command.

```
A******************************************************************************
A*   TO COMPILE:
A*      CRTDSPF FILE(XXXLIB/FIG1131DS)
A******************************************************************************
AAN01N02N03T.Name++++++RLen++TDpBLinPosFunctions+++++++++++++++++++++++++++++++
A                                        DSPSIZ(24 80 *DS3)
A                                        CF03(03)
A          R SFLRECORD                   SFL
A            LIBRARYNAM    10A  O  7  2
A            PROGRAMNAM    10A  O  7 14
A            DCREATEMDY     8A  O  7 27
A            DCREATETIM     4Y 00  7 36EDTWRD(' : ')
A            PGMOWNER      10A  O  7 43
A          R SFLCONTROL                  SFLCTL(SFLRECORD)
A                                        SFLSIZ(0024)
A                                        SFLPAG(0012)
A                                        OVERLAY
A  21                                    SFLDSP
A  22                                    SFLDSPCTL
A  23                                    SFLCLR
A  24                                    SFLEND(*MORE)
A                                      1 25'Programs with Service Program'
A                                        DSPATR(HI)
```

Figure 11.31: The FIG1131DS display file (part 1 of 2).

378

```
A                                        DSPATR(UL)
A                                     6  2'Library'
A                                        DSPATR(HI)
A                                        DSPATR(UL)
A                                     6 14'Program'
A                                        DSPATR(HI)
A                                        DSPATR(UL)
A                                     3  2'Requested Service Program:'
A            TARGETNAME   10A  O  3 29
A            TARGETLIB    10A  O  3 40
A                                     4  2'Search parameters:'
A            SEARCHOBJ    10A  O  4 29
A            SEARCHLIB    10A  O  4 40
A                                     6 44'Owner'
A                                        DSPATR(HI)
A                                        DSPATR(UL)
A                                     6 27'Created'
A                                        DSPATR(HI)
A                                        DSPATR(UL)
A                                     6 37'Time'
A                                        DSPATR(HI)
A                                        DSPATR(UL)
A            R FMT1
A                                    22  3'F3=Exit'  COLOR(BLU)
```

Figure 11.31: The FIG1131DS display file (part 2 of 2).

```
*********************************************************************
*   TO COMPILE:
*       CRTBNDPGM PGM(XXXLIB/FIG1132RG)
*********************************************************************
FFilename++IPEASFRlen+LKlen+AIDevice+.Keywords++++++++++++++++++++++++Comments
FFIG1131DS CF   E                  WORKSTN
F                                             SFILE(SFLRECORD:SflRcdNbr)
FQSYSPRT   O    F   132             PRINTER OFLIND(*INOA) USROPN

DName+++++++++++ETDsFrom+++To/L+++IDc.Keywords++++++++++++++++++++++++Comments
D GeneralDs       DS
D  InputSize             113    116B 0
D  ListOffset            125    128B 0
D  ListNbr               133    136B 0
D  EntrySize             137    140B 0
D InputDs         DS
D  UserSpace                     20
D TarNamLib       S              20
D TargetName      S              10
D TargetLib       S              10
D PrintOrDsp      S               1
D SrvListDs       DS
```

Figure 11.32: The FIG1132RG RPG program (part 1 of 5).

379

```
D PgmNameLib              1    20
D  ProgramNam                  10    OVERLAY(PgmNameLib:1)
D  LibraryNam                  10    OVERLAY(PgmNameLib:11)
D SrvPgmNam              21    30
D SrvPgmLib              31    40
D ErrorDs         DS                 INZ
D  BytesProvd             1     4B 0 INZ(116)
D  BytesAvail             5     8B 0
D  MessageId              9    15
D  Err###                16    16
D  MessageDta            17   116
D               DS                 INZ
D  StartPosit             1     4B 0
D  StartLen               5     8B 0
D  SpaceLen               9    12B 0
D  NbrEntries            29    32B 0
D  LenEntry              37    40B 0
D  NbrReturn             41    44B 0
D  MaxEntries            45    48B 0
D  ReceiveLen            49    52B 0 INZ(100)
D SrchNamLib      S           20
D SpaceAtrib      S           10
D SpaceValue      S            1
D SpaceAuth       S           10
D SpaceText       S           50
D SpaceReplc      S           10
D FormatName      S            8
D TotalNbr        S            7  0
D SflRcdNbr       S            4  0
D DoRrn           S            4  0
D Index           S            4  0
D               DS
D  Receiver                   100
D  PgmOwner                    10    OVERLAY(Receiver:28)
D  CrtDatTim                   13    OVERLAY(Receiver:49)
D   CreateYMD                   6  0 OVERLAY(CrtDatTim:2)
D   CreateTime                  4  0 OVERLAY(CrtDatTim:8)
D  SourceFile                  10    OVERLAY(Receiver:62)
D  SourceLib                   10    OVERLAY(Receiver:72)
D LibLstCon       C                  CONST('*LIBL     ')
D DateCreate      S            D     DATFMT(*YMD)
D CreateMDY       S            D     DATFMT(*MDY)
D DCreateMDY      S            8

CL0N01Factor1+++++++Opcode&ExtFactor2+++++++Result++++++++Len++D+HiLoEq......
C     *ENTRY      PLIST
C                 PARM                      SrchNamLib
C                 PARM                      TarNamLib
C                 PARM                      PrintOrDsp
C                 EVAL        UserSpace = ('BNDSPC    QTEMP')
C                 EVAL        TargetName = TarNamLib
C                 EVAL        TargetLib = %SUBST(TarNamLib:11:10)
C                 EVAL        SearchObj = SrchNamLib
```

Figure 11.32: The FIG1132RG RPG program (part 2 of 5).

```
C                       EVAL      SearchLib = %SUBST(SrchNamLib:11:10)
 *  Create user space
C                       CALL      'QUSCRTUS'
C                       PARM                    UserSpace
C                       PARM      *BLANKS       SpaceAtrib
C                       PARM      2048          SpaceLen
C                       PARM      *BLANKS       SpaceValue
C                       PARM      '*CHANGE'     SpaceAuth
C                       PARM      *BLANKS       SpaceText
C                       PARM      '*YES'        SpaceReplc
C                       PARM                    ErrorDs
 *  List service programs in all programs to the user space
C                       CALL      'QBNLPGMI'
C                       PARM                    UserSpace
C                       PARM      'PGML0200'    FormatName
C                       PARM                    SrchNamLib
C                       PARM                    ErrorDs
C                       EVAL      StartPosit = 1
C                       EVAL      StartLen = 140
 *  Retrieve user space general information
C                       CALL      'QUSRTVUS'
C                       PARM                    UserSpace
C                       PARM                    StartPosit
C                       PARM                    StartLen
C                       PARM                    GeneralDs
C                       EVAL      StartPosit = 1
C                       EVAL      StartLen = InputSize
 *  Retrieve user space detail information
C                       CALL      'QUSRTVUS'
C                       PARM                    UserSpace
C                       PARM                    StartPosit
C                       PARM                    StartLen
C                       PARM                    InputDs
C                       EVAL      UserSpace = ('BNDSPC    QTEMP')
C                       EVAL      StartPosit = ListOffset + 1
C                       EVAL      StartLen = EntrySize
 *  Retrieve the list by walking through the user space
C                       DO        ListNbr
C                       CALL      'QUSRTVUS'
C                       PARM                    UserSpace
C                       PARM                    StartPosit
C                       PARM                    StartLen
C                       PARM                    SrvListDs
C                       IF        (SrvPgmNam = TargetName)
C                       IF        (TargetLib = '*ANY')
C                                 or (SrvPgmLib = *blanks)
C                                 or (SrvPgmLib = TargetLib)
C                       EXSR      GETPROGRAM
C                       EVAL      SflRcdNbr = SflRcdNbr + 1
C                       WRITE     SFLRECORD
C                       ENDIF
C                       ENDIF
C                       EVAL      StartPosit = StartPosit + EntrySize
```

Figure 11.32: The FIG1132RG RPG program (part 3 of 5).

```
C                         ENDDO
C                         IF        PrintOrDsp = 'D'
C                         EXSR      DISPLAY
C                         ELSE
C                         EXSR      PRINT
C                         ENDIF
C                         EVAL      *InLr = *ON
C        GETPROGRAM       BEGSR
C                         CALL      'QCLRPGMI'
C                         PARM                    Receiver
C                         PARM                    ReceiveLen
C                         PARM      'PGMI0100'    FormatName
C                         PARM                    PgmNameLib
C                         PARM                    ErrorDs
C        *YMD             MOVEL     CreateYMD     CreateMDY
C                         MOVE      CreateMDY     DCreateMDY
C                         EVAL      DCreateTim = CreateTime
C                         ENDSR
C        DISPLAY          BEGSR
C                         IF        SflRcdNbr > 0
C                         EVAL      *In21 = *ON
C                         ENDIF
C                         EVAL      *In22 = *ON
C                         EVAL      *In24 = *ON
C                         WRITE     FMT1
C                         EXFMT     SFLCONTROL
C                         ENDSR
C        PRINT            BEGSR
C                         OPEN      QSYSPRT
C                         EXCEPT    HEADING
C                         EVAL      DoRrn= SflRcdNbr
C                         DO        DoRrn         Index
C        Index            CHAIN     SFLRECORD                           68
C                         IF        *In68 = *OFF
C                         EXCEPT    DETAIL
C                         ENDIF
C                         ENDDO
C                         ENDSR

O..............N01N02N03Field+++++++++YB.End++PConstant/editword/DTformat++++
OQSYSPRT    E            HEADING        3 02
O          OR    OA
O                                             5 'DATE:'
O                        UDATE          Y     14
O                                            75 'PAGE:'
O                        PAGE           Z     80
O                                            48 'Programs with Service'
O                                          +001 'Programs'
O          E             HEADING        1
O          OR    OA
O                                            30 'Requested Service Program'
O                        TargetName           42
O                        TargetLib            54
```

Figure 11.32: The FIG1132RG RPG program (part 4 of 5).

```
O          E          HEADING      3
O          OR   OA
O                                 30 'Search Parameters........'
O                     SearchObj   42
O                     SearchLib   54
O          E          HEADING      1
O          OR   OA
O                                 12 'Library'
O                                 27 'Program'
O                                 47 'Created On'
O                                 54 'Time'
O                                 63 'Owner'
O          EF         DETAIL       1
O                     LibraryNam  15
O                     ProgramNam  30
O                     DcreateMDY  47
O                     DcreateTim  54
O                     PgmOwner    68
```

Figure 11.32: The FIG1132RG RPG program (part 5 of 5).

```
/*==============================================================*/
/* To compile:                                                  */
/*                                                              */
/*         CRTCMD    CMD(XXX/SERPGMUSAG) PGM(XXX/FIG1132RG)      */
/*                   SRCMBR(FIG1133CM)                           */
/*                                                              */
/*==============================================================*/
          CMD       PROMPT('Service Program Useage')
          PARM      KWD(SEARCH) TYPE(QUAL) MIN(1) PROMPT('Search +
                    Program:')
          PARM      KWD(FOR) TYPE(QUAL1) MIN(1) PROMPT('Find +
                    Program:')
          PARM      KWD(DSPPRINT) TYPE(*CHAR) LEN(1) RSTD(*YES) +
                    DFT(D) VALUES(D P) PROMPT('Display or +
                    Print:')
QUAL:     QUAL      TYPE(*GENERIC) LEN(10) DFT(*ALL) SPCVAL((*ALL))
          QUAL      TYPE(*NAME) LEN(10) DFT(*LIBL) +
                    SPCVAL((*LIBL) (*CURLIB)) PROMPT('Library')
QUAL1:    QUAL      TYPE(*NAME) LEN(10)
          QUAL      TYPE(*NAME) LEN(10) DFT(*LIBL) +
                    SPCVAL((*LIBL) (*CURLIB) (*ANY)) +
                    PROMPT('Library')
```

Figure 11.33: The SERPGMUSAG command.

THE MODULE USAGE (MODUSAG) COMMAND

What we have always referred to as programs in the OPM became *modules* when we went to ILE. One or more modules are used to make a program under ILE.

Whatever confusion you may have over this issue will be cleared up when you get to chapter 13. Once you have read that chapter, it will become apparent that you are going to need some way to identify which programs use a particular module (depending on how you choose to do your program binding). We have written a tool that will allow you to identify all programs that use a particular module. We call it the Module Usage (MODUSAG) command.

The MODUSAG command shows all programs that use a specified module. You specify the generic program name to search (or *ALL) and the library. You indicate the module name and library you are interested in researching. In addition, you have the option of printing or displaying the results of the search.

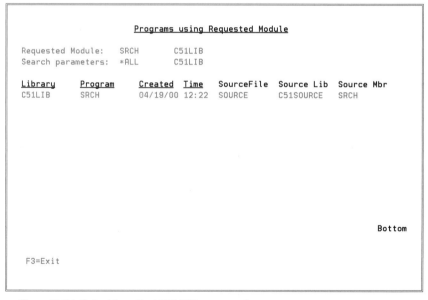

Figure 11.34: Output from the MODUSAG command.

You can see an example of the output from the MODUSAG command in Figure 11.34. The display file, RPG program, and the MODUSAG command can be seen in Figures 11.35 through 11.37, respectively.

You will find this command useful when you have more than one program using the same module. If you then need to make a change to the module, it would be useful to know the other programs that need to be recompiled in order to see the changed module. Again, the need for this tool is predicated on how you will be performing your program binding, which is discussed in chapter 13.

```
A*****************************************************************************
A*  TO COMPILE:
A*     CRTDSPF FILE(XXXLIB/FIG1135DS)
A*****************************************************************************
AAN01N02N03T.Name++++++RLen++TDpBLinPosFunctions+++++++++++++++++++++++++++++
A                                           CF03(03)
A              R SFLRECORD                  SFL
A                LIBRARYNAM   10A  0  7  2
A                PROGRAMNAM   10A  0  7 14
A                DCREATEMDY    8A  0  7 26
A                DCREATETIM    4Y 00  7 35EDTWRD('  :  ')
A                SOURCEFILE   10   0  7 42
A                SOURCELIB    10   0  7 54
A                SOURCEMBR    10   0  7 66
A              R SFLCONTROL                 SFLCTL(SFLRECORD)
A                                           SFLSIZ(0024)
A                                           SFLPAG(0012)
A                                           OVERLAY
A   21                                      SFLDSP
A   22                                      SFLDSPCTL
A   23                                      SFLCLR
A   24                                      SFLEND(*MORE)
A                                         1 25'Programs using Requested Module'
A                                           DSPATR(HI)
A                                           DSPATR(UL)
A                                         6  2'Library'
A                                           DSPATR(HI)
A                                           DSPATR(UL)
A                                         6 14'Program'
A                                           DSPATR(HI)
A                                           DSPATR(UL)
A                                         3  2'Requested Module:'
A                TARGETNAME   10A  0  3 22
A                TARGETLIB    10A  0  3 33
A                                         4  2'Search parameters:'
A                SEARCHOBJ    10A  0  4 22
A                SEARCHLIB    10A  0  4 33
```

Figure 11.35: The FIG1135DS display file (part 1 of 2).

```
A                                   6 26'Created'
A                                     DSPATR(HI)
A                                     DSPATR(UL)
A                                   6 35'Time'
A                                     DSPATR(HI)
A                                     DSPATR(UL)
A                                   6 42'SourceFile'
A                                     DSPATR(HI)
A                                   6 54'Source Lib'
A                                     DSPATR(HI)
A                                   6 66'Source Mbr'
A                                     DSPATR(HI)
A        R FMT1
A                                  22  3'F3=Exit'  COLOR(BLU)
```

Figure 11.35: The FIG1135DS display file (part 2 of 2).

```
*****************************************************************************
*  TO COMPILE:
*     CRTBNDPGM PGM(XXXLIB/FIG1136RG)
*****************************************************************************
FFilename++IPEASFRlen+LKlen+AIDevice+.Keywords++++++++++++++++++++++Comments
FFIG1135ds CF  E                  WORKSTN
F                                          SFILE(SFLRECORD:SflRcdNbr)
FQSYSPRT   O   F  132             PRINTER OFLIND(*INOA) USROPN

DName++++++++++++ETDsFrom+++To/L+++IDc.Keywords++++++++++++++++++++++Comments
D GeneralDs        DS
D  InputSize              113    116B 0
D  ListOffset             125    128B 0
D  ListNbr                133    136B 0
D  EntrySize              137    140B 0
D InputDs          DS
D  UserSpace                      20
D TarNamLib       S               20
D TargetName      S               10
D TargetLib       S               10
D PrintOrDsp      S                1
D                  DS
D ModListDs                      508
D  PgmNameLib             1        20
D   ProgramNam                    10     OVERLAY(PgmNameLib:1)
D   LibraryNam                    10     OVERLAY(PgmNameLib:11)
D  ModuleName                     10     OVERLAY(ModListDs:21)
D  ModuleLib                      10     OVERLAY(ModListDs:31)
D  SourceFile                     10     OVERLAY(ModListDs:41)
D  SourceLib                      10     OVERLAY(ModListDs:51)
```

Figure 11.36: The FIG1136RG RPG program (part 1 of 5).

```
D  SourceMbr                       10     OVERLAY(ModListDs:61)
D  CrtDatTim                       13     OVERLAY(ModListDs:81)
D   CreateYMD                       6  0  OVERLAY(CrtDatTim:2)
D   CreateTime                      4  0  OVERLAY(CrtDatTim:8)
D ErrorDs          DS                     INZ
D  BytesProvd              1       4B 0   INZ(116)
D  BytesAvail              5       8B 0
D  MessageId               9      15
D  Err###                 16      16
D  MessageDta             17     116
D                  DS                     INZ
D  StartPosit              1       4B 0
D  StartLen                5       8B 0
D  SpaceLen                9      12B 0
D  NbrEntries             29      32B 0
D  LenEntry               37      40B 0
D  NbrReturn              41      44B 0
D  MaxEntries             45      48B 0
D SrchNamLib       S             20
D SpaceAtrib       S             10
D SpaceValue       S              1
D SpaceAuth        S             10
D SpaceText        S             50
D SpaceReplc       S             10
D FormatName       S              8
D TotalNbr         S              7  0
D SflRcdNbr        S              4  0
D DoRrn            S              4  0
D Index            S              4  0
D DateCreate       S              D      DATFMT(*YMD)
D CreateMDY        S              D      DATFMT(*MDY)
D DCreateMDY       S              8


CLON01Factor1+++++++Opcode&ExtFactor2+++++++Result+++++++Len++D+HiLoEq......
C     *ENTRY        PLIST
C                   PARM                        SrchNamLib
C                   PARM                        TarNamLib
C                   PARM                        PrintOrDsp
C                   EVAL      UserSpace = ('MODSPACE   QTEMP')
C                   EVAL      TargetName = TarNamLib
C                   EVAL      TargetLib = %SUBST(TarNamLib:11:10)
C                   EVAL      SearchObj = SrchNamLib
C                   EVAL      SearchLib = %SUBST(SrchNamLib:11:10)
C   * Create user space
C                   CALL      'QUSCRTUS'
C                   PARM                        UserSpace
C                   PARM      *BLANKS           SpaceAtrib
C                   PARM      2048              SpaceLen
C                   PARM      *BLANKS           SpaceValue
C                   PARM      '*CHANGE'         SpaceAuth
C                   PARM      *BLANKS           SpaceText
```

Figure 11.36: The FIG1136RG RPG program (part 2 of 5).

```
C                      PARM      '*YES'          SpaceReplc
C                      PARM                      ErrorDs
 *   List all programs matching search criteria to user space
C                      EVAL      UserSpace = ('MODSPACE  QTEMP')
C                      CALL      'QBNLPGMI'
C                      PARM                      UserSpace
C                      PARM      'PGML0100'      FormatName
C                      PARM                      SrchNamLib
C                      PARM                      ErrorDs
C                      EVAL      StartPosit = 1
C                      EVAL      StartLen = 140
 *   Retrieve user space general information
C                      EVAL      UserSpace = ('MODSPACE  QTEMP')
C                      CALL      'QUSRTVUS'
C                      PARM                      UserSpace
C                      PARM                      StartPosit
C                      PARM                      StartLen
C                      PARM                      GeneralDs
C                      EVAL      StartPosit = 1
C                      EVAL      StartLen = InputSize
 *   Retrieve user space detail information
C                      EVAL      UserSpace = ('MODSPACE  QTEMP')
C                      CALL      'QUSRTVUS'
C                      PARM                      UserSpace
C                      PARM                      StartPosit
C                      PARM                      StartLen
C                      PARM                      InputDs
C                      EVAL      StartPosit = ListOffset + 1
C                      EVAL      StartLen = EntrySize
 *   Retrieve the list by walking through the user space
C                      DO        ListNbr
C                      EVAL      UserSpace = ('MODSPACE  QTEMP')
C                      CALL      'QUSRTVUS'
C                      PARM                      UserSpace
C                      PARM                      StartPosit
C                      PARM                      StartLen
C                      PARM                      ModListDs
C                      IF        (ModuleName = TargetName)
C         *YMD         MOVEL     CreateYMD       CreateMDY
C                      MOVE      CreateMDY       DCreateMDY
C                      EVAL      DCreateTim = CreateTime
C                      EVAL      SflRcdNbr = SflRcdNbr + 1
C                      WRITE     SFLRECORD
C                      ENDIF
C                      EVAL      StartPosit = StartPosit + EntrySize
C                      ENDDO
C                      IF        PrintOrDsp = 'D'
C                      EXSR      DISPLAY
C                      ELSE
C                      EXSR      PRINT
C                      ENDIF
```

Figure 11.36: The FIG1136RG RPG program (part 3 of 5).

```
C                   EVAL      *InLr = *ON
C       DISPLAY     BEGSR
C                   IF        SflRcdNbr > 0
C                   EVAL      *In21 = *ON
C                   ENDIF
C                   EVAL      *In22 = *ON
C                   EVAL      *In24 = *ON
C                   WRITE     FMT1
C                   EXFMT     SFLCONTROL
C                   ENDSR
C       PRINT       BEGSR
C                   OPEN      QSYSPRT
C                   EXCEPT    HEADING
C                   EVAL      DoRrn= SflRcdNbr
C                   DO        DoRrn       Index
C       Index       CHAIN     SFLRECORD                        68
C                   IF        *In68 = *OFF
C                   EXCEPT    DETAIL
C                   ENDIF
C                   ENDDO
C                   ENDSR

O.............N01N02N03Field+++++++++YB.End++PConstant/editword/DTformat++..
OQSYSPRT   E              HEADING       3 02
O          OR    OA
O                                            5 'DATE:'
O                         UDATE         Y   14
O                                           75 'PAGE:'
O                         PAGE          Z   80
O                                           48 'Programs with Modules'
O          E              HEADING       1
O          OR    OA
O                                           30 'Requested Module:'
O                         TargetName        42
O                         TargetLib         54
O          E              HEADING       3
O          OR    OA
O                                           30 'Search Parameters........'
O                         SearchObj         42
O                         SearchLib         54
O          E              HEADING       1
O          OR    OA
O                                           12 'Library'
O                                           27 'Program'
O                                           46 'Created On'
O                                           53 'Time'
O                                           67 'SourceFile'
O                                           80 'Source Lib'
O                                           93 'Source Mbr'
O          EF             DETAIL        1
O                         LibraryNam        15
```

Figure 11.36: The FIG1136RG RPG program (part 4 of 5).

389

```
O                          ProgramNam        30
O                          DcreateMDY        46
O                          DcreateTim        53
O                          SourceFile        67
O                          SourceLib         80
O                          SourceMbr         93
```

Figure 11.36: The FIG1136RG RPG program (part 5 of 5).

```
/*===========================================================*/
/* To compile:                                               */
/*                                                           */
/*          CRTCMD    CMD(XXX/MODUSAG)      PGM(XXX/FIG1136RG) */
/*                    SRCMBR(FIG1137CM)                       */
/*                                                           */
/*===========================================================*/
           CMD       PROMPT('Module Useage)')
           PARM      KWD(SEARCH) TYPE(QUAL) MIN(1) PROMPT('Search +
                       Program:')
           PARM      KWD(FOR) TYPE(QUAL1) MIN(1) PROMPT('Find +
                       Program:')
           PARM      KWD(DSPPRINT) TYPE(*CHAR) LEN(1) RSTD(*YES) +
                       DFT(D) VALUES(D P) PROMPT('Display or +
                       Print:')
QUAL:      QUAL      TYPE(*GENERIC) LEN(10) DFT(*ALL) SPCVAL((*ALL))
           QUAL      TYPE(*NAME) LEN(10) DFT(*LIBL) +
                       SPCVAL((*LIBL) (*CURLIB)) PROMPT('Library')
QUAL1:     QUAL      TYPE(*NAME) LEN(10)
           QUAL      TYPE(*NAME) LEN(10) DFT(*LIBL) +
                       SPCVAL((*LIBL) (*CURLIB) (*ANY)) +
                       PROMPT('Library')
```

Figure 11.37: The MODUSAG command.

390

THE WORK WITH FIELDS (WRKFLD) COMMAND

Although it may be used for a variety of other things as well, we originally wrote the Work with Fields (WRKFLD) command as a tool to help convert legacy systems into systems capable of handling the 21st century. It became apparent to us that there were no tools available to help programmers identify where the date fields in their systems were. To address this issue, we wrote the WRKFLD command.

The WRKFLD command allows you to display a subfile of all programs that contain a field with a specified length or name. For instance, if the size of your date fields are generally six digits with zero decimal positions, you can use this command to list every program that has a six-digit field and no decimal positions in it.

On the other hand, if all date fields in your system have DAT or DTE in the field name, we have provided a wild-card search capability. If all of your date fields have the characters DAT (or any characters you specify), you can filter the search to include only programs with field names that have the specified characters embedded in them.

When the subfile of program names is displayed, you can edit, browse, or print the source members that include the search criteria you specified. We designed this command to work on either OPM or ILE programs.

Due to the nature of this type of application, you must first build a work file over the programs before you can search for a field. The BLDWRKFLD command will build the work file for you. The command works by compiling a source member into the QTEMP library and directing its output to a file.

The BLDWRKFLD command may take some time to complete, so we have ensured that it runs in batch. If you run the command interactively, it will submit itself to batch.

Note: When you run the build command, you must be sure to have the library that contains the source to all of the utilities in your library list.

When you are running the WRKFLD command, you can elect to search for fields based on field characteristics (size and decimal positions) and field name. When you are specifying the field name, you can use an asterisk (*) as a wild card character, as we have done in Figure 11.38. As you can see, any field with six digits and no decimal positions that happen to have the characters DAT anywhere in the field name will be displayed in the subfile. Note that the date and time the command was run (and the work file was built) is prominently displayed on the screen.

```
                              Work with Fields

        Holding file to search in. . . . . . . HOLDFILE    Created: 19:26  4/30/2000
          Library of holding file . . . . . . WORKLIB
        Size of search field . . . . . . . .   00006 00
        Only include field named . . . . . .  _____


        Type options, press enter.
           1=Edit source   2=Browse   6=Print


        Opt  Field     Program    Opt  Field     Program
         ▮   OUTRECLEN FG1108RG    _    CRTTIME   FG1152RG
         _   UDATE     FG1108RG    _    OUTRECLEN FG1152RG
         _   WHEN      FG1115RG    _    SFFSIZ    FG1152RG
         _   CREATEYMD FG1132RG    _    SVDDATE   FG1152RG
         _   UDATE     FG1132RG    _    SVDTIME   FG1152RG
         _   CREATEYMD FG1136RG    _    TIME6     FG1152RG
         _   UDATE     FG1136RG    _    JOBNBR    FG1157RG
         _   TIMEFIELD FG1144RG    _    DATE6     FG1165RG
         _   UDATE     FG1144RG    _    MLCDAT    FG1165RG
         _   CRTDATE   FG1152RG    _    MLCHGD    FG1165RG
                                                             More...
        F3=Exit     F12=Previous
```

Figure 11.38: Output from the WRKFLD command.

Figures 11.39 through 11.41 represent the physical files required for the BLDWRKFLD and WRKFLD commands. Figure 11.42 shows the code for the BLDWRKFLD command. Figures 11.43 and 11.44 represent the CL and RPG programs behind the BLDWRKFLD command.

```
A*******************************************************************************
A*   TO COMPILE:
A*      CRTPF FILE(XXXLIB/FIELDSPF) SRCMBR(FIG1139)
A*******************************************************************************
AAN01N02N03T.Name++++++RLen++TDpBLinPosFunctions++++++++++++++++++++++++++++++++
A          R FIELDSREC
A            FIELDNAME     10         COLHDG('FIELD NAME')
A            PROGRAMNAM    10         COLHDG('PROGRAM NAME')
A            NBRDIGITS      5 0       COLHDG('NBR OF DIGITS')
A            NBRDECIMLS     2 0       COLHDG('NBR OF DECIMALS')
A            SOURCELIB     10         COLHDG('SOURCE LIB')
A            SOURCEFILE    10         COLHDG('SOURCE FILE')
A            CREATEDATE     8         COLHDG('CREATED DATE')
A            CREATETIME     4         COLHDG('CREATED DATE')
A          K NBRDIGITS
A          K NBRDECIMLS
```

Figure 11.39: The FIELDSPF physical file.

```
A***************************************************************************
A*  TO COMPILE:
A*     CRTPF FILE(XXXLIB/SPLDTAILE) SRCMBR(FIG1140)
A***************************************************************************
AAN01N02N03T.Name++++++RLen++TDpBLinPosFunctions+++++++++++++++++++++++++++++
A          R ILESPLRCRD
A            ILBLANK9        9        COLHDG('BLANKS')
A            ILFLDNAME      10        COLHDG('FIELD NAME')
A            ILFILLER8       8        COLHDG('FILLER')
A            ILFLDSIZE      10        COLHDG('FIELD SIZE')
A            ILFILLER       95        COLHDG('FILLER')
```

Figure 11.40: The SPLDTAILE physical file.

```
A***************************************************************************
A*  TO COMPILE:
A*     CRTPF FILE(XXXLIB/SPLDTAOPM) SRCMBR(FIG1141)
A***************************************************************************
AAN01N02N03T.Name++++++RLen++TDpBLinPosFunctions+++++++++++++++++++++++++++++
A          R OPMSPLRCRD
A            PMBLANK8        8        COLHDG('BLANKS')
A            PMFLDNAME      10        COLHDG('FIELD NAME')
A            PMFILLER2       2        COLHDG('FILLER')
A            PMFLDTYPE      10        COLHDG('FIELD TYPE')
A            PMFILLER      102        COLHDG('FILLER')
```

Figure 11.41: The SPLDTAOPM physical file.

```
/*==============================================================*/
/* To compile:                                                  */
/*                                                              */
/*        CRTCMD     CMD(XXX/BLDWRKFLD) PGM(XXX/FIG1143CL)      */
/*                   SRCMBR(FIG1142CM)                          */
/*                                                              */
/*==============================================================*/
          CMD        PROMPT('BUILD WORK FIELDS')
          PARM       KWD(SRCFILE) TYPE(NAME1) MIN(1) +
                     PROMPT('Source File Name:')
          PARM       KWD(HOLDFILE) TYPE(NAME1) MIN(1) +
                     PROMPT('Holding File Name:')
NAME1:    QUAL       TYPE(*NAME) LEN(10)
          QUAL       TYPE(*CHAR) LEN(10) DFT(*LIBL) SPCVAL((' ' +
                     *LIBL)) CHOICE('Name, *LIBL') +
                     PROMPT('Library Name:')
```

Figure 11.42: The BLDWRKFLD command.

393

```
/******************************************************************************/
/*    TO CREATE:                                                            */
/*        CRTCLPGM PGM(XXXLIB/FIG1143CL)                                    */
/******************************************************************************/
PGM   (&SRCIN  &HLDIN)

             DCL     VAR(&SRCIN) TYPE(*CHAR) LEN(20)
             DCL     VAR(&HLDIN) TYPE(*CHAR) LEN(20)
             DCL     VAR(&SRCLIB) TYPE(*CHAR) LEN(10)
             DCL     VAR(&HLDFIL) TYPE(*CHAR) LEN(10)
             DCL     VAR(&HLDLIB) TYPE(*CHAR) LEN(10)
             DCL     VAR(&SRCFIL) TYPE(*CHAR) LEN(10)
             DCL     VAR(&SRCTYP) TYPE(*CHAR) LEN(10)
             DCL     VAR(&MEMBR) TYPE(*CHAR) LEN(10)
             DCL     VAR(&JOBTYPE) TYPE(*CHAR) LEN(1)
             DCL     VAR(&MSGDTA) TYPE(*CHAR) LEN(512)
             DCL     VAR(&MSGID) TYPE(*CHAR) LEN(7)

             CHGVAR  &SRCFIL VALUE(%SST(&SRCIN 1 10))
             CHGVAR  &SRCLIB VALUE(%SST(&SRCIN 11 10))
             CHGVAR  &HLDFIL VALUE(%SST(&HLDIN 1 10))
             CHGVAR  &HLDLIB VALUE(%SST(&HLDIN 11 10))

     /*  MAKE SURE SOURCE FILE/LIBRARY EXISTS            */

             CHKOBJ  OBJ(&SRCLIB/&SRCFIL) OBJTYPE(*FILE)
             MONMSG  MSGID(CPF0000) EXEC(DO)
             RCVMSG  MSGDTA(&MSGDTA) MSGID(&MSGID)
             SNDPGMMSG  MSGID(&MSGID) MSGF(QCPFMSG) MSGDTA(&MSGDTA)
             RETURN
             ENDDO

             IF      (&SRCIN = &HLDIN) THEN(DO)
             SNDPGMMSG  MSGID(CPF9898) MSGF(QCPFMSG) MSGDTA('Source FILE/LIBRARY
                        AND holding FILE/LIBRARY cannot be the same name.')
             RETURN
             ENDDO

     /*  IF NOT RUNNING IN BATCH, SUBMIT IT AND GET OUT  */

             RTVJOBA  TYPE(&JOBTYPE)
             IF       COND(&JOBTYPE *EQ '1') THEN(DO)
             SBMJOB   CMD(CALL PGM(FIG1143CL) PARM(&SRCIN &HLDIN)) +
                        JOB(BLDWRKFLDS)
             SNDPGMMSG  MSGID(CPF9898) MSGF(QCPFMSG) MSGDTA('JOB +
                        BLDWRKFLDS has been submitted +
                        to batch.') MSGTYPE(*DIAG)

             GOTO     ENDPGM
             ENDDO

     /*  CREATE TEMPORARY WORK FILE FOR COMPILES  */
```

Figure 11.43: The FIG1143CL CL program (part 1 of 2).

```
             CHKOBJ     QTEMP/FLDSPOOL *FILE
             MONMSG     MSGID(CPF9801) EXEC(DO)
             CRTPF      FILE(QTEMP/FLDSPOOL) RCDLEN(132) +
                          OPTION(*NOSRC) MAXMBRS(*NOMAX) +
                          SIZE(*NOMAX) LVLCHK(*NO)
             ENDDO
             CLRPFM     QTEMP/FLDSPOOL

             CHKOBJ     &HLDLIB/&HLDFIL *FILE
             MONMSG     MSGID(CPF9801) EXEC(DO)
             CRTPF      FILE(&HLDLIB/&HLDFIL) SRCFILE(SOURCE) +
                          SRCMBR(FIG1139) SIZE(*NOMAX) LVLCHK(*NO)
             ENDDO
             CLRPFM     &HLDLIB/&HLDFIL
             OVRDBF     FILE(FIELDSPF) TOFILE(&HLDLIB/&HLDFIL)

   /*  GET THE FIRST SOURCE MEMBER TO COMPILE  */

             RTVMBRD    FILE(&SRCLIB/&SRCFIL) MBR(*FIRSTMBR) +
                          RTNMBR(&MEMBR) SRCTYPE(&SRCTYP)
             MONMSG     MSGID(CPF3049) EXEC(GOTO ENDPGM)
             GOTO       FIRST

LOOP:
             RTVMBRD    FILE(&SRCLIB/&SRCFIL) MBR(&MEMBR *NEXT) +
                          RTNMBR(&MEMBR) SRCTYPE(&SRCTYP)
             MONMSG     MSGID(CPF3049) EXEC(GOTO ENDPGM)
FIRST:
             IF         COND((&SRCTYP *NE 'RPG') *AND (&SRCTYP *NE +
                          'RPGLE')) THEN(GOTO CMDLBL(LOOP))

             ADDPFM     FILE(QTEMP/FLDSPOOL) MBR(&MEMBR)
             MONMSG     MSGID(CPF0000)
             OVRDBF     FILE(QSYSPRT) TOFILE(QTEMP/FLDSPOOL) MBR(&MEMBR)
             IF         COND(&SRCTYP *EQ 'RPG') THEN(DO)
             CRTRPGPGM  PGM(QTEMP/&MEMBR) SRCFILE(&SRCLIB/&SRCFIL) +
                          OPTION(*NOGEN *SRC) GENOPT(*XREF)
             ENDDO
             IF         COND(&SRCTYP *EQ 'RPGLE') THEN(DO)
             CRTRPGMOD  MODULE(QTEMP/&MEMBR) SRCFILE(&SRCLIB/&SRCFIL)
             MONMSG     MSGID(RNS9309)
             ENDDO
             OVRDBF     FILE(FLDSPOOL) TOFILE(QTEMP/FLDSPOOL) MBR(&MEMBR)
             CALL       FIG1144RG  (&SRCTYP &SRCLIB &SRCFIL)
             RMVM       FILE(QTEMP/FLDSPOOL) MBR(&MEMBR)
             MONMSG     MSGID(CPF0000)
             GOTO       LOOP

ENDPGM:

             DLTOVR     *ALL
ENDPGM
```

Figure 11.43: The FIG1143CL CL program (part 2 of 2).

```
        ************************************************************************
        *  TO COMPILE:
        *     CRTBNDRPG PGM(XXXLIB/FIG1144RG)
        ************************************************************************
        *
        FFilename++IPEASFRlen+LKlen+AIDevice+.Keywords+++++++++++++++++++++++++Comments
        FFldspool  IF   F  132         Disk    INFDS(InfoDs)
        FFieldsPf  O    e             Disk


        DName+++++++++++ETDsFrom+++To/L+++IDc.Keywords+++++++++++++++++++++++++Comments
        DSplDtaOpm       E DS                  EXTNAME(SplDtaOpm)
        DSplDtaILE       E DS                  EXTNAME(SplDtaILE)
        DSpoolType         S            10
        DSourceLib         S            10
        DSourceFile        S            10
        DWorkNumber        S             3 0
        DWrkDigits         S             5
        DFldLen1           S             1
        DFldLen2           S             2
        DTimeField         S             6 0
        DInfoDs            DS
        D MemberName               129   138
        DDateDs            DS
        DWorkDate                         D
        D Year4                           4    OVERLAY(WorkDate:1)
        D Month                           2    OVERLAY(WorkDate:6)
        D Day                             2    OVERLAY(WorkDate:9)


        CL0N01Factor1+++++++Opcode&ExtFactor2+++++++Result++++++++Len++D+HiLoEq......
        C         *ENTRY      PLIST
        C                     PARM                   SpoolType
        C                     PARM                   SourceLib
        C                     PARM                   SourceFile
        C         *MDY        MOVE      UDATE        WorkDate
        C                     TIME                   TimeField
        C         1           SETLL     FLDSPOOL
B1      C         SpoolType   Caseq     'RPG'        ProcessOpm
        C         SpoolType   Caseq     'RPGLE'      ProcessILE
E1      C                     ENDCS
        C                     Eval      *inlr = *ON
        * Process original program model source members
        C         PROCESSOPM  BEGSR
B1      C                     DOU       *in50 = *ON
        C                     READ      FLDSPOOL     SplDtaOpm          50
B2      C                     IF        *in50
        C                     LEAVE
E2      C                     ENDIF
        * Filter out none field name records
B2      C                     IF        PmBlank8 <> *blanks
        C                     ITER
E2      C                     ENDIF
B2      C                     IF        PmFldName = *BLANKS
        C                     ITER
E2      C                     ENDIF
```

Figure 11.44: The FIG1144RG RPG program (part 1 of 3).

```
        C                    MOVEL     PmFldType      TST2                    2
B2      C                    IF        (Tst2 <> 'A(') and
        C                              (Tst2 <> 'P(') and
        C                              (Tst2 <> 'B(') and
        C                              (Tst2 <> 'S(')
        C                    ITER
E2      C                    ENDIF
        *  Strip out size of field digits and decimals
        C                    EVAL      WrkDigits = *blanks
        C                    eval      NbrDigits = 0
        C                    eval      NbrDecimls = 0
B2      C                    If        Tst2 = 'A('
        C          ')'       Scan      PmFldType:3   G             2 0    02
        C                    Eval      WrkDigits = %SUBST(PmFldType:3:(G-3))
X2      C                    else
        C          ','       Scan      PmFldType:3   F             2 0    01
B3      C                    If        *in01 = *on
        C                    Eval      WrkDigits =  (%SUBST(PmFldType:3:(F-3)))
        C          ')'       Scan      PmFldType:F   G                    02
B4      C                    If        *in02 = *on
        C                    Eval      WorkNumber = (G-F) - 1
B5      C                    If        WorkNumber = 1
        C                    Eval      FldLen1 = %subst(IlFldSize:G+1:1)
        C                    MOVE      FldLen1        NbrDecimls
X5      C                    ELSE
        C                    EVAL      FldLen2 = %subst(IlFldSize:G+1:2)
        C                    MOVE      FldLen2        NbrDecimls
E5      C                    ENDIF
E4      C                    ENDIF
E3      C                    ENDIF
E2      C                    ENDIF
        * Right justify and replace blanks with 0's
B2      C                    IF        WrkDigits <> *blanks
        C                    EVAL      WrkDigits = %Trimr(WrkDigits)
        C          ' ':'0'   XLATE     WrkDigits      WrkDigits
        C                    Move      WrkDigits      NbrDigits
E2      C                    ENDIF
        C                    EVAL      FieldName = PmFldName
        C                    EVAL      ProgramNam = MemberName
        C                    EVAL      CreateDate = Year4 + Month + Day
        C                    MOVEL     TimeField      CreateTime
        C                    WRITE     FieldsRec
E1      C                    ENDDO
        C                    ENDSR
        C     PROCESSILE     BEGSR
B1      C                    DOU       *in50 = *ON
        C                    READ      FLDSPOOL       SplDtaILE             50
B2      C                    IF        *in50
        C                    LEAVE
E2      C                    ENDIF
        * Filter out none field name records
B2      C                    IF        ILBlank9 <> *blanks
        C                    ITER
E2      C                    ENDIF
```

Figure 11.44: The FIG1144RG RPG program (part 2 of 3).

```
B2   C                  IF      ILFldName = *BLANKS
     C                  ITER
E2   C                  ENDIF
     C                  EVAL    WrkDigits = *blanks
     C                  MOVEL   IlFldSize     TST2          2
     C                  MOVEL   IlFldSize     TST3          3
B2   C                  IF      (Tst2 <> 'A(') and
     C                          (Tst2 <> 'P(') and
     C                          (Tst2 <> 'B(') and
     C                          (Tst2 <> 'S(') and
     C                          (Tst3 <> 'DS(')
     C                  ITER
E2   C                  ENDIF
     * Strip out field size digits and decimals
     C                  EVAL    NbrDecimls = 0
B2   C                  IF      (Tst2 = 'A(') or (Tst3 = 'DS(')
B3   C                  IF      Tst2 = 'A('
     C                  EVAL    F = 3
X3   C                  ELSE
     C                  EVAL    F = 4
E3   C                  ENDIF
     C        ')'       SCAN    IlFldSize:F   G               2 0    02
     C                  EVAL    WrkDigits = %SUBST(IlFldSize:F:(G-F))
E2   C                  ENDIF
     C                  EVAL    F = 3
     C        ','       SCAN    IlFldSize:F   G               2 0    01
B2   C                  IF      *in01 = *on
     C                  EVAL    WrkDigits = %SUBST(IlFldSize:F:(G-F))
     C        ')'       SCAN    IlFldSize:G   H               2 0    02
B3   C                  IF      *in02 = *on
     C                  EVAL    WorkNumber = (H-G) - 1
B4   C                  IF      WorkNumber = 1
     C                  EVAL    FldLen1 = %subst(IlFldSize:G+1:1)
     C                  MOVE    FldLen1       NbrDecimls
X4   C                  ELSE
     C                  EVAL    FldLen2 = %subst(IlFldSize:G+1:2)
     C                  MOVE    FldLen2       NbrDecimls
E4   C                  ENDIF
E3   C                  ENDIF
E2   C                  ENDIF
     * Right justify the size field and replace *blanks with 0s
B2   C                  IF      WrkDigits <> *blanks
     C                  EVAL    WrkDigits = %Trimr(WrkDigits)
     C        ' ':'0'   XLATE   WrkDigits     WrkDigits
     C                  Move    WrkDigits     NbrDigits
E2   C                  ENDIF
     C                  EVAL    FieldName = IlFldName
     C                  EVAL    ProgramNam = MemberName
     C                  EVAL    CreateDate = Year4 + Month + Day
     C                  MOVEL   TimeField     CreateTime
     C                  WRITE   FieldsRec
E1   C                  ENDDO
     C                  ENDSR
```

Figure 11.44: The FIG1144RG RPG program (part 3 of 3).

Figures 11.45, 11.46, 11.47, and 11.48 are the display file, RPG program, CL program, and command that comprise the WRKFLD command.

```
A*******************************************************************************
A*  TO COMPILE:
A*     CRTDSPF FILE(XXXLIB/FIG1145DS)
A*******************************************************************************
AAN01N02N03T.Name++++++RLen++TDpBLinPosFunctions++++++++++++++++++++++++++++++++
A                                        DSPSIZ(24 80 *DS3)
A                                        CF03(03)
A                                        CF12
A              R FORMAT2                 SFL
A                SFLSELECT    1A  B 12  7DSPATR(HI)
A                HDNSRCLIB   10A  H
A                HDNSRCFIL   10A  H
A                FIELDNAME   10A  O 12 11
A                PROGRAMNAM  10A  O 12 22
A              R FORMAT2C                SFLCTL(FORMAT2)
A                                        SFLLIN(0005)
A                                        SFLSIZ(0040)
A                                        SFLPAG(0020)
A                                        ROLLUP(27)
A                                        OVERLAY
A  21                                    SFLDSP
A                                        SFLDSPCTL
A  25                                    SFLCLR
A  41                                    SFLEND(*MORE)
A                RRNRCD       4S OH      SFLRCDNBR
A                                      1 30'Work with Fields'
A                                        DSPATR(HI)
A                                        DSPATR(UL)
A                                      5  4'Size of search field . . . . . . .-
A                                          .'
A                                      9 23'2=Browse'
A                                        COLOR(BLU)
A N21                                     DSPATR(ND)
A                                      9 34'6=Print'
A                                        COLOR(BLU)
A N21                                     DSPATR(ND)
A                                      9  7'1=Edit source'
A                                        COLOR(BLU)
A N21                                     DSPATR(ND)
A                                      8  3'Type options, press enter.'
A                                        COLOR(BLU)
A N21                                     DSPATR(ND)
A                                     11  6'Opt'
A                                        DSPATR(HI)
A N21                                     DSPATR(ND)
```

Figure 11.45: The FIG1145DS display file (part 1 of 2).

```
A                                     11 11'Field'
A                                        DSPATR(HI)
A N21                                     DSPATR(ND)
A                                     11 22'Program'
A                                        DSPATR(HI)
A N21                                     DSPATR(ND)
A                                      3  4'Holding file to search in. . . . .-
A                                          .'
A           SEARCHFILE    10A  B  3 41
A 21                                      DSPATR(PR)
A                                      4  5'Library of holding file . . . . . -
A                                          .'
A           SEARCHLIB     10A  B  4 41
A 21                                      DSPATR(PR)
A           SRCHDIGITS     5D 0B  5 43CHGINPDFT
A                                        CHECK(RZ)
A 21                                      DSPATR(PR)
A           SRCHDECIML     2D 0B  5 49CHGINPDFT
A                                        CHECK(RZ)
A 21                                      DSPATR(PR)
A                                      3 54'Created:'
A N60                                     DSPATR(ND)
A           HOLDDATE       8Y 0O  3 69EDTWRD('  /  /    ')
A N60                                     DSPATR(ND)
A           HOLDTIME       4Y 0O  3 63EDTWRD('  :  ')
A N60                                     DSPATR(ND)
A                                     11 36'Opt'
A                                        DSPATR(HI)
A N21N61                                  DSPATR(ND)
A                                     11 41'Field'
A                                        DSPATR(HI)
A N21N61                                  DSPATR(ND)
A                                     11 52'Program'
A                                        DSPATR(HI)
A N21N61                                  DSPATR(ND)
A           FILTERNAME    10A  B  6 41
A 21                                      DSPATR(PR)
A                                      6  4'Only include field named . . . . .-
A                                          .'
A           R FORMAT1
A                                     23  4'F3=Exit'
A                                        COLOR(BLU)
A                                     23 16'F12=Previous'
A                                        COLOR(BLU)
```

Figure 11.45: The FIG1145DS display file (part 2 of 2).

```
     ********************************************************************
     *  TO COMPILE:
     *     CRTBNDPGM PGM(XXXLIB/FIG1146RG)
     ********************************************************************
     FFilename++IPEASFRlen+LKlen+AIDevice+.Keywords+++++++++++++++++++++++++Comments
     FFig1145DS CF   E                    WORKSTN
     F                                                 SFILE(Format2:RelRecNbr)
     F                                                 INFDS(InfoDs)
     FFIELDSPF   IF   E             K DISK             USROPN

     DName+++++++++++++ETDsFrom+++To/L+++IDc.Keywords+++++++++++++++++++++++++Comments
     DOverrideC        c                    'OVRDBF FILE(FIELDSPF) TOFILE('
     DSearchSize       S              7
     DSaveFile         S             21
     DHoldFile         S             21
     DCommand          S             55
     DCommandLen       S             15 5
     DRelRecNbr        S              4 0
     DTestWild         S              1
     DOkToGoON         S              1
     DIndex            S              2 0
     DWildSearch       S             10
     DTestField        S             10
     DDataField        S             10
     DX                S              2 0
     DI                S              2 0
     DSearchLen        S              2 0
     DFound            S              2 0
     DEight            S              8 0
     DIsoDate          S                D    datfmt(*iso)
     DUsaDate          S                D    datfmt(*usa)
     DInfoDs           DS
     D FirstLine                378    379B 0

     CL0N01Factor1+++++++Opcode&ExtFactor2+++++++Result+++++++++Len++D+HiLoEq......
     C                   DOU       *IN03 = *on
     C                   SETOFF                                           216061
     C                   WRITE     FORMAT1
     C                   EXFMT     FORMAT2C
     C                   IF        *in03 = *on
     C                   GOTO      endpgm
     C                   ENDIF
     * Clear the subfile
     C                   EVAL      *in25 = *on
     C                   WRITE     Format2C
     C                   EVAL      *in25 = *off
     C                   EVAL      RelRecNbr = 0
     * Override to requested fields holding file
     C                   EVAL      Holdfile=%Trim(SearchLib) +
     C                                '/' + SearchFile
     C                   IF        Holdfile <> Savefile
     C                   IF        SaveFile <> *blanks
     C                   CLOSE     FIELDSPf
```

Figure 11.46: The FIG1146RG RPG program (part 1 of 4).

```
     C                     ENDIF
     C                     EVAL      Command = OverrideC +
     C                                         %Trim(HoldFile) + ')'
     C                     CALL      'QCMDEXC'
     C                     PARM                     Command
     C                     PARM      55             CommandLen
     C                     OPEN      FIELDSPf
     C                     ENDIF
     C                     EVAL      SaveFile = HoldFile
     C         SizeKey     KLIST
     C                     KFLD                     SrchDigits
     C                     KFLD                     SrchDeciml
     *   Read requested records
     C         SizeKey     SETLL     FIELDSPf
     C                     DOU       *IN27 = *OFF
     C                     EVAL      X = 0
B1   C                     DOU       (*In41 = *on) or (X = 20)
     C         SizeKey     READE     FIELDSPF                      41
B2   C                     IF        *In41 = *ON
     C                     LEAVE
E2   C                     ENDIF
     C                     IF        FilterName <> *blanks
     C                     MOVEL     FilterName     TestWild
     C                     IF        TestWild = '*'
     C                     EXSR      WildSR
     C                     IF        OkToGoOn <> 'Y'
     C                     ITER
     C                     ENDIF
     C                     ENDIF
     C                     EVAL      Found = 0
     C                     EVAL      SearchLen = 0
     C                     IF        OkToGoOn <> 'Y'
     C         '*'         CHECKR    FilterName     Found
     C                     IF        Found <> 0
     C                     EVAL      SearchLen = Found - 1
     C         SearchLen   SUBST     FilterName:1  TestField
     C         SearchLen   SUBST     FieldName:1   DataField
     C                     IF        DataField <> TestField
     C                     ITER
     C                     ENDIF
     C                     ENDIF
     C                     ENDIF
     C                     IF        FieldName <> FilterName
     C                                 and TestWild <> '*'
     C                                 and SearchLen = 0
     C                     ITER
     C                     ENDIF
     C                     ENDIF
     C                     EVAL      RelRecNbr = RelRecNbr + 1
     C                     EVAL      HdnSrcLib = SourceLib
     C                     EVAL      HdnSrcFil = SourceFile
     C                     EVAL      RrnRcd = RelRecNbr
     C                     EVAL      X = X + 1
```

Figure 11.46: The FIG1146RG RPG program (part 2 of 4).

402

```
      C                     WRITE     FORMAT2
E1    C                     ENDDO
      * Only display subfile if records were written
B1    C                     IF        RelRecNbr <> 0
      C                     EVAL      *in21 = *on
      C                     ENDIF
      * Display heading for secondary columns if enough records
B1    C                     IF        RelRecNbr > 20
      C                     EVAL      *in61 = *on
      C                     ENDIF
      C                     MOVE      CreateDate     Eight
      C         *ISO        TEST(D)                  Eight              68
      C                     IF        *IN68 = *OFF
      C         *ISO        MOVE      Eight          IsoDate
      C                     MOVE      IsoDate        UsaDate
      C                     MOVE      UsaDate        HoldDate
      C                     Else
      C                     MOVE      *zeros         HoldDate
      C                     ENDIF
      C                     MOVE      CreateTime     HoldTime
      C         Reshow      TAG
      C                     EVAL      *in60 = *on
      C                     WRITE     FORMAT1
      C                     EXFMT     FORMAT2C
      C         *INKC       CABEQ     *ON            ENDPGM
      C                     ENDDO
      * Back up and input new request
      C                     IF        *INKL = *ON
      C                     ITER
      C                     ENDIF
      * Look for requests to edit,view, or print the source members
B2    C                     DOU       *in55 = *On
      C                     READC     FORMAT2                           55
B3    C                     IF        *in55 = *ON
      C                     LEAVE
E3    C                     ENDIF
B3    C         SflSelect   CASEQ     '1'            SOURCE
B3    C         SflSelect   CASEQ     '2'            SOURCE
B3    C         SflSelect   CASEQ     '6'            SOURCE
E3    C                     ENDCS
      C                     MOVE      ' '            SflSelect
      C                     UPDATE    FORMAT2
      C                     EVAL      RRNRCD = RelRecNbr
E2    C                     ENDDO
B2    C                     IF        Looked = 'Y'
      C                     MOVE      ' '            Looked             1
      C                     GOTO      RESHOW
E2    C                     ENDIF
      C                     ENDDO
      C         ENDPGM      TAG
      C                     EVAL      *inlr = *ON
      * Call program to edit,view or print the requested source member
      C         SOURCE      BEGSR
```

Figure 11.46: The FIG1146RG RPG program (part 3 of 4).

```
C                      CALL       'FIG1147CL'
C                      PARM                  HdnSrcLib
C                      PARM                  HdnSrcFil
C                      PARM                  ProgramNam
C                      PARM                  SflSelect
C                      MOVE       'Y'        Looked
C                      ENDSR
 * Look for wildscan if search field
C        WILDSR        BEGSR
C                      EVAL       OkTOGoON = 'Y'
C        '*'           SCAN       FilterName:2  Found
C                      IF         Found <> 0
C                      EVAL       Index = Found - 2
C        Index         SUBST(P)   FilterName:2  WildSearch
C        ' '           CHECKR     WildSearch    I
C        WildSearch:I  SCAN       FieldName                        05
C                      IF         *in05 = *oFF
C                      EVAL       OkTOGOON = 'N'
C                      ENDIF
C                      ENDIF
C                      ENDSR
```

Figure 11.46: The FIG1146RG RPG program (part 4 of 4).

```
/****************************************************************************/
/*    TO CREATE:                                                            */
/*        CRTCLPGM PGM(XXXLIB/FIG1147CL)                                    */
/****************************************************************************/
          PGM          PARM(&TOLIB &TOFILE &PASMBR &FUNC)

          DCL          VAR(&PASMBR) TYPE(*CHAR) LEN(10)
          DCL          VAR(&TOLIB)  TYPE(*CHAR) LEN(10)
          DCL          VAR(&TOFILE) TYPE(*CHAR) LEN(10)
          DCL          VAR(&FUNC)   TYPE(*CHAR) LEN(1)
          DCL          VAR(&OPTION) TYPE(*CHAR) LEN(1)

          IF           COND(&FUNC *EQ '1') THEN(DO)
          CHGVAR       &OPTION '2'
          ENDDO
          IF           COND(&FUNC *EQ '2') THEN(DO)
          CHGVAR       &OPTION '5'
          ENDDO
          IF           COND(&FUNC *EQ '6') THEN(DO)
          CHGVAR       &OPTION '6'
          ENDDO
          STRSEU       SRCFILE(&TOLIB/&TOFILE) SRCMBR(&PASMBR) +
                         TYPE(*SAME) OPTION(&OPTION)

          ENDPGM
```

Figure 11.47: The FIG1147CL CL program.

```
/*================================================================*/
/* To compile:                                                    */
/*                                                                */
/*          CRTCMD        CMD(XXX/WRKFLD) PGM(XXX/FIG1146RG)       */
/*                        SRCMBR(FIG1148CM)                        */
/*                                                                */
/*================================================================*/
          CMD           PROMPT('WORK FIELDS')
```

Figure 11.48: The WRKFLD command.

THE DISPLAY FILE DESCRIPTION (DSPFILDSC) COMMAND

As an AS/400 programmer, you are already intimately familiar with a very useful tool called the Display File Description (DSPFD) command. It will tell you almost everything there is to know about a particular file. If you want to know the auxiliary storage ID, the preferred storage unit, or the coded character set ID, it's all displayed at the push of a button and a couple of roll keys. Want to know if the file allows read, write, update, or delete operations? How about the access path size, or the file level identifier? All this information is displayed every time you run the command. And that is just the problem: *information overload*. You get screen after screen of information about the file, whether you want it or not. How often do you really care about data space activity? (Once in a blue moon, maybe.)

Ninety percent of the time we use the DSPFD command, we are only looking for a couple of pieces of information. If we are writing records to a file, it is the number of records in the file and maybe the file size that interests us. Other times (like when a file gets a level check error), it is the record size and the file creation information that is most useful. When tracking down problems, we occasionally need to know if the file has journalling turned on and, if so, the name of the journal. But that is about it. It is unusual that we need to see any more information than that.

It is for those reasons that we created our own "slimmed down" version of the DSPFD command. For want of a different, but accurate command name, we call our new command DSPFILDSC. An example of the output of this command is shown in Figure 11.49, while the parameters needed to run it are shown in Figure 11.50.

What It Won't Do

For the purposes of our DSPFILDSC command, we chose to totally ignore display files. When we need to look at a display file, we use IBM's DSPFD command. With display files, we are typically only looking for the "restore display," "defer write," "keep," and "assume" display file attributes. If you try to run DSPFILDSC on a display file, you will get an error message instead.

Another of our tool's limitations is in the way it handles multiple member files. Because we are not big fans of multiple member files, we did not include code to display information about more than one member at a time. You can display any individual member in a multiple member file (by specifying the member name), but we do not provide you with a member list.

The same is true with multiple format logical files. While our systems do employ multiple format logical files, we chose not to address multiple format members with our command. You can look at any individual format in a multiple format logical, but you must specify the member name.

What It Will Do

Our DSPFILDSC command *will* provide you with a single screen of accurate and pertinent information about any physical or logical file. In addition, the command will show you a couple of things DSPFD does not. The owner of the file is displayed (along with the creation information), which can be really useful when you are dealing with object authority issues. When displaying the key fields for your file, we also show the size and description of each of the key fields. We have found these additions to be useful on more than one occasion.

How It Works

There are three components that make up our DSPFILDSC command, which is shown in. Figure 11.50. The RPG IV driver program that appears in Figure 11.52 uses five main APIs to gather the necessary information about the specified file. (Refer to chapter 9 if you need help deciphering any of the APIs used with this tool.) The associated display file used by the RPG IV program to present the information is shown in Figure 11.51.

```
                      Display File Description

Physical File  . . . . .   INSUR        Insurance Company Master File
  Library . . . . . . . .   C51FILES
                                        File Type. . . . . . .    PF
Level check. . . . . . .   No           Member name. . . . . .    INSUR
Records in file. . . . .   000001549    Number of members. . . .  01
Deleted records in file.   000000024
File size. . . . . . . .   000888832    Record Format. . . . . .  INSREC
Owned by . . . . . . . .   QPGMR        Number of Formats. . . .  01
Created by . . . . . . .   LORI         Record length. . . . . .  000471
Created. . . .  12/15/99 03:58 PM       Number of fields . . . .  0098
Saved. . . . .  04/28/00 11:13 PM       Initial member size. . .  *NOMAX
Source file. . . . . .     FILES        Currently journaled. . .  No
  Library . . . . . . . .   C51LIB      Current or last journal.
                                          Library . . . . . . . .

   Key Field        Size   Text
   01  INNUM       000005 P Insurance ID


                                                              Bottom

   F3=Exit
```

Figure 11.49: The DSPFILDSC output screen.

```
/*==============================================================*/
/* To compile:                                                  */
/*                                                              */
/*          CRTCMD      CMD(XXX/DSPFILDSC) PGM(XXX/FIG1152RG) +  */
/*                      SRCFILE(XXX/SOURCE)                      */
/*                                                              */
/*==============================================================*/
            CMD         PROMPT('Display File Description')

            PARM        KWD(FILE) TYPE(QUAL) MIN(1) PROMPT('File')
            PARM        KWD(FORMAT) TYPE(*CHAR) LEN(10) DFT(*FIRST) +
                        PROMPT('Member name')
            PARM        KWD(RCDFMT) TYPE(*NAME) DFT(*FIRST) +
                        SPCVAL((*FIRST)) PROMPT('Record format')

QUAL:       QUAL        TYPE(*NAME) LEN(10)
            QUAL        TYPE(*NAME) LEN(10) DFT(*LIBL) +
                        SPCVAL((*LIBL)) PROMPT('Library')
```

Figure 11.50: The DSPFILDSC command.

```
A*******************************************************************
A*  TO COMPILE:
A*     CRTDSPF FILE(XXXLIB/FIG1150DS) SRCFILE(XXXLIB/QDDSSRC)
A*******************************************************************
A                                       CF03
A           R SFLRCD                    SFL
A             SFFLD       10A  O 18  9
A             SFTEXT      38A  O 18 29
A             SFKEY        2A  O 18  5
A             SFFSIZ       6  00 18 20
A             SFTYPE       1   O 18 27
A           R SFLCTL                    SFLCTL(SFLRCD)
A                                       SFLSIZ(0012) SFLPAG(0004)
A                                       SFLDSPCTL  OVERLAY
A  21                                   SFLDSP
A  25                                   SFLCLR
A  53                                   SFLEND(*MORE)
A                                     1 28'Display File Description'
A                                     3  2'Physical File  . . . . .'
A             OUTFILENAM  10A  O  3 28
A             OUTLIBNAME  10A  O  4 28
A                                     5 43'File Type. . . . . . . .'
A             OUTTYPE      5A  O  5 70
A                                     6 43'Member name. . . . . . .'
A             OUTMEMBER   10A  O  6 70
A             OUTRECLEN    6Y 00 11 70
A                                     9 43'Record Format. . . . . .'
A             OUTFORMAT   10A  O  9 70
A                                    12 43'Number of fields . . . .'
A             NBRFLDS      4Y 00 12 70
A                                    17  5'Key'
A                                    17  9'Field'
A                                    17 29'Text'
A             FILDSC      40A  O  3 40
A                                     7 43'Number of members. . . .'
A             NBRMBR       2S 00  7 70
A                                    13 43'Initial member size. . .'
A             MBRSIZ       8A  O 13 70
A                                     6  2'Level check. . . . . . .'
A             LVLCHK       3A  O  6 28
A                                     7  2'Records in file. . . . .'
A             NBRRCD       9S 00  7 28
A                                     8  2'Deleted records in file.'
A             NBRDLT       9S 00  8 28
A             LSTSVD       8A  O 13 19
A             CRTTIM       8A  O 12 28
A             SVDTIM       8A  O 13 28
A                                    11 43'Record length. . . . . .'
A                                    14 43'Currently journaled. . .'
A             JRNLD        3A  O 14 70
A                                    15 43'Current or last journal.'
A             JRNNAM      10A  O 15 70
A                                    16 43' Library . . . . . . . .'
```

Figure 11.51: The DSPFILDSC DDS (part 1 of 2).

```
A              JRNLIB        10A  0 16 70
A              CRTDAT         8A  0 12 19
A                                  12  2'Created. . . .'
A                                  11  2'Created by . . . . . . .'
A              CRTBY         10A  0 11 28
A                                  10  2'Owned by . . . . . . . .'
A              OWNER         10A  0 10 28
A                                  13  2'Saved. . . . .'
A                                  14  2'Source file. . . . . . .'
A              SRCFIL        10A  0 14 28
A                                  15  3'Library . . . . . . . .'
A              SRCLIB        10A  0 15 28
A                                   4  2' Library . . . . . . . .'
A                                  17 22'Size'
A                                   9  2'File size. . . . . . . .'
A              FILSIZ         9S 00  9 28
A                                  10 43'Number of Formats. . . .'
A              NBROFFMTS      2S 00 10 70
A            R FMT1
A                                  23  4'F3=Exit'  COLOR(BLU)
```

Figure 11.51: The DSPFILDSC DDS (part 2 of 2).

```
**********************************************************************
*  TO COMPILE:
*    CRTBNDRPG PGM(XXXLIB/FIG1152RG) SRCFILE(XXXLIB/QRPGLESRC)
**********************************************************************
FFig1151ds CF   E            WORKSTN
F                                     SFILE(SFLRCD:RelRecNbr)

D AR            S              1    DIM(4096)
D AKEY          S             10    DIM(120)
D Data          S             50
D DateField     S              d
D DoNbrKeys     S              5 0
D EntryFmt      S             10
D FileFormat    S              8
D FileLib       S             20
D FormatType    S             10
D I             S              7 0
D J             S              2 0
D ListFormat    S              8
D MemberName    S             10
D MessageTyp    S             10
D MessageQue    S             10
D MsgF          S             20    inz('QCPFMSG    QSYS        ')
D MultFmt       S              1
D ObjectType    S             10
D OverRide      S              1
D ReceiveVr2    S            300
```

Figure 11.52 : The DSPFILDSC program (part 1 of 7).

```
D RelRecNbr       S                   4  0
D S               S                   7  0
D SpaceAttr       S                  10
D SpaceAuth       S                  10
D SpaceRepl       S                  10
D SpaceText       S                  50
D SpaceVal        S                   1
D SpacePoint      S                   *
D System          S                  10
D TimeFld         S                   t
D Time6           S                   6  0
D UserSpace       S                  20     inz('FILSPC    QTEMP     ')

D ObjDs           DS                300
D  Owner                      53    62
D  CrtDatTim                  65    77
D   CrtDate                   66    71  0
D   CrtTimE                   72    77
D  SrcFil                    151   160
D  SrcLib                    161   170
D  SavDatTim                 194   206
D   SvdDate                  195   200  0
D   SvdTimE                  201   206  .
D  CrtBy                     220   229
D GenDs           DS                140     Based(GenDsPoint)
D  OffsetHdr                 117   120B 0
D  OffsetList                125   128B 0
D  NbrInList                 133   136B 0
D  SizeEntry                 137   140B 0
D HeaderDs        DS                 44     Based(HeadPoint)
D  OutFileNam                  1    10
D  OutLibName                 11    20
D  OutType                    21    25
D  OutFormat                  31    40
D  RecordLen                  41    44B 0
D ListDs          DS                 82     Based(ListPoint)
D  SfFld                       1    10
D  SfType                     11    11
D  BufferOut                  13    16B 0
D  FieldLen                   21    24B 0
D  Digits                     25    28B 0
D  Decimals                   29    32B 0
D  FieldDesc                  33    82
D ErrorDs         DS                116     INZ
D  BytesPrv                    1     4B 0 inz(116)
D  BytesAvl                    5     8B 0
D  MessageId                   9    15
D  ERR###                     16    16
D  MessageDta                 17   116
D ReceiveVar      DS               4096
D  FileType                    9     9
D  Attribs                    10    10
D  NbrOfMbrs                  48    49B 0
D  NbrOfFmts                  62    63B 0
D  FilDsc                     85   124
```

Figure 11.52 : The DSPFILDSC program (part 2 of 7).

```
D   DBFileOff              317    320B 0
D   DBPhyOff               365    368B 0
D   DBJrnOff               379    382B 0
D ReceiveMbr      DS              240
D   OutMember              29     38
D   NbrRcd                 141    144B 0
D   NbrDlt                 145    148B 0
D   OrgSiz                 149    152B 0
D   PathSiz                153    156B 0
D   SizMult                233    236B 0
D   PthMult                237    240B 0
D PhysicInfo      DS              15
D   InitSize               12     15B 0
D FindSelDs       DS              139
D   OtherStuff             1      116
D   NbrOfKeys              117    118B 0
D   KeyOffset              136    139B 0
D KeyDataDs       DS              10
D   DependKey              1      10
D JournalInf      DS              22      inz
D   Jrnnam                 2      11
D   JrnLib                 12     21
D   JrnYesNo               22     22
D                 DS
D   SpaceLen               1      4B 0
D   ReceiveLen             5      8B 0
D   MessageKey             9      12B 0
D   MsgDtaLen              13     16B 0
D   MsgQueNbr              17     20B 0

C     *Entry        Plist
C                   Parm                    FileLib
C                   Parm                    MemberName
C                   Parm                    EntryFmt
 * Retrieve object description (verify exists, get object owner)
C                   Call     'QUSROBJD'
C                   Parm                    ReceiveVr2
C                   Parm     300            ReceiveLen
C                   Parm     'OBJD0300'     FileFormat
C                   Parm                    FileLib
C                   Parm     '*FILE'        ObjectType
C                   Parm                    ErrorDs
 *  If file doesn't exist, send message and get out
C                   If       MessageId <> *BLANKS
C                   Exsr     SndMsg
C                   Goto     End
C                   EndIf
c                   Movel    ReceiveVr2     ObjDs
c                   If       CrtDatTim <> *blanks
c     *ymd          Move     CrtDate        DateField
c     *mdy          Move     DateField      CrtDat
c                   Move     CrtTime        Time6
c     *HMS          Move     Time6          Timefld
c     *USA          Move     Timefld        CrtTim
c                   Endif
```

Figure 11.52 : The DSPFILDSC program (part 3 of 7).

411

```
c                     If        SavDatTim <> *blanks
c        *ymd         Move      SvdDate      DateField
c        *mdy         Move      DateField    LstSvd
c                     Move      SvdTime      Time6
c        *HMS         Move      Time6        Timefld
c        *USA         Move      Timefld      SvdTim
c                     Endif
 *  Retrieve file description information
C                     Exsr      RtvFd
 *  If not a physical or logical, get out
C                     If        MessageId <> *blanks
C                     Exsr      SndMsg
C                     Goto      End
C                     EndIf
 *  Retrieve member description information
C                     Exsr      RtvMbr
 *  Create the user space
C                     Exsr      CrtSpace
 *  List fields to user space
C                     Call      'QUSLFLD'
C                     Parm                   UserSpace
C                     Parm      'FLDL0100'   ListFormat
C                     Parm                   FileLIb
C                     Parm                   EntryFmt
C                     PARM      '1'          OverRide
C                     Parm                   ErrorDs
c                     Eval      HeadPoint = GenDsPoint + OffsetHdr
c                     Eval      NbrFlds = NbrInList
c                     Exsr      Loddta
c                     Eval      OutRecLen = RecordLen

c                     Write     Fmt1
C                     Exfmt     SflCtl
C        End          Tag
C                     Eval      *InLR = *ON

C        RtvFd        Begsr
 *  Get file information into ReceiveVar
C                     Call      'QDBRTVFD'
C                     Parm                   ReceiveVar
C                     Parm      4096         ReceiveLen
C                     Parm                   FileLib
C                     Parm      'FILD0100'   FileFormat
C                     Parm                   FileLib
C                     Parm                   EntryFmt
C                     Parm      '0'          OverRide
C                     Parm      '*LCL'       System
C                     Parm      '*EXT'       FormatType
C                     Parm                   ErrorDs
C        MessageId    Cabne     *blanks      EndGet
C                     MoveA     ReceiveVar   AR(1)
c                     TestB     '0'          Attribs          90
c                     If        *in90
c                     Move      'Yes'        LvlChk
c                     Else
```

Figure 11.52 : The DSPFILDSC program (part 4 of 7).

412

```
C                    Move       'No '           LvlChk
C                    Endif
C                    TestB      '2'             FileType                90
C                    Move       NbrOfMbrs       NbrMbr
C                    If         *in90 = *off
C                    Eval       I = DBPhyOff
C                    MoveA      AR(I)           PhysicInfo
C                    If         InitSize = 0
C                    Movel      '*NOMAX'        MbrSiz
C                    Else
C                    Move       InitSize        MbrSiz
C                    Endif
C                    Endif
C                    Movel      'No'            Jrnld
C                    If         DbJrnOff <> *zeros
C                    Eval       I = DBJrnOff
C                    MoveA      AR(I)           JournalInf
C                    If         JrnYesNo = '1'
C                    Movel      'Yes'           Jrnld
C                    Endif
C                    Endif

C                    Eval       I = DBFileOff
C                    DO         NbrofFmts
C                    MoveA      AR(I)           FindSelDs
C                    Eval       S = (KeyOffset + 1)
*    Do for number of key fields
C                    Do         NbrOfKeys
C                    MoveA      AR(S)           KeyDataDs
C                    Eval       J = (J + 1)
C                    MoveA      DependKey       AKEY(J)
C                    Eval       S = (S + 32)
C                    EndDO
C                    EVAL       I = (I + 160)
C                    ENDDO
C       EndGet       Tag
C                    EndSR
*
C       RtvMbr       BegSR
C                    Call       'QUSRMBRD'
C                    Parm                       ReceiveMbr
C                    Parm       240             ReceiveLen
C                    Parm       'MBRD0200'      FileFormat
C                    Parm                       FileLib
C                    Parm                       MemberName
C                    Parm       '0'             OverRide
C                    Eval       filsiz = (Orgsiz * SizMult) +
C                                         (PathSiz * PthMult)
C                    EndSR
C       SndMsg       BegSR
*    Send error message
C                    Call       'QMHSNDPM'
C                    Parm                       MessageId
C                    Parm                       MSGF
C                    Parm                       FileLib
```

Figure 11.52 : The DSPFILDSC program (part 5 of 7).

```
C                    Parm      20             MsgDtaLen
C                    Parm      '*DIAG'        MessageTyp
C                    Parm      '*'            MessageQue
C                    Parm      2              MsgQueNbr
C                    Parm                     MessageKey
C                    Parm                     ErrorDs
C                    EndSR

c     Loddta         Begsr
c                    Eval      *in25 = *on
c                    Write     Sflctl
c                    Eval      *in25 = *off
c                    Eval      *in52 = *off
c                    Eval      RelRecNbr = 0
*     Do for number of key fields
c                    Eval      DoNbrKeys = NbrOfKeys * NbrofFmts
C                    Do        DoNbrKeys      I
*     Write the record to the subfile
C                    Exsr      Writer
C                    EndDO
c                    Endsr

C     Writer         BegSR
c                    Eval      ListPoint = GenDsPoint + OffsetList
*     Search list of fields to get size and description of key field
C                    Do        NbrInList
C                    If        AKEY(I) = SFFLD
c                    Move      I              Sfkey
C                    MoveL     FieldDesc      SFTEXT
C                    Eval      RelRecNbr = (RelRecNbr + 1)
C                    Eval      *IN21 = *ON
c                    If        Digits <> *zeros
c                    Move      Digits         sffsiz
c                    Else
c                    Move      FieldLen       sffsiz
C                    Endif
C                    Write     SflRcd
C                    Leave
C                    EndIf
c                    Eval      ListPoint = ListPoint + SizeEntry
C                    EndDO
c                    if        RelRecNbr > 0
c     RelRecNbr      Chain     SflRcd                         90
c                    Eval      *in53 = *on
c                    Update    SflRcd
c                    Endif
C                    EndSR
c     CrtSpace       Begsr
C                    Call      'QUSCRTUS'
C                    Parm                     UserSpace
C                    Parm      *BLANKS        SpaceAttr
C                    Parm      4096           SpaceLen
C                    Parm      *BLANKS        SpaceVal
C                    Parm      '*CHANGE'      SpaceAuth
C                    Parm      *BLANKS        SpaceText
```

Figure 11.52 : The DSPFILDSC program (part 6 of 7).

```
C               Parm      '*YES'      SpaceRepl
C               PARM                  ErrorDs
  * Retrieve pointer to user space
  c             Call      'QUSPTRUS'
  c             Parm                  UserSpace
  c             Parm                  SpacePoint
  c             Parm                  ErrorDs
  c             Eval      GenDsPoint = SpacePoint
  c             Endsr
```

Figure 11.52 : The DSPFILDSC program (part 7 of 7).

SCAN JOBLOG (SCNJOBLOG) COMMAND

The job log is probably the first place you go when you are troubleshooting a problem with an interactive job. When you ask the user how an error was found, you will likely be greeted with a blank stare or some sort of incoherent mumbling—and that's understandable. After all, this is your world, not theirs.

If the job that ended in an error is no longer active, you can use one of several ways to locate the spooled output files for the job and then display the QPJOBLOG file. The Display Spooled File (DSPSPLF) command is not overly helpful in analyzing a job log, but it does have a find capability, which comes in handy when you are looking for the cause of an error.

On the other hand, if the interactive job is still active, you need to use the DSPJOBLOG command to view it. However, we personally find DSPJOBLOG woefully inadequate when we are trying to analyze long-running interactive jobs; the command lacks any kind of rudimentary find capability and other features that would be useful for analyzing a job log for a long-running job.

What you really want is to be able to filter out nonessential informational messages quickly from a largely unintelligible job log. You want the ability to look only at error messages in the job log that are greater than a given severity level. You could then roll quickly through the "more interesting" messages until you find one pertinent to the problem. You should then be able to turn off the filter and read the complete job log, starting at that point. We also thought it would be nice to have one command to locate the job log with the same consistent interface, regardless of whether the job is active.

Those needs led us to write the Scan Job Log (SCNJOBLOG) command. Figure 11.53 shows the output of the command. The source for it is shown in Figure 11.54. Figure

11.55 refers to the CL program, Figure 11.56 refers to the DDS source, and Figure 11.57 refers to the RPG program. When running SCNJOBLOG, you supply the job name whose job log you want to scan. This parameter defaults to *, which is the IBM default that instructs the command in question to use the current job. You can enter the name of any interactive or batch job; if your job log file name has been overridden to something other than QPJOBLOG, you can enter the actual name in the optional parameter, FILENAME.

Our initial idea was to make this utility work like DSPSPLF. However, extracting different types of information from a single control field required too much code, so we separated the control field into several fields, as shown in Figure 11.53. The control fields are designed to provide most of the same functions as the control fields of DSPSPLF.

```
                               Scan Job Log Spooled File
Control:   _ Direction: _ Increment: 000                 File:     QPJOBLOG      Job. . . .  QPADEV0007
Find:      ______________ From: 001                      Column:      1          User . . .  DOUG
Severity:  _                                                                     Number . .  274285
*...+....1....+....2....+....3....+....4....+....5....+....6....+....7....+....8....+....9....+....0....+....1....+....2....+....3
 5769SS1 V4R4M0 990521                  Display Job Log                  CPU35    04/30/00 12:22:04        Page   1
  Job name . . . . . . . . . . :   QPADEV0007     User  . . . . . . :   DOUG        Number . . . . . . . . . . . :   274285
  Job description  . . . . . . :   RONJOBD        Library . . . . . :   RON
MSGID      TYPE                    SEV  DATE      TIME      FROM PGM      LIBRARY     INST    TO PGM      LIBRARY     INST
CPF1124    Information             00   04/30/00  09:20:19  QWTPIIPP      QSYS        05E5    *EXT                    *N
                                     Message . . . . :   Job 274285/DOUG/QPADEV0007 started on 04/30/00 at 09:20:19
                                       in subsystem QINTER in QSYS. Job entered system on 04/30/00 at 09:20:19.
CPF2451    Information             40   04/30/00  09:20:19  QMHCHMSQ      QSYS        07C3    *EXT                    *N
                                     Message . . . . :   Message queue DOUG is allocated to another job.
                                     Cause . . . . . :   If this message was received when trying to sign on, the
                                       most probable cause is that you are already signed on to another work
                                       station. (A message queue can be placed in break or notify mode in only one
                                       job at a time.) The message queue could also have been allocated by the
                                       Allocate Object (ALCOBJ) command or the Receive Message (RCVMSG) command.
                                       Recovery  . . . :   Determine what job has allocated the message queue
                                                                                                               More...

 F3=Exit
```

Figure 11.53: The SCNJOBLOG output screen.

You input the control code in the field labeled Control and press Enter. For instance, you can go to the bottom of the job log by entering a B and return to the top by entering a T. You can window left or right by using the code W in conjunction with a positive or negative number indicating the increment you desire. To move to the right, enter a plus (+) in the Direction field. To move to the left, enter a minus (-). If you are trying to reposition the screen without keying W, the Increment field indicates the number of lines to move up or down. If you leave the Direction field blank and enter only an increment value, you will go directly to that line (as opposed to advancing that number of lines from the current position).

The FIND field allows you to scan the job log for a particular phrase. The From field allows you to designate that each line is searched beginning at a particular column. The find function works a little differently than the control field in the DSPSPLF command in that the subfile is built with the complete message containing the search phrase. This is the case even if that message spans multiple lines, so you end up with a subfile containing all messages that contain the search phrase. With DSPSPLF, the find function stops at each occurrence of the search phrase.

If you enter a value in the SEVERITY field, only messages that have a severity level equal to or greater than that value are displayed. This allows you to roll quickly through a long job log, viewing only important messages. When you reach the section that is pertinent to your problem, zero out the Severity field to see all messages starting from that point.

This command provides more capabilities and a more consistent user interface for viewing job logs. Even if you write perfect code that never contains bugs (like us, for instance), your users will likely still find some unintended "feature" in a program that necessitates viewing a job log. Nonetheless, this tool should make it a little easier to find out what they did in their world to wreak havoc in yours.

```
/* TO CREATE:                                                    */
/*    CRTCMD CMD(XXXLIB/SCNJOBLOG) PGM(XXXLIB/FIG1155CL)         */
/*==============================================================*/
            CMD         PROMPT('SCAN JOBLOG SPOOLED FILE')
            PARM        KWD(JOBNAM) TYPE(JOB1) DFT(*) SNGVAL((* *)) +
                          CHOICE('Name') PROMPT('Job name')
            PARM        KWD(FILENAME) TYPE(*CHAR) LEN(10) +
                          DFT(QPJOBLOG) CHOICE('NAME') +
                          PMTCTL(*PMTRQS) PROMPT('File name')
            PARM        KWD(FILENUMBER) TYPE(*CHAR) LEN(5) +
                          DFT(*ONLY) SPCVAL((*ONLY *ONLY) (*LAST +
                          *LAST)) CHOICE('NAME') PMTCTL(*PMTRQS) +
                          PROMPT('File number')
JOB1:       QUAL        TYPE(*NAME) LEN(10)
            QUAL        TYPE(*NAME) LEN(10) PROMPT('User')
            QUAL        TYPE(*CHAR) LEN(6) RANGE(000000 999999) +
                          PROMPT('Number')
```

Figure 11.54: The SCNJOBLOG command.

```
/**********************************************************************
/*   TO CREATE:
/*        CRTCLPGM PGM(XXXLIB/FIG1155CL) SRCMBR(FG1155CL)
/**********************************************************************
      PGM PARM(&JOB &FILENAME &FILENBR)
      DCL VAR(&JOB) TYPE(*CHAR) LEN(26)
      DCL VAR(&JOBNAM) TYPE(*CHAR) LEN(10)
      DCL VAR(&JOBUSR) TYPE(*CHAR) LEN(10)
      DCL VAR(&JOBNBR) TYPE(*CHAR) LEN(6)
      DCL VAR(&FILENAME) TYPE(*CHAR) LEN(10)
      DCL VAR(&FILENBR) TYPE(*CHAR) LEN(5)
      DCL VAR(&ICREATED) TYPE(*CHAR) LEN(1)
      DCL VAR(&MSGDTA) TYPE(*CHAR) LEN(512)
      DCL VAR(&MSGID) TYPE(*CHAR) LEN(7)
            CHGVAR    VAR(&JOBNAM) VALUE(%SST(&JOB 1 10))
            CHGVAR    VAR(&JOBUSR) VALUE(%SST(&JOB 11 10))
            CHGVAR    VAR(&JOBNBR) VALUE(%SST(&JOB 21 6))
            IF        COND(&JOBNAM *EQ '*') THEN(DO)
            RTVJOBA   JOB(&JOBNAM) USER(&JOBUSR) NBR(&JOBNBR)
            ENDDO
            CRTPF     FILE(QTEMP/JOBLOGPF) RCDLEN(132)
            MONMSG    MSGID(CPF5813 CPF7302)
            CPYSPLF   FILE(&FILENAME) TOFILE(QTEMP/JOBLOGPF) +
                        JOB(&JOBNBR/&JOBUSR/&JOBNAM) SPLNBR(&FILENBR)
            MONMSG    MSGID(CPF0001 CPF3342 CPF3301 CPF3340) +
                        EXEC(GOTO CMDLBL(DONE))
            MONMSG    MSGID(CPF3303 CPF3309) EXEC(DO)
            DSPJOBLOG JOB(&JOBNBR/&JOBUSR/&JOBNAM) OUTPUT(*PRINT)
            CPYSPLF   FILE(&FILENAME) TOFILE(QTEMP/JOBLOGPF) +
                        SPLNBR(*LAST)
            MONMSG    MSGID(CPF3303) EXEC(GOTO DONE)
            CHGVAR    VAR(&ICREATED) VALUE('Y')
            ENDDO
            OVRDBF    FILE(JOBLOGPF) TOFILE(QTEMP/JOBLOGPF)
            CALL      PGM(FIG1157RG) PARM(&JOBNAM &JOBUSR &JOBNBR +
                        &FILENAME)
            DLTOVR    FILE(JOBLOGPF)
            IF        COND(&ICREATED = 'Y') THEN(DO)
            DLTSPLF   FILE(&FILENAME) SPLNBR(*LAST)
            ENDDO
            GOTO      ENDPGM
DONE:
            RCVMSG    MSGTYPE(*LAST) MSGDTA(&MSGDTA) MSGID(&MSGID)
            SNDPGMMSG MSGID(&MSGID) MSGF(QCPFMSG) MSGDTA(&MSGDTA)
ENDPGM:
      ENDPGM
```

Figure 11.55: The SCNJOBLOG CL driver program.

```
     ****************************************************************
     *  TO COMPILE:
     *     CRTDSPF FILE(XXXLIB/FIG1156DS) SRCMBR(FG1156DS)
     ****************************************************************
     A                                        DSPSIZ(27 132 *DS3)
     A                                        CA03 PRINT
     A             R SFLRCD                    SFL
     A               SFLINE       130A  O  6  2
     A  50                                     DSPATR(HI)
     A               HDNRRN         5S OH
     A             R SFLCTL                    SFLCTL(SFLRCD) OVERLAY
     A                                         SFLSIZ(0030) SFLPAG(0015)
     A                                         PAGEDOWN(95) PAGEUP(96)
     A  21                                     SFLDSP
     A  22                                     SFLDSPCTL
     A  25                                     SFLCLR
     A  91                                     SFLEND(*MORE)
     A               POSRRN         4S OH      SFLRCDNBR(*TOP)
     A                                       1 49'Scan Job Log Spooled File'
     A                                         DSPATR(HI)
     A                                       2  2'Control:'
     A               CNTRL          1A  B   2 14DSPATR(UL)
     A                                      2110'Job. . . .'
     A               JOBNAM        10A  O   2122
     A                                       3  2'Find:'
     A               SRCHFL        20A  B   3 14DSPATR(UL) CHECK(LC)
     A               STRFND         3Y OB   3 41DSPATR(UL) RANGE(1 132)
     A                                      3110'User . . .'
     A               JOBUSR        10A  O   3122
     A               FILSEV         2A  B   4 14DSPATR(UL)
     A                                      4110'Number . .'
     A                                       4  2'Severity:'
     A               OUTCOL       130A  O   5  2DSPATR(HI)
     A                                       3 83'Column:'
     A               W              3Y OO   3 94EDTCDE(Z)
     A                                       3 35'From:'
     A               DIRECTION      1   B   2 28
     A               INCREMENT      3Y OB   2 41
     A                                       2 17'Direction:'
     A                                       2 30'Increment:'
     A                                       2 83'File:'
     A               SPLFILE       10   O   2 94
     A               JOBNBR         6   O   4122
     A             R FORMAT1
     A                                      23  3'F3=Exit'   COLOR(BLU)
```

Figure 11.56: The SCNJOBLOG DDS.

419

```
*******************************************************************
*  TO COMPILE:
*     CRTBNDRPG PGM(XXXLIB/FIG1157RG)  SOURCE(XXXLIB/QRPGLESRC)
*******************************************************************

FFilename++IPEASFRlen+LKlen+AIDevice+.Keywords+++++++++++++++++++++++++++
fJobLogPf  if   f 132       disk     infds(joblds)
fFig1156Ds cf   e           workstn
f                                    infds(info) sfile(sflrcd:rrn)

DName++++++++++++ETDsFrom+++To/L+++IDc.Keywords++++++++++++++++++++++++++++
d EP              s              3 0
d filtercnt       s              5 0
d FilterOK        s              2
d FoundOne        s              1
d FP              s              3 0
d Hi              s              1   inz(x'22')
d L               s              3 0
d NewL            s              3 0
d Nm              s              1   inz(x'20')
d P               s              4 0 inz(1)
d PrimeRrn        s              5 0
d Rrn             s              5 0
d SavSev          s              2   inz('00')
d SflIndex        s              5 0 inz(15)
d W               s              3 0 inz(1)
d X               s              5 0
d Xx              s              5 0
d Aryc            s              1   dim(130)
d Column          C                  '*...+....1....+....2....+....3+
d                                    ....+....4....+....5....+....6+
d                                    ....+....7....+....8....+....9+
d                                    ....+....0....+....1....+....2+
d                                    ....+....3'
d InRec           ds           132
d InData                       132
d InAry                          1   dim(132) overlay(InData:1)
d Position1                      1   overlay(InData:1)
d MsgId                          7   overlay(InData:1)
d Type                          11   overlay(InData:12)
d Blank1                        35   overlay(InData:1)
d Other                         78   overlay(InData:38)
d Severity                       2   overlay(InData:36)
d Space1                         4   overlay(InData:38)
d Blank2                         8   overlay(InData:42)
d Other1                        78   overlay(InData:42)
d Info            ds
d  Sfbin              378     379b 0
d JoblDs          ds
d  JblRrn             397     400b 0

CLON01Factor1+++++++Opcode&ExtFactor2+++++++Result++++++++Len++D+HiLoEq
c     *entry        Plist
```

Figure 11.57: The SCNJOBLOG program (part 1 of 6).

```
c                   parm                    Jobnam
c                   parm                    Jobusr
c                   parm                    JobNbr
c                   parm                    SplFile
c                   eval      FilSev = '00'
c         1         setll     JobLogPf
c                   exsr      LoadSf

c                   Dou       *inkc = *on
c         Rrn       Comp      *zeros                              21
c                   eval      *in22 = *on
c                   write     Format1
c                   exfmt     SflCtl
c                   if        *inkc = *On
c                   goto      end
c                   endif
c                   setoff                                       2122
 * If roll forward requested
c                   if        *in95
c                   exsr      loadsf
c                   iter
c                   endif
 * If roll backward requested
c                   if        *in96
c         1         chain     SflRcd                             68
c         HdnRrn    chain     JoblogPf    Inrec                  68
c                   exsr      clearsf
c                   exsr      Rollback
c                   exsr      loadsf
c                   iter
c                   endif
 * If control value entered
c                   if        Cntrl <> *blanks Or Increment <> *zeros
c                   exsr      ExtractCnt
c                   iter
c                   endif

c                   if        SrchFl <> *blanks
c                   exsr      Clearsf
c         1         setll     JobLogPf
c                   exsr      LoadSf
c                   iter
c                   endif
c                   if        filsev <> SavSev
c         Sfbin     chain     Sflrcd                             68
c         HdnRrn    setll     Joblogpf
c                   eval      SavSev = filsev
c                   exsr      Clearsf
c                   exsr      LoadSf
c                   iter
c                   endif
c                   enddo
```

Figure 11.57: The SCNJOBLOG program (part 2 of 6).

```
c     End           tag
c                   eval        *inlr = *on

* Clear the subfile
c     ClearSf       Begsr
c                   eval        *in25 = *on
c                   write       SflCtl
c                   eval        Rrn = 0
c                   eval        *in25 = *off
c                   eval        PosRrn = 1
c                   endsr
* Rollback through subfile
c     RollBack      Begsr
c                   eval        xx = *zeros
c                   DoU         xx >= SflIndex
c                   Readp       Joblogpf       Inrec            6
c                   If          *in68
c     1             setll       Joblogpf
c                   leave
c                   endif

* If primary record type, check filter
c                   If          Blank1 <> *blanks AND
c                               Blank2 <> *blanks AND
c                               Position1 <> *blanks
* If skiping this message, zero filter count
c                   if          FilSev <> '00' AND
c                               Severity < FilSev
c                   eval        filtercnt = *zeros
c                   endif
* Add count of minor message lines to do index
c                   eval        xx = xx + filtercnt
c                   eval        filtercnt = *zeros
c                   endif
c                   eval        filtercnt = filtercnt + 1
c                   enddo
c                   endsr

c     LoadSf        Begsr
c                   if          Strfnd = 0
c                   eval        Strfnd = 1
c                   endif
c                   eval        xx = *zeros
c                   DoU         xx >= SflIndex
c                   Read        JobLogPf       InRec            91
c                   If          *in91 = *on
c                   leave
c                   endif
c                   eval        *in50 = *off
* If primary record type, check filter
c                   If          Blank1 <> *blanks AND
c                               Blank2 <> *blanks AND
c                               Position1 <> *blanks
```

Figure 11.57: The SCNJOBLOG program (part 3 of 6).

```
C                    eval      *in50 = *on
C                    eval      PrimeRrn = JblRrn
C                    if        FilSev <> '00'
C                    if        Severity < FilSev
C                    eval      filterOK = 'NO'
C                    else
C                    eval      filterOK = 'OK'
C                    endif
C                    endif
C                    endif
 * Ignore records less than the filtered severity level
C                    if        FilSev <> '00' AND
C                              filterOK = 'NO'
C                    iter
C                    endif
 * If search requested, see if line contains search criteria
C                    if        SrchFl <> *blanks
C                    eval      *in51 = *on
C                    exsr      Search
C                    if        foundone = *off
C                    iter
C                    else
C      PrimeRrn      setll     Joblogpf
C                    Exsr      WriteMsg
C                    iter
C                    endif
C                    endif

C                    exsr      WriteRec
C                    Enddo
C                    movea     Column        Aryc(1)
C                    movea(p)  Aryc(W)       Outcol
C                    Endsr

C      Writemsg      Begsr
C                    DoU       xx >= SflIndex
C                    Read      JobLogPf      InRec              91
C                    If        *in91 = *on
C                    leave
C                    endif
C                    eval      *in50 = *off
 * Ignore page heading records
C                    if        Position1 = *blanks AND
C                              Blank1 <> *blanks
C                    iter
C                    endif
 * Ignore spooled file heading records
C                    if        (MsgId = 'MSGID') AND (Type = 'TYPE')
C                    iter
C                    endif
 * If next primary record type, we're done with this message
C                    If        Blank1 <> *blanks AND
C                              Blank2 <> *blanks AND
```

Figure 11.57: The SCNJOBLOG program (part 4 of 6).

```
c                            Position1 <> *blanks
c                   If        PrimeRrn <> JblRrn
c                   Readp     JobLogPf      InRec                     91
c                   leave
c                   else
c                   eval      *in50 = *on
c                   endif
c                   endif
c                   exsr      Search
c                   if        *in68 = *on
c                   movel     Hi            InAry(FP)
c                   eval      InAry(EP) = NM
c                   endif
c                   exsr      WriteRec
c                   enddo
c                   Endsr

c     WriteRec      Begsr
c                   eval      rrn = rrn + 1
c                   eval      xx = xx + 1
c                   eval      Hdnrrn = Jblrrn
c                   movea(p)  InAry(W)      SfLine
c                   write     SflRcd
c                   eval      *in50 = *off
c                   if        xx = 1
c                   eval      PosRrn = Rrn
c                   endif
c                   endsr
c     Search        Begsr
c                   eval      *in68 = *off
c     ' '           checkr    SrchFl        L
c                   if        Strfnd + L > 132
c                   eval      NewL = (Strfnd + L) - 132
c                   eval      L = L - NewL
c                   if        L <= 0
c                   eval      L = 1
c                   endif
c                   endif
c     SrchFl:L      scan      InRec:Strfnd  FP                        68
c                   if        *in68 = *on
c     ' '           checkr    InRec:Fp      FP
c     ' '           scan      InRec:FP      EP                        68
c                   eval      Fp = Fp - 1
c                   if        Fp <= 0
c                   z-add     1             Fp
c                   endif
c                   endif
c                   Eval      Foundone = *in68
c                   Endsr

c     ExtractCnt    Begsr
c                   select
c                   When      Cntrl = 'T'
```

Figure 11.57: The SCNJOBLOG program (part 5 of 6).

```
c      1           setll    JobLoGPf
c                  eval     Cntrl = *blanks
c                  When     Cntrl = 'B'
c      *hival      setgt    JobLoGPf
c                  exsr     RollBack
c                  eval     Cntrl = *blanks
c                  When     Cntrl = 'W'
c      SfBin       chain    SflRcd                              68
c      HdnRrn      setll    JobLogPf
c                  select
c                  when     direction = *blanks
c                  eval     W = Increment
c                  when     Direction = '+'
c                  eval     W = W + Increment
c                  when     Direction = '-'
c                  eval     W = W - Increment
c                  endsl
c                  eval     Cntrl = *blanks
c                  When     Cntrl = *blanks
c      SfBin       chain    SflRcd                              68
c                  select
c                  when     direction = *blanks
c                  eval     PosRrn = Increment
c                  when     Direction = '+'
c                  eval     PosRrn = HdnRrn + Increment
c                  when     Direction = '-'
c                  eval     PosRrn = Hdnrrn - Increment
c                  endsl
c      PosRrn      setll    JobLogPf
c                  eval     Cntrl = *blanks
c                  endsl
c                  exsr     clearsf
c                  exsr     loadsf
c                  endsr
```

Figure 11.57: The SCNJOBLOG program (part 6 of 6).

FIND SOURCE (FNDSRC) COMMAND

IBM's Analyze User Object (ANZUSROBJ) command is great for telling you when source is missing or identifying cases when source members do not match the compiled object. But then what? The source code for the compiled object is no longer where it is supposed to be. Where did it go? This command might be helpful when you are trying to answer this question.

The Find Source (FINDSRC) command will locate all source members that match a specific set of search criteria. You can see a representation of the FINDSRC command in Figure 11.58. It was designed to search for qualified source members across all source files in a library, a user library list, or in all libraries and source files on the entire system. You

425

may optionally search for a specific member name, partial member name, and/or search the text description.

As shown in Figure 11.58, the first parameter on the command is for member name. You can enter a full member name to search all source files for. This field supports wild-card searches, which allows you to search for any member that contains certain characters. For our example, we used *PRT*, which found all source members that included PRT anywhere within the source member name. PRT* would yield all source members whose name begins with the characters PRT. Our example also included source members whose program text description included the word *print*. As you can see, we specified both member name search (in the member name field) and text search to achieve the results shown in Figure 11.59. If either of the search criteria was met, that member was added to the displayed subfile shown in Figure 11.59.

Our example also could have used the file name parameter, which allows you to filter the search by a specific source file name. Or we could have further qualified the search to look only in a specific library, use the library list of the job, or look in all libraries on the system.

Scouting out the Surrounding Terrain

The FINDSRC command in Figure 11.60 has been configured to call the FIG1161RG RPG IV program found in Figure 11.61. This program reads a systems file named QADBXREF, which is a file in QSYS that contains one record for every file on your entire AS/400 system. The advantage to using this file, as opposed to using an API, is speed. We will discuss the downsides to this methodology a little later.

If the search specified in the FINDSRC command is performed by the library list of the job, the FIG1162CL CL program in Figure 11.62 is called to retrieve the job's user library list. In this case, the library list of the job is loaded into an array and all source files found within the library list of the job are then read.

Once a source file is found, the FIG1161RG program passes control to the CL program shown in FIG1163CL, which will list all members in the source file into an outfile named ALLMBRS. This program then calls the FIG1165RG program to process the records in the ALLMBRS outfile.

There are three things you need to be aware of if you choose to use this utility as is. The first potential drawback is in the area of authority and maintenance. You must have authority to the QADBXREF file in QSYS to compile the FIG1161RG program. Also, if IBM ever changes the QADBXREF file in some future release of OS/400, you might have to recompile this program.

Second, the FIG1165RG program will not compile if the ALLMBRS file does not exist. You must create the file prior to compiling the FIG1165RG program by keying the following command:

```
DSPFD Somelib/Somefile TYPE(*mbrlist) OUTPUT(*OUTFILE)
OUTFILE(Somelib/ALLMBRS) )
```

And third, be aware of the size of the libraries you are attempting to search. We elected to make this an interactive display program. All edits were removed in the interest of brevity. This leaves the door wide open for the "locking up" of a workstation for a significant period of time. If your application libraries are very large, you may wish to take the steps necessary to make this a batch print program instead.

```
                        FIND SOURCE MEMBERS (FINDSRC)

Type choices, press Enter.

Member . . . . . . . . . . . . > AGING        Name
File name  . . . . . . . . . . > *ALL         Name, *ALL
  Library  . . . . . . . . . . >   *ALL       Name, *USRLIBL, *ALL
Search text for: . . . . . . .  _____




                                                             Bottom
 F3=Exit   F4=Prompt   F5=Refresh   F12=Cancel   F13=How to use this display
 F24=More keys
```

Figure 11.58: The FNDSRC prompt.

```
                    Find Source Member

        Source File:     SOURCE
        Source Library:  CORBASE


                    Create    Change
        Member      Date      Date      Text
        AGINGNEW    09/24/99  12/31/98  Aging program
        AGINGO      09/24/99  12/31/98  Aging program
        AGINGOLD    09/24/99  06/03/98  Aging program
        AGINGONEW   09/24/99  01/04/99  Aging program
        AGINGOOLD2  09/24/99  11/03/98  Aging program
        AGINGO0998  09/24/99  09/18/98  Aging program
        AGINGO998   09/24/99  09/18/98  Aging program




                                                                Bottom


        F3=Exit
```

Figure 11.59: The FNDSRC output screen.

```
/* TO CREATE:                                                      */
/*    CRTCMD CMD(XXXLIB/FINDSRC) PGM(XXXLIB/FIG1161RG)             */
/*===============================================================*/
            CMD        PROMPT('FIND SOURCE MEMBERS')
            PARM       KWD(MEMBER) TYPE(*CHAR) LEN(10) +
                         CHOICE('Name') PROMPT('Member')
            PARM       KWD(FILLIB) TYPE(FL1) MIN(0) CASE(*MONO) +
                         CHOICE('Name') PROMPT('File name')
            PARM       KWD(TXTSRCH) TYPE(*CHAR) LEN(20) +
                         CHOICE('Name') PROMPT('Search text for:')
FL1:        QUAL       TYPE(*NAME) LEN(10) DFT(*ALL) +
                         SPCVAL((*ALL *ALL))
            QUAL       TYPE(*NAME) LEN(10) DFT(*USRLIBL) +
                         SPCVAL((*USRLIBL *USRLIBL) (*ALL *ALL)) +
                         PROMPT('Library')
```

Figure11.60: The FNDSRC command.

```
*********************************************************************
*  TO COMPILE: (signed on as QSECOFR)
*     CRTBNDRPG PGM(XXXLIB/FIG1161RG)  SOURCE(XXXLIB/QRPGLESRC)
*     USRPRF(*OWNER) ALWNULL(*YES)
*********************************************************************
fQadbxref  if   e         k disk
d File          s            10
d Lib           s            10
d LibFile       s            20
d Member        s            10
d Message       s            60
d Prtdsp        s             1
d TxtDsc        s            20
d UseLib        s            10
d X             s             3 0
d NowCon        c               'Now searching file '
d               ds
d Libl                       275
d Alibl                       11     overlay(Libl:1) dim(25)
d               ds
d Dbfllb                      20
d Dbxfil                      10     overlay(dbfllb:1)
d Dbxlib                      10     overlay(dbfllb:11)
D ErrorDs       DS           116     INZ
D  BytesPrv             1      4B 0
D  BytesAvl             5      8B 0
D  MessageId            9     15
D  ERR###              16     16
D  MessageDta          17    116
D               DS                   inz
D  MsgQueNbr            1      4B 0
D  MessageKey           5      8B 0
D  MsgDtaLen            9     12B 0
c     *entry      plist
c                 parm                     member
c                 parm                     LibFile
c                 parm                     TxtDsc
c                 move      Libfile    Lib
c                 movel     Libfile    File
c                 select
c                 when      Lib = '*ALL'
c     *loval      setll     Qadbxref
c                 when      Lib = '*USRLIBL'
c                 call      'FIG1162CL'
c                 parm                     Libl
c                 movel     Alibl(1)   UseLib
c     UseLib      setll     Qadbxref
c                 eval      x = 1
c                 when      File <> '*ALL'
c     GetKey      Klist
c                 Kfld                     lib
c                 Kfld                     File
c     GetKey      setll     Qadbxref
```

Figure 11.61: The FNDSRC driver program (part 1 of 3).

```
c                 other
c       Lib       setll     Qadbxref
c                 endsl
c                 dou       *in41 = *on
c                 select
c                 When      Lib = '*ALL'
c                 read      Qadbxref                            41
c                 if        File <> '*ALL' AND
c                           DbxFil <> File
c                 iter
c                 endif
c                 when      Lib = '*USRLIBL'
c                 read      Qadbxref                            41
c                 if        *in41 = *off AND
c                           Dbxlib <> Alibl(x)
c                 eval      x = x + 1
c                 if        Alibl(x) = *blanks
c                 leave
c                 endif
c                 movel     Alibl(x)       UseLib
c       UseLib    setll     Qadbxref
c                 read      Qadbxref                            41
c                 endif
c                 if        File <> '*ALL' AND
c                           DbxFil <> File AND
c                           *in41 = *off
c                 iter
c                 endif
c                 When      File <> '*ALL'
c       GetKey    reade     Qadbxref                            41
c                 Other
c       Lib       reade     Qadbxref                            41
c                 endsl
c                 if        *in41 = *off
c                 if        Dbxatr = 'PF'
c                           and Dbxtyp = 'S'
c                 exsr      sndmsg
c                 call      'FIG1163CL'
c                 parm                          Member
c                 parm                          Dbfllb
c                 parm                          TxtDsc
c                 if        Member = '*LR'
c                 leave
c                 endif
c                 endif
c                 endif
c                 enddo
c                 eval      *inlr = *on
*
C       SNDMSG    BEGSR
C                 EVAL      BytesPrv = 116
C       'QCPFMSG' CAT       'QSYS':3       MSGF
c                 eval      MessageId = 'CPF9898'
c                 eval      Message = NowCon + DbxFil +
```

Figure 11.61: The FNDSRC driver program (part 2 of 3).

```
C                                   ' in library ' + DbxLib
*  Send status message
C                     CALL      'QMHSNDPM'
C                     PARM                   MessageId
C                     PARM                   MSGF          20
C                     PARM                   Message
C                     PARM      60           MsgDtaLen
C                     PARM      '*STATUS'     MessageTyp    10
C                     PARM      '*EXT'        MessageQue    10
C                     PARM      1             MsgQueNbr
C                     PARM                   MessageKey
C                     PARM                   ErrorDs
C                     ENDSR
```

Figure 11.61: The FNDSRC driver program (part 3 of 3).

```
/********************************************************************
/*   TO CREATE:
/*       CRTCLPGM PGM(XXXLIB/FIG1162CL) SRCFILE(XXXLIB/QCLSRC)
/********************************************************************
PGM         (&LIBL)
            DCL       VAR(&LIBL) TYPE(*CHAR) LEN(275)
            RTVJOBA   USRLIBL(&LIBL)
ENDPGM
```

Figure11.62: The CL program used to retrieve library list.

```
/********************************************************************
/*   TO CREATE:
/*       CRTCLPGM PGM(XXXLIB/FIG1163CL) SRCFILE(XXXLIB/QCLSRC)
/********************************************************************
PGM         (&MEMBER &LIBFILE &TXTDSC)
            DCL       VAR(&LIBFILE) TYPE(*CHAR) LEN(20)
            DCL       VAR(&TXTDSC) TYPE(*CHAR) LEN(20)
            DCL       VAR(&MEMBER) TYPE(*CHAR) LEN(10)
            DCL       VAR(&LIB) TYPE(*CHAR) LEN(10)
            DCL       VAR(&FILE) TYPE(*CHAR) LEN(10)

            CHGVAR    VAR(&LIB) VALUE(%SST(&LIBFILE 11 10))
            CHGVAR    VAR(&FILE) VALUE(%SST(&LIBFILE 1 10))

            DSPFD     FILE(&LIB/&FILE) TYPE(*MBRLIST) +
                        OUTPUT(*OUTFILE) OUTFILE(QTEMP/ALLMBRS)
            OVRDBF    FILE(ALLMBRS) TOFILE(QTEMP/ALLMBRS)
            CALL      PGM(FIG1165RG) PARM(&MEMBER &FILE &LIB +
                        &TXTDSC)

            DLTOVR    ALLMBRS
ENDPGM
```

Figure 11.63: The FNDSRC CL driver.

```
*************************************************************************
*   TO COMPILE:
*      CRTDSPF  FILE(XXXLIB/FIG1164DS)  SOURCE(XXXLIB/QDDSSRC)
*************************************************************************
A                                       DSPSIZ(24 80 *DS3) CA03
A          R SFLRCD                      SFL
A            MLNAME     10A  O  8  4
A            CHGDAT      8      8 15
A            CRTDAT      8      8 25
A            MLTXT      40A  O  8 35
A          R SFLCTL                      SFLCTL(SFLRCD)
A                                        SFLDSP SFLDSPCTL OVERLAY
A                                        SFLSIZ(0024) SFLPAG(0012)
A  91                                    SFLEND(*MORE)
A                                      1 24'Find Source Member' DSPATR
A                                      3  4'Source File:'
A                                      4  4'Source Library:'
A            SFFILE     10  O  3 21
A            SFLIB      10  O  4 21
A                                      7  4'Member' COLOR(BLU)
A                                      6 16'Create' COLOR(BLU)
A                                      6 26'Change' COLOR(BLU)
A                                      7 16'Date'   COLOR(BLU)
A                                      7 26'Date'   COLOR(BLU)
A                                      7 35'Text'   COLOR(BLU)
A          R FORMAT1
A                                     23  3'F3=Exit' COLOR(BLU)
```

Figure 11.64: The FNDSRC DDS.

```
*************************************************************************
*   TO COMPILE:
*      CRTBNDRPG PGM(XXXLIB/FIG1165RG)  SOURCE(XXXLIB/QRPGLESRC)
*************************************************************************
fAllMbrs   if   e           disk
fFig1164Ds cf   e           workstn
f                                       sfile(sflrcd:rrn)
d Begin          s              1
d ChgDat         s              8
d CrtDat         s              8
d Date6          s              6  0
d EndFld         s              1
d F1             s              3  0
d F2             s              3  0
d File           s             10
d FldDsc         s             50
d I              s              3  0
d IsoDate        s               d   datfmt(*iso) inz
d Lib            s             10
```

Figure 11.65: The FNDSRC program (part 1 of 4).

432

```
d L1              s              3  0
d Member          s             10
d MemberIn        s             10
d OK              s              1
d posit           s              3  0
d Rrn             s              4  0
d S1              s              3  0
d TxtDsc          s             20
d TxtS            s              3  0
d WldSrc          s             10
d Low             c                    'abcdefghijklmnopqrstuvwxyz'
d Upr             c                    'ABCDEFGHIJKLMNOPQRSTUVWXYZ'
d                 ds
d M1MTxt                        50
d M1Txt                         40      overlay(m1MTxt:1)

c       *entry     Plist
c                  Parm                      MemberIn
c                  Parm                      File
c                  Parm                      Lib
c                  Parm                      TxtDsc

c                  eval      Member = MemberIn
 * Check for wild card lookups
c                  exsr      Wildsr

c       1          setll     AllMbrs
c                  Read      AllMbrs                              91
c                  Dow       *in91 = *off
c                  eval      OK = 'N'
c                  if        member <> *blanks
c                  exsr      chknam
c                  endif
c                  if        ((Ok <> 'Y') AND (TxtDsc <> *blanks))
c                  exsr      chkdsc
c                  endif
c                  if        Ok = 'Y'
c                  move      M1Chgd         Date6
c       *ymd       move      Date6          IsoDate
c       *mdy       move      IsoDate        ChgDat
c                  move      M1CDat         DAte6
c       *ymd       move      Date6          IsoDate
c       *mdy       move      IsoDate        CrtDat
c                  eval      rrn = rrn + 1
c                  write     SflRcd
c                  endif
c                  Read      AllMbrs                              91
c                  Enddo
c                  if        Rrn > 0
c                  movel     file           Sffile
c                  movel     lib            Sflib
c                  write     Format1
c                  exfmt     SflCtl
```

Figure 11.65: The FNDSRC program (part 2 of 4).

433

```
c                    if        *inkc = *on
c                    eval      MemberIn = '*LR'
c                    endif
c                    endif
c                    eval      *inlr = *on
C        WILDSR       BEGSR
c        Low:Upr      Xlate     Member         Member
* Check name for wildcard search
c                    eval      F1 = 0
c                    eval      F2 = 0
c        '*'         scan      Member:1       F1
c                    if        F1 <> 0
c                    eval      S1 = F1 + 1
c                    if        S1 <= 10
c        '*'         scan      member:S1      F2
c                    endif
* If no second wildcard
c                    if        F2 = 0
* If wildcard in first position, target field must end with search ch
c                    if        F1 = 1
c                    eval      Begin = 'N'
c                    eval      EndFld = 'Y'
c        ' '         checkr    member         I
c                    eval      L1 = I - 1
c        L1          subst     member:2       WldSrc
c                    else
*   target field must begin with search characters
c                    eval      L1 = F1 - 1
c        L1          subst     member:1       WldSrc
c                    eval      Begin = 'Y'
c                    eval      EndFld = 'N'
c                    endif
* There is a second wildcard
c                    else
c                    eval      L1 = F2 - 2
c        L1          Subst     member:S1      WldSrc
c                    eval      Begin = 'N'
c                    eval      EndFld = 'N'
c                    endif
* There are no wild cards in the search field
c                    else
c        ' '         checkr    member         L1
c                    movel     member         WldSrc
c                    eval      Begin = 'N'
c                    eval      EndFld = 'N'
c                    endif
c                    movel     WldSrc         Member
c                    endsr
c        chknam      begsr
c                    eval      *in05 = *off
c                    select
c                    when      begin = 'Y'
c        wldsrc:l1   scan      mlname:1       posit                    05
```

Figure 11.65: The FNDSRC program (part 3 of 4).

```
   * if search successful, but field didn't start with search characters,
   *   search unsuccessful
   c                    if        ((*in05 = *on) AND (posit <> 1))
   c                    eval      *in05 = *off
   c                    endif
   *   must end with search characters
   c                    when      endfld = 'Y'
   c        ' '         checkr    mlname          s1                      01
   c                    if        *in01 = *off
   c                    eval      s1 = 10
   c                    endif
   c                    sub       11              s1
   c                    eval      s1 = s1 + 1
   c                    if        s1 >= 11
   c    wldsrc:11       scan      mlname:s1                               05
   c                    endif
   *   search characters can be anywhere
   c                    when      ((begin = 'N') AND (endfld = 'N'))
   c    wldsrc:11       scan      mlname                                  05
   c                    endsl
   *   if search was successful, indicate this
   c                    if        *in05 = *on
   c                    move      'Y'             ok
   c                    endif
   c    endchk          endsr
   c    ChkDsc          Begsr
   c    Low:Upr         Xlate     TxtDsc          TxtDsc
   c        ' '         CheckR    TxtDsc          TxtS
   c    Low:Upr         Xlate     MlMtxt          FldDsc
   c    TxtDsc:Txts     Scan      FldDsc                                  05
   c                    if        *in05 = *on
   c                    eval      Ok = 'Y'
   c                    endif
   c                    endsr
```

Figure 11.65: The FNDSRC program (part 4 of 4).

FINAL WORDS ABOUT TOOLS IN THE TOOLBOX

It is our position that you simply cannot have too many tools in your toolbox.

If a tool can improve your productivity enough that the amount of time it saves surpasses the amount of time you spent developing it, the development time was time well spent. If a tool eliminates or helps reduce certain errors from getting into production, implementation of the tool should be seriously considered.

12

WORKING WITH
DATE AND TIME DATA TYPES

If you have read any of our prior materials through the years, you already know we were proponents of using the date type as a viable solution for solving the Y2K "bug." We have written volumes of material on the subject that have been widely distributed in books, articles, white papers, and even published on IBM's AS/400 resource Web pages.

And even though the Y2K issue has long since been put to bed, the date and time data types are still extremely valuable in the overall scheme of things. The advantages are many and the downsides are few. We would like to use this chapter to further champion this cause and, hopefully, convince more of you to use these valuable tools.

THE DATE AND TIME DATA TYPES

This chapter will introduce you to the date and time data types. Our objective is both to convince you of their value and to teach you how to take advantage of them. We will give you some sample code to replace your old, clunky, RPG date and time routines. We will teach you how to convert your data so it will incorporate the new date and time data types. And we will investigate both the performance and storage issues surrounding these very special data types.

Even though date and time data types have been around since V2R1M1, we had to wait until V3R1 before we could begin using them in RPG. The good news is that it may have been worth the wait. These data types ensure data integrity and are fully integrated into the DB2 UDB for the AS/400.

Data elements may be designated as having *date* and *time* data types when they are defined in DDS or RPG IV Definition Specifications. Along with these new data types, we also have been introduced to a series of new RPG IV op codes designed to help us manipulate dates and times. Sophisticated routines to manipulate dates and times are a thing of the past. As you will see, complicated routines to increment or decrement dates or times have gone the way of the dinosaurs, too.

IT'S ELEMENTARY

The date data type allows you to store data in a number of six- and eight-digit date formats (Table 12.1), all of which include the century. The date separator is automatically stored with your data, making the field appear to be six, eight, or ten characters in length. The number and style of the separator character that appears depends on the chosen date format, as seen in Table 12.1.

Table 12.1: An Example of Date Data Types.

Format	DATFMT Parameter	Separator Character	Field Length	Example
Month, Day, Year	*MDY	/	8	12/31/00
Day, Month, Year	*DMY	/	8	31/12/00
Year, Month, Day	*YMD	/	8	00/21/31
Julian	*JUL	/	6	00/366 [1]
International Standards Organization	*ISO	-	10	2000-12-31
IBM USA Standard	*USA	/	10	12/31/2000
IBM European Standard	*EUR	.	10	31.12.2000
Japanese Industrial Standard Christian Era	*JIS	-	10	2000-12-31

[1] The Julian date of 00/366 is a valid translation of December 31, 2000, because 2000 is a leap year.

438

The time data type allows you to store data in a variety of eight-character time formats (Table 12.2). As with the date data type, the time separator is automatically stored with your data, making the field appear to be eight characters in length. The number and style of the separator character that appears depends on the specified TIMFMT parameter. Valid parameter entries can be seen in Table 12.2.

Table 12.2: An Example of Time Data Types.

Format	TIMFMT Parameter	Separator Character	Field Length	Example
Month, Day, Year	*HMS	:	8	16:00:00
International Standards Organization	*ISO	.	8	16.00.00
IBM USA Standard	*USA	:	8	4:00 PM
IBM European Standard	*EUR	.	8	16.00.00
Japanese Industrial Standard Christian Era	*JIS	:	8	16:00:00

One of the cool things about the date and time data types is how they conserve storage. Regardless of the time or date formats chosen, DB2 UDB for the AS/400 stores the date data type fields in only 4 bytes on disk and the time type fields in only 3 bytes. In the case of a date field, this happens to be the same amount of storage required to store a six-digit date in packed format. So as you convert your six-digit date fields from numeric or packed data types to the date data types, you will not notice any increase in DASD utilization.

WHAT YOU SEE IS NOT ALWAYS WHAT YOU GET!

Do not be confused by the fact that all the programming tools that show you file contents (DSPFFD, DSPPFM, and RUNQRY, for example) will show you the date and time fields as if they were just simple alphanumeric fields. All of the "packing" and "unpacking" of the date fields happens under the covers in OS/400, at a level you will not see. This can sometimes be a difficult concept to grasp. All your tools are telling you that the field defined with the date or time data type is taking 8 or 10 bytes of storage in your file, but this is not the case. No matter how your dates and times are currently stored, converting your dates to the new date data types will not require you to purchase additional DASD.

APPLES AND APPLES

Date and time fields are compared based on their *chronological* value. You can compare a date stored in month-day-year format to a date stored in Julian date format without performing any kind of conversion and still get your desired results. This also holds true with fields defined with the time data type. This fact is important because it means you will not need to convert the various date and time fields before comparing them with values stored in your database.

If you take a look at the examples in Table 12.1, you can see that all of the data examples point to the same date, December 31, 2000. Dates do not need to be in the same date format for you to do comparisons or to work with them. The system knows that an *ISO date of 2000-12-31 is equal to an *MDY date of 12/31/00.

DECIDING ON A FORMAT

Because date fields *are* stored and compared based on their chronological value, you may even want to store dates within the database in a month-day-year format. Doing so means you would not need to convert the date when you print it on a report. As a matter of fact, you would not even need to use an edit code or an edit word when printing dates. Fields defined with a date data type will print with the date separator characters (seen in Table 12.1) already in place.

But before you run off to reformat all of your date fields into month-day-year format, you need to be aware that the six-digit date fields (*YMD and *MDY) *only* cover the years from 1940 to 2039. When talking about fields defined with a date data type, the years between 1940 and 2039 are referred to as a *date window*. In the case of the default AS/400 date window, the system automatically assumes that the two-digit years between 40 and 99 belong in the 20th century and the years between 00 and 39 belong in the 21st century. As shown in Figure 12.1, a date of 12/31/96 is interpreted as being 12/31/1996, because the two-digit year of 96 is greater than or equal to 40. A date of 12/31/20 is interpreted as being 12/31/2020, because the two-digit year is less than 40.

```
96 is => 40, therefore 12/31/96 = 12/31/1996
20 is  < 40, therefore 12/31/20 = 12/31/2020
```

Figure 12.1: Examples of date windowing logic.

440

The reason for this anomaly is the way IBM employed its *date windowing* algorithms as they apply to the six-digit date. The system automatically assumes that when this format is used, the two-digit years between 40 and 99 are for the 20th century and the years between 00 and 39 belong in the 21st century. Consequently, the system-defined *LOVAL for a date field differs, depending on the chosen date format. If a date is defined with the eight-digit *ISO format type, *LOVAL is going to be 0001-01-01. If a date field is defined with the six-digit *YMD format, *LOVAL is going to be 40/01/01, and so on.

Using the date window should work well for most transaction dates, but it may be unacceptable in systems that perform some type of forecasting function or that record birth dates, many of which would obviously be prior to 1940. Unless you are putting together a brand new system, odds are pretty good that you have dealt with this potential problem long before now. For dates in which the century is ambiguous, you must use a format that includes the century, such as *ISO or *USA.

There is one more potential pitfall regarding defining dates and times (in your database) with formats other than the *ISO default. The "gotcha" is in the area of performance. Because the time and date data types are interchangeable within your HLL programs, the system will automatically convert all dates and times to the same data type when your program is running. Want to guess which data type the system defaults to when running your programs? You guessed it. Your programs will convert dates and times to the *ISO data type.

From a performance standpoint, you are left with two logical choices: (1) define the dates and times in your database with the *ISO format, or (2) use the Date Format (DATFMT) keywords in the Header or File Specifications. When these keywords are specified, you can tell your program to use the specified format as the program default in place of the *ISO format. To attain the best performance, you would have to specify the DATFMT keyword in each program that uses the file. There is an easy way to do this using the RPGLEHSPEC or DFTLEHSPEC data areas. The option of using these data areas is fully described in chapter 5.

FROM SOUP TO NUTS

Because Date and Time fields are entirely interchangeable with other date fields, the conversion from one type to another is as simple as a MOVE operation. For example, moving a date stored in the *ISO format to a date field defined with a *MDY date format (or any other format, for that matter) requires a simple RPG IV MOVE operation. The conversion of the data will be performed for you automatically.

Let's look at an example. Say a sales date is defined in your database file as an International Standards Organization (*ISO) date data type. If the field in your database was named SalesDate and you were to move that field to an output field on a screen, it would appear with the separator characters and display as 2000-12-31. But if you were to move the SalesDate field into the DateOfSale output field as defined in Figure 12.2, it would appear on the screen as 12/31/00.

Even though the SalesDate date field was read from the database as an *ISO date, we allowed the MOVE operation to reformat the field for us when we used *MDY in Factor 1 of the Calculation Specification. The end result was that the century digits were dropped (using windowing technology) and the date was formatted into the *MDY format we saw in Table 12.1.

That is pretty cool, but think about this: The result field in the MOVE operation in Figure 12.2 could be defined as either an eight-character alphanumeric field *or* a six-digit numeric field. Yes, you read that correctly. If the result field is an eight-character alphanumeric field, the separator characters will be automatically inserted. If the result field is defined as a six-digit numeric field, the result of the MOVE operation would appear without the separator characters. If our SalesDate field from our database was 2000-12-31, and it was moved to an alphanumeric field, as in the example in Figure 12.2, the result would be 12/31/00. But if the same MOVE operation was performed and the DateOfSale was defined as a six-digit numeric field, the result would have been 123100!

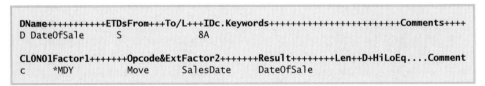

```
DName++++++++++++ETDsFrom+++To/L+++IDc.Keywords+++++++++++++++++++++++++++Comments++++
D DateOfSale      S              8A

CL0N01Factor1+++++++Opcode&ExtFactor2+++++++Result++++++++Len++D+HiLoEq....Comment
C     *MDY         Move     SalesDate      DateOfSale
```

Figure 12.2: Changing the output format of date fields.

Let's look at another example. Figure 12.3 shows two date fields defined with RPG IV Definition Specifications. The first field, named MDY_Date, is defined as a standalone field (as indicated by the "S" in positions 24-25), which has a date data type (indicated with the "D" in position 40). The optional Date Format (DATFMT) keyword tells the system that the date format of the field used is the *MDY format (see Table 12.1). The second field, named USA_Date, is also defined with a date data type, but the chosen date format is the *USA format.

As you can see in Table 12.1, the *MDY date format does not include the century. The date December 31, 2000, appears as 12/31/00. But because fields defined with the date data type are interchangeable, a simple MOVE operation will add or strip the century from your dates. Just because the date field in your database includes the century does not mean you want to output the century digits. The example in Figure 12.3 shows an example of using the MOVE operation to add the century digits to a date field.

```
DName+++++++++++ETDsFrom+++To/L+++IDc.Keywords+++++++++++++++++++++++++++++Comments
d MDY_Date          S             D    Datfmt(*MDY)

d USA_Date          S             D    Datfmt(*USA)

CLON01Factor1+++++++Opcode&ExtFactor2+++++++Result++++++++Len++D+HiLoEq...Comments
c                   MOVE      MDY_Date      USA_Date
```

Figure 12.3: Example of date windowing in a Move operation.

If the value of MDY_Date in Figure 12.3 is 12/31/00 and you perform the MOVE operation, the value of the USA_Date field becomes 12/31/2000. The two digits that represent the century are added to your date field automatically! On the other hand, if the initial value of the MDY_Date field is 12/31/99, the end result of the MOVE operation to the USA_Date field is 12/31/1999. This is an example of using the date windowing methodology to achieve the desired results.

A Rose by Any Other Name

Date and time data fields are very particular about data validity. If you define a field as a date or time data type, the system expects to see a valid date or time in that field. If there is any question about the content of the data you are going to place in a date or time field, you should use the TEST op code, which is described below, to check the field prior to placing it in the date field. If you think you can just leave zeros in a date or time field, forget it. The system will insist that you only allow valid dates and times in fields defined with a date or time data type (a nasty runtime error will occur if the data is deemed invalid).

The TEST op code tests a date, time, or timestamp field for validity according to the indicated data type. The field being tested is stored in the Result field and cannot be a date, time, or timestamp element. When you use the TEST op code on a numeric or alphanumeric field, you must indicate the data type you are testing for in the op code extender field (T for time and D for Dates). The desired field format (as seen in Table 12.1 and

12.2) must be indicated in Factor 1. All of the criteria required for the indicated data type must be met or the test will fail. For example, when you are testing alphanumeric fields, the keyed data must include the separator characters that coincide with the format indicated in Factor 1 or the data will be deemed invalid.

In Figure 12.4, the %ERROR built-in function is going to return a positive response if the data in the numeric Date field does not represent a valid date in the month-day-year format specified in Factor 1. You will note that in our example, we employed the %ERROR built-in function to display our error message. The reason this technique is important is because display files do not do an adequate job of supporting the date and time data types (more on this later). When dates are entered, you will need to validate the data prior to putting it into fields with a date or time data type. Failure to do so will result in a nasty little runtime error referred to as a *Date* or *Timestamp error*.

```
CLON01Factor1+++++++Opcode&ExtFactor2+++++++Result+++++++++Len++D+HiLoEq...Comments
C     *MDY        Test(DE)               Date
C                 If         %Error
 * your error message routine goes here
C                 EndIf
```

Figure 12.4: Validating a six-digit numeric date.

Please note the operational extender for the TEST op code used in Figure 12.4. Didn't we just tell you that the operational extender for the TEST op code was "D" for dates and "T" for times? Well, yes we did. But that statement is only true if you wish to use error indicators (as seen in Figure 12.5). On the other hand, if you wish to employ the %ERROR built-in function, you will need to modify your operational extender of the TEST op code. This means you will need to use an operation extender of "DE" for dates and "TE" for times.

When thinking about coding date and time input fields, you need to consider whether you want to use a numeric field or an alphanumeric field. Both can be used and both can be validated using the new TEST op code. A numeric input date is easy to code because there are no separator characters to contend with. But if you choose to use an alphanumeric input field, there may be some additional work required on your part.

In Figure 12.5, we use an example of the code required to test an alphanumeric date field that will be keyed as month-day-year, as specified in Factor 1 of the TEST op code statement. The trick with the TEST op code is that if the date is not keyed in the exact format the code in Factor 1 specifies, indicator 99 (in our example in Figure 12.5) is going to be turned on. *This includes separator characters!* So an alphanumeric date keyed as 120100 or 12-01-00 would not be considered valid when used with the code in Figure 12.5. The operator would have to key December 1, 2000, as 12/01/00 because a slash (/) is the appropriate separator character for the *MDY date format (as we saw in Table 12.1).

```
CLON01Factor1+++++++Opcode&ExtFactor2+++++++Result+++++++++Len++D+HiLoEq...Comments
c     *MDY          TEST(D)               AlfaDate                99
```

Figure 12.5: Validating a six-digit alphanumeric date.

READIN, RITIN, AND RITHMATIC

One of the best things about working with the new date and time data types is the RPG IV op codes that are designed specifically for these data types. There are three op codes (as illustrated in Table 12.3) that allow you to perform a variety of date and time manipulation functions. It should be noted that these op codes were designed to work with the date, time, and timestamp data types that are all part of the DB2/400 database.

Table 12.3: New Op Codes for Date and Time Manipulation.

Op Code	Purpose
ADDDUR	Adds the duration specified in Factor 2 to a date or time field and places the outcome of the operation in the Result field. Factor 2 contains both the number to add as well as the duration type you want to add.
EXTRCT	Extracts part of a date, time, or timestamp field and places the outcome in the Result field. The second part of Factor 2 is used to designate what type of information you want to extract.
SUBDUR	Subtracts a duration (specified in Factor 2) from a date or time field and places the outcome of the operation in the result field.

WHAT IS THE DOWNSIDE?

You knew it sounded too good to be true, didn't you? The bad news about the date and time data types was that as of V3R1 of OS/400 (when the date and time data types were initially made available to RPG IV), they were not originally supported for display files.

This support has since been added, but we do not feel that the implementation used could be categorized as a smashing success. Display files still do not do a good job of handling dates and times in regard to flexibility of output format or handling null values. Where they do excel is in the area of data validation. You do not need to worry about whether a date or time field is valid. If the date or time made it as far as your RPG IV program, it is most certainly valid.

In our experiences, we have elected to keep the dates on our display files as six-digit numeric fields. The edit for the date field has to be done in the RPG module using this methodology, but we have not found that to be much of an obstacle, as you will see in our next example.

We put together a simple RPG IV program (Figures 12.6 and 12.7) that will test dates keyed at a workstation. The program will accept input and send back a message indicating whether the keyed date was valid (see Figure 12.8). It will also allow the operator to press F6 to add a day to the date currently displayed, or press F5 to subtract a month. While this program is not very useful, it does give us a chance to see how a few of the new date op codes function.

```
A*******************************************************************************
A*  TO COMPILE:
A*     CRTDSPF FILE(XXXLIB/FIG1206DS)
A*******************************************************************************
AAN01N02N03T.Name++++++RLen++TDpBLinPosFunctions++++++++++++++++++++++++++++++++
A             R FORMAT1
A                                             CF03
A                                             CF05
A                                             CF06
A                                       1 30'Date Test'
A                                             DSPATR(HI)
A                                       9 29'Date:'
A             DATE         6D 0B        9 35
A  98                                         ERRMSG('You keyed a Valid Date!')
A  99                                         ERRMSG('Invalid Date!')
A                                      22  5'F3=Exit'
A                                             COLOR(BLU)
A                                      22 15'F5=Subtract a month'
A                                             COLOR(BLU)
A                                      22 37'F6=Add a day'
A                                             COLOR(BLU)
```

Figure 12.6: The FIG1206DS display file.

```
********************************************************************
*   TO COMPILE:
*      CRTBNDRPG PGM(XXXLIB/FIG1207RG)
********************************************************************
FFilename++IPEASF.....L.....A.Device+.Keywords++++++++++++++++++++++++++++++++Comments
FFIG1206DS CF    E               Workstn


DName+++++++++++ETDsFrom+++To/L+++IDc.Keywords++++++++++++++++++++++++++++++++Comments
d Workdate          S               D   Datfmt(*MDY)

CLON01Factor1+++++++Opcode&ExtExtended-factor2+++++++++++++++++++++++++++++++Comments
C                   DOU       *Inkc = *on
C                   EXFMT     Format1
C                   MOVEA     '00'           *In(98)
C       *MDY        TEST(D)                  Date                    99
C                   IF        %Error
* Test failed, date is invalid. Display error message
C                   ITER
C                   ENDIF
* If no function keys were pressed, just send the message
C       *Inke       IFEQ      *off
C       *Inkf       ANDEQ     *off
C                   EVAL      *In98 = *on
C                   ITER
C                   ENDIF

C                   MOVE      Date           WorkDate
C                   SELECT
* If F5 was pressed, decrement date and re-display screen
C                   WHEN      *Inke = *on
C                   SUBDUR    1:*M           WorkDate
* If F6 was pressed, increment date and re-display screen
C                   WHEN      *Inkf = *on
C                   ADDDUR    1:*D           WorkDate
C                   ENDSL
C                   MOVE      WorkDate       Date
C                   ENDDO

C                   EVAL      *Inlr = *on
```

Figure 12.7: The FIG1207RG RPG IV program.

The display file in Figure 12.6 has a six-digit numeric field called DATE. We added two error messages that will be used to reflect whether the keyed date was valid. The program in Figure 12.7 first tests the date field to see if it is valid based on the *MDY format specified in Factor 1 of the TEST op code.

You can see an example of the output from our simple program in Figure 12.8.

447

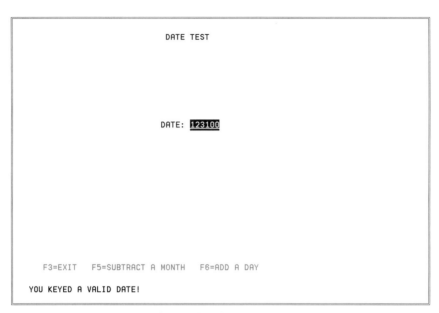

```
                         DATE TEST




                 DATE: 123100




        F3=EXIT   F5=SUBTRACT A MONTH   F6=ADD A DAY

    YOU KEYED A VALID DATE!
```

Figure 12.8: Example of the FIG1207RG RPG IV program.

If the date keyed is valid and function key F5 is pressed, the Subtract Duration (SUBDUR) op code is used to subtract one month from the date currently on the screen. If the date test is passed and function key F6 is pressed, the Add Duration (ADDDUR) op code is used to increment the displayed date by one day. In both of the examples for these op codes, the value to increment or decrement, as well as the duration interval for which the date is to be changed, is specified in Factor 2.

Valid duration intervals for date data types include *D or *DAYS (days), *M or *MONTHS (months), and *Y or *YEARS (years). Other duration types are *H or *HOURS (hours), *MN or *MINUTES (minutes), *S or *SECONDS (seconds), and *MS or *MSECONDS (microseconds).

You will notice in Figure 12.7 that we had to move the DATE field to a field defined with a date type before we could perform the ADDDUR or SUBDUR operations. While TEST must be performed on fields that are not defined with a date or time data type, the ADDDUR, SUBDUR, or EXTRCT op codes only work on fields that are defined as date or time fields.

DATE ARITHMETIC

As you have surmised by now, all of those fancy RPG II and RPG III routines we developed through the years to validate dates, calculate follow-up dates, or detect how old a particular transaction is are no longer of any value. Do not lament the fact that they have become extinct, however, because the replacement routines are simple and very easy to code.

In Figure 12.9, we wanted to calculate a 15-day follow-up date. After applying the code in this example, the resulting follow-up date in the FollowDate field would be 15 days after the date specified in the Factor 1 Date field. We no longer need to worry about whether the results of our actions will cause a change in the month or year. The system now handles all of that for you!

```
CLON01Factor1+++++++Opcode&ExtFactor2+++++++Result++++++++Len++D+HiLoEq...Comments
c       Date        ADDDUR   15:*DAYS      FollowDate
```

Figure 12.9: Calculating a 15-day follow-up date.

Figure 12.10 illustrates how you would calculate the age of a particular sales transaction. By moving the current system date (stored in month-day-year format) into a date data type work field we called Today, we are able to use the new field in our date math calculations.

```
DName+++++++++++ETDsFrom+++To/L+++IDc.Keywords+++++++++++++++++++++++++Comments++++
D Today         S                D    Datfmt(*MDY)
D DaysOld       S                4 0
D MonthsOld     S                4 0
D YearsOld      S                4 0

CLON01Factor1+++++++Opcode&ExtFactor2+++++++Result++++++++Len++D+HiLoEq...Comments
c                   Move     Udate         Today
c       Today       SUBDUR   SaleDate      DaysOld:*Days
c       Today       SUBDUR   SaleDate      MonthsOld:*M
c       Today       SUBDUR   SaleDate      YearsOld:*Y
```

Figure 12.10: Calculating the age of a transaction.

If our System Date format (DATFMT) was *YMD, we would also want to define Today as *YMD, or place *YMD in Factor 1 of our MOVE operation. You can use the Display Job (DSPJOB) command to tell what your system default is. You can use the Change Job

449

(CHGJOB) command if you want to change it for the current session, or the DATEEDIT Control Specification keyword within your program.

When using the MOVE op code for dates or times, there is one rule you need to remember: The format specified in Factor 1 of the MOVE operation is used to describe the field the system knows the least about. In other words, if the field in Factor 2 is not defined as a date or time data type, it will be defined by the format specified in Factor 1. If the Result field is not defined with a date or time data type, the format in Factor 1 is used to describe that field instead.

In our example in Figure 12.10, the SaleDate field in our database file could be in any format, as long as it is a date data type. The SaleDate field in our file might be in *YMD or *ISO format, but it will not affect the math, because each date is evaluated on its chronological value.

Finding the last day of the month has been made easy, as you can see in Figure 12.11. We took the current date and reset it to the beginning of the month. By using a data structure to overlay the Today date field with the day portion (CurrentDay) of the date, we were able to reset the date by simply moving '01' to the CurrentDay field. Note that we specified that the overlap position begins in the fourth position of the field because the *MDY format is stored as MM/DD/YY.

```
DName+++++++++++ETDsFrom+++To/L+++IDc.Keywords+++++++++++++++++++++++++++++Comments++++
D                       DS
D Today                           D   Datfmt(*MDY)
D  CurrentDay                  2      Overlay(Today:4)

D EndofMonth       S              D   Datfmt(*MDY)

CLON01Factor1+++++++Opcode&ExtFactor2+++++++Result++++++++Len++D+HiLoEq...Comments
C                  Move     Udate           Today
C                  Move     '01'            CurrentDay
C       Today      ADDDUR   1:*Months       EndOfMonth
C                  SUBDUR   1:*Days         EndOfMonth
```

Figure 12.11: Finding the last day of the month.

Once we reset the date to the beginning of the current month, we used the ADDDUR op code to add one month to the date so the result would be the first day of next month. Then we simply used the SUBDUR op code to subtract one day from the date to get the desired result. This relieves us from having to keep track of leap years or how many days are in each month.

450

DATE FORMATTING

As we have mentioned, if you define a field in your database file as a date data type, it will appear and print in the format specified in the DDS (including the separator characters). So if the sales date in your transaction file was defined in an *ISO format, it will print and display as YYYY-MM-DD. For example, a sales date of December 1, 2000, would appear as 2000-12-01 if you were to print the field in a report or view it on the screen. Note that no edit code is required when the date is printed or displayed, because the separator character is now part of the field.

But this can cause problems if your screens and reports were all designed to output a six-digit date field. Reworking all of the screens and reports to fit the new field sizes could require a great deal of work just to get you back to where you were in the first place. And what if your program specifications called for using a slash (/) as a separator character instead of a dash (-)? And wouldn't those same specifications probably require that dates be month-day-year instead of year-month-day?

Rather than redesign your reports and screens, we recommend that you simply move the date fields from your database file to a date field defined with the desired format prior to printing or displaying them.

Using the scenario we just described, let's say that our sales date is defined in our database file as an *ISO date data type. If we were to print the sales date of December 1, 2000, as defined, it would appear as 2000-12-01. But if we were to move the SalesDate field into the DateOfSale output field, as defined in Figure 12.12, it would appear as 12-01-00. If we wanted it to appear as 12/01/00, we would define the DateOfSale field with a date format of *MDY/ or *MDY (a slash is the default separator for the *MDY format).

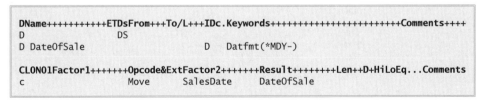

```
DName++++++++++++ETDsFrom+++To/L+++IDc.Keywords++++++++++++++++++++++++++Comments++++
D                      DS
D DateOfSale                    D    Datfmt(*MDY-)

CLON01Factor1+++++++Opcode&ExtFactor2+++++++Result++++++++Len++D+HiLoEq...Comments
c                   Move        SalesDate       DateOfSale
```

Figure 12.2: Changing the output format of date fields.

By performing this simple MOVE operation prior to output, we have eliminated the need to redefine our print or display output. Our database will be able to handle the change in century (because the date is stored with the century digits), but our output does not need

451

to be redesigned. The date of January 1, 2000, will appear as 01/01/00, but people look-ing at a report will know that a sales date of 01/01/00 represents the year 2000 and not the year 1900.

Once again, changing date formats is a simple MOVE operation when you are using fields with date data types. Moving a date defined with an *MDY (month-day-year) format to a date defined with a *YMD (year-month-day) format involves a simple MOVE operation.

Finding the day of the week can be simple too. The code in Figure 12.13 is used to calcu-late the day of the week by subtracting a base date of January 1, 1901, from the date you are calculating the day of the week for.

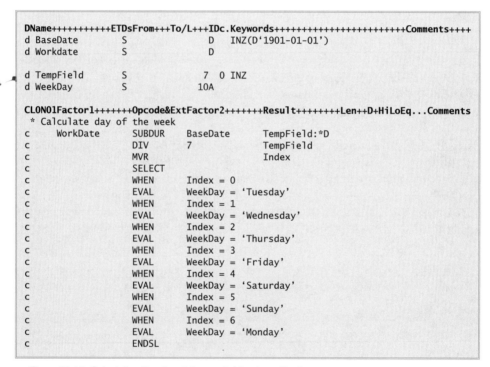

```
DName++++++++++ETDsFrom+++To/L+++IDc.Keywords++++++++++++++++++++++++++Comments++++
d BaseDate         S              D    INZ(D'1901-01-01')
d Workdate         S              D

d TempField        S              7  0 INZ
d WeekDay          S            10A

CLON01Factor1++++++++Opcode&ExtFactor2+++++++Result++++++++Len++D+HiLoEq...Comments
* Calculate day of the week
c       WorkDate       SUBDUR    BaseDate     TempField:*D
c                      DIV       7            TempField
c                      MVR                    Index
c                      SELECT
c                      WHEN      Index = 0
c                      EVAL      WeekDay = 'Tuesday'
c                      WHEN      Index = 1
c                      EVAL      WeekDay = 'Wednesday'
c                      WHEN      Index = 2
c                      EVAL      WeekDay = 'Thursday'
c                      WHEN      Index = 3
c                      EVAL      WeekDay = 'Friday'
c                      WHEN      Index = 4
c                      EVAL      WeekDay = 'Saturday'
c                      WHEN      Index = 5
c                      EVAL      WeekDay = 'Sunday'
c                      WHEN      Index = 6
c                      EVAL      WeekDay = 'Monday'
c                      ENDSL
```

Figure 12.13: Calculating the day of the week (simple method).

The key to calculating the day of the week in Figure 12.13 is to define a base date where you know what the day of the week is. In our example, we defined a base date of Tues-day, January 1, 1901. We then used the SUBDUR op code to subtract the base date from the WorkDate variable. The result of this operation is the number of days since the base date, which is then divided by 7 (the number of days in a week). The remainder of the division operation is the number of days after Tuesday.

While this method is simple, it may not be flexible enough for your needs. It assumes that the input date is already in a date data type.

The program in Figure 12.14 uses APIs to calculate the day of the week from a wide variety of date input pictures (as seen in Table 12.4). It first uses the CEEDAYS API to convert the input date to a Lilian date. The program then uses the CEEDYWK API to convert the Lilian date to the day of the week. The input date, the picture format describing the input date (see Table 12.4), and the day of the day of the week to be returned to the calling program are the three parameters used in this program. If you need to use other date formats that are not included in the table, refer to the *System API Reference* manual (SC41-3801-00) for a complete description of the formats the CEEDAYS API can handle.

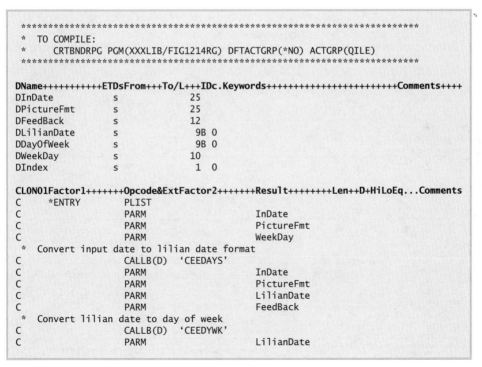

```
*****************************************************************************
*   TO COMPILE:
*      CRTBNDRPG PGM(XXXLIB/FIG1214RG) DFTACTGRP(*NO) ACTGRP(QILE)
*****************************************************************************


DName+++++++++++ETDsFrom+++To/L+++IDc.Keywords+++++++++++++++++++++++++Comments++++
DInDate           s              25
DPictureFmt       s              25
DFeedBack         s              12
DLilianDate       s               9B 0
DDayOfWeek        s               9B 0
DWeekDay          s              10
DIndex            s               1  0


CL0N01Factor1+++++++Opcode&ExtFactor2+++++++Result++++++++Len++D+HiLoEq...Comments
C     *ENTRY        PLIST
C                   PARM                     InDate
C                   PARM                     PictureFmt
C                   PARM                     WeekDay
*   Convert input date to lilian date format
C                   CALLB(D)  'CEEDAYS'
C                   PARM                     InDate
C                   PARM                     PictureFmt
C                   PARM                     LilianDate
C                   PARM                     FeedBack
*   Convert lilian date to day of week
C                   CALLB(D)  'CEEDYWK'
C                   PARM                     LilianDate
```

Figure 12.14: Calculating the day of the week (industrial strength) (part 1 of 2).

453

```
C                   PARM                    DayOfWeek
C                   PARM                    FeedBack
c                   move      DayOfWeek     Index
  *  Convert index field to day of week description
c                   SELECT
c                   WHEN      Index = 0
c                   EVAL      WeekDay = 'Error'
c                   WHEN      Index = 1
c                   EVAL      WeekDay = 'Sunday'
c                   WHEN      Index = 2
c                   EVAL      WeekDay = 'Monday'
c                   WHEN      Index = 3
c                   EVAL      WeekDay = 'Tuesday'
c                   WHEN      Index = 4
c                   EVAL      WeekDay = 'Wednesday'
c                   WHEN      Index = 5
c                   EVAL      WeekDay = 'Thursday'
c                   WHEN      Index = 6
c                   EVAL      WeekDay = 'Friday'
c                   WHEN      Index = 7
c                   EVAL      WeekDay = 'Saturday'
c                   ENDSL
c                   eval      *inlr = *on
```

Figure 12.14: Calculating the day of the week (industrial strength) (part 2 of 2).

Table 12.4: Some of the Date Input Pictures Allowed for Program FIG1214RG.

Date Input Picture	Sample Input Date	Description
YYMMDD	001201	Must include all six digits of the date (including leading zeros).
YYYYMMDD	20001201	Same as above, except the entire year, including century, is specified.
YYYY-MM-DD	2000-12-1	Eight-digit date is specified with the dash (-) as the separator character. Leading zeros are not mandatory for month and day.
MMDDYY	120100	Month-day-year six-digit date format; requires leading zeros on month and day.
MM/DD/YY	12/01/00	Same as above, except slash (/) is included as the separator character. Leading zeros on month and day must be specified.
ZM/ZD/YY	12/1/00	Same as above, except leading zeros on month and day may be suppressed.

454

*Table 12.4: Some of the Date Input
Pictures Allowed for Program FIG1214RG. (continued)*

Date Input Picture	Sample Input Date	Description
MM/DD/YYYY	12/01/2000	Eight-digit date is specified with the slash (/) as the separator character. Leading zeros are required on month and day.
DD.MM.YY	01.12.00	Six-digit day-month-year format with the decimal (.) as the separator character. Leading zeros are required on month and day.
DD MMM YY	01 DEC 00	Date is entered as day-month-year. Day is entered as two-digit numeric (including leading zeros). Month is entered as the three-character abbreviation. Year is entered as two-digit numeric.
DD Mmmmmmmmmm YY	01 December 00	Day-month-year format. Day is entered as two digits (leading zeros included). Month is specified as the full ten-character description (including blanks). Year is specified as two-digit numeric.
ZD Mmmmmmmmmz YY	1 December 00	Same as above, except leading zeros and trailing blanks are suppressed.
Mmmmmmmmmz ZD, YYYY	December 1, 2000	Same as above except input date is specified as month-day-year. A comma is specified to separate day and year, and the year is specified as four digits (including the century).
YY.DDD	00.336	Julian date with the decimal (.) as the separator character.
YYDDD	00366	Same as above, except no separator characters.

USING DATA TYPES TO FORMAT OUTPUT

Even if your legacy data does not include date or time data types, you still can take advantage of data types and built-in functions to format your output. To illustrate this fact, we wrote a little utility that can be used to edit numbers, dates, and times so they can be output to an alphanumeric field. This is often required when you are bringing data to the screen or to print.

To illustrate how our utility works, we wrote a small DDS window program (see Figure 12.15). The display file in Figure 12.16 and the ILE RPG Module in Figure 12.17 are used to produce the output you see in Figure 12.15. When the FIG1217RG program is called, the window you see in Figure 12.15 is displayed. The objective of this sample program is to key an input date, input time, or amount along with an "output description code" (seen in Tables 12.5 and 12.6) and press Enter. The result is that the formatted data will be displayed and presented in the bottom of the window, as in Figure 12.15. If the code you key is not valid with the type of input you keyed, an error message will be displayed.

The output description code for dates can be seen in Table 12.5. Our utility supports several of the more popular date data type formats as well as a few of our own, which we added just for fun. For the most part, time fields are usually output in far less exciting flavors (see Table 12.5).

Numeric output is often needed in a wide variety of formats, so we chose to have our little utility support most of the numeric edit codes supported by IBM Output Specifications or DDS Printer Files. The codes and sample output can be seen in Table 12.6. And just for kicks, we also allow you to add a floating dollar sign to the numeric output.

Let's talk about how the code works. The FIG1218RG program (Figure 12.18) accepts five fields as input. These five input fields are described in a single external data structure named FIG1219DS (see Figure 12.19). For the uninitiated, an external data structure is simply a physical file that holds no data per se, but is used to describe a block or grouping of data (parameters in our case). (External Data Structures are described in detail in chapter 8.) If you look at the code in the FIG1217RG program (Figure 12.17), you can see how we used the external data structure to call the FIG1218RG program. The FIG1218RG program reformatted the data and passed the results back in the parameters described by the external data structure.

When the FIG1218RG program is called, it checks to see if any input date was sent to the program. If the program determines that a date was sent, it checks the date for validity. The program expects the date to be passed as six digits in an mmddyy format. September 30, 1999, would be passed as 093099. If the date is deemed to be invalid, an error message is issued to that effect and control is returned to the calling program. On the other hand, if the date is deemed valid, the program reformats the date depending on the output description code passed to the program (valid codes can be seen in Table 12.5). Once again, invalid format codes will result in an error and control will be passed back to the calling program. If both the date and output description code are valid, the data will be appropriately formatted and control will be passed to the calling program. If you look at the code, you will see that using the MOVE operation and date data type performs much of the formatting task.

When required to find the day-of-the-week, the program uses the method we described previously in this chapter. The program simply subtracts a base date (defined in the definition specifications) from the input date. The result of the subtraction operation is divided by 7 (number of the days in the week), and the remainder is used as a single-digit index field for our compile time array named DAYS.

If an input time is passed, the utility essentially works as it would with an input date. There are only two flavors of time fields supported (see Table 12.5). Once again, the program uses the time data type to perform its formatting functions.

In the case of a numeric input field, we used the Edit Code (%EDITC) built-in function to apply the edit code to the numeric input field. When the floating dollar sign is requested, the program uses the EVAL statement with the %TRIM parameter to trim (remove) the blanks and concatenate the dollar sign to the desired output. Once the output is properly formatted, the value is returned to the calling program.

```
  KEY OPTIONS, PRESS ENTER..

  INPUT DATE........ 093000  INPUT AMOUNT... 000000000
  INPUT TIME........ 000000  EDIT CODE...... _
  OUTPUT DESCRIPTION. *ALF   FLOATING DOLLAR _ ($)

      Saturday, September 30, 2000

F3=EXIT F12=PREVIOUS
```

Figure 12.15: Sample output from FIG1217RG.

457

Table 12.5: Format Parameters
Describing the Desired Output for Dates and Times.

Format	Format Parameter	Example
Numeric Month, Day, Year	*MDY	12/31/99
Numeric Day, Month, Year	*DMY	31/12/99
Numeric Year, Month, Day	*YMD	99/21/31
Alphanumeric Month, Day, Year	*AMDY	December 31, 1999
Alphanumeric Month, Day, Year including the day of the week	*ALF	Friday, December 31, 1999
Day of the Week	*DOW	Friday
International Standards Organization	*ISO	16:24:32
IBM USA Standard	*USA	04:24 PM

Table 12.6: Edit Codes
Describing the Desired Output for Numeric Fields.

Code	Commas	Print Zero Balance?	Sign	Other	Sample
1	Yes	Yes	None		9,999.99
2	Yes	No	None		9,999.99
3	No	Yes	None		9999.99
4	No	No	None		9999.99
A	Yes	Yes	CR		9,999.99CR
B	Yes	No	CR		9,999.99CR
C	No	Yes	CR		9999.99CR
D	No	No	CR		9999.99CR
J	Yes	Yes	-		9,999.99-
K	Yes	No	-		9,999.99-
L	No	Yes	-		9999.99-
M	No	No	-		9999.99-
X				Remove plus sign	00099999
Y				Date field edit	9/99/99
Z				Zero Suppress	999999

458

```
A*******************************************************************
A*  TO COMPILE:
A*     CRTDSPF FILE(XXXLIB/FIG1216DS)
A*******************************************************************
A                                         CA03 CA12
A          R WINDOW
A                                         WINDOW(5 10 10 55 *NOMSGLIN *NORSTC-
A                                         SR)
A                               2  2'Key options, press Enter..'
A                                         DSPATR(HI) COLOR(BLU)
A                              10  1'F3=Exit'  COLOR(BLU)
A                              10  9'F12=Previous' COLOR(BLU)
A                               4  2'Input Date.........'
A                               5  2'Input Time.........'
A                               4 30'Input Amount...'
A                               5 30'Edit Code......'
A                               6 30'Floating Dollar'
A            OUTPUTDATA    50A  O  8  4DSPATR(HI)
A            INPUTDATE      6Y OB  4 22DSPATR(HI) CHECK(RZ)
A            INPUTTIME      6Y OB  5 22DSPATR(HI) CHECK(RZ)
A            INPUTNBR       9S 2B  4 46DSPATR(HI) CHECK(RZ)
A            EDITCODE       1A  B  5 46DSPATR(HI UL)
A            DOLLAR         1A  B  6 46DSPATR(HI UL)
A                               6 48'($)'
A                               6  2'Output Description.'
A            OUTPUTDESC     5A  B  6 22DSPATR(HI UL)
A*
A          R DUMMY
A                                         KEEP ASSUME
A                               1  3' '
```

Figure 12.16: Display DDS for the data format window module.

```
*******************************************************************
*  TO COMPILE:
*     CRTBNDRPG PGM(XXXLIB/FIG1217RG) DFTACTGRP(*NO) ACTGRP(QILE)
*******************************************************************

fFg1216Ds  cf   e           workstn

d Parameters    e ds               extname(FormatDS)

d CowsCumHom     s         1      inz(*off)

c              clear                 Window
* Processing Loop
c              dou        CowsCumHom = *On
c              clear                 OutPutDesc
```

Figure 12.17: RPG module for the data format window module (part 1 of 2).

459

```
c                  exfmt      Window
c                  clear                   OutPutData

c                  If         *InKC OR *InKL
c                  Leave
c                  EndIF

c                  If         Editcode <> *blanks
c                  If         Dollar = '$'
c                  Eval       OutputDesc = EditCode + Dollar
c                  else
c                  Eval       OutputDesc = EditCode
c                  Endif
c                  Endif

c                  Call       'FG1218RG'
c                  Parm                    Parameters
c                  enddo
 *
c                  eval       *inlr = *on
```

Figure 12.17: RPG module for the data format window module (part 2 of 2).

```
*****************************************************************************
*   TO COMPILE:
*       CRTBNDRPG PGM(XXXLIB/FIG1218RG) DFTACTGRP(*NO) ACTGRP(QILE)
*****************************************************************************

d Months          s             11      dim(12) ctdata perrcd(6)
d Days            s              9      dim(7)  ctdata perrcd(7)
 *
d Parameters      e ds                  extname(FormatDS)
d  EditCode                      1      Overlay(OutputDesc:1)
d  Currency                      1      Overlay(OutputDesc:2)
 *
d                 ds                     inz
d WorkDate              1      10d      datfmt(*iso)
d  WorkDay             9      10
d  WorkMonth           6       7
d  WorkIndex           6       7 0
d  WorkYear            1       4
 *
d BaseDate        s              d      inz(d'1901-01-04')
d Index           s              3 0    inz
d TempField       s              7 0    inz
d WorkTime        s              t      timfmt(*hms)
 *
```

Figure 12.18: RPG module for formatting data (part 1 of 4).

```
c       *entry          plist
c                       parm                    Parameters

 * If an input date is specified, validate the date
c                       If        InputDate > 0
c       *mdy            test(d)                 InputDate              68
c                       If        *in68
c                       Eval      OutputData = 'Invalid Input Date'
c                       Else
c       *mdy            Move      InputDate      WorkDate
c                       Select
c                       When      OutPutDesc = '*MDY'
c       *mdy            Movel     WorkDate       OutputData
c                       When      OutPutDesc = '*DMY'
c       *dmy            Movel     WorkDate       OutputData
c                       When      OutPutDesc = '*YMD'
c       *ymd            Movel     WorkDate       OutputData
c                       When      OutPutDesc = '*AMDY'
c                       Move      WorkMonth      Index
c                       Eval      OutputData = %Trim(months(WorkIndex)) +
c                                 ' ' + Workday + ', ' + WorkYear
c                       When      OutPutDesc = '*ALF'
c                       Exsr      DowSr
c                       Eval      OutputData = %Trim(days(Index)) +
c                                 ', ' + %Trim(months(WorkIndex)) +
c                                 ' ' + Workday + ', ' + WorkYear
c                       When      OutPutDesc = '*DOW'
c                       Exsr      DowSr
c                       Eval      OutputData = %Trim(days(Index))
c                       Other
c                       Eval      OutputData = 'Invalid Description'
c                       EndSl
c                       EndIf
c                       Return
c                       Endif

 * If an input time is specified, validate the time
c                       If        InputTime > 0
c       *hms            test(t)                 InputTime              68
c                       If        *in68
c                       Eval      OutputData = 'Invalid Input Time'
c                       Else
c       *hms            Move      InputTime      WorkTime
c                       Select
c                       When      OutPutDesc = '*HMS'
c       *hms            Movel     WorkTime       OutputData
c                       When      OutPutDesc = '*USA'
c       *usa            Movel     WorkTime       OutputData
c                       Other
c                       Eval      OutputData = 'Invalid Description'
c                       EndSl
```

Figure 12.18: RPG module for formatting data (part 2 of 4).

```
c                 EndIf
c                 Return
c                 Endif

 * If an input amount is specified, validate the edit code
c                 If         InputNbr <> 0
c                 Select
c                 When       EditCode = '1'
c                 Eval       OutputData = %EditC(InputNbr : '1')
c                 When       EditCode = '2'
c                 Eval       OutputData = %EditC(InputNbr : '2')
c                 When       EditCode = '3'
c                 Eval       OutputData = %EditC(InputNbr : '3')
c                 When       EditCode = '4'
c                 Eval       OutputData = %EditC(InputNbr : '4')
c                 When       EditCode = 'A'
c                 Eval       OutputData = %EditC(InputNbr : 'A')
c                 When       EditCode = 'B'
c                 Eval       OutputData = %EditC(InputNbr : 'B')
c                 When       EditCode = 'C'
c                 Eval       OutputData = %EditC(InputNbr : 'C')
c                 When       EditCode = 'D'
c                 Eval       OutputData = %EditC(InputNbr : 'D')
c                 When       EditCode = 'J'
c                 Eval       OutputData = %EditC(InputNbr : 'J')
c                 When       EditCode = 'K'
c                 Eval       OutputData = %EditC(InputNbr : 'K')
c                 When       EditCode = 'L'
c                 Eval       OutputData = %EditC(InputNbr : 'L')
c                 When       EditCode = 'M'
c                 Eval       OutputData = %EditC(InputNbr : 'M')
c                 When       EditCode = 'X'
c                 Eval       OutputData = %EditC(InputNbr : 'X')
c                 When       EditCode = 'Y'
c                 Eval       OutputData = %EditC(InputNbr : 'Y')
c                 When       EditCode = 'Z'
c                 Eval       OutputData = %EditC(InputNbr : 'Z')
c                 Other
c                 Eval       OutputData = 'Invalid Edit Code'
c                 EndSl

 * Apply a floating dollar sign, if applicable...
c                 If         Currency = '$'
c                 Eval       OutputData = '$' + %Trim(OutputData)
c                 Else
c                 Eval       OutputData = %Trim(OutputData)
c                 EndIf
c                 Return
c                 Endif

c                 eval       *inlr = *on
 *
```

Figure 12.18: RPG module for formatting data (part 3 of 4).

```
*****   subroutine: "dowsr"   ****************************************
***   calculate day of the week from month/day/year   ***************
csr   Dowsr        begsr
* Day is Friday when index = 1, Saturday when the index is 2, etc..
c      WorkDate      SubDur    Basedate        Tempfield:*D
c                    Div       7               Tempfield
c                    mvr                       Index
c                    add       1               Index
csr                  endsr
*
** Months
January    February   March      April     May       June
July       August     September  October   November  December
** Days
Friday   Saturday Sunday   Monday    Tuesday   WednesdayThursday
```

Figure 12.18: RPG module for formatting data (part 4 of 4).

```
*************************************************************************
*  TO COMPILE:
*    CRTPF FILE(XXXLIB/FORMATDS) SRCMBR(FG1219PF)
*************************************************************************
A          R FMTDS                      TEXT('Format Data Structure')
A            INPUTDATE     6S 0          TEXT('Input Date')
A            INPUTTIME     6S 0          TEXT('Input Time')
A            INPUTNBR      9S 2          TEXT('Input Number')
A            OUTPUTDESC    5A            TEXT('Description of Output')
A            OUTPUTDATA    50A           TEXT('Output Data')
```

Figure 12.19: Externally Described Data Structure for formatting data.

DATE CONVERSION

Speaking of conversion... What would you think if we told you that the system can convert the date fields in your database files from non-date data types to date data types for you? Well, it can, and we are going to show you how.

The Change Physical File (CHGPF), Alter Table (ALTTBL), and Copy File (CPYF) commands can all be used to automatically convert your database date fields. For the purposes of our example here, though, we are going to describe how to do this using the CPYF command.

Any programmer who has worked on the AS/400 for a while is familiar with the CPYF command. It is great for performing a variety of copy functions, but you are probably aware that it will not usually allow you to convert the data type of fields. One exception to this rule, however (as long as you follow a very specific set of rules), is when you are converting dates in your database files to fields that have a date data type.

Let's look at an example of how the CPYF command can be used to convert the data type of your date fields. Figure 12.20 shows us an example of the DDS of a sales transaction file.

```
A*****************************************************************************
A*  TO COMPILE:
A*     CRTPF FILE(XXXLIB/FIG1220PF) SRCMBR(FIG1220PF)
A*****************************************************************************
AANO1NO2NO3T.Name++++++RLen++TDpBLinPosFunctions+++++++++++++++++++++++++++++
A                                        UNIQUE
A             R TRANSREC                 TEXT('Sales Transactions')
A               TRCUSTNO     5A          TEXT('Customer Number')
A               TRSALEDATE   6S 0        TEXT('Sales Date')
A               TRTRANSNO    5S 0        TEXT('Sales Transaction ID#')
A               TRSKU#       23A         TEXT('SKU Number')
A               TRAMOUNT     7S 2        TEXT('Sales Amount')
  *
A             K TRCUSTNO
A             K TRSALEDATE
A             K TRTRANSNO
```

Figure 12.20: DDS for FIG1220PF transaction file with a six-digit date field.

The DDS in Figure 12.20 defines a simple Sales Transaction file. We have defined a customer number, sales date, transaction ID number, SKU number, and transaction amount. Note that the TRSALEDATE field is defined as a six-digit, numeric, signed field.

In Figure 12.21, we have taken the same Sales Transaction file definition and modified it so the TRSALEDATE field would be defined with a date data type. For our example, we chose to use the *ISO format. However, we could use any of the date data type formats we saw in Table 12.1 and still end up with our desired results.

In our examples, we are converting a sales transaction file with the six-digit date (FIG1220PF) to a new file (FIG1221PF), which we created with a sales date defined with an *ISO date data type. Note that the differences between the two files are the size, data type, and default value of the TRSALEDATE field.

```
A*******************************************************************
A*  TO COMPILE:
A*     CRTPF FILE(XXXLIB/FIG1221PF) SRCMBR(FIG1221PF)
A*******************************************************************
AAN01N02N03T.Name++++++RLen++TDpBLinPosFunctions++++++++++++++++++++++++++++
A                                    UNIQUE
A          R TRANSREC                TEXT('Sales Transactions')
A            TRCUSTNO     5A         TEXT('Customer Number')
A            TRSALEDATE   L          DATFMT(*ISO)
A                                    DFT('0001-01-01')
A                                    TEXT('Sales Date')
A            TRTRANSNO    5S 0       TEXT('Sales Transaction ID#')
A            TRSKU#       23A        TEXT('SKU Number')
A            TRAMOUNT     7S 2       TEXT('Sales Amount')
 *
A          K TRCUSTNO
A          K TRSALEDATE
A          K TRTRANSNO
```

Figure 12.21: DDS for FIG1221PF Sales Transaction file with a date data type.

For our purposes, the date in the FIG1220PF file was stored in a YYMMDD (year-month-day) format. This is important because it has a direct bearing on how the CPYF command will work.

We created a sample CL program in Figure 12.22 that will be used to convert our file without the date data type (FIG1220PF) to the new file with the date data type (FIG1221PF). Because we perform a CHGJOB command in this CL program (we will explain why shortly), it is important to submit this job rather than run it interactively. Failure to do so could result in subsequent interactive jobs that do not perform as expected.

```
/*****************************************************************************/
/*   TO CREATE:                                                              */
/*        CRTCLPGM PGM(XXXLIB/FIG1222CL)                                     */
/*****************************************************************************/
PGM
            CHGJOB      DATFMT(*YMD)
            CPYF        FROMFILE(FIG1220PF) TOFILE(FIG1221PF) +
                          MBROPT(*REPLACE) FROMRCD(1) FMTOPT(*MAP)
ENDPGM
```

Figure 12.22: CL program to convert a six-digit numeric date to *ISO date data type.

Figure 12.23 reflects what the data in our sample sales transaction file might look like. Note that the data in the column titled trsaledate shows our dates formatted as YYMMDD (year-month-day). The sales date in the first record, January 15, 1996, appears as 960,115 (note that query added the extra comma to our six-digit numeric field in an attempt to make it easier to read).

```
                            Display Report
                                      Report width . . . . . :      68
     Position to line  . . . . .  ____      Shift to column  . . . . . .
     Line     ....+....1....+....2....+....3....+....4....+....5....+....6....+...
              TRCUSTNO  TRSALEDATE  TRTRANSNO  TRSKU#                   TRAMOUNT
     000001   1000         960,115          1  00056405578902130456821  1,500.00
     000002   1000         960,119          4  56408798701234564021131    895.00
     000003   1001         960,120         15  56408798732165490780322    805.00
     000004   1001         960,120         17  21345054897012345648970    950.00
     000005   1002         960,120          7  54089790812318654987012  1,325.00
     000006   1005         960,115          6  87089798701234564078966  1,725.33
     000007   1005         960,121          8  56456489789012316549821  1,880.25
     000008   1010         960,118          9  56408798321045897634156    155.00
     000009   1010         960,118         12  54098780456105645644506    909.00
     000010   1010         960,120          2  56405487905315879012213    211.15
     000011   1010         960,120          6  78901231657498078970123    753.33
     000012   1010         960,120         14  87098756410321546548970    500.50
     000013   1010         960,120         18  54089702314567804564022    750.00
     000014   1010         960,120         21  54870231549870545640822     69.96
     000015   1010         960,121         16  54089703131564087086454    800.48
     000016   1011         960,115         10  79802134564897083213215    649.60
                                                                          More...
     F3=Exit      F12=Cancel      F19=Left      F20=Right      F24=More keys
```

Figure 12.23: Example of FIG1220PF sales data prior to conversion.

Prior to conversion, the data reflected in Figure 12.23 was stored in the FIG1220PF physical file. The CL conversion program in Figure 12.22 converted the data in the FIG1220PF physical file and placed the results in the FIG1221PF physical file. Figure12.24 shows the results after our conversion program was run.

Note that the same sales date (under the column titled TRSALEDATE in Figure 12.17), January 15, 1996, now displays as 1996-01-15. The CPYF command in our FIG1222CL conversion program automatically added the century and the date separator characters for us when the copy was performed!

Now that we have piqued your interest, note that there are some pretty strict rules that *must* be adhered to if you are going to use this method to convert your database files (see Table 12.7).

466

```
                             Display Report
                                    Report width . . . . . :        68
      Position to line  . . . . .  ____      Shift to column  . . . . . .
      Line    ....+....1....+....2....+....3....+....4....+....5....+....6....+...
            TRCUSTNO  TRSALEDATE  TRTRANSNO  TRSKU#                    TRAMOUNT
      000001  1000     1996-01-15         1  00056405578902130456821  1,500.00
      000002  1000     1996-01-19         4  56408798701234564021131    895.00
      000003  1001     1996-01-20        15  56408798732165490780322    805.00
      000004  1001     1996-01-20        17  21345054897012345648970    950.00
      000005  1002     1996-01-20         7  54089790812318654987012  1,325.00
      000006  1005     1996-01-15         6  87089798701234564078966  1,725.33
      000007  1005     1996-01-21         8  56456489789012316549821  1,880.25
      000008  1010     1996-01-18         9  56408798321045897634156    155.00
      000009  1010     1996-01-18        12  54098780456105645644506    909.00
      000010  1010     1996-01-20         2  56405487905315879012213    211.15
      000011  1010     1996-01-20         6  78901231657498078970123    753.33
      000012  1010     1996-01-20        14  87098756410321546548970    500.50
      000013  1010     1996-01-20        18  54089702314567804564022    750.00
      000014  1010     1996-01-20        21  54870231549870545640822     69.96
      000015  1010     1996-01-21        16  54089703131564087086454    800.48
      000016  1011     1996-01-15        10  79802134564897083213215    649.60
                                                                        More...
      F3=Exit       F12=Cancel      F19=Left      F20=Right    F24=More keys
```

Figure 12.24: Example of FIG1221PF sales data after conversion.

Table 12.7: Rules Regarding
Date Conversion Using the CPYF Command.

Rule	Description
No packed dates allowed.	While the CPYF command works great when converting six-digit numeric signed fields, it will give you an error if you try to use packed fields. If your dates are packed, simply change your DDS so the fields are signed numeric, recompile, and copy the file with packed dates into the one that no longer has packed dates. You will then be ready to convert to a file with the date data types.
Alphanumeric dates require separator characters.	The CPYF command *will* convert alphanumeric data into fields with a date data type, but the pre-converted data *must* include the separator characters that match the date format of the date data type to which you are converting.

Table 12.7: Rules Regarding
Date Conversion Using the CPYF Command (continued).

Rule	Description
Specify a default value for the new date data type.	If your DDS for the new date data type does not have a default value specified (see Figure 12.21), the system will automatically use the current date as the default date when it experiences a mapping error. A pre-converted date with zeros in it will experience a mapping error when it is copied to a field with a date data type (zeros are not a valid value in date data fields), and the current date will be placed in the converted data. Imagine an accounts receivable detail file with payment dates that are zero being converted into a new file with all of the payment dates filled in with the current date. What a mess!
The date format of your session must match the date format of the file you are trying to convert.	You will note that, in our sample conversion program (Figure 12.22), we performed a CHGJOB command to change the date format to *YMD (year-month-day). That is because the format of our pre-converted date field was in the *YMD format. The CPYF command will not perform the conversion if the session date format and the pre-converted date format do not match. If you are unlucky enough to have two date fields in the same file that have *different* date formats, you will need to perform your conversion in multiple passes (changing the DDS of your file to a date data type for one date, performing the conversion, and then repeating the process for the next date). Use the DSPJOB command to see what your session date format is currently. The safest method is to simply perform the CHGJOB command every time you convert a file, regardless of your default setting.
The name of the new field with the date data type must match the name of the one without the date data type.	This one is rather obvious. If you use the *MAP option of the CPYF command, the system uses the field names to map the data. If the field names do not match, no mapping can occur.
Copy the records in arrival sequence.	Anytime you perform a CPYF function, you should copy the records using the arrival access path unless there is a compelling reason not to. By specifying the FROMRCD(1) parameter in the CPYF command, as we did in Figure 12.22, the system will copy the records in arrival sequence instead of by key. You will notice that performance is considerably better than when you copy a file using a keyed access path.

In our sample conversion program (Figure 12.22), we chose to use two different source members to describe our sample sales transaction file. This is probably not practical in most programming environments.

A better approach for the purposes of conversion would be to move the physical file to a different library using the Move Object (MOVOBJ) command, recompile the DDS for the file (assuming it has been updated with the date data type), and then run your conversion program. In this scenario, the CPYF command in the conversion program would be a little different than the one we used in Figure 12.22. This is because the file names would be the same, although they would be qualified with the library name.

You should not expect good performance with this type of conversion. It will help significantly if you copy the file using the arrival sequence access path, but anytime you use the *MAP option on the CPYF command, you are looking at a pretty slow process.

DATA TYPE PERFORMANCE

When the date and time data types were made available to High Level Languages (HLLs) for the first time with V3R1, much was made about performance. The general view was that performance for the date and time data types was not good. We had decided to use the date data type to solve our Y2K woes, and this made us very concerned. We decided to take matters into our own hands and run our own performance tests. As you read the following text, bear in mind that these tests were done several years ago, and performance for the data types has been enhanced on subsequent releases of the OS/400 operating system. The following paragraphs describe what we found.

We created four identical data files with date fields in them. Each file contained three date fields, as well as several other fields. With exception of the format of the date fields, all of the files had identical data. Each file was populated with 100,000 identical records.

Just for kicks, we also created two other files to run our tests on. The first file was a logical file over one of our date files, but the date fields were excluded from the logical view of the file. All other fields were included in the view. A second file was also created that only had one date field instead of the three date fields.

By running our tests over all six files, we felt that we might be able to come up with a reasonably diverse set of runtime scenarios.

We then ran our tests on two separate AS/400s: a V3R2 CISC box and a V3R7 RISC box. Each test was run in batch in a dedicated environment. Our test was the only job running when our statistics were gathered.

The first test (as seen in Figures 12.25 and 12.26) simply read each file and recorded the length of time required to read the entire file. The timer began after each file was already open and the record pointer was set. The timer ended when the last record was encountered. Files were read by relative record number and not by key.The first four files were essentially the same, with the exception of the format of the dates. The fifth file was the logical file with no dates defined, and the sixth file had only one date field per record instead of three.

Our tests did not reveal that there were dramatic differences between the various read times. On our V3R2 CISC box, the read time varies from 3:37 to 5:32. The difference was much less dramatic on our V3R7 RISC box, with runtimes from 1:39 to 2:16. As expected, the files without the date data type performed the best. The *MDY date data type was the worst.

The *ISO date data type performed the best of the date data types. This is because the system converts all date data types to *ISO to work with within the program, and then converts them back as needed. This is why the date fields with various date data types appear as equals within your program (much like numbers defined as packed, binary, and numeric). Because there is less conversion work to perform, *ISO performed the best in our tests.

Type of Date	Time In	Time Out	Duration
Non Dates	07:48 PM	07:52 PM	3:37
*ISO Date	07:26 PM	07:30 PM	4:38
*USA Date	07:43 PM	07:48 PM	5:20
*MDY Date	07:37 PM	07:43 PM	5:32
*ISO Logical	07:30 PM	07:33 PM	3:06
Single *ISO	07:33 PM	07:37 PM	3:40

Figure 12.25: Reading dates on a V3R2 CISC box.

Type of Date	Time In	Time Out	Duration
Non Dates	06:44 PM	06:46 PM	1:39
*ISO Date	06:35 PM	06:36 PM	1:56
*MDY Date	06:40 PM	06:42 PM	2:14
*USA Date	06:42 PM	06:44 PM	2:16
*ISO Logical	06:36 PM	06:38 PM	1:31
Single *ISO	06:38 PM	06:40 PM	1:38

Figure 12.26: Reading dates on a V3R7 RISC box.

The real performance hit with the date data type appears when you change the format of the date from one format to another.

Our tests involved the same date files and test scenarios as before, except that right after reading a record from the file, we converted the field to an eight-character/digit output field so the date field would appear as mm/dd/yy. This is generally one of the most common things you would do with a date field you wished to output.

We read the files with the date data type and then simply did a move to an eight-character output field. By using *MDY in factor one of our MOVE operation, the program automatically converted the date from the format in which it was stored to mm/dd/yy.

In the case of the file with the non-date data types, we reformatted the dates in two different ways. In the first case, we used several MOVE operations to extract the year into a single field and then the month and day into a single field. We then used MOVE operations to put the fields back together in a mmddyy format.

The next case simply multiplied the date against 100.0001 to change it from yymmdd (as it was in the data file) to mmddyy, making it ready for output. Note that these tests were run prior to Y2K, when this operation still worked for six-digit dates.

We found it interesting that the percentage of difference in our test results was considerably greater on the V3R2 CISC box than on the V3R7 RISC box. While the difference between the conversion of the dates ranged from 1:45 to 5:30 on the RISC box, it ranged from 3:41 to 15:42 on the CISC box! That is a range of 314 percent and 426 percent, respectively.

Note also that the conversion of the non-date data types differed significantly between the two systems, as shown in Figures 12.27 and 12.28. Deciphering the date using the multiplication method took nearly twice as long on the CISC box as using MOVE operations.

Type of Date	Time In	Time Out	Duration
*ISO Date	06:17 PM	06:31 PM	13:20
*USA Date	06:56 PM	07:11 PM	15:23
*MDY Date	06:40 PM	06:56 PM	15:42
Non Dates	07:11 PM	07:15 PM	3:41
100.0001	07:15 PM	07:22 PM	6:32

Figure 12.27: Changing date formats on the CISC box.

Type of Date	Time In	Time Out	Duration
*ISO Date	06:12 PM	06:16 PM	4:43
*MDY Date	06:20 PM	06:25 PM	5:28
*USA Date	06:25 PM	06:31 PM	5:30
Non Dates	06:31 PM	06:33 PM	1:46
100.0001	06:33 PM	06:35 PM	1:45

Figure 12.28: Changing date formats on the RISC box.

As we have already stated, performance of the RISC systems and the OS/400 operating system have been greatly enhanced since the time these tests were run. But the performance data is still worth noting, because it affects the way you will design your database. If you are going to use the date data type in your database design, it is probably best to use the *ISO data type. This is because it is the default standard your ILE RPG modules will convert your date fields to when working with your data.

THE DATING GAME

We hope this chapter has helped give you a feel for working with the date and time data types. The data type is a valuable tool that will ensure the data in your database is valid. It may not be correct, but it *will* be valid. The operations that are designed to work with the data type are powerful, flexible, and easy to use. Go ahead and give it a try. Once you work with data types, you will not want to work any other way.

13

ILE CONCEPTS

There has been a lot of confusion over the announcement of RPG IV and the Integrated Language Environment (ILE). Because they were announced in the same time frame, many MIS professionals were confused into thinking that they were one and the same. In reality, the two are distinctly different.

RPG IV is simply the newest generation of the RPG programming language. ILE, on the other hand, is not a programming language at all. It is an environment that was designed to enhance (speed up) calls between programs, especially if the programs are created with different languages. In the Original Program Model (OPM), programs have been able to call other programs that were created in different languages, but the performance has always been less than desirable. With ILE, you have the option of creating the program so it will run as fast as if called programs were simply subroutines of the calling program.

To begin with, we need to understand two new concepts that are introduced with ILE. The first is the concept of *binding*. Binding is the process the compiler goes through when modules are linked together to create a program. As with most everything on the AS/400, binding comes in more than one flavor. We will cover the types of binding later in the chapter.

The second concept we need to understand is *activation groups*. An activation group is a subset of a job that is used to control the resources of that job. You may not be aware of this, but all jobs run in an activation group—even OPM programs! Activation groups can be used to control memory, file overrides, commitment control, and more. We will take a good look at activation groups later in this chapter.

In addition to these two main concepts, there are some other new concepts that support them. These include *modules*, *service programs*, *exports*, *imports*, *program interfaces*, and even a new language—*binder language*. We will cover all of these topics, and maybe a few more. Let's begin our journey through ILE by discussing the basic building block of programs—*modules*.

MODULES

This may come as a shock to some of you, but we do not write programs anymore. Instead, we write nice, neat, little modules. The theory behind this is that modules are generally smaller than programs, making coding, testing, and debugging easier to accomplish. A module is not a program. You cannot execute a module directly. Instead, we tell the system to gather these modules into a program (or a service program) that can be executed. Once the program has been created, the modules used to create the program are no longer needed or used. The module can then be deleted to save disk space.

In simple terms, a module is like a program you cannot run. It is produced with the ILE compiler, but it is nonexecutable. It is a building block for programs, with the compiler bringing modules together to create programs.

EXPORTS

Modules can contain *procedures* that are available to other ILE objects. A procedure is a set of instructions that performs a task and returns to the caller. Procedures that exist in one module, but are available to other ILE objects, are called *exports*.

A data item (field) can also be made available to ILE objects outside the module. It also can be called an *export*. Use the keyword EXPORT on the Data Definition Specification to designate a field as an export.

Exports are identified by name and type (procedure or data).

IMPORTS

Items that have been exported from one module can be imported to another. An *import* is simply a reference to a procedure or data item not defined in the current module.

Imports are identified by name and type.

Exporting a data item from one program and importing it into another performs the same function as passing the data as parameters from one program to another. However, we do not recommend using export/import to pass data! Maintenance on programs that use this technique is much more difficult. Because it is not readily apparent that data is being passed, it should be avoided.

Modules are created from your source code using the Create XXX Module (CRTXXXMOD) command, where XXX represents the programming language. To create an RPG module, you run the CRTRPGMOD command.

PROGRAMS

Programs are created using the Create Program (CRTPGM) command. Note that you do not specify a language when creating a program. This is because programs can be created from modules that in turn were created using different programming languages. (We are only going to cover ILE RPG/400 characteristics.)

If your program has only one module, you can use the Create Bound RPG (CRTBNDRPG) command instead of the CRTPGM command. This command combines the Create Module (CRTMOD) and the CRTPGM commands into a single step. The module is created in the QTEMP library, used in the compilation of the program, and then discarded.

As with OPM programs, ILE programs have only one program entry point (PEP). PEPs are coded in modules, and programs can consist of more than one module. As a result programs could conceivably have more than one PEP. Because this is not allowed, you control which PEP is used via the ENTMOD parameter on the CRTPGM command. You designate which module is used as the entry point. All other PEPs in other modules in the program are ignored (as program entry points).

BINDING

As we have already said, programs are created through the process of binding modules together. By using a parameter on the CRTPGM command, you can list each module that needs to be included in the program. As a convenient alternative, you can specify that the binder search a *binder directory* to find the modules that need to be included in the program.

A binding directory is a list of modules and service programs that you may need when you are creating a program. You can create a directory of all modules that provide a similar function (math, for instance). Then you simply specify the math function binding directory, and the binder will go find the ones you used.

There are two methods of binding: bind by copy and bind by reference. The choice of which method you use can have an enormous impact on performance and maintenance.

Bind by Copy

When a program is compiled, all of the modules identified on the module parameter of the CRTPGM command are copied into the created program. The binding directory is searched if there are any unresolved imports. If a match is found that provides a corresponding export, that module is also copied into the program. Physical addresses the system needs to access these parts are established when the program is compiled.

Bind by copy creates a program that executes very quickly. In fact, all of the called modules that have been bound to the program will execute almost as quickly as if they were coded as subroutines. But this speed is bought at the expense of maintenance.

Because of the maintenance considerations involved, bind by copy is best suited for code used in only one or two programs.

Bind by Reference

When a program is compiled, no copying of modules is performed. Instead, symbolic links to the service programs that provide the services are saved in the program. These symbolic links are converted to the real addresses the system needs when the program is activated.

Bind by reference is best suited for code used in a lot of programs, such as utility functions, or for general application functions.

Service Programs

A service program is a collection of procedures (programs or modules) that are directly accessible by other ILE programs. They provide common services other programs may need. For those of you who are familiar with Microsoft Windows concepts, they are similar in concept to Dynamic Link Libraries (DLLs).

Some of the characteristics of a service program are:

- One or more modules (from any language) are copied to make a service program.

- No Program Entry Procedure is associated with a service program. PEPs in modules that are contained in the service program are ignored.

Suppose for a minute that you have different modules that perform different math functions. One module does addition, another square roots, and still another percentage calculations. All of these modules could be pulled into a single service program to provide math functions. Thereafter, any program that needs a math function only needs to access the service program to gain access to the required function.

But why shouldn't a program that needs a math function call the corresponding module directly? Why go through a service program to access the function? Doesn't this just add another layer of complexity? The answer to all of these questions lies in one dreaded word: maintenance. But before we can show you how adding another layer of complexity actually simplifies maintenance, we must briefly examine how programs are put together.

Modules are bound to programs using the bind-by-copy method. Service programs are bound to programs using the bind-by-reference method. Modules that are bound into programs using the bind-by-copy method will be much more difficult to maintain than those that are bound by reference. Think about it for a minute. Suppose one little line of code needs to be changed in a module. If that module has been bound by copy into 50 other programs, you will need to find all those other programs and then recompile them.

Service programs are not bound by copy into other programs. As a result, it is possible to make a change to a service program and not be required to recompile all the programs that access it. If all you are doing is fixing a bug or changing some logic in the program, you will not have to recompile any of the programs that use the service program. This is true as long as you do not change the *public interface* to the program in a way that makes it incompatible with the existing programs. The public interface to a service program consists of the names of the exported procedures and data items accessible to other ILE programs.

The system uses these procedures and data items to generate what is called a *signature*. A signature provides a quick and easy method to validate the public interface to a service program. If you add procedures to a service program, this would normally change the signature, and any programs that access that service program would have to be recompiled. But through the use of a binder language, you can tell the system to keep multiple signatures (both the new one as well as any previously generated signature). Then you do not need to recompile any of the existing programs that access the service program (unless you want them to access the new procedure added to the service program).

BINDER LANGUAGE

The binder language consists of a small set of commands that define the exports for a service program. You enter these commands into a source member (type BND) using SEU. This member is not compiled. The default file for the member is QSRVSRC.

To create a service program, you use the Create Service Program (CRTSRVPGM) command. One of the parameters available on this command is EXPORT/SRCFILE/SRCMBR. This parameter directs the binder to a source file and member that contain the binder statements the binder will use to generate one or more signatures for the program.

It is possible to change this parameter to *ALL, in which case all symbols are exported from the service program and no binder language is necessary. This option is the easiest to use but can be a nightmare to maintain. If the order or number of exports changes (due to maintenance of the service program), the signature would change and all programs or service programs that use the changed service program would have to be recompiled. This is why *ALL is not the default on the CRTSRVPGM command.

THE COMMANDS

The commands available in the language we need to concern ourselves with are Start Program Export (STRPGMEXP), End Program Export (ENDPGMEXP), and EXPORT. Let's examine each command in detail, after which you should be an expert binder language programmer.

The STRPGMEXP command identifies the beginning of a list of exports from a service program. One of the parameters of this command is PGMLVL (program level), which accepts either the *CURRENT or *PRV value. This parameter allows us to define multiple export lists, each with a STRPGMEXP command and a corresponding ENDPGMEXP command. This is the secret to maintaining multiple signatures (multiple lists of exports).

There can be only one STRPGMEXP(*CURRENT) statement in the member, but there can be multiple STRPGMEXP(*PRV) statements.

One of the other parameters on the STRPGMEXP command is level check (LVLCHK), which performs the same function as level checking for files. Turn this off, LVLCHK(*NO), and no signature checking will be performed. If you go there, beware. The maintenance you save now by turning this off will undoubtedly have to be repaid in triplicate later, when users begin to experience runtime errors.

There is one other parameter on the STRPGMEXP command: SIGNATURE. This allows you to explicitly specify a signature for the program. The default is *GEN, which causes the binder to generate a signature based on the export statements.

There are two instances in which you might consider specifying your own signature.

- The binder could generate a duplicate signature if two export blocks have the same exports in the same order. But you know that the two interfaces are not really compatible (if they have a different number of parameters, for example) and should not generate the same signature.

- The binder could generate a new signature when you want it to remain the same. For instance, you change the name of a procedure, but it is still the same function.

The EXPORT command identifies the symbol name to be exported from the service program. An *export* is either a program or data to which the service program provides access. You should note that if the exported symbol contains lowercase letters, the symbol should be enclosed in apostrophes (''). Otherwise, the symbol name is converted to all uppercase letters.

The ENDPGMEXP command simply identifies the end of the list of exports.

Figure 13.1 shows a sample of the binder language program. Originally, this service program contained two exports: Program1 and Program2. A third program, Program3, has been added, and a new signature has been generated with it. Because the original signature is still being maintained (STRPGMEXP PGMLVL(*PRV)), any programs that were compiled using this service program and expecting two exports will still work and do not have to be recompiled. If you do recompile any of the programs that use this service program, they will get a signature assigned based on the current three exports.

```
STRPGMEXP PGMLVL(*CURRENT) LVLCHK(*YES)
EXPORT SYMBOL(Program1)
EXPORT SYMBOL(Program2)
EXPORT SYMBOL(Program3)
ENDPGMEXP
STRPGMEXP(PGMLVL(*PRV)
EXPORT SYMBOL(Program1)
EXPORT SYMBOL(Program2)
ENDPGMEXP
```

Figure 13.1: Sample binder language program.

SERVICING THE SERVICE PROGRAM

You have now created a service program that contains several modules and shipped it out to all of your customers. One of those customers complains about a problem in module number 6, which you quickly locate and correct. To recompile that service program on all of your accounts' machines means you have to send them the source for every modules. Obviously, this could become a time-consuming and expensive endeavor. All you really want to do is ship module number 6 and update the service program to include the corrected module. That is exactly what the Update Service Program (UPDSRVPGM) command allows you to do.

The UPDSRVCMD command will not work on programs that have been compiled with *NO specified on the Allow Update (ALWUPD) parameter. Why you would want to shut this fantastic function down is beyond us, but you can if you want to.

For most quick fixes, the command is very simple. You specify the module or modules being replaced. Only existing modules with the same name will be replaced. You cannot use the command to add new modules to a service program.

Sometimes, the update function is not so simple. There are extra parameters on the command to account for these times. Let's examine them.

Parameter Definitions:

RPLLIB: Replacement Library. Allows you to specify how to handle the update when more that one module contained in the service program has the same name. The default for this parameter is *ONLY, and an error will be generated if the same name appears more than once in the module list. FIRST (use the first module found with this name) or *MODULE (use the module that comes from the same library as the specified module) are two other options available.

BNDSRVPGM: Bound Service Programs. If you have changed the number of imports or exports in the module being updated, you may need more service programs to resolve them. This parameter allows you to specify additional service programs that will be bound to this service program to handle those imports.

BINDIR: Binding Directory. Provides another method of specifying modules or service programs that will handle extra imports.

CASCADING REFERENCES

When a service program is activated, all programs that are in the service program are also activated. This can cause a major performance hit, however, so be aware.

Let's go back to our example of the math service program. Let's assume that this service program uses modules to add, divide, multiply, and so on. If we run a program that calls the module to add, the system will also have to load all of the modules to subtract, divide, multiply, and so on into memory when the program is run, whether or not we are using them.

Even worse, if any math modules that are not being used happen to call other modules, they will also be loaded into memory. Those unneeded modules could reference other unneeded modules, and this could go on and on. Hence the term "cascading references."

TIPS FOR GOOD SERVICE

Use a naming convention with a common prefix. This will help prevent modules with the same name from being in different programs. It will also make it easier to specify modules generically on the module parameter of the CRTPGM command.

Keep the number of programs that use a particular module low. We recommend that modules not be copied into multiple programs. If a module must be used by more than one program, put the module in a service program.

Use the binder language for all service programs. Although you can create service programs without using the binder language, maintenance will be much simpler if you do.

You must continue (or start, if you are not already doing so) to use shared file opens in your programs. We discussed this in chapter 1, but we cannot stress the importance of this enough.

LIP SERVICE

Congratulations! In an industry that is defined as service, you have mastered the fine art of service programs. In the process, you have added another language to your ever-growing list of languages. Never mind that there are only three statements in the language. It is the size of the list that matters.

Service programs are an important aspect of ILE. They should be used both when you are creating new applications and when you are converting existing OPM applications to ILE.

ACTIVATION GROUPS

An *activation group* is a substructure of a job into which all programs are activated. It has two main functions. It is a method of grouping system resources (static variables, dynamic storage, and open files, for example) needed to run the programs. This separation of resources effectively isolates a set of programs from other users on the system. This is great if your AS/400 runs software from different vendors (and whose doesn't?). It is also a method of cleaning up storage (that used to be done when a program ended, but it is now done when an activation group ends).

An activation group is created when the first program that needs the activation group is called. Thereafter, any programs that use the same activation group will use the same resources.

When you create a program, you specify the activation group in which the program is to run. You use the ACTGRP parameter on the CRTPGM or CRTSRVPGM commands to accomplish this. This parameter allows three options.

- You name the activation group. This allows you to isolate your application from others.

- The system names the activation group. You specify ACTGRP(*NEW) for this option, which indicates to the system that it needs to generate a new activation group whenever this program is called. The system will assign a unique name to the activation group.

- Use the activation group of the calling program. You specify ACTGRP(*CALLER) for this option. The system will never generate a new activation group, but will instead use the activation group of the program calling this program.

Default Activation Group

The default activation group is created whenever an OS/400 job is started. This is the default activation group used by all OPM programs.

It is also possible (but not intended) for ILE programs to run in this default activation group. If you specify ACTGRP(*CALLER) when you create the ILE program and then call the program from a program that is already running in the default activation group (OPM program), the ILE program will run in the default activation group. This situation should be avoided because the default activation group cannot be deleted.

Named Activation Group

A named activation group is created by explicitly naming the activation group in which the program is to run. This is done via the ACTGRP parameter of the CRTPGM command.

Named activation groups are persistent. This means they exist until the end of the job or until they are explicitly destroyed. Because they are persistent and there is tremendous overhead involved in creating activation groups, this is the recommended option to use when creating programs.

New Activation Group

The other option available for activation groups is ACTGRP(*NEW). New activation groups are not persistent. Every time a program with this option is called, a new activation group is created and named by the system. When the program ends, the activation group is destroyed. If the program is called again, a new activation group is created. The act of creating (and to some degree destroying) activation groups is a resource hog. If you are continually doing this, you will notice a response problem.

Because *NEW activation groups are not persistent, this is an excellent option to use when you are testing program changes.

SCOPING

Activation groups support another concept called *scoping*. There is a new parameter on the Open Database File (OPNDBF) and Open Query File (OPNQRYF) commands, called OPNSCOPE, that can be used to limit your file resources to an activation group. There is an OVRSCOPE parameter on all OVRXXXF commands to do the same thing. This means that file overrides used in one activation group will not be used if you call another program that runs in another activation group.

Scoping can have a big effect on commitment control. Commitment control has been with us for a long time. It is a method for controlling a block of file updates so, if an error occurs while updating one of the files in the block, none of the updates will actually take effect.

Let's say Program A presents a screen for the user to enter some information and then updates five files based on the information entered. The program updates file 1, then updates file 2, and then an error occurs. If the updates are performed under commitment control, the changes that were made to files 1 and 2 would be undone or "rolled back" to their original state. This is true with both ILE programs and OPM.

Now let's complicate matters a little bit and say that after updating files 1 and 2, and before updating the other files, Program A calls Program B. Program B also is under commitment control and executes some code that ends the commit block. What happens to the updates that were performed to file 1 and 2 in Program A? In OPM, the updates are committed and, if an error occurs during the update to file 3, the updates to file 1 and 2 will not be rolled back. In ILE, because the commitment control was scoped to an activation group, the end commit block in Program B will not affect the commitment control in Program A. The new Commit Scope (CMTSCOPE) parameter on the Start Commitment Control (STRCMTCTL) command can be used to control scoping.

Another important aspect of activation groups to be aware of is the way activation groups control memory allocation. In OPM, storage is released when a program ends with the Last Record indicator ON. In ILE, the storage is not released until the activation group ends.

The Reclaim Resource (RCLRSC) command will not clean up the storage left by a program, but Reclaim Activation Group (RCLACTGRP) will. However, you cannot run the RCLACTGRP command from within the activation group you are attempting to reclaim (there just had to be a catch, didn't there?).

ILE Be Good

ILE has introduced us to some new concepts. Some of these we can choose to ignore and some we cannot. Creating service programs may not be necessary for every shop. On the other hand, every program runs in an activation group, so you cannot get around understanding these critters.

As it exists today, ILE simply sets the stage for the future. Programs created by different vendors in different languages that provide interconnected functions (with sub-second response) could be a not-too-distant reality. Hopefully, we have given you a good understanding of the concepts. It is up to you to take it from here.

14

ILE PROCEDURES

Procedures come in two flavors: main procedures and subprocedures. By definition, a main procedure is a procedure that can be specified as the program entry procedure (PEP). It is the procedure that receives control when the program is first called. It is defined in the main source section starting with the H specification and proceeding through to the O specifications. Back in the days of OPM RPG, we used to refer to this as an RPG program.

A subprocedure is specified after the main source section (or after an H specification that contains the NOMAIN keyword). They begin and end with a P (Prototype) specification. In between the P specifications, they can only use D (Data definition) and C (Calculation) specifications.

Despite the fact that procedures are distinctly different from subprocedures, we have found that the two terms are used interchangeably in general use. When programmers refer to procedures, they usually mean subprocedures. Do not be confused by the commingling of the two terms. We may be guilty of the same infraction throughout this chapter.

SUBPROCEDURES VS. MAIN PROCEDURES

Subprocedures differ from and are better than main procedures in the following ways:

Local Variables Are Supported

A local variable is a variable that is only seen within the procedure it is defined within. It is not visible to other subroutines or mainline code. This reduces risk of error and makes modular code much easier to maintain!

You define a local variable (like all other variables) on a D specification. But the D specification is placed inside the subprocedure, after the P specification. This placement of the D specification is what defines the variable as local to the procedure.

The Call Interface Must Be Prototyped

Prototyping refers to defining the procedure interface within the calling program. The compiler will then match the definition in the calling program with the procedure interface definition defined in the procedure. Any errors will be caught at compile time, not during runtime.

The prototype contains other information, as well. It contains the name of the program or procedure to execute (and therefore whether a program or procedure is being called). It also can contain keywords that indicate whether information about the interface should be passed from the calling program to the procedure, whether a parameter is optional, whether the parameter is to be passed by reference or value, and more. We will cover these keywords in more depth later in this chapter.

You Can Pass Parameters to a Subprocedure by Value

The normal method of passing parameters on the AS/400 is to pass a value by reference. What is actually passed to the called program is a pointer to the parameter data, not the parameter data itself. This methodology is what allows a called program to change the parameter and have it automatically reflected in the calling program.

Prototyping subprocedures allows you to define parameters that can be passed by value. Using the VALUE keyword indicates that you want the value of the parameter, not a pointer to the data, to be passed to the called program.

You Can Call a Subprocedure from within an Expression

Subprocedures can be called directly from within an RPG expression. You can call a subprocedure from any of the freeform opcodes: DO, IF, WHEN, etc. For instance, if you have a subprocedure called Exists, as seen in Figure 14.1, the freeform program statement would execute a call to the Exists subprocedure.

```
CLON01Factor1+++++++Opcode&ExtFactor2+++++++Result++++++++Len++D+HiLoEq
C                 if        Exists(PrintName:'*DEVD') = 'Y'
```

Figure 14.1: Freeform expression executing the Exists subprocedure.

Now that we have discussed some of the advantages of using procedures, let's see how to code one. Figure 14.2 shows the code for a subprocedure named Exists. The Exists subprocedure is designed to test, using the Retrieve Object Description API (QUSROBJD), for the existence of any given object. If the object exists, the Exists subprocedure will return a "Y". If the object is not found, the subprocedure will return an "N".

The Exists subprocedure is designed to be called by any program that needs to validate the existence of an object. Because the Exists subprocedure is going to be called by more than one program, it is best to bind the code into a service program. While a service program does not execute quite as fast as when you are binding the procedure directly into the calling program, it does provide better maintenance flexibility. We will discuss how to create service programs later in the chapter.

Note the use of the NOMAIN keyword in the H specification of the source code in Figure 14.2. This keyword tells the compiler not to embed any of the RPG cycle code into the module, which makes for a smaller object.

Our Exists subprocedure begins with the P specification that contains the character B in the declaration type field (position 24). Note that the EXPORT keyword is also coded on this line. This indicates that the procedure can be called from other modules. Next comes the definition for the procedure interface. A declaration type of PI designates it as the procedure interface. Because there is also a field definition on the same line, it indicates that the procedure will return a value. The length of the value returned is the length of the field defined on the Procedure Interface line, in this case a 1-byte field.

Every field definition following the first procedure interface line that does not contain a declaration type is, by definition, a parameter to the subprocedure. This subprocedure accepts three, 10-byte parameters: Object, ObjectType, and ObjectLib.

The CONST keyword indicates that the parameter is to be passed by read-only reference. This means that the calling program can code the parameter as a literal, a field, or an expression. The OPTIONS(*NOPASS) keyword on the OBJECTLIB parameter indicates that this parameter does not have to passed to this subprocedure.

One of the first things the subprocedure does is test to see if the caller specified the library. We use the %PARMS built-in function to see if the parameter was passed. If the parameter was passed, we use it. Otherwise, we default to the use of the library list. Next we call the Retrieve Object Description (QUSROBJD) API to retrieve information about the requested object. If the object cannot be found, an error will be returned in the ErrorDs data structure. (See chapter 9 for complete description of this API.) If no error was returned from the API, we set the valid flag field to "Y". Otherwise, we set it to "N".

The RETURN op code ends the subprocedure and returns control to the caller. The value in factor 1 (Valid) will be returned to the caller. This can be a field or an expression.

The subprocedure then ends with another P specification, this time with an E as the declaration type. We have included the subprocedure name on this line, but the name is not required. The B and E declaration types work in conjunction to define the subprocedure, much like the BEGSR/ENDSR op codes.

```
HNOMAIN
 *
 *  procedure name:    Exists
 *
 *  procedure function: Return Y/N field based on objects existence.

 * GetAcro prototype
D/copy *libl/prsource,Exists

P  Exists       B               export
d  Exists       PI         1
d  Object                  10    const
d  ObjectType              10    const
d  ObjectILib              10    const options(*nopass)
```

Figure 14.2: Sample code for the Exists subprocedure (part 1 of 2).

```
d ReceiveVar      s             100
d ReceiveLen      s               9b 0 inz(100)
d ObjdFormat      s               8    inz('OBJD0100')
d ObjectLib       s              20    inz('          *LIBL     ')
d ObjectTypF      s              10
d Valid           s               1
D ErrorDs         DS            116    INZ
D BytesPrv              1         4B 0 inz(116)
D BytesAvl              5         8B 0 inz(0)
D MessageId            9         15
D ERR###              16         16
D MessageDta          17        116
  *

c                    movel    Object       ObjectLib
c                    eval     ObjectTypF = ObjectType
c                    if       %parms = 3
c                    move     ObjectILib   ObjectLib
c                    endif
  * Attemp to retrieve object description
C                    CALL     'QUSROBJD'
C                    PARM                  ReceiveVar
C                    PARM                  ReceiveLen
C                    PARM                  ObjdFormat
C                    PARM                  ObjectLib
C                    PARM                  ObjectTypF
C                    PARM                  ErrorDs

c                    select
  * If not authorized, then object exists
c                    when     MessageId = 'CPF9821'
c                    eval     Valid = 'Y'
  * Otherwise, error trying to get object description, means not valid
c                    when     MessageDta <> *blanks
c                    eval     Valid = 'N'
c                    other
c                    eval     Valid = 'Y'
c                    endsl

c                    return   Valid
P Exists          E
```

Figure 14.2: Sample code for the Exists subprocedure (part 2 of 2).

PARAMETER KEYWORDS

Now that we have seen a simple subprocedure in action, let's take a closer look at some of the prototyping parameter keywords.

CONST – Pass by read only reference.

Used to pass literals and expressions. The parameter must not be changed by the called program or subprocedure. The compiler may copy the parameter to a temporary field and actually pass the address of the temporary field.

DATFMT(Fmt) - Indicates the format of the date parameter.

Indicate the format in parenthesis. Indicate separator character with inmost parenthesis. Use any valid date format, such as *YMD (year month day), *MDY (month day year).

EXPORT - The subprocedure may be accessed from outside the module.

An exported subprocedure can be used outside the program or service program it is bound to. If you do not specify this keyword, the subprocedure is hidden from outside use. You could code subprocedures that are only used by other procedures within a service program. This is similar to encapsulation in object-oriented terminology.

EXTPGM(Pgm Name) – This parameter represents the external name of the program whose prototype is being defined.

Pass the name of the program being called in parenthesis. Any parameters passed along with this must be passed by reference. The subprocedure cannot define a return value if this keyword is used.

EXTPROC(Proc Name) – The external procedure name of the procedure whose prototype is being defined.

Specify either the name of the subprocedure or a procedure pointer. If specifying a name, the case of characters counts.

NOOPT – No optimization is to be performed.

Used mainly in exception handling to ensure that the value of the field is the latest assigned value. All data items in OPM are implicitly defined as NOOPT. If you are creating a prototype to call an OPM program, you should use NOOPT on all parameters.

OPDESC - pass operational descriptors.

Information about the parameters being passed will be sent to the subprocedure. Use the Retrieve Operational Descriptor (CEEDOD) API to retrieve the information (such as length) about the parameter. Valid only if passed by reference.

OPTIONS - Specifies different parameter passing options.

*NOPASS: The parameter does not have to be specified (passed) when calling the subprocedure. If used, all subsequent parameters must also contain *NOPASS. The subprocedure must be coded in such a way as to not use the parameter if it was not passed in.

*OMIT: This special value can be used to indicate that the parameter should be ignored. It is not allowed when passing by value. It's useful when you have multiple parameters and any of the middle parameters are optional, but subsequent parameters are not.

*VARSIZE: Indicates the parameter can be shorter or longer than defined in the prototype. Not valid when passing by value. The subprocedure must ensure that it only accesses as much data as was passed. Use the OPDESC keyword or, for variable-length fields, use the %LEN built-in function.

*STRING: Null terminated character value. Can pass a pointer or a character expression. If passing an expression, the system will create a temporary field and pass a pointer to that field. This parameter is useful when talking to C programs.

*RIGHTADJ: Right adjust character fields.

PROCPTR – The parameter is a procedure pointer.

Because you can call a program via a procedure pointer (as opposed to using its name), you can pass this pointer as a parameter to another program. That program can call the program the procedure pointer is pointing to without ever knowing its name.

VALUE - Parameter is passed by value.

Parameters are normally passed by reference on the AS/400. This means that a pointer to the data is passed, not the actual data itself. This keyword changes that paradigm. The actual data is passed.

VARYING - Parameter has a variable length format.

Can eliminate the need for the subprocedure to use OPDESC to retrieve the length of the data passed in. Procedure can use the %LEN built-in function to retrieve the actual length of the data.

Now, let's see some more subprocedures in action.

Figure 14.3 shows the code for the SndErrMsg subprocedure, and Figure 14.4 shows the code the for RmvErrMsg subprocedure. The purpose of these subprocedures is to send error messages to your message log and remove them after they have been displayed on the screen. The idea is to show multiple error messages in an error message subfile, with embedded data in any message that needs it. Figure 14.5 shows how to use these subprocedures together to accomplish this task. We will begin with the SndErrMsg subprocedure.

You pass in the error message number and, optionally, the data to be embedded into the text of the message. You can also pass in the message file name and library.

Because it will be called from most interactive programs that perform editing on entry fields, the subprocedure in Figure 14.3 is intended to be bound into a service program. As a result, we use the NOMAIN keyword on the H specification. This strips the RPG cycle from the module.

Now we code the prototype statement. You can see that this procedure does not return a value because no field is defined on the PR definition statement. It does use the OPDESC keyword, which means that information about the used parameters will be passed from the calling program to this subprocedure. We will cover how to get that information a little later.

Next comes the list of parameters. All parameters are defined with the CONST keyword so they will be passed by read-only reference. Therefore, this procedure should not alter any of the parameters.

The first parameter is the message ID. It is a 10-byte field that contains the key to record in the message file we want to display on our screen.

The second parameter is the data that is to be embedded into the message. It is defined as a 32,766-byte field with the OPTIONS (*VARSIZE) keyword. This means the actual size of the parameter can vary each time the subprocedure is called. This is important because

494

each message might be defined with a different size message data field. We also use the option *NOPASS, which means this parameter is optional. This is also important because some messages may not use message data at all.

The next three parameters are also optional. We will default the correct values for each parameter that is not passed to the procedure.

We then begin the subprocedure with a P specification with the data definition type of B. Because this line also has the EXPORT keyword, this subprocedure can be called from outside the service program we will bind it to. Next comes the procedure interface statements, which must match (and do match) the prototype statements.

Then we define the default variables to be used in place of any parameter that is not passed to the subprocedure. We also define the fields that will be passed to the Send Program Message (QMHSNDPM) API. This API will do the work of sending the message to the message queue. (Refer to chapter 9 for information about how this API works.)

The next code you see is the prototype for the CEEDOD API. This API works in conjunction with the OPDESC keyword in order to retrieve information about the parameter. It wants six 10-byte integer parameters and one 12-byte parameter. Note that we have not named any of the parameters except the first and sixth. We are not required to name any parameter on a prototype statement. In fact, the compiler ignores any name you give it. Only the attributes and keywords are important. We named them for documentation purposes only.

In the Calculation Specifications, we are using the %PARMS built-in function to determine how many parameters are actually passed to the subprocedure. If we have more than one, we need to know the length of the message data field. So we call CEEDOD using the number 2 to indicate that we are interested in information about the second parameter passed to us. The API will return the length of the parameter in the field we have named INLEN. We then pass that information along to the QMHSNDPM API along with the message ID and message data fields. The message queue and message queue number fields tell the system how far up the call stack to send the message. The RETURN statement ends the subprocedure.

```
HNOMAIN
 *
 *  procedure name:   SndErrMsg
 *
 *  procedure function: Send a program message wrapper 4 QMHSNDPM API.

d  SndErrMsg       PR                          opdesc
d  PMsgId                          10          const
d  PMsgData                        32766       const options(*varsize:*nopass)
d  PMsgInType                      10          const options(*nopass)
d  PMsgFile                        10          const options(*nopass)
d  PMsgLib                         10          const options(*nopass)

P  SndErrMsg       B                           export
d  SndErrMsg       PI                          opdesc
d  MsgInId                         10          const
d  MsgInData                       32766       const options(*varsize:*nopass)
d  MsgInType                       10          const options(*nopass)
d  MsgFile                         10          const options(*nopass)
d  MsgLib                          10          const options(*nopass)

d  DefMsgFile      s               10          inz('QCPFMSGF  ')
d  DefMsgLib       s               10          inz('QSYS      ')
d  DefMsgType      s               10          inz('*DIAG     ')
d  MsgFileLib      s               20
d  MsgData         s                           like(MsgInData)
d  MsgDtaLen       s                6 0
d  MsgId           s               10
d  MsgKey          s                9b 0
d  MsgQueue        s               10
d  MsgQueNbr       s                9b 0
d  MsgType         s               10
d  Release         s               10

D  ErrorDs         DS                          INZ
D  BytesProv                1      4B 0 inz(116)
D  BytesAval                5      8B 0
D  MessageId                9      15
D  Err###                  16      16
D  MessageDta              17      116
 *_____-*
 * Prototype for CEEDOD (Retrieve operational descriptor)
 *_____
D  CEEDOD          PR
D  ParmNum                         10I 0 CONST
D                                  10I 0
D                                  10I 0
D                                  10I 0
D                                  10I 0
D  InLen                           10I 0
D                                  12A   OPTIONS(*OMIT)

 * Parameters passed to CEEDOD
```

Figure 14.3 : The SndErrMsg procedure (part 1 of 2).

```
D DescType        S              10I 0
D DataType        S              10I 0
D DescInfo1       S              10I 0
D DescInfo2       S              10I 0
D InLen           S              10I 0
D HexLen          S              10I 0
 *

c                 move     MsgInId        MsgId

c                 if       %parms > 1
c                 callp    CEEDOD(2          :DescType:DataType:
c                          DescInfo1 : DescInfo2: Inlen:
c                          *OMIT)
c                 clear                   MsgData
c                 move     Inlen          MsgDtaLen
c                 eval     MsgData = %subst(MsgInData:1:MsgDtaLen)
c                 else
c                 clear                   MsgDtaLen
c                 clear                   MsgData
c                 endif

c                 if       %parms >= 3
c                 eval     MsgType = MsgIntype
c                 else
c                 eval     MsgType = DefMsgType
c                 endif

c                 if       %parms >= 4
c                 movel    MsgFile        MsgFileLib
c                 else
c                 movel    DefMsgFile     MsgFileLib
c                 endif

c                 if       %parms >= 5
c                 move     MsgLib         MsgFileLib
c                 else
c                 move     DefMsgLib      MsgFileLib
c                 endif

C                 CALL     'QMHSNDPM'
C                 PARM                    MsgId
C                 PARM                    MsgFileLib
C                 PARM                    MsgData
C                 PARM                    MsgDtaLen
C                 PARM                    MsgType
C                 PARM     '*'            MsgQueue
C                 PARM     1              MsgQueNbr
C                 PARM                    MsgKey
C                 PARM                    ErrorDs

c                 return
P  SndErrMsg      E
```

Figure 14.3 : The SndErrMsg procedure (part 2 of 2).

497

The RMVERRMSG procedure is intended to remove messages from your program message queue. This is so they will not be shown on subsequent writes to your message control subfile. See Figure 14.5 for an example of how this procedure is used in a calling program.

By now, you should be able to look at this procedure and know what is going on with it. It accepts one optional parameter by way of OPTIONS(*NOPASS). It is passed by read-only reference because of the use of the CONST keyword. The parameter is the message ID to remove, and it defaults to *ALL if the message ID was not passed in.

The purpose of the procedure is to call the QMHRMVPM API and tell it to remove the indicated message (or all messages) from the message queue.

```
HNOMAIN
*
*   procedure name:    RmvErrMsg
*
*   procedure function: Remove program messages wrapper 4 QMHRMVPM API.
*                       Usually used to clear previously displayed
*                       error messages.

d  RmvErrMsg       PR
d  PRmvId                       10      const options(*nopass)

P  RmvErrMsg       B                    export
d  RmvErrMsg       PI
d  RmvId                        10      const options(*nopass)

d  DefRmvMsg       s            10      inz('*ALL     ')
d  CallStack       s            10      inz('*         ')
d  CallStackC      s           9b 0 inz(1)
d  RmvKey          s             4
d  RmvMsg          s            10

D  ErrorDs         DS                   INZ
D  BytesProv             1      4B 0 inz(116)
D  BytesAval             5      8B 0
D  MessageId             9     15
D  Err###               16     16
D  MessageDta           17    116
*

c                   if        %parms >= 1
c                   move      RmvId          RmvMsg
c                   else
```

Figure 14.4: The RmvErrMsg procedure (part 1 of 2).

```
c                    move      DefRmvMsg    RmvMsg
c                    endif

C                    CALL      'QMHRMVPM'
C                    PARM                   CallStack
C                    PARM                   CallStackC
C                    PARM                   RmvKey
C                    PARM                   RmvMsg
C                    PARM                   ErrorDs

c                    return
P  RmvErrMsg     E
```

Figure 14.4: The RmvErrMsg procedure (part 2 of 2).

Figure 14.5 shows an example of how these procedures would be used in a program that edits input screens. A loop is established to process the input screen. If an error is encountered, the message subfile is written to the screen to show the messages in the message queue. Then the input screen is shown and processed. The RmvErrMsg procedure is called to remove any messages that might have been issued the last time the loop was executed. Then the edits are performed, and the SndErrMsg procedure is called for each error found. After all the editing is done, and if any errors were found, the MSGCTL subfile is shown again with the new messages. (See chapter 2 if you need more information on coding error message subfiles.)

```
FDisplay1  cf   e            workstn

 * Send error message prototype
d  SndErrMsg     PR                     opdesc
d  PMsgId                      10       const
d  PMsgData                 32766       const options(*varsize:*nopass)
d  PMsgInType                  10       const options(*nopass)
d  PMsgFile                    10       const options(*nopass)
d  PMsgLib                     10       const options(*nopass)

 * Remove error message prototype
d  RmvErrMsg     PR
d  PRmvId                      10       const options(*nopass)

c                    movel     '*'          Pgmq
c                    dow       *in40 = *off

 * Display error message subfile
c                    if        *in40 = *on
```

Figure 14.5: Example of using SndErrMsg/RmvErrMsg procedures (part 1 of 2).

```
C                       WRITE     MSGCTL
c                       endif

 * Display screen asking for input
c                       exfmt     SomeScreen
c                       eval      *in40 = *off

c                       if        *in03 = *off
 * Clear any existing messages in message queue
c                       callp     RmvErrMsg

 * Test for errors
c                       if        Fld1 > 100
c                       eval      *in40 = *on
 * Send error message
c                       callp     SndErrMsg('USR0453':Fld1)
c                       endif
c                       endif

c                       enddo
c                       eval      *inlr = *on
```

Figure 14.5: Example of using SndErrMsg/RmvErrMsg procedures (part 2 of 2).

Let's take a look at another subprocedure. RPG IV has an EVAL statement that essentially left justifies a field. As of V4R4, it has also has an EVALR statement, which will right justify a field. But it does not have an EVALC statement to center a field. Figure 14.6 shows the code for a subprocedure that will do just that. We have chosen to name the subprocedure CENTERFLD rather than EVALC because we figure IBM will eventually get around to providing this capability, and EVALC would be the obvious choice for it to use.

This subprocedure accepts any length field and returns the field with its data centered. You can see that this subprocedure uses the EXPORT keyword so it can be called from outside the module to which it is bound. It also uses the OPDESC keyword so information about the actual parameters used will be passed automatically from the caller. See the SndErrMsg subprocedure for a description of the OPDESC keyword.

The CEEDOD API is used to get the actual length of the field passed in. We then use CHECKR op code to find out how many non-blank characters are in the field. Simple math gives us the number of characters to offset the data within the field, and the %SUBST built-in function allows us to adjust the data the required number of characters. That is all there is to the subprocedure.

500

```
HNOMAIN
 *
 *  procedure name:    CenterFld
 *
 *  procedure function: Return a centered field.

d  CenterFld     PR          32766     opdesc
d   FieldToCtr               32766     options(*varsize)

P  Centerfld     B                     export
d  CenterFld     PI          32766     opdesc
d  FieldToCtr                32766     options(*varsize)

 *_____*
 * Prototype for CEEDOD (Retrieve operational descriptor)
 *_____
D CEEDOD         PR
D ParmNum                    10I 0 CONST
D                           10I 0
D                           10I 0
D                           10I 0
D                           10I 0
D                           10I 0
D                           12A   OPTIONS(*OMIT)

 * Parameters passed to CEEDOD
D DescType       S           10I 0
D DataType       S           10I 0
D DescInfo1      S           10I 0
D DescInfo2      S           10I 0
D InLen          S           10I 0
D HexLen         S           10I 0

d  X             s            5 0
d  y             s            5 0
d  z             s            5 0
d  Returnfld     s                  like(FieldToCtr)
 *

C                CALLP     CEEDOD(1          :DescType:DataType:
C                          DescInfo1 : DescInfo2: Inlen:
C                          *OMIT)
c                eval      X = InLen

c      ' '       checkr    FieldToCtr:X  Y
c                eval      z = ((X - y) / 2) + 1

c                eval      %subst(ReturnFld:z:Y) =
c                          %subst(FieldToCtr:1:Y)

c                return    ReturnFld
P  CenterFld     E
```

Figure 14.6 : CenterFld procedure.

COMPILING

It is perfectly acceptable to code a subprocedure inside the source member that uses it. In fact, it is a good idea to replace your subroutines with subprocedures in order to take advantage of prototyping parameters, and local variables. However, if the subprocedure is going to be used by more than one program, you should put it in a service program and bind the service program to the calling program. All of the procedures in this chapter use the NOMAIN keyword in the header specification, which implies they are subprocedures that should be accessed through service programs.

To compile any of the subprocedures in this chapter, use the CRTRPGMOD command to create the module. To create the SndErrMsg procedure, you would enter:

```
CRTRPGMOD MODULE(SOMELIB/SNDERRMSG) SRCFILE(SOMELIB/QRPGLESRC)
```

You would run the same command to create the RmvErrMsg module. Once the two modules were created, you would want to bind them into a service program. Figure 14.7 shows the parameters for the Create Service Program (CRTSRVPGM) command. This is a classic example of binding programs that perform similar functions into one service program. (See Chapter 1 for the performance implications regarding service programs.)

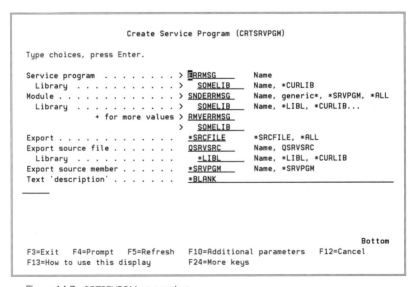

```
                         Create Service Program (CRTSRVPGM)

            Type choices, press Enter.

            Service program  . . . . . . . >  ERRMSG       Name
              Library  . . . . . . . . . . >    SOMELIB    Name, *CURLIB
            Module . . . . . . . . . . . . >  SNDERRMSG    Name, generic*, *SRVPGM, *ALL
              Library  . . . . . . . . . . >    SOMELIB    Name, *LIBL, *CURLIB...
                        + for more values >  RMVERRMSG
                                          >    SOMELIB
            Export . . . . . . . . . . . .    *SRCFILE     *SRCFILE, *ALL
            Export source file . . . . . .    QSRVSRC      Name, QSRVSRC
              Library  . . . . . . . . . .     *LIBL       Name, *LIBL, *CURLIB
            Export source member . . . . .    *SRVPGM      Name, *SRVPGM
            Text 'description' . . . . . .    *BLANK
            _____


                                                                        Bottom
            F3=Exit   F4=Prompt   F5=Refresh   F10=Additional parameters   F12=Cancel
            F13=How to use this display       F24=More keys
```

Figure 14.7 : CRTSRVPGM parameters.

```
                    Create Bound RPG Program (CRTBNDRPG)

  Type choices, press Enter.

  Program  . . . . . . . . . . . . >  USEERRMSG     Name, *CTLSPEC
    Library  . . . . . . . . . . >    SOMELIB       Name, *CURLIB
  Source file  . . . . . . . . .      QRPGLESRC     Name, QRPGLESRC
    Library  . . . . . . . . . .      *LIBL         Name, *LIBL, *CURLIB
  Source member  . . . . . . . .      *PGM          Name, *PGM
  Generation severity level  . . .    10            0-20
  Text 'description' . . . . . . .    *SRCMBRTXT

  Default activation group . . . . >  *NO           *YES, *NO
  Activation group . . . . . . . .    QILE          Name, QILE, *NEW, *CALLER
  Binding directory  . . . . . . . >  DIRNAME       Name, *NONE
    Library  . . . . . . . . . . .    *LIBL         Name, *LIBL, *CURLIB...
              + for more values
                                      *LIBL


                                                                  Bottom
  F3=Exit   F4=Prompt   F5=Refresh   F10=Additional parameters   F12=Cancel
  F13=How to use this display        F24=More keys
```

Figure 14.8 : The CRTBNDRPG command.

BINDING DIRECTORY

A binding directory is a list of objects. When compiling a program, the compiler will search this list to find the objects it needs to compile the program. When you create the modules for the procedures, you put them in a library. You then run the Add Binding Directory Entry (ADDBNDDIRE) command to add the module to the list of objects the compiler will consider for use. If the binding directory does not already exist, you can create it with the Create Binding Directory (CRTBNDDIR) command.

ACTIVATION GROUP CONSIDERATIONS

When you create the program that calls the procedure, you need to change a couple of the default parameters. Table 14.2 shows the parameters for the CRTBNDRPG command you could use to create the program. You cannot create a program that uses procedures into the default activation group (see chapter 13 for more information about activation groups). You must change the default for the DFTACTGRP parameter from *YES to *NO. Because of this change, you must also enter the ACTGRP parameter. We have chosen to use the named activation group QILE, which is the default for this parameter if you specify DFTACTGRP(*NO). See chapter 1 for an explanation of the various strategies you can employ regarding activation groups.

PUTTING HEADER SPECIFICATIONS INTO YOUR PROGRAMS

There are a couple of techniques you can use to ensure your programs are always compiled into the correctly named activation group. You can code a header specification that contains the keywords DFTACTGRP(*NO) and ACTGRP(NAME) in every program. If you used /COPY to bring in the correct header specification into every program, this would further ensure consistency in every program. But it means you have to modify every program that needs it.

Another option is to use the RPGLEHSPEC data area. If you put the keywords in this data area, all you have to do is recompile the program. The header specification will be pulled into your program automatically. You can create this data area in any library and make it any size you choose. The drawback here is if you already have a header specification coded in the program, the keywords will not be pulled into the program. If you use a data area to bring in a header specification, you must ensure that only valid keywords are in the data area.

If the compiler does not find a header specification in the program, or the RPGLEHSPEC data area in the library list, it will look for another data area called DFTLEHSPEC in the QRPGLE library. If it finds this data area, it will use the header specifications found there.

THE SUBPROCEDURE ADDICTION

Warning! Subprocedures are addictive. Once you start coding them, you won't be able to quit. But unlike cigarettes, subprocedures are actually good for you! Start taking advantage of the options they provide. Using expressions to call the procedure, prototyping parameters, passing by value, and local variables are all capabilities that are now at your fingertips. Go ahead and try it. We guarantee you will like it.

APPENDIX:
ABOUT THE CD-ROM

The CD-ROM that accompanies this book contains source code for many of the figures. Table A.1 represents a cross-reference for the figures and files on the disc.

Table A.1: Disc Cross-Reference Information.

Figure	File Name	Description
2.8	FG208DS	DDS for "Customer Subfile"
2.9	FG209RG	RPG Program for "Customer Subfile"
2.10	FG210DS	DDS for State Lookup Window Subfile
2.11	FG211RG	RPG for State Lookup Window Subfile Program
2.12	FG212DS	DDS for Message Subfile
2.13	FG213RG	RPG for Message Subfile
2.15	FG215	DDS for Physical File PRINTER
2.16	FG216	DDS for Logical File PRINTERS
2.17	FG217DS	DDS for Printer Lookup
2.18	FG218RG	RPG Specifications for Printer LOOKUP

Table A.1: Disc Cross-Reference Information (continued).

Figure	File Name	Description
3.3	FG303DS	Sample DDS for Menu Bar in Figures 3.1 and 3.2
3.4	FG304RG	RPG Program to Present a Menu Bar
3.7	FG307RG	RPG for the System Request Window
3.8	FG308DS	DDS for the System Request Window
6.2	FG602RG	Using QCMDEXC to Run OPNQRYF from within an RPG Program
6.3	FG603RG	Using QCMDEXC to Override Printer Attributes
6.4	FG604DS	Customer List Prompt Screen Display File
6.6	FG606RG	Using QCMDEXC to Submit Jobs from within an RPG Program
6.7	FG607RG	RPG API Program to Validate Printer Existence
6.8	FG608RG	RPG Running C Functions to Call AS/400 Commands
6.9	FG609RG	Prototyping C Functions to be used within RPG programs
7.3	FG703RG	Using Sort Array (SORTA) to Resequence Array Elements
7.4	FG704RG	Multicolumn Customer Phone List Using Arrays to Format Output
9.2	FG902RG	Sample of the Retrieve Object Description API
9.3	FG903RG	Sample RPG Program to Validate Object Existence
9.4	FG904RG	Sample RPG Program Using the Send Program Message (QMHSNDPM) API
9.5	FG905DS	DDS for the MSGEX RPG Program Using the QMHSNDPM Send Program Message API
9.6	FG906RG	RPG Program to Create a User Space
9.7	FG907RG	RPG Program to Retrieve User Space
9.10	FG910RG	RPG Program to Retrieve File Access Paths
9.11	FG911DS	DDS for the DSPPATH Command
9.12	FG912CM	DSPPATH Command
9.13	FG913RG	Move Spool File Entries
9.14	FG914RG	Validate/Encrypt Passwords
11.2	FG1102CM	DSPPATH Command to Display File Access Paths
11.3	FG1103DS	DSPPTH Display File
11.4	FG1104RG	DSPPTH RPG Program
11.6	FG1106CM	Display Field (DSPFLD) Command
11.7	FG1107DS	Display Fields Display File
11.8	FG1108RG	Display Fields RPG Program

Table A.1: Disc Cross-Reference Information (continued).

Figure	File Name	Description
11.9	FG1109CM	RGZPFFLTR Command Source
11.10	FG1110RG	RGZPFFLTR RPG Program
11.11	FG1111CL	RGZPFFLTR CL Program
11.13	FG1113CM	FNDDSPLF Command
11.14	FG1114DS	FNDDSPLF Display File
11.15	FG1115RG	FNDDSPLF RPG Program
11.19	FG1119CM	BLDOBJREF Command
11.20	FG1120CL	BLDOBJREF CL Program
11.21	FG1121RG	BLDOBJREF RPG Program
11.22	FG1122CL	BLDOBJREF CL Program
11.23	FG1123CL	BLDOBJREF CL Program
11.24	FG1124CL	BLDOBJREF CL Program
11.25	FG1125CL	BLDOBJREF CL Program
11.26	FG1126RG	WRKOBJREF RPG Program
11.27	FG1127DS	WRKOBJREF Display File
11.28	FG1128	WRKOBJREF Work File
11.29	FG1129CM	WRKOBJREF Command
11.31	FG1131DS	Display Service Program Usage Display File
11.32	FG1132RG	Display Service Program Usage RPG Program
11.33	FG1133CM	Display Service Program Usage Command
11.35	FG1135DS	Display Module Usage Display File
11.36	FG1136RG	Display Module Usage RPG Program
11.37	FG1137CM	Display Module Usage Command
11.39	FG1139	Work with Fields Physical File
11.40	FG1140	Work with Fields Physical File
11.41	FG1141	Work with Fields Physical File
11.42	FG1142CM	BLDWRKFLD Command
11.43	FG1143CL	BLDWRKFLD CL Program
11.44	FG1144RG	BLDWRKFLD RPG Program
11.45	FG1145DS	WRKFLD Display File
11.46	FG1146RG	WRKFLD RPG Program
11.47	FG1147CL	WRKFLD CL Program

Table A.1: Disc Cross-Reference Information (continued).

Figure	File Name	Description
11.48	FG1148CM	WRKFLD Command
11.50	FG1150CM	DFD Command
11.51	FG1151DS	Display File Description Display File
11.52	FG1152RG	Display File Description RPG Program
11.54	FG1154CM	SCNJOBLOG Command
11.55	FG1155CL	Scan Job Log CL Program
11.56	FG1156DS	Scan Job Log Display File
11.57	FG1157RG	Scan Job Log RPG Program
11.60	FG1160CM	FNDSRC Command
11.61	FG1161RG	Find Source Members Driver RPG Program
11.62	FG1162CL	Find Source Member CL Program
11.63	FG1163CL	Find Source Member CL Program
11.64	FG1164DS	Find Source Member Display File
11.65	FG1165RG	Find Source Member RPG Program
12.6	FG1206DS	Date Test Display File
12.7	FG1207RG	Date Test RPG Program
12.13	FG1213RG	Find Day of the Week RPG Program (simple method)
12.14	FG1214RG	Find Day of the Week RPG Program (industrial strength)
12.16	FG1216DS	Data Formatting Display File
12.17	FG1217RG	Data Formatting RPG Program
12.18	FG1218RG	Date Testing RPG Program
12.19	FG1219PF	Date Testing External Data Structure
12.20	FG1220PF	Converting Date Data Types – "FROM" DDS
12.21	FG1221PF	Converting Date Data Types – "TO" DDS
12.22	FG1222CL	Date Data Type Conversion CL Program
14.02	FG1402RG	Send Program Message Wrapper Procedure
14.03	FG1403RG	Remove Program Message Wrapper Procedure
14.04	FG1404RG	Example using SNDPGMMSG Procedure
14.05	FG1405RG	Centering Text Within a Field Procedure

The source code for files used in the examples is also on the CD-ROM.

FILE: CUSTOMER   Customer File

FILE: PRINTER   Printer Description File

FILE: PRINTERS   Printer File by Description

FILE: REQUEST   Request File

FILE: STATES   States Description File

TRANSFERRING THE SOURCE

The companion CD-ROM includes source code for program samples and utilities listed in this appendix. You will need a PC and PC Support (or another file-transfer utility) to transfer the source to the AS/400. In addition, your system needs the RPG compiler.

To transfer the source, follow these steps:

1. Sign on to the AS/400 with a user profile that has *PGMR user class.

2. If you want, create a library to contain all the software you are about to install. For example, you could call it POWERRPG for ease of identification:

```
CRTLIB LIB(POWERRPG)
```

3. Create a source physical file called SOURCE in the library of your choice. You *must* name this file SOURCE:

```
CRTSRCPF FILE(POWERRPG/SOURCE) RCDLEN(112) TEXT('Power
RPG/IV source')
```

where POWERRPG is the name of the library selected.

4. Transfer all source code to the source file just created. The preceding cross-reference table is provided to allow you to match the figures in the book to the file names found on the diskette.

COMPILING THE POWER TOOLS

Almost all of the objects in chapter 11 can be created automatically by running the MAKECL program.

Compile the MAKECL program as follows:

```
CRTCLPGM PGM(POWERRPG/MAKECL) SRCFILE(POWERRPG/SOURCE)
SRCMBR(MAKECL)
```

To run the MAKECL program, submit the following to the job queue:

```
CALL MAKECL PARM('POWERRPG')
```

There are only two objects that could not be compiled by the MAKECL program that must be compiled by QSECOFR. The FG1110RG RPG program is part of the Reorganize Physical File Filter (RGZPFFLTR) command, which references the QADBXREF file. This file resides in library QSYS and may only be accessed by QSECOFR. The other program that makes use of this file is the FG1161RG program that is part of the Find Source command.

To compile these programs, sign on as QSECOFR and key:

```
CRTBNDRPG PGM(POWERRPG/FIG1110RG) USRPRF(*OWNER) ALWNULL(*YES)
SRCFILE(POWERRPG/SOURCE) SRCMBR(FG1110RG)

CRTBNDRPG PGM(POWERRPG/FIG1161RG) USRPRF(*OWNER) ALWNULL(*YES)
SRCFILE(POWERRPG/SOURCE) SRCMBR(FG1161RG)
```

COMPILING THE REST OF THE SOURCE

Some of the source members on the CD-ROM that are not from chapter 11 can be compiled individually. In these instances, you will find instructions on how to compile each source member in the first few lines of each source member itself. For the most part, the compiles are very straightforward.

In the example below, POWERRPG represents the name of the library where the source members reside and XXX is the name of the source member to compile.

For CL programs:

```
CRTCLPGM PGM(POWERRPG/XXX) SRCFILE(POWERRPG/SOURCE)
```

For display files:

```
CRTDSPF FILE(POWERRPG/XXX) SRCFILE(POWERRPG/SOURCE)
```

For RPG programs:

```
CRTBNDRPG PGM(POWERRPG/XXX) SRCFILE(POWERRPG/SOURCE)
```

INDEX

Note: Boldface numbers indicate illustrations.

Note: Boldface numbers indicate illustrations.

518

E

Note: Boldface numbers indicate illustrations.

Note: Boldface numbers indicate illustrations.

Note: Boldface numbers indicate illustrations.

Other Best-sellers of Related Interest

The Modern RPG IV Language— Second Edition

by Robert Cozzi, Jr.

Now you can exploit all the enhanced functionality that IBM has built into RPG IV. The long awaited update to Cozzi's masterpiece on RPG IV shows how to take full advantage of the powerful features and functions added to the language since 1996. If you program in RPG IV, this book will be indispensable to your productivity and your career.

The Modern RPG IV Language—Second Edition takes you through the language from the very foundations to the most advanced techniques. At the core of this book are the chapters on built-in functions (BIFs) and op codes. Cozzi details each BIF and provides valuable information on more than 30 op codes and provides a syntax table that gives you the information you need at a glance, plus an explanation of the hows and whys of usage. And this isn't just a book on theory and rules; Cozzi includes over 100 charts and tables that show you how the rules apply. He also includes samples of the functions and operations in real-life code—more than 350 individual examples! 592 pages. Level: Novice, Intermediate, and Advanced.

❏ BOOK 5005 ....$99
ISBN 1-58347-002-6

Subfiles in RPG IV: Rules, Examples, Techniques, and Other Cool Stuff

by Kevin Vandever

This book begins with easy-to-understand explanations of subfile concepts and then goes on to offer a bounty of practical examples, advanced techniques, and other cool stuff never before seen in subfile books. It is a comprehensive resource you will use over and over as you advance from basic subfile usage to gurulike mastery of subfile programming.

For each topic, the book offers concepts, explanations, and practical examples you can use as templates for further development. The templates are fully functioning programs that include both DDS and RPG IV code—from basic single-page display subfiles to powerful techniques such as recursion, data queues, and embedded SQL. As an added bonus, each example is included on an accompanying CD-ROM, ready to copy to your AS/400.

The book includes a free CD-ROM with sample source code. 288 pages. Level: Novice, Intermediate, and Advanced.

❏ BOOK 5018 ....$79
ISBN 1-58347-003-4

Introduction to RPG IV

by Robert Cozzi, Jr.

Now you can come up to speed quickly on the basics of programming in RPG IV, the modern, modular AS/400 programming language that has gained acceptance worldwide. All you need is this easy-to-follow book from Bob Cozzi, the world's leading authority on RPG programming. Rich with practical examples and sample code, this book provides step-by-step guidance for writing structured programs in RPG IV. You'll find out how to create simple, powerful programs with just a few lines of code.

Completely up-to-date with all new RPG IV features, this book tells you everything you need to understand the modern constructs of RPG IV, including figurative and named constants, operation extenders, and free-format expressions. You'll discover how to perform basic programming tasks, such as opening files, processing data, communicating with the user, controlling work flow, and calling other programs. You'll even learn how to set up a development environment, including the integration of RPG IV and DDS! This book opens the door to the world of programming in RPG IV. 304 pages. Level: Novice.

❏ BOOK 577 ....$59
ISBN 1-883884-46-2

Re-engineering RPG Legacy Applications

by Paul Tuohy

Now you can use IBM's recent enhancements to the AS/400, OS/400, and RPG to immediately increase the reliability of your legacy applications, improve programmer productivity, and build a firm basis for the future of your business. This book and companion CD-ROM provide a tutorial aimed at showing you how to modernize your applications by taking you through the re-engineering of a sample application step-by-step. Author Paul Tuohy covers conversion of RPG IV programs as well as re-engineering them to take full advantage of RPG IV and ILE. He also covers triggers, referential integrity, and APIs so that your applications can take advantage of all the new technology that is available today. This book will be a valuable aid as you evaluate your legacy applications and then move into re-engineering.

Putting your company's IT resources in a condition of stasis while technology moves on can be a costly business mistake. It is possible and profitable to derive some of the benefits of new technology from within a legacy application. Best of all, re-engineering gives you the opportunity to learn new programming concepts and acquire new skills. 528 pages. Level: Intermediate to Advanced.

BOOK 5009 ....$99
ISBN 1-58347-006-9

Complete CL

The Definitive Control Language Programming Guide—Third Edition

by Ernie Malaga and Ted Holt

This new and updated version of the classic 1992 book brings together the solid basics of CL and the newest innovations to this mainstay programming language.

When you have completed this book, you will be able to write simple and advanced CL programs, understand the strengths and limitations of the CL language, develop a good CL coding style, and avoid common mistakes when writing CL. You will learn to manipulate strings with built-in functions and operators, code looping, and decision structures; make procedures communicate with one another via messages; make CL procedures communicate with users; and use data queues and data areas. You also will learn to understand and use overrides effectively, process display and database files, use APIs, and effectively use the QTEMP library. You will be able to avoid the pitfalls of adopted authorities, understand security issues, convert S/36 operational control language (OCL) and S/38 CL to native CL, and much more. If you are responsible for AS/400 application development or if you are an operator or programmer responsible for AS/400 operations, you won't want to be without this book. 496 pages. Level: Novice to Intermediate.

❏ BOOK C5001 .... $79
ISBN 1-883884-58-6

5 Easy Ways to Order!

 FAX this order form to 760-931-9935, 24 hours a day, 365 days a year.

 MAIL your order to 5650 El Camino Real, Suite 225, Carlsbad, CA 92008.

 EMAIL your order to *custsvc@ midrangecomputing.com*.

 PHONE toll-free 1-800-477-5665 (Mon. to Fri., 6 a.m. to 5 p.m. PST).

 ONLINE ordering is available at *www.mc-store.com*.

Open Query File Magic!

A Complete Guide to Maximizing the Power of OPNQRYF—Second Edition

by Ted Holt

OPNQRYF (Open Query File) is the most powerful, most complex, and least documented command in the CL language. You can use it to sort and summarize data, but it can also do much more for you. It allows you to create new fields and assign values to them, perform complex joins of multiple files, create new files with existing and calculated fields, select records (even based on summarized data), and much more! This book explains the ins and outs of OPNQRYF from the basic operations through the most complex mapping and selection parameters. Ted Holt, long known for his ability to teach and show by example, makes the often-complex rules of OPNQRYF easy to understand. He shows you not only the how of OPNQRYF but also the when (when you should use certain functions and parameters to make more powerful and flexible applications for your users) and the why (why you should choose certain options in specific situations).

This book is reorganized to make it more useful not only as a learning tool but also as a reference for ongoing value. 304 pages. Level: Intermediate to Advanced.

 ❏ BOOK 590 ....$69
ISBN 1-883884-57-8

CL Programming for the AS/400—Second Edition

by Greg Veal

Learning CL programming has never been easier, thanks to *CL Programming for the AS/400—Second Edition*, the enhanced version of Greg Veal's 1992 best-seller.

Completely updated for V4R4, this book has new, comprehensive information on CL in the ILE, and each of its 14 chapters has been refined to include comparisons of important concepts from the ILE and Original Program Model (OPM) perspectives. Learning the material will be easy as you progress through the more advanced concepts using examples of real-world programs just like those that support user applications and system operations in many companies. In addition, review questions at the end of each chapter will allow you to self-test your knowledge. An optional instructor's guide with progressive lab assignments, exercise hints, and sample solutions is also available. Whether for self-study or formal classroom education, *CL Programming for the AS/400—Second Edition* is the perfect resource for learning CL programming. 368 pages. Level: Novice, Intermediate, and Advanced.

❏ BOOK 5007 .... $69
ISBN 1-58347-004-2

Other Best-sellers of Related Interest

The AS/400 & Microsoft® Office Integration Handbook

by Brian Singleton with Colleen Garton

This book takes a detailed look at how you can integrate applications in the Microsoft Office 97 product suite with data from your AS/400. Unravel secrets such as how to use your AS/400's output with your PC's data formatting tools or how to make attractive, professional reports with AS/400 data the easy way. Learn the secret of using visual query tools to point and click the creation of sophisticated information output and how to analyze and summarize the detailed (and often cumbersome) reports from your AS/400. Discover how you can combine the presentation capabilities of Microsoft Office with the database capabilities of the AS/400 to provide your company with the best of both worlds.

In the first sections of the book, Singleton introduces you to the essential knowledge you need to use Client Access as you integrate AS/400 data with the Microsoft Office applications. He covers installing and configuring Client Access, how to provide a seamless method of AS/400 integration with Microsoft Office using ODBC, the network drive functionality of Client Access, and the Client Access data transfer function. He also covers TCP/IP's FTP file transfer function and how to use it to bring data from the AS/400 to your PC.

The remaining sections of the book cover the veritable Swiss Army knife functions of Microsoft Office. 320 pages. Level: Novice, Intermediate, and Advanced.

  ❑ BOOK 587...$79
    ISBN 1-883884-49-7

AS/400 Associate System Operator Certification Study Guide

by Steve Murray
Rochester Community and Technical College

This is the first study guide designed specifically for AS/400 professionals preparing for IBM's Associate System Operator certification exam. This guide takes you through the basics of AS/400 operation from concepts to work management, providing the help you need to successfully complete the IBM Associate System Operator certification exam 000-052. Hands-on lab exercises reinforce the chapter topics and prepare the reader to operate an AS/400 system. Whether you need individual or group operator training, you will find this book to be an excellent resource. 384 pages. Level: Novice to Intermediate.

  ❑ BOOK 5010...$119
    ISBN 1-58347-007-7

AS/400 Professional System Operator Certification Study Guide

by Steve Murray, Rochester Community and Technical College, and IBM's Partners in Education

Here is a fast and easy way to learn advanced AS/400 operations concepts and prepare for IBM test 000-053 (AS/400 Professional System Operator). All you need is *AS/400 Professional System Operator Certification Study Guide*. Developed by Midrange Computing and Rochester Community and Technical College in cooperation with IBM's AS/400 professional certification program, this book takes you through all the aspects of AS/400 operations required to pass this IBM test.

Steve Murray will show you the necessary concepts of advanced operations through a step-by-step tutorial on each topic, followed by hands-on lab exercises that will reinforce what was learned in the text. Whether you are preparing for IBM test 000-053 or are in need of individual or group operator training, you will find this book to be an excellent resource.

An instructor's manual is also available for this text. 544 pages. Level: Novice.

  ❑ TEXTBOOK 5019 ....$129
    ISBN 1-58347-014-X

Client Access/400 Expert Reader

by Joe Hertvik

Now you have one source for intelligent answers to difficult questions about building an AS/400-centric network: *Client Access/400 Expert Reader*. Edited by Joe Hertvik, this book brings together the best solutions to appear in the *Client Access/400 Expert* technical journal, now known as *Midrange Network Expert*. If you are responsible for network-to-AS/400 connectivity, you must have this book!

Written by more than 25 different AS/400 networking experts, the articles are categorized by major subject headings and are completely indexed so they're easy to find. Instead of just reprinting the articles, Hertvik has updated them to reflect current knowledge. He has also added a series of editor's notes that expand on the knowledge in many of the pieces. As a result, all of the material in this book is relevant to the environment you work in today. 464 pages. Level: Novice, Intermediate, and Advanced.

  ❑ BOOK 589...$89
    ISBN 1-883884-60-8

Other Best-sellers of Related Interest

The AS/400 Programmer's Handbook, Volume II

by Mark McCall

Now you can avoid countless hours of wading through IBM's technical manuals trying to find out how a technique needs to be coded. This book and CD-ROM contain more than 70 prototypical techniques and coding examples that you can use and adapt for hundreds of applications. From system APIs to SQL, the material encompasses the most useful and powerful features of the AS/400.

Like the original *AS/400 Programmer's Handbook*, this new book gives you a leg up on your application development tasks by providing you with dozens of elegant solutions you may have heard about but not yet put into practice.

Author Mark McCall begins each section with a thorough discussion of each topic. He then shows and explains several examples from real-life applications-code that's downloadable from the companion CD-ROM and ready to include in your applications. He tells you both *what* the example does and *how* it works, all in a programmer-to-programmer style that makes you feel like you have a mentor sitting right beside you. 400 pages. Level: Novice, Intermediate, and Advanced.

❑ BOOK 5017 ....$69
ISBN 1-58347-012-3

The AS/400 Programmer's Handbook

A Toolbox of Examples for Every AS/400 Programmer
by Mark McCall

Now you can eliminate hours of time spent researching complex programming techniques. This handy desktop guide provides programming examples for nearly every AS/400 development task you face. No more rummaging around in old code to find and modify a technique you need for a new application. No more writing routines from scratch. This book and companion diskette put dozens of prototypical techniques at your fingertips.

You get more than 70 examples of essential programming techniques using CL, RPG III, RPG IV, command creation, and User Interface Manager (UIM) panel groups. All of the code examples from the book are included on the companion diskette—ready for you to upload into your development library.

Spiral-bound so it lays flat on your desk, *The AS/400 Programmer's Handbook* is the first place to turn whenever you need help remembering or understanding a coding technique. 400 pages. Level: Novice, Intermediate, and Advanced.

❑ BOOK 585 ....$59
ISBN 1-883884-48-9

Application Development: Managing the Project Life Cycle

by Mark Hoffman and Ted Beaumont

Written by two consultants who have spent more than 30 years developing applications and managing project life cycles, this book is about real-world AS/400 application development. It focuses on a world where not every program gets into production without a bug, where the scope of projects changes with the winds, where projects run over-time and over budget, and where users couldn't care less about the new application being forced on them by MIS—in short, a whole world where Murphy's Law prevails. The authors not only give you good techniques for real-world application development management, they also include charts, worksheets, and checklists that will help you manage your projects. Make sure your concepts get out of the manager's office and into the practices of those involved in getting the work done. Includes a diskette and a project management program that runs on the AS/400. 275 pages. Level: Intermediate.

❑ BOOK 573 ....$59
ISBN 1-883884-45-4

7 Client/Server Applications in Visual Basic

by Mark McCall

Imagine building an addition to your home with all the tools and materials you need right at hand and, better yet, the framing already in place! That's what it's like to develop and implement powerful, effective client/server applications with this new book and companion diskette. You'll start writing effective client/server apps immediately—guaranteed! Author Mark McCall has been developing client/server applications in his shop for years. He's done all the front-end grunt work for you. All you need to build powerful, production-quality client/server applications is Visual Basic, a PC attached to an AS/400, and this book!

Instead of simply discussing technical theories, this book provides seven working example applications as learning tools for you to understand, use, and, ultimately, build upon. It's a paint-by-numbers approach that lets you "color in" the template code to fit your organization's unique development needs—all the time learning as you go. These templates are far more than just code snippets—they are complete applications with error handling and production-quality user interface design. Best of all, every one of the techniques used in the applications is explained in full detail. 439 pages. Level: Novice to Intermediate.

❑ BOOK 569..$99
ISBN 1-883884-42-X

Other Best-sellers of Related Interest

The AS/400 Owner's Manual for V4

by Mike Dawson

Midrange Computing's all-time bestselling manual is now V4R2-ready! Designed for AS/400 professionals at all levels, *The AS/400 Owner's Manual for V4* walks you through hundreds of AS/400 tasks from the perspective of how most shops actually work. Cutting through the dozens of parameters and options of AS/400 commands, *The AS/400 Owner's Manual for V4* takes you directly to the results you need. Offering much more than brief, to-the-point instructions, it also includes valuable descriptions that examine why AS/400 managers, administrators, operators, and programmers do certain things on the machine and how the AS/400 works internally. This edition is completely up-to-date for Version 4 of OS/400 and contains a new chapter about the Internet and TCP/IP. Wire-bound and concise, *The AS/400 Owner's Manual for V4* is the perfect workstation tool for anyone who does AS/400 operations, administration, or management. 464 pages. Level: Novice, Intermediate, and Advanced.

❏ BOOK 5000 ....$59
ISBN 1-58347-001-8

Java® Application Strategies for the AS/400

An Introduction to AS/400 Java Development Strategies for RPG Programmers

by Don Denoncourt

At last! Here's a book that lays out real-world strategies for the development of AS/400 Java applications! *Java Application Strategies for the AS/400* is the new book written specifically for RPG programmers to help them understand the structure and intent of the Java programming language as well as why Java applications developed with the structure techniques used in RPG applications are doomed to fail.

You will learn about the structure and the intent of the Java programming language and standard strategies for object-oriented design (OOD), strategies for interoperating Java applications with your legacy applications, and strategies and frameworks for the development of business classes. You will also find out how to develop Java GUIs complete with a replacement paradigm for AS/400 subfiles.

The book includes a FREE companion CD-ROM that contains the source code presented in the book, the complete source for Midrange Computing's object-to-relational framework classes, and a .jar file that contains the package of Java classes for Midrange Computing's object-to-relational classes. 448 pages. Level: Novice, Intermediate, and Advanced.

❏ BOOK 591 ....$79
ISBN 1-883884-61-6

5 Easy Ways to Order!

FAX

this order form to
760-931-9935,
24 hours a day, 365
days a year.

MAIL

your order to
5650 El Camino Real,
Suite 225, Carlsbad,
CA 92008.

EMAIL

your order
to *custsvc@
midrangecomputing.
com.*

PHONE

toll-free
1-800-477-5665
(Mon. to Fri., 6 a.m. to
5 p.m. PST).

ONLINE

ordering is
available at
www.mc-store.com.

For a complete list of titles, call **1-800-477-5665** or visit our Web site at *www.midrangecomputing.com.*

Multimedia CD-ROM

FastTrak to AS/400® System Operations
by Gary Patterson

This interactive presentation blends audio, video, and hands-on instruction into a multisensory learning experience that teaches the basics of IBM AS/400 operations. It is designed for novice to intermediate operators and others who need a firm foundation in AS/400 operations, including system administrators, programmers, help desk staff, and managers.

When you have completed this multimedia presentation, you will understand AS/400 system management, printing, basic work management, database journaling, and basic AS/400 security. You will be able performing such tasks as handling AS/400 messages, starting and stopping the system, managing system values, and managing communication lines, devices, and controllers. You also will be able to back up and restore libraries, objects, and the entire system; manage disk space and reduce DASD usage; manage and apply PTFs; install operating system upgrades and licensed programs; utilize the AS/400's automated operations facilities; and monitor the performance of individual jobs and the system as a whole. You even will be able to troubleshoot and solve system problems. In addition, this presentation will teach you timesaving tips and techniques that you can apply right away. If you are an AS/400 system operator, system administrator, programmer, or manager seeking a comprehensive in-house training solution for teaching basic AS/400 operations, this multimedia presentation is for you! 6 to 8 hours. Level: Novice to Intermediate.

 Multimedia CD C6612...$199
ISBN: 1-58347-336-X

FastTrak to AS/400® and PC Data Integration
by Brian Singleton

This interactive tutorial quickly and thoroughly teaches you various methods of making your PCs and AS/400s interact and exchange data. Brian Singleton has updated, enhanced, and expanded his previous Microsoft integration presentations to help you create a seamless connection between your AS/400 and the Microsoft Office product suite.

Walking through this tutorial will help you understand and use the most efficient transfer method for the job and control the interaction process from the AS/400 or from the PC. You will find out how to use Office applications to create killer Web pages from AS/400 data—automatically—and execute SQL statements on your AS/400 without the SQL Development Kit. You will be able to use Microsoft Word to create form letters, mailing labels, envelopes, and other documents; pull AS/400 data into Microsoft Excel for use in reports; create Excel charts that are updated as AS/400 data changes; design a simple data warehouse using powerful Excel PivotTables; get long field names

into Excel when retrieving data; and generate complex reports in Access with zero code. You also will find out how to exchange documents with OV/400 and write Visual Basic For Applications macros to retrieve AS/400 data—including code snippets—exactly the way you want.

Your productivity will soar as you employ the time-saving techniques described in this presentation. You'll learn how to optimize PC-to-AS/400 interactions, reducing wait time; call PC programs from AS/400 jobs and call AS/400 jobs from the PC; understand your options for scheduling automatic updates; and automate nightly report-generating processes using tools you already have. You will even learn how to secure your AS/400 from unwanted access.

If you need to integrate Microsoft applications and live data from the AS/400, this presentation is for you. 6 to 8 hours. Level: Novice to Intermediate.

 MULTIMEDIA CD C6613 ....$149
ISBN: 1-58347-337-8

FastTrak to Java on the AS/400®
by Don Denoncourt

Using hands-on instruction, this interactive tutorial teaches you the various methods of developing Web applications with Java. Walking through this tutorial will help you understand the three basic Java deployment options: browser-based applets, client/server style applications, and the server-side Java of servlets and JavaServer Pages. You also will learn how to test servlets and JavaServer Pages on Windows with Sun's free Java Server Web Development Kit. You will know what AS/400 program products need to be installed to support server-side Java applications and what optimization techniques are available for AS/400-based Java applications.

Once you have learned these fundamentals, you will be able to develop your first server-side Java application using servlets. You will then develop your first server-side Java application using JavaServer Pages. You will be able to separate presentation logic from programming logic and set up a server-side Java development and test environment on your PC. You will also be able to choose among six ways to invoke legacy AS/400 programs from Java and know which method of integrating Java with RPG and COBOL works best in various scenarios. You even will be able to build Web subfiles with HTML and JavaServer Pages!

If you're an AS/400 programmer who needs to extend legacy applications to the Internet, this tutorial will provide you with the best techniques for integrating Java and legacy AS/400 programs. 6 to 8 hours. Level: Intermediate to Advanced.

 Multimedia CD C6614...$149
ISBN: 1-58347-338-6

Midrange Computing Publications

Midrange Computing

Enhance your skills as an midrange professional and keep current with all the emerging technology—hardware, software, and accessories. Think of our staff of midrange experts as your own personal consultants, constantly tackling the problems you face and reporting back to you with the solutions you need. Look at the editorial lineup of *Midrange Computing*:

- Don Denoncourt is a professional Java and C++ software developer.
- Ted Holt, senior technical editor for RPG IV programming, is a renowned expert on legacy RPG applications and programming products.
- Joe Hertvik, editor of the *Midrange Network Expert* technical journal, is a leading industry expert on connectivity to the AS/400.

Magazine 001
One-year, 12-issue subscription $129

Midrange Network Expert

Midrange Network Expert (formerly *AS/400 Network Expert)* covers the vast uncharted territory where Windows NT, UNIX, Novell NetWare, Lotus Notes and Domino, and a number of different workstation clients and peripherals meet the AS/400. You'll find out how to hook everything and anything up to the AS/400 to benefit your organization.

Each page of *Midrange Network Expert* is packed with easy-to-understand, hands-on, step-by-step guidance designed to help you meet the challenge of integrating your AS/400 into your network. You'll get solid AS/400 networking solutions that are guaranteed to help you get more done and stand out from the crowd.

Magazine 011
One-year, six-issue subscription............................$89

Midrange Technology SHOWCASE

Midrange Technology SHOWCASE helps you make sense of the new products for the IBM midrange market—at absolutely no charge. Here is just some of what you'll get:

- News & Analysis: in-depth coverage and commentary on events and trends in the midrange arena
- Hardware, Software & Services: comprehensive coverage of innovative midrange products and vendor services, including beat news, product reviews and comparisons, and case studies
- Focus: monthly spotlight on current technologies impacting IT operations
- Internet & E-Business: Information about developing Internet applications and e-commerce solutions
And much more!

Magazine 031   FREE SUBSCRIPTION (available in United States only)

Go to *www.mc-store.com/astecshow.html* and complete the questionnaire to subscribe.

ResourceCD

Get more than 10 years' worth of *Midrange Computing* back issues on one easy-to-search, easy-to-share CD, plus information from *Midrange Network Expert* and *AS/400 NetJava Expert*. *ResourceCD* is powered by the sophisticated search-and-view capabilities of Adobe Acrobat Reader, which is provided free of charge on the disc. You can conduct powerful searches, scan documents quickly, and then zoom in on the details you need. You'll save even more time by uploading useful utilities directly from the disc, with all of the program code already keyed in and ready to go.

Keep the solutions coming all year long by subscribing to *ResourceCD Quarterly Updates*. Each quarter, you'll receive the latest three issues of *Midrange Computing* magazine on CD-ROM.

ResourceCD 102 ....$129

Both ResourceCD and Quarterly
Updates 103 ....$189

ORDER FORM

5 Easy Ways to Order!

BILL TO:

Name _____

Title _____

Company _____

Address _____

City _____ State _____ ZIP _____

FAX
this order form to 760-931-9935,
24 hours a day, 365 days a year.

MAIL
your order to 5650 El Camino Real,
Suite 225, Carlsbad, CA 92008.

EMAIL
your order to *custsvc@
midrangecomputing.com.*

PHONE
toll-free 1-800-477-5665
(Mon. to Fri., 6 a.m. to 5 p.m. PST).

ONLINE
ordering is available at *www.
mc-store.com.*

SHIP TO (if different from above):

Name _____ Title _____

Company _____

Address _____

City/State/ZIP _____

ITEMS ORDERED:

Item No.	Description	Price	Quantity	Total Price
			Subtotal	

ADDITIONAL INFORMATION:

Daytime Phone (required to process order):

(_____) _____ - _____

Fax (_____) _____ - _____

Email _____

Add 7.75% sales tax (CA residents only), 6.25% sales tax (TX residents only),
or 6% sales tax (NJ residents only). No state tax on magazines and technical
journals. Residents of Canada add 7% GST (for printed materials only).

Shipping—$6.25 per item (ground, continental United States only).
No shipping charged for magazines and technical journals.

Total

* Note: All prices are United States only. Please call for orders and prices
outside the United States. Prices subject to change.

BILLING INFORMATION:

☐ Payment Enclosed (Make check payable to Midrange Computing.)
CREDIT CARD: ☐ VISA ☐ MasterCard ☐ American Express ☐ Discover

Card # _____ Exp. Date _____

BILL ME: P.O. # _____

Signature (required) _____

VISA **MasterCard** **AMERICAN EXPRESS Cards** **DISCOVER NOVUS**

Priority code: YUWBZ